P9-DBO-674

HOMELAND SECURITY LAW AND POLICY

ABOUT THE EDITOR

WILLIAM C. NICHOLSON is a nationally known expert in homeland security law and policy. He serves as an Adjunct Professor at Widener University School of Law, where he conceived and instructs a course entitled "Terrorism and Emergency Law." Bill also serves as an Adjunct Professor at the University of Delaware, where he teaches his "Homeland Security Law and Policy" course. He previously served as General Counsel to the Indiana State Emergency Management Agency (SEMA), Indiana Department of Fire and Building Services (DFBS) and Public Safety Training Institute (PSTI) as well as seven related boards and commissions in the public safety arena, including the Indiana Emergency Response Commission and Indiana Emergency Medical Services Commission. Bill has published numerous articles and has spoken nationwide on terrorism and emergency law issues. Among his recent notable publications are a book, *Emergency Response and Emergency Management Law*, Charles C Thomas Publisher, Ltd. (2003), and a major law review article, "Legal Issues in Emergency Response to Terrorism Incidents Involving Hazardous Materials: The Hazardous Waste Operations and Emergency Response ("HAZWOPER") Standard, Standard Operating Procedures, Mutual Aid and the Incident Command System," *Widener Symposium Law Journal*, Volume 9, Number 2, 294 (2003). Bill received several awards for his contributions while serving as General Counsel to the Indiana State Emergency Management Agency.

Bill is also a member of the Editorial Board for *Best Practices in Emergency Services: Today's Tips for Tomorrow's Success* as well as the Editorial Board for *Journal of Emergency Management.*

His awards include *Distinguished Hoosier* from Indiana Governor Frank O'Bannon, *Honorary Emergency Medical Technician* from the Indiana Emergency Medical Services Commission, and *Army Material Command, Command Counsel Team Project Award* presented by General John G. Coburn, Commanding General of Army Material Command, for "exemplary service as a member of the U.S. Army Soldier and Biological Command's Chemical Stockpile Emergency Preparedness Program's Memoranda of Agreement and Memorandum of Understanding Team." He is a member of the Wilmington, DE, Local Emergency Planning Committee and the Wilington, Delaware, Anti Terrorism Committee. He is admitted to practice in Oregon, Indiana, and the District of Columbia. Bill Nicholson earned a B.A. from Reed College in Portland, OR, and a Juris Doctor from Washington and Lee University's School of Law in Lexington, VA.

He may be reached at wcnicholson@widener.edu

HOMELAND SECURITY LAW AND POLICY

Edited by

WILLIAM C. NICHOLSON

Widener University School of Law
Wilmington, Delaware

With a Foreword by

SENATOR JOSEPH BIDEN

CHARLES C THOMAS • PUBLISHER, LTD.
Springfield • Illinois • U.S.A.

Published and Distributed Throughout the World by

CHARLES C THOMAS • PUBLISHER, LTD.
2600 South First Street
Springfield, Illinois 62704

This book is protected by copyright. No part of
it may be reproduced in any manner without written
permission from the publisher. All rights reserved.

© 2005 by CHARLES C THOMAS • PUBLISHER, LTD.

ISBN 0-398-07582-4 (hard)
ISBN 0-398-07583-2 (paper)

Library of Congress Catalog Card Number: 2005041701

With THOMAS BOOKS *careful attention is given to all details of manufacturing
and design. It is the Publisher's desire to present books that are satisfactory as to their
physical qualities and artistic possibilities and appropriate for their particular use.*
THOMAS BOOKS *will be true to those laws of quality that assure a good name
and good will.*

Printed in the United States of America
JW-R-3

Library of Congress Cataloging-in-Publication Data

Homeland security law and policy / edited by William C. Nicholson; with a foreword by
  Joseph Biden.
    p. cm.
  ISBN 0-398-07582-4–ISBN 0-398-07583-2 (pbk.)
    1. Terrorism–United States–Prevention. 2. National security–United States. 3. National
security–Law and legislation–United States. 4. Emergency management–United States. 5.
War and emergency legislation–United States. 6. Civil rights–United States. I. Nicholson,
William C.

HV6432.H664 2005
363.32′0973–dc22   2005041701

This book is dedicated with appreciation to the warriors who defend us on foreign soil and the emergency responders and emergency managers who daily confront homeland security's challenges.

CONTRIBUTORS

Ann Strack Angelheart, Ph.D.

Dr. Angelheart is a graduate of the University of Florida, where she earned her B.A., M.A. and Ph.D. in Geography, with Specializations in Economic Geography and Natural Hazards. She has taught at the University of North Carolina at Charlotte and the University of Florida. Her publications include "Business Response to Natural Disaster: A Case Study of the Response by Firms in Greenville, North Carolina, to Hurricane Floyd."

Senator Joseph R. Biden, Jr.

Senator Biden is the senior senator for the state of Delaware. One of the most respected voices on national security and civil liberties, Senator Biden has earned national and international recognition as a policy innovator, effective legislator and party spokesperson on a wide range of key issues. He is the top Democrat on both the Senate Foreign Relations Committee and the Judiciary Subcommittee on Crime, and is a central player on some of the most important issues facing the nation, from crime prevention and constitutional law to international relations and arms control.

Louise K. Comfort, Ph.D.

Louise K. Comfort is a professor of Public and International Affairs at the University of Pittsburgh. She teaches in the field of public policy analysis, information policy, organizational theory, and policy design and implementation. She holds degrees in political science from Macalester College (B.A.) University of California at Berkeley (M.A.), and Yale University (Ph.D.). She is Principal Investigator, Interactive, Intelligent, Spatial Information System (IISIS) Project, 1994–present: http://www.iisis.pitt.edu. She has served as Principal Investigator/Project Coordinator on 21 funded research projects; coinvestigator on seven funded research projects; team leader on two field research teams and team member on six field research teams. She has conducted field research on information processes in disaster operations following earthquakes in Mexico City, 1985; San Salvador, 1986; Ecuador, 1987; Whittier Narrows, California, 1987; Armenia, 1988; Loma Prieta, 1989; Costa Rica, 1991; Erzincan, Turkey, 1992; Killari, India, 1993; Northridge, California, 1994; Hanshin, Japan, 1995; Izmit, Turkey, 1999; Nantou County, Taiwan, 1999; and Gujarat, India, 2001.
Recent publications related to Homeland Security include: "Rethinking Security: Organizational Fragility in Extreme Events." 2002. *Public*

Administration Review. Vol. 62, Special Issue (September): 98–107. "Governance under Fire: Organizational Fragility in Complex Systems." 2002. In *Governance and Public Security*. Syracuse, NY: Campbell Public Affairs Institute, Maxwell School of Citizenship and Public Affairs, Syracuse University, pp. 113–127. "Managing Intergovernmental Response to Terrorism and Other Extreme Events." 2002. *Publius*. Vol. 32, No. 4 (Fall): 29–50, and "Assessment of Homeland Security Initiatives: Commonwealth of Pennsylvania." 2003. Invited paper. Century Foundation Study on Homeland Security at the State Level. Century Foundation, New York, New York. Submitted February 16, 2003. Published June 25, 2003.

Frank J. Costello, Esq.

Frank Costello is a managing partner of Zuckert, Scoutt & Rasenberger, L.L.P., a Washington, D.C., law firm with 40 years of experience in handling regulatory, international, legislative, and litigation matters, primarily in transportation industries. The firm's aviation practice encompasses virtually every aspect of that industry. Mr. Costello currently serves as chairman of the Aviation Committee of the American Bar Association's Section of Public Utility, Communications, and Transportation Law. Mr. Costello is admitted to practice in the District of Columbia. He is a graduate of Dartmouth College (1965) and the Georgetown University Law Center (1970).

William R. Cumming, Esq.

Mr. Cumming is the principal in the Vacation Lane Group, a nonprofit think tank dedicated to expanding knowledge of emergency management and homeland security in a democratic context. He was employed for 34 years by the federal government in various capacities. He retired from the FEMA Office of General Counsel after working there from 1979 to 1999. He previously served in the Office of the General Counsel in the Department of Housing and Urban Development and as a tax law specialist and legal advisor in various sections of the Internal Revenue Service. While on active duty with the United States Army, Mr. Cumming commanded and inspected nuclear weapons units. He received his J.D. from the University of Virginia and his B.A. in History and International Relations magna cum laude from Lehigh University.

Michael Donohue

Michael Donohue is a fourth-year evening division student at the Widener University School of Law. A member of the Widener Moot Court Honor Society and Delaware Journal of Corporate Law, Mr. Donohue has served as a Law Clerk for Pennsylvania Attorney General Gerald J. Pappert's Philadelphia regional office of the Bureau of Consumer Protection since May of 2002. The "Dirty Bomb" was originally conceived and presented during

Professor William C. Nicholson's popular Terrorism and Emergency Law class taught at Widener University School of Law.

Monica Teets Farris, Ph.D.

Dr. Monica Teets Farris is Senior Postdoctoral Research Associate at the Center for Hazards Assessment, Response, and Technology (CHART) at the University of New Orleans and teaches a hazards policy course in the College of Urban and Public Affairs. She received her M.A. from Louisiana State University and Ph.D. from the University of New Orleans, both in Political Science, the latter with a public policy specialization. Her current research includes examining benefits of utilizing Web-based emergency planning and response, and ways in which GIS-based risk assessment processes affect community participation and risk reduction outcomes. Dr. Farris recently participated in a postassessment of the emergency response effort in Washington, D.C., following Hurricane Isabel and is currently the project manager of a FEMA-funded study of flood mitigation from a community sustainability perspective and a FEMA Disaster Resistant University grant recently awarded to UNO. She has publications forthcoming in the *International Journal of Risk Assessment and Management* and the *Journal of Coastal Research.*

Keith Feigenbaum

Keith Feigenbaum is a graduate of James Madison University, where he received a B.A. in Journalism/French. Mr. Feigenbaum is now a second-year student at the Widener University School of Law. He previously worked as a National Security Policy Analyst at Science Applications International Corporation at the Pentagon.

Gregory M. Huckabee, Esq.

Gregory M. Huckabee is an Associate Professor of Business Law and Director, International Programs at the University of South Dakota School of Business. He received his A.B. in 1972, M.B.A. in 1974, and J.D. in 1976 from Gonzaga University in Spokane, WA. Commissioned in R.O.T.C. in 1974, he entered active duty in 1976 and served for 27 years as a Regular Army Judge Advocate. He received an LL.M. in 1984 from The Judge Advocate General's School in Charlottesville, VA; an M.S. in 1988 in Education from Jacksonville State University in Jacksonville, AL; an M.A. in 1991 in Congressional Studies from The Catholic University of America in Washington, D.C.; and an LL.M. in 1994 from The George Washington University National Law Center in Washington, D.C. He served as the Legal Advisor for the 2001 Presidential Inauguration DoD Joint Task Force, the 2001 National Scout Jamboree DoD Joint Task Force, and the Staff Judge Advocate of the WMD First U.S. Army Joint Response Task Force-East 1997–2003.

Professor Leslie Gielow Jacobs

Leslie Gielow Jacobs has been a member of the University of the Pacific, McGeorge School of Law Faculty since 1992. Her legal scholarship, focusing on constitutional law, particularly free speech, and government action, has appeared in law journals at Yale, Michigan, Northwestern, Illinois, Ohio State, UC Davis, Rutgers, Tulane, Florida, and Indiana. Professor Jacobs is most recently applying her constitutional law expertise to the areas of bioterrorism and infectious disease law. Her most recent article, addressing the constitutionality of "sensitive but unclassified" secrecy clauses attached to government-funded scientific research will appear in the first volume of the *National Security Law Journal.* She has also coauthored with Dean Elizabeth Rindskopf Parker an article titled, "Government Information Controls and Scientific Inquiry," which appears in the second volume of *Biosecurity and Bioterrorism: Biodefense Strategy, Practice, and Science,* and an entry on United States bioterrorism defense policy that will appear in the *Encyclopedia of Bioterrorism Defense,* forthcoming from J. Wiley & Sons, Inc. She leads McGeorge's Bioterrorism, National Security, and Public Health Law Initiative, one of whose goals is encouraging introduction of bioterrorism and public health law issues into the law school curriculum. Professor Jacobs served as a law clerk to the late Associate Justice Lewis F. Powell, Jr. and to Judge Louis F. Oberdorfer (U.S. District Court, District of Columbia). She also practiced with two San Francisco law firms and taught at the University of California, Davis Law School before joining the faculty at University of Pacific, McGeorge School of Law. Professor Jacobs received her B.A. from Wesleyan University and her J.D. magna cum laude from the University of Michigan Law School.

Eva Lerner-Lam

Eva Lerner-Lam has 27 years of experience in transportation planning, operations, research and policy making. Founder and president of the Palisades Consulting Group, Inc. (www.palisadesgroup.com), she leads many national technical committees focused on transportation security. She has served in several key public sector positions, including Director of Planning and Operations for the San Diego Metropolitan Transit Development Board and Member of the New Jersey Transit Corporation Board of Directors, and has received numerous professional awards and honors. She is a graduate and past trustee of Princeton University, and earned a Master's degree in Civil Engineering/Transportation Systems Division from the Massachusetts Institute of Technology.

Kristin S. Nolan
Kristin S. Nolan is a fourth-year evening division student at the Widener University School of Law. "The USA PATRIOT Act, Money Laundary, and Suspicious Activities Reports from Financial Institutions" was originally conceived and presented during Professor William C. Nicholson's Popular Terrorism and Emergency Law class taught at Widener University School of law.

Robert W. Smith, Ph.D.

Dr. Smith is the Director of the Master of Public Administration program at Clemson University. He received his M.P.A. and Ph.D. in Public Administration from the University at Albany (SUNY). He was a former senior budget official for the New York State Division of the Budget (12 years) and former Regional Director for U.S. Senator Daniel Patrick Moynihan. He has numerous publications and has performed research in the areas of public budgeting and administrative ethics.

Richard T. Sylves, Ph.D.

Dr. Sylves is a Professor of Political Science and International Relations and Senior Policy Fellow of the Center on Energy and Environmental Policy, both at the University of Delaware. He has published extensively on disaster policy and emergency management. He has researched presidential disaster declarations for more than fifteen years and he has coedited (with William L. Waugh) two books on disaster management in the United States. He is completing a book on presidential disaster declarations with State University of New York Press. From 1995–1999, Sylves completed two research grant projects for the U.S. Federal Emergency Management Agency's Higher Education Project. One was on the "Political and Policy Basis of U.S. Emergency Management," (now available from FEMA/DHS online) and "The Economic Dimensions of Disaster." He regularly publishes articles regarding emergency management. He has worked with William L. Waugh on several studies of disaster management in the United States, he has served on the National Academy of Science (NAS) panel, "Estimating the Costs of Natural Disasters," and he today serves as an appointed member of the NAS Natural Disasters Roundtable. In 1998, Sylves completed a NOAA-Sea Grant Project Report on federally declared disasters employing Excel data analysis and ArcView 3.0 GIS mapping.

Frances L. Edwards, Ph.D., CEM

Dr. Edwards is the Director of the Office of Emergency Services for the City of San José, California. She is responsible for public education programs, the city's Emergency Operations Plan, Emergency Operations Center, and the RACES and CERT programs involving over 1,400 volunteers. She was named "Public Official of the Year" by *Governing* Magazine in 2002. Dr. Edwards was recently named by *San Jose Magazine* as one of the "Power 100" in the Silicon Valley. Her most recent publications are *Saving City Lifelines*, (Mineta Transportation Institute, 2003), on terrorism and transportation, and *First to Arrive: State and Local Response to Terrorism*, (MIT Press, 2003) on media relations.

FOREWORD

The term "homeland security" was virtually unused in the United States before September 11, 2001, but the attacks of that day have forced all of us to rethink our relationships abroad, the missions of federal, state, and local governments here at home, and the best way to "provide for the common defense." *Homeland Security Law and Policy* frames those discussions in a unique and incredibly helpful way, and its publication is extremely timely.

At the federal level, many changes have been made to address the nation's vulnerabilities. Antiquated statutes have been rewritten so that law enforcement and intelligence investigators can better share critical information. We are well into the second year of operations for the third-largest federal agency, the Department of Homeland Security. This reorganization—the most ambitious attempt to redraw the federal bureaucracy in fifty years—is an attempt to merge together twenty-two formerly distinct agencies, an effort that has not yet entirely borne fruit. Congress is considering ways to reorganize itself to better fund and oversee our homeland security operations. Efforts to share intelligence and information among all levels of government and with the private sector are underway, yet those projects as well are not yet completed.

More explosive detection systems, advanced checkpoint X-ray devices, and explosive trace detection systems are at work in over 400 airports around the country. A biometric-based entry-exit program has been implemented at our borders. More cargo containers are being inspected. Radiation detectors have been installed in some areas to check for nuclear weapons or radioactive materials that can be used to make dirty bombs. Risk assessments at some chemical plants have been conducted, and billions of dollars have been appropriated for the country's first responders.

However, many challenges remain. We inspect only a tiny fraction of all cargo containers entering the United States. Too few resources are directed toward securing our most vulnerable and critical infrastructures: rail lines, chemical plants, and surface transportation modes. The Coast Guard protects over 95,000 miles of shoreline with an aging fleet and workforce the size of a large city's police department. The number of customs inspectors is unchanged since 9–11. The FBI is in the midst of a massive transformation, but it has not increased its overall number of special agents. Its information technology—so low-tech on 9–11 that the FBI resorted to overnight delivery services to obtain current photographs of al Quaida suspects—remains woefully unsuited to a great investigative agency.

At the local level, too little has been done in the nearly four years since we were attacked. The number of uniformed local law enforcement personnel is dropping in many areas of the country. Commission after commission has reported on the problems facing our first responders: no routine access to critical intelligence, poor preparedness to deal with a chemical or biological attack, underequipped and underfunded agencies across the nation, and a lack of interoperable communications gear.

Our country long ago determined that federal expenditures for national defense are necessary and appropriate, but we have not yet had a national conversation on how to effectively fund the homeland security improvements experts tell us are necessary. Today, state and local governments are being asked to shoulder a fiscal burden that many believe ought to be a federal responsibility. Yet in important respects the federal government remains on the sidelines. The Department of Homeland Security has not yet issued a plan to protect our critical infrastructures, nor have standards been set to guide cities and states in their preparedness efforts.

As I write this, Congress is in the midst of rare August hearings to consider the recommendations of the 9–11 Commission to reform our intelligence agencies and wage a more effective war on terrorism. For these reforms to succeed, and in order to truly create a safer America, the public must be informed on homeland security policy. All levels of government will benefit from an engaged electorate so that tough decisions can be made on homeland security and the war on terror. *Homeland Security Law and Policy* will help educate students on the choices facing the nation, and I compliment Professor Nicholson for his contribution to the debate.

Senator Joseph R. Biden, Jr.
Wilmington, Delaware
August 2004

INTRODUCTION

The United States of America faced a watershed moment on September 11, 2001. The terrorist attacks shocked our nation into the realization that a major hazard existed for which preparedness was insufficient. The overwhelming nature of the challenges involved in making our country safe from future terrorist attacks soon became apparent. The debate over what constitutes the challenges and how the country can best respond to them has been ongoing since the day of the attacks.

Homeland Security Law and Policy has as its goal the presentation of a broad range of legal and policy issues that face our country as we grapple with the new reality of terrorism. The subject matter is very extensive, encompassing the entire range of activities in the American economy and government. Complete coverage of all aspects of the matter is, therefore, not possible in a volume such as this. Rather than provide superficial treatment of every issue, therefore, in-depth consideration of an assortment of key topics was deemed to be the best approach. So, for example, all types of transportation policy are not included. Rather, mass transit and aviation policy issues provide a focus for the subject matter. Similarly, bioterrorism and "dirty bombs" supply the means to discuss issues related to Weapons of Mass Destruction.

The reader will note a number of thematic topics that recur at various points in the text. Some of the most controversial spring from challenges to traditional concepts of federalism as the national government assumes control of matters once the province of state and local governments. Decisions on funding and personnel priorities coming from Washington affect all emergency responders to a much greater extent than ever before. Multiple perspectives on important policy issues illuminate them in important ways.

The first test the nation faces is the basic one of defining what is meant by homeland security. The text opens with consideration of this issue, from the strictly legal and pedagogical perspectives. Subsequent chapters also address the issue as it applies directly to their subject matter.

The immediate response to the 9–11 attacks came from our existing structure of emergency responders and emergency managers. The roots of homeland security in the Federal Emergency Management Agency's (FEMA's) hazardous materials responsibilities provide a context for the subsequent development of the discipline. The changes in FEMA's priorities after it became part of the new Department of Homeland Security (DHS) illustrate the new pressures that homeland security duties have put on the federal government, and highlight the difficult choices that must be made when needs outstrip resources. The internal debate over whether the "all-hazards" approach or a strong terrorism concentration is the proper path captures an ongoing policy dispute. The process by which DHS is adopting the National Response Plan (NRP) and the National Incident Management System (NIMS) demonstrates the difficulties in creating truly national policies and getting buy-in from the affected stakeholders. The choice among different legal avenues for their adoption illustrates the intersection of law and policy options.

Homeland security decisions made in Washington, DC have far-reaching impacts on state and local governments, who often find themselves saddled with unfunded mandates when the federal government decides that an issue must be tackled nationwide. The cascading effects of federal choices on other government partners show the far-reaching nature of these policy selections.

As new challenges arise, new or revised structures often come into place to allow a cooperative approach to common problems. The government, private sector, and higher education can create promising partnerships, as shown in the case study on that subject. From the federal side, the Department of Defense (DoD) possesses more assets that can be brought to bear in the event of a disaster than any other entity. Utilizing these advantages requires understanding a range of legal matters, as well as some institutional history.

In the immediate aftermath of the 9–11 attacks, the Congress enacted strong new statutes designed to more fully protect the nation from terrorist attacks. Many observers decried the effect of these laws on civil liberties, and campaigned for less intrusive alternatives. On the other side of the fence, supporters argued that even more steps were needed to fully protect us from potential terror attacks. Comparison of the attitudes of the two groups allows an interesting exploration of the underlying policy choices. Some parts of the new laws were less controversial: controlling money laundering and, thusly, preventing the financing of terrorist entities was a generally well-accepted step. While reporting requirements increased, strict limitations on sharing the information resulted in acceptance by the general public.

The transportation industry continues to be a potential target for terrorists, as it offers potential victims in concentrated numbers. Perhaps the most challenging aspect of transportation is mass transit, the vehicles that take people to and from work every day. Providing meaningful security for mass transit is very difficult, because the numbers of people using the system preclude detailed inspections of all passengers. The March 11, 2004, terrorist attacks on subways in Madrid, Spain, illustrate how devastating a strike on mass transit might be. Terrorists using passenger airliners as flying bombs carried out the 9–11 attacks. The airline industry therefore faces very close scrutiny as it undergoes extensive security reforms. The evolution of aviation security policy provides an interesting view of the changing nature of the terrorist threat.

Al Quaida leader Osama Bin Laden has said, "If it is true that I have acquired [chemical or nuclear] weapons, I thank God who has made it possible. And if I seek to procure such weapons, it is a duty." The reality of this threat makes the possible use of weapons of mass destruction (WMD) perhaps the most frightening aspect of terrorism. One thorny issue that confronts those considering proactive steps to address the enormous threat of WMD is how much to spend and where to spend it. The overwhelming nature of potential WMD effects and competing priorities mean that there will literally never be sufficient resources to completely address the issue. Many bioterrorism preparedness steps, for example, will increase readiness for a variety of public health hazards. Others, however, are specific to WMD and have limited or nonexistent application to other risks. Sometimes, the best preparedness steps must take place before the event occurs, as with administration of medication to lessen the effect of radiation poisoning. Unfortunately, the widespread availability of radioactive elements to enhance the effect of conventional explosives, turning them into "dirty bombs," means that a possible detonation could occur anywhere and anytime.

In the immediate aftermath of the September 11, 2001 attacks, the nations of the world were virtually unanimous in their support of the United States and the war on Al Quaida, the group that masterminded the blows. Following our invasion of Iraq, however, other nations around the world have been far less helpful. Understanding U.S. policy decisions that resulted in the Iraqi invasion and other nations' attitudes toward that conflict sheds light on potential steps that may assist us in finding more allies in the war on terror. Domestically, some leaders have rethought our commitment to Iraq and criticized the process that led the nation down that road. President Bush continues to pursue the war vigorously despite questions from critics. The decisions of policymakers regarding the war in Iraq, in all probability, will result in the war on terror's most lasting international legacy.

Americans want to avoid any repeat of the 9–11 attacks. To that end, the 9–11 Commission investigated the precursor events in detail, with the goal of recommending steps to make our nation safer in the future. Their report contains significant proposals for reorganization of American intelligence assets. The Commission focuses on the need to unify all aspects of our intelligence efforts, from management to analysis. Response from the executive branch and Congress was quickly forthcoming, in the form of new executive orders and sweeping legislative proposals. The outcome of the policy discussions exemplified by these documents will determine the future of our intelligence agencies and, in large part, will dictate our vulnerability to future attacks.

The future of homeland security will involve both domestic and international aspects. Our nation is currently engaged in a war on terror with no readily apparent exit strategy. The commitment to Iraq appears to be a deep one, with all involved aware of the potential downsides of failure. Here in the United States, the high levels of funding over the past few years for terrorism preparedness reportedly will decline significantly in the next few years. The danger to our nation from terrorists as well as more mundane natural and manmade hazards will continue. Homeland security law and policy issues will continue to be with us, but whether the current high level of attention to these matters will persist is uncertain. Understanding and debating these vital subjects will assist future leaders in making wise choices when their turn comes to decide the direction of our national strategy.

William C. Nicholson
Wilmington, Delaware
October 2004

ACKNOWLEDGMENTS

My thanks to Senator Joseph Biden for his leadership and insight into homeland security matters. Our nation and the state of Delaware both benefit every day from his wise guidance and informed perspectives on homeland security policy issues, both foreign and domestic. I wish to thank the nationally renowned authors who kindly submitted the excellent materials contained in this book, including: Keith Feigenbaum; Robert W. Smith; William R. Cumming; Richard T. Sylves; Frances L. Edwards; Louise K. Comfort; Monica Teets Farris; Gregory M. Huckabee; Kristin S. Nolan; Eva Lerner-Lam; Frank J. Costello; Ann Strack Angelheart; Professor Leslie Gielow Jacobs; and Michael P. Donohue. I am grateful to the Honorable Birch E. Bayh, a great and wise mentor, and to Senator Evan Bayh, in whose gubernatorial administration I had the honor to serve. My appreciation to those who encouraged and fostered my interest in this subject matter include: former Director of the Indiana State Emergency Agency (SEMA) and current Indiana State Police Superintendent Melvin J. Carraway; former SEMA Director Patrick R. Ralston; SEMA Deputy Director Phillip K. Roberts; the Honorable Melanie George; and many other current and former emergency response and emergency management friends both in Indiana and in Delaware. My gratitude to my friend LTC Stephen T. Udovich USAR for sharing information on the obligations and rewards of life as a regular Army officer, member of the National Guard, and now Army reserves. Steve was notified in early October 2004 to deploy to Iraq to train a battalion of the Iraqi National Guard. My prayers focus on Steve and his two young sons, Ethan and Adam, as well as my good buddy and former snake eater SGM Gaetano A. Gravino, Sr. DEANG, who is serving as a security consultant in Iraq. I join the nation in thanking all of our warriors serving in harm's way. Thanks to John R. Powers, Ph.D. for his guidance on emergency management issues and leadership of the innovative FirTH Alliance and CCRI. A special word of gratitude to B. Wayne Blanchard, Ph.D., C.E.M., and his able assistant Barbara L. Johnson for their dedicated devotion to the FEMA Emergency Management Higher Education Project. They have created the proper atmosphere for incubation and growth of emergency management and related academic pursuits, including homeland security programs, in institutions of higher learning across the United States. Their work is largely responsible for the ongoing professionalization of emergency management in the United States.

My greatest thanks and all my love go, as always, to my wife Nancy, who keeps my homeland happy and my heart secure.

W.C.N.

CONTENTS

Page

Foreword – Senator Joseph Biden xiii
Introduction xv
Acknowledgments xix

Section I Homeland Security and Emergency Management 3

**Chapter 1 Part 1: Defining Homeland Security and
Terrorism: Legal Enactments** 5
Keith Feigenbaum
   I.   Federal Definitions 5
   II. State Responses 7
   III. Conclusion 8

**Part 2: Defining "Homeland Security": Content
and Context Grounded in the Curricula** 10
Robert W. Smith
   I.   Basis for the Analysis 10
   II. Homeland Security as Defined in the
        Literature 11
   III. Homeland Security in the Classroom 12
   IV. Sampling the Syllabi 13
   V.   A Grounded Theory Approach: What the
        Courses Tell Us 15
   VI. Cataloging the Courses 16
        A. Homeland Security Courses 16
        B. Emergency Management or
            Preparedness 17
        C. Military-Oriented Courses 17
        D. Terrorism and National Security Courses 17
        E. Technical or Specialized Courses 17
   VII. Sorting Through Definitions 18
   VIII. Concluding Points 19
   IX. Synthesizing a Definition 19

**Chapter 2 FEMA's Place in Policy, Law, and Management:
A Hazardous Materials Perspective 1979–2003** 23
William R. Cumming and Richard T. Sylves
   I.   Overview 23

II.   Disasters Resulting from Intentional or
      Accidental Acts of Humans 24
      A. The Policy-Making Process 24
      B. Executive Orders 25
      C. Emergency Management's Roots 25
      D. Humanitarian Aid Versus Technical
          Prowess 26
      E. Prelude to Homeland Security 27
III. Early FEMA and HAZMAT 27
      A. Generalists Versus Specialists 28
      B. FEMA Staffing, Powers, and Primary
          Accountability 29
      C. FEMA's Clientele 29
IV.   FEMA and Nuclear Power Emergencies.......... 30
      A. Early History 30
      B. Meese Memorandum: National
          System for Emergency
          Coordination 31
      C. Risk Analysis and Nuclear Power
          Emergencies 31
      D. Reagan's Preemptive Ruling 31
      E. Clinton, Bush, and Nuclear Power
          Emergencies 32
 V.   FEMA, Love Canal, Bhopal, and
      Chernobyl 32
VI.   FEMA and Hazardous Materials
      Emergencies from Reagan to Clinton 33
VII. FEMA HAZMAT and Fire Jurisdiction:
      The United States Fire Administration 34
      A. USFA and the Reagan Era 35
      B. Hazardous Materials Transportation 35
      C. USFA in the Clinton and
          Bush Era 36
VIII. FEMA and Nuclear Attack
      Emergencies 36
IX.   FEMA and the Chemical Weapons
      Disposal Program 37
 X.   FEMA and Terrorism Consequence
      Management 39
XI.   FEMA and Major Oil Spills 40
XII. FEMA HAZMAT in the Clinton-Witt
      and Bush-Allbaugh Eras 41
XIII. Conclusion 42

Chapter 3   **FEMA'S Changing Priorities since**
                   September 11, 2001 56
                   William C. Nicholson
      I.   All Hazards 57
      II.   Mitigation 57
      III. Responder Training 58
           A.   FEMA Emergency Management Higher Education
               Project 59
           B.   National Fire Academy 59
           C.   Loss of the National Emergency
               Training Center 60
           D.   Destruction of Key Infrastructure 60
      IV. Funding Decisions Point to the Future 61
      V.   Conclusion 62

Chapter 4   **The Shape of Emergency Response and
                   Emergency Management in the Aftermath of the
                   Homeland Security Act of 2002: Adopting the
                   National Response Plan (NRP) and the
                   National Incident Management System (NIMS)** 68
                   William C. Nicholson
      I.   Why the NRP and NIMS? 69
      II.   Creating a National Response Plan and
           National Incident Management System 70
            A.   Comprehensive Content 70
           B.   Challenging Deadlines 70
           C.   NRP 1 and NIMS 1 70
      III. Creation of the Initial National Response Plan 71
           A.   State and Local Governments and
                Responders Weigh In 71
           B.   The Initial National Response Plan 72
      IV. Subsequent NRP Versions:
           Ever More Comprehensive Plans 73
      V.   NIMS 2 and the Adopted NIMS: More Detail for
           Responders and Emergency Managers 78
            A.   Preparedness Issues 78
           B.   The NIMS Integration Center and
                Responder Certification Issues 78
           C.   NFPA 1600: Another Important Standard
                for Emergency Management 80
                1.   Incorporating NFPA 1600:
                     The Emergency Management
                     Accreditation Program 81

        2. NFPA 1600 and ICS 82

        3. NIMS and NFPA 1600 Planning
            Standards 82

    D. Mutual Aid Concerns 83

    E. Implementing NIMS 84

  VI. NRP and NIMS as Rulemaking 85

 VII. Conclusion 87

Section II Local and Regional Perspectives 109

**Chapter 5 Homeland Security from the Local
Perspective** 111

Frances L. Edwards

    I. Local Government Terrorism Preparedness
      Before 9-11 111

   II. The Warning: Mass Destruction 114

  III. Local Government's Response to
      Terrorism After 9-11 117

  IV. Federal Legislation's Impact on Local
      Government Homeland Security Systems 120

   V. All Hazards Emergency Management and
      the Move to DHS 123

  VI. Funding: Promises and Reality 126

 VII. Urban Area Security Initiative (UASI):
      The Federal/Local Connection–Reverting
      to a Process that Worked? 128

VIII. The Future of Local Homeland
      Security Policy 129

  IX. Where Do We Go From Here? 132

   X. Conclusion 133

**Chapter 6 Homeland Security Initiatives and Emergency
Management in Metro Areas: The Pennsylvania
Perspective** 137

Louise K. Comfort

    I. Maintaining Security in Interdependent Systems .. 137

   II. Domestic Preparedness for Extreme Events 138

  III. Homeland Security Initiatives After
      September 11, 2001 139

    A. Formation of the Pennsylvania Office of
        Homeland Security 139

    B. Report of Governor's Task Force
        on Security 139

    C. Funding Issues and Budgetary Constraints ... 140

D.   Search for Workable Strategies Within
Constraints 141
E.   Continuing Debate over Priorities for Action ... 141
IV.   Obstacles, Dilemmas, and Opportunities for
Enhancing Security 141
A.   Obstacles 141
B.   Dilemmas 141
C.   Opportunities 142
V.   An Emerging Strategy for Homeland Security 142

Section III   Partnering for Homeland Security 147

**Chapter 7   New Partnerships for Homeland Security, Policy
Development, and Application: Government,
Private Sector, and Higher Education** 149
Monica Teets Farris
I.   Shifts in Disaster Management Strategies 149
II.   Changes in Technology 151
III.   Partnerships with Universities 151
IV.   Partnering with Private Industry 152
V.   Case Study 153
VI.   Conclusion 155

**Chapter 8   Partnering with the Department of Defense for
Improved Homeland Security** 159
Gregory M. Huckabee
I.   The Pecking Order 160
II.   When Does the Flag Go Up? 163
A.   Immediate Response 163
B.   Declaration of a National Disaster
when Requested by a State 164
C.   Unilateral Presidential Action 165
D.   Emergencies Involving Federal
Primary Responsibility 165
III.   How Does DoD Play Friendly? 165
A.   The Organization: Why Me? 165
B.   Command Structure: Who Is On First? 166
C.   Train to Fight: DoD Loves the
Lead Federal Agency (LFA) 167
D.   The Battle: Bring on the Impossible 167
IV.   DoD Law Enforcement Actions: When a
Sheriff is Needed 169
A.   The Insurrection Act: When the Party
Gets Out of Hand 169

      B.   Chemical-Biological WMD: When Gas
         and Bugs Get Loose 170
      C.   Transactions Involving Nuclear Materials:
         When Dr. Strangelove Visits 170
      D.   Execution of Quarantine and Health Laws:
         The Unthinkable 170
      E.   Emergency Authority: When All
         Else Fails 170
      F.   Military Purpose Doctrine: Duty, Duty,
         Always Duty 171
      G.   Indirect DoD Law Enforcement Support:
         Back-up 171
  V. Conclusion 172
  VI. Summary 172

Section IV Civil Rights Issues 177

**Chapter 9 Insatiable Appetite: The Government's
Demand for New and Unnecessary Powers
After September 11** 179
An American Civil Liberties Union Report
   I. The Ever-Expanding Arsenal 180
      A.   The USA PATRIOT Act 181
      B.   Spying on Americans 183
      C.   Detention of Noncitizens 183
      D.   Detention of Citizens 184
      E.   Dragnet Questioning and Fingerprinting
         of Immigrants 185
      F.   Military Tribunals 185
      G.   Attorney-Client Privilege 186
      H.   New Secrecy Measures 186
   II. Additional Measures on the Horizon 188
      A.   Surveillance 188
      B.   State and Local Insatiable Appetites 189
   III. Challenges to American Values 189
      A.   The Threat to Patriotic Dissent 189
      B.   The Threat to Liberty 190
      C.   The Threat to Equality 191
      D.   The Threat to Constitutional Checks
         and Balances 192
      E.   The Threat to Open Government 192
      F.   The Threat to the Rule of Law 193
   IV. Conclusion 194

Chapter 10 Antiterrorism Investigations and the Fourth Amendment After September 11, 2001 197
Testimony of Paul Rosenzweig
    I.   Fourth Amendment Principles 198
    II. Overarching Principles 198
    III. "Data Mining"–Total Information Awareness Today 200
       A. Data Analysis 200
       B. Data Collection: Structural Limitations 202
       C. Data Collection: Legal Limitations 204
    IV. FBI Investigative Guidelines 206

Chapter 11 The USA Patriot Act, Money Laundering, and Suspicious Activity Reports from Financial Institutions 209
Kristin S. Nolan
    I.   What Is Money Laundering? 209
    II. What Is Terrorism? 210
    III. How Are Money Laundering and Terrorism Related? 211
    IV. Regulatory Framework 212
    V. How Does Preventing Money Laundering Prevent Terrorism? 212
    VI. Preventing Both and Violations of the Right to Privacy: Suspicious Activity Reports 213
    VII. Conclusion 216

Section V Challenges for Transportation 223

Chapter 12 Mass Transit and Homeland Security: Policy Issues 225
Eva Lerner-Lam
    I.   Why Is Public Transit Security a Challenge? 225
       A. The "Open" Nature of Public Transit Makes It an Attractive Target 225
       B. Multi-Jurisdictional Environments Require Aggressive Coordination, Cooperation, and Funding 225
       C. Multimodal Interactions Can Increase Vulnerability and Consequences 226
    II. Types of Public Transit Security Threats 226

III. Public Transit Security Policy 227
   A. A "Systems Approach" 227
   B. "Safety *and Security* First" 227
   C. Collaboration and Coordination 227
   D. Role of Technology 227
   E. Transit as a First Responder 228
IV. Key Strategies 228
   A. Prepare 228
   B. Prevent 229
   C. Respond 229
   D. Recover 229
V. Transit Initiatives 229
VI. Challenges and Future Policy Directions 230
   A. Federal 230
   B. Regional and State 230
   C. Local 230
   D. Technology Interoperability Challenges 231
VII. Conclusion 231

Chapter 13 Post-9-11 Challenges for Aviation Security 234
   Frank J. Costello
   I. A Brief History of U.S. Aviation Security 234
   II. The Legal Framework 237
      A. The Authority of the Federal Government to
         Regulate Aviation Security 237
      B. The Federalized Screening Process 238
      C. The Security Responsibilities of Private
         Parties 238
      D. International Legal Obligations 240
      E. Privacy 241
   III. Conclusion 244

Section VI Weapons of Mass Destruction 251

**Chapter 14 Natural Disasters and Weapons of Mass
   Destruction: Policy Issues and Implications** 253
   Ann Strack Angelheart
   I. The Changing Dynamics of Disaster Response . . . 253
   II. Change in Disaster Impacts 254
      A. Politics and Media in American
         Disaster Recovery 254
      B. The American Military and
         Domestic Disaster Recovery 256

    C. Who Pays? 256
  III. When Terrorism Creates a Disaster 257
    A. Fear and Communication 258
    B. Preventing Terrorism and Protecting
      the Public 259
  IV. Conclusion 259

Chapter 15 Bioterrorism Defense: Current Components and
**   Continuing Challenges** 262
    Leslie Gielow Jacobs
  I. The Context 262
  II. The Components 263
  III. The Continuing Challenges 264
    A. Detecting and Deterring Biological
      Weapons Development and Use 264
    B. Achieving Nonproliferation 266
    C. Preparing to Respond to a Bioterrorism
      Attack 267
    D. Risk Assessment and Resource Allocation 268
  IV. Conclusion 268

Chapter 16 Understanding the "Dirty Bomb" and Its Policy
**   Implications** 275
    Michael P. Donohue
  I. The Dirty Bomb 275
    A. Nature of the Dirty Bomb 275
    B. Makings of a Dirty Bomb 276
  II. Potential Effects of a "Dirty Bomb"
    Detonation 278
  III. Response to a "Dirty Bomb" 278
    A. Governmental 278
    B. Cleanup 279
    C. Medical Treatment 280
  IV. Conclusion 280

Section VII Foreign Policy Aspects of Homeland Security 287

Chapter 17 Two Years Later: World Opinion; Foreign
**   Views of U.S. Darken since Sept. 11** 289
    Richard Bernstein
  I. Bush as Salesman 290
  II. Trying to Define "Threat" 291
  III. A Residue of Goodwill 292

Chapter 18   GOP Congressman: War was a Mistake 294
Representative Doug Bereuter (R.-Nevada)
  I.   Apparent Intelligence Failures 294
  II. Skewing of Intelligence to Justify the War? 295
  III. Preparations for War and the Aftermath 295

Chapter 19   President Bush Discusses Iraq 298

Section VIII   Future Challenges for Homeland Security 303

**Chapter 20   Restructuring Management of National
              Security Intelligence** 305

**Part 1:   HOW To Do It? A Different Way of Organizing
           the Government** 305
  I.   Unity of Effort Across the Foreign-Domestic
       Divide 306
       A. Joint Action 306
       B. Combining Joint Intelligence and
           Joint Action 307
  II. Unity of Effort in the Intelligence Community 310
       A. The Need for a Change 310
           1.   Members of the U.S. Intelligence
                Community 310
           2.   Departmental Intelligence Agencies 310
       B. Combining Joint Work with Stronger
           Management 312
       C. Unity of Effort in Managing Intelligence 314
  III. Unity of Effort in Sharing Information 316
  IV. Unity of Effort in the Congress 318
       A. Strengthen Congressional Oversight of
           Intelligence and Homeland Security 318
       B. Improve the Transitions Between
           Administrations 319
  V.   Organizing America's Defenses in the
       United States 320
       A. The Future Role of the FBI 320
       B. Creating a New Domestic Intelligence
           Agency Has Other Drawbacks 320
       C. Homeland Defense 322

**Part 2:   Executive Orders Issued in Response to
           the 9-11 Commission Report** 324
       Executive Order 13354 of August 27, 2004 324
       National Counterterrorism Center 324

Executive Order 13355 of August 27, 2004 327
Strengthened Management of the Intelligence
Community 327
Executive Order 13356 of August 27, 2004 330
Strengthening the Sharing of Terrorism Information to
Protect Americans 330

**Part 3: 9-11 Commission Report Implementation
Legislation.** 333

Chapter 21 The Future of Homeland Security 338
William C. Nicholson

Appendices
Appendix A Homeland Security-oriented Websites 343

Appendix B List of Acronyms 349

Appendix C Legal Authorities and References for the
National Response Plan (NRP) 352

Appendix D Overview of Initial Federal Involvement
Under the *Stafford Act* 364

Appendix E State Definitions of Terrorism 365

Appendix F Author's Update for Chapter 3 374

Index 375

HOMELAND SECURITY LAW AND POLICY

Natural hazards continue in a time of terrorism. ORANGE BEACH, AL–The vast fury of Hurricane Ivan's 130 mph winds and 30-foot swells. Hurricane Ivan passed directly over Orange Beach. September 16, 2004. FEMA photo by Butch Kinerney.

Section I

HOMELAND SECURITY AND EMERGENCY MANAGEMENT

Chapter 1

PART 1: DEFINING HOMELAND SECURITY AND TERRORISM: LEGAL ENACTMENTS

KEITH FEIGENBAUM

On November 25, 2002, President George W. Bush signed into law the Homeland Security Act of 2002,[1] thus moving various governmental agencies under one roof with one poorly defined goal: homeland security. A preliminary challenge was writing legally binding definitions of terrorism and homeland security.

Prior to September 11, 2001, only piecemeal definitions of terrorism existed in legislation. These related to the destruction of aircraft or aircraft facilities, violence at international airports, biological weapons, arson and bombings, hostage taking, and assassinations, among a variety of other serious offenses.[2] Meanwhile, what we now consider homeland security was better known as homeland defense prior to September 11.[3] As of yet, there is no consensus on the meanings of terrorism and homeland security, although legislation has been enacted with varying definitions of these expressions.

This part of the chapter examines the definitions that have been enacted into law or published with the goal of setting boundaries to these expansive terms. In his concurring opinion in *Jacobellis v. Ohio*, Supreme Court Justice Potter Stewart wrote on the term obscenity: "I shall not today attempt further to define the kinds of material I understand to be embraced within that shorthand description. . . . *But I know it when I see it.*"[4] It is tempting to take a similar approach to defining terrorism and homeland security, yet elements of both the federal government and state governments have gone a few steps further.

I. FEDERAL DEFINITIONS

When we see people walk into cafeterias with bombs strapped to their bodies, that's terrorism. When we see people fly airplanes into fully occupied buildings, that's terrorism. When people in the name of revolution go and cut off the hands and arms of little children in a village to terrorize them, that's terrorism. That's what we need to stop. That's what this campaign is about. If we can delegitimize those tactics for political purposes, we will have won our campaign against terrorism.[5]
— *Ambassador F.X. Taylor, U.S. Coordinator for Counterterrorism*

The notion of defending the homeland from outside threats and responding to catastrophes within our borders is nothing new. The U.S. Constitution gives Congress the power to "provide for calling forth the Militia to execute the laws of the Union, suppress Insurrections and repel Invasions."[6] Following the Revolutionary War, militias were formed to respond to real and perceived threats from Great Britain, Spain, and France, each of which retained territories in North America and maintained navies that preyed on U.S. merchant ships.[7] The Army set out to defend the homeland

---

Note: Keith Feigenbaum is a second-year student at the Widener University School of Law. He previously worked as a National Security Policy Analyst at Science Applications International Corporation at the Pentagon.

from fortified positions near our harbors, while also protecting settlers and traders engaged in the country's westward expansion.[8] Meanwhile, the Navy sought to control the sea lanes, thus projecting U.S. might overseas and protecting the country's economic interests.[9]

These early efforts at securing the homeland are best termed "homeland defense," an expression that gained new meaning following the Japanese attack on Pearl Harbor in 1941 (the first foreign assault on U.S. soil since the War of 1812). The United States responded to that attack on service members and civilians with renewed efforts by the Navy to patrol the seas, defending against enemy submarines with help from the Army Air Force.[10] In following decades, the North American Air Defense Command was formed to respond to the Soviet nuclear threat. This threat spawned Americans to engage in civil defense efforts that, in part, consisted of building backyard bomb shelters and engaging in air raid drills in schools.[11]

Today, homeland defense and civil defense have essentially merged, both in the way the country sets out to protect itself and in the country's lexicon. The President's *National Strategy for Homeland Security* defines homeland security as "a concerted national effort to prevent *terrorist* attacks within the United States, reduce America's vulnerability to *terrorism*, and minimize the damage and recover from attacks that do occur."[12] (Emphasis added.) The Homeland Security Act sets out the broader goals for a Department of Homeland Security, which include disparate agencies like the Federal Emergency Management Agency and the U.S. Customs Service (formerly part of the Department of the Treasury) that work toward common goals:

- Prevent terrorist attacks within the United States;
- Reduce the vulnerability of the United States to terrorism;
- Minimize the damage, and assist in the recovery, from terrorist attacks that do occur within the United States;
- Carry out all functions of entities transferred to the Department, including by acting as a focal point regarding natural and manmade crises and emergency planning;
- Ensure that the functions of the agencies and subdivisions within the Department that are not

related directly to securing the homeland are not diminished or neglected except by a specific, explicit Act of Congress;
- Ensure that the overall economic security of the United States is not diminished by efforts, activities, and programs aimed at securing the homeland; and
- Monitor connections between illegal drug trafficking and terrorism, coordinate efforts to sever such connections, and otherwise contribute to efforts to interdict illegal drug trafficking.[13]

The President's *National Strategy for Homeland Security*[14] and the Homeland Security Act[15] demonstrate that the overriding goal in homeland security is to prevent and respond to terrorism, without actually defining the term. The Federal Bureau of Investigation (FBI) defines terrorism as "the unlawful use of force or violence against persons or property to intimidate or coerce a government, the civilian population, or any segment thereof, in furtherance of political or social objectives."[16] This definition, while helpful in focusing attention on the elements of terrorism, is not legally binding, as it has never been enacted into statute or regulation or adopted by court decision.

Even prior to September 11, the FBI separated terrorism into two types: domestic and international. The FBI defines domestic terrorism as involving "groups or individuals whose terrorist activities are directed at elements of our government or population without foreign direction."[17] Examples of domestic terrorism include the 1995 bombing of the Murrah Federal Building in downtown Oklahoma City, OK, allegedly by U.S. citizens. Before September 11, the Oklahoma City bombing was the most deadly terrorist attack on U.S. soil, killing 169 men, women, and children.[18]

According to the FBI, international terrorism involves "groups or individuals whose terrorist activities are foreign-based and/or directed by countries or groups outside the United States or whose activities transcend national boundaries."[19] The terrorist attacks of September 11 and the 2000 bombing of the Navy destroyer USS *Cole* in the Yemeni port of Aden are examples of international terrorism.[20] The FBI defines a "terrorist act" as an attack against a single target (e.g., a building or physical structure, an aircraft, etc.), whereas the term "terrorist incident" is used to describe the overall concerted terrorist attack.[21] A terrorist incident may consist of multiple terrorist acts.

The FBI definitions have since been augmented and codified in the U.S. Code. Now, the term "international terrorism" means activities that:

(A) involve violent acts or acts dangerous to human life that are a violation of the criminal laws of the United States or of any State, or that would be a criminal violation if committed within the jurisdiction of the United States or of any State;

(B) appear to be intended—
  (i) to intimidate or coerce a civilian population;
  (ii) to influence the policy of a government by intimidation or coercion; or
  (iii) to affect the conduct of a government by mass destruction, assassination, or kidnapping; and

(C) occur primarily outside the territorial jurisdiction of the United States, or transcend national boundaries in terms of the means by which they are accomplished, the persons they appear intended to intimidate or coerce, or the locale in which their perpetrators operate or seek asylum;

The term "domestic terrorism" means activities that:

(A) involve acts dangerous to human life that are a violation of the criminal laws of the United States or of any State;

(B) appear to be intended—
  (i) to intimidate or coerce a civilian population;
  (ii) to influence the policy of a government by intimidation or coercion; or
  (iii) to affect the conduct of a government by mass destruction, assassination or kidnapping; and

(C) occur primarily within the territorial jurisdiction of the United States.[22]

These definitions are reflected in parts of the USA PATRIOT Act,[23] the Homeland Security Act,[24] and the Department of the Treasury definitions of terrorism.[25] Each piece of legislation defines terrorism, in short, as a violent or dangerous act intended to intimidate or coerce a civilian population, to influence the policy of a government by intimidation or coercion, or to affect the conduct of a government by mass destruction, assassination, kidnapping, or hostage-taking. The evolution of this language reveals that a consensus among federal agencies has come about only in recent years.

II. STATE RESPONSES

Some states encountered terrorism prior to September 11 and were home to state emergency management offices. Few, however, had sought to define homeland security or terrorism until after September 11. In the aftermath of the attacks, very few states created their own definitions of the term homeland security, although many have enacted legislation that adopted the federal definition (18 states) or their own meaning for terrorism.

Only two states have adopted definitions of homeland security: Alabama and Washington. The Alabama Homeland Security Act of 2003 defines homeland security as "the development,

coordination, and implementation of a state policy to secure the State of Alabama from terrorist threat or attack. The term includes efforts to detect, prepare for, prevent, protect against, share intelligence where applicable, respond to, and recover from terrorist attacks within the State of Alabama."[26] In its Statewide Homeland Security Strategic Plan, Washington cites the *National Strategy for Homeland Security*[27] and adds its own spin on homeland security:

The preparation for, prevention of, deterrence of, preemption of, defense against, and response to threats and aggressions directed towards U.S. territory, sovereignty, domestic populations, and infrastructure; as well as crisis management, consequence management, and other domestic civil support.[28]

Alabama and Washington employ different terminology in their definitions, but there is consensus as to what homeland security involves: preparation for, prevention of, protection against, response to, and recovery from threats of terrorism and terrorist acts. While Alabama and Washington are the only states to have memorialized their notions of homeland security, all states have formally recognized the threat to the homeland, with each state creating a homeland security office or commission to address terrorism-related threats.[29]

As stated earlier, eighteen states have adopted the federal definition of terrorism.[30] The remaining states have adopted some notion of terrorism as acts intended to intimidate, coerce, influence, and affect the civilian population or the government, as described in 18 U.S.C. § 2331.[31] Some states, such as California, have gone no further in their definitions, favoring broad language. California defines terrorism as "any unlawful harm, attempted harm, or threat to do harm to, any state employee, state property, or the person or property of any person on the premises of any state-occupied building or other property leased or owned by the state."[32]

In contrast, Washington, D.C., takes a narrow approach, specifying those acts that "intimidate" or "coerce" civilians or the government. The broadness of the intimidation language is troubling. The nonviolent protests of the Civil Rights movement of the 1960s would fall within its ambit. Had this law been in effect during that period, our nation might conceivably still be bearing the burden of segregation and Jim Crow laws that limited the opportunities and contributions of many of our citizens. The District of Columbia also includes murder in the first degree; placing obstructions upon or displacement of railroads; murder of law enforcement officer or public safety employee; murder in the second degree; manslaughter; kidnapping and conspiracy to kidnap; assault with intent to kill only; mayhem or maliciously disfiguring; arson; malicious burning, destruction, or injury of another's property, if the property is valued at $500,000 or more; or an attempt or conspiracy to commit any of the [above] offenses.[33]

Illinois goes a step further in its definition of terrorism, including an act that "disables or destroys the usefulness or operation of any communications system . . . ," or one that "disables or destroys the usefulness or operation of a computer network. . . ."[34] Other acts of terrorism defined in the Illinois statute include those intended to damage ground, air, or water transportation; the production or distribution of electricity, gas, oil, or other fuel; the treatment of sewage or the treatment or distribution of water; or controlling the flow of any body of water, among others.[35] Nebraska, like California, has taken a broader approach to its definition:

A person commits terroristic threats if he or she threatens to commit any crime of violence: (a) With the intent to terrorize another; (b) With the intent of causing the evacuation of a building, place of assembly, or facility of public transportation; or (c) In reckless disregard of the risk of causing such terror or evacuation.[36]

What each state holds in common is it recognition that terrorism, however defined, is a threat for which the civilian populations and state governments must prepare. As stated in Washington's Statewide Homeland Security Strategic Plan, "terrorist organizations remain committed to death and destruction within our borders. . . . Only by concerted action can we reduce our vulnerabilities and defend against further domestic attacks."[37]

III. CONCLUSION

At its essence, homeland security means protecting our way of life against those who threaten it, or wish to destroy it. While the United States is a nation that has always fought to defend the homeland and preserve our way of life against such threats, the threat of terrorism is redefining the environment in which we must respond. By defining homeland security and terrorism, we are taking steps to identify the threat and defeat it, rather than allowing the terms to delineate themselves through further, perhaps ever more damaging, examples of killing and destruction of property.

ENDNOTES

1. Homeland Security Act, Public Law 107-296, H.R. 5005, Sec. 2, 2002.
2. "Antiterrorism and Effective Death Penalty Act of 1996," 18 USC § 2332b, P-L 104-132 (2004).
3. Jenkins, Brian Michael, "Perspectives on Terrorism: Where I draw the line," *Christian Science Monitor*, www.csmonitor.com, 2004.
4. *Jacobellis v. Ohio*, 378 U.S. 184 (1964).
5. Http://usinfo.state.gov/topical/pol/terror/ataglance1.htm
6. U.S. CONST. art. I, _ 8, cl. 15.
7. Garamone, Jim, "A Short History of Homeland Defense," American Forces Press Service, http://www.defenselink.mil/news/Oct2001/n10252001_200110252.html, 10/25/01.
8. *Id.*
9. *Id.*
10. *Id.*
11. *Id.*
12. *National Strategy for Homeland Security*, Office of Homeland Security, The White House, July 2002, *Introduction*, Page 2, http://www.whitehouse.gov/homeland/book/nat_strat_hls.pdf
13. Homeland Security Act, Public Law 107-296, H.R. 5005, §2, 2002.
14. *National Strategy for Homeland Security*, Office of Homeland Security, The White House, July 2002, *Introduction*, Page 2, http://www.whitehouse.gov/homeland/book/nat_strat_hls.pdf
15. Homeland Security Act, Public Law 107-296, H.R. 5005, Sec. 2, 2002.
16. Federal Bureau of Investigation, "Terrorism in the United States: 1999," http://www.fbi.gov/publications/terror/terror99.pdf, 1999.
17. Http://www.fema.gov/hazards/terrorism/terror.shtm
18. Http://www.cnn.com/US/OKC/bombing.html
19. Http://www.fema.gov/hazards/terrorism/terror.shtm
20. Http://usinfo.state.gov/topical/pol/terror/00101204.htm
21. Http://www.usdoj.gov/ag/annualreports/pr2002/pdf/Section01.pdf
22. 18 U.S.C. § 2331 (2004).
23. Uniting and Strengthening America by Providing Appropriate Tools Required to Intercept and Obstruct Terrorism (USA PATRIOT) Act of 2001, H.R. 3162, Sec. 802.
24. Homeland Security Act of 2002, Public Law 107-296, H.R. 5005, Sec. 2.
25. 31 C.F.R. § 595-97 (2004), Executive Order 13224 - "Blocking Property and Prohibiting Transactions with Persons Who Commit, Threaten to Commit, or Support Terrorism" (Department of the Treasury).
26. Alabama Homeland Security Act of 2003, ALA. CODE § 31-9A-3 (2003).
27. *National Strategy for Homeland Security*, Office of Homeland Security, The White House, July 2002, *Introduction*, Page 2, http://www.whitehouse.gov/homeland/book/nat_strat_hls.pdf
28. "The Washington Statewide Homeland Security Strategic Plan," http://emd.wa.gov/3-map/a-p/hlssp/wa-st-hlssp-04.pdf, p. 71 (2004).
29. National Conference of State Legislatures, "State Offices of Homeland Security," http://www.ncsl.org/programs/legman/nlssa/sthomelandoffcs.htm, accessed 05/19/04.
30. 18 U.S.C. § 2331 (2004).
31. "Domestic terrorism" means activities that (A) involve acts dangerous to human life that are a violation of the criminal laws of the United States or of any State; (B) appear to be intended (i) to intimidate or coerce a civilian population; (ii) to influence the policy of a government by intimidation or coercion; or (iii) to affect the conduct of a government by mass destruction, assassination, or kidnapping; and (C) occur primarily within the territorial jurisdiction of the United States.
32. CAL. GOV'T CODE § 8549.2 (2004).
33. D.C. CODE ANN. § 22-3152 (2003).
34. 720 ILL. COMP. STAT. 5/29D-10 (2004).
35. *Id.*
36. NEB. REV. STAT. § 28-311.01 (2003).
37. "The Washington Statewide Homeland Security Strategic Plan," http://emd.wa.gov/3-map/a-p/hlssp/wa-st-hlssp-04.pdf, Executive Summary, p. 3 (2004).

PART 2: DEFINING "HOMELAND SECURITY": CONTENT AND CONTEXT GROUNDED IN THE CURRICULA

ROBERT W. SMITH

The purpose of this chapter is to develop a definition of homeland security based on the content and context of a purposeful sample of graduate and undergraduate courses ranging from emergency management, preparedness and planning, to terrorism and disaster response, to homeland security and national security at selected four-year colleges and universities in the United States.[1] The reasons for this exploratory study stem from definitional questions raised by both practitioners and academics about a) the variety of course descriptions and treatments of homeland security; b) the quandary posed by this definitional imprecision; and c) possible implications of this ambiguity for the substantive curriculum in the respective disciplines.[2]

This chapter is not meant to be an exhaustive study that catalogs all courses on homeland security nor will it be an exhaustive synthesis of all syllabi in the field. Instead this chapter establishes a framework for guiding future research in the field by establishing a conceptual definition grounded by what is being taught in homeland security courses.

I. BASIS FOR THE ANALYSIS

To begin this type of grounded analysis, it is important to offer some a priori observations about the genre of courses that teach, treat, or evaluate homeland security:

1. There has been a widespread recognition of courses that treat homeland security as a major theme (many begun as a response to the terrorist events of September 11, 2001);
2. The content of these courses are only loosely coupled under the term homeland security; and
3. Many of these courses have either been newly added to the curriculum, or have long been offered as part of a specialized knowledge base but without any substantive contribution to defining homeland security.

In some respects, even the articulation of these a priori observations may encourage practitioners and academicians to move beyond a rather instrumental definition and toward development of a fuller conceptual definition of homeland security. These a priori observations lead to a general research question posited in this chapter: What is homeland security?

Note: Robert W. Smith is the Director of the Master of Public Administration program at Clemson University. He received his M.P.A. and Ph.D. in Public Administration from the University at Albany (SUNY). He was a former senior budget official for the New York State Division of the Budget (12 years) and former Regional Director for U.S. Senator Daniel Patrick Moynihan. He has numerous publications and has performed research in the areas of public budgeting and administrative ethics.

II. HOMELAND SECURITY AS DEFINED IN THE LITERATURE

The coverage of the Congressional response to the terrorist attacks of September 11, 2001, reveals an early struggle with what would constitute homeland security.[3] It was clear that Congress and the federal government were poised to take action as part of a comprehensive counterterrorism effort. The use of the term counterterrorism seems the closest to capture the intent of early efforts to both investigate and respond to domestic terrorism in the United States. However, news accounts in the period reveal a much broader context for the effort beyond counterterrorism. The ensuing discussions revolved around institutional capabilities and the organizational and interjurisdictional issues that would result in a comprehensive strategy to make sure a catastrophic attack like that of September 11 would not occur again.

In the most lucid account of the chronology and evolution of the term, Kelly points out the evolutionary nature of homeland security.[4] One of the more public pronouncements of homeland security can be traced to President Bush's Executive Order 13228 in 2001, which created the Office of Homeland Security.[5] That definition identifies ". . . the mission of homeland security as implementation of a comprehensive national strategy to secure the U.S. from terrorist threats or attacks."[6] Kelly outlines how National Security Strategies from 1996 through 2000 under President Clinton included concepts such as counterterrorism, drug trafficking, organized crime, and environmental and security concerns.[7] However, it was under the *National Security Strategy* in 2000 that identified "emerging threats to our homeland. . . ."[8]

The U.S. Army on a separate track issued a white paper entitled *Supporting Homeland Defense* and offered a definition of ". . . protecting our territory, population and critical infrastructure at home by deterring and defending against foreign and domestic threats, supporting civil authorities for crisis and consequence management and helping . . . to ensure the survivalbility . . . of national assets."[9] This definition was more inclusive and called for infrastructure protection and overlapping responsibilities of jurisdictions (both civilian and military) for coordinating homeland security.

It has been acknowledged that it was U.S. Deputy Secretary of Defense John Hamre who used the term homeland security for the first time–interchangeable with homeland defense.[10] The U.S. Army in turn published the *Army Homeland Security Strategic Planning Guidance Document.* A new definition was offered as "those active and passive measures taken to protect the population, area and infrastructure of the United States, its possessions, and territories by deterring, defending against, and mitigating the effects of threats, disasters, and attacks; supporting civil authorities in crisis and consequence management; and helping ensure the availability, survivability, and adequacy of critical national assets."[11]

This definition focused on two distinct orientations: homeland defense and domestic support. These orientations are reflected in the Joint Chiefs of Staff definition of homeland security as follows: "The preparation for, prevention of, deterrence of, preemption of, defense against, and response to threats and aggressions directed toward U.S. territory, sovereignty, domestic population, and infrastructure; as well as crisis management, consequence management and other domestic civil support."[12] It is clear that this definition also includes a managerial dimension that casts homeland security as part and parcel of broader emergency management and preparedness efforts.

Although these definitions have a tradition in either a military or emergency management context, more recent iterations of the meaning of homeland security clearly show the problematic nature of defining the term. In July 2002, the *National Strategy for Homeland Security* revolved around three elements: a national effort to prevent terrorist attacks in the United States; a reduction in U.S. vulnerability to terrorism; and a minimization of damage and then recovery from attacks that do occur.[13] At some levels this is a telling evolution because the definition implies a coordinated (and intergovernmental) national effort to address homeland security, a recognition that risk and vulnerability assessment are crucial components, and that it is unlikely the efforts will stop all forms of terrorism.

What this recent definition implies is that the federal government takes the lead in intelligence and warning systems, border security, traditional counterterrorism efforts, infrastructure protection, disaster management, and emergency response but with the support of state and local jurisdictions. In addition, the definition embraces risk assessment, concern for individual liberty, priority of national safeguards, attention to all program areas that improve security, an emphasis on budgetary resources, a focus on performance, and mission and organizational responsibilities. What this means is that the evolution of a definition has come full circle to become devolution where it is almost impossible to precisely define homeland security without including all the possible components. Therefore, how can practitioners train and academics teach such courses?

III. HOMELAND SECURITY IN THE CLASSROOM

It also is instructive to provide some brief background on the evolution of such courses as part of the curricula examined in this chapter. Teaching about terrorism or emergency management is certainly not new. Indeed, specialized courses have been offered over the years.[14] However, the content of such classes has been largely in terms of understanding terrorism as a phenomenon, how and why terrorists operate, or technical aspects related to terrorist planning and implementation.

Because the United States is geographically separated from the international community by both the Atlantic and Pacific oceans, Americans have long believed themselves to be set apart from the repercussions of international terror. Not until September 11, 2001, when international terrorists flew hijacked commercial aircraft into the World Trade Center and the Pentagon, did the American public realize the importance of homeland security and the imminence of its implementation. Before this point in time, homeland security was not a recognized term from either an instrumental or conceptual viewpoint.

Yet, as of June 2002, a CBS News Poll indicated that 70 percent of Americans were in support of the creation of a Homeland Security Department, and 66 percent responded that such an agency would increase the strength of the fight on terrorism.[15] Anecdotal evidence suggests that this positive assessment was rendered despite a general lack of knowledge about what homeland security really meant.

The resulting consolidation of twenty-two separate federal domestic agencies into the Department of Homeland Security (DHS) in 2003 demonstrated the U.S. government's resolve to invigorate and maintain a strong defense to ward off future domestic terrorist crises. With such dramatic government reorganization, it was clear that homeland security was elevated to the top of the public policy agenda in the United States. But, it is again interesting to note that there was little coverage and consideration given to what was actually meant by homeland security.

At the same time, government agencies responsible for homeland security and academic institutions now had to confront how best to deliver homeland security services and prepare current and future administrators for their duties and roles in homeland security agencies.[16] Aside from technical training to emergency management, health officials, law enforcement and military or National Guard personnel, typically offered as emergency management or disaster preparedness training, there has been little guidance available for what a curriculum in homeland security and related programs should look like. Yet, as an emerging national priority, homeland security education and training for leaders, public officials, and citizens has also been elevated in priority.[17]

Although courses focusing on the narrow theme of homeland security were not in abundance until after September 11, 2001, courses on terrorism as a political or sociological phenomenon have been offered for many years.[18] Similarly, emergency management courses have also been offered, although the scope of these courses have markedly changed in the last few years to focus not only on traditional EMS topics (e.g., earthquake or tornado response), but also on the response to biological and chemical weapons attacks and emergencies resulting from terrorist activities within U.S. domestic borders.

Homeland security may not have been a specialization in the curriculum in the past because there was not a standard body of knowledge on which instructors could readily base a curriculum. More to the point, the Federal Emergency Management Agency (FEMA) only recently added a prototype course in emergency management with a focus on homeland security.[19] In addition, many instructors themselves did not have the requisite expertise to teach the full range of topical coverage now required in these classes. One notable exception may be intelligence, emergency response, or counterterrorism experts teaching courses as visiting or adjunct instructors, or as guest lecturers addressing the threat of domestic terrorism as part of another course (e.g., national security, global terrorism, etc.). However, definitional issues remained. Were these courses emergency management courses with a module on homeland security or were these terrorism courses now cast as homeland security courses?

Prior to the creation of the Department of Homeland Security, few homeland security courses were offered in colleges or universities. The establishment and organization of DHS has provided an institutional impetus and a framework for developing a homeland security curriculum (including counterterrorism), extended emergency management response, intelligence gathering, border and airport protection, and disaster assistance. At the governmental level, early experience with homeland security technical education and training was largely decentralized to the many federal agencies responsible for some aspect of homeland security. An ever-increasing number of consulting firms now offer specialized training or courses in homeland security to fill the gap.[20]

Given the imprecise or multifaceted nature of the definition of homeland security, the varied approaches employed to teach homeland security, and the fact that there has not been much in the way of scholarly or pedagogical examination of such courses, this chapter seeks to fill a gap in our understanding of what is being taught in homeland security courses. In order to answer this research question, available course syllabi were reviewed for topical coverage, the stated objectives and goals of the course, and the actual definitions of homeland security. Developing a conceptual definition of homeland security as grounded in the actual syllabi used to teach such courses is an important first step toward answering the research question.

IV. SAMPLING THE SYLLABI

The research design employed in this chapter involved a three-tiered strategy. The first approach was to initiate a random Web-based survey of courses bearing the title (search term) "Homeland Security," followed by a more purposeful sample of courses listed on the FEMA Website."[21] The unit of analysis for the study was course syllabi. Initially, the search was directed to identify specific graduate-level homeland security courses regardless of discipline. To maximize the sample size, yet another sampling iteration included other courses that were offered at the undergraduate and graduate levels. After recognizing that this sample would yield a limited number of courses, the search was expanded to include courses where homeland security was a substantive topic but the course title did not necessarily contain the term homeland security.

This purposeful sampling logic facilitated identification of the largest possible number of homeland security courses pertinent for developing a conceptual definition. The rationale for purposeful sampling is the gathering of information in an effort to determine the characteristics of a population (in this case the syllabi). Patton provides a more detailed explanation of the logic of purposeful sampling.[22] After the initial round of random sampling, purposeful sampling was utilized, driven by the a priori theory to guide the subsequent data gathering.[23] When dealing with a potentially new genre of courses on homeland security, syllabi were added to the sample after initial sampling pointed to key terms, topics, or definitions that led to a further refinement of the sample and courses germane to the study of homeland security.

From a starting sample size of approximately 100 course syllabi that fit this sampling logic, the courses were sorted according to the following typology:

I. Courses Entitled as or Specific to Homeland Security
II. Courses as an Extension of Emergency Management (inclusive of disaster preparedness)
III. Military-Oriented Courses
IV. Homeland Security Treated in Terrorism or National Security Courses
V. Technical/Professional Courses

After sorting the syllabi at this level, there were fifty-seven courses that were included in the next stage of analysis. See Table 1.1 for a table of the sampled courses used to determine a definition of homeland security.

Table 1.1
SAMPLING OF COURSES CURRENTLY OFFERED AT THE UNIVERSITY LEVEL

Sample Course by College or University	Course Name	Content Analysis Focus
I. Homeland Security Courses		
University of Delaware	Homeland Security Law and Policy	Terrorism, evolving legal standards, foreign policy implications, nature of Islam, structure at local-state-federal levels
Regent University	Protecting the Homeland: Terrorism Threats and National Security	National security, terrorism
Tufts University	Proliferation/Counter proliferation and Homeland Security	National security, weapons proliferation
University of Arizona	Governance and Security and the Response to Terrorism	Terrorism, law, and organization
University of Central Oklahoma	Homeland Security	Terrorism and mobilization
Virginia Tech	Design, Implementation, and Evaluation of Homeland Security	Evaluation and implementation
Georgetown University	U.S. Homeland Security	Terrorism, counterterrorism, history, law, organization
II. Emergency Management and Preparedness Courses		
CalState–Bakersfield	Emergency Management and Homeland Security	EMS
Santa Monica College	Emergency Management of Terrorism	EMS, law enforcement, contingency planning, terrorism
Cal State–Fullerton	Emergency Management	EMS, preparedness, mitigation, recovery
University of North Texas	Terrorism and Emergency Management	Counterterrorism, terrorism, EMS
Arizona State University	Terrorism, WMD, and Contemporary Issues	Disaster management, terrorism, WMD

Table 1.1 (*Continued*)

Sample Course by College or University	Course Name	Content Analysis Focus
III. Military-Oriented Courses		
National War College	Homeland Security	Asymmetric warfare, terrorism, counterterrorism, law, consequence management
Air War College	Homeland Security: Protect, Prevent, and Recover	Risk assessment, intelligence, national security
IV. Terrorism and National Security Courses		
Troy State University	National Security Policy	National security policy, terrorism, mass destruction, asymmetric warfare
Villanova University	National Security Policy	National security, terrorism
Harvard University	American National Security Policy	National security, terrorism, WMD, peacekeeping
V. Technical/Specialized Courses		
Widener University School of Law	Terrorism and Emergency Law Seminar	Emergency response, emergency management, terrorism, civil liberties
Southern Methodist University	Homeland Security Seminar	Terrorism, attack, assessment, and abatement
John Jay College: City University of New York	Terrorism Seminar	Terrorism, counterterrorism, immigration
Indiana University School of Law	Seminar in International Law: Homeland Security	Legal foundations, civil liberties
Princeton University	Terrorism and Homeland Security	Terrorism, organizational response

V. A GROUNDED THEORY APPROACH: WHAT THE COURSES TELL US

The second stage of analysis used a grounded theory paradigm, applying a content analysis technique to the descriptions of the course, topical/unit coverage, and the use of terminology in the syllabi.[24] The purpose of content analysis was to identify key phrases and descriptors using an open coding scheme that describes the phenomenon being studied. In this case, open coding identified terms, concepts, and threads in the syllabi related to homeland security. The next step of axial coding further refines these descriptors and starts to assemble the data into groups of similar concepts that form broader categories (of courses) that can be further evaluated. Finally, key conceptual labels emerge from the analysis. They are used to

systematically describe the phenomena being studied. The third column of Table 1.2 reflects the construction of core conceptual labels revealed in the axial coding stage. In the open coding stage, there were 33 terms that emerged from the syllabi as significant topical coverage in the courses. Axial coding identified 12 key concepts that serve as the basis for constructing core categories to help understand the homeland security curriculum and pedagogy. See Table 1.2 for a tabular presentation of the content analysis of topical course coverage and description of homeland security. The third and final stage of the analysis was to assign conceptual labels that could be linked to a definition of homeland security derived from the syllabi.

Table 1.2
SUBJECTS ADDRESSED IN UNIVERSITY LEVEL COURSES

Open Coding	<20	20<	Axial Coding	Core Categories for Definition
Federalism	X			
State Coercion		X		
Civil Society		X	Impact on Society	*
Legal Constraints		X	Legal Environment	*
Organization Theory		X	Organizational Roles	*
Contingency Planning	X		Planning	*
Budget Processes		X		
Organizational Analysis DHS		X	Agency Focus DHS	*
Consequence Management	X			
Civil Liberties		X	Civil Liberty v. Security	
Legislation: The USA PATRIOT Act		X		
Policy Theory		X	Policy Implications	*
Policy Design		X		
Catastrophic Threat	X			
First Responders	X			
Infrastructure Protection	X		Protection of Assets	*
Emergency Management	X			
Sociology of Disasters		X		
Emergency Preparedness	X		Emergency Response	*
Border/Port Control		X		
Counterterrorism		X	Response to Terrorism	*
Asymmetric Warfare	X			
WMD	X			
Cyber Attack	X			
Intelligence Activities		X	Significance of Intelligence Activity	
Deterrence Theory	X			
Terrorism	X		Understanding Terrorism	
Risk Assessment	X		Calculating Risk	*
Vulnerability Assessment	X			
Security Policy		X	Overall Security Policy	*
Military Response	X		Military Role	*
Rogue States		X		
Law Enforcement Role		X		

VI. CATALOGING THE COURSES

Courses offered under the moniker of homeland security since 2002 have fallen primarily into the following categories:

A. Homeland Security Courses

Today's homeland security courses focus not only on threats of domestic terrorism in the United States, but they also encompass other topics beyond terrorism. Many curricula include discussion concerning the controversy surrounding the creation of DHS, as well as the organization of the department and the implications of its considered in many of these courses. These courses incorporate a variety of themes and concepts to define homeland security: the study of terrorism and counterterrorism efforts, the emergency response to terrorist activities/events, preparedness and mitigation of disasters, risk assessment of terrorist threats, law enforcement response and planning, monitoring, and detection of terrorist threats, legal constraints and framework for addressing terrorism, and national state and local and international coordination.

B. Emergency Management or Preparedness

As previously noted, although emergency management courses have been offered for some time, they have been reinvented to focus on a wider variety of topics. Emergency management courses are making the transition from traditional topics in EMS to teaching first responders to an emergency scene to handle biological, chemical, and nuclear weapons attacks and emergencies. Courses also cover terrorism as technique and process. As a result, many homeland security courses still function as emergency management courses. These courses incorporate a variety of themes and concepts to define homeland security including: mutual aid and co-lateral support, HAZMAT incident management, contingency plan coordination, critical infrastructure preparedness, GIS and simulation applications, crisis communications, business and industry interface, vulnerability assessment and risk analysis, resources allocations, nature of terrorism, medical response, regulatory environment, organizational and legal analysis, and emergency preparedness paradigms.

C. Military-Oriented Courses

Military institutions have placed a premium on the importance of teaching national security and terrorism courses in the past. With the creation of DHS and more imminent domestic threats, however, these courses have shifted their focus to include the bureaucratic and organizational issues of the DHS and the mobilization of defense capabilities. This emphasis is demonstrated by the creation of a first of a kind master's degree program in homeland security offered by the Naval Postgraduate School in 2003.[25] These courses incorporate a variety of themes and concepts to define homeland security including: the study of terrorism, asymmetric warfare, consequence management, detection of threats, proliferation of nuclear and biological weapons, electronic surveillance and other intelligence capabilities, the USA PATRIOT Act and legal parameters, border/port control and trade issues, Department of Homeland Security, public health system response, critical infrastructure assets, and domestic use of military NORTHCOM (Northern Military Command charged with homeland security) responsibilities.

D. Terrorism and National Security Courses

Of the more long-standing courses that have been around in a variety of programs, there have been courses exploring terrorism or courses on national security policy. Although these courses are much broader in scope than just homeland security, they are more on the forefront of addressing homeland security as a response to growing domestic terror events and articulation of a national policy. These courses treat the topic of homeland security and include: history of terrorism, weapons of mass destruction, military contingencies, risk assessments, concept of vital security, security politics, decision making, rogue states, asymmetric warfare, interventionalism, noncombatants, death squads, dissident groups, terrorism as a political method, covert action, state terrorism, suicide bombings, state-sponsored terrorism, ethnic and religious terrorism, counterterrorism, and legal framework of response.

E. Technical or Specialized Courses

Seminars relating to the increased threats to homeland security have also been implemented at many institutions of higher education and may or may not be credit-bearing courses. Many seminars employ speakers from the highest levels of government to provide participants with comprehensive, up-to-date information relating to homeland security. Another type of course is more specialized where one component of homeland security is examined (e.g., weapons of mass destruction, risk assessment and homeland security, Islamic terrorists, etc.). While many seminars are targeted to traditional students, others are organized for practitioners or analysts to ensure the understanding of homeland security. Typical definitions of homeland security in these types of seminars range from descriptors of: domestic versus international terrorism, the culture of terrorism, profiling terrorists, economic impact of terrorism, building security and management, airport security, community emergency response teams, legal issues, civil liberties, crime scene management, incident preparedness, personal protective equipment, decontamination procedures, and mass fatalities incidents.

VII. SORTING THROUGH DEFINITIONS

First, it is clear that homeland security courses play a variety of roles in the curriculum. One genre of courses is taught as specific homeland security courses where the subject is treated in a focused fashion with an orientation toward counterterrorism. Homeland security is also taught as part of emergency management or preparedness courses where it is treated as another type of disaster or emergency situation. As such, these courses cast homeland security in the broader context of planning, and incident management tailored to terrorist-type emergencies. Another group of courses in homeland security are long-established courses in such traditional formats as terrorism or national security-type courses. However, this necessarily prevents a fuller treatment of the more specialized knowledge areas that comprise homeland security.

Other courses, mostly taught in military academies or security institutes, focus the curriculum on national security, risk assessment, and the military response to terrorist threats. Finally, there is a genre of courses that can be considered special courses or seminars on homeland security. These courses typically are issue-focused (be that civil liberties or incident-related) and do not necessarily offer a comprehensive treatment of homeland security. By their very nature they are "short" courses and convey a limited set of specialized knowledge (e.g., first responder protocol).

The actual content analysis performed on the syllabi reveals that despite the descriptor of "homeland security," many courses still retain a familiar focus on core functions in public affairs. Even a cursory review of the content terms presented in Table 1.2 suggest that concepts of federalism, civil liberties, the legal imperative, organization theory, policy design, and the budget processes speak to the treatment of homeland security as requiring a much broader field of knowledge.

Somewhat surprising was the absence of some of the more technical topics (e.g., weapons of mass destruction, intelligence activity, etc.) that might be expected to play more of a role in courses on homeland security. The first responder, disaster, and incident management focus of some homeland security courses solidly grounds the course as an emergency management course, but subsumes the treatment of homeland security.

Therefore, content analysis of a purposeful sample of homeland security courses reveals numerous concepts, threads, and topics that make it difficult to accurately construct one inclusive definition of homeland security. This quandary poses real implications for the knowledge base imparted in these courses. The very real issue for instructors of homeland security concerns what core competencies must be included in the standard curriculum.

In many respects homeland security is no different from any other course in political science or public administration. Indeed, there are many ways to teach Introduction to American Politics, but there is probably some agreement on the coverage of the Constitution, and institutions of government. Similarly, in public administration it is probably fair to say that an organization theory class can be taught any number of ways, yet there should be a common thread tied to the orthodoxy of theorists, human relations school, and others. The point is simply that the quandary over clarity of definition imposes some real constraints on development of a broader curriculum and an understanding of what these courses should convey in terms of knowledge and training.

This definitional quandary is nowhere better evidenced than in the Congressional Budget Office's (CBO) 2004 Executive Budget Brief attempting to explain funding for homeland security in 2004. Essentially the CBO has used three types of definitions for describing activities and programs receiving funds as homeland security. The standard definition is stated as "a concerted national effort to prevent terrorist attacks within the United States, reduce America's vulnerability to terrorism, and minimize the damage and recover from attacks."[26] At the same time, the CBO makes distinctions in defining international versus domestic terror activities. They also include some military activities and include emergency preparedness and response as part of their definition.

The Department of Homeland Security itself identifies what constitutes homeland security through six distinct mission areas.[27] The six areas are intelligence and warning, border and transportation security, domestic counterterrorism, protection of infrastructure, defense against catastrophic threat, and emergency preparedness and response. The DHS provides a useful template for developing a conceptual definition from the course syllabi examined in this study.

VIII. CONCLUDING POINTS

There are two distinct observations that can be made about the courses included in this abbreviated study. First, there are numerous courses offered on homeland security but there is very little agreement about what constitutes homeland security as a curriculum. Some 61 areas of topical coverage or course focus are identified in the 57 syllabi included in this study. The range of topics mined from the syllabi suggests that there is little agreement on a definition for homeland security but also speaks to a broader issue of what the substantive content of such courses should be. Standardization of course content may or may not be desirable. Just like many courses there is certainly more than one way to teach a class.

Second, the content of the syllabi is not exclusive to one primary field; instead topical coverage (e.g., federalism or civil liberties) seems to be heavily grounded in a variety of disciplines. At some levels this may suggest an interdisciplinary focus for many courses on homeland security.

IX. SYNTHESIZING A DEFINITION

Because of the exploratory nature of this research and the purposeful sample employed, it is difficult to draw any definitive conclusions from this chapter. However, it seems appropriate to discuss some implications of this study for the future of homeland security courses and to offer a definition gleaned from the curricula to guide further research.

With respect to directions for future research, this study should be replicated more systematically and with a broader and more rigorous sampling strategy. Casting a broader net that would examine all courses offered on homeland security would be instructive. Possible alternate methodologies could include mailing questionnaires to randomly selected schools to inquire about homeland security courses. It is hoped that this research will start a discussion in the broader public affairs community about the role of homeland security courses given the illusive nature of the topical coverage delivered through these courses.

However, there is sufficient data in this sample of courses to construct a conceptual definition of homeland security. This definition is derived from an analysis of the content terms extracted from the syllabi in a traditional grounded theory analysis. The terms (see Table 1.2) are assembled into a key statement or definition of what the data tell the researcher. The syllabi suggest that **homeland security is a system of emergency preparedness that requires military and civilian response to perceived, potential, or imminent terrorist threats against U.S. citizens and interests at home**. At many levels this definition is not earth-shattering, but it does capture the inherent nature of homeland security as a discipline or area of study closely aligned with emergency management. Moreover, this definition recognizes the interface between military and civilian authorities and places the appropriate emphasis on recognition

of the terrorist-driven nature of homeland security. If these component statements are accurate or obvious, it is still not clear that this is what is being taught under the rubric of homeland security.

It is clear there is a demand for these courses, but the demand outpaces the recognition of agreement over what should be taught in these classes. This chapter offers a ground floor or baseline to begin this debate. Any future debate or research should help improve on the delivery of these courses and better integrate or link homeland security to the overall curricula. In the absence of this work, and a more precise definition of homeland security, the question about what we are really teaching in such courses remains unanswered.

ENDNOTES

1. The initial sample was directed at courses offered through MPA/MPS programs. Because numbers were small, the sample was expanded to include graduate and undergraduate offerings in related disciplines.
2. See Kelly Gyenes, "Rhetorics of Terrorism, Homeland Security at Richmond." December 19, 2003. <http://www.cnn.com/2003/ALLPOLITICS/12/18/elec04.richmond/>. See also Jessie Seyfer, "School offers training for 'homeland security' jobs." January 13, 2003. <http://www.mercurynews.com/mld/mercurynews/news/local/4934708.htm>. See also Eric Kelderman, "College programs follow the money." August 8, 2003. <http://www.gazette.net/200332/weekend/a_section/172253-1.html>.
3. McCutcheon, Chuck. "Defining Homeland Security," *CQ Weekly*, September 29, 2001, at (http://library2.cqpress.com/cqweekly/document.php?id.)
4. Kelly, Patrick. 2002. "Defining Homeland Security." *Military Intelligence Professional Bulletin*, 28(3): 10–15.
5. Executive Order 13228 of October 8, 2001, *Establishing the Office of Homeland Security and the Homeland Security Council.*
6. Executive Order 13228 (2001).
7. Kelly (2002).
8. United States Department of the Army. 2000. *Army Homeland Security Strategic Planning Guidance.* Washington, DC: U.S. Department of the Army.
9. United States Department of the Army, 1999. *Army Homeland Security Strategic Planning Guidance.* Washington, DC: U.S. Department of the Army.
10. Kelly (2002).
11. United States Department of the Army. 2001. *Army Homeland Security Strategic Planning Guidance.* Washington, DC: U.S. Department of the Army.
12. United States Department of the Army. 2002. *Joint Chiefs of Staff Homeland Security Definitions.* Washington, DC: Department of the Army.
13. Caudle, Sharon. 2003. "Homeland Security: A Challenging Environment." *The Public Manager,* Spring 2003: 19–22.
14. The School for National Security Executive Education, a component of the National Defense University, has offered "U.S. Foreign Policy in an Age of Global Terrorism," and "The Global War on Terrorism."
15. See http://www.cbsnews.com/stories/2002/06/21/opinion/polls/main512974.shtml
16. FEMA provides courses on emergency preparedness and response for emergency personnel and the public through: Emergency Management Institute, Noble Training Center, EENET, Community Emergency Response Teams, Master Trainer Program, National Fire Academy, and EMI Independent Study Courses.

17. The Naval Postgraduate School (Monterey, CA) was one of the first schools develop a master's degree curriculum in homeland security.
18. George Mason University's "Theory and Politics of Terrorism."
19. See http://training.fema.gov/emiweb/edu/high news.asp
20. Government Institutes (www.govinst.com) offers the course, "Security Vulnerability Analysis Workshop for Hazardous Materials Managers." InfoSec Institute (www.infosecinstitute.com) offers the course, "SCADA Security: Protecting our Homeland Security."
21. The sample was gathered using four Internet search engines.
22. Patton, Michael. 1990. *Qualitative Evaluation and Research Methods* (2nd ed.). London: Sage Publications.
23. See Strauss, Anselm, & Juliet Corbin, 1990. *Basics of Qualitative Research: Grounded Theory Procedures and Techniques.* London: Sage Publications, for a discussion of this research strategy.
24. For a thorough discussion of grounded theory and the use of content analysis, see Anselm Strauss and Juliet Corbin, eds. *Grounded Theory in Practice.* Thousand Oaks, CA: Sage Publications, 1997.
25. See Joe Naviatil, "NPS Offering Master's Degree in Homeland Defense," *Naval Supply Corps Newsletter.* May–June 2003, 66(1), 50.
26. See http://www.cbo.gov/showdoc.cfm?index=5414& sequence=0
27. See Office of Management and Budget 2003 Report to Congress on Combating Terrorism at http://www.whitehouse.gov/omb/inforeg/2003_ combat_terr.pdf

DISCUSSION QUESTIONS

1. The lack of a universally accepted definition of terrorism may lead to overly broad and even abusive interpretations of the term. In what ways have abuses already occurred and how can future abuses be prevented?
2. What is the utility of using similar, though slightly different, wording to define international terrorism and domestic terrorism in a world where terrorism transcends the nation–state?
3. While some state legislatures were quick to pass antiterrorism legislation in the months and years following September 11, 2001 (and still others already had laws on the books to deal with terrorist incidents), others have yet to codify any antiterrorism or homeland security measures. What dangers arise from this apparent reluctance to address current threats to each state?
4. Federal homeland security efforts have been center stage in the news media in recent years. What role should the states play in the monumental task of securing the homeland (i.e., borders, airports, ports of entry, shipping lanes, etc.)?
5. Which is the preferred approach to defining terrorism: that of ("any unlawful harm, attempted harm, or threat to do harm to, any state employee, state property, or the person or property of any person on the premises of any state-occupied building or other property leased or owned by the state"), or that of Washington, D.C. (those acts that "intimidate" or "coerce" civilians or the government)? Explain your answer.
6. How would you define homeland security? What are its essential elements?
7. When and how did homeland security become a common/accepted term?
8. Is homeland security a public policy? What is the difference, if any, between public policy and law regarding homeland security?
9. Who is responsible for homeland security at the federal level? State level? Local level?
10. What agencies of government and other organizations are responsible for formulating and implementing homeland security?
11. What should be the primary focus of a course on homeland security?
12. What elements of our syllabus are most interesting to you, and why?
13. Rank in order the five most important terms from Table 1.2, Column 1 (Open Coding). Explain your choices. Do the same for

the terms in Table 1.2, Column 4 (Axial Coding).

14. Review the types of courses presented in Table 1.1. Design a rough draft of a course syllabus on homeland security.

15. Should homeland security be taught as a broad-based course or as a specialized or technical course?

16. Describe the relationship between homeland security and emergency management.

Chapter 2

FEMA'S PLACE IN POLICY, LAW, AND MANAGEMENT: A HAZARDOUS MATERIALS PERSPECTIVE 1979–2003

WILLIAM R. CUMMING and RICHARD T. SYLVES

I. OVERVIEW

This chapter reviews the evolution of FEMA's hazardous materials-related duties to develop insights from a portion of FEMA's policy, law, and management history. FEMA historically had four separate cultures: (1) a disaster culture, (2) a flood insurance culture, (3) a HAZMATS culture, including civil defense, and (4) a national security culture. This chapter discusses the HAZMATS culture specifically. It shows that FEMA's HAZMATS history was shaped by major disasters, by presidential and congressional actions, by the programmatic decisions of its directors, and by the outcomes of its interaction with other federal departments and agencies. This study builds on the premises discussed in an earlier article, "FEMA's Path to Homeland Security" published in Issue 2 of Volume 1 of the *Journal of Homeland Security and Emergency Management*. That article discussed four themes. First, presidents, aided by their respective FEMA directors, sometimes had to decide whether or not to address new types of "technological" or "human-caused" disaster. These decisions set policy precedents that often imposed new obligations on FEMA. Second, FEMA was a combatant in many bureaucratic "turf" wars. FEMA officials were often pitted against others in competing agencies over "who was in charge." Third, the nature of FEMA's work had both "humanitarian" and "technical" characteristics, posing a dilemma for FEMA officials who had to decide job assignments and position qualifications for those hired to serve as managers and line workers in the agency. Fourth, FEMA's HAZMAT story is a prelude to the era of homeland security.

The following is a policy analysis, jurisdictional overview, and targeted management study of the U.S. Federal Emergency Management Agency (FEMA) from its organizational birth in 1979 to its absorption into the new Department of Homeland Security on March 1, 2003 (see Note 1). It would be impossible to cover the entire range of FEMA's jurisdictional and managerial responsibilities during its existence as an independent agency (1979–2003). Instead, the focus is on how FEMA came to gradually shoulder more responsibility for addressing emergency management aspects of hazardous materials (HAZMAT). Presidents from Jimmy Carter to George W. Bush have come to augment and clarify FEMA's responsibilities. They often did so through executive orders, reorganizations, budgeting, and policy initiatives, many of which became law. Congress too added HAZMAT-related work to FEMA's plate, this through law, resolutions, committee oversight, and budgeting.

Hazardous materials may appear to be an overly narrow lens through which to examine the dynamics of FEMA's role in policy, law, and public management.[1] HAZMATS involve chemicals and radiological materials and so this subject distinctly overlaps weapons of mass destruction (WMD) issues. FEMA's current struggle for position in the Department of Homeland Security involves disputes over jurisdiction of WMD programs. FEMA's original disaster programs encompassed few HAZMAT duties. The agency assumed more HAZMAT authority, however, as a result of its role in the 1978–1980 Love Canal hazardous substance contamination controversy, the 1981 explosion of hexane gas in the city of Louisville, Kentucky, and later through the Radiological Emergency Preparedness (REP) program. When the Soviet nuclear power plant explosion at Chernobyl occurred, the American reaction was to give FEMA more HAZMAT authority. Likewise, in 1984 in the aftermath of the Bhopal, India, methyl isocynate disaster, FEMA gained more HAZMAT emergency responsibilities. FEMA inherited a wide range of duties with regard to "civil defense against nuclear attack" from its predecessor the Civil Defense Preparedness Agency (1972–1979). These responsibilities involved radiation detection, monitoring, decontamination of personnel, and health/safety considerations similar to those in hazardous materials detection, cleanup, and health/safety. FEMA and the U.S. Army entered into an arrangement in 1988 for FEMA to provide various off-post emergency management services to the Army for its Chemical Weapons Stockpile Disposal Program, renamed Chemical Stockpile Emergency Preparedness Program (CSEPP) in 1992. FEMA's preparation, planning, and training for accidental or terror-caused releases of radioactive materials from civilian nuclear power plants, most particularly the off-site (outside plant grounds) consequences of such incidents, paralleled or overlapped FEMA's other HAZMAT obligations.

Over its 24-year history, FEMA addressed the consequences of major oil spills, various chemical releases and explosions, the site management and recovery from major acts of terrorism perpetrated inside the United States, as well as conducting federal emergency management of a steadily increasing number and variety of natural disasters. For example, Presidents Clinton and Bush assigned FEMA the job of supporting state and local pesticide spraying to abate the spread of West Nile Virus. In early February 2003, President Bush asked FEMA to coordinate the collection of *Columbia* space shuttle debris and reimburse states that incurred costs in searching for, securing, and recovering the debris.

Both of these latter assignments carried hazardous substance control obligations.

Over FEMA's organizational life span, the president and Congress assigned the agency direct authority for, or coordinating authority for, many new and often unanticipated national calamities. Many, if not most, of these calamities drew on FEMA's experience and expertise in helping people, communities, local governments, and states cope with disasters, including HAZMAT incidents.

In 2002, Public Law [P.L.] 107-296 established the Department of Homeland Security (DHS). Title V of that law set forth within DHS the new Emergency Preparedness and Response directorate (EP&R). President Carter's Reorganization Plan No. 3 of 1978 conceived FEMA and the Homeland Security Act of 2002, signed by President George W. Bush on November 25, 2002, ended the agency's existence as an independent federal agency reporting to the president and moved its personnel, property, equipment, and programs into DHS effective March 1, 2003. Thus, FEMA's official organizational life as an independent agency began April 1, 1979, and ended March 1, 2003. Under Title V of the Homeland Security Act of 2002, DHS inherited FEMA in its entirety and most of the old FEMA now composes DHS-EP&R. Owing to a directive approved by DHS Secretary Tom Ridge in August 2003, FEMA retains its name while operating within DHS. Under the Homeland Security Act, FEMA is a part of the Emergency Preparedness and Response Directorate (EP&RD).

This examination demonstrates that policy, law, management history, and disasters shaped FEMA's HAZMAT role. Presidential and congressional actions, the decisions of its directors, and outcome of FEMA's interaction with other federal departments and agencies also heavily influenced FEMA's HAZMAT role. This chapter outlines the agency's organizational change, its disaster management assignments, and the actions of some of its directors.

II. DISASTERS RESULTING FROM INTENTIONAL OR ACCIDENTAL HUMAN ACTS

A. The Policy-Making Process

Several themes flow simultaneously in this work. First, FEMA's HAZMAT history demonstrates

that the president and other policymakers, FEMA directors, and other federal officials regularly had to decide how to manage new types of "technological" or "human-caused" disaster. Ordinarily, the policy-making process assumes that policymakers identify a problem. If it is definable as a "public problem," lawmakers begin a process of policy formation in which various solutions to the problem are put forward, often in the form of legislative measures. Various lawmakers and political interests establish positions on these measures and a process of coalition building takes place among legislators. The president, and various officials of the executive branch, may engage in this policy formation and policy adoption process by proposing measures, exercising political influence in the legislative process, or contributing to the congressional hearing process. Legislators ultimately vote on proposed measures to address the problem and once a policy is adopted as the outcome of a final vote, often through enactment of a law, institutional resources and spending authority are provided to implement the law. This is the textbook idealization of the policy process.[2] Many federal laws have emerged by way of this general process over the years. For some acute and unforeseen disasters or emergencies, however, the conventional policy process is often too slow, too cumbersome, and too costly. Presidential executive orders sometimes provide the president and the federal government with a high-speed, rapid response alternative to the conventional policy creation process.

B. Executive Orders

Sometimes presidents issued executive orders directing FEMA to manage some new type of emergency or disaster. This approach was often faster than waiting for Congress to enact a law on the subject. Congress has vested in the president authority to delegate certain statutory authority among executive branch organizations through executive orders. Executive orders signed by the president provide an interpretive or operational basis for agency action, as well as delegating presidential authority.[3] It should be noted that delegation does not preclude the president from acting on his own pursuant to statutory or implied authority. See generally, 3 U.S.C. Section 301.

Presidents have regularly used executive orders to shape FEMA authority, to steer the agency to fulfill various public purposes or policy goals, and to draw it into various multi-agency work assignments and planning endeavors. Executive orders,

however, carry no inherent budget authority. Consequently, presidents may sometimes issue them with little expectation that federal agencies will be able to accomplish fully what they stipulate.

Once a president issues an executive order, department and agency heads must fight to obtain from the Office of Management and Budget (OMB) and Congress the budget authority necessary to implement the order. These public managers must address their own, their agency's, or congressional, priorities as well. They therefore must fit executive order assignments into the priorities of the department or agency they manage. From 1979 to 2003, FEMA's list of statutes, executive orders, and National Security presidential directives never exceeded 50. In contrast, some federal departments and agencies must cope with hundreds of statutes, executive orders, and presidential directives. For a list of executive orders reflecting FEMA's HAZMAT role, see Appendix A.

In turn, presidents, in conjunction with Congress, sometimes used reorganization authority to reconfigure FEMA to address new types of disaster. Admittedly, some human-caused disasters are only new because they have recently come to assume national significance or because they are new to generations of leaders who have not experienced them in the past. Since 1950, the federal government, through a succession of agencies including FEMA (since 1979), has regularly addressed great numbers and varieties of natural disasters, usually under a presidential declaration.

C. Emergency Management's Roots

On May 2, 1953, President Eisenhower introduced distinctive federal emergency management when he issued the first presidential declaration of major disaster (DR #1) to address tornado damage in four counties of Georgia. In the months following his January 1953 inauguration, Eisenhower reorganized a diffuse set of disaster relief programs, assigned to federal agencies whose respective jurisdictions rarely involved disaster relief, into a new Office of Civil Defense in the Department of the Army. In a major study of presidential emergency authority, the McKinsey Company examined presidential authority in the civil defense and civilian defense mobilization system and concluded that the president needed vast flexibility to deal with arrangements for emergencies in this area. Congress agreed, and the eventual result was the promulgation of Reorganization Plan No. 1 of 1958, a plan that withdrew authority from the Secretary of Defense and the independent Federal Civil Defense Administration and vested authority in the president. (See 5 U.S.C. Section 901.) As it happens, much of that authority was then delegated back to the Secretary of Defense, but the principle of presidential flexibility was established. The Office of Civil Defense and Defense Mobilization was established in the Defense Department but was later reorganized again as a separate bureau reporting to the Secretary of Defense and an Executive Office of the White House organization the Office of Emergency Planning, later Office of Emergency Preparedness. In 1972, the Secretary of Defense took the civil defense function away from the Secretary of the Army and created a civilian agency in the Defense Department named the Defense Civil Preparedness Agency (DCPA). DCPA existed from 1972 to 1979, when FEMA was established.[4] Civil defense against nuclear attack was a paramount concern in the 1950s and 1960s. DCPA was to promote civil defense and domestic emergency management as complementary concerns.[5]

The federal role in addressing natural disasters has frequently been controversial. This has often been the case when presidents declined governors' requests for declarations of major disaster or emergency. Presidents, from Eisenhower to Bush, have issued turndowns on grounds that the governor-requested "disaster" event did not warrant a presidential declaration. This might occur if the president and his advisors did not judge that the event was of sufficient magnitude, if they thought it could be addressed adequately with state and local resources, if it did not meet the criteria by which federal disaster managers determined need for a declaration, or if it did not conform to accepted categories of disaster types.

Human-caused disasters, emergencies, or calamities sometimes result from failures of various technologies (i.e., dam failures, nuclear reactor malfunctions, hazardous substance releases, etc.), and involve most all of the same controversies as encountered in natural disasters. However, human-caused disaster and technology-caused disaster often pose problems of identifying liability and possible negligence; confronting terrorism, sabotage, arson, or other crimes; and addressing matters of environmental protection. Technological disasters often reveal excessive human dependence on vulnerable infrastructure, much of it serving "lifeline" needs. Modern presidents and Congress frequently asked FEMA to address new types of human- or technology-caused disasters. Many of these assignments stem from flexible FEMA legal authority in hazardous materials emergency management duties.

D. Humanitarian Aid Versus Technical Prowess

The nature of FEMA's work has both humanitarian and technical characteristics. Throughout its 23-year history, those who appointed FEMA officials and those FEMA officials who had to define the agency's public service positions, qualifications, and work assignments (as well as recruiting and selecting workers) faced a dilemma. Should FEMA be managed and staffed by generalist public managers, often schooled in the social sciences or the humanities? Or, should FEMA be managed and staffed by technical specialists, educated in the physical or biological sciences, or in engineering fields? In the broad realm of hazardous materials, FEMA leaders had to regularly choose between using generalists and using technical specialists.

If FEMA leaders opted to rely mostly on generalists, generalist managers might be capable of serving humanitarian goals well. They might also be highly politically responsive in periods when elected officials demand expedited emergency services or recovery resources. Putting generalists ahead of technical specialists, however, might also mean that policymakers would assign technical management of the problem, with commensurate jurisdictional authority and resources, to another federal agency possessing the appropriate scientific and engineering expertise rather than FEMA. Conversely, if FEMA leaders chose technical specialists rather than generalists, the agency's scientific and engineering recommendations and training might be more credible and its in-house emergency response better suited to manage disasters in accord with scientific rationalism. Technical specialists, when compared with generalists, however, may be less able to address humanitarian disaster assistance, less able to work compatibly in the intergovernmental world of domestic disaster management, and less able to fulfill presidential obligations of public responsiveness.

E. Prelude to Homeland Security

The short history of FEMA represents the prelude to post-9-11 homeland security. During the 1980s and 1990s, a gradual but increasingly serious increase in human-caused disasters, some caused by acts of terrorism, moved the U.S. government toward acknowledging that federal emergency management had to consider that threats from outside the nation could produce disasters or emergencies domestically. The 1993 World Trade Center (WTC) bombing perpetrated by foreign terrorists was not the first attack on American homeland by foreign nationals. The 1993 WTC bombing reminded Americans, however, that they were vulnerable to attack by terrorists. The 1995 bombing of Oklahoma City's Alfred P. Murrah Federal Building, although committed by Americans, drew FEMA further into the terrorism consequence management business.[6]

The American catastrophe of the September 11, 2001, terror attacks removed the distinction between conventional domestic disaster management and defense against foreign attack. President Bush's Homeland Security Presidential Directive

HSPD-5 issued on February 28, 2003, states, "The Assistant to the President for Homeland Security and the Assistant to the President for National Security Affairs shall be responsible for interagency policy coordination on domestic and international incident management, respectively, as directed by the President. The Assistant to the President for Homeland Security and the Assistant to the President for National Security Affairs shall work together to ensure that the United States domestic and international incident management efforts are seamlessly united."[7]

Modern homeland security highlights the overlap or coincidence of domestic emergency management and terrorism consequence management at home. Homeland security in the former era of civil defense against nuclear attack sometimes required an odd and conflictive marriage of civil defense duties and conventional domestic emergency management of natural disasters. Owing to the range of weapons and instruments potentially available to modern terrorists and the damage these might cause, modern antiterror emergency management under homeland security and conventional disaster management may actually complement each other much more than civil defense and domestic emergency management did during the Cold War. In addition, odd as it may seem, many hazardous materials emergency management duties and many homeland security obligations intertwine with one another.

III. EARLY FEMA AND HAZMAT

When FEMA began operation, it had few programs, functions, or activities that pertained to hazardous materials emergencies. During its first years, FEMA housed two directorates with HAZMAT duties: Plans and Preparedness (1979–1981) as well as Mitigation and Research (1979–1981). At that time, most of FEMA's HAZMAT work involved emergency preparedness (i.e., training, resources, and personnel), hazard mitigation, emergency response, and disaster recovery. The only hazardous materials authority FEMA inherited from its progenitors involved: (1) radiological hazards relating to nuclear strategic missile attack, and

(2) National Fire Academy training of management cadre on matters of hazardous materials. One of FEMA's tasks was to improve state and local government capability to respond directly to hazardous materials incidents or events, something policymakers never asked FEMA's predecessor organizations to do. Capability refers to augmenting, training, and educating personnel, conducting emergency response exercises, increasing necessary resources, and advancing emergency planning.

The so-called Clean Water Act (initially the Federal Water Pollution Control Act of 1972), the Resource, Conservation and Recovery Act, and the Toxic Substance Control Act (RCRA), all enacted in 1976, assigned considerable emergency response and cleanup duties to the U.S. Environmental Protection Agency (EPA) and the U.S. Department of Transportation (DOT), but not to FEMA's predecessor agencies. Until the late 1970s, few envisioned that hazardous materials and toxic substance incidents would eventually demand federal emergency management services and resources. Arguably, even fewer anticipated that HAZMAT expertise and incident management would later provide an introduction for federal government response to biological and chemical warfare attacks, and radioactive contamination from so-called dirty bombs, or RDDs (Radiological Dispersal Devices), all defined now as weapons of mass destruction.

In the late 1970s, President Carter's Reorganization Project staff, and the professional staffs of the House and Senate committees, exercising reorganization oversight, worked to reform federal emergency management. They neglected to directly address the emergency management implications of hazardous materials incidents, a subject that would soon have dramatic effects on FEMA and its

operations. Congressional hearings that took place during FEMA's 1978–1979 gestation period made no mention of the agency's role in hazardous materials incidents. At this time, FEMA's fledgling, senior management, unintentionally and without fully appreciating the significance of what was occurring, also failed to anticipate the importance of hazardous materials issues.

President Carter's Executive Order (E.O.) 12127 moved elements of Commerce, Housing, and Urban Development (HUD) (the Federal Insurance Administration specifically), and the Office of Science and Technology Policy into FEMA. That order also transferred to FEMA several statutory functions previously delegated to other federal departments. Carter's E.O. 12148, issued July 20, 1979, completed Reorganization Plan No. 3 of 1978 by transferring presidential authority vested in certain offices of the Department of Defense (DoD), HUD (Federal Disaster Assistance Administration), and General Services Administration (Federal Preparedness Agency) to FEMA.

The four provisions of Carter's E.O. 12148 presented next, encapsulate a broad range of FEMA's duties.

PARTIAL TEXT OF SECTION 2 OF EXECUTIVE ORDER 12148

Section 2. Management of Emergency Planning and Assistance

2-101. The Director of the Federal Emergency Management Agency shall establish federal policies for, and coordinate, all civil defense and civil emergency planning, management, mitigation, and assistance functions of Executive agencies.

2-102. The Director shall periodically review and evaluate the civil defense and civil emergency functions of the executive agencies. In order to improve the efficiency and effectiveness of those functions, the Director shall recommend to the

President alternative methods of providing federal planning, management, mitigation, and assistance.

2-103. The Director shall be responsible for the coordination of efforts to promote dam safety, for the coordination of natural and nuclear disaster warning systems, and for the coordination of preparedness and planning to reduce the consequences of major terrorist incidents.

2-104. The Director shall represent the President in working with state and local governments and private sector to stimulate vigorous participation in civil emergency preparedness, mitigation, response, and recovery programs.

A. Generalists Versus Specialists

From September 1979 to January 1981, Director John Macy led FEMA (see Appendix A). Macy had gained considerable esteem as chairman of the

federal Civil Service Commission throughout the presidency of Lyndon Johnson and during Richard Nixon's first term. Macy held several strong personal beliefs about public management at the federal level. First, Macy preferred generalists—meaning staff without technical credentials, whether earned from education, experience, or both–over specialists. Second, Macy believed that independent agencies in the executive branch, including the one he was directing, were an affront to Cabinet government. Macy had been part of the Executive Office of the President (EOP) staff tasked with designing President Richard Nixon's Super Cabinet proposal. Under the scheme ultimately proposed, even small Cabinet organizations would report to the president through an appropriate department, such as State, Justice, Defense, Treasury, or Health-Education-Welfare. Nixon's Super Cabinet proposal never came to be.

A few FEMA officials had worked previously in the White House Office of Emergency Planning, then the White House Office of Emergency Preparedness (OEP) from 1962 to 1973. Many in this group believed that the OEP organizational concept was superior because it entailed location in the Executive Office of the White House. Macy had dealt with OEP as chairman of the Civil Service Commission. Macy helped Nixon phase out the OEP under reorganization in 1973. OEP had an excellent staff with major political connections at the White House level. At FEMA, however, Macy preferred recruiting nonpolitical managers and staff. He inherited, however, several presidentially appointed, Senate-confirmed Carter appointees, all with strong reservations about independent agencies like FEMA. Many had previously been high-ranking officials in Cabinet departments.

B. FEMA Staffing, Powers, and Primary Accountability

FEMA, even at its staffing high watermark, approximated only 3,000 Full-Time Equivalent (FTE) employees; FTE is an Office of Management and Budget construct meaning one person working one full year. FEMA's regular workforce was never much larger than were the respective workforces of many small Cabinet bureaus. If FEMA's cadre of Disaster Assistance Employees (DAEs), intermittently employed temporaries, is included as when the agency is under full activation, FEMA's total workforce never exceeded 6,000.

FEMA was an independent agency with coordinative authority, major intergovernmental obligations, and significant disaster assistance duties and resources. FEMA was not, however, a regulatory agency. It possessed a wisp of regulatory authority in the rules, conditions, and mandates it applied through its disaster assistance, intergovernmental emergency management subsidization, and flood insurance programs. Because it lacked significant regulatory power, FEMA leaders may have concluded that managers who were technical specialists in scientific or engineering fields were less central to the agency's missions than were managers who were expert in administrative procedure, who could operate in complex intergovernmental and interagency settings, and who understood the political significance of their work.[8]

Students of government often ask whether a federal agency better serves, or is more responsive to, the president or the Congress. It is fair to say that FEMA was always more of a president-serving agency than a Congress-serving agency. FEMA's strategic role in the presidential disaster declaration process and the president's direct authority to approve or turn down governor requests for declarations, gave this diminutive agency a high profile at the White House. In addition, presidents have come to rely on FEMA to address in an expedited manner various problems or anomalies they choose to define as disasters or emergencies.

Nonetheless, FEMA always had a support base in Congress. Most lawmakers deeply appreciated FEMA's role in providing postdisaster relief and recovery assistance, particularly when they and the public perceived it as well managed. Nevertheless, successive FEMA leaderships attempted to minimize their contacts with Congress. FEMA leaderships were often highly defensive in their dealings with Congress. They reacted defensively to congressional proposals calling for FEMA to take on new programs, functions, or activities, unless the president concurred with the proposals. FEMA officials rarely submitted new authorizing language to Congress.

C. FEMA's Clientele

FEMA has built mutually beneficial alliances with various organizations preoccupied with specific forms of disaster. For example, the influential earthquake interest community has close ties with various program offices of FEMA. Likewise, the hurricane community, the flood community, and the tornado communities, to name a few, have considerable vested interests in various FEMA units. However, Birkland and others have demonstrated that these hazard-specific interests often compete with one another, sometimes to the detriment of FEMA's all-hazards emergency management obligations.[9]

Many of FEMA's clientele interests have been ambivalent about what FEMA does for them. Moreover, some of these interests lack political influence in Congress or use whatever political capital they have to seek benefits unrelated to FEMA or disaster management. However, since 9-11, many interests have been drawn to FEMA, and now DHS, owing to new terrorism-related laws, new security obligations, and to the accompanying infusion of vast sums of federal funding.

IV. FEMA AND NUCLEAR POWER EMERGENCIES

In late March of 1979, the Three Mile Island (TMI) Nuclear Power Station Unit #2, a Nuclear Regulatory Commission (NRC) licensed facility, began to experience a series of malfunctions and operating problems that resulted in uncontrolled releases of radioactive gases and the partial meltdown of the unit's reactor core. The TMI calamity quickly became a major embarrassment for the Carter administration, as many inside and outside government judged NRC's handling of the emergency as bungled or incompetent. TMI spotlighted the need for improved federal emergency management, particularly with respect to emergency planning and response outside the grounds of nuclear utility complexes.

A. Early History

FEMA opened its doors as an independent agency on April 1, 1979, only a few days after the start of the TMI incident. President Carter entrusted FEMA with assuming many response and recovery duties. When the Senate confirmed John Macy's appointment in August of 1979, several high-level commissions recommended that his agency lead preparedness off-site in the event of incidents at fixed nuclear power stations. This development was an important expansion of FEMA's then-limited hazardous materials area duties.

Mitch Rogovin conducted the Carter administration's review of the J.K. Kemeny Commission Report–Report of the President's Commission on the Accident at Three Mile Island. Rogovin did not complete his report in time for the NRC to respond to it through its own TMI report. As a result, NRC was unable to defend against the transfer of many of its radiological emergency preparedness planning duties to FEMA brought about by Carter's E.O. 12148. NRC's management of the TMI incident and presidential dissatisfaction with NRC resulted in a considerable amount of jurisdiction over radiological emergency preparedness around nuclear power plants moving from the NRC to FEMA.

On December 10, 1979, President Carter issued a memorandum designating FEMA as the agency to which he intended to transfer off-site response for fixed nuclear power plants. President Carter did not issue an implementing document to effect this change, however, and the FEMA leadership did not ask for one. Congress never redrafted the Atomic Energy Act of 1954, and its subsequent amendments, to reflect FEMA's new off-site nuclear power plant emergency assignment. Even now the Atomic Energy Act, while referencing health and safety, does not mention emergency planning or response. These omissions resulted in years of bureaucratic turf battles and litigation between FEMA and NRC over which organization would be in charge of both off-site risk management and emergency planning around various nuclear facilities, among them the controversial Shoreham (Long Island, NY) and Seabrook (New Hampshire) nuclear power stations. This disagreement was not fully resolved until the litigation ran its course in the early 1990s. This dispute stands as a classic example of the type of who's-in-charge conflicts that FEMA endured.

The formal commitment of FEMA to the informal Carter assignment occurred when Macy signed a Memorandum of Understanding (MOU) with NRC's chairperson.[10] It went into effect on November 3, 1980. FEMA published the first Federal Radiological Emergency Response Plan (FRERP) to comply with a presidential assignment in Carter's E.O. 12241, National Contingency Plan, dated September 29, 1980. The original aim of those who devised the FRERP was to set out the roles of various federal departments and agencies when a release of radionuclides (as depositional material or airborne particles) from fixed nuclear power plants endangers the public.

In 1985, during the Reagan presidency, a new Federal Radiological Emergency Response Plan emerged (see Note 2). It encompassed most of the Carter era MOU. Under Carter E.O. 12241 of 1980 and Reagan E.O.12657 of 1988 (see below), FEMA has off-site responsibilities for the consequences of accidents at Nuclear Regulatory Commission (NCR) licensed fixed nuclear power plants. NRC has on-site responsibilities, together with the facility owner, for the consequences of accidents at these nuclear power plants (see Note 3).

B. Meese Memorandum: National System for Emergency Coordination

Attorney General Edwin Meese II, as chair of President Reagan's Domestic Policy Council, issued a memorandum on January 19, 1988. Titled the National System for Emergency Coordination (NSEC), the Meese memorandum assigned specific agencies lead roles in addressing certain types of disasters. The memo gave FEMA the lead for natural disasters and the Department of Justice the lead for dealing with terrorism events. For hazardous materials, however, Department of Energy (DOE) was given the energy lead. DOE and DOD led in nuclear weapon events or reactor-related incidents where one or the other department was the owner or operator. EPA was lead agency for pollution emergencies (including chemical accidents), and NRC was the prime mover for nuclear power plant events.

As the NSEC assigned NRC the on-site lead for nuclear power incidents and accidents, FEMA officials initially concluded that their entire FRERP role had been eliminated.[11] This confusion among FEMA's most senior officials reflects a dilemma

that they regularly faced. Was FEMA to engage only in humanitarian aspects of emergency response to nuclear incidents, or was it supposed to also address the scientific and engineering dimensions of nuclear safety?

C. Risk Analysis and Nuclear Power Emergencies

During the 1980s, the NRC and FEMA disagreed about which agency should determine nuclear power emergency risk and safety. After lengthy administrative adjudication of the Shoreham (NY) and Seabrook (NH) nuclear power cases, the Reagan administration determined that NRC would get the job. In many respects, determination of nuclear accident risk involves engineering fault analysis and statistical probabilities, especially those regarding threats to public health. Determination of nuclear safety may consider risk studies, but the decision regarding what is safe or unsafe involves a value judgment. In a democracy, important value judgments often require public consent and consent is customarily the work of elected representatives of the people. Because the NRC could decide what is safe or unsafe, FEMA's role in nuclear power off-site emergency planning was diminished.

D. Reagan's Preemptive Ruling

President Reagan assigned FEMA added radiological planning and preparedness responsibilities on November 18, 1988, through E.O. 12657, Federal Emergency Management Agency Assistance in Emergency Preparedness Planning at Commercial Nuclear Power Plants. Reagan's ruling amended the FRERP and directed FEMA to ensure adequate off-site planning when state and local governments fail to adequately plan, prepare or respond to a nuclear power plant accident.

This Reagan policy initiative augmented and clarified FEMA's nuclear power emergency management duties. As a policy instrument, it helped the Reagan administration deter antinuclear challenges aimed at undermining nuclear plant operator licensing. Over much of the 1980s, antinuclear power interests hoped that they could convince state, and especially local, government officials with jurisdiction in nuclear plant emergency planning zones (EPZs) to resist, or withhold cooperation, in producing FEMA-NRC acceptable emergency plans and/or maintaining FEMA-NRC required response capacity.[12] These people reasoned that nuclear utilities without approved and maintained off-site emergency response plans could not obtain or retain their NRC-approved operator licenses. The Reagan executive order allowed nuclear utilities and cooperating governments to devise nuclear power emergency response plans substitutable for those needed from uncooperative states and localities. The Department of Energy principally drafted that executive order.[13] By May of 1992, a new Federal Response Plan (FRP) helped to substantially resolve the FEMA-NRC dispute.

E. Clinton, Bush, and Nuclear Power Emergencies

In 1993, President Clinton's new director of FEMA, James Lee Witt, declared that he interpreted the language of Carter E.O. 12148, Federal Emergency Management in Sections 2-101, 2-102, 2-103, 2-104, and 2-201, as assigning the director of FEMA responsibilities in technological emergencies, such as nuclear power plant emergencies. He reinforced this claim by referring to FEMA's assignments in Clinton's E.O. 12241, E.O. 12580, and E.O. 12657, mandated September 5, 1993 (see Note 4).

For FEMA (and today DHS), however, and by inference for serving presidents, a significant nuclear emergency problem remains unresolved. The Price-Anderson Act of 1956 and its later

amendments do not explain how FEMA (or DHS today) is to handle citizen claims filed after a nuclear power incident. If a nuclear power plant incident produces life and property damage in the future, and if the president issues a declaration of major disaster for the incident, the Stafford Act of 1988 and its amendments provide no guidance to FEMA or DHS regarding how to compensate citizen claims or allocate disaster relief. One attempt at resolving these issues is NUREG-1447. This document was issued after the Presidential Commission on Response to a Catastrophic Nuclear Accident reported to Congress that the Disaster Relief Act of 1974, as amended by Public Law 100-107, had no applicability to such an event.

Another issue before the NRC and FEMA involved the storage of potassium iodide, used by people in nuclear power radiological emergencies to help displace the buildup of radioactive strontium in the thyroid gland. NRC made the issue a subject of formal rulemaking. FEMA did not make protective action decisions on evacuation from or re-entry to contaminated areas under formal rulemaking. According to NRC adjudicative case law, however, FEMA was required to give recommendations. These functions are by law the specific responsibility of DOE, EPA, HHS, Department of Agriculture, and the NRC. Again, therefore, FEMA is obliged to address matters of science, this time medical science, in its emergency management work. Public Law 107-188 mandates that the federal government distribute potassium iodide tablets to people living within a 20-mile circumference around each NRC-regulated nuclear power plant.

V. FEMA, LOVE CANAL, BHOPAL, AND CHERNOBYL

In 1979–1980, FEMA became involved in events at Love Canal, a neighborhood in Niagara Falls, New York. An abandoned and largely forgotten subsurface hazardous waste dump situated under an elementary school and a subdivision of homes began to leach substances alleged to have caused major illness and birth defects among those in the Love Canal community. This eventually led President Jimmy Carter to issue a series of

presidential emergency declarations, and ultimately a declaration of major disaster, pursuant to the Disaster Relief Act of 1974, Public Law 93-288, for the contamination of property.

The early awkward response to Love Canal by New York state authorities, FEMA, and other federal agencies led to years of litigation. Nevertheless, Love Canal motivated the federal government, particularly FEMA, EPA, and public health authorities, to develop methods for responding to these types of events. In 1980, during the waning days of the Carter administration, the president and Congress approved the so-called Superfund law.[14] President Carter also issued Executive Order 12316.[15] Both Superfund and E.O. 12316 were in part a result of FEMA's poor early performance in addressing the issues raised by Love Canal.

Since 1980, the Superfund program has mushroomed. Today it accounts for about one-third of EPA's FTE positions, many of them occupied by scientists and engineers. Superfund remains at this writing EPA's largest and most expensive program. Superfund jurisdiction never enlarged FEMA as it did EPA, and this may stand as an example of FEMA generalists losing out to EPA technical specialists.

Ironically, Director Macy initially saw no role for FEMA in addressing the nation's Superfund sites. He insisted that this activity did not belong in FEMA because in his view it was not an emergency management program.

Under the Disaster Relief Act of 1974 (P. L. 93-288) and the Robert T. Stafford Disaster Relief and Emergency Assistance Act of 1988 (P. L. 101-107), legal officials of FEMA's Office of General Counsel and attorneys at the Department of Justice took legal action against Occidental Petroleum, a firm that absorbed Hooker Chemical, the party responsible for disposing the largest share of hazardous materials into Love Canal. The federal government eventually recovered disaster moneys FEMA had paid out at Love Canal over the period 1979–1983 from responsible parties.

Love Canal represents federal emergency management's introduction to hazardous materials contamination emergencies. Federal, state, and local government reaction to the incident was highly improvised. Various public health, environmental protection, and emergency management agency officials had to either assume new, or redefine their old, jurisdiction in a manner that met public needs but minimized their agency's liability.

VI. FEMA AND HAZARDOUS MATERIALS EMERGENCIES FROM REAGAN TO CLINTON

FEMA's State and Local Programs Support (SLPS) Directorate carried out a variety of HAZMAT duties under the Disaster Relief Act of 1974, P. L. 93-288. In the early 1980s, however, government lawyers and judges consistently interpreted the statute to mean that FEMA authority did not directly apply to hazardous materials incidents, despite FEMA's role in the Love Canal hazardous waste controversy. It was therefore ironic that President Ronald Reagan's very first declaration of major disaster came in 1981 after an explosion of hexane, a substance accidentally discharged into the sewers of Louisville, Kentucky, by the Ralston Purina Company. The incident caused extensive damage and posed an environmental and health hazard. The declaration called for FEMA to provide and coordinate immediate federal disaster relief.

FEMA's Office of General Counsel and the Department of Justice eventually succeeded in using the Disaster Relief Act of 1974 (P. L. 93-288)

to compel Ralston Purina to reimburse FEMA for its expenses in the cleanup and repair. In the Stafford Act of 1988, Congress allowed recovery against persons causing or aggravating a disaster but only when gross negligence (undefined) caused or aggravated the emergency or disaster. FEMA never used this authority, however, to seek monetary recovery or injunctive relief. In other words, FEMA did not use the Stafford Act to prosecute (through the Attorney General) persons or corporations alleged to have caused or aggravated disasters or emergencies.

Regardless, from 1981 to 1990, FEMA was responsible for the temporary and permanent relocation of citizens forced to evacuate owing to hazardous materials releases. This authority was contingent upon cross-delegation from EPA. In 1990, the Bush administration transferred these duties from FEMA to EPA.

In 1984, a Union Carbide facility in Bhopal, India, released the toxic gas, methyl isocynate, into the air. At the time of the release, Union Carbide provided little warning of the release to the surrounding population. The poisonous gas is estimated to have killed over 2,000 people. Many thousands more suffered major injuries. News of the disaster sparked intense international and American interest. The event impelled Congress and the president to enact into law the Superfund Amendments and Reauthorization Act of 1986, or SARA. The Emergency Planning and Community Right to Know Act of 1986 (EPCRA), under SARA Title 3, outlines FEMA's emergency duties in hazardous substance release (see Note 7). SARA Title 3 augmented FEMA's responsibilities in emergency management of, and planning for, actual or potential releases of hazardous chemicals.

From 1981 to 1994, FEMA chaired the Preparedness and Training Committees of the National Response Team (NRT) for the departments and agencies listed in the National Contingency Plan. FEMA continued NRT membership under Reagan E.O. 12580. FEMA's job was to support development of state and local government expertise in the generic functions of emergency planning, preparedness, response, and recovery operations and disaster mitigation. This work helped state and local governments address the consequences of civil emergencies, such as those that result from major chemical releases (see Note 8).

By the mid-1980s, the Times Beach, Missouri, dioxin contamination, revelations about other abandoned toxic waste dumps, and America's reaction to the Bhopal, India, air toxin disaster carved out a substantial role for FEMA in hazardous substance emergency response and recovery. The Chernobyl nuclear power plant disaster in the Ukraine region of the former Soviet Union also underscored the need for improved radiological HAZMAT capabilities and preparedness in the United States.

VII. FEMA HAZMAT AND FIRE JURISDICTION: THE UNITED STATES FIRE ADMINISTRATION

From 1982 to 1992, FEMA's HAZMATS programs were primarily the job of its SLPS Directorate and its United States Fire Administration (USFA). The SLPS Directorate of FEMA operated from September 1981 to November 1993. USFA, the object of this section, predates and postdates FEMA. USFA had its genesis in the former Fire Prevention and Control Administration (FPCA) of the Department of Commerce under the Fire Prevention and Control Act of 1974 (see Note 5). That law, whose main aim was to advance the work of the Fire Services, was the product of long effort by Senator Warren Magnuson of the state of Washington and chairman of the Senate Commerce Committee. Headed by Howard Tipton for most of its Commerce years, the USFA represented a specific clientele group, America's fire service community. USFA has continuously conducted hazardous materials training courses at its National Fire Academy. These courses serve federal, state, and local emergency responders and others.

USFA, from its inception, had a fire claims program to reimburse local firefighters for their firefighting efforts at federal facilities and on federal lands. Under the Disaster Relief Act of 1974, P.L. 93-288, FPCA and later USFA only possessed emergency management authority for reimbursement of firefighting costs on federal land (see 44 CFR Part 151). After enactment of the Stafford Act of 1988, USFA could provide fire suppression assistance under fire suppression declarations (see 44 CFR part 204). The aim was always to supplement state and local government firefighting efforts. Other offices of FEMA, not USFA, handled the agency's bread-and-butter major disaster, or emergency, work.

Fire service interests hoped that FPCA, and then USFA, would establish the legitimacy and prestige of federal fire training and education. Fire service leaders expected USFA to garner national reputation and prestige, a kind of seal of approval, which they could confer on local fire service personnel who had completed training at their Emmitsburg, Maryland, facility. The aim was to parallel the reputation and status enjoyed by local law enforcement personnel who completed training in the FBI's highly respected program at Quantico, Virginia.

A. USFA and the Reagan Era

Unfortunately, FPCA officials made two powerful enemies that would punish USFA in the 1980s. The first was Edward Rollins, who would become a principal campaign consultant for President Ronald Reagan and later a senior Reagan White House official. Rollins, owing to his personal frustration with USFA leadership, was anxious to terminate USFA. He found powerful allies at the Office of Management and Budget (OMB). Senior OMB officials had long held the view that fire protection, training, and response was a local issue that under any definition of federalism was not an appropriate activity for the federal government. They overlooked the fact that the Department of Defense has 30,000–50,000 military and civilian firefighters, and that the Forest Service, the Bureau of Land Reclamation, and National Park Service all retain at various times many thousands of firefighters.

Rollins and OMB officials succeeded in zero budgeting USFA funding in Reagan budget submissions for federal fiscal years 1982 and 1984. Anticipating USFA's termination, Reagan administration FEMA officials dispersed many USFA workers to other offices within the agency. USFA and the fire service community had enough friends and supporters in Congress to prevent USFA budget termination in both fiscal years. Congress consistently found ways to restore funds to USFA's budget.

USFA was never larger than 25 FTE and its National Fire Academy never exceeded 150 FTEs. Yet, USFA and the fire service community fended off powerful opposition in the Reagan era. Although politically weak on the presidential level and often impeded by organizational competitors, USFA continued to develop hazardous materials-related courses and materials.

B. Hazardous Materials Transportation

In another dispute, the Hazardous Materials Transportation Act of 1977 (HMTA) (Title 49 U.S. Code) created a system of preemptive federal regulation for the movement of hazardous materials throughout the United States. The Commerce Clause of the Constitution was the legal basis of this statute and the measure allowed federal implementing agencies to preempt state or local laws determined to be in conflict with HMTA regulations. Under its HMTA authority, the DOT issued many preemption orders geared to overturn state and local hazardous materials laws judged to burden interstate commerce. Over time, DOT often re-delegated its HMTA authority back to the states under approved plans.

FEMA carries some HMTA responsibilities. The USFA and the SLPS components of FEMA became embroiled in a hazardous materials transport controversy in the 1980s. The controversy began when the state of Ohio sued to overturn DOT preemption of its laws on the basis that the federal government had failed to provide adequate training in emergency response to responders in that state who would have to meet the imposed HMTA obligations.

In the same period, in an effort to establish a federal protocol, the Technical Hazards Division of FEMA's SLPS Directorate contracted for a study of emergency response to radiological materials incidents occurring in transport. It was FEMA's job to train emergency responders to handle such incidents. The study, referred to as the Bradford contract, caused a huge controversy. Fire community members repudiated the study. They alleged that it contained erroneous technical advice. Congressional hearings ensued and lawmakers ridiculed FEMA for its technical ineptness. The dispute demonstrated poor intra-agency coordination and unclear lines of authority within FEMA at the time. By a strange twist, the Department of Justice used the discredited study and USFA's hazardous materials training offerings and documents (put forward by the fire community to challenge the study) to successfully block Ohio's efforts to gain a restraining order.

In November of 1990, President Bush signed into law the Hazardous Materials Transportation Uniform Safety Act (HMTUSA) P.L. 101-615. HMTUSA called for a comprehensive update of the National Contingency Plan (see Note 10). FEMA continues hazardous materials transport emergency training and planning today.

C. USFA in the Clinton and Bush Era

From 1990 to 1993, the USFA operated all of FEMA's hazardous materials training programs. In November of 1993, the Clinton administration, as part of Clinton-Witt FEMA reorganization, transferred USFA training for nonfire hazardous materials emergency response to FEMA's Preparedness, Training, and Exercises (PTE) Directorate. FEMA's Emergency Management Institute (EMI), long part of the SLPS, and later PTE, directorates, continued its own hazardous materials curriculum in accord with standards embodied in DOT's Hazardous Materials Transportation grants program.

The United States Fire Administration is the only FEMA Directorate, besides the Federal Insurance Administration, to outlast independent agency FEMA, retaining its name and people in the new Department of Homeland Security. USFA's fortunes may have improved in the aftermath of the 9-11 terror attacks. The heroic efforts of New York City firefighters in and around the World Trade Center on 9-11, their tragic losses stemming from the collapse of the towers, plus the superlative work of Arlington County (VA) and other northern Virginia and District of Columbia firefighters after the terror attack on the Pentagon, won widespread public and political support for the nation's fire services. USFA is a key federal component of the nation's fire service training and education. USFA has long maintained a memorial to fallen firefighters at its Emmitsburg, Maryland, facility. President George W. Bush visited the memorial in late 2001 to attend a commemorative service in honor of the firefighters lost in the 9-11 terror attacks.

Subsequent events, however, show that the firefighting community still has many stakeholders fighting to take control of its destiny. "[I]n the Washington bureaucracy, budgets and table of organizations mean power, or lack thereof. The fire service is not a power player within DHS. Its voice is weak, buried under layers of bureaucracy"[16] . . . DHS has not responded urgently to congressional testimony from fire chiefs from around the country painting a bleak picture of response capabilities. Nor does it seem to have paid much attention to reports from organizations such as The Council of Foreign Relations, a New York-based nonpartisan research group. In its preparedness report *Emergency Responders: Drastically Underfunded, Dangerously Unprepared*, the council stated that "the U.S. remains dangerously ill-prepared to handle a catastrophic attack on American soil."[17]

VIII. FEMA AND NUCLEAR ATTACK EMERGENCIES

The old pre-FEMA Defense Civil Preparedness Agency in the Department of Defense had the job of radiological preparedness, planning, and response resulting from strategic nuclear attack. In jurisdictional terms, the president possessed all the authority under the Federal Civil Defense Act of 1950, P.L. 81-920, and could simply re-delegate DCPA's authority to FEMA. This President Carter did and from 1979 to 1981, the radiological emergency programs of the former DCPA went to FEMA's Associate Director for Plans and Preparedness.

FEMA's duties in the realm of nuclear attack emergencies appear in Carter E.O. 12148, although later measures preempted this order. Next are two key provisions of the Carter order:

2-203. For purposes of this Order, "civil emergency" means accidental, natural, man-caused, or wartime emergency or threat thereof, which causes or may cause substantial injury or harm to the population or substantial damage to or loss of property.

2-204. In order that civil defense planning continues to be fully compatible with the Nation's overall strategic policy, and in order to maintain an effective link between strategic nuclear planning and nuclear attack preparedness planning, the development of civil defense policies and programs by the Director of the Federal Emergency Management Agency shall be subject to oversight by the Secretary of Defense and the National Security Council.

On January 27, 1981, FEMA also entered into a Memorandum of Understanding with the Department of Defense and the Department of

Energy regarding Nuclear Weapon Accidents and Nuclear Weapon significant incidents.

In the fall of 1981, with Reagan administration approval, the newly formed FEMA State and Local Programs Support Directorate took on these and other nuclear attack emergency duties. FEMA's SLPS Directorate encompassed several offices: among them the Office of Natural and Technological Hazards, which handled Radiological Emergency Planning. Richard W. Krimm, a seasoned public manager, headed this office during Reagan's first term. The FEMA leadership placed Krimm, a manager with no technical or scientific credentials, in charge of a program that often required an understanding and application of scientific and engineering knowledge. Krimm's appointment was typical of the FEMA leadership penchant for preferring generalist and experienced public managers rather than scientists and engineers who were expert in understanding the nature of hazardous materials damage, threats, or cleanup.

For a time, owing to regular underfunding of the Radiological Preparedness Program, Krimm had to draw staff and resources from the National Flood Insurance Program to continue the work of his office. Krimm was constantly waging a multifront bureaucratic turf war to save his programs from a Reagan FEMA leadership more intent on converting offices like Krimm's into instruments of national defense policy. U.S.–Soviet relations were tendentious over most of the Reagan presidency. The Reagan administration used FEMA to improve civil defense against nuclear attack. This was a tactic aimed at matching Soviet efforts in civil defense and a stratagem intended to intimidate Soviet leaders by convincing them that the United States might carry out a first strike against them with nuclear weapons if sufficiently provoked.[18]

The Office of Natural and Technological Hazards (ONT) operated from 1981 to 1985 and its Technical Hazards Division carried on from 1985 to 1993 (see Note 6). From 1985 to 1989, the Natural Hazards Division was positioned in the Federal Insurance Administration. ONT became a fundamental part of the Mitigation Directorate established in November of 1993 by Director Witt (see Appendix B). Thus, the people and programs of FEMA's ONT, a key hazardous materials emergency management office, were pressed to assume nuclear attack emergency responsibilities even as they were compelled to manage other HAZMAT concerns and even as they sustained budget and staff cuts.

IX. FEMA AND THE CHEMICAL WEAPONS DISPOSAL PROGRAM

FEMA's jurisdiction over hazardous materials in the Reagan era sometimes expanded in a civil-military context even as its jurisdiction over domestic, nonmilitary hazardous materials issues was challenged, underfunded, or ignored. Retired Army General Julius Becton directed FEMA from November 1985 to June 1989. On August 3, 1988, Director Becton and the Secretary of the Army negotiated an agreement through which FEMA would lead the off-post activity of the Chemical Stockpile Disposal Program, renamed the Chemical Stockpile Emergency Preparedness Program (CSEPP) in 1992.

Much of FEMA's off-post chemical weapons disposal program work involved identifying routes by which to transport old chemical weapons to permanent disposal facilities, securing mutual agreement with state and local governments to use these routes, and winning the cooperation of state and local jurisdictions in providing security and emergency support if necessary. Many of these weapons were old military ordnance that were deteriorating, outmoded, scheduled for permanent disposal under America's treaty obligations, and sometimes unsafe.

The formal FEMA-Army Memorandum of Understanding took effect in 1988. Although later modified, the original agreement failed to identify the legal basis for FEMA's authority in the program. On top of this, a FEMA staff-level review usually precedes the signing of such agreements. No thorough staff-level review took place before FEMA and the U.S. Army signed the MOU. Therefore, most of FEMA's senior management had not signed on to the agreement before it took effect and FEMA had no clear legal authority under which to fulfill its obligations under the MOU. In other words, many unconsulted FEMA managers had to later decide how their offices or programs would relate to chemical weapons disposal obligations taken on by Becton. In addition, FEMA needed to secure a clear grant of authority to backstop its chemical weapons disposal program duties. Here again, FEMA encountered a who's-in-charge controversy. Given FEMA's role as primary emergency management interface with state and local governments, a role in this program that made political sense if FEMA was to be viewed as the principal stop for state and local governments, FEMA should have to be invested with more authority in this program. However, technical considerations and an unusual standard of safety, one requiring "Maximum Protection of the Public," made the program administratively controversial for FEMA.

Chemical and Bio-Weapon Emergency

In November of 1990, during Operation Desert Shield, President George Bush signed an executive order declaring a national emergency stemming from what he judged to be an unusual and extraordinary threat to the national security posed by proliferation of chemical and biological weapons. This national emergency executive order remains in effect at this writing. The Gulf War also accelerated adoption of the Federal Response Plan (FRP). FEMA issued an internal memorandum detailing its emergency response readiness during the Gulf War, mandating use of the FRP to respond to terrorist events.[19]

The Chemical and Biological Weapons and Warfare Elimination Act of 1991 had the twin purposes of preventing the proliferation of chemical and biological weapons among other nations and, by example, it called on America to destroy its arsenal of chemical and biological weapons. The law's Chapter 32 of Title 50 (War and National Defense) presents the "Chemical and Biological Warfare Program." Title 50 contains the authorization for destruction of the chemical weapons stockpile of the United States. The United States is to fulfill this obligation by the year 2008 pursuant to International Conventions and obligations, some

dating as far back as the 1920s. The Chemical Demilitarization Program established under Chapter 32 is a combined effort of DoD and FEMA. DoD leads on-post activities and FEMA leads off-post activities in cooperation with state and local governments. The federal government has scheduled the CSEPP program for termination by FY 2011 under international treaty arrangements.

On September 30, 1993, President Clinton signed E.O. 12868[20] titled "Measures to Restrict the Participation by United States Persons in Weapon Proliferation Activities." In it, President Clinton declared that the proliferation of nuclear, biological, and chemical weapons, and the means of delivering them constitute an unusual and extraordinary threat to the national security, foreign policy, and economy of the United States, and he declared a further national emergency remains in effect. Clinton's order applies in the case of subversion of chemical or biological weapons in America's stockpile or disposal process. Significant in both the Bush and Clinton executive orders is the obvious linkage of U.S. chemical and biological weapons disposal and matters of foreign threat from these weapons. In both respects, there was a place for sound federal emergency management. These activities represent harbingers of post-September 11 homeland security duties.

FEMA's chemical weapons disposal program regularly encountered spending authority problems. This was because the federal government funds the entire chemical weapons stockpile disposal program exclusively through an annual appropriation to the Department of Defense. In the early 1990s, FEMA sought from Congress, with Bush OMB approval, a specific line item appropriation for its chemical weapons disposal program work. If approved, it would have appeared in the broad Veterans Affairs, HUD, and Independent Agencies Appropriation that contains most of FEMA's budget lines. Owing to congressional, largely Alabama delegation, displeasure with FEMA's handling of this work at the time, legislators proposed slashing FEMA's chemical weapons disposal program funds by 40 percent. In reaction, FEMA and the Bush administration made a hasty retreat by withdrawing their request for a dedicated appropriation for FEMA. As a result, FEMA (and DHS-EP&RD today) continued to rely solely on transfers of funding from DoD to pay for its CSEPP program implementation costs.

FEMA's associate director signed a new FEMA/Department of the Army MOU for Preparedness, Training, and Exercises for CSEPP on October 8, 1997, but like the original MOU, it made no mention of FEMA's role in emergency response. The aim of the second MOU was to facilitate grant assistance to state and local governments under CSEPP. In 1998, President Clinton signed the Strom Thurmond National Defense Authorization Act for Fiscal Year 1999, P.L.

105-261, a measure that assigned FEMA lead agency designation for managing the off-site consequences of a CSEPP chemical weapons incident lead (see Note 9).

Today, FEMA statutory authority in CSEPP resides in the FY99 Defense Authorization Act. Under that law FEMA's CSEPP authority holds until 2007. FEMA's CSEPP appropriations, which the agency distributed to states with CSEEP sites, continued to originate in the annual DoD appropriation, not the Homeland Security Department Appropriation Act.[21]

X. FEMA AND TERRORISM CONSEQUENCE MANAGEMENT

In the late 1980s, FEMA officials still did not consider terrorism or hazardous materials significant in the agency's work. Yet, Carter E.O. 12148, signed in July of 1979, assigned FEMA a "consequences of terrorism" role. Terrorism and technological emergencies are sometimes inseparable. Under Reagan E.O. 12656, §101, and other authority, technological emergencies are those that may seriously degrade or threaten the national security of the United States and may trigger national security plans or deployment of national security assets. President Reagan issued E.O. 12656 pursuant to the president's authority under the National Security Act of 1947, as amended, 50 U.S.C. §§404-405, the Federal Civil Defense Act of 1950 (enacted July 1950 and repealed in November 1994 by P. L. 103-337) and the Defense Production Act of 1950, as amended. In April of 1995, President Clinton issued Presidential Decision Directive (PDD) 39 (see House Document 105-29) and in May of 1998, PDD-62. Those measures declared that any terrorist use of, or threat to use, weapons of mass destruction (WMD) will be considered automatically to involve the federal government's "preeminent responsibility and authority."

FEMA had participated in mid- to late-1980s terrorism exercises, principally TRANSBORD I, II, and III. The scenario in TRANSBORD III is illustrative, and the drill had much in common with the major TOPOFF II terrorism exercise played in May 2003. Conducted by respective Canadian and American federal, state, provincial, and local officials, TRANSBORD III modeled

a terrorist seizure and eventual explosion of a barge containing chlorine, a poisonous gas, at a point not far from Detroit, MI, and Windsor, Canada. FEMA's players never documented the lessons they learned from the exercise. FEMA management made no changes in its operations owing to the experience of the exercise. Some of FEMA's lack of enthusiasm for counterterrorism may have stemmed from bureaucratic conflicts and the closed-shop behavior of many Federal Bureau of Investigation (FBI) officials who believed counterterrorism was the exclusive domain of their agency.

As indicated, FEMA has regularly faced encroachment on its jurisdiction from competing federal agencies. For example, in 1990, EPA published a document entitled "Response Capabilities for a Chemical/Biological Incident." EPA officials referred to the Meese Memorandum but they failed to mention, or integrate it with, 40 CFR Part 300, the National Contingency Plan for Oil Spills and Hazardous Materials Releases, commonly referred to as the National Contingency Plan (NCP), promulgated pursuant to E.O. 12560, as amended. One would expect FEMA to publish such a document, not EPA. In a concession that they may have overstepped their bounds, EPA officials alleged that their "Response Capabilities" publication has been overtaken by the updated 40 CFR Part 300.[22] While the original EPA document may have some redeeming value as a guide to EPA's own incident command role, EPA has never made the document available and never rescinded its publication by announcement in the *Federal Register*. As a second example of interloping, the FBI published a document elucidating law enforcement incident command for chemical and biological emergencies and crisis response, again without significant FEMA consultation. The FBI and FEMA did manage to publish the counterterrorism CONPLAN in 1998, despite these disagreements.

A Joint Resolution of Congress (P.L. 103-160) signed into law in November of 1993, required FEMA to improve its emergency response planning for chemical and biological incidents. The resolution maintained, "It is the sense of Congress that the President should strengthen Federal interagency emergency planning by the Federal Emergency Management Agency and other appropriate Federal, State, and local agencies for development of a capability for early detection and warning of and response to: (1) potential terrorist use of chemical or biological agents or weapons; and (2) emergencies or natural disasters involving industrial chemicals or the widespread outbreak of disease." FEMA's failure to act on this resolution led policymakers preparing so-called Nunn-Lugar-Domenici legislation in 1996 to assign the job of federal interchange with state and local governments to another federal agency (Title XIV of the Defense Authorization Act for FY97, Public Law 104-201).

As late as 1994, significant factions within FEMA's Response and Recovery Directorate continued to argue against major disaster declarations for human-caused events. They did not oppose,

however, emergency declarations for human-caused events. Presidents issue emergency declarations to mobilize rapid federal assistance to facilitate life safety, rescue, and emergency response. Conceivably, if factional reluctance held sway, this could have affected FEMA's operational response to both terrorism events and technological emergencies. The Robert T. Stafford Act of 1988 clearly states that the president may issue declarations of major disaster or emergency regardless of cause, for events producing fire, flood, or explosion (terms undefined). Since the Oklahoma City bombing in 1995, FEMA officials now collectively support declarations of major disaster for human-caused disasters. By the mid-1990s, internal FEMA factional resistance to the practice of rolling human-caused emergency declarations into declarations of major disaster dissipated as a practical and legal matter.

FEMA was trusted with few technical responsibilities in national emergencies. As late as 2003, FEMA's role in all federal response plans did not include the technical aspects of hazard identification and assessment for chemical, biological, or radiological accidents or events. FEMA did not stockpile, and did not provide, protective equipment for monitoring or for decontaminating people or property affected by chemical-biological-radiological exposure. At one time under its RADEF instrumentation program, FEMA did provide monitoring devices for radiological incidents to the states, but the federal government terminated that program long ago.

XI. FEMA AND MAJOR OIL SPILLS

Releases of oil or hazardous materials in manufacture, transport, or use that violate federal regulations sometimes require emergency response and recovery operations by government. The National Contingency Plan addresses the assignment of federal agency duties in such events (see Note 11). FEMA was an original signer of the NCP. Federal law does not classify oil as a hazardous substance. Nonetheless, major oil spills often require emergency response and recovery aimed at cleanup, damage compensation, and environmental restoration. Oil spill disasters and hazardous materials

disasters require many of the same emergency management skills and resources.

President Reagan, under authority provided in the Superfund Act of 1980, declared that the NCP "shall provide for a National Response Team (NRT)." NRT is composed of representatives of appropriate federal departments and agencies for national planning and coordination of preparedness and response actions. Regional Response Teams are the regional counterparts of the NRT. These teams plan and coordinate regional preparedness and response actions. The former SLPS

Directorate chaired both the Preparedness and Training Committees of the National Response Team, established by E.O. 12580 (see Note 12).

Under the National Contingency Plan, the lead federal agency On-scene Commander (OSC) refers to the EPA or Coast Guard senior official at the site of an incident. The NCP calls for use of incident command procedures at sites of hazardous materials release. The plan requires FEMA to manage humanitarian and financial assistance needed in oil spills or hazardous materials incident response and recovery. The plan anticipates a technical response that includes decontamination and monitoring as well as application of safe re-entry procedures for decontaminated areas. There is no direct funding under the Superfund Act of 1980, or the Superfund Amendments and Reauthorization Act of 1986, or the transportation legal authorities for humanitarian relief such as mass population aid, sheltering, feeding, and medical care. The EPA, the Coast Guard, and DOT have no jurisdictional or budget authority to undertake these kinds of emergency response.

In March of 1989, the *Exxon Valdez,* a very large crude oil carrier or supertanker, ran aground in Alaska's Prince William Sound, causing massive punctures of the vessel's hull and creating a colossal oil spill. When White House and Congressional people asked FEMA headquarters to respond to the oil spill disaster, FEMA officials resisted. FEMA officials determined that under the Stafford Act of 1988, the agency lacked legal authority to provide assistance. They also expressed concern that if their agency helped, FEMA might not recover its disaster relief expenditures if the

Department of Justice filed a civil or criminal recovery action for monetary damages against Exxon Corporation. At the time, Senate Appropriations Committee members requested and received an opinion for the record, which explained FEMA's declination.

The litigation surrounding the federal cases involving *Exxon Valdez* discovery and Freedom of Information Act (FOIA) requests to FEMA compelled FEMA officials to disclose its Alaskan oil spill role. President Bush assigned FEMA some oil spill work under E.O. 12580, which the agency pursued through its participation on the NRT RRTs (see Note 13).

While Bush's E.O. 12580, as amended, still reflects a population relocation and NRT role for FEMA, the agency's relocation role became obsolete as of October 31, 1990. The Bush administration gave that role to EPA. EPA now uses the U.S. Army Corps of Engineers for population relocation.

The original NCP blurred the distinction between incident command and consequences management. The federal government substantially clarified the differences in NCP revisions of September 1994. The revisions gave EPA incident command leadership for hazardous materials incidents occurring on land and the Coast Guard incident command leadership for hazardous materials releases transpiring in or along waterways.

FEMA continues its role on the NRT and on the RRTs under Bush E.O. 12580. FEMA continued to provide coordination and program assistance to lead and supporting departments or agencies under the NCP and FRERP.

XII. FEMA HAZMAT IN THE CLINTON-WITT AND BUSH-ALLBAUGH ERAS

In the Clinton-Witt era of the 1990s, FEMA moved more assertively into disaster mitigation work and hazard risk assessment. This course steered the agency more directly into matters of science and engineering. New technologies, such as geographical information systems, remote sensing, smaller computers that are more portable, information systems technology, and so on helped to automate federal emergency management. Yet, jurisdictional turf wars in other realms continued

to raise the question, "Who is in charge?" That question tormented each cohort of FEMA officials in their relationships with officials of other departments and agencies.

In September of 1993, FEMA Director James Lee Witt, with Clinton administration assent, created the Preparedness, Training, and Exercise (PTE) Directorate. PTE absorbed the Radiological Emergency Preparedness (REP) Program, the Chemical Stockpile Emergency Preparedness

Program, and hazardous materials assignments. Clinton's E.O. 12241 gave FEMA's PTE Directorate duties in the Federal Radiological Emergency Response Plan.

FEMA Director James Lee Witt mandated integration of the FRP and FRERP in a decision document dated September 5, 1993. Those inside FEMA were slow to merge the two plans. As mentioned, in failing to resolve issues such as the interplay between the Price-Anderson Act and the Robert T. Stafford Act, confusion continued regarding postaccident, postdeclaration payments of citizen claims by federal agencies (see Note 14).

On January 31, 1995, Director Witt issued Policy Statement No. 1-95, regarding FEMA's informal adoption of the FRP by the director. It stated officially that FEMA should use the principles of the Incident Command System (ICS) in all of its response efforts. Those in FEMA working with Urban Search and Rescue plans and CSEPP had already agreed to use ICS. The NCP for Hazardous Materials, the FRERP, and the Meese Memorandum all mandated use of ICS. The FRP also adopted "Incident Command." FEMA deserves much credit for promoting, and diffusing use of, the Incident Command System across all realms of federal emergency response.

From June 2001 to May 2002, PTE functions were part of the Response and Recovery Directorate. After May of 2001, FEMA Director Joseph Allbaugh, a former chief of staff to Texas Governor George W. Bush and a trusted Bush campaign manager, temporarily dispatched these functions to the Office of National Preparedness in FEMA.[23] Allbaugh later returned them to the Response and Recovery Directorate (RRD). On March 1, 2003, when the Department of Homeland Security (DHS) absorbed FEMA, the RRD was broken

into two offices and both went into the DHS Emergency Preparedness and Response (EP&R) Directorate. However, those who organized DHS placed the Office of National Preparedness in Border and Immigration Security, a unit entirely separate from and unrelated to the EP&R directorate.

President Bush issued Homeland Security Presidential Directive/HSPD-5 on February 28, 2003. Its purpose was, "To enhance the ability of the United States to manage domestic incidents by establishing a single, comprehensive national incident management system." Paragraphs 3 and 4 of the directive concisely explain the marriage of conventional disaster management and terrorism consequence management (see Note 15).

Particularly remarkable is Paragraph 11 of the directive. To paraphrase, it calls for the Assistant to the President for Homeland Security (today the Secretary of DHS) and the Assistant to the President for National Security Affairs to manage "interagency policy coordination on domestic and international incident management," respectively, as directed by the president (see Note 16). The aim is "to ensure that the United States domestic and international incident management efforts are seamlessly united." Section 15 calls for a National Emergency Management System, which is to include a core set of concepts, principles, terminology, and technologies covering the incident command system, multiagency coordination systems, unified command, training, qualifications, certification, and incident information collection, tracking, and reporting. The directive called for "stand up" of NIMS by June 1, 2003 (see Note 17). (On March 1, 2004, the final version of the National Incident Management System [139 pp.] was issued by DHS.)

XIII. CONCLUSION

Presidents have regularly augmented or refashioned FEMA authority through executive orders. They did so to steer the agency to fulfill various new public purposes or policy goals, and to draw it into various multiagency work assignments and planning endeavors. FEMA directors also played

a major role in determining duties and obligations the agency would take on or forgo.

Over the period 1978 to early 1979, President Jimmy Carter used his powers of reorganization to create FEMA and Congress offered no objection. The Three Mile Island nuclear power plant incident in March of 1979 convinced Carter that the Nuclear Regulatory Commission was not up to the job of managing nuclear power emergencies outside utility grounds. He decided to assign much of this kind of work to his new FEMA, subject to cooperation with the NRC. Carter issued several hazardous materials emergency declarations for Love Canal, and ultimately declared a disaster there. The Carter presidency ended in January of 1981 shortly after President Carter signed Superfund into law. All of this rapidly introduced FEMA to the world of hazardous materials emergency management.

President Reagan served from January 1981 to January 1989. Reagan's first presidential disaster declaration was for a hexane explosion in the sewers of Louisville, Kentucky. Love Canal and the Louisville hexane incident, among others, pressed Reagan era FEMA officials to conclude that their interpretation of the Disaster Relief Act of 1974 (P.L. 93-288) was incorrect: Human-caused disasters and technological hazards were indeed part of FEMA's domain. The Reagan administration also had to cope with the Times Beach, Missouri, dioxin contamination and America's reaction to the Bhopal, India, hazardous substance tragedy in 1985. The Bhopal disaster impelled Congress and the Reagan administration to enact the Superfund Amendments and Reauthorization Act, a measure that called for local emergency planning committees and community right-to-know protections for those residing near dangerous chemical facilities. The 1986 Chernobyl nuclear power plant disaster in the Soviet Union pressed the Reagan administration to reassess nuclear safety emergency planning around U.S. nuclear power stations.

President Reagan signed the Robert T. Stafford Disaster Relief and Emergency Assistance Act (P.L. 101-107) on November 23, 1988. The Stafford Act continues to stand as a milestone in the history of federal emergency management and it had many implications in hazardous materials-related emergency management. When Stafford became law most FEMA senior officials–unless they had personal experience working with oil, hazardous substance, or radiological emergencies and plans– remained uncertain regarding FEMA's role in technological emergencies. During the Reagan era, FEMA assumed a role in the Chemical Weapons

Stockpile Disposal Program. The Reagan administration played a major role in reforming federal emergency management assignments through the Meese Memorandum and through executive orders concerning emergency planning and preparedness around commercial nuclear power plants. These measures strongly effect federal emergency management today.

President George H.W. Bush served from January 1989 to January 1993. On January 24, 1991, Wallace E. Stickney, the Bush FEMA director, signed a memorandum regarding FEMA's Emergency Response Readiness. That memorandum stipulated that the Federal Response Plan was the single plan by which FEMA would provide direct and indirect financial and technical assistance to state and local governments and their citizens or other eligible applicants. The Federal Response Plan provides a system of federal humanitarian relief applicable whether or not a presidential declaration of major disaster or emergency is in effect.

The Bush administration officially issued the FRP in May 1992 and the Clinton administration completed a comprehensive revision of the plan in April 1999. The RFP has evolved into an all-hazard document. It began as a "Plan for a Federal Response for Natural Disasters," which in turn became the "Plan for a Federal Response to a Catastrophic Earthquake" in 1987 pursuant to the Earthquake Hazards Reduction Act of 1977, as amended (42 U.S.C. §7701 et seq.) The FRP did not necessarily replace other federal emergency plans. Representatives of 26 other federal departments or agencies and the American Red Cross follow the FRP.

President William J. Clinton served from late January 1993 until late January 2001. Clinton's appointment of James Lee Witt as director of FEMA, and Clinton's strong interest in matters of disaster policy, helped improve both the substance and image of FEMA operations. Owing to President Clinton's support, the White House political office and key staff regularly protected and defended FEMA, something seldom done by White House staffs of previous presidents. Clinton's HAZMAT legacy encompasses matters of chemical weapons disposal, hazardous materials emergency management, and HAZMAT disaster mitigation initiatives.

George W. Bush became president in late January of 2001. Bush and his FEMA Director Joseph Allbaugh brought about several internal, though questionably effective, reorganizations of FEMA. The Bush-Allbaugh FEMA diminished the Clinton administration's organizational emphasis on disaster mitigation. President Bush came to depend heavily on FEMA to address natural disasters as well as human-caused or technology-caused calamities. The terror attacks of 9-11 redefined the entire mission of the Bush administration and the result was a complete merger of federal emergency management with homeland security (counterterrorism) efforts.

The absorption of FEMA into the Department of Homeland Security may not represent the end of FEMA, although some are extremely worried about the way the unification has taken place.[24] Establishment of DHS ended FEMA's status as an independent federal agency reporting directly to the president. FEMA lost authority for certain activities owing to the Homeland Security Act and to reorganization measures as it was incorporated into DHS. These activities and functions primarily involve telecommunication functions.[25] Because of deficiencies in the way DHS was created, the department's broadest and most flexible statutory authority, particularly the Stafford Act, FEMA leadership has a shot at being a major player in the department. Chronic understaffing, if not addressed, however, means that FEMA composes less than 2 percent of DHS staff, and is thus vulnerable to being overlooked.

The vestiges of FEMA now are only a part of a federal Cabinet-level department. FEMA's primary preparedness grant programs have been drastically cut.[26] The result may be a much reduced role for traditional emergency management at the state and local level, funding for which has historically been provided by FEMA.[27] Administrative authority for the Assistance for Firefighters Grant Program (FIRE Grant Program) has moved to the Office of Domestic Preparedness, leading many in the fire service to question the administration's commitment to their needs.[28]

In a way, however, FEMA Director Macy's desire to move FEMA from independent agency status to that of a full Cabinet-level department may have been finally fulfilled. Bureaucratic clout is not necessarily permanent, and only the competence and knowledge of FEMA's own staff will ultimately determine whether it continues or is terminated. With 170,000 employees and some 22 major federal agencies and programs offices, DHS appears to manifest a strong bias against FEMA. This is in part because so few top DHS appointees and staff understand FEMA's past roles, strengths, and weaknesses.

Owing to the Homeland Security Act of 2002, the DHS Emergency Preparedness and Response Directorate (encompassing the bulk of the old FEMA) does have some new authority and new staff. Whether those new functions and staff remain in DHS and FEMA remains to be seen. Already the pharmaceutical stockpile function is scheduled to return to HHS. Moreover, while the secretary of DHS has assumed the role played by FEMA directors, and also enjoys more presidential access, a greater role in matters of national security policy, management authority over vast areas of border control, customs, immigration, emergency health, and more. The secretary of DHS, heading the third largest department of the federal government, is today a "super-FEMA director" able to work on the same plain as secretaries of other Cabinet-level departments.[29]

FEMA directors and other officials regularly had to decide how to manage new types of technological or human-caused disaster. Many FEMA leaders were reluctant to extend their agency's duties into strange new realms related to human-caused or technology-caused disasters. FEMA leaders needed time to decide on what FEMA's role would be in various hazardous materials and oil spill emergencies. The agency faced a long-running struggle to establish its place in nuclear power emergency response. Conversely, the agency may have moved into chemical weapons transport emergency management prematurely. FEMA's role in terrorism consequence management evolved from its experience in hazardous materials management, nuclear power emergency planning, and nuclear attack emergency planning. FEMA's role in oil spill emergencies, bio- or chemical attack, and postterror attack victim compensation remains muddled or unclear.

FEMA's work has both humanitarian and technical characteristics, posing a dilemma for FEMA officials who had to decide job assignments and position qualifications for those hired to serve as managers and line workers in the agency. With few exceptions, FEMA has elected to emphasize humanitarian work rather than technical work. When FEMA conducted its humanitarian work well–particularly when elected officials and the public were satisfied with FEMA's handling of disaster relief–generalist, politically responsive agency management seemed to be a wise course of action. Hazardous materials-related emergencies, however, often involve complex matters of science and engineering, areas of expertise poorly represented in the ranks of FEMA.

FEMA's story has been a prelude to post-September 11 homeland security. FEMA's management of human-caused and technology-caused emergencies and disasters, as well as its management of natural disasters, prepared its people for the era of terrorism consequence management. Ironically, FEMA's disaster management authority and experience significantly counterweighted its small staff size, relative to several other very large agencies moved into DHS. FEMA's hazardous materials management history evolved through different presidents, different FEMA leaders, and frequent reorganizations. For FEMA people, disasters, or emergencies, some almost unimaginable, often triggered presidential declarations of major disaster or emergency, new laws, new executive orders, new directives, and new policies that they had to address. FEMA's hazardous materials emergency management legacy may fairly be said to reside in the organizational heart of the Department of Homeland Security today.

NOTES

Reader Notes

Note 1: William R. Cumming worked for the U.S. FEMA Office of General Counsel from 1979 to 1999. Richard T. Sylves is a professor of Political Science and International Relations at University of Delaware and has published extensively on disaster policy and emergency management.

Note 2: The Federal Radiological Emergency Response Plan (FRERP) appeared 50 Fed. Reg. 46542 on November 8, 1985, and was republished as a notice on May 8, 1996, at 61 Fed. Reg. 20944-70. The FRERP has never been codified in the Code of Federal Regulation (CFR), although a correction was published on June 5, 1996, at 61 Fed. Reg. 28583-84. Over the years, FEMA officials delegated administration of the FRERP to several of its directorates: (1) the Plans and Preparedness Directorate from signing until October 1981; (2) the State and Local Programs Support Directorate from 1981 to November 1993; (3) the Preparedness, Training, and Exercises Directorate from November 1993 to June 2001; and, (4) the Response and Recovery Directorate from June 2001 until March 1, 2003. For a brief period during 2002, the Office of National Preparedness, an independent organization within FEMA, had jurisdiction over the Radiological Emergency Preparedness Program.

Note 3: The FRERP is not the only technical response plan for radiological releases that might affect the public. NRC uses another plan called the National Contingency Plan (40 CFR Part 300). NCP applies to nonpower plant NRC licensees who might produce radiological releases likely to threaten the public. EPA leads primary response under the NCP if a party releases nonlicensed radiological materials.

Note 4: These 1993 orders involve administrative procedures aimed at eliminating confusion between the Federal Response Plan (FRP) and the Federal Radiological Emergency Response Plan (FRERP). In a related development, FEMA published in the *Federal Register* at 63 Fed. Reg. 48222 (September 9, 1998) the Draft Final Recommendations of the Radiological Emergency Preparedness (REP) program Strategic Review. FEMA coordinated its radiological role through the Federal Radiological Preparedness Coordinating Committee (FRPCC) and the NRC/FEMA Steering Committee described respectively at 44 CFR Part 351 and 56 Fed. Reg. 9459 (March 6, 1991) and publishes and distributes appropriate guidance and technical materials with NRC concurrence. The FRPCC appears as well in the Hazardous Materials Transportation Authorization Act of 1994, at 49 U.S.C. §5101. NRC uses the Hazardous Materials NCP to respond to incidents involving NRC licensees not building or operating fixed nuclear power stations. FEMA's response duties were managed by its Preparedness, Training, and Exercises Directorate.

Note 5: The key laws that sustain USFA are the Federal Fire Prevention and Control Act of 1974, as further amended by the Hotel and Motel Fire Safety Act of 1990 (P.L. 101-391) and Arson Prevention Act of 1994 (P.L. 103-254) and Firefighters' Safety Study Act (P.L. 101-446). These are codified at 15 U.S.C. §2201 et seq. (see 44 CFR Parts 150-152).

Note 6: ONT was led at various times by Senior Executives Richard Sanderson, Dennis Kwiatkowski, Dr. Joan Steyart, Ph.D., and Craig Wingo, P.E., and retired Army Col. Joseph D. Schwarzkop. Ann Martin, Delburt Kohl, Russell Salter, Vanessa Quinn, and W. Craig Conklin were principal FEMA senior civil servants who administered these hazard programs under various organizational schemes. Schwarzkop, Wingo, Quinn, and Conklin remain with the Department of Homeland Security, although not all in technical hazards programs, while the others have left or retired.

Note 7: EPCRA, also known as SARA Title III, 42 U.S.C. §11001 et seq., is a closely related authority. EPCRA mentions FEMA's emergency duties at 42 United States Code §11005(a).

Note 8: The key executive orders relating to Hazardous Materials for FEMA included Carter E.O. 12148, as amended; E.O. 12241; E.O. 12580, as amended, and E.O. 12657. For Hazardous Materials incidents with National Security Emergency implications, see Reagan E.O. 12656, as amended.

Note 9: FEMA cited as its authority Carter E.O. 12148 and the Emergency Planning and Community Right to Know Act of 1986. FEMA also cited §611 of the Stafford Act of 1988. The Army referred to §1412 of P.L. 99-145 (which also mentioned FEMA as an optional funding organization for state and local governments with reimbursement by the Army) and P.L. 104-201 (DoD Authorization Act for FY 96) for

Integrated Product and Process Teams (IPTS) under the program. The Army also cited E.O. 12580 (which also mentions FEMA in §1, 2, and 9). The Stafford Act specifically mentions that DoD is eligible for predeclaration assistance, something relevant to CSEPP emergencies. DoD has no up-to-date implementing regulations, see 32 CFR Part 501-502.

Note 10: This statute was recast as part of the complete recodification of Title 49 of the United States Code and now appears at 49 U.S.C. §5101 et seq. FEMA was referenced in the statute.

Note 11: The NCP appears in the Code of Federal Regulations (CFR) at 40 CFR Part 300. Relatedly, FEMA published the Draft Final Recommendations of the Radiological Emergency Preparedness (REP) program Strategic Review in the *Federal Register* at 63 Fed. Reg. 48222 (September 9, 1998).

Note 12: Later, E.O. 12777, updated the NCP, and those original committees were superseded by a Response Committee, a Technology Committee, and a Preparedness Committee, all under the Co-Chair of EPA and the U.S. Coast Guard. The Coast Guard is now part of the Department of Homeland Security, and so one co-chair agency of the NCP is in DHS.

Note 13: The National Oil and Hazardous Substances Pollution Contingency Plan (the "NCP") was originally issued with FEMA concurrence pursuant to Reagan E.O. 12316, August 14, 1981, revoked by Reagan E.O. 12580, January 23, 1987. That latter executive order remains in effect. GHW Bush E.O. 12777, October 18, 1991, and Clinton E.O. 13016, August 1996, both significantly amended the NCP. In September 1994, the National Contingency Plan was republished at 40 CFR Part 300 clarifying the incident command leadership role of the EPA and the Coast Guard vis-à-vis the consequence management lead role for FEMA.

Note 14: See for example the conflict in official FEMA positions on the use of the Robert T. Stafford Act (pre-enactment of present Title VI) in NUREG 1457, Resources Available for Nuclear Power Plant Emergencies Under the Price-Anderson Act and the Robert T. Stafford Disaster Relief and Emergency Assistance Act, dated July 1992, issued by NRC (asserts that the Act may be used citing Title V of the Act), and the Report of the President's Commission on Catastrophic Nuclear Accidents (pursuant to E.O. 12658) (stating the Act has no applicability to such an event). See also NRC correspondence dated March 25, 1992. NUREG 1447 also addresses this issue but until the attorney general definitively interprets the two statutory schemes that allow for off-site relief and damages, no real answer exists.

Note 15: In Paragraphs 6 and 7 of Homeland Security Presidential Directive HSPD-5, President George W. Bush conveys more about how disaster management is to be addressed as "domestic incident management." "(6) The Federal Government recognizes the roles and responsibilities of state and local authorities in domestic incident management. Initial responsibility for managing domestic incidents generally falls on state and local authorities. The Federal Government will assist state and local authorities when their resources are overwhelmed, or when Federal interests are involved. The Secretary will coordinate with State and local governments to ensure adequate planning, equipment, training, and exercise activities. The Secretary will also provide assistance to State and local governments to develop all-hazards plans and capabilities, including those of greatest importance to the security of the United States, and will ensure that State, local, and Federal plans are compatible. (7) The Federal Government recognizes the role that the private and nongovernmental sectors play in preventing, preparing for, responding to, and recovering from terrorist attacks, major disasters, and other emergencies. The Secretary will coordinate with the private and nongovernmental sectors to ensure adequate planning, equipment, training, and exercise activities and to promote partnerships to address incident management capabilities."

Note 16: The National Homeland Security Strategy issued on July 6, 2002, called for merger of the Federal Response Plan, National Contingency Plan for Oil Spills and Hazardous Materials Releases, and the Federal Radiological Emergency Response Plan. Then on February 28, 2003, the president signed (issued) Homeland Security Presidential Directive HSPD-5, naming the Secretary of Homeland Security as the incident manager for all federal responses, ordering the creation of the National Incident Management System [NIMS] and a National Response Plan, and further implementing the Homeland Security Strategy of July 6, 2002.

Note 17: Paragraph 18 of HSPD-5 states, "All Federal departments and agencies will use the NIMS in their domestic incident management and emergency prevention, preparedness, response, recovery, and mitigation activities, as well as those actions taken in support of State or local entities. The heads of Federal departments and agencies shall participate in the NRP, shall assist and support the Secretary in the development and maintenance of the NRP, and shall participate in and use domestic incident reporting systems and protocols established by the Secretary."

Endnotes

1. "A Review of Federal Authorities for Hazardous Materials Accident Safety," December 1993, EPA 550-R-93-002, from U.S. EPA.
2. James E. Anderson, "Policy Implementation," Ch. 6, pp. 213–270, in *Public Policymaking: An Introduction.* 3rd. ed. Boston: Houghton-Mifflin, 1997.
3. Phillip J. Cooper. *By Order of the President: The Use and Abuse of Executive Direct Action.* Lawrence, KS: University of Kansas Press, 2002.
4. For a discussion of these organizations see the CRS report dated April 18, 1978, entitled "Emergency Preparedness and Disaster Assistance: Federal Organizations and Programs."
5. For a history of organizations involved in civil defense go to www.disaster-time.com.
6. The 1984 Olympics in Los Angeles and the 1996 Olympics in Atlanta impacted FEMA and its involvement in domestic terrorism preparedness and response.
7. The implementation document, the "National Incident Management System" 139 pp., was issued on March 1, 2004, by DHS.
8. Haddow, George and Jane Bullock. *Introduction to Emergency Management.* Amsterdam, Netherlands: Butterworth-Heinemann, 2003.
9. Birkland, Thomas A. *After Disaster: Agenda Setting, Public Policy, and Focusing Events.* Washington, D.C.: Georgetown University Press, 1997.
10. 45 Fed. Reg. 82713.
11. See NRC letter dated January 13, 1989, and DOE letter dated December 20, 1988.
12. Sylves, Richard T. "Nuclear Power Emergency Planning: Politics of the Task." *International Journal of Mass Emergencies and Disasters.* 2(1984): 185–196.
13. E.O. 11130, the executive order on executive orders, allows any federal department or agency to draft suggested new or amended language for an executive order subject to OMB review. The

attorney general determines whether the final draft of the executive order is appropriate in law.

14. Comprehensive Environmental Response, Compensation, and Liability Act (CERCLA) 42 U.S.C. § 9604 (2004).
15. Now totally replaced by Reagan E.O. 12560 as amended.
16. Harvey Eisner, Editor-in-Chief *Firehouse Magazine*, Editorial, FIRE CHIEF (Feb 1, 2004). Found online at: http://firechief.com/ar/firefighting_editors_editorial/index.htm.
17. Council on Foreign Relations, "Emergency Responders: Drastically Underfunded, Dangerously Unprepared," http://www.cfr.org/pdf/Responders_TF.pdf, page 2, July 29, 2003.
18. See National Security Decision Directive 47 (1982) and 188 (1985) http://www.colorado.edu/hazards/wp/wp107/appendixa.html

19.

FEDERAL EMERGENCY MANAGEMENT AGENCY
WASHINGTON, D.C. 20472

January 24, 1991

MEMORANDUM FOR: ALL FEMA EMPLOYEES

FROM: Wallace E. Stickney
                 Director
SUBJECT: FEMA's Emergency Response Readiness

Events in the Middle East have made readiness a watch word throughout the world. Accordingly, we have reviewed and tested our plans, our communications system, and procedures for support to state and local emergency response operations. We found that some requirements and systems need updating and clear decisions needed to be made. To ensure FEMA's capability to support the full scope of emergency response, and best support the state and local response plans which we helped develop, I have determined that the Federal Response Plan (for Public Law 93-288, as amended) will be used if needed. We use all or parts of this plan on a regular basis and it is the process with which states are most familiar. The State and Local Programs and Support and National Preparedness Directorates are cooperating in finetuning this capability, and I am pleased with their progress.

Our readiness review identified some areas of FEMA in need of additional improvement. These areas include the Continuity of Operations Plan and other routinely used management tools. We are taking this opportunity to address these areas as well to assure a fully integrated response capability. I appreciate your assistance in the longer term planning required to achieve these improvements. We will be a much better agency next month than we were last month!

To date there is no known specific threat against any facility or person. However, because of the war in the Middle East, the potential exists that a terrorist act could occur. FEMA, like most other departments and agencies, has taken steps to enhance security in this building and in all field activities. In addition, security awareness of personnel has been encouraged through security advisories both local and nationwide. We feel confident that should a specific threat become identified, we will be provided information to make available to all FEMA employees. Moreover, should a threat exist anywhere in the country, we are confident that we and the state officials will be advised of this by those agencies tasked with law enforcement aspects of national security.

FEMA's readiness to respond to major emergencies is an important responsibility for all of us. I know we all want to offer our talents to FEMA when needed. Extra assistance could be required were a major technological or natural disaster to occur. Please let your supervisor know if you would like to volunteer to assist, should we need to implement the federal response plan.

I appreciate your support in these times. Our task without question, is to execute our assigned programs and emergency operations. We know our responsibilities. We have reviewed, practiced, tested, and updated our procedures. We will continue to hone our skills and be prepared to do our best when called. I am confident that if we all simply do our jobs well, we will ensure that the Federal Government will provide the support that the state and local governments need, when and if required.

20. 58 Fed. Reg. 51749.

21. The Department of Homeland Security Appropriation is now one of the fourteen appropriations acts that fund the federal government. The first such statute was Public Law 108-90, October 1, 2003. It is perhaps the most significant Congressional consolidation so far with respect to the Department besides the Homeland Security Act of 2002.

22. EPA, like FEMA, administers an array of statutes. The problem is that each statutory scheme has its own standards of enforcement and emergency response. Thus, it is virtually impossible to know in advance exactly how EPA will respond to an unexpected event. See, for example, enforcement guidance published in the *Federal Register* on May 30, 1991, at 56 Fed. Reg. 24393.

23. A White House Press Release on May 8, 2001, announced ONP creation within FEMA. In effect ONP was designated the lead federal office federal interchange with state and local governments on matters of terrorism. Events of 9-11 effectively ended the assignment and the clout of the office.

24. "Former Director of FEMA Testifies Before Subcommittee on National Security, Emerging Threats and International Relations and the Subcommittee on Energy Policy, Natural Resources and Regulatory Affairs" (Found on the Web at http://www.allhands.net/pn//modules.php?op=mo dload&name=News&file=article&sid=592&mode= thread&order=0&thold=0.) "[FEMA] has been buried beneath a massive bureaucracy whose main and seemingly only focus is fighting terrorism and while that is absolutely critical, it should not be at the expense of preparing for and responding to natural disasters. While the likelihood of another terrorist attack on our land may be inevitable, it is an absolute certainty that our country will experience more natural disasters and there is no question that some will be catastrophic. It is not a matter of "if," it is a matter of when and where."

25. See E.O. 12472, and 47 CFR Parts 11, 67, 201–212.

26. Karin Fischer, "Anti-Terrorism Focus Could Hurt State Cuts Would Affect Ability to Respond to Natural Disasters," *Charleston (WV) Daily Mail P1C* (February 27, 2004). "State officials, however, are alarmed at reductions in grants that help pay for the salaries of emergency services staff. The appropriation for the Emergency Management Performance Grants would decrease by $9 million, and states would face limitations on the share that would go to pay personnel."

27. Shaun Waterman, *Analysis: Fear of Being Eclipsed by Terror*, UPI (March 19, 2004). "Of the plethora of federal grants that fund state and local emergency management activities, only one–the Emergency Management Performance Grant–has historically covered the wage costs of this personnel-intensive business. The Bush administration's proposed 2005 budget cuts the allocation for that program by 5 percent, but–far more damagingly, say critics–caps the amount that can be spent on salaries at one-quarter of any grant. The fact is, if no source of funding is available for these posts, the temptation will always be to save money (by cutting them) and make those (emergency management) duties someone else's responsibility–give it to the fire department, or the police."

28. FIRE Grants Moved to ODP, Funded at $750 Million, *Fire Chief on Line News & Trends* (Sep 18 2003). "[T] he IAFC and many other fire service organizations have fought the transfer of the FIRE Grants to the Office of Domestic Preparedness, saying the program that has become critical to equipping fire departments might be lost in other first responder grant programs. . . . Randy Bruegman, immediate past president of the International Association of Fire Chiefs . . . recently warned that moving the program to ODP would mean the end of the FIRE grant program as we know it. He still holds by that prediction. I still believe that's true, said Bruegman, chief of the city of Fresno Fire Department." Found on the Web at: http://firechief.com/ar/firefighting_fire_grants_ moved_2/index.htm (Last consulted March 9, 2004). See also Harvey Eisner, Editor-in-Chief, *Firehouse Magazine*, Editorial, *Fire Chief* (Feb 1, 2004). Found online at: http://firechief. com/ar/firefighting_editors_editorial/index.htm "As a weak USFA minimizes the fire service, so is it minimized by moving administration of the FIRE Act into the Office of Domestic Preparedness, which resides within the DHS Borders and Transportation Directorate and has no connections with the fire service. This is a politically calculated move, the only goal of which is to repurpose existing appropriations for basic fire department needs into the Homeland Security Department's WMD bureaucracy."

29. The results of TOPOFF II in May 2003, and under HSPD-5, suggest that the DHS Secretary should not be assigned the job of Incident Commander.

APPENDIX A: DIRECTOR OF FEMA TERMS OF OFFICE

Carter Administration:
April 1, 1979–August 1979----------------Gordon Vickery
Acting FEMA Director and United States Fire Administrator
September 1979–January 1981----------------John W. Macy, Jr.
FEMA Director, Confirmed by Senate

Reagan Administration:
February 1981–March 1981----------------Bud E. Gallagher
Acting FEMA Director and Director Special Facility Berryville, VA

April 1981----------------John C. McConnell
Acting FEMA Director and Associate Director for Plans and Preparedness

May 1981–August 1985----------------Louis O. Guiffrida
FEMA Director, Confirmed by Senate
Reagan Appointee

September 1985–October 1985----------------Robert H. Morris
Acting FEMA Director and Deputy Director

November 1985–June 1989----------------Julius W. Becton, Jr.
FEMA Director, Confirmed by Senate

G.H.W. Bush Administration:
July 1989–May 1990----------------Robert H. Morris
Acting FEMA Director and Deputy Director

June 1990–August 1990----------------Jerry Jennings
Acting FEMA Director and Deputy Director

September 1990–January 1993----------------Wallace E. Stickney
FEMA Director, Confirmed by Senate

Clinton Administration:
February 1993–March 1993----------------William C. Tidball
Acting FEMA Director and Chief of Staff

April 1993–January 2001----------------James L. Witt
FEMA Director, Confirmed by the Senate
G.W. Bush Administration:

February 2001–March 1, 2003----------------Joseph M. Allbaugh
FEMA Director, Confirmed by Senate

March 2003–to present----------------Michael Brown
Undersecretary for the Emergency Preparedness and Response Directorate, Department of Homeland Security

KEY DIRECTORATES OR ADMINISTRATIONS OF THE FEDERAL EMERGENCY MANAGEMENT AGENCY 1979–2003 (LISTED CHRONOLOGICALLY FROM 1979)

1. Federal Insurance Administration, 1979–2003

No technological hazards programs, functions, or activities

2. United States Fire Administration, 1979–2003

Responsible for training nonfederal first responders (fire) for HAZMATs. Terrorism response added by the Antiterrorism and Effective Death Penalty Act of 1996, P. L. 104-132, 18 U.S.C. Section 1189. (This authority was funded through appropriations passed through to FEMA by the Department of Justice.)

3. Disaster Response and Recovery Directorate, 1979–1981

Natural hazards response by charter but assigned recovery duties under declarations for Love Canal hazardous substance incident and Louisville, Kentucky, hexane explosion.

4. Plans and Preparedness Directorate, 1979–1981

Civil defense planning and grants largely oriented to radiological response to nuclear strategic attack. Briefly housed Radiological Emergency Planning.

5. Mitigation and Research Directorate, 1979–1981

Focused on all-hazards and housed research portion of civil defense budget. Its budget reached $14M in some years before repeal of Federal Civil Defense Act in 1994.

6. Training and Fire Directorate, 1981–1983

Encompassed USFA, item 2. Note that the Fire Prevention and Control Act of 1974 clearly established authority to train for HAZMAT response.

7. National Preparedness Directorate, 1981–1993

This Directorate was responsible for national security planning in FEMA with particular emphasis on industrial mobilization and use of the military to support domestic response activity when required. This directorate housed FEMA's antiterrorism or counterterrorism response planning.

8. State and Local Preparedness and Support Directorate, 1981–1993

Responsible for the remnants of civil defense planning and for grants to state governments. It handled the REP and CSEEP programs, under MOU's with Department of the Army and the Nuclear Regulatory Commission. Also home of FEMA representative to the National Contingency Plan for Oil Spills and Hazardous Materials Releases. See E.O. 12580.

9. Emergency Operations Directorate, 1981–1986

Responsible for Continuity of Government (COG) and COOP Continuity of Operations Planning (COOP).

10. Response and Recovery Directorate 1993–2003

Responsibility for the Federal Response Plan promulgated 1992 with Emergency Support Function 11, applicable for HAZMATs.

11. Preparedness, Training, Exercises Directorate 1993–2001

Responsible for REP, CSEEP, and HAZMATs planning but not actual emergency response operations.

12. Mitigation Directorate 1993–2001

Responsibility for natural hazards only.

13. Information Technology Services Directorate 1994–2003

No HAZMATS responsibility albeit for communications (See Emergency Support Function 5 of FRP)

14. Insurance and Mitigation Directorate 2001–2003

No responsibility for hazardous materials or terrorism.

INFORMAL CITATIONS FOR LEGAL AUTHORITIES PARTIALLY DELEGATED TO THE EMERGENCY PREPAREDNESS AND RESPONSE DIRECTORATE (DHS) FORMERLY FEMA

Statutes

Atomic Energy Act of 1954, as amended, 42 U.S.C. §2011 et seq. (Authority for Radiological Preparedness Program. See 44 CFR Parts 350-354. There is no mention of FEMA or DHS in the Atomic Energy Act).

Comprehensive Environmental Response, Compensation and Liability Act of 1980 (CERCLA), as further amended by Superfund Amendments and Reauthorization Act of 1986 (SARA), 42 U.S.C. §9615 et seq. (See 40 CFR Part 300).

Defense Production Act of 1950, as amended, 50 U.S.C. App. §2061, et seq. (See 15 CFR Part 700 and 44 CFR Parts 320-336).

Department of Defense Authorization Act for 1986, § 1412 (Public Law 99-145; 99 Stat.747), as amended by Public Law 101-510, both codified as 50 U.S.C. §1521 (Authority for CSEPP).

Earthquake Hazards Reduction Act of 1977, as amended most recently by Public Law 105-47 (October 1, 1997), 42 U.S.C. §7701 et seq. (See 44 CFR Parts 361 & 362).

Emergency Planning and Community Right to Know Act of 1986, as amended, 42 U.S.C. §11001 et seq. (Authority for hazard materials planning and disclosure. See 40 CFR Part 300.).

Federal Fire Prevention and Control Act of 1974, as further amended by the Hotel and Motel Fire Safety Act of 1990 (Public Law 101-391) and Arson Prevention Act of 1994 (Public Law 103-254) and Firefighters' Safety Study Act (Public Law 101-446) all codified at 15 U.S.C. §2201 et seq. (See 44 CFR Parts 150-152).

Great Lakes Planning Assistance Act of 1988, Title II of Public Law 100-707, 33 U.S.C. §426p. note. (See 44 CFR Part 207).

Hazardous Materials Transportation Act, as further amended by Hazardous Materials Transportation Uniform Safety Act of 1990, both codified at 49 U.S.C. §5101 et seq. (Hazardous materials planning and training).

Homeland Security Act of 2002, Public Law 107-296, November 25, 2002, 6 U.S.C.

Multihazard Research, Planning, and Mitigation Act, Public Law 96-472, 42 U.S.C. §5195 note.

National Dam Safety Program Act, 33 U.S.C. §467 et seq.

Robert T. Stafford Disaster Relief and Emergency Assistance Act, as amended, 42 U.S.C. §5121 et seq. (See 44 CFR Parts 206 & 300).

Stewart B. McKinney Homeless Assistance Act, as amended, 42 U.S.C. §11311 et seq. (Emergency food and shelter program).

National Flood Insurance Act of 1968, as further amended by Flood Disaster Protection Act of 1973, and National Flood Insurance Reform Act of 1994, all codified at 42 U.S.C. §4001 et seq. (See 44 CFR Parts 59-79).

Executive Orders

Executive Order 11988 of May 24, 1977, as amended, Floodplain Management, 3 CFR, 1977 Comp., p. 117, 42 U.S.C. §4321 note p.191. (See 44 CFR Part 9).

Executive Order 12127 of March 31, 1979, Federal Emergency Management Agency, 3 CFR, 1979 Comp., p. 376. (Implements Reorg. Plan No. 3 of 1978).

Executive Order 12148 of July 20, 1979, as amended, Federal Emergency Management, 3 CFR, 1979 Comp., p. 412. (Implements Reorg. Plan No. 3 of 1978).

Executive Order 12241 of September 29, 1980, National Contingency Plan [Radiological Emergencies], 3 CFR, 1980 Comp., p. 282. (Note: Source of FRERP).

Executive Order 12580 of January 23, 1987, as amended, Superfund Implementation, 3 CFR, 1987 Comp., p. 193 (Note: Amended by E.O. 12777 of October 18, 1991, and further amended by E.O. 13016 of August 28, 1996). (See 40 CFR Part 300).

Executive Order 12656 of November 18, 1988, Assignment of Emergency Preparedness Responsibilities, 3 CFR, 1988 Comp., p. 585.

Executive Order 12657 of November 18, 1988, Federal Emergency Management Agency Assistance in Emergency Preparedness Planning at Commercial Nuclear Power Plants, 3 CFR, 1988 Comp., p. 611. (See 44 CFR Part 352).

Executive Order 12673 of March 23, 1989, Delegation of Disaster Relief and Emergency Assistance Functions, 3 CFR, 1989 Comp., p. 309. (See 44 CFR Part 206).

Executive Order 12699 of January 5, 1990, Seismic Safety of Federal and Federally Assisted or Regulated New Building Construction, 3 CFR, 1990 Comp., p. 269.

Executive Order 12742 of January 8, 1991, National Security Industrial Responsiveness, 3 CFR, 1991 Comp., p. 309.

Executive Order 12919 of June 3, 1994, National Defense Industrial Resources Preparedness, 3 CFR, 1994 Comp., p. 901. (See 15 CFR Part 700, 44 CFR Parts 321-336).

Executive Order 12941 of December 1, 1994, Seismic Safety of Existing Federally Owned or Leased Building, 3 CFR, 1994 Comp., p. 955.

HAZARDOUS MATERIALS LEGAL AUTHORITIES PARTIALLY DELEGATED TO THE EMERGENCY PREPAREDNESS AND RESPONSE DIRECTORATE (DHS) FORMERLY FEMA

Statutes

Atomic Energy Act of 1954, as amended, 42 U.S.C. §2011 et seq. (Authority for Radiological Preparedness Program. See 44 CFR Parts 350-354. There is no mention of FEMA or DHS in the Atomic Energy Act).

Comprehensive Environmental Response, Compensation and Liability Act of 1980 (CERCLA), as further amended by Superfund Amendments and Reauthorization Act of 1986 (SARA), 42 U.S.C. §9615 et seq. (See 40 CFR Part 300).

Department of Defense Authorization Act for 1986, § 1412 (Public Law 99-145; 99 Stat.747), as amended by Public Law 101-510, both codified as 50 U.S.C. §1521 (Authority for CSEPP).

Emergency Planning and Community Right to Know Act of 1986, as amended, 42 U.S.C. §11001 et seq. (Authority for hazard materials planning and disclosure. See 40 CFR Part 300).

Federal Fire Prevention and Control Act of 1974, as further amended by the Hotel and Motel Fire Safety Act of 1990 (Public Law 101-391) and Arson Prevention Act of 1994 (Public Law 103-254) and Firefighters' Safety Study Act (Public Law 101-446) all codified at 15 U.S.C. §2201 et seq. (See 44 CFR Parts 150-152).

Hazardous Materials Transportation Act, as further amended by Hazardous Materials Transportation Uniform Safety Act of 1990, both codified at 49 U.S.C. §5101 et seq. (Hazardous materials planning and training).

Homeland Security Act of 2002, Public Law 107-296, November 25, 2002, 6 U.S.C.

Robert T. Stafford Disaster Relief and Emergency Assistance Act, as amended, 42 U.S.C. §5121 et seq. (See 44 CFR Parts 206 & 300).

Executive Orders

Executive Order 12148 of July 20, 1979, as amended, Federal Emergency Management, 3 CFR, 1979 Comp., p. 412. (Implements Reorg. Plan No. 3 of 1978).

Executive Order 12241 of September 29, 1980, National Contingency Plan [Radiological Emergencies], 3 CFR, 1980 Comp., p. 282. (Note: Source of FRERP).

Executive Order 12580 of January 23, 1987, as amended, Superfund Implementation, 3 CFR, 1987 Comp., p. 193 (Note: Amended by E.O. 12777 of October 18, 1991, and further amended by E.O. 13016 of August 28, 1996). (See 40 CFR Part 300).

Executive Order 12657 of November 18, 1988, Federal Emergency Management Agency Assistance in Emergency Preparedness Planning at Commercial Nuclear Power Plants, 3 CFR, 1988 Comp., p. 611. (See 44 CFR Part 352).

Executive Order 12673 of March 23, 1989, Delegation of Disaster Relief and Emergency Assistance Functions, 3 CFR, 1989 Comp., p. 309. (See 44 CFR Part 206).

DISCUSSION QUESTIONS

1. The original organization design for FEMA was for an all-hazards organization. In approving the reorganization, the Senate worried that the disaster function of doling out funds to state and local government would become a reckless give-away program, undermining mitigation, and dominating the agency's programs, functions, and operations to the extent that other programs,

functions, and activities would be disregarded by management.

Discuss your position on FEMA's organizational design based on your readings and experience. Have any of the Senate's concerns proven to be valid?

2. Technical response refers to the following functions: (1) detection of hazards; (2) monitoring of hazards; (3) issuance of PARs (Protective Action Recommendations) to the public; (4) making evacuation or shelter in place decisions; (5) making reentry decisions; and (6) supervision of remediation efforts and cleanup. Given that technical response functions were never officially housed in FEMA but rather in agencies like EPA and NRC, did FEMA lack the ability to provide effective coordination and oversight of other agencies' technical response capability? Is there a role for FEMA-style generalists in hazardous materials emergency management?

3. To some degree, FEMA served as the critical civil/military interface with the Department of Defense (DoD) during the period before the creation of the Department of Homeland Security. How well did FEMA do as an intermediary between the military and people they dealt with on the state, local, and community level?

4. Please identify and discuss FEMA hazardous materials policies and functions that set the stage for modern bioterror and WMD threats. Given FEMA's record in these domains, should the remnants of the agency now in the Department of Homeland Security be trusted with bioterror and WMD emergency management responsibilities today?

5. What role did FEMA have in applied research issues impacting emergency management? Should it have been different?

Chapter 3

FEMA'S CHANGING PRIORITIES SINCE SEPTEMBER 11, 2001

WILLIAM C. NICHOLSON

In the aftermath of the September 11, 2001, terrorist attacks on our nation, much has changed for emergency responders and emergency managers in the United States. The federal government's response to those events also altered the infrastructure that supports these key public safety players.

In the immediate aftermath of the attacks, the Federal Emergency Management Agency swung into action, fulfilling its role under the Federal Response Plan (FRP),[1] which was at that time the way the federal government made available its full resources for response to catastrophic events. The FRP's Terrorism Annex,[2] established pursuant to Presidential Decision Directive (PDD) 39,[3] provided the structure for federal response to all types of terrorism incidents. As outlined in the Terrorism Annex, PDD 39 required the FBI to be the lead agency during crisis management, or the immediate aftermath of the event, with the twin goals of apprehending the people behind the attack and preventing future terrorism incidents.[4] The Terrorism Annex tasked FEMA with leadership during consequence management as the response and recovery effort proceeded.[5]

On June 6, 2002, President Bush proposed a new Department of Homeland Security. The result was an extensive alteration to the federal approach to terrorism and all other emergency events. The Homeland Security Act of 2002 Public Law 107-296 (HS Act),[6] unifies domestic preparedness for terrorism by uniting law enforcement entities concerned with this threat. As introduced, the proposed law contained President Bush's goals for the Department of Homeland Security. Although the Congress intended to have significant impact on the proposed department, the president's approach was adopted almost without change. Some members of Congress worried about preserving the nonlaw enforcement roles of federal agencies transferred to the new department.[7] Others expressed concern about the relative lack of congressional control over the proposed agency's budget.[8] Their concerns that the major federal reorganization needed to be carefully performed resulted in some delay in putting the new department in place.

Signed into law by President Bush on November 25, 2002, the HS Act significantly revises the national approach to terrorism and all other emergency events.[9] The HS Act's most visible effect was creation of DHS by uniting 170,000 federal workers from 22 agencies into a single organization. In the wake of DHS's creation, the leviathan has swallowed FEMA, a relatively tiny agency.[10] Under President Clinton, FEMA was an independent agency, whose director had direct access to the White House. Former FEMA Director James Lee Witt believes that the lack of direct access that FEMA enjoyed as a cabinet-level agency will result in significantly decreased effectiveness in fulfilling FEMA's role.[11]

On February 28, 2003, President Bush issued Homeland Security Presidential Directive 5 (HSPD 5).[12] HSPD 5 deals with crisis management and consequence management as a single, integrated task rather than as two separate functions,[13] thus superseding PDD 39. HSPD 5 also requires federal regulation of homeland security responders.[14]

Joining DHS has resulted in the agency losing numerous employees, who describe extreme dissatisfaction over the DHS structure and their roles within it.[15] Professional staff are reportedly being replaced by ignorant, politically connected newcomers, even as key functions are being outsourced to contractors, again based on political connections.[16] The mind-set has changed at FEMA, where employees now must compete for their jobs with outside political contractors to prove that they can do the task more cheaply.

Cheapest, however, is not always best. Some functions are so central to an agency's mission that the capacity to perform them must be maintained internally, even if this results in added costs. Such an approach is particularly appropriate where, as with FEMA, rapid performance of agency functions is closely tied to public safety and delay would most likely result in greater loss of life and increased property damage.

I. ALL HAZARDS

Some observers worried that formation of an enormous organization like DHS might result in a bureaucratic nightmare. Many emergency responders thought that DHS would focus on law enforcement needs to the detriment of other emergency response groups. FEMA's future, in particular, worried some observers. FEMA has historically been the nation's first defense against all types of hazard. As written, DHS's mission in the HS Act is all about terrorism. For DHS as a whole, previous emphasis on preparation for all-hazards emergency preparedness and response fell out of favor.

FEMA leaders continue to talk a good game about all-hazards preparedness, but they are competing against people with law enforcement backgrounds who see terrorism as DHS's only mission.[17] Funding decisions illustrate that traditional emergency management priorities take a back seat to terrorism under the Bush administration.[18] Key policymakers worry that lowered national preparedness for these most likely hazards may result in increased danger to the nation.[19]

Some emergency management experts warned soon after DHS's formation that FEMA's all-hazards role might be diluted or changed into a solely terrorism preparedness and response organization.[20] Such an approach would lessen FEMA's traditional emphasis on natural disasters.[21] This matter first arose when DHS's primary mission was decreed by the HS Act to be "(A) prevent terrorist attacks within

the United States; (B) reduce the vulnerability of the United States to terrorism; and (C) minimize the damage, and assist in the recovery, from terrorist attacks that do occur within the United States."[22] To be sure, the HS Act tasks the Undersecretary for Preparedness and Response with preparing for[23] and responding to[24] "terrorist attacks, major disasters, and other emergencies," but burying this language in the HS Act rather than making it part of the DHS's mission indicates that these tasks are incidental to the department's primary mission of dealing with terrorism.

Experienced emergency responders and emergency managers worried that this perspective on the part of the administration might result in an unbalanced pouring of funds into antiterrorism,[25] despite the fact that natural disasters have to date had a far greater financial impact on the nation. Wildfires, earthquakes, and floods will not go away just because hazards other than terrorism are lower on the federal priority list. Further, despite the administration's priorities, experience continues to demonstrate that the major threat worldwide has been natural and manmade (but not intentional) hazards. In 2002, manmade disasters accounted for 16 percent of total insured losses, while natural catastrophes comprised the remaining 84 percent.[26] In 2003, over 60,000 lives were lost, 41,000 of which occurred as a result of the Bam, Iran, earthquake.[27]

II. MITIGATION

Historically, some of the nation's most cost-effective expenditures have been for mitigation, a term that applies to removing or lessening the

effect of likely risks: "Mitigation is the cornerstone of emergency management. It's the ongoing effort to lessen the impact disasters have on people's lives and property through damage prevention and flood insurance."[28] FEMA's Mitigation Division's "overall mission is to protect lives and prevent the loss of property from natural hazards."[29] Under the Clinton administration, mitigation study[30] and funding received high priority. FEMA performed analysis of the costs and benefits of hazard mitigation,[31] including studies focused on the benefits to the private sector.[32] The reason for this effort was monetary—FEMA spent $21 billion on disaster relief between 1989 and 1998, compared to $4 billion during the 10 years preceding.[33] When one peruses the contents of the FEMA Mitigation Division Website,[34] two characteristics are immediately apparent. First, the site contains many excellent resources on mitigation strategy and implementation. Second, these resources date almost exclusively from the tenure of James Lee Witt as head of FEMA under President Clinton.

Under the Bush administration, the online link to the National Mitigation Strategy has been disconnected.[35] Other choices made by the Bush administration tell the tale of mitigation's declining importance from their perspective. They gave notice through funding choices beginning in 2001 that mitigation was a low priority. The administration cancelled Project Impact, an extremely successful program designed to help local governments partner with the private sector to mitigate natural hazards.[36] Both pre- and postdisaster mitigation, key elements of the "cycle of emergency management," have been severely curtailed.[37] Important mitigation requests continue to go unfunded,[38] unnecessarily exposing the nation to significant economic losses.

Concentrating on terrorism funding at the expense of other forms of mitigation and preparedness would repeat what are generally agreed

to have been mistakes made by federal emergency management in the 1980s.[39] At that time, preparation for a nuclear war devoured over 75 percent of emergency management resources,[40] with the result that state and local resources were inadequate for significant natural disasters.[41] One expert is more optimistic, pointing out that funding tends to follow the most newsworthy and recent disaster, and stating that the next significant event could be a natural disaster.[42] The potential problem with such a funding approach, however, is that it is reactive rather than proactive, limiting the effect of lessons learned.[43]

HSPD 5 does make reference to all-hazards preparedness.[44] The December 17, 2003, publication of HSPD 8 "National Preparedness"[45] further illustrates that all-hazards are somewhere on the administration's agenda. HSPD 8 specifies a "national domestic all-hazards preparedness goal." It defines "all-hazards preparedness" as "preparedness for domestic terrorist attacks, major disasters, and other emergencies."[46] Although the administration speaks well regarding all-hazards preparedness, however, funding tells the true tale of where priorities lie.

Some emergency managers believe that DHS is in the process of destroying a FEMA structure of cooperation and mutual trust among all levels of government.[47] Indeed, the situation has grown so worrisome that former FEMA Director James Lee Witt recently proposed restoring FEMA's status as an independent agency.[48]

In the aftermath of Florida's being hit by multiple hurricanes in the months of August and September of 2004, the agency has received high marks for the quality of its responses. Some argue, however, that the prime motivation for this good service to the citizens of Florida is political, motivated by the proximity of the 2004 election.[49]

III. RESPONDER TRAINING

As mentioned earlier, HSPD 5 requires federal regulation of homeland security responders.[50] One of FEMA's historic missions has been support of emergency responders through training. Under the aegis of FEMA, the National Fire Academy (NFA) has for years offered the finest training for our nation's firefighters.[51] Similarly, the Emergency

Management Institute (EMI)[52] has offered the best training for emergency managers. The FEMA Emergency Management Higher Education Project has, over the last 11 years, nurtured college and university programs for emergency management. These resident, outreach, and distance learning programs all originate from the National

Emergency Training Center (NETC) facility in Emmitsburg, MD.

In the three years after 9–11, funding for preparedness increased by 990 percent compared with the three years before the attacks.[53] Unfortunately, however, Congress did not perform any needs assessment before sending out the funds.[54] Rather, the lawmakers treated the sudden opportunity to spend $13.1 billion as a huge pork barrel, providing funding based on political clout rather than any measured need.[55] Funding for the important NFA and EMI programs did not increase.

In the wake of the 9–11 attacks, the training mission of FEMA has altered considerably. At this crucial point in our nation's history, arguably DHS is not fully addressing the needs our firefighters and emergency managers. When one considers all the funds being expended on training and equipping first responders (whose numbers now include emergency managers), this statement sounds completely wrongheaded. Close examination of the facts underlying the Bush administration's approach to responder funding and training facilities, however, reveals a disturbing trend. The Homeland Security Act of 2002, which created DHS, divided the responsibility for training emergency responders, giving duties to two groups. The Office of Domestic Preparedness (ODP), located in the Transportation Security Administration (TSA) was given the mission of preparing responders for terrorism events. Training for all other hazards remained with the Undersecretary for Emergency Preparedness and Response (EPR). Among the agencies that were brought into EPR is FEMA, which historically was responsible for training for all-hazards.

Despite the demonstrated excellence of FEMA's training efforts, however, DHS is in the process of dismantling the finest emergency responder training infrastructure in the federal government. Apparently, DHS has unilaterally required the United States Fire Administration (USFA), the National Fire Academy (NFA), and the Emergency Management Institute (EMI) to return all budget allocations NOT directly impacting students. This means that the classes at NFA and EMI will continue, but all curriculum development ceases. It also means that any funding for products or services that does not result in direct student benefit is to be returned to DHS.[56]

A. FEMA Emergency Management Higher Education Project

In 1995, when the FEMA Higher Ed Project commenced, there were five emergency management (EM) curricula at the collegiate level. As of 2004, such programs are up and running at 110 institutions of higher learning. Projected growth is significant, with an additional 96 institutions developing or investigating EM programs, including 31 at the associate level, 35 at the bachelor level, and 30 at the graduate level. The FEMA Higher Education Project has achieved a record of unparalleled success, delivered for a minimal outlay of funds.[57]

The Higher Ed Project creates emergency management training curricula for nationwide dissemination. Terrorism education as well as more likely natural and manmade hazards training have been included among its courses since well before 9–11. Rather than building on the Project's success, however, DHS has reduced its funding by two thirds between 2002 and 2004.

B. National Fire Academy

In support of firefighters across our nation, the National Fire Academy makes available a wide variety of services to firefighters. These include:

1. Provides 8000 campus seats per year for advanced residential training at NETC.
2. Develops firefighting curricula.
3. Facilitates meetings of national concern, such as those discussing national credentialing standards for firefighters.
4. Maintains national statistics of fires that often lead to recalls of products.
5. Shares nine campus courses each year with state fire training systems.
6. Provides three additional six-day courses for the FEMA region.
7. Supplies a mechanism to review and enter state curricula into the national market.
8. Facilitates the exchange of curriculum and data between and among state and local fire departments.

9. Offers Train the Trainer courses to promptly move curricula into the hands of the frontline firefighters whose efficiency and safety are supported by evolving standards.
10. Maintains records of individuals from each state and shares the demographics with the state fire training systems.
11. Fosters and maintains communications among the state fire training community.
12. Educates firefighters in the states to a level beyond that of nondegree granting institutions.
13. Identifies and targets fire prevention efforts in areas of priority.
14. Focuses program activities on mutually agreed upon national priorities such as firefighter line of duty deaths (LODD).
15. Makes available valuable research publications at no cost.
16. Provides a venue and logistic support for the Assistance to Firefighters grant program.
17. Develops and provides public fire and life safety education programs and Public Service Announcements.
18. Provides emergency management training for local, state, and federal emergency managers.
19. Serves as the training agency for all of FEMA.
20. For firefighters, the greatest emotional connection of all is that the National Fire Academy is home of the National Fallen Firefighter Monument and annual memorial service.[58]

C. Potential Alternative Uses for the National Emergency Training Center

In what may be an indication of coming changes, installation of a reinforced security fence around the National Emergency Training Center may indicate that DHS has a secret, unpublicized agenda for the NETC. One is hard pressed to believe that the fence was put in place for the protection of firefighters and career civilian bureaucrats. Apparently, someone from the newly constituted DHS noted the facility at Emmitsburg, MD, and determined that it would be better used for purposes other than training firefighters and emergency managers. NETC's pastoral setting is strategically situated between Camp David and Site R. The fence and reduced funding for the entities contained at the site are indications that NETC may lose its Emmitsburg location. This may mean that the National Fire Academy, Emergency Management Institute, and FEMA Higher Ed Project may soon be but a fond memory in the hearts and minds of our nation's firefighters and emergency managers.[59]

If this situation continues to evolve without strong input from the legislature that should be providing oversight to DHS, the end may be near for the National Emergency Training Center. The potential disassembly of our federal fire and emergency management training structure poses significant danger to the nation.

D. Damage to Key Infrastructure

Over the years since the NETC was founded in 1979, there have been many changes to our national fire academy and federal fire focus. Most were in development of capacity to serve our firefighters and their communities. Unfortunately, the value of firefighters and the municipal level of defense of our communities are apparently not properly appreciated by DHS: "The value of firefighters and the municipal level of defense of our communities are not paramount among the DHS folks that I interact with. The ODP Director and Deputy Director have articulated that they do not view state fire academies as meeting the advanced needs of terrorism preparation and response."[60]

Federal fire programs make a significant contribution to national preparedness for all hazards, including terrorism. Indeed, the fire service will usually be the first responders to terrorist events, since they will generally be reported as explosion, fire, or HAZMAT release of undetermined origin. Unfortunately, in the bureaucratic maze that is Washington, budgets and table of organizations equate to power. The fire service is clearly not a powerful part of DHS. DHS has failed to respond in a significant manner to congressional testimony from fire chiefs who paint a gloomy picture of current response capabilities.

Meanwhile, volunteer and paid fire personnel must find their own sources for funding to pay for attending classes at Emmitsburg, since DHS will not cover any expenses for attendees to NFA training. This is a short-sighted failure to utilize the best training DHS offers, while at the same time ODP pours money into unproven training initiatives.

DHS appears to be systematically dismantling FEMA's proven, robust structure, which has provided support to the fire and emergency management communities since 1980.

IV. FUNDING DECISIONS POINT TO THE FUTURE

Since its creation, many within DHS have been engaged in a monumental turf war over funding and power. The tug of war has revolved around the central mission of DHS. Those within ODP see prevention of terrorism as the agency's prime mission, an approach that naturally results in the primacy of their organization. Others, however, believe that a more balanced approach makes more sense.

"It's a competing balance inside the Department [of Homeland Security]," DHS Undersecretary and FEMA head Michael Brown says. "The department has two missions. One is to prevent terrorism. The other is to prepare the country for all hazards. My job is to convince and show and lead by example that the all-hazard approach fits into their terrorism prevention."[61] Former FEMA Director James Lee Witt is less optimistic about the outcome of the competition: "[FEMA] has been buried beneath a massive bureaucracy whose main and seemingly only focus is fighting terrorism and while that is absolutely critical, it should not be at the expense of preparing for and responding to natural disasters."[62]

Funding decisions clearly illustrate the Bush administration's response to the challenge. President Bush's 2005 budget proposal illustrates the administration's one-dimensional approach to emergency preparedness. It transfers, reduces, or eliminates grants geared specifically to local and state efforts directed at all-hazards dangers—such as floods, wildfires, and blizzards—into programs focused solely on terrorism. Observers question funding decisions that reflect a "myopic focus on terrorism."[63]

Emergency managers in state and local governments see their budgets and, in some cases, their very survival being squeezed by what some say is a narrow-minded focus on terrorism. Recently, the Bush administration attempted to cut funding for Emergency Management Performance Grants (EMPGs),[64] including specific limitations on the amount that could be spent on personnel. Many

federal grants finance state and local emergency management activity, but only the EMPG focuses on the salary costs of the personnel-intensive activity. The Bush administration's proposed 2005 budget cut the EMPG allocation by 5 percent—a decrease of $9 million. It also put a ceiling on the amount that can be spent on salaries at one-quarter of any grant. This personnel limitation is the greatest danger to the future of emergency management. One knowledgeable observer estimated that over half the nation's 4,000 emergency management jobs might be lost.[65] If there is no funding for these positions, local governments may try to save money by abolishing them and moving emergency management duties to another body, such as the fire department or the police. The effect of eliminating emergency management would be to recreate the interservice rivalries that emergency management, as the honest broker coordinating preparedness efforts, largely eliminates. Congress later in the budget process, restored EMPG funding and deleted the limitation on personnel costs.

Emergency managers and firefighters[66] in particular believe that funding for terrorism comes at the expense of their programs.[67] Firefighters have expressed concern that "[I]n the Washington bureaucracy, budgets and table of organizations mean power, or lack thereof. The fire service is not a power player within DHS. Its voice is weak, buried under layers of bureaucracy. . . ."[68] The Bush administration decided to transfer to the Office of Domestic Preparedness,[69] which is responsible for terrorism preparedness,[70] the Assistance for Firefighters Grant Program (FIRE Grant Program).[71] "This is a politically calculated move, the only goal of which is to repurpose existing appropriations for basic fire department needs into the Homeland Security Department's WMD bureaucracy. . . ."[72] Randy Bruegman, chief of the city of Fresno Fire Department and immediate past president of the International Association of Fire

Chiefs, warned that moving the program to ODP would mean "the end of the FIRE Grant program as we know it."[73]

These choices clearly support ODP while choking the life out of other programs. Other indications that ODP has won the turf battle over funding and power within DHS abound. The 50-state fire training systems recently were informed that a Computer-Based Hazardous Materials/Weapons of Mass Destruction (HAZMAT/WMD) Operations curriculum development effort that was virtually complete for pilot delivery was cancelled indefinitely. Further, 2004 funding allocation for Training Resource and Data Exchange (TRADE) was

withdrawn as part of a greater effort to turn back $11 million to the parent organization, the Department of Homeland Security.[74]

In reality, local responders in some parts of the nation may well be more poorly financed than before the advent of DHS and the enormous increases in funding since September 11, 2001. "While money for homeland security has grown, regular state and federal funding for police and fire operations continues to be cut as both state legislatures and the Bush administration try to control growing budget deficits. In order to get the homeland security money, states and localities must frame their needs in terms of terrorism."[75]

V. CONCLUSION

The cost of response and recovery from natural hazards continues to increase. Their economic impact exceeds that of terrorism by many magnitudes. Decisions by the Bush administration have resulted in decreased funds for all-hazards mitigation and preparedness, even as funding for antiterrorism efforts has skyrocketed. The effect on FEMA has been a change in the way that the agency does business. Once vital mitigation and preparedness programs have been left to wilt, while terrorism-related efforts increase markedly.

Unfortunately, as the current approach to preparedness demonstrates, lessons like those of the 1980s are frequently taught but rarely learned. Paradoxically, despite much greater levels of preparedness spending, the failure to bring a more balanced set of priorities to DHS funding and training may well result in a nation that is, overall, at significantly greater risk for loss of lives and property damage than it was prior to September 11, 2001.

The future for FEMA's mitigation efforts may well be affected by the high costs of responding to the devastating fall 2004 hurricane season.

Watchdogs may question the result of funding terrorism at the expense of other mitigation and preparedness efforts. The 2004 hurricane season underlines former FEMA Director James Lee Witt's statement that "While the likelihood of another terrorist attack on our land may be inevitable, it is an absolute certainty that our country will experience more natural disasters and there is no question that some will be catastrophic. It is not a matter of "if" it is a matter of when and where."

The vast majority of Americans favor homeland security and eliminating the threat of terrorism on American soil. The nation also understands that since September 11, 2001, American society has changed significantly. It is frequently said that the nation is fighting a different kind of war that calls for new federal priorities and initiatives. At the same time that these realities must be managed, however, it is important not to lose perspective. Emergency managers must recall the mistakes of the past to avoid repeating them, while at the same time creating new and better tools to ensure the security of our homeland.

ENDNOTES

1. FEDERAL EMERGENCY MANAGEMENT AGENCY, THE FEDERAL RESPONSE PLAN (1999). The FRP establishes a process and structure for the systematic, coordinated, and effective delivery of federal assistance to address the consequences of any major disaster or emergency declared under the Robert T. Stafford Disaster Relief and Emergency Assistance Act, as amended (42 USC 5121, *et seq.* (2002)).

2. FRP TERRORISM ANNEX at 2 (1999). The purpose of this annex is to ensure that the Federal Response Plan (FRP) is adequate to respond to the consequences of terrorism within the United States, including terrorism involving WMD.

3. Presidential Decision Directive ("PDD") 39, Policy on Counterterrorism, (June 21, 1995).

4. Id. PDD-39 reaffirms existing federal lead agency responsibilities for counterterrorism, which are assigned to the Department of Justice (DOJ), as delegated to the FBI, for threats or acts of terrorism within the United States. The FBI as the lead for crisis management will involve only those federal agencies required and designated in classified documents. The Directive further states that FEMA with the support of all agencies in the FRP, will support the FBI in Washington, DC, and at the event scene until the attorney general transfers lead agency responsibility to FEMA. FEMA retains responsibility for consequence management throughout the federal response.

5. Id.

6. Homeland Security Act of 2002, H.R. 5005, 107th Cong. (2002) (enacted) [hereinafter HS Act].

7. David Firestone, *Congress to Begin Debating a Domestic Security Agency, New York TIMES*, July 8, 2002, A-1. "Many in Congress are concerned that the changes ahead will represent more than just a different phone number or letterhead for the agencies they oversee. If the Coast Guard, for example, moves from the Transportation Department to the Homeland Security Department, will its basic mission of ensuring maritime safety and mobility shift more toward defense? Several coastal state representatives are preparing to fight such a move. Members from farm states are similarly worried about moving the Animal and Plant Health Inspection Service out of the Agriculture Department."

8. Id. ". . . Congressional appropriations leaders, accustomed to deciding how the government will spend its money, have protested the administration's proposal that the department be able to shift money among its divisions without their approval."

9. William C. Nicholson, "Integrating Local, State and Federal Responders and Emergency Management: New Packaging and New Controls," *Journal of Emergency Management 15*, 15 (Fall 2003).

10. "Former Director of FEMA Testifies Before Subcommittee on National Security, Emerging Threats and International Relations and the Subcommittee on Energy Policy, Natural Resources and Regulatory Affairs" (March 24, 2004) (Found on the Web at http://www.all-hands.net/pn// modules.php?op=modload&name=News&file=article&sid=592&mode=thread&order=0&thold=0. "I hear from emergency managers, local and state leaders, and first responders nearly every day that the FEMA they knew and worked well with has now disappeared. In fact one state emergency manager told me, 'It is like a stake has been driven into the heart of emergency management.' . . . FEMA has been buried beneath a massive bureaucracy whose main and seemingly only focus is fighting terrorism and while that is absolutely critical, it should not be at the expense of preparing for and responding to natural disasters."

11. Id. "[T]he FEMA director has lost cabinet status and with it the access and the close relationship with the president and cabinet affairs. I assure you that we could not have been as responsive and effective during disasters as we were during my tenure as FEMA director, had there been layers of federal bureaucracy between myself and the White House. Just one degree of separation is too much, when time is of the essence and devastating events are unfolding rapidly."

12. Homeland Security Presidential Directive 5, Subject: Management of Domestic Incidents, The White House, February 28, 2003. http://www.whitehouse.gov/news/releases/2003/02/20030228-9.html

13. HSPD 5, paragraph 3.

14. HSPD 5, paragraph 16.

15. Jon Elliston, *SAN FRANCISCO BAY GUARDIAN* (CA) (Sept 15–21, 2004 issue) "*FEMA-AGENCY PROFILE: Disaster In The Making.*"

16. Id.

17. Robert Block, *WALL STREET JOURNAL*, "*Identity Crisis–Hurricane Tests Emergency Agency at Time of Ferment: Now Under Homeland Security, FEMA Has Lost Clout, Managers on Ground Say: Terrorist With 145 MPH Winds*" (August 16, 2004). "According to [DHS Under Secretary Michael] Brown and other insiders, a quiet battle is underway within the Homeland Security Department. On one side are former law enforcement officials, advocating secrecy, tight security, and intelligence as the key to minimizing the trauma of any terrorist attack. On the other are firefighters and emergency managers who emphasize collaboration, information sharing, public awareness, and mitigation efforts to reduce the impact of disasters."

18. Id. "Since the Sept. 11 attacks, state emergency managers have faced a sharp reduction in federal funding to help them prepare for natural calamities, while resources earmarked to counterterrorism

have soared. Federal grants supporting states' antiterrorism plans have jumped to more than $3 billion this year from $221 million in 2001. During the same period, FEMA's principal grant program to state and local emergency management has been cut by Congress at White House urging by some $90 million, to $180 million."

19. Karin Fischer, "Anti-Terrorism Focus Could Hurt State Cuts Would Affect Ability to Respond to Natural Disasters," *Charleston (WV) Daily Mail,* P1C (February 27, 2004). "[Senator Robert] Byrd and [WV Office of Emergency Services director Steve] Kappa are concerned President Bush's budget proposal transfers, reduces, or eliminates grants geared specifically to local and state response efforts for 'all-hazards' dangers—such as floods, wildfires, and blizzards—into programs geared directly to responding to terrorism attacks."

20. William L. Waugh, Jr., Ph.D. "The 'All-Hazards' Approach Must be Continued" 2 *Journal of Emergency Management 1,* 11 (Fall 2003).

21. George D. Haddow and Jane A. Bullock, INTRODUCTION TO EMERGENCY MANAGEMENT, 241 (2003). "As emergency management systems focus their efforts on preparing for and responding to terrorist events, these efforts should not diminish their capabilities or capacity for dealing with natural hazards."

22. HS Act §101.

23. HS Act § 501(1).
    SEC. 501. UNDERSECRETARY FOR EMERGENCY PREPAREDNESS AND RESPONSE.
    In assisting the Secretary with the responsibilities specified in section 101(b)(2)(D), the primary responsibilities of the Under Secretary for Emergency Preparedness and Response shall include (1) helping to ensure the preparedness of emergency response providers for terrorist attacks, major disasters, and other emergencies;

24. HS Act § 501(3):
    (3) providing the Federal Government's response to terrorist attacks and major disasters, including–
    (A) managing such response;

25. William C. Nicholson, *Emergency Response and Emergency Management Law,* pp. 236–238 (2003).

26. Swiss re: Facts and Figures on Global Insurance, Insured Losses by Category, 2002. Found on the Web at: http://www.swissre.com/INTERNET/pwswpspr.nsf/fmBookMarkFrameSet?ReadForm&BM=../vwAllbyIDKeyLu/MPDL-5WFEAH?OpenDocument).

27. SIGMA No. 1 (2004) *Natural Catastrophes and Man-Made Disasters in 2003: Many Fatalities, Comparatively*

Modest Insured Losses," In 2003, the ". . . [t]otal damage attributable to [natural catastrophes was approximately $70 billion . . . [while] [t]otal damage caused by manmade disasters amounted to $15 billion." Found on the Web at: http://www.swissre.com/INTERNET/pwswpspr.nsf/fmBookMarkFrameSet?ReadForm&BM=../vwAllbyIDKeyLu/MPDL-5WFEAH?OpenDocument.

28. FEMA Website at http://www.fema.gov/fima/

29. FEMA Website at http://www.fema.gov/fima/aboutfima.shtm

30. Federal Emergency Management Agency, National Mitigation Strategy: Partnerships for Building Safer Communities, (Washington, DC: Government Printing Office, 1995). (No longer found online at the FEMA Website.)

31. "Report on Costs and Benefits of Natural Hazard Mitigation," found on FEMA Website at: http://www.fema.gov/pdf/library/haz_cost.pdf.

32. "Protecting Business Operations Second Report on Costs and Benefits of Natural Hazard Mitigation" (August 1998) found on FEMA Website at: http://www.fema.gov/pdf/library/haz_pbo.pdf.

33. Id. "The Federal Emergency Management Agency's (FEMA) expenditures for disaster relief between 1989 and 1998 totaled over $21 billion. For the ten years previous to 1989, the total expenditures were only $4 billion."

34. FEMA Website at http://www.fema.gov/fima/

35. See missing link at bottom of page on FEMA Website at http://www.fema.gov/library/prepandprev.shtm#mit

36. Jon Elliston, SAN FRANCISCO BAY GUARDIAN (CA) (Sept 15–21, 2004 issue) *"FEMA-AGENCY PROFILE: Disaster In The Making."* ". . . since 2001, key federal disaster mitigation programs, developed over many years, have been slashed and tossed aside. FEMA's Project Impact, a model mitigation program created by the Clinton administration, has been canceled outright."

37. Id. "Federal funding of postdisaster mitigation efforts designed to protect people and property from the next disaster has been cut in half, and now communities across the country must compete for predisaster mitigation dollars."

38. Id. "In North Carolina, a state regularly damaged by hurricanes and floods, FEMA recently refused the state's request to buy backup generators for emergency support facilities. And the budget cuts have halved the funding for a mitigation program that saved an estimated $8.8 million in recovery costs in three eastern N.C. communities alone after 1997's Hurricane Floyd. In Louisiana, another state

vulnerable to hurricanes, requests for flood mitigation funds were rejected by FEMA this summer."

39. Bullock and Haddow, "The Future of Emergency Management," 2 *Journal of Emergency Management* No. 1, 19, 22 (Fall 2003). "To abandon the all-hazards approach would be repeating the mistake the EM community made in the 1980s."

40. Id.

41. Id.

42. Telephone Interview with Rick D. Schlegel, EAI Corporation, Deputy Program Manager, Incident Command Responder Course, Anniston, AL (March 8, 2004). "I wouldn't be too worried about the current emphasis on terrorism. We've just gone back to the days of the cold war. This is cyclic. Whatever wheel is squeaking the loudest gets the grease. For example, in the past, when we would have a mass fatality incident, suddenly there was lots of money for mass fatality preparedness. Previously, the all-hazards approach was the big thing—now it's terrorism. The wheel will turn around again when we see a problem with a natural disaster that we could have been better prepared for."

43. Bullock and Haddow, "The Future of Emergency Management" 2 *Journal of Emergency Management* No. 1, 19, 22 (Fall 2003). "To abandon the all-hazards approach would be repeating the mistake the EM community made in the 1980s. . . . The result was that federal, state, and local capacities to respond to natural disasters were severely diminished. As Hurricanes Hugo, Iniki, and Andrew vividly demonstrated, state and local capacities were quickly overcome. The federal government response under FEMA was disorganized and late."

44. HSPD 5 mandates addressing all hazards. HSPD 5 at paragraph 16. "[The NRP] shall integrate Federal Government domestic prevention, preparedness, response, and recovery plans into one all-discipline, all-hazards plan." HSPD 5 at paragraph 6. "The Secretary will also provide assistance to State and local governments to develop all-hazards plans and capabilities, including those of greatest importance to the security of the United States, and will ensure that State, local, and Federal plans are compatible."

45. Homeland Security Presidential Directive 8, Subject: National Preparedness, The White House, December 17, 2003. http://www.whitehouse.gov/news/releases/2003/12/20031217-6.html

46. HSPD 8 at 1.

47. "Former Director of FEMA Testifies Before Subcommittee on National Security, Emerging Threats and International Relations and the Subcommittee on Energy Policy, Natural Resources and Regulatory Affairs" (March 24, 2004) (Found on the Web at http://www.all-hands.net/pn//modules.php?op=modload&name=News&file=article&sid=592&mode=thread&order=0&thold=0).

48. Id. "I firmly believe that FEMA should be re-established as an independent agency, reporting directly to the president—but allowing for the secretary of homeland security to task FEMA to coordinate the federal response and perform its historical duty of consequence management following a terrorist or any other kind of disastrous event."

49. Jon Elliston, *San Francisco Bay Guardian* (CA) (Sept 15–21, 2004 issue) *"FEMA-AGENCY PRO-FILE: Disaster In The Making."* "As storms continue to batter the Panhandle, no one would call Florida lucky. But with national elections just around the corner, the hurricanes could scarcely have hit at a better time or place for obtaining federal disaster assistance. 'They're doing a good job,' one former FEMA executive says of the Bush administration's response efforts. 'And the reason why they're doing that job is because it's so close to the election, and they can't f*** it up, otherwise they lose Florida—and if they lose Florida, they might lose the election.'"

50. HSPD 5 at paragraph 16.

51. For links to NFA training opportunities, see http://training.fema.gov/

52. For links to EMI training opportunities, see http://www.training.fema.gov/emiweb/

53. Amanda Ripley, "How We Got Homeland Security Wrong," *Time Magazine*, p. 32 (March 29, 2004). "Since the Sept. 11 attacks, about $13.1 billion has surged into state coffers from the Federal Government—sorely needed money that has gone for police, fire, and emergency services to help finance equipment and training to prevent and respond to terrorist attacks. That is a 990% increase over the $1.2 billion spent by the Federal Government for similar programs in the preceding three years."

54. Id. ". . . the vast majority of the $13.1 billion was distributed with no regard for the threats, vulnerabilities, and potential consequences faced by each region."

55. Id. "With no clear direction from the feds, state officials have been engaged in a perverse competition for antiterrorism dollars. . . . In some ways, it is a familiar story: of state officials understandably guarding their piece of the pie, of rural localities getting disproportionate help from the government. But this money is not for roads; it is the first

demonstration of how America will protect its citizens in a new kind of war. Bogged down in emotion and opportunism, the debate is leading to dangerous gaps in the preparedness of our most vulnerable communities."

56. Communication from Adam Piskura, President, North American Fire Training Directors, May 28, 2004. See http://www.naftd.org/ for more information on the organization.

57. See High Ed Presentation at http://www.training.fema.gov/emiweb/downloads/highedbrief_course2.ppt

58. Communication from Adam Piskura, President, North American Fire Training Directors, May 28, 2004. See http://www.naftd.org/ for more information on the organization.

59. Id.

60. Id.

61. Robert Block, *WALL STREET JOURNAL*, "Identity Crisis–Hurricane Tests Emergency Agency At Time of Ferment: Now Under Homeland Security, FEMA Has Lost Clout, Managers on Ground Say: Terrorist With 145 MPH Winds" (August 16, 2004), "According to [DHS Undersecretary Michael] Brown and other insiders, a quiet battle is underway within the Homeland Security Department. On one side are former law enforcement officials, advocating secrecy, tight security and intelligence as the key to minimizing the trauma of any terrorist attack. On the other are firefighters and emergency managers who emphasize collaboration, information sharing, public awareness, and mitigation efforts to reduce the impact of disasters."

62. "Former Director of FEMA Testifies Before Subcommittee on National Security, Emerging Threats and International Relations and the Subcommittee on Energy Policy, Natural Resources and Regulatory Affairs" (March 24, 2004) (Found on the Web at http://www.all-hands.net/pn//modules.php?op=modload&name=News&file=article&sid=592&mode=thread&order=0&thold=0)

63. Shaun Waterman, "Analysis: Fear of Being Eclipsed by Terror," UPI (March 19, 2004). "[E]mergency managers over the country . . . working in state and local governments to plan and prepare their communities for the worst, feel their budgets and in some cases their very existence being squeezed by what some say is a myopic focus on terrorism."

64. Karin Fischer, "Anti-Terrorism Focus Could Hurt State Cuts Would Affect Ability to Respond to Natural Disasters," *CHARLESTON (WV) DAILY MAIL* P1C (February 27, 2004). "State officials, however, are alarmed at reductions in grants that help pay for the salaries of emergency services staff. The appropriation for the Emergency Management Performance Grants would decrease by $9 million, and states would face limitations on the share that would go to pay personnel."

65. "Former Director of FEMA Testifies Before Subcommittee on National Security, Emerging Threats and International Relations and the Subcommittee on Energy Policy, Natural Resources and Regulatory Affairs" (Found on the Web at http://www.all-hands.net/pn//modules.php?op=modload&name=News&file=article&sid=592&mode=thread&order=0&thold=0.

66. Harvey Eisner, Editor-in-Chief *Firehouse Magazine*, Editorial, *FIRE CHIEF* (Feb 1, 2004). Found online at: http://firechief.com/ar/firefighting_editors_editorial/index.htm. DHS has not responded urgently to congressional testimony from fire chiefs from around the country painting a bleak picture of response capabilities. Nor does it seem to have paid much attention to reports from organizations such as The Council of Foreign Relations, a New York-based nonpartisan research group. In its preparedness report *Emergency Responders: Drastically Underfunded, Dangerously Unprepared*, the council stated that "the U.S. remains dangerously ill-prepared to handle a catastrophic attack on American soil."

67. Shaun Waterman, "Analysis: Fear of Being Eclipsed by Terror," UPI (March 19, 2004). "Of the plethora of federal grants that fund state and local emergency management activities, only one–the Emergency Management Performance Grant–has historically covered the wage costs of this personnel-intensive business. The Bush administration's proposed 2005 budget cuts the allocation for that program by 5 percent, but–far more damagingly, say critics–caps the amount that can be spent on salaries at one-quarter of any grant. The fact is, if no source of funding is available for these posts, the temptation will always be to save money (by cutting them) and make those (emergency management) duties someone else's responsibility–give it to the fire department, or the police."

68. Harvey Eisner, Editor-in-Chief *Firehouse Magazine*, Editorial, *FIRE CHIEF* (Feb 1, 2004). Found online at: http://firechief.com/ar/firefighting_editors_editorial/index.htm

69. HS Act § 502.
SEC. 502. FUNCTIONS TRANSFERRED.
In accordance with title VIII, there shall be transferred to the Secretary the functions, personnel, assets, and liabilities of the following entities–(2) the

Office for Domestic Preparedness of the Office of Justice Programs, including the functions of the Attorney General relating thereto

70. Press release, *Department of Homeland Security Announces Opening of Assistance to Firefighters Grant Program Application Period*, (March 2, 2004). Found on the Web at: http://www.dhs.gov/dhspublic/display?content=3271. "ODP [is] the principal Federal agency responsible for the preparedness of the United States for acts of terrorism, including coordinating preparedness efforts at the Federal level, and working with all State, local, tribal, parish, and private sector emergency response providers on all matters pertaining to combating terrorism, including training, exercises, and equipment support."
71. Id.
72. "FIRE Grants Moved to ODP, Funded at $750 Miillion," *Fire Chief on Line News & Trends* (Sep 18 2003) "[T] he IAFC and many other fire service organizations have fought the transfer of the FIRE Grants to the Office of Domestic Preparedness, saying the program that has become critical to equipping fire departments might be lost in other first responder grant programs. . . ." Found on the Web at: http://firechief.com/ar/firefighting_fire_grants_moved_2/index.htm. See also Harvey Eisner, Editor-in-Chief *Firehouse Magazine*, Editorial, *FIRE CHIEF* (Feb 1, 2004). Found online at: http://firechief.com/ar/firefighting_editors_editorial/index.htm "As a weak USFA minimizes the fire service, so is it minimized by moving administration of the FIRE Act into the Office of Domestic Preparedness, which resides within the DHS Borders and Transportation Directorate and has no connections with the fire service."
73. Id.
74. Communication from Adam Piskura, President, North American Fire Training Directors, May 28, 2004. See http://www.naftd.org/ for more information on the organization.
75. Amanda Ripley, "How We Got Homeland Security Wrong," *TIME MAGAZINE*, p. 32 (March 29, 2004).

DISCUSSION QUESTIONS

1. Which type of hazard do you think is more important, terrorism or natural hazards, and why?
2. The author makes the point that FEMA's mitigation efforts for natural hazards are receiving less funding than antiterrorism. What do you think the proper priorities for funding are, and why?
3. Discuss the importance of the fact that terrorists have a specific intent to inflict casualties and kill a maximum number of people compared to acts of nature being without ill will. How should this affect our national priorities?
4. Analyze the chapter's evaluation of responder training funding decisions. Where do you think training funding priorities should lie, and why?
5. What is the importance of the Emergency Management Performance Grant?
6. Do you agree with former FEMA Director Witt that FEMA should regain its status as a Cabinet-level independent agency? Explain your answer.
7. Overall, do you believe that FEMA has benefited by the creation of DHS? List benefits and costs to FEMA.
8. List the stakeholder communities that FEMA serves. Do you believe that FEMA's stakeholder communities have benefited from the creation of DHS, and why?

Chapter 4

THE SHAPE OF EMERGENCY RESPONSE AND EMERGENCY MANAGEMENT IN THE AFTERMATH OF THE HOMELAND SECURITY ACT OF 2002: ADOPTING THE NATIONAL RESPONSE PLAN (NRP) AND THE NATIONAL INCIDENT MANAGEMENT SYSTEM (NIMS)*

WILLIAM C. NICHOLSON

The concept of incident command (more recently and commonly referred to as incident management)[1] dates back to the early 1970s, when a group of forward-looking California fire department and federal agency leaders began work on a new system to coordinate, deploy, and maintain the large resources needed to fight major wildland fires.[2] The success of the newly created incident management system (IMS) led to its being adopted by a variety of players, including law enforcement, public health, public works, and the private sector.[3] Emergency management groups also embraced the system,[4] and recommended in 2000 that all levels of government utilize it for response to Weapons of Mass Destruction (WMD) events.[5] Credentialing bodies have universally accepted IMS as the pattern for integrating emergency response.[6] Despite IMS's demonstrated value, however, not all emergency response groups have adopted it.[7] Concern that the nation needed a universal approach to management of incidents led the Congress, in the Homeland Security Act of 2002, Public Law 107-296 (HS Act),[8] to require adoption of IMS.[9] In response to the congressional mandate, during the summer of 2003 the Department of Homeland Security (DHS) released a National Response Plan and National Incident Management System (NRP 1 and NIMS 1)[10] to emergency response groups as well as state and local government representatives.[11]

Concerned stakeholders voiced several criticisms of the NRP 1 and NIMS 1.[12] The language in the documents confused many observers.[13] The text appeared to create new structures that could have the effect of complicating emergency response and coordination of resources.[14] Some experienced emergency management professionals worried that the focus rested too heavily on terrorism, with a consequent lessening of the all-hazards[15] approach to risk management.[16] In particular, they were bothered that natural hazards did not appear to receive sufficient emphasis.[17] The NRP 1 and NIMS 1 incorporated problematic approaches to emergency responder issues.[18] Emergency response organizations as well as representatives of state and local governments believed that their input should have been part of the process of creating the documents from their inception.[19] Instead, DHS only asked for their feedback after several drafts had been created and circulated internally at the agency.[20] Some affected constituencies worried that this history boded ill for any attempts to try to rectify what many viewed as badly flawed blueprints for national preparedness and response.[21]

DHS solicited input from affected groups, sending out preliminary versions of the NRP and NIMS.[22] August 1, 2003, was the date set by the agency for receipt of feedback from interested parties.[23] So emphatic and critical was the response that DHS rapidly put together an NRP/NIMS State and Local

---

* This article's original publication is in *The Widener Law Review*, Issue 12, Vol. 2 (forthcoming Spring 2006).

Working Group in an attempt to obtain state and local endorsements without which the effort could not succeed.[24] The Group first met to discuss the NRP line by line during the week of August 11, 2003.[25] The Initial National Response Plan (INRP) issued September 30, 2003, resulted from their efforts.[26] In September, the group met again, this time to go over NIMS 1.[27] The result of the second meeting was a significantly revised National Incident Management System–Coordination Draft (NIMS 2), which was issued for comment on December 3, 2003.[28] On March 1, 2004, the first anniversary of the Department of Homeland Security,[29] DHS Secretary Tom Ridge announced publication of an adopted version of NIMS (adopted NIMS).[30]

On February 24, 2004, DHS released to state homeland security advisors and other homeland security partners[31] a reworked National Response Plan Draft #1 (NRP Draft #1).[32] Subsequently, DHS put out a number of additional draft versions of the NRP. These include NRP Draft #2, issued April 28, 2004,[33] and the NRP "Final Draft" issued on June 30, 2004. The document has steadily grown in size as different stakeholders have provided feedback.[34] Despite its nomenclature, the NRP "Final Draft" is not the same as the adopted document.[35]

DHS finally adopted and issued the NRP on November 16, 2004. The NRP will be reviewed during its first year of existence and reissued if necessary.[36] Following that first year, it will be revised and reissued every 4 years or more frequently if the Secretary of DHS deems it advisable.[37]

This chapter analyzes both the content of the revisions to the NRP and NIMS and the processes employed to make the changes.

I. WHY THE NRP AND NIMS?

When finalized, the NRP and NIMS will be the end product of a process that began with the passage of the HS Act. Signed into law by President George W. Bush on November 25, 2002, the HS Act considerably alters the national approach to terrorism and all other emergency events.[38] The HS Act's most visible effect was creation of DHS by uniting 180,000 federal workers from 22 agencies into a single organization.[39] As written, the mission of DHS in the HS Act revolves around terrorism.[40] A further challenge posed by the law was therefore how to combine the efforts of DHS with those of state and local governments as well as emergency responders into a truly national system reaching beyond terrorism for all hazards emergency preparedness and response.[41]

Some observers worried that creation of DHS might be a bureaucratic nightmare.[42] The new organization, some feared, might be rife with infighting, inflexible, and sluggish in responding to events.[43] Emergency responders were concerned that DHS would focus on law enforcement needs.[44] Such anxiety seemed reasonable because acts of terrorism, which are crimes,[45] were the impetus for creation of DHS.[46] NRP 1 and NIMS 1 were viewed as logical outgrowths of an agency insensitive and unresponsive to the needs of the nonlaw enforcement responders it was tasked with serving.[47]

On February 28, 2003, President Bush put out marching orders for the implementation of the HS Act. On that date, he issued Homeland Security Presidential Directive 5 (HSPD 5).[48] HSPD 5 instructed all federal agencies to take specific steps for planning and incident management.[49] The HSPD 5 also mandated setting emergency responder performance standards and established sanctions for responders who fail to conform to those standards.[50]

HSPD 5's major goal is making certain that all levels of government operate in concert in an efficient and effective manner, utilizing a single, comprehensive approach to domestic incident management.[51] To achieve this objective, it treats crisis management and consequence management as a single, integrated task rather than as two separate functions.[52] The previous dual approach was established by Presidential Decision Directive 39,[53] which is superseded by HSPD 5. The Directive identifies the lead agencies for terrorism events and other major disasters.[54] As required by the HS Act,[55] HSPD 5 commands that DHS create and enforce standards for emergency responders. HSPD 5 specifies consequences for those responders who do not comply with federal regulation of their activities beginning in Federal Fiscal Year 2005.[56]

HSPD 5 directs all federal agencies to collaborate with DHS to establish a National Response

Plan (NRP) and a National Incident Management System (NIMS).[57] HSPD 5 also sets out a timetable for those actions.[58] NIMS is the operational part of the NRP.[59] In this fashion, authority for creation of the NRP Draft #1 and the adopted NIMS flows from the HS Act through HSPD 5 to DHS.[60] The way in which DHS utilized this authority is a fascinating glimpse into the formation of policy that directly affects all levels of our federal system.

II. CREATING A NATIONAL RESPONSE PLAN AND NATIONAL INCIDENT MANAGEMENT SYSTEM

A. Comprehensive Content

HSPD 5 instructs the Secretary of DHS to "integrate Federal Government domestic prevention, preparedness, response, and recovery plans into one all-discipline, all-hazards plan,"[61] the NRP. The NRP must use NIMS to "provide the structure and mechanisms for national-level policy and operational direction for Federal support to State and local incident managers and exercise of direct Federal authorities."[62] Every federal agency has to embrace and play a part in the NRP and adopt NIMS.[63]

HSPD 5 contains specific requirements for the content of the NRP and NIMS. Included are: protocols for operating under different threat levels; incorporation of existing federal plans such as the National Oil and Hazardous Substances Pollution Contingency Plan—usually referred to as the National Contingency Plan (NCP)[64] (which is the federal approach to hazardous materials response), and the Federal Radiological Emergency Response Plan (FRERP);[65] development of other plans as needed; a consistent approach to information gathering and reporting as well as for providing recommendations to senior federal officials; and "rigorous requirements" for ongoing improvements from testing, exercising, incident experience, and new information and technologies.[66] Given this laundry list of new standards, one should not be surprised that NRP 1 and NIMS 1 ended up as comprehensive documents.

B. Challenging Deadlines

HSPD 5 required the Secretary of DHS, by April 1, 2003 (two months after its issuance), to "develop and publish the initial version of the NRP, in consultation with other Federal departments and agencies."[67] The Presidential Directive does not mention, or apparently even contemplate, involvement by responder groups or state and local government representatives in the NRP development process. In contrast, HSPD 5 directed the Secretary, by June 1, 2003 (four months after its issuance), to consult with state and local governments as well as other federal departments and agencies to "develop a national system of standards, guidelines, and protocols to implement the NIMS" and establish a mechanism for ongoing management and maintenance of NIMS, including regular consultation with the above-named stakeholders.[68] By September 1, 2003, the Secretary was required to review existing authorities and regulations and recommend revisions to the president that would enable full implementation of the NRP.[69] The challenging scope required for the NRP and NIMS combined with the very short deadlines imposed by President Bush in HSPD 5 led responsible officials at DHS to create an interagency task force to write the documents.[70] DHS Secretary Ridge selected Admiral James M. Loy, Undersecretary of Transportation, to be the NRP Task Force Director.[71]

The task of organizing the first drafts from the task force was contracted out to the RAND Corporation[72] through the Transportation Security Administration (TSA). The time pressure and complexity of the job doubtless influenced the decision to bring RAND on board. One truism that applies to all levels of government is that there are never enough hands to promptly accomplish all tasks with which the organization is entrusted.

C. NRP 1 and NIMS 1

RAND reportedly did a good job of creating documents that faithfully reflected the task force's interpretation of HSPD 5's requirements.[73] From the perspective of DHS, NRP 1 and NIMS 1 were merely "straw men," created as a vehicle to draw comment and very much in draft form.[74] State and local government representatives and responders, perhaps because they were not involved in the documents' creation, worried that NRP 1 and NIMS 1 would be very close to the final product.[75] They viewed the products as unhelpful, seeing them as creating a muddle of entities, terms, and acronyms and submerging existing, commonly accepted vocabulary beneath an impenetrable layer of new terminology.[76] NIMS 1 described itself and NRP 1 as "new paradigms" for domestic incident management.[77] One source within the Federal Emergency Management Agency (FEMA), however, characterized NRP 1 as "Just the old FRP [Federal Response Plan] with the names changed."[78]

Emergency management has historically been described as being composed of four phases—mitigation, preparedness, response, and recovery.[79] While the four-phase cycle is not perfect, it does offer a global approach to disasters and a common vocabulary for emergency management and government leaders.[80] NRP 1 changed the accepted four phases in the cycle of emergency management into five domains of incident management activities: awareness, prevention, preparedness, response, and recovery.[81] The four phases of emergency management under NIMS 1, therefore, were in the future to be referred to as five domains of incident management. This name change could have proven to be somewhat bewildering to emergency responders, who have grown used to the term incident management as applying to the more evolved management approach to incident command at the scene of events.[82]

NIMS 1 sought to establish local, state, and federal emergency Prevention and Preparedness Councils (PPCs): "PPCs integrate awareness, prevention, and preparedness activities into a unified structure that provides an ongoing multi-agency coordinating system (MACS) for all potential and impending hazards."[83] NIMS 1 included multiple complex charts illustrating how the system was projected to work in the field.[84] The PPC was projected to be the preparedness complement to the Emergency Operations Center (EOC).[85]

MACS was planned to incorporate national and regional EOCs.[86] MACS was to provide "standardized mechanisms for managing the flow of financial and physical resources before, during, and after an incident occurs."[87] Wise resource management has always been one of the primary goals of the incident command system.[88] The multiagency coordinating group (MAC Group) was conceived as an entity that would:

1. Prioritize among incidents and associated resource allocations;
2. Deal with conflicting agency policies; and
3. Give strategic guidance and direction to EOCs.[89]

MACS "operates at all levels, across all domains, for all contingencies."[90]

The PPO and MAC Group were two aspects of NIMS 1 to which responders most strongly objected. From the local level, one authority inquired, "Why are we creating a new layer of bureaucracy?" calling attention to the fact that "The EOC already has a group called Situation Analysis that constantly reviews incoming information on the disaster or emergency. The EOC also has a group called Resource Management that identifies resources and allocates them as needed. Adding MACS just adds another layer of organization that is not needed. Haven't the writers of the NRP ever worked in a State or Local EOC? . . . All MACS will do is slow down the process of getting critical resources to priority emergency situations!"[91]

III. CREATION OF THE INITIAL NATIONAL RESPONSE PLAN

A. State and Local Governments and Responders Weigh In

In August and September, the NRP/NIMS Working Group met to go over NRP 1 and NIMS 1.[92] Aware of the need for buy-in from these partners in preparedness, DHS officials with whom they met welcomed their feedback on the documents.[93] The agency's people quickly realized that the texts were seriously flawed in the eyes of the audience that would have to live with them on a daily basis.[94]

To their credit, the folks from DHS rolled up their sleeves ands went back to the drawing board. Toward the end of August or early September, Bob Stephan, Special Assistant to Secretary Ridge, came on board to coordinate revision of the documents to respond to the states' and locals' concerns. Mr. Stephan and his team decided to go back to basics on the NRP, and produce a new NIMS containing more detail than NIMS 1.[95] Their efforts resulted in the INRP and NIMS 2.

B. The Initial National Response Plan

Following their receipt of the NRP/NIMS Working Group's input, DHS released an Initial National Response Plan (INRP) on October 10, 2003.[96] This "initial" document is actually at least the eleventh revision of the NRP.[97]

The NRP/NIMS Working Group and their partners at DHS deserve considerable credit for their efforts. The INRP is a significant improvement on its predecessor.[98] The plan's size has been reduced, from fifty pages to eleven pages. Compared to NRP 1, the INRP is a "bare bones" interim document.[99] The reason for the change was Mr. Stephan's realization that a document was needed that would promptly put into operational terms the Secretary's responsibilities under HSPD 5 as the senior official for domestic emergency response. His goal was to "lock and cock the Secretary's responsibilities."[100]

One change in the documents is the somewhat greater sensitivity they demonstrate for state and local government partners; the new text treats them as equals in the pursuit of homeland security.[101] The INRP specifies that interaction between newly created federal structures like the Homeland Security Operations Center (HSOC)–a federal EOC–and analogous state, local, and tribal organizations will be "developed and coordinated collaboratively with other affected entities and published in a separate document."[102] The INRP requests state governments to report to the HSOC (again, according to mutually agreed-on procedures) the activation of state EOCs, announcements of declarations at the state or local level, and activation of interstate mutual aid agreements.[103]

Another essential feature of the INRP is its willingness to build on the many plans that are already present at the federal level.[104] The INRP's purpose was to coordinate these existing frameworks, acting as a "bridging document" between the NRP Draft #1 and documents such as the Federal Response Plan (FRP), the U.S. Government Interagency Domestic Terrorism Concept of Operations Plan, and the National Contingency Plan.[105] The INRP provided that, until the final NRP was fully in place, existing policies and procedures would remain in effect.[106] The DHS Secretary in cooperation with other federal, state, nongovernmental, tribal, and local partners has developed the NRP Draft #1 as a next step toward a final NRP.[107]

The INRP eliminates almost all of the pointless new jargon to which many observers objected in previous iterations, including the "Preliminary Framework for the NIMS."[108] As mentioned, NRP 1 eliminated the well-known four phases of emergency management–mitigation, preparedness, response, and recovery–in favor of five domains of incident management activities: awareness, prevention, preparedness, response, and recovery.[109]

For many responders, the most troublesome part of NRP 1 was the Secretary's responsibility under Training and Continuous Improvement to "Ensure rigorous requirements for continuous improvements through a national system to plan, equip, train, exercise, test, and evaluate and to provide standards and credentialing for homeland security."[110] This requirement of HSPD 5 is addressed in the adopted NIMS.[111]

Postevent activities are more easily comprehended than in NRP 1, including authorizing the DHS Secretary to appoint a Principal Federal Official (PFO) for oversight and coordination of federal activities.[112] The PFO will not be the only federal contact, however, with state, local, and tribal officials, the media and the private sector for incident management.[113] Requests for and deployment of federal assistance will be executed as the FRP and other existing plans have required in the past.[114] A Joint Field Office will incorporate the Joint Operations Center, the Disaster Field Office, and other entities into a one-stop shop for contact with federal entities.[115]

The INRP encompasses significant improvements on a living document. Albert Ashwood, the National Association of Emergency Managers representative to the Working Group, summed up: "We have a document that's in draft form. We're going to have to be continually looking at it. . . . It must be recalled that this is a work in progress."[116] The NRP/NIMS Working Group deserves much praise for its hard work to rescue an approach that was flawed in many ways. Their assistance has benefited DHS significantly, and will continue to do so through the consulting process.

IV. SUBSEQUENT NRP VERSIONS: EVER MORE COMPREHENSIVE PLANS

The NRP Draft #1[117] and later versions of the NRP in some ways hearken back to NRP 1[118] but overall analysis reveals that their roots lie much more in the Federal Response Plan. It is a much longer document than the INRP.[119] The documents were created to embody the direction of HSPD 5 to ". . . integrate Federal Government domestic prevention, preparedness, response, and recovery plans into one all-discipline, all-hazards plan."[120] The evolving NRP Draft #1, however, reveal greater sensitivity to the concerns voiced in the aftermath of NRP 1's release.[121]

NRP 1 made no reference to the National Guard, a shortcoming that the later NRP Drafts address.[122] The later NRP Drafts task state-controlled (not federally called up) army and air national guard units with primary duties of supporting their states during civil emergencies.[123] The NRP Drafts contemplate using the Guard to support federal law enforcement activities when called to federal duty.[124] They also posit that the Guard will assist state law enforcement efforts when it has been called to service as a state-level resource.[125] The documents mention the controls placed on military forces by the *Posse Comitatus* Act,[126] but interpret the act not to apply to Guard units on state service.[127] This interpretation of the *Posse Comitatus* Act is generally endorsed by legal scholars,[128] who also point out that state law may limit the Guard's use while on state service.[129]

NRP 1 also does not mention emergency medical services (EMS). The NRP Draft #1 recognizes EMS as an "incident management component,"[130] but only mentions EMS once in the entire document. That limitation continues in the NRP Final Draft.[131] The specifics for EMS are, however, laid out in an attached annex as Emergency Support Function #8,[132] in a manner similar to the Federal Response Plan.

NRP 1 also discusses the governor's role only very briefly.[133] The NRP Draft #1 expands significantly on NRP 1's language regarding the governor's role.[134] Under NRP 1, the governor "is responsible . . . to prepare for and to respond to manmade incidents, including terrorism, natural disasters, and other contingencies . . .", while the NRP Draft #1 requires that he or she "is responsible . . . to prevent, prepare for, to respond and recovery [sic] from incidents involving all hazards including terrorism, natural disasters, accidents, and other contingencies." Adding prevention and recovery to the governor's responsibilities reflects their nature under state law.[135] The NRP Draft #1 also contains stronger language regarding promotion of mutual aid agreements (moving from "may encourage" in NRP 1[136] to "encourages" in the NRP Draft #1.[137]) The NRP Draft #1 includes detailed reference to federal procedures for governors to request assistance[138] under the Stafford Act.[139]

Gone are the five "domains" of incident management posited in NRP 1.[140] The language reverts to the "phases"[141] of an incident. Further, the phases include those familiar to emergency management–mitigation, preparedness, response, and recovery–and adds a new phase, prevention.[142] Adding prevention makes sense, as the term refers to the law enforcement piece of DHS's responsibilities,[143] a duty that was not borne by traditional emergency management.[144] The NRP Draft #1 also addresses other concerns regarding terminology and structure. The multiagency coordinating system (MACS),[145] which was conceived of as the heart of incident management,[146] is not present in the NRP Draft #1.[147] Likewise, its multiagency coordinating group (MAC Group)[148] is not present in the adopted NIMS. The local, state, and federal emergency Prevention and Preparedness Councils[149] that were to be the basic underlying structures for MACS[150] are a thing of the past. The NRP Draft #1 approaches the matter from a functional perspective, concentrating on tasks that must be performed rather than creating new structures.[151]

Some concerns regarding terminology remain. The definition of preparedness does not include the terms training and exercising,[152] thus differentiating it from the traditional FEMA concept familiar to emergency managers.[153] Indeed, training and exercising are not found in the definitions of any of the phases of incident management,[154] as delineated in the NRP Draft #1.[155]

Unlike NRP 1, the NRP Draft #1 contains an indication in the table of contents[156] that significant reference materials would be added. Of assistance to emergency managers and responders, these materials include Emergency Support Functions Annexes[157] (contained in a separate document distributed with the NRP Draft #1). Other information that is due to be added later included Support Annexes[158] (including Legal)[159] and Hazard Specific Incident Annexes.[160] The revival of Emergency Support Functions and Hazard Specific Annexes hearkens back to the Federal Response Plan.[161] A useful tool for attorneys is the existing portion of the Authorities and References Section,[162] which includes federal authorities for actions under the NRP Draft #1.

Adoption of the National Response Plan

The National Response Plan was finally adopted in November 2004.[163] The NRP is effective upon issuance, with a phased implementation process during the first year. During the first 120 days of this implementation process, the Initial NRP (INRP), Federal Response Plan (FRP), U.S. Government Domestic Terrorism Concept of Operations Plan (CONPLAN), and Federal Radiological Emergency Response Plan (FRERP) are to remain in effect.

Implementation Phases for the National Response Plan[164]

• **Phase I—Transitional Period (0 to 60 days):**
This 60-day timeframe is intended to provide a transitional period for departments and agencies and other organizations to modify training, designate staffing of NRP organizational elements, and become familiar with NRP structures, processes, and protocols.

• **Phase II—Plan Modification (60 to 120 days):**
This second 60-day timeframe is intended to provide departments and agencies the opportunity to modify existing federal interagency plans to align with the NRP and conduct necessary training.

• **Phase III—Initial Implementation and Testing (120 days to 1 year):**
Four months after its issuance, the NRP is to be fully implemented, and the INRP, FRP, CONPLAN, and FRERP are superseded. Other existing plans remain in effect, modified to align with the NRP. During this timeframe, the Department of Homeland Security (DHS) will conduct systematic assessments of NRP coordinating structures, processes, and protocols implemented for actual Incidents of National Significance (defined on page 4 of the NRP), national-level homeland security exercises, and National Special Security Events (NSSEs). These assessments will gauge the plan's effectiveness in meeting specific objectives outlined in Homeland Security Presidential Directive-5 (HSPD-5).

At the end of this period, DHS will conduct a 1-year review to assess the implementation process and make recommendations to the Secretary on necessary NRP revisions. Following this initial review, the NRP will begin a deliberate 4-year review and reissuance cycle.

The NRP encourages private sector entities, particularly those who represent critical infrastructure or key resources, to develop suitable emergency response and business continuity plans and information-sharing and incident-reporting protocols. These should be created to address their business's unique requirements, and be coordinated with regional, state, and local emergency response plans and information-sharing networks. These structures should be in harmony with the NRP Base Plan and supporting annexes.[165]

Structure of the National Response Plan

The NRP's structure continued to evolve, becoming in the process more similar to the Federal Response Plan.[166] DHS had the goal of impacting the existing state and local structure as little as possible in the NRP.[167]

The **Base Plan** describes a national approach to domestic incident management designed to incorporate the efforts and resources of federal, state, local, tribal, private sector, and nongovernmental organizations. The Base Plan comprises planning assumptions, roles and responsibilities, concept of operations, preparedness guidelines, and plan maintenance instructions.

Appendixes provide other relevant, more detailed supporting information, including terms, definitions, acronyms, authorities, and a compendium of national interagency plans. They include:

- Glossary of Key Terms
- List of Acronyms
- Authorities and References
- Compendium of National/International Interagency Plans
- Overview of Initial Federal Involvement Under the Stafford Act
- Overview of Federal-to-Federal Support in Non-Stafford Act Situations

The **Emergency Support Function (ESF) Annexes** specify the missions, policies, structures, and responsibilities of federal agencies for managing resource and program support to states and federal agencies or other entities during Incidents of National Significance. The ESF Annexes consist of:

ESF	Scope
ESF #1–Transportation	• Federal and civil transportation support • Transportation safety • Restoration/recovery of transportation infrastructure • Movement restrictions • Damage and impact assessment
ESF #2–Communications	• Coordination with telecommunications industry • Restoration/repair of telecommunications infrastructure
	• Protection, restoration, and sustainment of national cyber and information technology resources
ESF #3–Public Works and Engineering	• Infrastructure protection and emergency repair • Infrastructure restoration • Engineering services, construction management • Critical infrastructure liaison
ESF #4–Firefighting	• Firefighting activities on federal lands • Resource support to rural and urban firefighting operations
ESF #5–Emergency Management	• Coordination of incident management efforts • Issuance of mission assignments • Resource and human capital • Incident action planning • Financial management
ESF #6–Mass Care, Housing, and Human Services	• Mass care • Disaster housing • Human services
ESF #7–Resource Support	• Resource support (facility space, office equipment and supplies, contracting services, etc.)
ESF #8–Public Health and Medical Services	• Public health • Medical • Mental health services • Mortuary services
ESF #9–Urban Search and Rescue	• Life-saving assistance • Urban search and rescue

ESF #10–Oil and
Hazardous Materials
Response

- Oil and hazardous materials (chemical, biological, radio-logical, etc.) response
- Environmental safety and short- and long-term cleanup

ESF #11–Agriculture
and Natural Resources

- Nutrition assistance
- Animal and plant disease/pest response
- Food safety and security
- Natural and cultural resources and historic properties protection and restoration

ESF #12–Energy

- Energy infrastructure assessment, repair, and restoration
- Energy industry utilities coordination
- Energy forecast

ESF #13–Public Safety
and Security

- Facility and resource security
- Security planning and technical and resource assistance
- Public safety/security support
- Support to access, traffic, and crowd control

ESF #14–Long-term
Community Recovery
and Mitigation

- Social and economic community impact assessment
- Long-term community recovery assistance to states, local governments, and the private sector
- Mitigation analysis and program implementation

ESF #15–External Affairs

- Emergency public information and protective action guidance
- Media and community relations

- Congressional and international affairs
- Tribal and insular affairs

The **Support Annexes** provide guidance and describe the methods and administrative obligations needed to assure efficient and effective achievement of NRP incident management objectives. The Support Annexes are described next.

Support Annexes

- **Financial Management** provides guidance for NRP implementation to ensure that incident-related funds are provided expeditiously and that financial management activities are conducted in accordance with established law, policies, regulations, and standards.
- **International Coordination** provides guidance for carrying out responsibilities regarding international coordination in support of the federal response to domestic Incidents of National Significance.
- **Logistics Management** describes the framework within which the overall NRP logistics management function operates. It also outlines logistics management responsibilities and mechanisms for integrating federal, state, local, and tribal resource providers.
- **Private-Sector Coordination** outlines processes to ensure effective incident management coordination and integration with the private sector, including representatives of the nation's Critical Infrastructure/Key Resources (CI/KR) sectors and other industries.
- **Public Affairs** describes interagency incident communications procedures designed to enable the coordination and dissemination of timely public information during Incidents of National Significance.
- **Science and Technology** provides guidance and mechanisms to ensure that all levels of government can leverage the nation's science and technology resources efficiently and effectively in the management of Incidents of National Significance.
- **Tribal Relations** describes the policies, responsibilities, and concept of operations for

effective coordination and interaction with tribal governments and communities during Incidents of National Significance.

- **Volunteer and Donations Management** provides guidance on volunteer and donations management functions related to Incidents of National Significance.
- **Worker Safety and Health** details processes to ensure coordinated, comprehensive efforts to identify responder safety and health risks and implement procedures to minimize or eliminate illness or injuries during incident management and emergency response activities.[168]

The **Incident Annexes** address contingency or hazard situations requiring specialized application of the NRP. The Incident Annexes describe the missions, policies, responsibilities, and coordination processes that govern the interaction of public and private entities engaged in incident management and emergency response operations across a spectrum of potential hazards. These annexes are typically augmented by a variety of supporting plans and operational supplements. The Incident Annexes are new to the adopted NRP, and should provide much-needed guidance for state and local responders in their responses to the referenced types of event. The Incident Annexes are described next.

Incident Annexes

- The **Biological Incident Annex** describes incident management activities related to a biological terrorism event, pandemic, emerging infectious disease, or novel pathogen outbreak.
- The **Catastrophic Incident Annex** establishes the strategy for implementing and coordinating an accelerated national response to a catastrophic incident.
- The **Cyber Incident Annex** establishes procedures for a multidisciplinary, broad-based approach to prepare for, remediate, and recover from catastrophic cyber events impacting critical national processes and the national economy.
- The **Food and Agriculture Incident Annex** describes incident management activities related to a terrorist attack, major

disaster, or other emergency involving the nation's agriculture and food systems.

(To be published in a subsequent version of the NRP.)

- The **Nuclear/Radiological Incident Annex** describes incident management activities related to nuclear/radiological incidents.
- The **Oil and Hazardous Materials Incident Annex** describes incident management activities related to certain nationally significant oil and hazardous materials pollution incidents.
- The **Terrorism Incident Law Enforcement and Investigation Annex** describes law enforcement and criminal investigation coordinating structures and processes in response to a terrorist event.[169]

In keeping with its status as a national plan, the NRP requires incident management and emergency response plans to incorporate its approach to their subject matter. Specifically, they must include, to the extent authorized by law:

- Principles and terminology of the NIMS;
- Reporting requirements of the NRP;
- Linkages to key NRP organizational elements (such as the Interagency Incident Management Group (IIMG), National Response Coordination Center (NRCC), Regional Response Coordination Center (RRCC), Joint Field Office (JFO), etc.); and
- Procedures for transitioning from localized incidents to Incidents of National Significance.[170]

Although a Legal Support Annex was to have been issued in the NRP as indicated by its inclusion in the table of contents for the NRP Draft #1,[171] this element does not appear in the document, nor did it appear in the contents of NRP Final Draft. Such guidance would have been particularly welcome to attorneys at all levels of government, who for the most part have been flying blind when the time came to advise on legal issues during incidents.[172] Both they and their business counterparts need all the information they can get regarding incident management, an issue that will likely become ever more prominent in their legal practices.[173]

V. NIMS 2 AND THE ADOPTED NIMS: MORE DETAIL FOR RESPONDERS AND EMERGENCY MANAGERS

The NRP/NIMS Working Group meeting that resulted in the INRP was the first of an ongoing series of conferences.[174] A subsequent conference addressed NIMS 1, and they produced yet another document responsive to concerns of state and local representatives.[175] NIMS 2 is a much more detailed document than is the INRP.[176] Hence, the adopted NIMS is very close in content to NIMS 2,[177] in contrast to differences between the INRP, the NRP Draft #1, and the adopted NRP.

A. Preparedness Issues

Perhaps the most interesting and significant parts of the adopted NIMS deal with preparedness.[178] Adopted NIMS's Chapter III–Preparedness lays out a "preparedness cycle" that includes:

1. planning;
2. training;
3. equipping;
4. exercising;
5. evaluating; and
6. taking action to correct or mitigate.[179]

Emergency managers can take heart from changes between NIMS 1, NIMS 2, and the adopted NIMS. While the former attempted to create a completely new structure,[180] the latter two documents recognize the importance of FEMA's established all-hazards approach to preparedness.[181] Despite the funding issues mentioned earlier regarding the primacy of terrorism, the adopted NIMS clearly anticipates that it will apply to all hazards.[182] The adopted NIMS recognizes the fact that different jurisdictions have evolved different preparedness organizations.[183] It specifies, however, that when preparedness must take place across jurisdictions, organizations should be multijurisdictional in nature.[184] This pronouncement dovetails with the adopted NIMS's heavy emphasis on mutual aid agreements, discussed in more detail next.[185]

The roles of preparedness organizations and the nature of preparedness programs are laid out in some detail.[186] Plans need to address the elements of the preparedness cycle enumerated earlier.[187] Planning must include emergency operations plans, procedures for implementing the plans, preparedness plans (including training and exercising), mitigation plans, and recovery plans.[188] Training and exercises (to federal standards) must be run to ensure continual improvement in all-hazards incident management nationwide.[189] Personnel qualifications[190] and equipment[191] must be standardized to enable integration of different entities. For all aspects of preparedness, publications management is a key element, as it provides consistent standards and promotes interoperability.[192]

B. The NIMS Integration Center and Responder Certification Issues

As mentioned, HSPD 5 requires federal regulation of homeland security responders.[193] These standards will be enforced through funding cuts for noncompliant entities.[194] Although such cuts could have begun in FFY 2005, DHS issued guidance for compliance in FFY 2005 that puts off such steps.[195]

The adopted NIMS requires "establishing guidelines, protocols, and standards for planning, training and exercises, personnel qualification and certification, equipment certification, and publication management."[196] National level preparedness standards will be "maintained and managed" through a multijurisdictional, multidisciplinary center, using a collaborative process.[197] To accomplish this goal, the adopted NIMS sets up a NIMS Integration Center (NIC),[198] which was referred to as the Management and Maintenance Center under NIMS 2.[199]

The NIC's nature is outlined in very general terms in the adopted NIMS.[200] Mr. Stephan expressed concern that the NIMS needed to be produced and useful as quickly as possible.[201] The discussions between stakeholders on how to put together the Integration Center are able therefore to progress in parallel with the NIMS revision.[202] The result should be more rapid deployment of two mature documents, rather than prolonged consideration of a single text.[203] In early 2004, a cross-department working group with outreach to other interested parties began to flesh out the Integration Center.[204] They came up with a detailed concept of operations and staffing requirements for the NIC.[205] One aspect of specialized support for the Integration Center will be legal staff, possibly on detached duty from the DHS Office of General Counsel.[206]

On April 7, 2004, Secretary Ridge signed a memorandum prepared by Bob Stephan approving a Management Directive establishing the NIMS Integration Center.[207] Attached to the memorandum were a detailed Concept of Operations and Staffing Plan for the NIC as well as a Proposed Budget for FFY 2004. Interestingly, the NIC is to be housed in the Emergency Preparedness and Response Directorate (EP&R),[208] which was originally tasked in the HS Act with drafting the NRP,[209] of which NIMS is the operational section. As mentioned previously, the various versions of the NRP were actually drawn up under the auspices of the TSA. Putting the NIMS Center under EP&R may signal that DHS is returning to the stated intent of the HS Act, as well as that the diminution of FEMA's role (discussed at greater length in Chapter 3) may be at an end.

The goal for the NIMS Integration Center is not to be a federal Big Brother creating impassible barriers to entry for responders.

This NIMS Center is not going to be a bunch of guys pushing it out to the field. It's going to be participatory development. And in many cases, the NIMS Center may not even be the organization that actually develops the standards—it may be a professional association, but then the NIMS Center can take that and put a stamp of approval on it . . . and help promulgate it.[210]

Changes in NIMS standards and other corrective actions may be proposed by a variety of entities, including local, state, tribal, federal, private sector, and professional organizations.[211] Ultimate authority for alteration in NIMS standards rests with the Secretary of DHS.[212] In other words, other interested groups may propose modifications, and their input is advisory only.

As suggested by Mr. Stephan, some responder organizations have already begun the process of putting together proposed standards for federal homeland security responders. In keeping with a congressional mandate, the U.S. Fire Academy and DHS held a series of meetings to develop national fire service credentialing standards for federally declared disasters, with the goal of improving multiagency coordination and response effectiveness.[213] One guideline that the group emphasized was the need to operate within the framework of existing state credentialing systems, rather than imposing a new layer of bureaucracy. This would be a voluntary system.[214] The last meeting of the USFA group took place on December 11, 2003—about a week after the release of NIMS 2.[215]

Dealing with the proposed USFA standards may be an early test of the Integration Center. The proposal that the federal standards be voluntary would appear to conflict with the clear mandate for standard setting contained in the adopted NIMS.[216] The adopted NIMS anticipates that jurisdictions may continue to credential personnel for operation within their boundaries, but states that "Personnel that are certified for employment in support of an incident that transcends interstate jurisdictions through the Emergency Management Assistance Compacts System will be required to meet national qualification and certification standards."[217] In common with other advocates for the incident management system, Mr. Stephan particularly emphasizes the need for common standards and vocabulary when responding to incidents involving Weapons of Mass Destruction or other particularly dangerous substances.[218]

One potential effect of the multitiered (federal and other jurisdictions) credentialing system may be uneven levels of protection for different parts of the nation due to authorization of federal, state, tribal, and local training authorities.[219] Those with federal credentials will receive federal grant funds for equipment and training, whereas responders with other levels of certification will be denied those funds, as required by HSPD 5.[220] Further, Homeland Security Undersecretary Michael Brown recently stated that DHS will make contributions to first-responder salaries in partnership with state and local governments.[221]

Less affluent and rural jurisdictions that do not have federally certified responders will be forced to pay their all expenses solely from local funds.[222]

This situation would compound challenges that currently face such entities.[223] As documented in the recent Council of Foreign Relations report on responder resources entitled "Emergency Responders: Drastically Underfunded, Dangerously Unprepared," current unfunded requirements total $98.4 billion.[224] Under the multitiered system,[225] local responders who are not a part of the federal certification system would suffer from increasingly inadequate funding. The outcome might be continuing deterioration of emergency response capabilities in those jurisdictions least able to afford the cost of preparedness.[226] One worries about volunteer services that have difficulty in recruiting members under current conditions.[227] These groups frequently report that any additional required training results in fewer new members and attrition of current members.[228] In the wake of new federal standards that require additional training, some local organizations might be forced to disband, leaving portions of the country bereft of emergency responders.[229]

Mr. Stephan does not agree:

> What we're looking for is not to force people to spend a whole lot of money. . . . We think we are building enough flexibility into the system. . . . [I]f you are a small podunk jurisdiction and can't afford a big computer system, you are going to have to update your manuals. . . . The key is we are building for a very broad system of users.[230]

The variety of circumstances faced by emergency response groups across the nation makes setting national standards a challenge. For example, firefighters in the industrialized northeast frequently confront fires or spills involving hazardous materials. West of the Mississippi River, in contrast, wildfires are a major concern.[231] Clearly, while both groups of firefighters have common aspects to their work for which common standards may be promulgated, there is no need to require everyone to know everything. Perhaps a national "basic firefighter" qualification with endorsements for further national standards such as HAZMAT or wildfire expertise might be a workable approach. Delayed compliance or waivers for organizations with demonstrable undue hardships might provide

limited safe harbors within the new regulatory framework. The details of how such a system might work will become clearer as the Integration Center's outlines take more definite shape.[232] Additional federal bureaucracy may be needed to enforce HSPD 5's funding penalties for noncompliant organizations and personnel. If the system as enacted has sufficient flexibility, the result could be a workable national model that is achievable by all.

C. NFPA 1600:[233] Another Important Standard for Emergency Management[234]

On April 29, 2004, the American National Standards Institute (ANSI) recommended to the 9-11 Commission that the National Fire Protection Association (NFPA) standard, "NFPA 1600 Recommended Practices for Disaster Management," be established as the national preparedness standard.

On July 22, 2004, the 9-11 Commission formally endorsed NFPA 1600, stating that they were encouraged by DHS Secretary Ridge's praise for it and specifying their preference that its adoption be promoted by DHS. The Commission further urged that compliance with NFPA 1600 be taken into account by the insurance and credit-rating industries in assessing a company's insurance rating and creditworthiness. The 9-11 Commission also believes that "compliance with the standard should define the standard of care owed by a company to its employees and the public for legal purposes."[235] Legislation has been introduced to enact the 9-11 Commission's recommendations.[236] The legislation endorses and adopts recommendations of 9-11 Commission virtually without change, including adoption of NFPA 1600. The bill specifically addresses the private sector, which it finds to be largely unprepared for terrorist attacks, due in part to a lack of widely accepted standards for private sector preparedness.[237] It states that DHS's mandate extends to working with the private sector, as well as government entities. The legislation would further establish a Private Sector Preparedness Program, amending the Homeland Security Act of 2002. The program would mandate DHS to promote a private sector "voluntary" preparedness program such as NFPA 1600. The teeth of the legislation is contained in a "Sense of Congress" finding that insurance and credit-rating industries should consider compliance with voluntary national preparedness standard, in assessing insurability and credit worthiness. This would be a congressional endorsement of the 9-11 Commission's recommendation. In this manner, the federal government is creating a system whereby business pressures will produce compliance with the NFPA 1600 standard.

NFPA 1600 sets up a shared set of norms for disaster management, emergency management, and business continuity programs. It also recognizes ways to exercise plans and makes available a listing of resource organizations within the fields of disaster recovery, emergency management, and business continuity planning. One vital aspect of NFPA 1600 is its requirement that all emergency management and business continuity programs must comply with all relevant laws, policies, and industry practices.[238]

1. Incorporating NFPA 1600: The Emergency Management Accreditation Program

The National Emergency Management Association (NEMA) has also endorsed NFPA 1600 as an appropriate standard for emergency management. As early as 1998, NEMA passed a resolution signaling its support of NFPA 1600.[239] The standard, along with other existing documents like the Capability Assessment for Readiness (CAR), provides the foundation for the Emergency Management Accreditation Program (EMAP).[240] The accreditation process includes application, self-assessment, on-site assessment by an outside review team, committee and commission review of compliance with the EMAP Standard, and re-certification every five years.

EMAP has moved rapidly from a concept first expressed in 1997 through pilot tests and assessments through certification of units of government, the first of which was awarded in 2003.

Emergency Management Accreditation Program Timeline

April 2002	EMAP opened for registration and for state applications
Summer-Fall 2002	Local pilot tests
2003	EMAP conducted 20 state/territorial baseline assessments
June 2003	Two states are conditionally accredited: Arizona and North Dakota
September 2003	First two jurisdictions receive EMAP accreditation: Florida and District of Columbia
January 2004	Continue state/territorial baseline assessments and begin conducting local on-site assessments for programs seeking accreditation

EMAP is supported by a large number of important players in emergency management, including the National Emergency Management Association, International Association of Emergency Managers, Federal Emergency Management Agency, U.S. Department of Transportation, Association of State Flood Plain Managers, Institute for Business and Home Safety, International Association of Fire Chiefs, National Association of Counties, National Association of Development Organizations, National Conference of State Legislatures, National Governors Association, National League of Cities, and the U.S. Environmental Protection Agency.

Although the program is voluntary, the fact that it is endorsed by such a wide variety of authorities means that EMAP is well on its way to becoming the *de facto* standard for emergency management in the United States. The more programs become accredited under the standard, the more likely a court will be to hold all emergency management to the norm. Accepted industry practices may move from *de facto* to *de jure* acceptance through common law adoption in the courts.[241] Clearly, potential liability could result from not performing to the standards set by EMAP. The wise emergency management program manager will take prompt steps to ensure that his or her program is accredited under EMAP.

2. NFPA 1600 and ICS

Use of ICS is required by both NFPA 1600[242] and NIMS.[243] The emergency manager is therefore obligated to ensure that it is utilized in emergency responses. The Hazardous Waste Operations and Emergency Response ("HAZWOPER") Standard[244] has been in existence for over twenty years. Its mandates for use of ICS are valuable, therefore, for the emergency manager thinking about how best to adopt ICS. The lessons learned over the past twenty-plus years from use of ICS at HAZMAT scenes will be invaluable for implementation of the standard in the wake NFPA 1600's and NIMS's requirements to do so.

3. NIMS and NFPA 1600 Planning Standards

The adoption of the NFPA 1600 emergency management standard discussed earlier, however, may well result in liability for negligently drafted plans. This is because the planning portion of NFPA 1600 details particular tasks. Several plans are mandated:

> **5.7.1*** The program shall include, but shall not be limited to, a strategic plan, an emergency operations/response plan, a mitigation plan, a recovery plan, and a continuity plan.[245]

The content of these plans is laid out with some particularity. The emergency response plan is described as follows:

> **1.7.2.2** The emergency operations/response plan shall assign responsibilities to organizations and individuals for carrying out specific actions at projected times and places in an emergency or disaster.[246]

All of the plans required by NFPA 1600 have several shared components:

> **5.7.3** Common Plan Elements.

> **5.7.3.1** The functional roles and responsibilities of internal and external agencies, organizations, departments, and individuals shall be identified.

> **5.7.3.2** Lines of authority for those agencies, organizations, departments, and individuals shall be established or identified.[247]

NFPA 1600 also requires other steps be taken that are a normal part of planning, such as hazard identification, risk assessment, and impact analysis.[248] As mentioned previously, NFPA 1600 also imposes a duty to adhere to current laws, policies, and industry practices.[249] This means that the requirements of NFPA 1600 are a moving target. Avoidance of liability for bad planning will therefore require constant attention to evolving standards.

In addition to the NFPA 1600 standard, the National Incident Management System (NIMS)[250] sets mandatory standards for emergency management programs that wish to receive federal funds, including Emergency Management Performance Grants (EMPGs),[251] after October 2004.[252] (This could have been a hollow threat, at least as far as the EMPGs were concerned, due to planned budget cuts in the program.[253] Thanks to congressional intervention the cuts did not materialize.) NIMS requires emergency operations plans (EOPs), corrective action and mitigation plans, and recovery plans.[254] NIMS's requirements for EOPs are rather extensive.

National Incident Management System Suggested Requirements for EOPs[255]

- Defines the scope of preparedness and incident management activities necessary for the jurisdiction.
- Describe organizational structures, roles and responsibilities, policies, and protocols for providing emergency support.
- Facilitate response and short-term recovery activities.
- Drive decisions long-term prevention and mitigation efforts or risk-based preparedness measures directed at specific hazards.
- Be flexible enough for use in all emergencies.
- Describe the purpose of the plan, situation and assumptions, concept of operations, organization and assignment of responsibilities, administration and logistics, plan development and maintenance, and authorities and references.

- Contain functional annexes, hazard-specific appendices, and a glossary.
- Predesignate jurisdictional and/or functional area representatives to the IC or UC to facilitate responsive and collaborative incident management.
- Include preincident and postincident public awareness, education, and communications plans and protocols.

NIMS establishes a national industry standard. NIMS frames its mandates as suggestions, using the term "should" rather than "must." The requirement of NFPA 1600 that plans must incorporate industry standards, however, will eventually make these voluntary elements mandatory. NIMS complements NFPA 1600, and sets the benchmark for planning. Failure to plan to its requirements may well result in liability.

NFPA 1600 and state laws require local emergency management to prepare and keep current a local disaster emergency plan for its area. Since 9-11, states have expanded their statutory schemes to include specific enactments addressing terrorism. In particular, states that list planning requirements frequently have added planning for terrorist events to their laws.[256] This is an example of the evolving nature of planning requirements. As experienced emergency managers say, the plan is never final, but rather a living document.

D. Mutual Aid Concerns

Mutual aid agreements (MAAs)[257] are a key element in helping organizations to work smoothly together.[258] They are mandated by a number of standards, including NFPA 1600[259] and NIMS.[260] Their importance to the EOP is obvious: They allow multiplication of resources. The proper contents for intra-state and inter-state mutual aid agreements are found on the National Emergency Management Association (NEMA) Website.[261]

Unlike much of the adopted NIMS,[262] the nature and contents of mutual aid agreements are strong suggestions only.[263] The reason for this is that the HSPD 5 provides for federal standards for such matters as responder qualification and certification,[264] but not for MAAs. These agreements are therefore matters to be decided independently by the different units of government that may be involved.[265]

The Emergency Management Assistance Compact (EMAC) is the benchmark for interstate agreements. Various states have adopted slightly differing versions of EMAC.[266] One issue that EMAC does not address is the credentialing of visiting emergency responders such as emergency medical technicians and doctors. This was reportedly a matter of such controversy when EMAC was written that the decision was made to allow each state to deal with the issue separately.[267] It is unfortunate that there is not a uniform national approach to this issue in EMAC.

For those who become federally certified under the authority of NIMS, nationwide credentialing will be a part of the package.[268] This approach will do a great deal to lessen potential confusion in the aftermath of an emergency or disaster.

The EMAC Web page also contains a model intrastate agreement.[269] Some states already have made provision for an intrastate agreement. For example, Indiana has an intrastate mutual aid program that applies to every political subdivision of the state that does not opt out by adopting an ordinance or resolution stating that it does so.[270]

Jurisdictions that request mutual aid assistance must be aware of potential legal claims that may arise from doing so. While the model agreements discussed here will cover issues like who is responsible for injuries to members of the assisting unit, case law indicates that the requesting entity may be responsible for their workers' compensation claims if they are injured during the response.[271]

Interestingly, the MAA contents list is the only place in the document where legal issues are directly addressed.[272] It specifies workers' compensation, treatment of liability and immunity, and recognition of qualifications and certifications as matters for inclusion in an MAA.[273] While these are vital legal issues, the lack of an overall approach to liability issues as a distinct hazard remains a shortcoming in virtually all emergency operations plans.[274] The proposed Legal Support Annex[275] to the NRP Draft #1 might have addressed this shortcoming. Past offerings focused on federal issues, without being of much help to state and local attorneys.[276]

The adopted NIMS requires that responders to interstate requests for assistance be federally certified.[277] In the national Emergency Management Assistance Compact (EMAC),[278] the issue of certifying visiting responders is left to the individual states. The challenges posed by the multitiered certification system include important legal issues that must be considered in the context of mutual aid.[279] First of all, an interstate agreement apparently may not validly be reached if one of its members is not federally certified pursuant to NIMS.[280] As a practical matter, however, emergency responders help those who need them, and respond to requests for assistance from their neighbors, regardless of legal consequences.[281] Mr. Stephan recognizes this reality:

> If you've got a mass casualty situation, you're going to try to get everyone in there you can [whether they are Federally certified or not]. On a local type of scene, probably not. That's going to have to be situationally dependent. Liability issues come up. If you are nationally certified, you're going to be able to fit in all the different scenarios—that's the best option.[282]

FEMA currently imposes requirements for formal MAAs in order to receive reimbursement for mutual aid expenses,[283] yet many groups do not enter into such pacts. This background indicates that increases in their use will continue to slowly grow,[284] but the mandate of the adopted NIMS will ensure more rapid growth.[285] Greater understanding of potential liabilities, including possible nullification of existing agreements and loss of Federal grant funds, may increase the use of MAAs.[286]

E. Implementing NIMS

On September 8, 2004, the DHS NIMS Integration Center (NIC) issued a letter to all state governors, with copies to State Administrative Agencies, State Emergency Management Directors, State Homeland Security Advisors, DHS Directorates and Offices, and the Homeland Security Advisory Council.[287] The letter outlines the background of NIMS, including issuance of HSPD 5, creation of NIMS in obedience to HSPD 5, adoption of NIMS by the federal government, and creation of the NIMS Integration Center. The document's bulk contains the steps required for states, territorial, tribal FFY 2005: October 1, 2004–September 30, 2005.

In keeping with its status as a national system, the letter states that, while some NIMS requirements are specific to local jurisdictions, the leadership role of the states is critical for full NIMS implementation. The correspondence specifies that FFY 2005 is a "start-up year" and that full NIMS compliance is not immediately required in order to receive grant funds. The NIC is currently working to identify all preparedness grant programs, whose continuance depends on NIMS compliance.

Minimum FY 2005 NIMS Compliance Requirements:

State and territory level efforts to implement the NIMS must include the following:

- Incorporating NIMS into existing training programs and exercises
- Ensuring that federal preparedness funding (including DHS Homeland Security Grant Program, Urban Area Security Initiative [UASI] funds) support NIMS implementation at the state and local levels (in accordance with the eligibility and allowable uses of the grants)
- Incorporating NIMS into Emergency Operations Plans (EOP)
- Promotion of intrastate mutual aid agreements
- Coordinating and providing technical assistance to local entities regarding NIMS
- Institutionalizing the use of the Incident Command System (ICS).

At the state, territorial, tribal, and local levels, jurisdictions should support NIMS implementation by:

- Completing the NIMS Awareness Course: "National Incident Management System (NIMS), An Introduction" IS 700
- Formally recognizing the NIMS and adopting the NIMS principles and policies
- Establish a NIMS baseline by determining which NIMS requirements you already meet

- Establishing a timeframe and developing a strategy for full NIMS implementation
- Institutionalizing the use of the Incident Command System (ICS).

In some jurisdictions, significant changes to law, including legislation, executive orders, ordinances, resolutions, or regulations, may be needed to comply with NIMS. The NIC will provide models for these enactments. This process will accelerate the devolution of power over responders and their sponsoring organizations from the state and local levels of the government to the federal sphere.

States are encouraged to achieve full NIMS compliance in FFY 2005. Those that do not do so will be required to leverage federal assistance funds to completely adopt NIMS during FFY 2006. Those that have not become fully NIMS compliant will not receive federal preparedness funds during FFY 2007. This time frame will be less onerous than the denial of federal preparedness funds to noncompliant entities in FFY 2005 authorized by HSPD 5. Units of government nonetheless continue to face a firm, albeit delayed, deadline for losing federal funds if they do not "voluntarily" comply with NIMS. Of course, the heart of NIMS is adoption of the Incident Command System (ICS), which the letter specifies must be consistent with the concepts and principles taught by DHS.

Even after the stakeholder input described above, support for NIMS is not universal.[288] Some responders reacted critically to the letter's rapid promulgation of NIMS, saying that NIMS lacks clarity and fails to provide sufficient training and funding for personnel.[289] "The start of fiscal year 2006 is too soon to begin to tie the receipt of federal terrorism-response grant funding to NIMS implementation," Los Angeles County Fire Chief Michael Freeman told a Congressional subcommittee. "The NIMS has 518 measurable requirements. It is unclear to us whether DHS will require implementation of all 518 or whether a percentage will be required or whether there will be a top 10," Freeman said. "Implementing all 518 requirements within the next year will be a Herculean and perhaps unreasonable task."[290] Freeman was referring to the NIMS Compliance Assurance Support Tool (NIMS CAST)[291] when he listed 518 requirements.

Deputy Associate Director David Kaufman of the DHS Office for Domestic Preparedness (ODP) recently stated that the NIMS Integration Center's determination of "what implementation and compliance means and all the rest" will take time. Therefore, Kaufman said, "We can't exactly require that compliance this month."[292]

On September 29, 2003, at a hearing before the Select Committee on Homeland Security's Emergency Preparedness and Response Subcommittee, Democrat Bennie Thompson of Mississippi said, "I am concerned that DHS is not providing additional grant funds to achieve these goals and that they are unfunded mandates. For example, I am not aware of any additional funding for state and local governments to train personnel on the NIMS, nor am I aware of any funding to revise and publish new emergency operations plans that are consistent with NIMS. It appears," Thompson said, "that DHS expects the states to leverage their general ODP grant funds for this purpose and choose between implementing NIMS and other equally pressing needs like specialized equipment, training, terrorism exercises, and enhanced security at critical infrastructure sites."[293]

VII. NRP AND NIMS AS RULEMAKING

The Administrative Procedure Act (APA) 5 USC §§551–706 establishes standards and procedures for federal rulemaking. The APA defines a rule as "the whole or a part of an agency statement of general or particular applicability and future effect designed to implement, interpret, or prescribe law or policy" or establish rules of practice. (5 USC §551(4)).[294] 44 USC §3502(1) defines agency as "any executive department, military department, Government corporation, Government controlled corporation, or other establishment in the executive branch of the Government. . . ."

DHS is an executive department. While typically plans are not rules,[295] the comprehensive character[296] of the NRP and NIMS, their universal applicability to all emergency preparedness and response activities,[297] and their future effect[298] are aspects that resemble rules. Especially convincing is the truth that at the NRP's and NIMS's heart is the all-encompassing implementation and direction of all-hazards homeland security rules for all levels of government.[299] The NRP, through the adopted NIMS, its operational section, institutes in minute detail emergency preparedness and response rules of practice for all levels of government.

The argument that the NRP and NIMS have the effect of a rule or regulation, and should therefore be issued as such, is quite convincing. It would be additionally classified as a "significant regulatory action" if the NRP (which may be viewed as including NIMS, which is described as its "operational" aspect) would be likely to result in a yearly economic effect of $100 million or more or adversely affect public health or safety.[300] To make the financial impact determination would necessitate a cost analysis, but given that homeland security annual expenditures between 2001 and March 2004 were $30.5 billion, the NRP's economic effect will most likely be well in excess of $100 million.[301] As the previous discussion of potential deleterious effects of the two-tiered system of emergency responders illustrates, an adverse affect on some segments of public safety is also a likely outcome of issuing the NRP.

As a significant regulatory action, Executive Order 12866 would require centralized regulatory review[302] of the NRP to determine, among other things, quantified potential costs and benefits from the rule, and who is likely to reap the benefits or bear the costs and a discussion of less costly alternatives that might achieve the same goals.[303] Although the NRP might be classified as an "emergency rule" and exempted from the timing of performing regulatory analysis,[304] this task must still be performed.[305]

The APA contains different types of rulemaking methods. The most common procedure, usually referred to as "informal" or "notice and comment" rulemaking, appears at 5 USC §553. The law requires three things:

1. prior notice, normally achieved through publication in the *Federal Register*;[306]
2. an opportunity to participate by interested persons through submission of written comments containing data, views, or arguments;[307] and

3. issuance of a final rule along with "a concise and general statement of . . . [the rule's] basis and purpose."[308]

DHS has specifically been granted rulemaking authority.[309] FEMA, a constituent agency of DHS, has such authority independently.[310] An interested party might petition DHS to issue the NRP and NIMS a rules[311] under either grant of rulemaking authority. Even if the agency were to decide not to promulgate the documents as a rule, it would be required to issue a statement of the reasoning behind such a decision.[312] The agency's decision not to issue a rule might then be appealed in court.[313] Such public participation in agency decision making is looked upon favorably by the courts.[314] Other interested persons might intervene in an appeal as well.[315]

One must note that the agency reportedly consulted extensively with attorneys during the adoption process.[316] Unlike the rest of the documents, however, where DHS consulted rather extensively with nonfederal government stakeholders, there is no indication whatever that attorneys outside DHS and the White House were consulted at any stage during the process of drafting and revision.[317] Knowledgeable outside attorneys who could have provided valuable input on the adoption process include members of the National Emergency Management Association Legal Counsels Committee, state and local emergency management attorneys, as well as law school academics and lawyers in private practice whose areas of expertise include emergency response and emergency management.

Requesting that the rule be issued pursuant to DHS's or FEMA's authority appears to make sense, given the HS Act's requirement that the Undersecretary for Emergency Preparedness and Response put together the NRP.[318] FEMA is a part of the Emergency Preparedness and Response Directorate (EPRD),[319] while the Transportation Security Administration (TSA), which is responsible for the NRP and NIMS,[320] is part of the Border and Transportation Security Directorate (BTSD).[321] Whether issued as a rule or not, DHS has violated the clear mandate of the HS Act by using the BTSD rather than EPRD as the vehicle for consolidating existing federal government emergency response plans into a single, coordinated national response plan.[322]

If DHS were to issue this material as a rule using the notice and comment rulemaking structure, the current approach would be flawed for several reasons. First, the NRP and NIMS were not published in the customary way as a Notice of Proposed Rule in the *Federal Register*. Rather, they were sent directly to a select number of interested parties.[323] Second, the "public comment" period does not contemplate the involvement of the general public, as illustrated by the limited release of the material.[324] Third, DHS's intent is to establish a final version of the NRP, as they did the Adopted NIMS, after internal federal executive agency analysis and some input from selected stakeholders.[325] The EO 12866 §6 Regulatory Analysis does not appear to be part of DHS's adoption plan.

When asked what lessons the NRP/NIMS adoption process holds for federal agencies that are often assumed to be inflexible and unresponsive, Bob Stephan said the following:

The only lesson there is that you have to seek the comments and you have to understand that they are important. The lion's share of what we're responsible for and what we are concerned about resides on the state and local jurisdictions. They have to be part of the solution, and they have to be part of the acceptance of whatever you're coming up with. In this whole security world, that is the constituency that you're concerned about. You have to find out how to reach out and touch the right partners from the political, governmental, and [emergency response and emergency management] discipline sides of the house.[326]

Although DHS is to be commended for opening the process to the extent it has, more access could well benefit the end product. Scrutiny of the NRP and NIMS using the rulemaking process would cast refreshing illumination on what has otherwise been an internal matter between DHS, other federal agencies, and a limited group of stakeholders. The documents would surely gain from receiving supplementary contributions from all interested parties, including the general public.

VII. CONCLUSION

Many emergency managers and responders were extremely concerned that the NRP and NIMS adoption process began without their views being heard.[327] For a considerable time, it appeared that DHS was headed down the wrong track in creating and imposing standards for those who are the frontline troops in all-hazards preparedness.[328]

To the surprise of many observers, DHS has proven to be fairly flexible and open to suggestions by the communities that the agency regulates pursuant to federal law.[329] The contributions of state, local, and tribal governments as well as emergency response groups have helped the agency to understand that cooperation and buy-in are essential for success in its mission.[330] The adopted NIMS provides a formalized structure for their ongoing feedback on regulatory and other issues of interest in the form of the NIMS Integration Center.[331] Still, the process has been significantly less inclusive than it might have been, with no avenue for involvement of the general public. Incorporating the requirements of NFPA 1600 will be yet another challenge. Buy-in from the regulated community is still not complete. Perhaps the greatest difficulty will lie in finding the financial resources needed to ensure compliance with the unfounded–and likely very expensive–mandates embodied in the NRP and NIMS.

One must recall that the final word on federal regulation of state and local responders and emergency managers comes from the DHS Secretary.[332] Further, the administration apparently possesses contradictory views of preparedness, paying lip service to all-hazards readiness while diverting funding away from emergency responders and emergency managers. While Secretary Ridge has shown himself to be sensitive to the concerns of the regulated communities, there is no assurance that such respect for these stakeholders' views will emanate from future holders of his office.

The Homeland Security Act of 2002 could be amended to give the concerned communities a formalized portion of control over the regulatory scheme with which they must abide. Such a change in the law would ensure that DHS continues to consider their perspectives and modify its practices to take them into account. A simpler approach that would afford a voice for all concerned would have been utilization of notice and comment rulemaking to enact the NRP and NIMS.

Making laws is commonly compared with making sausage–a process that, once observed, decreases one's appetite for the end product. The creation of the NRP and NIMS illustrates that this comparison applies equally to establishment of "voluntary" standards. Appetite aside, however, the importance of this effort cannot be overstated. Creating a uniform national approach to incident response and management will surely result in significantly increased safety for emergency responders and greater efficiency in resource management. In an era when disasters and emergencies appear to constantly increase in size and complexity, and multiple agencies must work together ever more frequently, seeking and achieving common standards is a most worthy goal.

ENDNOTES

1. Incident command is a system that uses a command model, while incident management uses a management model. Paul M. Maniscalco & Hank T. Christen, *Understanding Terrorism and Managing the Consequences*, 24 (2001). Experienced responder leaders, however, do not see a difference other than in terminology between the two. Scott Baltic, "ICS For Everyone," 3 *Homeland Preparedness Professional*, (1)22, (January/February 2004).

2. National Fire Service Incident Management System, *Model Procedures for Structural Firefighting, Second Edition* 1 (2000). See generally Scott Baltic, "ICS For Everyone," 3 *Homeland Preparedness Professional*, (1)20, (January/February 2004).

3. Pat West, Senior Editor, "NIMS: The Last Word on Incident Command?" *Fire Chief on Line* (March 5, 2004) Found at: http://firechief.com/ar/firefighting_nics_last_word/index.htm (Last consulted March 9, 2004). "What we've said now with the NIMS document is that it's not just a fire service issue. We're expanding (incident management) to include all the agencies involved in response to emergencies–beyond police, EMS, and fire–to include all the government agencies that will respond to a disaster as well as some private organizations."

4. "[T]he National Emergency Management Association adopted a position in September 1996 adopting the National Interagency Incident Management System and its Incident Command System (ICS) as the model for all risk/hazard response activities by state and local governments . . ." National Emergency Management Association Terrorism Committee, A Resolution Advocating the Incident Command/Management System for all WMD Operations by All Levels of Government, February 25–March 1, 2000.

5. *Id.*

6. William C. Nicholson, "Legal Issues in Emergency Response to Terrorism Incidents Involving Hazardous Materials: The Hazardous Waste Operations and Emergency Response ("HAZWOPER") Standard, Standard Operating Procedures, Mutual Aid and the Incident Command System," *Widener Symposium Law Journal*, (9)2, 295, note 116 at 309 (2003).

7. "Clearly, ICS is gaining momentum, though there's still a long road before it's a truly universal structure and language for managing incidents." Scott Baltic, "ICS For Everyone," 3 *Homeland Preparedness Professional*, (1)26, (January/February 2004).

8. Homeland Security Act of 2002, H.R. 5005, 107th Cong. (2002) (enacted) [hereinafter HS Act].

9. *Id.* at §501 (5) The HS Act requires "[b]uilding a comprehensive incident management system with Federal, state, and local government personnel, agencies, and authorities, to respond to . . . [terrorist] attacks and disasters."

10. Note on numbering: NRP 1 and NIMS 1 were actually not the first version of these texts, both of which underwent numerous internal revisions at DHS. They were, however, the first versions released outside the agency, hence the "1" reference.

11. William C. Nicholson, "The New (?) Federal Approach to Emergencies," 2 *Homeland Preparedness Professional*, (8)8, (August 2003).

12. See generally William C. Nicholson, "Integrating Local, State and Federal Responders and Emergency Management: New Packaging and New Controls," 1 *Journal of Emergency Management*, 15 (Fall 2003).

13. Martin Edwin Andersen, "Local Responders Howl at DHS Emergency Management Plan" *Congressional Quarterly Homeland Security–Local Response* (August 8, 2003).

14. "Comments on the National Incident Management System–July 1, 2003" submitted to DHS by Timothy L. Dunkle, Pennsylvania State Fire Training Administrator and Vice President–North American Fire Training Directors.

15. William C. Nicholson, *Emergency Response and Emergency Management Law*, 236–238 (2003).

16. William L. Waugh, Jr., "The 'All-Hazards' Approach Must Be Continued," 2 *Journal of Emergency Management*, (1)11, (Fall 2003).

17. "Comments on the National Incident Management System–July 1, 2003" submitted to DHS by Timothy L. Dunkle, Pennsylvania State Fire Training Administrator and Vice President–North American Fire Training Directors.

18. William C. Nicholson, "Integrating Local, State and Federal Responders and Emergency Management: New Packaging and New Controls," 1 *Journal of Emergency Management*, 15, 16–17 (Fall 2003).

19. *Id.* at 20.

20. *Id.*

21. *Id.* at 19.

22. *Id.* at 20.

23. *Id.* at 21.

24. *Id.* at 20.

25. Telephone interview with DHS employee requesting anonymity, August 2003.

26. Telephone interview with Albert Ashwood, Director, Oklahoma Department of Emergency Management. August 22, 2003.

27. Id.

28. National Incident Management System–Coordination Draft (NIMS 2), Department of Homeland Security (December 3, 2003).

29. *President Marks Homeland Security's Accomplishments at Year One*, White House Press Release (March 2, 2004) found on the Web at http://www.whitehouse.gov/news/releases/2004/03/20040302-2.html (last consulted March 4, 2004.)

30. *Department of Homeland Security Secretary Tom Ridge Approves National Incident Management System (NIMS)*, "NIMS gives all of our Nation's responders the same framework for incident management and fully puts into practice the concept of, 'One mission, one team, one fight,'" DHS Press Release (March 1, 2004) found on the Web at http://www.dhs.gov/dhspublic/display? content=3259 (last consulted March 4, 2004.)

31. NRP Base Plan DRAFT #1, *All Hands Community Newsletter*, No. 23, for Thursday, March 11, 2004.

32. Transmittal Letter, National Response Plan Draft 1 (February 25, 2004) "The NRP supercedes the Federal Response Plan (FRP), United States Government Interagency Domestic Terrorism Concept of Operations Plan (CONPLAN), and the Initial National Response Plan (INRP)." As this document was neither signed nor generally released, it too was not a final document.

33. NRP Draft #2 did not include a transmittal letter, instead stating that it is "To be developed."

34. NRP1 was 50 pages long. Draft #1 has 82 pages, while Draft #2 is 107 pages. The NRP "Final Draft" issued on June 30, 2004, is 121 pages long. The adopted NRP issued November 16, 2004, is 430 pages long, including all appendices and annexes.

35. EIIP Virtual Forum Presentation–September 15, 2004. "The National Response Plan: An Update." Statement by Associate Director Barbara Yagerman, Operations and Response Operations Integration Staff, Department of Homeland Security: "When the NRP is approved it will be posted on the DHS Website. There are differences in the final approved NRP and the draft that you may have seen."

36. NRP at x. "Within 1 year of its effective date, the Secretary of Homeland Secretary will conduct an interagency review to assess the effectiveness of the NRP, identify improvements, and provide recommendations regarding plan modifications and reissuance, if required."

37. NRP at 59. "Working toward continuous improvement, DHS is responsible for coordinating full reviews and updates of the NRP every 4 years, or more frequently if the Secretary deems necessary. The review and update will consider lessons learned and best practices identified during exercises and responses to actual events, and incorporate new information technologies. DHS will distribute revised NRP documents to the HSC for the purpose of interagency review and concurrence."

38. William C. Nicholson, "Integrating Local, State and Federal Responders and Emergency Management: New Packaging and New Controls," 1 *Journal of Emergency Management*, 15, 15 (Fall 2003).

39. *President Marks Homeland Security's Accomplishments at Year One*, "On March 1, 2003, approximately 180,000 personnel from 22 different organizations around the government became part of the Department of Homeland Security–completing the largest government reorganization since the beginning of the Cold War." White House Press Release (March 2, 2004) found on the Web at http://www.whitehouse.gov/news/releases/2004/03/20040302-2.html (last consulted March 4, 2004.)

40. HS Act §101.

    SEC. 101. EXECUTIVE DEPARTMENT; MISSION.

    (a) Establishment. There is established a Department of Homeland Security, as an executive department of the United States within the meaning of title 5, United States Code.

    (b) Mission. (1) The primary mission of the Department is to–

    (A) prevent terrorist attacks within the United States;

    (B) reduce the vulnerability of the United States to terrorism; and

    (C) minimize the damage, and assist in the recovery, from terrorist attacks that do occur within the United States.

41. *Id.* HSPD 5 mandates addressing all hazards. HSPD 5 at paragraph 16: "[The NRP] shall integrate Federal Government domestic prevention, preparedness, response, and recovery plans into one all-discipline, all-hazards plan." HSPD 5 at paragraph 6: "The Secretary will also provide assistance to State and local governments to develop all-hazards plans and capabilities, including those of greatest importance to the security of the United States, and will ensure that State, local, and Federal plans are compatible."

42. Jeffrey Manns, "LEGISLATION COMMENT: Reorganization as a Substitute for Reform: The Abolition of the INS," 112 *Yale Law Journal*, (145)151 (October 2002). "The creation of this superagency may result in little more, however, than forcing a host of agencies to order new letterhead and change their seals. Worse still, the Department of Homeland Security may become a bureaucratic juggernaut, whose unmanageability may magnify the shortcomings of each component agency."

43. Elishia L. Krauss, "Building a Bigger Bureaucracy: What the Department of Homeland Security Won't Do; Views You Can Use," *The Public Manager*, (1)32, 57 (March 22, 2003). "Unfortunately, with bureaucracy we only create more layers of inefficiency and bureaucratic red tape, instead of streamlining the processes and focusing resources directly on the mission. Specifically, homeland security requires an organization that is collaborative, quick acting, and efficient. These are not qualities inherent in federal bureaucracies."

44. "This [DHS, the NRP and NIMS] will be run by cops. It's a mechanism to get cops additional funding." Telephone interview with Adam Piskura, Director of Training, Connecticut Fire Academy,

President, North American Fire Training Directors, August 21, 2003.

45. Terrorism is a federal crime. *See generally* Note, "Responding To Terrorism: Crime, Punishment, and War," 115 *Harvard Law Review*, 1217, 1224 (2002). "[T]he United States has traditionally treated terrorism as a crime. The U.S. Code contains criminal statutes that define and establish punishments for terrorism."

46. William C. Nicholson, "Legal Issues in Emergency Response to Terrorism Incidents Involving Hazardous Materials: The Hazardous Waste Operations and Emergency Response ("HAZWOPER") Standard, Standard Operating Procedures, Mutual Aid and the Incident Command System," *Widener Symposium Law Journal*, (9)2, pp. 295, 305–306 (2003).

47. William C. Nicholson, "Integrating Local, State and Federal Responders and Emergency Management: New Packaging and New Controls," 1 *Journal of Emergency Management*, 15, 18–21 (Fall 2003).

48. Homeland Security Presidential Directive 5, Subject: Management of Domestic Incidents, The White House, February 28, 2003. http://www.whitehouse.gov/news/releases/2003/02/20030228-9.html

49. HSPD 5 Paragraph 3.

50. HSPD 5 Paragraph 17 b.

51. HSPD 5 Paragraph 3.

52. *Id.*

53. Presidential Decision Directive 39, U.S. Policy on Counterterrorism (June 21, 1995).

54. HSPD 5 Paragraph 21–23.

55. HS Act of 2002, SEC. 501. UNDERSECRETARY FOR EMERGENCY PREPAREDNESS AND RESPONSE.

    In assisting the Secretary with the responsibilities specified in section 101(b)(2)(D), the primary responsibilities of the Undersecretary for Emergency Preparedness and Response shall include–

    . . . (A) establishing standards and certifying when those standards have been met[.]

56. HSPD 5 Paragraph 20.

57. HSPD 5 Paragraph 19.

58. HSPD 5 Paragraph 17–20.

59. HSPD 5 Paragraph 16.

60. William C. Nicholson, "Integrating Local, State and Federal Responders and Emergency Management: New Packaging and New Controls," 1 *Journal of Emergency Management*, 15, 15 (Fall 2003).

61. HSPD 5 Paragraph 16.

62. *Id.*

63. HSPD 5 Paragraph 18.

64. 40 CFR §300 (2003).

65. 50 *Federal Register* 46542 (1985).
66. HSPD 5 Paragraph 16 a–d.
67. HSPD 5 Paragraph 17 a.
68. HSPD 5 Paragraph 17 b.
69. HSPD 5 Paragraph 17 c.
70. William C. Nicholson, "Integrating Local, State and Federal Responders and Emergency Management: New Packaging and New Controls," 1 *Journal of Emergency Management*, 3(15), 17 (Fall 2003).
71. Admiral Loy has since been promoted to be Deputy Secretary of DHS. He was sworn in for this position on December 4, 2003. http://www.dhs.gov/dhspublic/display?theme=11&content=2996
72. Martin Edwin Andersen, "Local Responders Howl at DHS Emergency Management Plan" *Congressional Quarterly Homeland Security–Local Response* (August 8, 2003). "According to sources familiar with the emergency planning process, the draft plan was prepared for the DHS by the RAND Corporation . . ."
73. Telephone interview with Bob Stephan, Assistant to Secretary Ridge, January 14, 2004.
74. *Id.*
75. William C. Nicholson, "Integrating Local, State and Federal Responders and Emergency Management: New Packaging and New Controls," 1 *Journal of Emergency Management*, 15, 21 (Fall 2003).
76. Martin Edwin Andersen, "Local Responders Howl at DHS Emergency Management Plan" *Congressional Quarterly Homeland Security–Local Response* (August 8, 2003). The NRP and NIMS create ". . . a welter of entities, terms, and acronyms and that existing, commonly accepted terminology is buried under a confusing layer of bureaucratese."
77. NIMS 1 at 4.
78. Telephone interview with FEMA employee wishing anonymity August 14, 2003.
79. *Principles of Emergency Management*, FEMA online course Number IS 230 Chapter 3: The Emergency Management Cycle at 3.1–3.2, found on the Web at http://training.fema.gov/EMIWeb/IS/is230lst.asp (last consulted March 4, 2004).
80. William L. Waugh, Jr., Ph.D. "The 'All-Hazards' Approach Must be Continued," 2 *Journal of Emergency Management*, (1)11, (Fall 2003). "The model of mitigation, preparedness, response and recovery has its problems, but it provides both a unifying approach to dealing with hazards and disasters and a common terminology for emergency managers and public officials."
81. NRP 1 at 6.
82. William C. Nicholson, "Legal Issues in Emergency Response to Terrorism Incidents Involving Hazardous Materials: The Hazardous Waste Operations and Emergency Response ("HAZWOPER") Standard, Standard Operating Procedures, Mutual Aid and the Incident Command System," *Widener Symposium Law Journal*, (9)2, pp. 295, 309 (2003).
83. NIMS 1 at 5.
84. NIMS 1 at 4, 8–12, 14–15.
85. NIMS 1 at 7. *Principles of Emergency Management*, FEMA online course Number IS 230 Chapter 3: The Emergency Management Cycle at 3.13., found on the Web at http://training.fema.gov/EMIWeb/IS/is230lst.asp (last consulted March 4, 2004). "The Emergency Operations Center (EOC) . . . is the central location from which all off-scene activities are coordinated. Senior elected and appointed officials are located at the EOC, as well as personnel supporting critical functions, such as operations, planning, logistics, and finance and administration. The key function of EOC personnel is to ensure that those who are located at the scene have the resources (i.e., personnel, tools, and equipment) they need for the response."
86. NIMS 1 at 30.
87. NIMS 1 at 6.
88. *Basic Incident Command System (ICS) Independent Study*, FEMA online course Number IS 195 Chapter 4: Incident Resource Management at 4.2, found on the Web at http://training.fema.gov/EMIWeb/IS/is195lst.asp (last consulted March 4, 2004). "The effective management of operational resources is a vital consideration in any incident."
89. NIMS 1 at 22.
90. NIMS 1 at 7.
91. "Comments on the National Incident Management System–July 1, 2003" submitted to DHS by Timothy L. Dunkle, Pennsylvania State Fire Training Administrator and Vice President–North American Fire Training Directors.
92. William C. Nicholson, "Integrating Local, State and Federal Responders and Emergency Management: New Packaging and New Controls," 1 *Journal of Emergency Management*, 15, 20 (Fall 2003).
93. "We've been able to channel our feedback through the state homeland security advisors to get the formal governmental piece, and they help us reach out further. We're also using the professional associations in the disciplines and the Homeland Security Advisory Council organization to help extend that outreach for us." Telephone interview with Bob Stephan, Assistant to Secretary Ridge, January 14, 2004.

94. William C. Nicholson, "Integrating Local, State and Federal Responders and Emergency Management: New Packaging and New Controls," 1 *Journal of Emergency Management*, 15, 20 (Fall 2003).

95. Telephone interview with Bob Stephan, Assistant to Secretary Ridge, January 14, 2004.

96. Keith Bea, "Overview of Components of the National Response Plan and Selected Issues," *CRS Report for Congress*, page 4, Dec. 24, 2003.

97. The National Response Plan, Initial Plan issued on May 14, 2003, was referenced in its file title as Version 10. Similarly, NIMS 2 is subtitled "Working Draft Version 7.1, December 3, 2003." Curiously, the NRP Draft #1 is referred to on its cover as "Draft # 1," although it is clearly the latest of numerous drafts.

98. "[T]he INRP represents a significant first step towards an overall goal of integrating the current family of Federal domestic prevention, preparedness, response, and recovery plans into a single all-discipline, all-hazards plan." Statement of Dr. Charles E. McQueary, Undersecretary for Science and Technology, Department of Homeland Security, before the Committee on House Science February 11, 2004.

99. Telephone interview with Bob Stephan, Assistant to Secretary Ridge, January 14, 2004.

100. *Id.*

101. NRP 1 uses the term partner or partnership five times. INRP discusses collaboration with state and local governments and anticipates working out procedures together with them.

102. INRP at 4.

103. INRP at 4.

104. INRP at 1.

105. "The NRP will replace the Federal Response Plan, U.S. Counterterrorism Concept of Operations Plan, and the National Contingency Plan. Other plans will be developed within the NRP as annexes to the NRP or we will change them to be consistent as appendices to the NRP." Telephone interview with Bob Stephan, Assistant to Secretary Ridge, January 14, 2004.

106. INRP at 1. "The current family of Federal incident management and emergency response plans remains in effect during this interim period, except as specifically modified by this document."

107. "What we're going to do is a comprehensive look . . . This will be the cornerstone for incident management and response." Telephone interview with Bob Stephan, Assistant to Secretary Ridge, January 14, 2004.

108. NRP 1 at 37–40.

109. "The NRP sets forth a new concept of a "response" plan by covering five domains: awareness, prevention, preparedness, response, and recovery." NRP 1 at 6.

110. NRP 1 at 21.

111. "Under the NIMS, preparedness is based on national standards for the qualification and certification of emergency response personnel. . . . Personnel that are certified for employment in support of an incident that transcends interstate jurisdictions through the Emergency Management Assistance Compacts System will be required to meet national qualification and certification standards." Adopted NIMS at 38.

112. INRP at 6–7.

113. INRP at 6.

114. INRP at 6–7.

115. INRP at 8.

116. Telephone interview with Albert Ashwood, Director, Oklahoma Department of Emergency Management, NEMA Representative at the Forum meeting. August 22, 2003.

117. The National Response Plan, Initial Plan issued on May 14, 2003, was referenced in its file title as Version 10. Curiously, the NRP Draft #1 is referred to on its cover as "Draft # 1," although it is clearly the latest of numerous drafts.

118. Comparison of the tables of contents reveals coverage of the same topics. NRP 1 at v-vi. NRP Draft #1 at i-iii.

119. NRP1 was 50 pages long. Draft #1 has 82 pages, while Draft #2 is 107 pages. The NRP "Final Draft" issued on June 30, 2004, is 121 pages long.

120. HSPD 5 paragraph 16.

121. NRP Draft #1 Transmittal Letter (found at beginning of NRP Draft #1, unnumbered). "This plan was developed through an inclusive interagency, interjurisdictional process incorporating the expertise and recommendations of Federal, State, local, tribal, and private sector stakeholders. . . . The successful implementation of this national plan will take the concerted efforts of all stakeholders."

122. The term is found five times in the NRP Draft #1. NRP Draft #1 at 37–39, 69.

123. NRP Draft #1 at 38.

124. NRP Draft #1 at 39.

125. *Id.*

126. 18 U.S.C. §1385 (2003).

127. NRP Draft #1 at 69. "The primary prohibition of the *Posse Comitatus* Act is against direct involvement by active duty military personnel (to include reservists on active duty and *National Guard personnel in federal service*) in traditional law enforcement

activities (to include interdiction of vehicle, vessel, aircraft, or other similar activity; a search or seizure; an arrest, apprehension, stop and frisk, or similar activity)." (Emphasis added.)

128. See, e.g. "The *Posse Comitatus* Act: A Principle in Need of Renewal," 75 *Washington University Law Quarterly*, 953, 964 (Summer, 1997). "Additionally, the PCA only applies to forces in federal service, and therefore, the National Guard is not limited by the PCA in its normal status of state service."

129. *Id.* at note 70.

130. NRP Draft #1 at 1–2. "The NRP incorporates the best practices and procedures from various incident management components–homeland security, emergency management, law enforcement, fire-fighting, public works, public health, and emergency medical services–and integrates them into a unified structure."

131. NRP Final Draft at 2.

132. Emergency Support Function #8, Public Health and Medical Services Annex, Draft: July 6, 2004.

133. NRP 1 at 12. As a state's chief executive, the governor is responsible for the public safety and welfare of the people of that state or territory. The governor:
   1. Is responsible for coordinating state and local resources to address effectively the full spectrum of actions to prepare for and to respond to man-made incidents, including terrorism, natural disasters, and other contingencies;
   2. Has extraordinary powers during a contingency to suspend authority, to seize property, to direct evacuations, and to authorize emergency funds;
   3. Plays a key role in communicating to the public, in requesting federal assistance, when state capabilities have been exceeded or exhausted, and in helping people, businesses, and organizations to cope with disasters; and
   4. May also encourage local mutual aid and implement authorities for the state to enter into mutual aid agreements with other states and territories to facilitate resource sharing.

134. NRP Draft #1 at 53. As a state's chief executive, the governor is responsible for the public safety and welfare of the people of that state or territory. The governor:
   1. Is responsible for coordinating state and local resources to address the full spectrum of actions to prevent, prepare for, to respond and recovery from incidents involving all hazards including terrorism, natural disasters, accidents, and other contingencies;
   2. Has extraordinary powers to suspend authority, to seize property, to direct evacuations, and to authorize emergency funds;
   3. Provides leadership and plays a key role in communicating to the public, and in helping people, businesses, and organizations to cope with the consequences of any type of domestic incident within the state;
   4. Encourages participation in local mutual aid and implements authorities for the state to enter into mutual aid agreements with other states and territories to facilitate resource sharing; and
   5. Requests federal assistance when state capabilities have been exceeded or exhausted.

135. See, e.g., Indiana Code IC 10-14-3-7
Declaration of purposes
Sec. 7.

   (b) It is also the purpose of this chapter and the policy of the state to:
   (4) clarify and strengthen the roles of the:
      (A) governor;
      (B) state agencies; and
      (C) local governments;
         in the prevention of, preparation for, response to, and recovery from disasters;

136. NRP 1 at 12.

137. *Id.*

138. NRP Draft #1 at 48, 67–68.

139. Robert T. Stafford Disaster Relief and Emergency Assistance Act, as amended (42 USC 5121, *et seq.* (2003)).

140. NRP 1 at 6.

141. NRP Draft #1 at 14. "IV. Phases of Incident Management Activities."

142. NRP Draft #1 at 14. "Domestic incident management activities addressed in the NRP span the event including prevention, preparedness, response, recovery, and mitigation."

143. NRP Draft #1 at 14. "Prevention involves actions to interdict, disrupt, preempt or avert a potential incident. This includes homeland security and law enforcement efforts to prevent terrorist attacks."

144. "The local Emergency Program Manager has the day-to-day responsibility of overseeing emergency management programs and activities. And most emergencies are handled at the local level without state or federal assistance. This role entails coordinating all aspects of a jurisdiction's mitigation, preparedness, response, and recovery capabilities." FEMA Independent Study Course IS 230–*Principles of Emergency Management* at 4.1. Found on

the Web at: http://training.fema.gov/EMIWeb/ IS/is230lst.asp (Last consulted March 10, 2004).

145. NRP 1 at 38–39.

146. NRP 1 at 38: "MACS is a combination of committees, facilities, equipment, personnel, procedures, and communications protocols integrated into a common interagency system with responsibility for coordinating and supporting incident operations. MACS establishes policies and priorities; allocates and tracks resources; and coordinates interagency and intergovernmental decisions. The MACS functions principally through Emergency Operations Centers and Emergency Prevention and Preparedness Councils."

147. It does, however, resurface in adopted NIMS at 26: "A multiagency coordination system is a combination of facilities, equipment, personnel, procedures, and communications integrated into a common system with responsibility for coordinating and supporting domestic incident management activities. The primary functions of multiagency coordination systems are to support incident management policies and priorities, facilitate logistics support and resource tracking, inform resource allocation decisions using incident management priorities, coordinate incident-related information, and coordinate interagency and intergovernmental issues regarding incident management policies, priorities, and strategies. Direct tactical and operational responsibility for conducting incident management activities rests with the Incident Command."

148. NIMS 1 at 5.

149. NRP 1 at 39. "Emergency Prevention and Preparedness Councils (EPPC) EPPCs are multiagency, multijurisdictional bodies established for preevent coordination. EPPCs are the principal mechanism through which to maintain and improve the NIMS."

150. NRP 1 at 38.

151. NRP at 14. "Under NIMS, Preparedness encompasses the full range of deliberate, critical tasks and activities necessary to build, sustain, and improve the operational capability to prevent, protect against, respond to, and recover from domestic incidents. Preparedness, in the context of an actual or potential incident, involves actions to enhance readiness and minimize impacts. This includes hazard mitigation measures to save lives and protect property from the impacts of terrorism, natural disasters, and other events." Adopted NIMS takes the same approach. Adopted NIMS at 26.

152. *Id.*

153. Preparedness includes three elements: planning, training, and exercising. George D. Haddow and

Jane A. Bullock, *Introduction to Emergency Management*, 115 (2003).

154. Arguably, training and exercising may be inferred from the preparedness definition's use of the language ". . . the full range of deliberate, critical tasks and activities necessary to build, sustain, and improve the operational capability to prevent, protect against, respond to, and recover from domestic incidents." NRP Draft #1 at 14. Omitting the terms, however, may indicate a failure to embrace the basics of emergency management. Clearly, training and exercising remain high on the DHS's list of priorities, as demonstrated by its citation (NRP Draft #1 at 53) to HSPD 5's requirement that the Secretary of DHS ". . . coordinate with State and local governments to ensure adequate planning, equipment, training, and exercise activities." HSPD 5 at paragraph 6.

155. NRP Draft #1 at 14–16. They do, however, constitute an important aspect of the adopted NIMS. Adopted NIMS at 37–38.

156. NRP Draft #1 at ii-iii.

157. Emergency Support Functions Draft. This document will be revised, as noted at its beginning: "Note: These are unedited outlines of the ESF Annexes. The agencies preparing these outlines did not have the draft Basic Plan to use as a reference. It is the intention of the Writing Team that any inconsistencies, gaps and other discrepancies will be corrected between this DRAFT and DRAFT #2 where the outlines will be expanded to full drafts."

158. NRP Draft #1 at ii-iii.

159. *Id.* The adopted NRP does not contain a legal annex.

160. *Id.*

161. Federal Response Plan (Interim) 1 (January 2003). "The Federal Response Plan . . . organizes the types of Federal assistance that a State is most likely to need under 12 Emergency Support Functions (ESFs), each of which has a designated primary agency . . ." Found on the Web at: http://www.fema.gov/ pdf/rrr/frp/frp2003.pdf Last consulted March 8, 2004).

162. NRP Draft #1 at 65–72.

163. The adopted NRP may be found on line at: http://www.rmfd.org/National%20Response%20 Plan%20-%20Approved-Unsigned%20 (16%20Nov%202004).pdf

164. National Response Plan at ix.

165. NRP at x.

166. FEDERAL EMERGENCY MANAGEMENT AGENCY, THE FEDERAL RESPONSE PLAN (1999).The FRP establishes a process and structure

for the systematic, coordinated, and effective delivery of federal assistance to address the consequences of any major disaster or emergency declared under the Robert T. Stafford Disaster Relief and Emergency Assistance Act, as amended (42 USC 5121, *et seq.* (2002)).

167. EIIP Virtual Forum Presentation–September 15, 2004. "The National Response Plan: An Update." Statement by Associate Director Barbara Yagerman, Operations and Response Operations Integration Staff, Department of Homeland Security: "Our goal was to preserve and mirror the existing structure of state emergency operations plans to the degree that we could. There are only three new ESFs, some modifications to a few of the ESFs. The new structures in the plan–the HSOC, the Joint Field Office, the Interagency Incident Management Group, primarily impact the federal partners."

168. NRP at xi.

169. NRP at xiii.

170. NRP at 60.

171. NRP Draft #1 at ii–iii.

172. See generally, Howard D. Swanson, "The Delicate Art of Practicing Municipal Law Under Conditions of Hell and High Water," 76 *North Dakota Law Review* 487 (2000) and Roger A. Nowadsky, "Lawyering Your Municipality Through a Natural Disaster or Emergency," 27 *Urban Law.* 9 (Winter, 1995).

173. Michael D. Brown, Acting Deputy Director, Chief Operating Officer and General Counsel, FEMA, Address "FEMA's Role in the Aftermath of 9-11 and Homeland Security" at Widener University School of Law (March 14, 2002) "This subject is not going away. The events of 9-11 are, unfortunately, likely to be the shape of things to come. All attorneys advising businesses [as well as emergency management government attorneys] are going to have to know how terrorism and emergency law works." Brown was nominated in January 2003 by President Bush to be Undersecretary for Emergency Preparedness and Response at DHS. http://www.fema.gov/about/bios/brown.shtm (Last consulted March 6, 2004).

174. Telephone interview with Albert Ashwood, Director, Oklahoma Department of Emergency Management, NEMA Representative at the Forum meeting. August 22, 2003.

175. Telephone interview with Bob Stephan, Assistant to Secretary Ridge, January 14, 2004.

176. NIMS 2 is 92 pages long, while the INRP is 11 pages long.

177. NIMS 2 is 92 pages long, while adopted NIMS is 139 pages long. Their contents have the same labels. The difference in overall length is due to the adopted NIMS containing three additional tabs in Appendix A: The Incident Command System. Those tabs are:

Tab 7–Predesignated Facilities and Areas
Tab 8–The Planning Process
Tab 9–Examples of ICS Forms.

Together, these tabs account for 26 of the additional 47 pages. The remaining 21 pages are spread through the document.

178. Adopted NIMS at 33–43.

179. Adopted NIMS at 35. "Individual jurisdictions establish programs that address the requirements for each step of the preparedness cycle (planning, training, equipping, exercising, evaluating, and taking action to correct and mitigate). These programs should adopt relevant NIMS standards, guidelines, processes, and protocols."

180. "Deep-sixing the current system [as done by NRP 1 and NIMS 1], the critics charge, amounts to 'reinventing the wheel,' in the words of one specialist." Martin Edwin Andersen, "Local Responders Howl at DHS Emergency Management Plan," *Congressional Quarterly Homeland Security–Local Response* (August 8, 2003).

181. Adopted NIMS at 3. "The NIMS integrates existing best practices into a consistent, nationwide approach to domestic incident management that is applicable at all jurisdictional levels and across functional disciplines in an all-hazards context."

182. Adopted NIMS at 1. "For purposes of this document, incidents can include acts of terrorism, wildland and urban fires, floods, hazardous materials spills, nuclear accidents, aircraft accidents, earthquakes, hurricanes, tornadoes, typhoons, war-related disasters, etc."

183. "The needs of the jurisdictions involved will dictate how frequently such [preparedness] organizations must conduct their business, as well as how they are structured." Adopted NIMS at 35.

184. "In those instances where preparedness activities need to be accomplished across jurisdictions, preparedness organizations should be multijurisdictional." Adopted NIMS at 35–36.

185. Adopted NIMS at 39.

186. Adopted NIMS at 33–42.

187. Adopted NIMS at 35–36.

188. *Id.*

189. "Incident management organizations and personnel at all levels of government, and within the private-sector and nongovernmental organizations, must be

appropriately trained to improve all-hazards incident management capability nationwide. Incident management organizations and personnel must also participate in realistic exercises–including multidisciplinary and multijurisdictional events and private-sector and nongovernmental organization interaction–to improve integration and interoperability." Adopted NIMS at 37.

190. "Under the NIMS, preparedness is based on national standards for the qualification and certification of emergency response personnel." Adopted NIMS at 38.

191. "A critical component of preparedness is the acquisition of equipment that will perform to certain standards, including the capability to be interoperable with similar equipment in other jurisdictions." Adopted NIMS at 39.

192. "Publication management for the NIMS includes development of naming and numbering conventions; review and certification of publications; methods for publications control; identification of sources and suppliers for publications and related services; and management of publication distribution." Adopted NIMS at 40.

193. HSPD 5 at paragraph 16.

194. HSPD 5 at paragraph 20.

195. See Appendix 1 to this chapter.

196. Adopted NIMS 2 at 33.

197. "The process for managing and maintaining the NIMS ensures that all users and stakeholders–including various levels of government, functional disciplines, and private entities–are given the opportunity to participate in NIMS Integration Center activities. To accomplish this goal, the NIMS Integration Center will be multijurisdictional and multidisciplinary and will maintain appropriate liaison with private organizations." Adopted NIMS at 59.

198. Adopted NIMS at 59–64.

199. NIMS 2 at 21.

200. Adopted NIMS at 59–64.

201. Telephone interview with Bob Stephan, Assistant to Secretary Ridge, January 14, 2004.

202. *Id.*

203. *Id.*

204. *Id.*

205. *Id.*

206. Telephone interview with Bob Stephan, Assistant to Secretary Ridge, January 14, 2004.

207. Memorandum for Secretary Tom Ridge from Bob Stephan (endorsed by Secretary Ridge), *NIMS Integration Center (NIC)*, Department of Homeland Security (April 7, 2004).

208. Id.

209. HS Act §501(6).

210. Telephone interview with Bob Stephan, Assistant to Secretary Ridge, January 14, 2004.

211. Adopted NIMS at 59:
Revisions to the NIMS and other corrective actions can be proposed by

- local entities (including their preparedness organizations; see Chapter III);
- State entities (including their preparedness organizations; see Chapter III);
- regional entities (including their preparedness organizations; see Chapter III);
- tribal entities (including their preparedness organization; see Chapter III);
- Federal departments and agencies;
- private entities (including business and industry, volunteer organizations, academia, and other nonprofit and nongovernmental organizations); and
- NIMS-related professional associations.

212. HSPD 5 at paragraph 15.

213. "National Fire Service Credentialing System" *U.S. Fire Administration Newsletter*, December 2003, Issue 3 (found on the Web at http://www.usfa.fema.gov/downloads/txt/newsletter12-03.txt) (Last consulted February 26, 2004).

214. *Id.* The process of credentialing involves the following elements:

- Identifying the standards that would be used as the basis for the credentials issued
- Certifying the individuals against these standards
- Reviewing the certifying bodies to ensure that their processes are valid
- Maintaining a record system that allows for identification of the individual and verification of the information contained on that identification.

215. *Id.* "The final credentialing meeting was held on Dec. 11, 2003."

216. "The NIMS Integration Center will be further responsible for . . . facilitating the development and publication of national standards, guidelines, and protocols for the qualification and certification of emergency responder and incident management personnel, as appropriate . . ." Adopted NIMS at 60.

217. Adopted NIMS 2 at 38.

218. Telephone interview with Bob Stephan, Assistant to Secretary Ridge, January 14, 2004.

219. NIMS 2 at 38. "Federal, State, local, and tribal certifying agencies; professional organizations; and

private organizations should credential personnel for their respective jurisdictions." Federalism considerations would seem to mandate such an approach.

220. HSPD 5 at paragraph 20.

221. Ted Leventhal, "Lawmakers Voice Concerns About Emergency Preparations," *National Journal's Technology Daily* (March 3, 2004). Found on the Web at: http://www.govexec.com/dailyfed/0304/030304tdpm2.htm (Last consulted March 10, 2004). "[Brown] said Homeland Security will contribute to first-responder salaries in partnership with state and local governments." Given the requirement for federal certification for federal funds as of FFY 2005, this promise clearly will apply to only federally certified first responders.

222. HSPD 5 at paragraph 20.

223. *Fire Fighters Give Bush Failing Grade on Anniversary of Creation of Dept. of Homeland Security,* International Association of Fire Fighters: News from Fire Fighters "The creation of the Department of Homeland Security was a step in the right direction. But one year after its creation, our nation's firefighters and emergency medical personnel are still operating with too few staff, outdated equipment and the need for training to appropriately and safely respond to all of the emergencies, disasters and possible acts of terrorism we need to be prepared for today. The result is that our communities are more vulnerable because of Bush's failure in Homeland Security." (February 27, 2004).

224. Council on Foreign Relations, "Emergency Responders: Drastically Underfunded, Dangerously Unprepared," http://www.cfr.org/pdf/Responders_TF.pdf, page 2, July 29, 2003.

225. Adopted NIMS at 38.

226. See notes 133–134 and accompanying text.

227. See generally Franklin Woodrow Wilson II, *Recruitment and Retention of the Volunteer: The Missing Piece of the Fire Service* (August 15, 2002). "The fire service recognizes the pressures placed on volunteers, but must find ways to make volunteer opportunities more doable. A fundamental change in the nature of some of its volunteer jobs is likely necessary in order to attract new, energetic professionals to volunteer in the fire service."

228. Reade Bush, TriData Corporation, *Special Presentation: Recruitment and Retention in the Volunteer Fire Service,* Report on The National Volunteer Fire Summit, National Fire Academy, Emmitsburg, Maryland (June 6, 1998). "Several factors underlie today's retention and recruitment problem in the volunteer fire service. It is a complex and multi-faceted problem. . . . [S]tringent training standards, leadership problems, and time constraints caused by increased family responsibilities–particularly in two-career families and single parent households–seem to be the most common roots . . ."

229. *Id.* "Many fire departments across the nation today are experiencing more difficulty with recruiting and retaining members than ever before. This is demonstrated by the decline in the number of active volunteer firefighters nationally, which is estimated to have dropped from 884,600 in 1983 to 815,500 in 1996, and by reports from fire departments in every region of the country . . . 43% of the U.S. population is protected by volunteer or mostly volunteer departments."

230. Telephone interview with Bob Stephan, Assistant to Secretary Ridge, January 14, 2004.

231. National Interagency Coordination Center, 2003 Statistics and Summary, US Large Fires January 1–December 31, 2003. Found on the Web at: http://www.nifc.gov/news/2003_statssumm/intro_summary.pdf. (Last consulted March 9, 2004).

232. Telephone interview with Bob Stephan, Assistant to Secretary Ridge, January 14, 2004.

233. NFPA 1600 (2004 Edition) may be accessed on the Web at: http://www.nasttpo.org/NFPA1600.htm

234. This material is adopted and incorporated from William C. Nicholson, Chapter 16: Legal Issues in Emergency Management, an online chapter in FEMA's *Introduction to Emergency Management,* found on the Web at http://www.training.fema.gov/emiweb/edu/introtoEM.asp

235. The 9/11 Commission Report 398 (2004) found on the Web at http://www.gpoaccess.gov/911/.

236. S.2774 *9-11 Commission Report Implementation Act* (Introduced September 7, 2004). Additional bills have been introduced in the House of Representatives.

237. S.2774, §806. Private Sector Preparedness.

238. NFPA 1600 §5.2 (2004 Edition).

239. NFPA 1600 Standard Resolution, found on the Web at http://www.nemaweb.org/?335.

240. EMAP Recent and Upcoming Activities, found on the Web at http://www.emaponline.org/What/Implementation/Description_Full.cfm.

241. Indeed, custom and usage within an industry need not be complete or general where improved safety standards, which EMAP provides for emergency management, are involved. See *TJ Hooper,* 60 F 2d 737 (2d Cir. 1932), certiorari denied, *Eastern Transportation Co. v. Northern Barge Corp.,* 287 US 662 (1932), where in 1932, despite the absence of statutes, regulations or even custom as to

radio-receiving sets, Judge Learned Hand found a vessel unseaworthy for lack of one. Two barges had been lost in a storm and the tugs and their tows might have sought shelter in time had they received weather reports by radio. This case may show which way the wind blows for the future of emergency management certification under EMAP.

242. NFPA 1600 §5.8.

243. NIMS at 1–2.

244. 29 C.F.R. §1910.120 (2004). The regulations provide that employees in close proximity to hazardous wastes must receive forty hours of off-site training and have three days of on-site field experience. 29 C.F.R. §1910.120(e)(3)(i). Employees occasionally on-site must receive twenty-four hours of off-site training and have one day of on-site field experience. 29 C.F.R. §1910.120(e)(3)(ii) & (iii). Supervisors must complete an additional eight hours of training on subjects such as employee safety and spill containment. 29 C.F.R. §1910.120(e)(4).

245. NFPA 1600 §5.7.1 (2004 Edition).

246. NFPA 1600 §5.7.2.2 (2004 Edition).

247. NFPA 1600 §5.7.3 (2004 Edition).

248. NFPA 1600 §5.3 (2004 Edition).

249. NFPA 1600 §5.2 (2004 Edition).

250. National Incident Management System may be accessed on the Web at: http://www.dhs.gov/interweb/assetlibrary/NIMS-90-web.pdf

251. EMPG description on the Web at: http://www.fema.gov/preparedness/empg.shtm

252. Homeland Security Presidential Directive 5, §20 Subject: Management of Domestic Incidents, The White House, February 28, 2003. http://www.whitehouse.gov/news/releases/2003/02/20030228-9.html

253. Shaun Waterman, "Analysis: Fear of Being Eclipsed by Terror," *UPI* (March 19, 2004). "Of the plethora of federal grants that fund state and local emergency management activities, only one–the Emergency Management Performance Grant–has historically covered the wage costs of this personnel-intensive business. The Bush administration's proposed 2005 budget cuts the allocation for that program by 5 percent, but–far more damagingly, say critics–caps the amount that can be spent on salaries at one-quarter of any grant. . . . "The fact is, if no source of funding is available for these posts, the temptation will always be to save money (by cutting them) and make those (emergency management) duties someone else's responsibility–give it to the fire department, or the police."

254. NIMS at 36–37.

255. NIMS at 36–37.

256. See, e.g., Fla. Stat. §252.34 (2004) emergency management responsibilities, Fla. Stat. §395.1056 (2004) requiring hospitals to plan for terrorism events.

257. "Mutual-aid agreements are the means for one jurisdiction to provide resources, facilities, services, and other required support to another jurisdiction during an incident. Each jurisdiction should be party to a mutual-aid agreement (such as the Emergency Management Assistance Compact) with appropriate jurisdictions from which they expect to receive or to which they expect to provide assistance during an incident. This would normally include all neighboring or nearby jurisdictions, as well as relevant private-sector and nongovernmental organizations." Adopted NIMS at 39.

258. William C. Nicholson, "Legal Issues in Emergency Response to Terrorism Incidents Involving Hazardous Materials: The Hazardous Waste Operations and Emergency Response ("HAZWOPER") Standard, Standard Operating Procedures, Mutual Aid and the Incident Command System," *Widener Symposium Law Journal*, (9)2, pp. 295, 315–317. (2003).

259. NFPA 1600 §5.6

260. NIMS at 39–40.

261. Found on the Web at http://www.emacweb.org/

262. See, e.g. adopted NIMS at 38 (certification and equipment standards).

263. "Each jurisdiction **should** be party to a mutual-aid agreement . . ." Adopted NIMS at 39, "At a minimum, mutual-aid agreements **should** include the following elements or provisions . . ." Adopted NIMS at 39–40. (Emphasis added).

264. HSPD 5 paragraph 15 provides: "The Secretary shall develop, submit for review to the Homeland Security Council, and administer a National Incident Management System (NIMS). . . . To provide for interoperability and compatibility among Federal, State, and local capabilities, the NIMS will include . . . qualifications and certification . . ."

265. The adopted NIMS recognizes this reality of the federal system when it specifies that "Authorized officials from each of the participating jurisdictions will collectively approve all mutual-aid agreements." Adopted NIMS at 39–40. Absent such ratification, the units of government are not bound to an agreement.

266. See, e.g., Indiana Code 10-14-6 Interstate Emergency Management and Disaster Compact (2004).

267. See, e.g., Indiana Code §§10-14-3-3 and 10-14-3-15(b) for one approach. Section 10-14-3-3 defines

"emergency management worker" as any full-time or part-time paid, volunteer, or auxiliary employee of:

(1) the state;
(2) other:
  (A) states;
  (B) territories; or
  (C) possessions;
(3) the District of Columbia;
(4) the federal government;
(5) any neighboring country;
(6) any political subdivision of an entity described in subdivisions (1) through (5); or
(7) any agency or organization;

performing emergency management services at any place in Indiana subject to the order or control of, or under a request of, the state government or any political subdivision of the state.

Sec. 15. (b) Any requirement for a license to practice any professional, mechanical, or other skill does not apply to any authorized emergency management worker who, in the course of performing duties as an emergency management worker, practices a professional, mechanical, or other skill during a disaster emergency.

268. NIMS at 46. "Personnel certification entails authoritatively attesting that individuals meet professional standards for the training, experience, and performance required for key incident management functions. Credentialing involves providing documentation that can authenticate and verify the certification and identity of designated incident managers and emergency responders."

269. Found on the Web at http://emacweb.org/docs/Wide%20Release%20Intrastate%20Mutual%20Aid.pdf

270. Indiana Code 10-14-3-10.6.

271. See, e.g., *Thomas v. Lisbon,* 550 A.2d 894 (S.Ct. Conn. 1988).

272. NIMS at 39–40.

273. Id.

274. William C. Nicholson, "Litigation Mitigation: Proactive Risk Management in the Wake of the West Warwick Club Fire," 1 *Journal of Emergency Management,* 14, 17–18 (Summer 2003).

275. NRP Draft #1 at iii. The table of contents indicated that a Legal Support Annex would be a part of the NRP Draft #1 eventually.

276. FEMA, through the Emergency Management Institute, taught a class to state and FEMA attorneys September 9–10, 1998 entitled "Course E709: Expediting Disaster Response and Recovery Pursuant to the Stafford Act." The course focussed on the federal side of emergency law. Subsequently, FEMA has worked to educate state-level attorneys through the National Emergency Management Association ("NEMA") Legal Counsels Committee during their twice-yearly meetings. Telephone interview with Tamara S. Little, Assistant Attorney General, State of Ohio, NEMA Legal Counsels Committee Chair (March 21, 2002).

277. "Personnel that are certified for employment in support of an incident that transcends interstate jurisdictions through the Emergency Management Assistance Compacts System will be required to meet national qualification and certification standards." Adopted NIMS at 38.

278. Public Law 104-321.

279. Adopted NIMS 2 at 38, William C. Nicholson, "Legal Issues in Emergency Response to Terrorism Incidents Involving Hazardous Materials: The Hazardous Waste Operations and Emergency Response ("HAZWOPER") Standard, Standard Operating Procedures, Mutual Aid and the Incident Command System," *Widener Symposium Law Journal,* (9)2, pp. 295, 315–317. (2003).

280. Since interstate responders under NIMS must be Federally certified (adopted NIMS at 38), it follows that both parties must be federally certified in order to reach a valid interstate mutual aid agreement under NIMS.

281. William C. Nicholson. *Emergency Response and Emergency Management Law,* note 50 page 109 (2003).

282. Telephone interview with Bob Stephan, Assistant to Secretary Ridge, January 14, 2004.

283. Federal Emergency Management Agency Response and Recovery Policy 9523.6 *Mutual Aid Agreements for Public Assistance* (1999). Found on the Web at http://www.fema.gov/rrr/pa/9523_6.shtm

284. Scott Baltic, "ICS For Everyone," 3 *Homeland Preparedness Professional* 1, 26 (January/February 2004).

285. Adopted NIMS at 38.

286. William C. Nicholson, *Emergency Response and Emergency Management Law,* 246–254 (2003).

287. See Appendix 1 at the conclusion of this chapter.

288. Joe Fiorill, "Emergency Responders Rap Federal Incident Management System," *Global Security Newswire* (September 30, 2004). "The decision to establish a National Incident Management System must be applauded," George Washington University professor Joseph Barbera, co-director of the university's Institute for Crisis, Disaster and Risk Management said. "The development process used in creating the NIMS document, however,

was not as open to professional input as many of us would have preferred. It is particularly unclear whether the NIMS development process provided a full hearing for the concerns and issues of acute-care medical and hospital professionals."

289. *Id.*

290. *Id.*

291. Deconstructed NIMS compliance requirements may be found online at: http://www.all-hands.net/pn/modules.php?op=modload&name=Downloads&file=index&req=viewdownload&cid=15&min=15&orderby=titleA&show=15

292. Joe Fiorill, "Emergency Responders Rap Federal Incident Management System," *Global Security Newswire* (September 30, 2004).

293. *Id.*

294. Parallel citations are found in Executive Order (EO) 12291 §1(a) (February 17, 1981) entitled "Federal Regulation," issued by President Reagan, in EO 12866 §3(d) (September 30, 1993) entitled "Regulatory Planning and Review," issued by President Clinton, and in FEMA rules at 44 CFR §1.2(a). EO 12291 was revoked by EO 12866 (September 30, 1993). EO 12866 was amended by EO 13250 (February 26, 2002).

295. The Federal Response Plan, for example, is not a rule. The National Contingency Plan 40 CFR §300 *et seq.* (2004), in contrast, was adopted as a rule. While it might seem simplistic to argue that the word "national" in the title of a plan should tilt the balance toward its being a rule, the fact is that any plan that is national in scope, affecting all levels of government and all Americans, would benefit from the input of the U.S.-wide stakeholder group and the public that will be affected by it, as contemplated by the APA.

296. HSPD 5 paragraph 1 states that its purpose, as implemented through the NRP and NIMS, is "To enhance the ability of the United States to manage domestic incidents by establishing a single, comprehensive national incident management system." See also NRP Draft #1 Transmittal Letter. "The incident management structures and processes outlined herein call for maximum integration and coordination at all levels of government and between the government and private entities . . ."

297. *Id.*

298. NRP Draft #1 at 1. "Given the complex 21st century threat environment, the nation can no longer rely on a patchwork quilt approach to incident management. These threats demand a tightly woven tapestry, with a clearly defined framework and processes that eliminate artificial distinctions and

barriers. The National Response Plan (NRP) and the National Incident Management System (NIMS) provide the framework and processes that weave all of the capabilities and resources of all of the jurisdictions, disciplines, and levels of government and the private sector into a cohesive, unified, coordinated, and seamless national approach to domestic incident management."

299. *Id.*

300. EO 12866 §3(f). (f) "Significant regulatory action" means any regulatory action that is likely to result in a rule that may:

(1) Have an annual effect on the economy of $100 million or more or adversely affect in a material way the economy, a sector of the economy, productivity, competition, jobs, the environment, public health or safety, or State, local, or tribal governments or communities. Referred to as a "major rule" by EO) 12291 §1(b)(1).

301. Remarks by the President on the one-year anniversary of the U.S. Department of Homeland Security, White House Office of the Press Secretary, found on the Web at: http://www.dhs.gov/dhspublic/display?content=3280 (Last consulted on March 13, 2004). "[We] have tripled federal funding for homeland security since 2001, to some $30.5 billion."

302. EO 12866 §6.

303. *Id.* at §6(C).

304. *Id.* at §6(D).

305. *Id.*

306. 5 USC §553(b).

307. 5 USC §553(c).

308. *Id.*

309. HS Act §102. SECRETARY; FUNCTIONS . . .

(b) Functions. The Secretary– . . .

(2) may promulgate regulations hereunder . . .

310. FEMA policies and procedures require at 44 CFR §1.4 (parallel citation at EO 12866 §6), among other things, "adequate information concerning the need for and consequences of proposed government action," cost benefit analysis, choice of the alternative involving the least net cost to society, and choice of the option that maximizes the aggregate net benefits to society. Further, FEMA policy requires public participation in rulemaking.

311. 5 USC §553(e) provides that: "Each agency shall give an interested person the right to petition for the issuance, amendment, or repeal of a rule."

312. 5 USC §553(e) does not give the public a right to compel an agency to perform a rulemaking proceeding, *see* WWHT, Inc. v. FCC, 656 F.2d 807, 813 (D.C. Cir. 1981); S. REP. NO. 752, 79th Cong., 1st Sess. 15 (1945), *reprinted in* ADMINISTRATIVE

PROCEDURE ACT: LEGISLATIVE HISTORY, S. DOC. NO. 248, 79th Cong., 2d Sess. 406–07 (1946) at 185, 201. The APA mandates that an agency denying a rulemaking request must give notice of the denial accompanied by a statement of the grounds for denial. *See* 5 U.S.C. §555(e) (2004). "Prompt notice shall be given of the denial in whole or in part of a written application, petition, or other request of an interested person made in connection with any agency proceedings. Except in affirming a prior denial or when the denial is self-explanatory, the notice shall be accompanied by a brief statement of the grounds for denial."

313. 5 USC §704.

314. Jim Rossi, "Participation Run Amok: The Costs of Mass Participation for Deliberative Agency Decisionmaking," 92 *Northwestern University Law Review* 173, 190 n.96 (Fall, 1997). (Citing National Resources Defense Council v. SEC, 606 F.2d 1031, 1046 n.18 (D.C. Cir. 1979).

315. Rule 24(a)(2) of the Federal Rules of Civil Procedure confers a right of intervention upon a person who "claims an interest relating to" the subject matter of the suit in which the person wants to intervene, provided that the disposition of the suit might "impair or impede" the person's ability to protect that interest and the interest is not "adequately represented" by a party to the suit.

316. EIIP Virtual Forum Presentation–September 15, 2004. "The National Response Plan: An Update." Statement by Associate Director Barbara Yagerman, Operations and Response Operations Integration Staff, Department of Homeland Security: "We worked closely with DHS and White House attorneys throughout the process, and we adhered to all requirements that they stipulated were appropriate."

317. *Id.*

318. HS Act §501(6) SEC. 501. UNDERSECRETARY FOR EMERGENCY PREPAREDNESS AND RESPONSE.

In assisting the Secretary with the responsibilities specified in section 101(b)(2)(D), the primary responsibilities of the Under Secretary for Emergency Preparedness and Response shall include . . . (6) consolidating existing Federal Government emergency response plans into a single, coordinated national response plan . . .

319. HS Act §502(1).

320. Martin Edwin Andersen, "Local Responders Howl at DHS Emergency Management Plan," *Congressional Quarterly Homeland Security–Local Response* (August 8, 2003).

321. HS Act §402(5).

322. HS Act §501(6).

323. NRP Base Plan DRAFT #1, *All Hands Community Newsletter* No. 23 for Thursday, March 11, 2004.

324. EO 12866 §6(A)(1) requires public participation. "Each agency shall (consistent with its own rules, regulations, or procedures) provide the public with meaningful participation in the regulatory process."

325. EIIP Virtual Forum Presentation–September 15, 2004. "The National Response Plan: An Update." Statement by Associate Director Barbara Yagerman, Operations and Response Operations Integration Staff, Department of Homeland Security: "The plan was developed in close coordination with the White House, the interagency team, and state and local stakeholders."

326. Telephone interview with Bob Stephan, Assistant to Secretary Ridge, January 14, 2004.

327. Pat West, Senior Editor, "NIMS: The Last Word on Incident Command?" *Fire Chief on Line* (March 5, 2004). Found at: http://firechief.com/ar/ firefighting_nics_last_word/index.htm (Last consulted March 9, 2004). "When this document was first written, it was written as if the federal government was going to respond to an automobile accident and take care of it, when the fact is, all emergencies are local. They start with local people and they end with local people. You may invite a whole lot of other people in the middle, but they start and end locally. But what we were able to do is we were able to take a document that was written from the federal perspective and influence it into what I believe is now a national perspective."

328. William C. Nicholson, "Integrating Local, State and Federal Responders and Emergency Management: New Packaging and New Controls," 1 *Journal of Emergency Management*, 15, 20 (Fall 2003).

329. *Id.* at 21.

330. William C. Nicholson, "The New Federalism in Homeland Security," 2 *Homeland Preparedness Professional*, 8, 8–10 (November/December 2003).

331. Adopted NIMS at 50.

332. Adopted NIMS at 50 "*The Secretary has ultimate authority and responsibility* for publishing revisions and modifications to NIMS-related documents, including supplementary standards, procedures, and other materials, in coordination with other Federal, State, local, tribal, and private entities with incident management and emergency responder responsibilities, expertise, and experience." (Emphasis added.)

DISCUSSION QUESTIONS

1. Describe how the NRP and NIMS adoption process evolved.
2. What is your opinion of the process by which the NRP and NIMS were adopted?
3. What is your opinion of the result of the NRP/NIMS adoption process?
4. How did the relationship between DHS and stakeholder groups change during the process of adopting the NRP and NIMS? What effect did the changing relationship have on the resulting documents?
5. What ends were served by utilizing so many drafts of the documents before finalizing them?
6. Compare the discussion of the INRP and the NRP as adopted. What differences do you see in the approaches of the two documents. Which do you think makes the most sense, and why?
7. What do you see as the biggest challenges facing the NIMS Integration Center? What suggestions do you have on how to address those challenges?
8. Discuss the situation of rural volunteer emergency response groups in the aftermath of NIMS. What do you see as their biggest potential difficulties in the NIMS era? How would you address those issues?
9. Read the September 8, 2004, letter giving instructions on how to comply with the NRP and NIMS for FFY 2005 attached as an appendix to this chapter. What is your reaction to the steps outlined therein?
10. What are the advantages and disadvantages to adopting the NRP and NIMS in the way it was done rather than through the Administrative Procedure Act?
11. Do you agree with the author's conclusion that adoption of common incident response and command standards is a worthy goal? Why or why not?

APPENDIX 1 NIMS COMPLIANCE LETTER

U.S. Department of
Homeland Security
Washington, DC 20528

September 8, 2004

Dear Governor:

In Homeland Security Presidential Directive (HSPD)-5, *Management of Domestic Incidents*, the President directed me to develop and administer the National Incident Management System (NIMS). The NIMS provides a consistent nationwide approach for Federal, State,[1] territorial, tribal, and local[2] governments to work effectively and efficiently together to prepare for, prevent, respond to, and recover from domestic incidents, regardless of cause, size, or complexity. On March 1, 2004, the Department of Homeland Security (DHS) issued the NIMS to provide a comprehensive national approach to incident management, applicable at all jurisdictional levels and across functional disciplines. HSPD-5 also required DHS to establish a mechanism for ongoing coordination to provide strategic direction for, and oversight of, the NIMS. To this end, the NIMS Integration Center (NIC) was established to support both routine maintenance and the continuous refinement of the NIMS.

All Federal departments and agencies are required to adopt the NIMS and use it in their individual domestic incident management and emergency prevention, preparedness, response, recovery, and mitigation activities, as well as in support of all actions taken to assist State or local entities. The NIC is working with Federal departments and agencies to ensure that they develop a plan to adopt NIMS and that all fiscal year (FY) 2005 Federal preparedness assistance program documents begin the process of addressing State, territorial, tribal, and local NIMS implementation.

This letter outlines the important steps that State, territorial, tribal, and local entities should take during FY 2005 (October 1, 2004–September 30, 2005) to become compliant with the NIMS.

The NIMS provides the framework for locals, tribes, territories, States, and the Federal Government to work together to respond to any domestic incident. Many of the NIMS requirements are specific to local jurisdictions. In order for NIMS to be implemented successfully across the nation, it is critical that States provide support and leadership to tribal and local entities to ensure full NIMS implementation. We are looking to you and your State Administrative Agency (SAA) to coordinate with the State agencies, tribal governments, and local jurisdictions to ensure NIMS implementation. Given the importance and urgency of this effort, Federal, State, territorial, tribal, and local entities should begin efforts to implement the NIMS, if such efforts are not already underway.

Implementation of and compliance with the NIMS is critical to ensuring full and robust preparedness across our nation. HSPD-5 established ambitious deadlines for NIMS adoption and implementation. FY 2005 is a start-up year for NIMS implementation and full compliance with the NIMS is not required for you to receive FY 2005 grant funds. Since FY 2005 is a critical year for initial NIMS adoption, you should start now by prioritizing your FY 2005 preparedness assistance (in accordance with the eligibility and allowable uses of the grant) to facilitate its implementation. The NIC is working with the Federal departments and agencies to identify all of preparedness assistance programs. The NIC will then provide this information to the States, territories, tribes, and local governments.

To the maximum extent possible, States, territories, tribes, and local entities are encouraged to achieve full NIMS implementation and institutionalization across the entire response system during FY 2005. This memorandum highlights the important features of NIMS implementation that should receive special emphasis in FY 2005, but does not represent all of the actions necessary to fully implement the NIMS.

The NIMS is the nation's first-ever standardized approach to incident management and response. The NIMS unifies Federal, State, territorial, tribal, and local lines of government into one coordinated effort. This integrated system makes America safer by establishing a uniform set of processes, protocols, and procedures that all emergency responders, at every level of government, will use to conduct response actions. This system ensures that those involved in emergency response operations understand what their roles are and have the tools they need to be effective.

This system encompasses much more than the Incident Command System (ICS), although ICS is a critical component of the NIMS. It also provides a common foundation for training and other preparedness efforts, communicating and sharing information with other responders and with the public, ordering resources to assist with a response effort, and for integrating new technologies and standards to support incident management. For the first time, all of the nation's emergency responders will use a common language, and a common set of procedures when working individually and together to keep America safe. The NIMS ensures that they will have the same preparation, the same goals and expectations, and most importantly, they will be speaking the same language.

MINIMUM FY 2005 NIMS COMPLIANCE REQUIREMENTS:

State and territory level efforts to implement the NIMS must include the following:

· **Incorporating NIMS into existing training programs and exercises**
· **Ensuring that Federal preparedness funding (including DHS Homeland Security Grant Program, Urban Area Security Initiative (UASI) funds) support NIMS implementation at the State and local levels** (in accordance with the eligibility and allowable uses of the grants)
· **Incorporating NIMS into Emergency Operations Plans (EOP)**
· **Promotion of intrastate mutual aid agreements**
· **Coordinating and providing technical assistance to local entities regarding NIMS**
· **Institutionalizing the use of the Incident Command System (ICS).**

At the State, territorial, tribal, and local levels, jurisdictions should support NIMS implementation by:

· **Completing the NIMS Awareness Course: "National Incident Management System (NIMS), An Introduction" IS 700**
This independent study course developed by the Emergency Management Institute (EMI) explains the purpose, principles, key components, and benefits of NIMS. The course also contains "Planning Activity" screens, allowing participants an opportunity to complete some planning tasks during the course. The planning activity screens are printable so that they can be used after the course is complete. The course is available online and will take between forty-five minutes to three hours to complete. The course is available on the EMI Web page at: http://training.fema.gov/EMIWeb/IS/is700.asp.

· **Formally recognizing the NIMS and adopting the NIMS principles and policies**
States, territories, tribes, and local entities should establish legislation, executive orders, resolutions, or ordinances to formally adopt the NIMS. The NIC will provide sample language and templates to assist you in formally adopting the NIMS through legislative and/or executive/administrative means.

• Establish a NIMS baseline by determining which NIMS requirements you already meet

We recognize that State, territorial, tribal, and local entities have already implemented many of the concepts and protocols identified in the NIMS. The 2004 DHS Homeland Security Grant Program encouraged grantees to begin utilizing the NIMS concepts, principles, terminology, and technologies. The NIC is developing the NIMS Capability Assessment Support Tool (NIMCAST). The NIMCAST is a Web-based self-assessment system that States, territories, tribes, and local governments can use to evaluate their incident response and management capabilities. This useful tool identifies the requirements established within the NIMS and can assist you in determining the extent to which you are already compliant, as well as identify the NIMS requirements that you are not currently meeting. As gaps in compliance with the NIMS are identified, States, territories, tribes, and local entities should use existing initiatives, such as the Office for Domestic Preparedness (ODP) Homeland Security grant programs, to develop strategies for addressing those gaps. The NIC will formally pilot the NIMCAST with a limited number of States in September. Upon completion of the pilot, the NIC will provide all potential future users with voluntary access to the system. Additional information about the NIMCAST tool will be provided later this year.

• Establishing a timeframe and developing a strategy for full NIMS implementation

States, territories, tribes, and local entities are encouraged to achieve full NIMS implementation during FY 2005. To the extent that full implementation is not possible during FY 2005, Federal preparedness assistance must be leveraged to complete NIMS implementation by FY 2006. By FY 2007, Federal preparedness assistance will be conditioned by full compliance with the NIMS. Again, in order for NIMS to be implemented successfully across the nation, it is critical that States provide support and leadership to tribal and local entities to ensure full NIMS implementation. States should work with the tribal and local governments to develop a strategy for statewide compliance with the NIMS.

• Institutionalizing the use of the Incident Command System (ICS)

If State, territorial, tribal, and local entities are not already using ICS, you must institutionalize the use of ICS (consistent with the concepts and principles taught by DHS) across the entire response system. The 9-11 Commission Report recommended national adoption of the Incident Command System (ICS) to enhance command, control, and communications capabilities. All Federal, State, territory, tribal, and local jurisdictions will be required to adopt ICS in order to be compliant with the NIMS. Additional information about adopting ICS will be provided to you by the NIC.

FY 2006 and FY 2007 Requirements:

In order to receive FY 2006 preparedness funding, the minimum FY 2005 compliance requirements described above must be met. Applicants will be required to certify as part of their FY 2006 grant applications that they have met the FY 2005 NIMS requirements. Additional information about NIMS compliance and resources for achieving compliance will be forthcoming from the NIC. In addition, FY 2005 Federal preparedness assistance program documents will address State and local NIMS compliance. The NIC Web page, www.fema.gov/nims, will be updated regularly with information about the NIMS and guidance for implementation. The NIC may be contacted at the following:

Gil Jamieson, Acting Director
NIMS Integration Center
500 C Street, SW
Washington, DC 20472
(202) 646-3850
NIMS-Integration-Center@dhs.gov
www.fema.gov/nims

Thank you for your support in implementing the NIMS. I look forward to continuing our collective efforts to better secure the homeland and protect our citizens and appreciate all of your hard work in this important endeavor.

Sincerely,
Tom Ridge

cc: State Administrative Agency
     State Emergency Management Director
     State Homeland Security Advisor
     DHS Directorates and Offices
     Homeland Security Advisory Council

ENDNOTES

1. As defined in the Homeland Security Act of 2002, the term "State" means any State of the United States, the District of Columbia, the Commonwealth of Puerto Rico, Guam, American Samoa, the Commonwealth of the Northern Mariana Islands, and any possession of the United States." 6 U.S.C. 101 (14)
2. As defined in the Homeland Security Act of 2002, Section 2(10): the term "local government" means "(A) county, municipality, city, town, township, local public authority, school district, special district, intrastate district, council of governments . . . regional or interstate government entity, or agency or instrumentality of a local government: an Indian tribe or authorized tribal organization, or in Alaska a Native village or Alaska Regional Native Corporation; and a rural community, unincorporated town or village, or other public entity." 6 U.S.C. 101(10)

Rockledge, FL September 9, 2004—Local, state, and federal employees and volunteers continue to work at the Emergency Operations Center for Brevard County. FEMA Photo by Jocelyn Augustino.

Section II

LOCAL AND REGIONAL PERSPECTIVES

Chapter 5

HOMELAND SECURITY FROM THE LOCAL PERSPECTIVE

FRANCES L. EDWARDS

Emergency management is usually defined as having four phases: mitigation, preparedness, response, and recovery.[1] Local government emergency managers have used these four phases to manage community capability to withstand emergencies and disasters. The programmatic work has evolved since World War II through a civil defense emphasis, to an all-hazards emphasis, and now to a time when terrorism prevention is taking center stage. The current challenge for local government emergency managers is to balance the emphasis on terrorism prevention with the demand for maintaining capability for natural hazard response. In the last 50 years there have been three terrorist attacks of note (World Trade Center, 1993; Murrah Building, 1995; and 9-11 attacks, 2001), yet there have been hundreds of damaging floods, dozens of significant hurricanes, and two major earthquakes in that same period.

All-hazards emergency management posits that preparing for any disaster that has significant community consequences provides a platform for response to any other major disaster. Thus, in California most communities prepare for earthquakes, whereas in Florida communities prepare for hurricanes, but in both cases a response to an explosion can be managed from the same Emergency Operations Plan and the same Emergency Operations Center.

Likewise in some ways mitigation has multiple benefits that are cumulative across the disaster spectrum. Community disaster preparedness education creates a population base that is self-supporting for the first hours of a disaster, regardless of its cause. Creation of a thorough risk analysis for the community provides first responders with predisaster knowledge of vulnerabilities. While prevention is situationally specific, such as preventing crime or preventing floods, mitigation crosses situations, such as the development of communications interoperability or Geographical Information System (GIS) maps that serve in any disaster. The current emphasis on prevention creates the investment limitations of a single disaster focus, while a return to the mitigation philosophy provides a broader-based use of funding for community protection.

I. LOCAL GOVERNMENT TERRORISM PREPAREDNESS BEFORE 9-11

Cities and counties in the United States have developed local programs for homeland security in the context of national civil defense. Beginning with the blackout wardens of World War II and continuing through the Cold War era, local volunteers and government staff members formed a

Note: Frances L. Edwards, Ph.D., CEM, is the director of the Office of Emergency Services for the city of San José, California. She is responsible for public education programs, the city's Emergency Operations Plan, Emergency Operations Center, and the RACES and CERT programs involving over 1,400 volunteers. She was named "Public Official of the Year" by *Governing* Magazine in 2002. Dr. Edwards was recently named by *San Jose Magazine* as one of the "Power 100" in the Silicion Valley. Her most recent publications are *Saving City Lifelines,* (Mineta Transportation Institute, 2003), on terrorism and transportation, and *First to Arrive: State and Local Response to Terrorism,* (MIT Press, 2003) on media relations.

partnership to ensure the safety of the American homeland. The threat was from external sources: enemy planes dropping bombs, surreptitious landings of saboteurs on beaches, or communications loss from electromagnetic pulse. The federal government led the way, providing Geiger counters and package hospitals, public information fliers on fallout shelters, siren systems for community warning, and funding for staff salaries in the Civil Defense Program.

By the 1970s the federal support shifted away from a wartime focus to all-hazards emergency management. The Federal Emergency Management Agency (FEMA) was created in 1979. The Robert T. Stafford Act clearly defined the all-hazards scope of FEMA's authority, and delineated federal financial support that would be available to communities beset by disaster. By 1996 the budget was $817 million for mitigation, preparedness, response, and recovery work funded by FEMA.[2]

The direct link between FEMA and local government activities was the Emergency Management Assistance program (EMA) that provided a portion of the salary and benefits for a full-time emergency manager in a community.[3] The program required the development and maintenance of an all-hazards emergency operations plan, an emergency operations center, and a community education program on topics appropriate to the location: earthquakes, hurricanes, or tornadoes, for example. EMA communities were required to conduct periodic threat analyses[4] and exercises of related coordination and response capabilities.

During this era the local communities planned for nuclear attack as well. The anticipated response for most communities was to shelter in place and wait for federal and military assistance. The main mitigation work was development of shielding for critical communications equipment from electromagnetic pulse, and the main preparedness work was the maintenance and exercising of the community's alerting and warning system, whether siren-based or media-based (Emergency Broadcasting System).[5] The federal government stocked fallout shelters with survival supplies, and public education included community-level surveillance by all Americans for sabotage against critical infrastructure.

In most states the health officer of any jurisdiction has powers to declare a medical emergency and order isolation of patients and quarantine of community members. Most of these laws were written during the public health emergencies of the early 1900s when contagious diseases reached epidemic proportions. The pandemic flu right after World War I, the arrival of plague in San Francisco at the beginning of the century, and the virulent seasonal outbreaks of childhood diseases such as pertussis generated public support for strict health measures. However, the general availability of antibiotics following World War II led to a gradual diminution of public interest in health regulations.

By mid-century, many laws changed governing personal behavior. For example, because the laws against public spitting, originally passed to stop the spread of tuberculosis, were most often being enforced against minorities, those laws were declared unconstitutional. In 1964 the Civil Rights Act strengthened the rights of individuals regarding probable cause and due process.[6]

Terrorism was a reality for Americans during this Cold War era. Organizations like the Weathermen and Symbionese Liberation Army disrupted communities with explosive devices, focusing especially on public safety staff, during the period of demonstrations against the war in Vietnam. Puerto Rican separatist groups perpetrated attacks on public infrastructure, even after a vote to remain a commonwealth was successful. The Unabomber mailed carefully handmade letter bombs to individuals he perceived as responsible for turning American society over to machines. Until Ted Kaczynski, the Unabomber, was arrested there was fear over unusual packages, which resulted in a special FBI training program for mailroom workers.[7]

Americans traveling abroad were warned of Irish Republican Army bombs in Great Britain and Cypriot separatists in the Mediterranean. The Red Brigades kidnapped government officials and threatened the public peace in Germany and Italy. Palestinian terrorists bombed Israeli targets, and Lebanese civil war groups created terror throughout the Middle East. In 1983, 300 people were killed when terrorists destroyed the American marine barracks at the Beirut Airport, and the French peacekeepers' residence in Beirut. The year ended with the tragic destruction of an airplane over Lockerbie, Scotland, caused by a bomb in a suitcase belonging to a terrorist's girlfriend.

New York City experienced a major international terrorist attack in 1993 when a militant Islamic group placed a truck bomb in the underground parking garage of the World Trade Center. The plan was to cause one tower to topple over into the other, bringing both down. Fortunately the bomb's engineering and placement did not result in the desired outcome. However, over 1,000 people were forced to evacuate the building after hours, leading to injuries, and many first responders reported respiratory distress while working at the scene. The FBI later discovered that cyanide had been included in the bomb as a "secondary device" aimed at killing the first responders. This event generated new training for law enforcement staff on dealing with explosive devices and being aware of the possibility of secondary devices. Fire department and emergency medical services personnel were given additional training on caring for the victims of bomb and blast events.

During the 1990s American cities hosting high-profile meetings began to develop more complex emergency response plans. For example, when San Diego hosted the Republican National Convention in 1996 they developed plans for sweeping venues for explosives, screening for weapons, and having heightened crowd surveillance during events. The G-7 Summit in Denver likewise generated new attention to potential terrorist activities designed to disrupt these significant meetings. By 1999 preparation for the turn of the millennium (Y2K) generated renewed interest in American groups known for terrorist activity. Militias and "Christian Identity" organizations focused their attention on antigovernment and race-based aggression. Threats against law enforcement involving Ricin, and threats to use biological materials, were more frequent, leading to aggressive prosecution by the FBI.

The 1996 Olympics in Atlanta were a catalyst for the development of their Metropolitan Medical Strike Team[8] and related federal coordination plans. The Department of Health and Human Services (DHHS) was able to plan the resources and systems needed to respond to a terrorist Weapons of Mass Destruction/Nuclear, Biological, Chemical (WMD/NBC) event. Local and national teams were trained, and decisions were made on the use of resources for victim care and mass fatality management. A bomb planted at one of the parks tested the effectiveness of the emergency response plans made by the community and the federal partners.

The pro-life movement in America developed a violent membership subset. Along with the firearms murders of physicians working in women's health clinics, aggressions against the clinic facilities began. Eric Rudolph began using bombs against both women's clinics and entertainment locations frequented by the gay community. These bombings in Georgia were notable for the placement of secondary devices, again aimed at public safety first responders. Larger cities developed specialized law enforcement units to handle explosive devices safely, and to investigate crimes using explosive devices.

In the mid-1990s, the Emergency Management Assistance (EMA) program changed to the Emergency Management Planning Grant (EMPG) program. The work required under the program was defined by the states to meet their unique natural hazards needs. The funds were no longer limited to personnel time, but were allocated to projects based on priorities set by the local government. The cycle of planning, training, and exercising could be altered to better meet local needs. Public education efforts shifted to home and personal preparedness for natural disasters, while the mitigation focus shifted to strengthening the built environment against natural hazards.

Still, the average American community did not see itself as a potential target for terrorist groups. Although bombings of laboratories at University of California (UC) Berkeley and People for the Ethical Treatment of Animals (PETA) attacks against an animal experiment at UC Irvine posed serious law enforcement challenges, the residents did not see themselves as at risk of terrorist attack in their home communities. In addition, most terrorist attacks within the United States were limited to improvised explosive devices of relatively small size: pipe bombs, letter bombs, and package bombs.

II. THE WARNING: MASS DESTRUCTION

In 1995 two events occurred weeks apart that changed the American view of terrorism, converting the concern to weapons of mass destruction (WMD), and adding the possibility of battlefield weapons to the urban environment. In April Aum Shinrikyo cult members released homemade Sarin in the Tokyo subway system at rush hour to try to stop a Tokyo Metropolitan Police Department investigation of their activities. Sarin is an organophosphate battlefield weapon, a nerve agent, a human pesticide. Immediate treatment with antidote is essential to save lives. In May Timothy McVeigh used a truck bomb loaded with at least 4,000 pounds of Animal Noise Force Organization (ANFO) to destroy the Alfred P. Murrah Federal Building in Oklahoma City. ANFO is used for agriculture and mining-related blasting work, and is available premixed. The individual ingredients–ammonium nitrate fertilizer and fuel oil–are readily available in most communities.

These two events stunned the U.S. Congress into recognizing that such attacks could be repeated in any American city. They also realized that the Cold War model of a passive local response and an active federal government/military response would not work. The victims rescued alive at the Murrah Building were all rescued by Oklahoma City Fire Department personnel and their local mutual aid partners, all within the first 17 hours after the blast. Federal response organizations arriving later assisted with recovery, but did not save any lives. Victims of nerve agent poisoning require antidote within minutes. Victims of a biological attack require vaccination or prophylactic antibiotics within hours of the first symptoms. Local first responders in public safety and health care need an awareness that such events might occur, and special training in handling victims of these unique events, so that they can begin the life-saving actions.

In 1996 Senators Nunn, Lugar, and Domenici cosponsored an amendment to the National Defense Authorization Act for Fiscal Year 1997 (P.L. 104-201) to create the Domestic Preparedness Program focused on "weapons of mass destruction/nuclear, biological, chemical (WMD/NBC)." The 25 largest U.S. cities, plus Anchorage, Alaska,

and Honolulu, Hawaii, because of their isolation, were offered contracts with the Department of Health and Human Services (DHHS) to create Metropolitan Medical Strike Teams (MMST) in their local communities.[9] Using the Sarin attack as the model, the initial MMSTs, in Washington, D.C., and Atlanta, Georgia, had been "enhanced hazardous materials teams,"[10] typically based in the fire department. Later program evolution resulted in more elements of the local government becoming an integral part of the terrorism preparedness and response plan, including law enforcement, public health, emergency services, emergency medical services, coroner and local medical care providers, both public and private. In 2000 DHHS amended the contracts to incorporate preparing to respond to a covert release of a biological agent, and changed the name to Metropolitan Medical Response Systems in recognition of the involvement of fixed medical resources.[11]

Through the Domestic Preparedness Program a new partnership was created between local governments and the federal government. Six federal agencies were assigned tasks to assist local governments in becoming prepared for possible WMD/NBC attacks in their communities. These six were divided into crisis management, those that would respond to the event to help in the field, and consequence management, meaning those that would respond to the Emergency Operations Center to help with the recovery. Department of Defense (DoD), Department of Health and Human Services (DHHS), and Department of Justice (DOJ) were the crisis management contingent.

The DoD provided train-the-trainer classes for first responders in "weapons of mass destruction/nuclear, biological, chemical (WMD/NBC)." These included information on terrorism awareness, terrorism response operations, use of the incident command system (ICS) in a terrorism event, WMD/NBC for hazardous materials teams, WMD/NBC for emergency medical services personnel (emergency medical technicians and paramedics), and a special course for hospital staff members. The DoD also provided a loaned equipment cache to support the continuation of this training.

The DHHS made a contract with the original 27 cities (eventually 122 cities) to provide a series of "deliverables" that included plans, staff training, and exercises. In turn the community would receive funding support for the acquisition of specified equipment, supplies, and pharmaceuticals to support the approved plans. DHHS provided a project officer to oversee the development of the plans and the acquisition of the materials. Part of the contract required that the WMD/NBC training become an ongoing part of the city's police and fire training cycles. There was no promise of sustainment funding, so pharmaceutical caches had to be self-sustaining through beneficial use rotation (as in public health infectious disease clinics), or dwindle as the expiration dates arrived.[12]

A critical element of the MMST program was the creation of the Strategic National Stockpile (SNS), a vendor-managed inventory of pharmaceuticals and medical equipment that could be deployed to assist a community attacked with WMD/NBC agents. The governor of any state under attack could request the delivery of the stockpile to that state. The state health department was responsible to coordinate with local health departments to break down and deliver the goods to the areas needing the materials to treat victims and provide prevention care to the community.

Local public health officers had to develop plans for the distribution of antibiotics and vaccinations to community members. They also had to work with hospitals to develop plans for the reception of victims into emergency departments and the definitive care of victims in hospitals. These plans included developing local surge capacity for bed space and staffing, the distribution of medical equipment and antidotes from the SNS, and protection of hospital facilities and staff from contamination or contagion.

The Public Health Officers Association recognized the need to update the existing isolation and quarantine laws. The Department of Justice undertook a study of constitutional issues related to isolation and quarantine in light of the strengthened probable cause and due process protections embodied in the Civil Rights Act of 1964. The Centers for Disease Control and Prevention (CDC) in 1999 commissioned the drafting of a model state law that would give new powers to local public health officers. The "Model State Emergency Health Power Act (MSEHPA) provided the basis for health officers to get governors to declare a "public health emergency," and use the state militia (National Guard) to enforce public health orders. The MSEHPA allowed for arrest, quarantine, and forcible vaccination of citizens. This model legislation was widely debated, but not released in draft until after 9-11.

The DOJ provided assistance in two forms. First, local offices of the FBI developed or enhanced their terrorism response unit. The lead staff in these units created Joint Terrorism Task Force (JTTF) organizations to bring in local law enforcement personnel for intelligence gathering and sharing. Although this greatly enhanced the level of information sharing between local and federal agencies, the dedicated officer became a new unfunded financial burden on local police departments. The large cities were asked to donate the time of an officer and a vehicle to this effort. While valuable and beneficial, economic conditions in America's largest cities made this added expense a budgetary challenge that many could not meet. Second, the DOJ offered the opportunity for competitive grants to enhance the WMD/NBC response equipment cache beyond the medically oriented materials permitted for purchase under the MMST/MMRS program. Winning communities could purchase personal protective equipment (PPE) for the bomb unit, and for individual patrol officers; interoperable communications equipment; and special equipment for WMD/NBC response.

Three other federal agencies were part of the Domestic Preparedness Program, assisting with the consequence management aspects. FEMA had the lead role, providing both access to the federal financial assistance,[13] and bringing the resources of the federal government to aid the damaged community through the Federal Response Plan (FRP). Organized along emergency support functions, the FRP provided the plan for the response of both full-time federal assets, such as the military units, and parttime/volunteer assets, such as the Disaster

Medical Assistance Teams (DMAT) and the Urban Search and Rescue (USAR) teams.

The Environmental Protection Agency (EPA) would oversee the immediate response and long-term cleanup of chemical or biological attacks. The EPA would provide a subject matter expert for the Planning/Intelligence Section of the Incident Command System, determine the characteristics of the site pollution, then mandate the appropriate PPE for those working in the area. They would also determine how debris would be handled, including how it had to be cleaned on-site, how and where it could be disposed of, and the ultimate cleaning and potential re-use of the site. EPA would also monitor the ongoing health of workers, including search dogs and other helper animals. They would interface with the local public health department for community disease surveillance possibly related to the attack, and support public education on risks and self-protection for the affected community.

The Department of Energy would serve the same functions as the EPA if the attack were by a nuclear device or radiological device (radiological dispersal device or "dirty bomb"). Public education would be especially important, as people have little accurate information about energetic materials and their health effects, and are therefore likely to become more frightened of such events.

The original 27 MMST communities committed a significant amount of local resources to augment the financial support provided by the federal partners. The original cities received only $350,000 from the DHHS contract, and about $300,000 in loaned equipment from DoD. There was no funding to support the staff time to take the training, either from the original federal train-the-trainer classes, or from the department-based follow-on training. The cost of overtime for staff training was actually one of the largest expenses associated with developing the MMSTs. For example, San Jose, California, invested over $1 million in local funds for staff overtime to train the police department in the first year of the program. Federal funds provided for planning and exercising did not cover any personnel costs incurred by the cities. In 2000 the original cities were provided with an additional $200,000 to support bioterrorism response planning and cache development,

some of which could be used to support staff time for those functions, but not for receiving training nor for participating in the exercises.

Following the antiwar bombings of the 1960s, and the women's health clinic attacks in the 1990s, many communities had developed bomb units, or Explosive Ordinance Disposal Units. These were most often placed in the police department, and often worked closely with active duty military units near their community. These units were brought into the MMST organization to search for secondary devices. A new level of training was required for the bomb units to cover the range of WMD/NBC agents. Because some explosive devices might be developed as dispersal devices for the biological or chemical agents, a new level of PPE was needed that would provide the traditional flak protection while also providing respiratory protection. The challenge of creating optics for both the self-contained breathing apparatus (SCBA) and the bomb-resistant face shield to provide a clear view for bomb dismantling resulted in the new dual suits being very expensive. Some communities were able to obtain funding for one or two SCBA bomb suits through the competitive DOJ grants, but others had to obtain the equipment at local expense. Cooling vests, extra air bottles, and other necessary accessory items usually had to be purchased at local expense due to grant funding limitations. The purchase of PPE for bomb dogs with federal grant funds was not originally permitted.

Most airports in the major cities of the United States are owned by local governments and operated under rules made by the Federal Aviation Administration (FAA). Since the hijackings of the 1970s, the FAA had mandated screening of passengers for weapons. Following the 1983 destruction of the Pan Am flight over Lockerbie, the security rules at airports became much more stringent. Federal requirements for security staffing increased, adding unreimbursed costs to airport operations. Passenger screening for parcels was implemented in the early 1990s. Later more stringent passenger screenings were begun, adding costs to the airports and inconvenience to the passengers.

Access to public buildings had become tighter after the murder of Supervisor Harvey Milk and

Mayor Muscone of San Francisco in the 1970s. Some buildings, including court facilities, used metal detectors and X-ray machines to screen persons and parcels entering the facility. Newer local government buildings were built with controlled access using proximity cards with readers tied to a computer system that recorded the name, entry, and exit time for each person. The added infrastructure cost was borne by local government.

FEMA had encouraged local communities to adopt the Community Emergency Response Team (CERT) program after the Northridge Earthquake of 1994. CERT, a 16-hour class series, emphasized the development of neighborhood-based emergency response capabilities that could provide immediate response in areas that were cut off from the community, or where first responders were unavailable due to high demands for services. Skills taught included home and personal preparedness, disaster fire suppression, household hazardous materials management, disaster medicine and psychology, and light search and rescue. FEMA paid for the expenses to attend train-the-trainer courses for city staff (but again not overtime for backfill), and provided the manuals for the community students who formed teams within their own neighborhoods. Other costs were to be covered from the EMPG funds, including staff teaching time and training materials.

In the late 1990s the MMST communities began to include terrorism awareness and preparedness information in the CERT program, lengthening it to 20 hours. The FBI provided a videotape for use with employees and the community. Shelter-in-place techniques were taught, and CERT members were encouraged to develop kits with materials to seal off their homes from chemical spills, smoke, or WMD/NBC attacks.

III. LOCAL GOVERNMENT'S RESPONSE TO TERRORISM AFTER 9-11

September 11, 2001, marked a watershed event in emergency management in the United States. The attack on the World Trade Center, the Pentagon, and yet another hijacked plane that was downed by its passengers, demonstrated a level of vulnerability that was unexpected. The response to this tragedy clearly demonstrated the importance of a well-understood emergency response plan; communications interoperability among police, fire and EMS; and a system for command and control that was well practiced. In most communities it is the emergency manager who is responsible for the development and exercising of the emergency operations plan. Emergency management was recognized as the lynchpin that holds together the diverse agencies that respond when disaster strikes.

Within a short time after the airplane-based attacks, letters containing weaponized[14] anthrax were delivered to news media and elected officials. Mail-handling facilities were contaminated, and secondary deaths resulted from mail sorting and handling.[15] Although FBI investigations pointed to a domestic source of the material,[16] no final conclusion was reached as to the sender or the motive. Initially assumed to be a domestic attack,[17] by the winter of 2003 new analysis suggested the possibility of an international attack.[18]

Physical and cybersecurity became keystones in the local effort to prevent terrorist attacks. Most communities developed a security department, either real or virtual, to evaluate the vulnerabilities of their community and facilities, and to recommend immediate and long-range fixes for the identified deficiencies. Brainstorming sessions brought together experts from police, fire, emergency services, general services, information technology, public works, environmental services, and transportation departments to review existing vulnerabilities and evaluate the cost-benefit of various mitigation techniques.

The tension between the need for public access to public buildings and the desire to protect people working in public buildings created difficult decisions. Some communities, such as San Diego, began stopping everyone at the city hall lobby and screening people and parcels with metal detectors and X-ray machines. Others chose to badge all employees. Some followed the high-tech industry's model of requiring a badge and an escort for all nonemployee visitors. Civil liberties issues were raised by employee groups when some governments proposed doing background checks

Table 5.1
2004 ESTIMATED ACCOUNTING OF HOMELAND SECURITY
COSTS SINCE 9/11/01 CITY OF SAN JOSE, CA

City Department/Area	Cost
AIRPORT	
Facilities, On-site Improvements, and Personnel	$13,000,000
POLICE DEPARTMENT	
Airport-related Overtime (unreimbursed)	$7,687,064
Training	$2,000,000
Equipment	$700,000
FIRE DEPARTMENT	
WMD Antidotes and Supplies	$128,000
WMD Task Force and Kits	$117,700
California Task Force 3	$72,000
Multiple Terrorist Response	$32,000
USAR Training	$2,000
OFFICE OF EMERGENCY SERVICES	
Emergency Planning	$75,000
Emergency Preparedness Training and Outreach	$50,000
Citywide Terrorism Response Exercises	$45,000
Safe Schools Terrorism Exercises	$55,000
Bioterrorism Tabletop Exercises	$20,000
Chemical Terrorism Tabletop Exercises	$20,000
Off-Airport Tabletop Exercises	$20,000
Hospital Personnel Decontamination Class	$1,000
INFORMATION TECHNOLOGY	
NIMDA Virus Response	$500,000
Internet Access/Filtering	$110,000
ITD Security Taskforce	$27,000
CMO Security Taskforce	$3,000
GENERAL SERVICES	
Building Access Control Systems and Alarms	$105,000
Employee ID Cards, Security Guard	$115,000
ENVIRONMENTAL SERVICES	
Water Pollution Control Plant and Muni-Water Utility Upgrades	$1,250,000
Total	$26,499,264

on nonsworn employees, especially those working on cyber systems.

The right of public access to city council meetings was evaluated as a factor in deciding that people attending public meetings could not be required to register or be limited in their ability to come and go from the meeting, such as through escorts. Police were then forced to develop plans for in-chambers surveillance of the audience and rapid protection of public officials during meetings. Public works projects were undertaken to separate the public portions of the building, such as the council chambers, from the business portions of the buildings where employees had some safety expectations. Back doors were locked, inconveniencing employees who were accustomed to easy access from the parking structure to their work location, or to outdoor smoking areas. Keys, access cards, and badges were issued at local expense. New buildings were designed with security in mind, including barriers to prevent vehicles from getting close to the building, air handler intakes in inaccessible spots, and access key-operated elevators to confine the public to specific floors. All of this costs money. (See Table 5.1.)

Federal agencies mandated some local government actions to prevent terrorist attacks on infrastructure. Airports were the first focus of new, and largely unfunded, federal mandates to local governments. In the first hours after the 9-11 attack all planes were grounded over American airspace. The immediate economic impact on local communities was staggering. Business travel stopped, causing all related industries to lose revenue. Local governments with airports saw sales tax revenues and hotel taxes drop significantly. Taxi services, hotels, and restaurants laid off employees. Airports lost parking revenue and airport terminal vendors were closed. When the flights were restarted the traveling public was flight averse for several years, perpetuating the economic losses. Some parking close to terminals was permanently closed. Only ticketed passengers could enter the gate areas, so vendors lost revenues from meeters and greeters, who began to avoid parking at all, and met their passengers at the curb.

The FAA created new regulations regarding screening of vehicles, passengers, and baggage at airports. New baggage screening machines were both costly and consumed significant space unavailable at most airports. Temporary shelters were erected at local expense, to be followed by new capital projects to provide permanent housing for the explosives detection and baggage screening equipment. New passenger screening machines and more stringent screening of carry-on items resulted in both a further consumption of formerly revenue-generating space, and long delays for passengers, making flying still less attractive.

Heightened airport security was visible immediately with armed and uniformed National Guard personnel highly visible at vehicle and passenger checkpoints and in terminals. Military presence at the airports was augmented by local police officers, and later the local police became completely responsible for security at passenger and vehicle screening points. Because there was neither time nor funding to enlarge the local police department to meet this demand, the cost of overtime soared. For example, in San Jose, California, the overtime cost of providing the additional police at the airport was $20 million from 9/11/2001 through March of 2003, barely 18 months.

The Transportation Security Administration (TSA), a new federal agency, was created in the wake of 9-11. Its goal was to develop a more efficient system of passenger screening based on a cadre of better paid, professional screeners at the nation's airports. Before 9-11 most passenger screening was performed by minimum-wage employees of contractors to the airlines, hired on the low-bidder system. Many screeners were not citizens and some spoke only rudimentary English. The new TSA hiring process required that applicants be citizens, and pass a background check and an English proficiency test. Yet more space was required at each airport for the mandated oversight staff of the TSA, including a TSA airport security director. In order to ensure thorough screening, additional metal detectors and X-ray lines were installed. After Richard Reed attempted to blow up his shoes aboard an airplane, shoe screening areas also had to be set aside. Airports developed most of this space by moving airport management staff off-site, and sacrificing revenue-generating vendor areas at terminals.

Bridges and tunnels were also required to heighten security of the critical portions of their facilities. Bridges were evaluated for weak points, which were then shielded or placed under surveillance. National Guard units were used to patrol critical bridges and tunnels. Surveillance of approaches and inspections of large trucks became routine. These expenses were paid for by the operating authority, usually a local government or a special district.

Mass transit systems were also required to evaluate their vulnerabilities and create mitigation programs. Air-monitoring devices to detect biological or chemical devices were installed in some systems. Surveillance cameras and security guards were added to other systems. Out-of-the-way areas like power generation stations and air handler systems were evaluated for shielding or heightened surveillance. Vehicle operators were given terrorism awareness training and equipped with better emergency communications equipment. Again the expenses were borne by the owner, usually the local government or a special district.

The EPA also created a security mandate for all providers of water service with more than three thousand customers. By mid-2003 drinking water agencies, both public and private, had to conduct a vulnerability study of all their facilities. They had to assess all risks to their facilities and make a plan for the mitigation of those risks. While all hazards were reviewed, the focus was on preventing tampering with drinking water services, rapid assessment of unwanted materials in the water, and prevention of the delivery of tainted water to consumers. The cost of both the vulnerability evaluation and report and the mitigation steps was borne by the water agency, frequently a local government agency or a locally funded special purpose government.

Hazardous materials users, including both private industry and public wastewater treatment facilities, received warning letters from local government emergency managers encouraging a heightened attention to security of the chemicals and treatment works. Businesses and operators added security guards, fencing, barriers, and surveillance cameras. Some wastewater treatment plants changed processes to eliminate the on-site storage of toxic chemicals, especially toxic gases.

IV. FEDERAL LEGISLATION'S IMPACT ON LOCAL GOVERNMENT HOMELAND SECURITY SYSTEMS

Presidential Decision Directive 39, "U.S. Policy on Counterterrorism, (6/21/95)" PDD 62, "Combating Terrorism, (5/22/98)," and PDD 63, "Critical Infrastructure Protection, (5/22/98)" laid the groundwork for the developing counterterrorism relationships between the local and federal governments. PDD-39 assigned consequence management to FEMA and crisis management duties to the FBI, thereby creating a planning relationship between local governments and these federal partners, as outlined in the MMST discussion earlier. PDD-62 assigned key health-related roles to DHHS, and PDD-63 broadly addressed the need to secure the nation's critical infrastructure, located in someone's local government jurisdiction.

On October 10, 2000, the president signed the Disaster Mitigation Act (DMA), P.L. 106-390, which embodied amendments to the 1988 Stafford Act. The two main purposes were to create a national program for predisaster hazard mitigation, and to streamline the administration of disaster relief. The act included funding to support the creation of predisaster hazard mitigation plans at the state and local government levels.

The goal of DMA 2000 was for every hazard-prone local government to develop plans to lessen the impact of future disasters on the community. Funds were to be used to inventory and map known hazards, including for the first time terrorism, and undertake a public education program to encourage private entities and individual citizens to join with local government in making changes. Future federal disaster reimbursements would be contingent on the development of the mitigation plans.

Although some funding was provided to local communities for creating the maps and plans, the amounts would not cover the cost of staff time to work on this federally prioritized program, delaying or supplanting work on different locally recognized needs. California communities selected to receive funding received $25,000 each, and were required to provide a 33 percent match, or about $8,000, to complete the program funding. This $32,000 would barely cover the cost of creating the multihazard GIS maps on which the plan was to be based. Although it can be argued that the community would benefit from the inventory and analysis of hazards, most hazard-prone communities are only too aware of the local hazards, and would prefer to use resources for CERT and other forms of public education to implement known mitigation measures rather than divert staff time to write another plan.

In January 2002 in his State of the Union message, President George W. Bush announced the creation of the Citizen Corps to offer Americans the opportunity to continue the community volunteerism that arose out of the 9-11 tragedy. The president invited people to become part of CERT, Neighborhood Watch, Volunteers in Police Service, and Medical Reserve Corps. These programs were often already in place in communities. The federal government would now provide funding to the states to assist with developing and improving these programs. A Citizen Corps Council under the sponsorship of a locally elected official would oversee the development of these programs.

Local governments with CERT programs in place were hoping for financial assistance with trainers' salaries, student materials, and student manual printing. Because the per capita funds were only passed through to the county in many states, the existing Citizen Corps programs often got no funding. Again the philosophy was that the communities with CERT programs in place did not need help, while those without programs did. As with the MMST program, the communities that had been active partners with the federal government got shortchanged, while those who had not made local investments were rewarded. Funding was diverted for the purchase of posters and generic fliers rather than being invested in staff salaries or student materials.

Competitive grants were also provided for starting Medical Reserve Corps. Interested agencies applied through the state, and DHS made the selections. Developing a Medical Reserve Corps requires creating solutions to a variety of complex legal, licensure, and insurance issues. Applications from public health departments that would be best equipped to manage these problems and ensure their integration with existing CERT programs were passed over in favor of nonprofit organizations with no experience managing licensed medical professionals. Senior citizens' clubs and faith-based groups were selected who used the funding for hiring consultants to try to make a plan. In most cases the first year's funds were completely consumed in trying to make a workable plan to try to recruit medical professionals, while never addressing the difficult issues. Second year funding went to similar groups. So far there are no successes, no functioning reserve units, nor even functional registration and use plans.

In March 2002, Homeland Security Presidential Directive 3 was issued that created the color code-based Homeland Security Advisory System. The intention was to provide a consistent method for interpreting to the public and government agencies the level of threat from terrorists that existed at a specific time. The color codes each represented a level of threat and an accompanying table of advice for actions to be taken by government agencies and the public. The American Red Cross created a set of public education materials with the focus on various elements of society: the individual, family, neighborhood, businesses, and schools.

The color codes also carried actions by other government agencies, such as TSA and the FAA.

The color codes probably had the greatest immediate and financial impact on local governments. First there were demands on emergency management personnel to make presentations on the code system. No training was provided to the emergency management community to meet these needs beyond the Red Cross materials on the Web.

Second, federal agencies mandated response actions to the various color codes that required additional local government staffing of key activities. The airports were required to limit parking when the code rose to orange, and to enhance public safety presence. Surveillance of key infrastructure and additional access control at public buildings were required. The cost of the related overtime and the loss of airport revenues were all the financial responsibility of the local governments. While homeland security funding was flowing for first responders, its use precluded the reimbursement of the out-of-pocket and off-budget expenses to state and local governments.

While color codes were announced without justification, local agencies had to simply comply with federal directives and manage through the financial burdens. The Orange Alert during the Iraq War was reimbursed through a special war appropriation. Data collected for that relatively brief period of less than one month demonstrated that increased costs for police and fire overtime alone exceeded $250,000. No reimbursement was available for lost airport revenues based on parking limitations, for the costs of critical infrastructure surveillance by civilian personnel, nor for the cost of heightened security around privately owned critical infrastructure, or hazardous materials facilities.

The initial color code was orange, and was then reduced to yellow, where it stayed until the Iraq War. After stating that orange and above would be regionalized and based on credible threats, the national level was raised to orange during the 2003 holiday season because of threats against Los Angeles, Las Vegas, New York City, and Washington, D.C. For most of the community the color codes have become the subject of jokes, and few individuals, families, or neighborhoods are any longer changing their behavior based on the color codes. Yellow is now perceived as normal.

The tragedy of 9-11 led to a reorganization of the federal government to create the new Department of Homeland Security, as discussed in Chapter 3. The Homeland Security Act of 2002, signed on November 25, 2002, provided the legal framework for the creation of the Department of Homeland Security. Several of the provisions had a direct impact in local government. First, there was no provision to provide funding for cities to be partners in the fight against terrorism, yet their cooperation and participation was essential. The bill structures the new relationships so that the federal agencies related to the states, and the programs and their funding would then trickle down to local governments as defined by each state. Significant lobbying by the National Sheriff's Association led to a preference to manage the local elements at the county sheriff's level, cutting out the nation's largest cities where the bulk of the population and choicest targets are located. The National League of Cities and U.S. Conference of Mayors began a vigorous lobbying campaign to help federal officials understand the vulnerabilities of the nation's cities and their need for dedicated funding for critical infrastructure protection.

Second, other provisions changed the legal relationships between local public health officers and the federal public health authorities. The anthrax letters of the fall of 2001 brought home clearly the crucial role of public health in terrorism prevention and response. Under the Reserve Clause of the Constitution,[19] vaccination and quarantine laws have been state-based regulations. The newly released draft of MSEHPA was introduced in state legislatures and adopted by more than half the states by November 2002 when the Homeland Security Act of 2002 was signed. However, some states refused to pass the model legislation, and others amended it to require informed consent to vaccination, and exemptions for medical and religious reasons.

Section 304 of the Homeland Security bill allows the Secretary of DHHS "to issue a declaration of health emergency after concluding that an actual or potential bioterrorist incident or other potential public health emergency warrants" the administration of vaccines or medications. The law provides for no exemptions and is expected to override state public health vaccine laws, which currently provide

exemptions.[20] This represents a tension between the Reserve Clause and an interpretation of the defense powers given to Congress in Section 8 of the Constitution. It also changes the powers of the local government public health officer, and may result in the imposition of federal authority at the local government level. Military involvement in the enforcement of the medical aspects of the Homeland Security Act is also possible.

The role of the military in preparing for and responding to a terrorist attack has been problematic since this problem was recognized. At the Hoover Institution National Security Forum in 1998 this issue was raised. Lewis Libby has suggested that while the military would be likely to play a key role in the response to any WMD/NBC event, the Defense Science Board study states that "legal authorities for a domestic military role in dealing with such contingencies (WMD/NBC terrorist attacks) are less well and less widely understood."[21] Deputy Secretary of Defense John Hamre has stated, "It's deeply rooted in American Constitutional democracy . . . that the Department of Defense only deals with threats outside the borders of the United States. If it's inside the borders of the United States, it is a law enforcement problem."[22] Warren Richey of the *Christian Science Monitor* has noted, "For nearly 125 years it has been illegal for any federal troops to be used directly in law enforcement actions within U.S. borders."[23] Governors have, and have used, the power to call out the state militias (National Guard) for assistance to local authorities in civil unrest.[24]

Local public officials still debate the proper role of local authority vis-à-vis federal authority in a WMD attack. Initial response will be undertaken by local first responders, who may not recognize the event as a terrorist attack for hours. Their first federal point of contact would be the FBI, who would investigate the attack as a crime. If the FBI determines that the event is a terrorist attack, they can request a Presidential Disaster Declaration, thereby opening to the community the Federal Response Plan assets. Regardless of federal actions, local police officials remain responsible for local civil peace regardless of the presence of federal officers. How would the tasks of responding to a terrorist attack be shared among the local, state, and federal partners?[25]

The events of 9-11 demonstrated that there is a role for each entity, but that the local authority must be, and be seen to be, in charge. As Mayor Rudi Giuliani noted about his role on 9-11 in *Leadership*, "I immediately devised two priorities. We had to set up a new command center. And we had to find a way to communicate with the people in the city."[26] The mayor's regular interviews demonstrated to the community that there was still order in government. "I assured people that I had spoken to the governor and the White House, that the city was being protected by our military, and that I'd observed the jets."[27]

Presently there are legal authorities that permit military support to civilian organizations,[28] and special Civil Support Teams (CST) have been created within the National Guard to provide for intelligence gathering on behalf of the DoD, and advice to local authorities, at WMD/NBC events.[29] Limits in the use of the active duty military inside the United States date from the post-Civil War era. *Posse Comitatus* Act (18 U.S.C. paragraph 1385) prohibits the use of military personnel "to execute the laws" except "under circumstances authorized by the Constitution or Act of Congress." This law has been understood at the local level to mean that the military will not be used as a law enforcement entity in a local community. However, because this is statutory limitation on the use of the military, it can be changed by Congress. However, Homeland Security Presidential Directive 5, section 16 suggests the possibility of the centralization of authority during terrorist events at the federal level. The National Response Plan is defined as ". . . for exercising direct Federal authorities and responsibilities, as appropriate."[30]

Some scholars have argued that existing statutes regarding the president's authority to wage war already modify the application of *posse comitatus* doctrine. For example, 10 U.S.C. paragraphs 331–333 was used in the desegregation of southern schools on the grounds of interference with the constitutional rights of citizens.[31] *Posse comitatus* may also not apply when a war or warlike condition exists on U.S. soil.[32] It is instructive to note that in Chief Justice William H. Rehnquist's book, *All the Laws But One: Civil Liberties in Wartime*, he endorses the doctrine of necessity in applying the military to the resolution of attacks: "It is neither desirable nor is it remotely likely that civil liberty will occupy as favored a position in wartime as it does in peacetime."[33]

Given these cautionary words, local civil authorities still do not anticipate the military supplanting local law enforcement powers. The Homeland Security Act of 2002 may make that assumption problematic in the area of public health. The new sweeping federal health authorities appear to be backed up precisely by the force of the military, marking a significant change in the balance of powers in public health between the local health officer, the states, and the federal health officials. And the enigmatic phrases of HSPD-5 (9) make clear the primacy of military and its chain of command when providing "civil support."

Section 501 defined the new role of FEMA as a part of the Department of Homeland Security. Included were the oversight of the MMST/MMRS program, as mentioned earlier, and the development of interoperability among first responders. This means that local governments can look to FEMA to assist with the sorting of frequency issues and spectrum problems. In the 1980s the FCC sold a significant amount of spectrum that had formerly been dedicated to public safety or amateur radio to commercial users, including pager and cell phone providers. This loss of spectrum creates significant problems in developing interoperable field communication systems. Local governments will benefit from having a single federal agency to advocate for needed changes to facilitate this life-saving capability.

V. ALL-HAZARDS EMERGENCY MANAGEMENT AND THE MOVE TO DHS

Postevent evaluations of the 9-11 attacks suggested that intelligence might have been available within the federal agencies that was inadequately analyzed and evaluated. At the federal level there was a desire to centralize the efforts of the diverse agencies that deal with various aspects of defense within the borders of the United States, with the goal of enhancing coordination and cooperation.

This entailed taking FEMA and incorporating it into a much larger new federal agency, the new Department of Homeland Security, whose creation is covered in detail in Chapter 3.

After more than 20 years of all-hazards emergency management, the local emergency management community was concerned when FEMA was moved to the Department of Homeland Security. For 20 years the professional emergency manager oversaw a program based on the four phases of emergency management: mitigation, preparedness, response, and recovery. Homeland Security seemed focused on only two phases exclusively: response, and a new fifth phase, prevention.[34]

A second concern was the inclusion of FEMA's well-organized program in the newly forming and evolving department. For the first year of the Department of Homeland Security's development it was unclear from week to week where former FEMA programs would be found. Funding for the traditional EMPG program was placed in the Border Security section along with all grant funds. MMST oversight moved from Department of Health and Human Services to Department of Homeland Security, and then from the former DHHS staff of the DHHS Office of Emergency Preparedness to FEMA staffers unfamiliar with the program's purpose and evolution.[35]

Terrorism awareness became a priority within local communities after the tragedy of 9-11. Local governments recognized that a local response capability was required to save lives. The MMST/MMRS communities increased the emphasis on training and equipment cache maintenance, while other cities began developing local capabilities on a regional basis, or in concert with statewide efforts. Terrorism awareness classes for public employees and for the community were offered to large audiences. While professional emergency managers provided guidance to the public on the development of home preparedness kits, vendors offered gas masks and pharmaceuticals of questionable value and appropriateness.

Well-meant directions from the Department of Homeland Security to stockpile duct tape for a shelter-in-place kit became grist for the humor mills on the Internet. Local emergency managers distributed more detailed information on developing and using a shelter-in-place kit, and the American Red Cross created terrorism-specific pages on its national public education Website. The structure already in place for distributing all hazards disaster preparedness information was useful in informing the public on terrorism preparedness. However, the message from the federal agencies seemed to be that terrorism was different, and the public began expecting unique or novel information on home preparedness. Professional emergency managers developed a strategy to integrate the new terrorism preparedness with the old all-hazards approach, pointing out that a chemical attack was a very bad hazardous materials event, and a biological attack was a very bad illness outbreak. This approach helped to calm the public, but it was not adopted at the national level.

The Department of Homeland Security provided some funding through FEMA channels to states to encourage local communities to add terrorism awareness to their CERT programs. They also provided planning funds to pay for updating the local Emergency Operations Plan with a Terrorism Annex, and a review of the Emergency Operations Center. These two important programs provide the paradigm of local government emergency management concern. The funds went from the federal government to the states on a per capita basis, but the funds were often passed along on some other basis, and often did not reach the first responders in the local community, but stayed at the county government level.

The Department of Homeland Security states that terrorism is to be added to the all-hazards approach to emergency management. However, the initial program conversions seem to suggest that homeland security will emphasize terrorism with the all-hazards approach in a secondary position. The Homeland Security Presidential Directives 5 and 8 suggest that prevention is to be the focus of local emergency management effort, a phase that applies only to terrorism and some technological accidents. Earthquakes and hurricanes are not preventable.

There is also a concern that the locus of responsibility may be shifting with the development of the homeland security philosophy. Under FEMA's guidance in the 1990s there was a strong trend toward the placement of the emergency management function in the executive branch of government, and directly under the chief executive. For example, FEMA Director James Lee Witt, formerly a local government official, had cabinet status in the Clinton administration. The state of California created the Governor's Office of Emergency Preparedness headed by a senior government leader, Bill Medigovich. The city of New York Office of Emergency Management is part of the office of the Mayor, as is the same office in San Francisco. The director of the Office of Emergency Services is a department head in the city of Los Angeles and the city of San Jose. These trends demonstrated that the role of emergency services was to carry out policy set by the elected officials, coordinating both uniformed and civilian elements of the local government.

While the Department of Homeland Security remains a cabinet-level department headed by Secretary Tom Ridge, formerly governor of Pennsylvania, the trend within states is toward placing Homeland Security within the law enforcement community. For example, California hired a retired FBI agent, George Vinson, as its first director of Homeland Security. New York City's Office

of Emergency Management is headed by a New York Police Department senior officer, John Odermatt. The result is a trend toward a law enforcement philosophy rather than an all-hazards approach to emergency management. The emphasis shifts to preventing terrorism and away from mitigating and preparing for all hazards. At the local government level this often translates to a law enforcement-dominated emergency management office, where mitigation is poorly understood, and nonterrorism hazards take a backseat to terrorism preparedness.

Although terrorism offers the possibility of terrible tragedies, natural hazards actually occur with distressing frequency. Recent American earthquakes have demonstrated the lives saved and property losses prevented through mitigation and preparedness programs.[36] Hurricanes and tornadoes demonstrate that retrofitting buildings and training the public saves lives. These seasonally recurring and cyclical natural events cannot be prevented and will recur. The greatest cost-benefit comes from maintaining the all-hazards focus within community emergency preparedness programs.

VI. FUNDING: PROMISES AND REALITY

The local emergency management program was, historically, supported by a combination of local and federal funding. The shift to the Department of Homeland Security has changed the way historically available funds are being allocated. The federal government seems to be eliminating all of the city/federal programs and replacing them with funds that have terrorism as its priority, and that are funneled through the states. Local emergency managers are naturally concerned that with law enforcement in strong leadership positions within homeland security at the federal and state levels, funding for law enforcement projects and equipment will get priority over fire, medical, and emergency medical projects. While public health departments have their own funding sources, the need to do joint planning and coordinated exercises may not be as clear to law enforcement as it is to fire and emergency management.

The most notable change is in the EMPG funding. This money formerly was channeled through the states to the local governments on a per capita basis. Communities could count on support for the maintenance of their emergency operations centers, their emergency operations plans, and their exercise programs to ensure local capability for response to the threats specific to the local community. Since 2003 all funds are sent to the states, and they determine the allocation of the funding among state agencies, counties, and cities. In 2004 it has been proposed that all grant programs be rolled together, potentially ending the historic federal support for emergency management at the local level.

Emergency management has always had a hard time competing against law enforcement and fire for local funds. Often the dedicated federal funding was all that kept local emergency - management offices financially supported. While the community appreciates emergency management after a disaster, its day-to-day role in preparedness is often denigrated because elected officials have found that emergency management support is not bankable at the polls. The average voter does not understand the role of emergency management, but they do understand the need for police officers and firefighters. Apparently the federal officials also fail to appreciate that without emergency management to coordinate the work of many city departments, the response to disasters would return to its previously fragmented pattern.

Another concern is the loss of the FEMA fire grants. Until 2004 communities could apply to FEMA for specific fire-related equipment and training, and receive 75% support for essential projects. Recently fire agencies have benefited from fire grants to improve personal protective equipment and communications system interoperability, important factors in terrorism response. After 2004 the FEMA fire grants are proposed to be rolled into the Homeland Security funding that is passed to the states. Individual states would then decide how to allocate these funds for a variety of homeland security programs. With the Department of Homeland Security's emphasis on law enforcement, the fire community is concerned that their needs may be overlooked, even though it is the fire service that actually responds to most of the natural and technological hazards that recur seasonally or cyclically in communities. And the role of the fire community in the 9-11 rescues will never be forgotten.

Finally, the COPS grants are also proposed for inclusion in the omnibus homeland security funding. These funds were first made available directly to communities to help fight crime through enlargement of the patrol force of the police departments. Later the projects were diversified to include various types of support equipment, including communication equipment for interoperability. Rather than respecting the right of the local community to evaluate its own needs and receive direct assistance, the program now changes the rubric from "all disasters are local" to "all disasters belong to the state."

The new system for allocating funds through the states has the probably undesired effect of punishing those communities that were the strongest partners with the federal government in the pre-9-11 period. Many of the MMST/MMRS communities invested significant local funds in staff overtime for training, and in sustaining the program during the years when they had little or no funding from DHHS.[37] The states are conducting local capability evaluations of communities and awarding funding based on gaps and needs. While this is laudable, maintenance of existing capability should have priority over attempting to create capability in communities that did not take the initiative to develop local resources when free training was readily available and grants for equipment could be accessed. These existing resources, such as MMST/MMRS, USARs, Bomb, hazardous materials teams, and other special units, are available to other, often smaller, communities through mutual aid at time of need. Allowing these resources to be eliminated due to local budget inadequacies while trying to create new units elsewhere is not a sensible use of scarce tax dollars.

The law enforcement focus is also obvious in the allocation of the homeland security funding passed through the states for 2003. (See tables 5.2 and 5.3) In Santa Clara county most of the funding was kept by the sheriff and the fire district chief. The only funds passed to local government were $550,000 for police radios for San Jose so their officers could participate in the new countywide interoperability project's frequencies. The MMST's request for $123,000 for pharmaceutical sustainment was denied.[38] The overtime funding included in the 2003 Homeland Security grants is under the control of the sheriff and not being provided to any local agency for use by any public safety staff. In Alameda county the sheriff kept all the funds. Thus, rolling the former FEMA and DOJ grants into the 2004 Homeland Security grant does not bode well for the needed sustainment and enhancement of local public safety emergency response capability.

Homeland Security officials justify the passage of the funds to the states on two grounds. First, it is the most efficient for the federal bureaucracy. They only have to write fifty checks instead of hundreds to individual cities. Second, it encourages statewide coordination and cooperation. The California experience cited here would suggest that experience has not borne out this supposition.

Table 5.2
HOMELAND SECURITY GRANT DISTRIBUTION
Through Operating Area Administering Authority–Santa Clara County As of July, 2004

State Funding Received Population: *	Total to Op Area: 1,731,422	Total to San Jose: 946,241	Percent to San Jose: 55%
FY 2001 State Domestic Prep Grant	$452,273	$0	0%
FY 2002 FEMA Supplemental EOP	$310,494	$110,000	35%
FY 2002 State Domestic Prep Grant	$733,168	$125,000	23%
FY 2003 State Homeland Security	$1,665,503	$0	0%
FY 2003 State Homeland Supplement	$3,927,836	$550,000	14%
FY 2003 EMPG Grant	$195,241	$75,919	39%
FY 2004 State Homeland Security (est)	$4,996,482	$30,544	.006%
FY 2004 EMPG (est)	$165,000	$64,350	39%
FY 2004 LETPP	$1,056,795	$127,000**	12%
Total to Op Area:	**$13,502,792**	**$1,082,813**	**8%**

The City of San Jose encompasses 55% of the total population of the County of Santa Clara and yet received only 8% of homeland security funds.
* State of California, Department of Finance, 2004, http://www.ci.san-jose.ca.us/planning/sjplan/data/population/e-5_2004.pdf
** Includes $112,000 in Red Alert reimbursement for December 2003 through January 2004

Table 5.3
HOMELAND SECURITY GRANT DISTRIBUTION BY PROFESSION
Santa Clara County
As of July 2004

Funding Received	Total to Law and Fire:	Total to Emer. Mgt:	Total Pub Health:*	Total
FY 2001 State Domestic Prep Grant	$452,273			$ 452,273
FY 2002 FEMA Supplemental EOP		$310,494		$ 310,494
FY 2002 State Domestic Prep Grant	$733,168			$ 733,168
FY 2003 State Homeland Security	$1,165,503		$500,000	$1,665,503
FY 2003 State Homeland Grant	$3,927,836			$3,927.836
FY 2003 EMPG Grant		$195,241		$ 195,241
FY 2004 State Homeland Security	$4,351,482	$145,000	$500,000	$4,996,482
FY 2004 EMPG		$165,000		$165,000
FY 2004 COPS/ECOMM	$4,660,000			$4,660,000
FY 2004 LETPP	$1,056,795			$1,056,795
Total to Op Area:	**$17,013,889**	**$ 1,148,903**	**$1,000,000**	**$19,162,792**
Percent of Total:	**89%**	**6%**	**5%**	

* Public Health also receives CDC and DHHS funding for Homeland Security external to these grants. It is estimated that Public Health received about $7 million in addition during this same period.

VII. URBAN AREA SECURITY INITIATIVE (UASI): THE FEDERAL/LOCAL CONNECTION–REVERTING TO A PROCESS THAT WORKED?

The USA PATRIOT Act, Public Law 108-7; Public Law 108-11 created the Urban Area Security Initiative (UASI) to "address the unique needs of large urban areas." In FFY 2003 the secretary of the Department of Homeland Security identified 30 urban areas deemed most at risk for terrorist attack. These urban areas were selected by a committee (made up of a cross-section of national leaders, including government and business leaders and the commissioners of professional sports) to be UASI areas. They used the C.A.R.V.E.R.[39] method of threat analysis to select the urban areas, with population only one factor. In some cases a major city was partnered only with its immediately surrounding county, such as Los Angeles city and Los Angeles county. In other cases the urban area definition was enlarged to include adjacent cities and counties, such as in San Francisco where the cities of San Jose and Oakland and the counties of Marin, San Mateo, Santa Clara, Alameda, and Contra Costa were included, along with the Golden Gate Bridge authority.[40]

The Department of Justice developed a secure Website where each of the participating communities entered data on its threat analysis, its current capabilities, and its needs or gaps. The participating jurisdictions and the state worked together to create a strategy for the enhancement of security within that community, based on the acknowledged threats. The strategy included specific goals to advance each element of the strategy.

Funding for each urban area was determined based on the threat analysis.[41] The urban areas developed governance that included the core city, core county and state that could vote on the final allocation of funds, an advisory committee representing the various professions concerned with homeland security, and a larger working group with representation from every participating jurisdiction. The goal is to ensure that there is a region-wide consensus on priorities for the enhancement of homeland security. The allocation of funds should support the priorities established through a consensus process, with the three-member voting body having the final allocation authority.

While the secret C.A.R.V.E.R. method seems to have unique features that skew scores away from population and economic impacts, and toward professional sports venues and heavy industry, the fact that the nation's largest urban areas have an opportunity to determine their own funding priorities is a step forward. Past federal/local partnerships, such as HUD block grants and the USAR and MMST/MMRS programs, have demonstrated a high degree of accountability and project success. In contrast, bleeding federal taxpayer dollars into state-controlled allocation programs without clear goals and objectives has not enhanced homeland security. Funds thus allocated have not reached first responders who actually rescue and treat the victims of disasters, whether natural or human caused.

The UASI program has been enlarged for 2004, adding some new communities and providing some differentiation in larger urban areas with unique subregions.[42] The 2004 grant announcement stated that the 2004 cities were selected based on "a formula that combines population, population density, critical infrastructure, and threat/vulnerability assessment."[43]

While this program has yet to spend any funds, the first year's deliberative approach appears to be a trend that would ensure future spending on more rational activities. Given the high correlation with the largest MMST/MMRS and USAR communities, the UASI program could generate the kind of coordinated strategy development and resource allocation that could truly result in enhanced homeland security for everyone.

VIII. THE FUTURE OF LOCAL HOMELAND SECURITY POLICY

"All disasters are local," as former FEMA director James Lee Witt often said. It is the local first responders and the local resources that save lives. Regional coordination and the development of regional and statewide mutual aid enable even small communities to meet their needs for security at a reasonable resource cost.

The future of homeland security has been mapped out in the Homeland Security Presidential Directives (HSPDs) issued since the beginning of 2003. These HSPDs provide guidance to the development of the new Department of Home-land Security and to its local and state partners. HSPD-5 marked the beginning of a national approach to local homeland defense. The purpose was "to enhance the ability of the United States to manage domestic incidents by establishing a single, comprehensive national incident management system."

The most immediate change from HSPD-5 is the change from the Federal Response Plan under FEMA as the instrument of federal response to disasters to a new National Response Plan.[44] This means that the separate plans for oil spills, nuclear responses, and similar specialized plans will now be integrated into one national plan under DHS, rather than scattered among a variety of agencies. This should make coordination easier for local government emergency managers who faced the problem of harmonizing the local response with a variety of uncoordinated federal programs.

The most troublesome aspect of the new NRP definition is the substitution of prevention for mitigation in the emergency preparedness rubric. Mitigation is only included in section 18, which applies to federal agencies. Natural hazards, and the damage they cause, in general are not preventable, but the damage often can be mitigated. Under recent administrations mitigation has been a proven benefit to communities (note Table 5.4). A national program to create "disaster-resistant communities" and "disaster-resistant universities" has proven its value in lives saved in earthquakes and hurricanes.[45] The loss of the term mitigation from the federal rubric also calls into question the role of mitigation overall in all-hazards emergency management. The DMA 2000 program has been extended to 2004 for document submission, and additional awards have been made for regional mitigation planning. Local emergency managers are left wondering what the expectations of the mitigation program will be by the time the regional work is completed in 2006.

A second major change in national emergency management practice is the introduction of

Table 5.4
SELECTED COST-BENEFIT DATA

Equipment Name	Replacement Cost ($)	Mitigation Cost ($)	Replacement Delivery Time	Replacement/Mitigation Cost Ratio
Non structural Retrofitting				
Blue M oven	1,000	27	4–6 wks	37
Lindberg Tube furnace	1,200	45	2–4 wks	27
Pentium 4, 1.3 GHz, 128 MB RD RAM with 15" monitor	1,287	66	5 days	20
HP Desk Jet Printer	750	11	1 wk	68

Source: Guna S. Selvaduray, *et al, Nonstructural Hazard Mitigation Retrofit of an Engineering Laboratory at San Jose State University*, 7th US National Conference on Earthquake Engineering, Boston, MA 7/21–25, 2002.

Deficiency	Replacement Cost ($)	Mitigation Cost ($)	Replacement Delivery Time	Unit Savings
Multi-Family Structural Retrofitting				
Tuck-under parking*	$45,000 per unit	$3,100 per unit	18 months post-quake	$41,900 per unit ***
Unbraced cripple walls*	$45,000 per unit	$3150 per unit	18 months post-quake	$41,850 per unit
URM–multi-family**	$45,000 per unit	$13,500 per unit	36 months inc demolition	$31,500 plus life safety value ****

Source: * Steven M. Vukazich, *Apartment Owners Guide to Earthquake Safety*, City of San Jose OES, 1998.
** City of San Jose URM Retrofit Program Report, April 1992 (updated to 1998 dollars).
*** Sixteen people died in the "tuck-under parking" Northwood Meadows Apartments after the Northridge Earthquake. (http://www.dailynews.com/Stories/0,1413,200%257E30561%257E1885379,00.html).
**** Six people died from URM failure in 1989 Loma Prieta earthquake (http://www.santacruzsentinel.com/special/specquake/quake8.htm); two people died from URM parapet failure in 2003 San Simeon earthquake (http://sfgate.com/cgi-bin/article.cgi?f=/c/a/2003/12/23/QUAKE.TMP).

the idea of a nationwide approach to emergency management command and control. In its first drafts the National Incident Management System (NIMS) was patterned after two systems in use for over 10 years in California. The first is the nationally recognized Incident Command System (ICS)[46] used by the fire service and taught at the National Fire Academy as the preferred method for command and control at emergencies and disasters. The Federal Emergency Management Agency has formally adopted FIRESCOPE ICS as the incident management system for federal disaster response operations. A number of other federal departments and agencies, including Environmental Protection Agency (EPA) and Occupational Health and Safety Administration (OSHA), have also adopted the FIRESCOPE ICS as their management method of choice.

The second is the Standardized Emergency Management System (SEMS), used in emergency operations centers (EOC) at the local, regional, and state levels in California. Based on ICS, SEMS brought the same concepts from the field into the EOC to ensure seamless coordination.[47] Government scholars have endorsed SEMS as representing "the most promising state-initiated program to enhance local capabilities." Features that were considered most significant included the development of substate regional coordination, the development of a disaster information system, and "the standardization of emergency management structures and functions. Whether these innovations diffuse to other states is a concern."[48]

HSPD-5 mandates the development of NIMS, "to ensure that all levels of government across the Nation have the capability to work efficiently and effectively together, using a national approach to domestic incident management."[49] While it is anticipated that California communities will be able to integrate the SEMS elements readily with the newly mandated NIMS, local governments in other states may find the application of NIMS yet another unfunded mandate. Local emergency response plans will have to be revised to conform to NIMS. Field-level operations plans will have to be coordinated with NIMS, and EOC staff will have to be trained to use the new system. The NRP and NIMS are discussed in much greater detail in Chapter 4.

HSPD-5 goes on to acknowledge that local and state governments retain principal responsibility for homeland security, and pledges the support of DHS for the development of appropriate plans and capabilities.[50] This commitment may guide the future of emergency management in new directions through the application of EMPG funding and mitigation program funding.

Clause 12 of the HDPS-5 mandates the collection of homeland security data nationally: "The Secretary shall provide standardized, quantitative reports to the Assistant to the President for Homeland Security on the readiness and preparedness of the Nation–at all levels of government–to prevent, prepare for, respond to, and recover from domestic incidents." The theme of developing measurable and attainable goals recurs in HSPD-8.[51] It seems clear that yet another version of the Capability Hazards Inventory Program (CHIP) will have to be created to accomplish this data collection. FEMA had been working on creating a new instrument called Capability Assessment for Readiness (CAR), but only the state version was released for review.

In an effort to encourage the standardization of emergency management readiness throughout the nation, FEMA entered into a joint venture with the International Association of Emergency Managers (IAEM) to create an evaluation tool. The result was Emergency Management Accreditation Program (EMAP)[52] that was used in 2003 for the first time. Florida and Washington, D.C., were the first two emergency management programs to be evaluated.[53] The EMAP was based on NFPA 1600, a tool developed by the National Fire Protection Association for use in businesses. Its applicability as an evaluation instrument for the effectiveness of government-level emergency management programs remains to be seen. However, Clause 12 would seem to support the application of EMAP.

Furthermore, HSPD-5 requires that, "The NRP will include rigorous requirements for continuous improvements from testing, exercising, experience with incidents, and new information and technologies."[54] While continuous improvement has long been the goal of emergency management, funding to enable the kind of change outlined in HDPS-5 has never been available to local governments. Homeland security funding streams will have to be specifically directed at developing and maintaining local government capabilities if this goal is to be realized.

The interim dates for the development of NIMS and NRP have passed, and various drafts have been circulated. The details of these documents remain a concern to local emergency managers, and the mechanism for the professional emergency management community to comment remains unknown. The evolution of these important documents should include an intentional participation by the professionals who must administer local- and state-level emergency management programs.

On December 17, 2003, HSPD-7 and 8 were issued to further elaborate the roles and priorities for homeland security planning. HSPD-7, which replaced PDD-62[55] focuses on the need to protect critical infrastructure from destruction: "Federal departments and agencies will identify, prioritize, and coordinate the protection of critical infrastructure and key resources in order to prevent, deter, and mitigate the effects of deliberate efforts to destroy, incapacitate, or exploit them. Federal departments and agencies will work with State and local governments and the private sector to accomplish this objective."[56]

Many communities contain facilities and materials that would make the development of WMD/NBC agents redundant. Since 9-11, local emergency managers have worked with law enforcement intelligence colleagues to develop lists of key facilities that require extra security during heightened alert status. The provisions of HSPD-7 would strengthen this effort, bringing to bear federal resources to ". . . identify, prioritize, and coordinate the protection of critical infrastructure and key resources with an emphasis on critical infrastructure and key resources that could be exploited to cause catastrophic health effects or mass casualties comparable to those from the use of a weapon of mass destruction."[57]

Local emergency managers have long worked with their counterparts in water, sanitation, telecommunications, information technology, and transportation to ensure the ongoing provision of essential services to the community even during disasters. The new federal program, which states an intention to develop infrastructure protection plans for specific sectors including these,[58] and emphasizing the importance of protection

cyberspace,[59] offers the opportunity to build on this existing web of relationships. However, without additional staff and funding for the needed mitigation work, this goal of national infrastructure protection will not be achieved. Again, federal funding could be targeted at critical communities and critical infrastructure to heighten both homeland security and the survivability of critical infrastructure after any disaster.

An important new initiative is the federal commitment to share information with state and local governments: "The Secretary, consistent with the Homeland Security Act of 2002 and other applicable legal authorities and presidential guidance, shall establish appropriate systems, mechanisms, and procedures to share homeland security information relevant to threats and vulnerabilities in national critical infrastructure and key resources with other Federal departments and agencies, State and local governments, and the private sector in a timely manner."[60]

HSPD-8 outlines the required "national domestic all-hazards preparedness goal, establishing mechanisms for improved delivery of Federal preparedness assistance to State and local governments, and outlining actions to strengthen preparedness capabilities of Federal, State, and local entities." It is defined as "a companion to HSPD-5, which identifies steps for improved coordination in response to incidents. This directive describes the way Federal departments and agencies will prepare for such a response, including prevention activities during the early stages of a terrorism incident."

During the hours after the 9-11 attacks the term first responders was used to refer to police, fire, and emergency medical personnel who had gone to the scenes of destruction to rescue and treat victims. It quickly became clear that this definition did not adequately describe all those professions that saved lives, both that day and historically. HSPD-8 offers a new definition: "The term first responder refers to those individuals who in the early stages of an incident are responsible for the protection and preservation of life, property, evidence, and the environment, including emergency response providers as defined in section 2 of the Homeland Security Act of 2002 (6 U.S.C. 101), as well as emergency management, public health, clinical care, public works, and other skilled support personnel (such as equipment operators) that provide immediate support services during prevention, response, and recovery operations."[61] This recognition of emergency management as part of the first responder community is critical to their maintaining a lead role in the development of future homeland security policies and plans. The inclusion of public works and skilled trades members recognizes their contribution to the rescues at the World Trade Center and Pentagon on 9-11.[62]

As an implementation document, HSPD-8 defines the delivery of assistance to state and local governments and first responders. This directive commits the federal agencies to timely delivery of assistance for preparedness and support for first responder preparedness for preventing and responding to major events.[63]

HSPD-8 also ties in with the UASI development of strategies, and the use of population, population density, and infrastructure when determining federal assistance for local communities. This consistency between HSPD-8 and UASI suggests both a concerted approach by the administration and a coordinated effort, which should lead to a more coherent outcome across jurisdictions: "Federal preparedness assistance will support State and local entities' efforts including planning, training, exercises, interoperability, and equipment acquisition for major events as well as capacity building for prevention activities such as information gathering, detection, deterrence, and collaboration related to terrorist attacks."[64]

IX. WHERE DO WE GO FROM HERE?

Future federal homeland security funding programs need to be developed with a more deliberative approach, based on clear goals developed from the HSPD-8 initiative. Even recognizing that there is a war going on and time is crucial, government must stop sacrificing sense for speed in the distribution of funding. Critical needs of first responders are going unmet as local officials develop spending plans designed for political benefits to themselves rather than meeting the needs of the residents of the nation's largest cities. Politics and egos have played a large part in the funding allocations since 9-11. Future allocations must be based on sensible, understandable threat and vulnerability analysis, undertaken in a confidential environment. This analysis must then become the basis for the allocation of scarce local, state, and federal homeland security tax dollars to meet the strategies developed and the articulated national security goals.

Dual use was a controversial local approach to homeland security in the early days of the MMST/MMRS program. However, it quickly became obvious to the six federal partner agencies that tools and systems with day-to-day applications would be more efficiently used in any response, including terrorism.[65] An Institute of Medicine study of the MMST/MMRS program deduced that "Communities that have strong systems in place rather than resources directed primarily at specific hazards . . . can respond better to unexpected events."[66] The development of these all-hazards systems is the key to emergency management success.

The dual use concept was eventually adopted by the DHHS in making the MMRS contracts. So DoD stopped requiring that communities accept Sarin detectors, and agreed that multi-gas detectors did the same job more effectively off the battlefield. The hazardous materials team would use the multi-gas detector at many local events, such as industrial accidents, and over time would become familiar with it and keep it maintained. A single-use item like a Sarin detector would get pushed to the back of the storage space, and its battery would die. When it was needed, no one would know where it was, once found no one would remember how to turn it on, and once the instruction manual was found the battery would be found to be dead.

This lesson should be carried over to terrorism response enhancement in the world of all-hazards emergency management. Funds spent on systems and equipment that will be used day to day, but that will also enhance response to a terrorist attack, are a better investment of scarce tax dollars. ICS and NIMS should be used at all events to enhance interdepartmental coordination at a local emergency event, and interagency coordination at the regional and wider levels. Improvements in public health, including childhood disease immunizations, disease surveillance systems, and public health education programs, provide a bulwark against disease, whether evolving from nature or created by terrorists. Regionalizing expensive specialized units like MMSTs and USARs, with financial support for the host agency, improves everyone's resource base without raising everyone's costs.

If emergency management is to be affordable into the future, the old all-hazards framework of mitigation, preparedness, response, and recovery needs to be retained. Prevention is just one form of mitigation that applies to a limited range of threats. The mitigation emphasis actually serves homeland security well, for, in fact, in an open society all terrorist attacks cannot be prevented. The lone suicide can always perpetrate an act of violence against others.

However, mitigation, including public education on surveillance and self-protection, and partnerships with the business community, can make the value of such attacks diminish over time. The Israeli example demonstrates that once the citizenry understands that the government is in control and prepared, a lot of the terror goes out of terrorism. In the end that is probably the best mitigation outcome of all.

X. CONCLUSION

The local government emergency manager is confronted with a series of competing demands, and a very limited source of local funding and federal assistance to meet those demands. Both the dual use and all-hazards focus help to stretch available resources to provide the broadest preparedness possible in a community. Federal assistance has taken two conflicting paths in the early 2000s. On the one hand the creation of the Citizen Corps brought together a variety of community-based volunteer opportunities with a dual use/all-hazards approach: Community Emergency Response Teams, Volunteers in Policing, Medical Reserve Corps, and Neighborhood Watch share an all-hazards focus. At the same time the emphasis on prevention of terrorism and providing equipment and resources to respond to terrorism cuts into the resources available for developing natural hazards response capabilities.

The homeland security effort has spread funding for equipment, and to a lesser extent for training, across the nation. However, $800,000 in heavy rescue equipment for two small towns outside of Dallas, Texas, and sideband sonar for Santa Clara county, California, with a 15-mile coastline of marsh and silt, seem unlikely to contribute significantly to either homeland security or disaster response. Emergency preparedness funding for all four phases should be focused on all-hazards capabilities. Unique equipment for specific disaster response should be justified based on local hazard/risk/vulnerability analysis. The focus must change from the postulated scenarios and once-in-a-lifetime concerns to the seasonal, annual, or cyclical damage that is the reality for most of the nation.

All disasters really are local. Securing the homeland means providing every resident with a sense of security against the hazards most likely to occur in their hometowns within their lifetimes. Washington, D.C., and New York City need a clear focus on terrorism as their worst-case disaster, but for the rest of the nation the greatest threat is still the cataclysms of Mother Nature.

RECOMMENDED READINGS

Drell, Sidney D., Sofaer, Abraham D. and Wilson, George D., editors. *The New Terror: Facing the Threat of Biological and Chemical Weapons,* Stanford, CA: Hoover Institution Press, 1999.

Federal Emergency Management Agency. "The Emergency Program Manager, IS-1." Washington, DC: U.S. Government Printing Office, 1993.

Giuliani, Rudolph W. Giuliani. *Leadership.* New York: Hyperion 2003.

"Homeland Security Presidential Directives 5,7,8," www.whitehouse.gov

Jenkins, Brian and Edwards-Winslow, Frances. *Saving City Lifelines: Lessons Learned in the 9-11 Terrorist Attacks,* San Jose, CA: Mineta Transportation Institute, 2003.

Kayyam, Juliette N. and Pangi, Robyn L., editors. *First to Arrive: State and Local Responses to Terrorism,* Cambridge, MA: The MIT Press, 2003

Manning, Frederick J. and Goldfrank, Lewis, editors. *Preparing for Terrorism.* Washington, DC: National Academy Press, 2002.

Mileti, Dennis S. *Disasters by Design.* Washington, DC: Joseph Henry Press, 1999.

Preston, Richard. *The Demon in the Freezer.* New York: Random House, 2002.

Rehnquist, William H. *All the Laws But One: Civil Liberties in Wartime.* New York: Knopf, 1998.

Sylves, Richard T. and Waugh, William L., Jr. *Disaster Management in the U.S. and Canada.* Springfield, IL: Charles C Thomas Publisher, Ltd, 1996.

Waugh, William. *Living with Hazards, Dealing with Disasters.* Armonk, NY: M.E. Sharpe, 2000.

Winslow, Frances E. "Planning for Weapons of Mass Destruction/Nuclear, Biological, and Chemical Agents: A Local/Federal Partnership," and Winslow, Frances E. and Walmsley, John, "Metropolitan Medical Strike Team Systems: Responding to the Medical Demands of WMD/NBC Events," in Ali Farazmand, *Handbook of Crisis and Emergency Management,* New York: Marcel Dekker, Inc. 2001.

ENDNOTES

1. United States, Federal Emergency Management Agency, The Emergency Program Manager, IS-1, Washington, District of Columbia, United States of America, U.S. Government Printing Office, 1993.

2. Richard T. Sylves, "Redesigning and Administering Federal Emergency Management," in Richard T. Sylves and William L. Waugh, Jr. *Disaster Management in the U.S. and Canada,* Springfield, IL: Charles C. Thomas Publisher, Ltd, 1996, p.7. Note Chapter 1 for an overview of FEMA's history and development.

3. Because the funds were disbursed to the states per capita, the percentage of the actual salary covered varied widely from state to state, with 100% available in Wyoming to less than 25% in California.

4. Initially the analysis was done by hand. In the 1990s several automated systems were used, ending with the Capability Hazards Inventory Program (CHIP). The data collected included the various hazards—natural and human-caused—and the population that would be at risk in each. For example, while the entire community would be at risk in an earthquake, only those living along waterways and in low-lying areas would be at risk in flash floods; or those downwind would be at risk in a hazardous materials accident at a fixed site.

5. The original Emergency Broadcast System (EBS) was designed to facilitate the immediate broadcast of messages from the president regarding a state of war. It was based on one key station in each community that would maintain specific equipment for the linkup with the president, and would hold periodic drills to make the public aware of the alert tone. This has evolved into the Emergency Alert System (EAS) that is an all-hazards broadcast capability involving all the broadcasters in the community. Access codes are provided to key emergency managers, and alerts, including crawls on television stations, can be triggered for community emergencies and disasters.

6. Presentation by Dr. John C. Yoo at the Hoover Institution National Security Forum, Stanford University, 1998.

7. The FBI guidance originally created in this era became an important training aid during the fall 2001 anthrax letters event. Poster available at http://www.fbi.gov/pressrel/pressrel01/mail3.pdf

8. This program is described on pages 114 and after.

9. Communities using the Incident Command System changed the name to Metropolitan Medical Task Force, because a strike team is a single resource, such as fire engines. A task force covers multiple skills and equipment.

10. Frederick J. Manning and Lewis Goldfrank, editors, *Preparing for Terrorism,* Washington, DC: National Academy Press, 2002, p. 25. See this resource for a comprehensive discussion of the MMST/MMRS program.

11. Manning and Goldfrank, p. 25–26.

12. For a complete description of the MMST program see Frances E. Winslow, "Planning for Weapons of Mass Destruction/Nuclear, Biological, and Chemical Agents: A Local/Federal Partnership," p. 677 ff, and Frances E. Winslow and John

Walmsley, "Metropolitan Medical Strike Team Systems: Responding to the Medical Demands of WMD/NBC Events," p. 259 ff, in Ali Farazmand, *Handbook of Crisis and Emergency Management*, New York: Marcel Dekker, Inc. 2001.

13. Under the Stafford Act paragraph 5170b. Essential Assistance (Sec 403), b., communities getting a Presidential Disaster Declaration could be reimbursed 75% of their eligible emergency response costs from FEMA.

14. Weaponized material has been prepared to be most deadly to humans. For example, the anthrax was milled to a specific size most easily inhaled and retained in the lungs of victims.

15. Guy Gugliotta, "Study: Anthrax Tainted Up to 5,000 Letters; Cross-Contamination Blamed for the Deaths of Two Women," *Washington Post*, May 14, 2002.

16. The anthrax material was identified genetically as a strain developed at the Ames, Iowa, research facility.

17. See Richard Preston, *The Demon in the Freezer*, New York: Random House, 2002, for a detailed description of the events of the fall 2001.

18. Bill Gertz and Rowan Scarborough, "Anthrax Terror," in *Washington Post*, December 26, 2003.

19. Amendment 10, U.S. Constitution.

20. Barbara Loe Fisher, "Power Grab by Federal Government Sets Stage for Forced Vaccination in America," National Vaccine Information Center, www.909shot.com/Issues/homeland%20security.htm, 2002, p. 4 of 5.

21. Lewis Libby, "Legal Authority for a Domestic Military Role in Homeland Defense," in Sidney D. Drell, Abraham D. Sofaer and George D. Wilson, editors, *The New Terror: Facing the Threat of Biological and Chemical Weapons*, Stanford, CA: Hoover Institution Press, 1999, p. 306.

22. *Ibid.*, p. 308

23. *Christian Science Monitor*, www.csmonitor.com, November 21, 2002, quoted at http://foi.missouri.edu/homelandsecurity/howwillthe.html

24. Paul D. Monroe, Jr., "Homeland Security and War Fighting: Two Pillars of National Guard Responsibility," in Juliette N. Kayyam and Robyn L. Pangi, editors, *First to Arrive: State and Local Responses to Terrorism*, Cambridge, MA: The MIT Press, 2003, Chapter 11.

25. Frances E. Winslow, "The First-Responders Perspective," in Drell et al., 1999, pp. 380–382.

26. Rudolph W. Giuliani, *Leadership*, New York: Hyperion, 2003, p. 6.

27. Giuliani, 2003, p. 16.

28. For a discussion of these see Monroe in Kayyem and Pangi, 2003, Chapter 11.

29. For details on the CSTs see http://www.globalsecurity.org/military/agency/army/wmd-cst.htm

30. HSPD-5, (16) (a).

31. Lewis in Drell et al., 1999, p. 318.

32. Lewis in Drell et al., 1999, p. 320.

33. William H. Rehnquist, *All the Laws But One: Civil Liberties in Wartime*, New York: Knopf, 1998, p. 224.

34. HSPD-5 changes the rubric. See the following discussion.

35. Homeland Security Act of 2002, Section 501, part (c).

36. Compare the relatively low loss of two lives in the Paso Robles earthquake of 6.5 magnitude on December 22, 2003, with the 28,000 dead in the Bam, Iran, earthquake of 6.6 magnitude, just days later on December 26, 2003. Even the Northridge earthquake on January 17, 1994, in the highly urban Los Angeles area resulted in only 57 deaths and 1,500 injuries. Mitigation steps such as building code enforcement and building retrofit account for most of the lives saved.

37. The original 1997 cities' contracts ended 9/30/01, and no sustainment funds were provided in FFY 2002. The FFY 2001 funds for most cities were $50,000, barely adequate to sustain the expiring pharmaceutical cache. As was mentioned earlier, all overtime for training was always a local expense.

38. While Congress required that the states pass through 80% of the funding to local government, each state defines local government differently. In California it can be the Operational Area, "all of the political jurisdictions within the geographical boundaries of a county" as defined in SEMS. Generally the cities provide all their own public safety services. The money was allocated to the states on a per capita basis. While San Jose is 55% of the population of the Santa Clara Operational Area, it received 8% of the total homeland security grant funding for 2001–2004, and this included the FEMA EMPG and Emergency Management funds that were distributed per capita, and the Orange Alert/Iraqi War overtime reimbursement that was based on actual expenditures.

39. C.A.R.V.E.R. is a classified method. It measures 6 factors to come up with comparative strengths and weaknesses between multiple sites. Its elements are: criticality; accessibility (to the throughout element); recoverability; vulnerability; effect on population; and recognizability as a target.

40. A list of 2003 UASI communities can be found at http://www.dhs.gov/interweb/assetlibrary/UASI_FY03_allocations.doc

41. Note that funding for airports is still allocated through FAA and TSA channels, and funding for

public health infrastructure comes through Centers for Disease Control and Prevention (CDC) and DHHS programs.

42. The list of 2004 UASI communities can be found at http://www.dhs.gov/interweb/assetlibrary/UASI_FY04_allocations.doc

43. http://www.cfda.gov/public/printfriendlyprog.asp?progid=1705

44. HSPD-5, (16).

45. Note footnote 36 and Table 5.2.

46. The Incident Command System uses five functions for command and control: command, operations, planning/intelligence, logistics, and finance. Further details and home studies are available at www.fema.gov

47. For a more detailed description of SEMS see Frances E. Winslow, "Intergovernmental Challenges and California's Approach to Emergency Management," in Sylves and Waugh, 1996, p. 120–121.

48. William L. Waugh, Jr. and Richard T. Sylves, "Intergovernmental Relations of Emergency Management," in Sylves and Waugh, 1996, p. 62–63.

49. HSPD-5, (3) and (15).

50. HSPD-5, (6).

51. HSPD-8, (6).

52. For details visit www.fema.gov or www.emaponline.org

53. http://www.emaponline.org/News/Accredited.htm

54. HSPD-5 (16) (d).

55. HSPD-7 (37).

56. HSPD-7 (8).

57. HSPD-7 (13).

58. HSPD-7 (15).

59. HSPD-7 (16).

60. HSPD-7 (28).

61. HSPD-8 (2) (d).

62. For a description of the role of transportation workers at the World Trade Center see Brian Jenkins and Frances Edwards-Winslow, *Saving City Lifelines: Lessons Learned in the 9-11 Terrorist Attacks*, San Jose, CA: Mineta Transportation Institute, 2003.

63. HSPD-8, (5).

64. HSPD-8, (11).

65. Winslow in Drell et al., 1999, p. 379–380.

66. Manning and Goldfrank, 2002, p. 38.

DISCUSSION QUESTIONS

1. Discuss the constitutional supports for the concept that all disasters are local. What roles in disaster response are covered? How might natural hazards events be different from terrorism?

2. Discuss the evolution of disaster response from a tornado watch through the community recovery from the disaster. List which local, regional, state, and federal organizations should be involved, and what role they play.

3. Federal funds are allocated to local communities by various methods, including per capita, block grants, state pass-throughs, and contracts. Discuss the relative benefits of each method as applied to emergency preparedness.

4. Discuss the relative importance of mitigation, preparedness, response, and recovery in emergency management. How are mitigation, prevention, and preparedness different? What is the current balance of effort and funding among the four phases?

5. Discuss the role of the emergency operations center. Why is it the key to successful emergency management? How does it support field services to the affected community? How does SEMS enhance this? What impact will NIMS have on EOCs?

Chapter 6

HOMELAND SECURITY INITIATIVES AND EMERGENCY MANAGEMENT IN METRO AREAS: THE PENNSYLVANIA PERSPECTIVE

LOUISE K. COMFORT

This chapter addresses the policy problem of integrating homeland security initiatives with emergency management policy and practice in metropolitan regions. As the events of September 11, 2001, vividly demonstrated, metropolitan regions are likely targets for terrorist threats. Yet, current emergency management plans and practices to support communication, coordination, and mobilization of resources for extreme events are least developed at the regional level. This chapter examines the complex issues involved in developing a regional approach to integrating homeland security initiatives with emergency management planning and practice for metro areas, using the context of Pennsylvania with its two major metropolitan regions, Pittsburgh and Philadelphia.

I. MAINTAINING SECURITY IN INTERDEPENDENT SYSTEMS

The challenge to public policymakers responsible for homeland security in metropolitan regions lies in recognizing the limits of their capacity to control a complex, dynamic public environment. This recognition compels them to build networks of collaboration and coordination with other agencies and organizations to detect threats and respond effectively to danger. This task requires skills of observation, communication, analysis, and integration that differ markedly from the traditional administrative skills of managing financial accounts and directing personnel performance. Uncertainty in political, economic, social, and cultural conditions at state, national, and international levels creates the potential for destabilizing actions intended to cause deliberate harm. Deliberate threats to security in metropolitan regions may not be isolated events, but represent a larger scheme intended to harm the nation or its global partners. Measures taken to reduce threats to security in metropolitan regions need to be set within a larger framework of action for maintaining security in a wider state and national context.

For example, interdependencies between the operating systems of any major metropolitan area–transportation, electrical power, communications, water, gas, and sewage distribution systems–may spread failure in any one system to failure across the set of systems, escalating a relatively minor incident into a catastrophic event. The interdependence among systems that creates efficiency under normal operating conditions is equally efficient in transmitting failure. As these operating systems cross jurisdictional boundaries,

---

Note: Originally submitted to the Special Session on "A Holistic Systems Approach to the Health and Management of Infrastructure," Workshop on Health Monitoring of Critical Infrastructure, Stanford University, Stanford, CA, September 14–17, 2003.

threats perpetrated in one state may spread damage to neighboring states. Security is a relative matter, and requires continual adaptation to incoming information regarding the degree of

perceived risk A design for enhancing security in metro regions needs to be integrated into the larger design for enhancing security in the states and the nation.

II. DOMESTIC PREPAREDNESS FOR EXTREME EVENTS

Concern for domestic security is not new. Three prior initiatives in assessing risk and developing strategies of preparedness and response capacity have contributed to the evolution of different perspectives regarding the most effective means to enhance domestic security. The three initiatives include:

- The Weapons of Mass Destruction training and education program for emergency responders initiated in 1998;
- The Y2K preparedness efforts in 1998–1999 to protect computational infrastructure that served not only public agencies, but also private and nonprofit organizations that perform vital commercial and community services; and
- The West Nile virus monitoring and tracking system implemented in 2000–2001 that involved health, agriculture, and environmental protection agencies in a systematic effort to locate and identify sources of contamination as well as to provide valid public information regarding protection from the disease.

These three initiatives each focused on different aspects of the problem of domestic security and evolved different approaches to assessing and responding to different types of threats. Consequently, the agencies that led these different initiatives, with their respective clienteles, perceived the problem of security differently and supported different strategies for risk reduction for the population and infrastructure of the state. Most public, private, and nonprofit managers, rather, are interpreting their responsibilities for increasing security measures in light of their own previous experience and perceived needs.

The first, and likely strongest, approach to enhancing security is that taken by the emergency response community. The Commonwealth of

Pennsylvania has been engaged since 1996 in a program of education and training in counterterrorism measures for emergency response personnel.[1] This effort continued under the Weapons of Mass Destruction program instituted in 1998 with the creation of nine regional task forces to counter terrorism in the state.[2] As the nine regional task forces have coalesced into distinct groupings of emergency managers and focused their attention on vulnerabilities in training and equipment, their primary concern has been the protection of emergency personnel in disaster operations and upgrading their equipment and skills to improve response to more dangerous types of events.

The second, and broader, initiative is that formed by public, private, and nonprofit agencies to upgrade the interdependent computational capacity of organizations that manage the operational infrastructure for an advanced economy and society with developed technical infrastructure. The partnerships initially formed during the extensive preparations to address the Year 2000 computer problem and are intersectoral. Working groups representing transportation agencies, businesses, banks, hospitals, schools, and community service organizations focused on strategies of action that identified interdependent relationships on a regional basis. Although public agencies exerted leadership in this effort, private companies were visible and strong participants in the partnership and nonprofit organizations such as universities, schools, and community organizations were also actively involved. The dominant perspective of the organizations that participated in these working groups was their focus on shared information infrastructure that enables the performance of interdependent functions in a technologically developed society.

The third initiative is that undertaken to monitor and inform public action in reference to the West

Nile virus health threat that first surfaced in Pennsylvania in 2000. The collaborative approach taken in the West Nile initiative is instructive, as it represents a systematic, scientific effort to collect information needed in order to base decisions affecting public health on valid evidence. Charged with protecting Pennsylvania citizens from the little-known West Nile virus, the DEP constructed a statewide geographic information system and established a monitoring system for reporting, accessing, and analyzing information regarding the observation of symptoms or indicators of the virus.[3] The appropriate use of information technology to tag, locate, and report evidence regarding the disease and its carriers supported the emergence of a multi-organizational response system to inform public

agencies, health institutions, and the general public regarding the appropriate actions to take to reduce risk of exposure to the virus, and after exposure, to learn what remedies were available. Key participants in this initiative included university research centers, hospitals, and commercial technology firms that represented a different group of organizations than those involved in first response operations.

Elements of each approach could be identified in the public debate regarding the agenda for emergency preparedness in Pennsylvania prior to September 11, 2001, but no clearly defined strategy was accepted collectively by all constituent groups. These three groups, each representing significant but specific interests in domestic security, operated largely independently.

III. HOMELAND SECURITY INITIATIVES AFTER SEPTEMBER 11, 2001

The traumatic events of September 11, 2001, crystallized the awareness of danger from deliberate attacks throughout the Commonwealth. Several actions were taken almost immediately after 9–11 to address homeland security issues within the Commonwealth. Other actions followed over the succeeding months, as the debate over priorities and funding allocations continued. These actions have framed the policy debate on homeland security in Pennsylvania in different ways, and have engaged or diminished the roles of constituent groups in this process.

A. Formation of the Pennsylvania Office of Homeland Security

When Mark Schweiker assumed the governorship of Pennsylvania on October 6, 2001, he quickly established the Commonwealth's Office of Homeland Security and formed the Task Force on Security to advise him on priorities for action. This task force, composed of thirteen members representing state and local agencies, was charged with assessing the current state of preparedness in Pennsylvania and identifying urgent needs.

The composition of the task force indicated the governor's initial perspective on security issues. Five of the thirteen members, or nearly 40 percent

of the total task force, represented emergency response organizations at municipal, county, and state jurisdictions, and David L. Smith, then-director of the Pennsylvania Emergency Management Agency, chaired the task force. The other members included representatives from state departments and the Public Utility Commission, but there were no representatives from the private sector or from the research universities and major nonprofit organizations of the state. The task force was asked to report its findings to the governor by November 19, 2001.

B. Report of Governor's Task Force on Security

The Task Force on Security submitted its report as requested.[4] The task force had reviewed the major areas of state action in reference to security, and offered a set of recommendations to the governor for enhancing the state's performance on security issues. Recommendations fell into four basic categories:

- Improving emergency response;
- Detecting and responding to attacks–chemical, biological, or cyber;
- Integrating radio communications systems;
- Training, education, and outreach.

The bulk of the report addressed issues in the first two categories. The third issue, integration of radio communications systems, focused on the technical aspects of communicating among the diverse radio systems used by state agencies, but did not address the equally difficult problem of integrating knowledge bases among the different state agencies to create a distributed electronic knowledge base regarding specific security issues for all state agencies.

Recommendations for training and education included a call to voluntary agencies such as the Red Cross and YMCA/YWCA to assist households in developing preparedness plans, but the task force focused primarily on activities to increase training and preparedness for first responders. Investment in training for different types of attacks was urged for immediate implementation.

The task force report, intended to serve as the basic document to guide state action in reference to homeland security, left several issues unresolved. The report did not clarify exactly what homeland security means, or how it differs from standard emergency preparedness and response activities. Key security issues such as intelligence gathering, sharing, and analysis received little attention in initiatives proposed for the state. With no clear definition of homeland security, officials at state, county, and municipal levels were left to interpret the term largely on the basis of their prior experience in emergency management and response.

Second, without a clear understanding of what actions constitute an increase in preparedness to meet security needs, there was little discussion of evaluating the initiatives to enhance performance of state and local organizations in reference to security threats. Without defined criteria for improved performance in security matters at municipal, county, and state levels of operations, actions taken are not likely to produce a coherent strategy at regional or state levels of operation.

Third, there was little discussion of the role of nonprofit or business organizations in the proposed recommendations, outside of a general exhortation to assist households and business organizations in developing emergency plans. These organizations represent a significant component of the state's intellectual and social infrastructure that could be mobilized to address security concerns.

The task force report provided a review of the Commonwealth's existing state of preparedness and offered a blueprint for areas that needed change. However, fulfilling the proposed set of recommendations on scant resources created a different set of problems for the Commonwealth, one that slowed action in meeting security needs and exacerbated already existing tensions among federal, state, county, and municipal agencies in terms of emergency preparedness and response.

C. Funding Issues and Budgetary Constraints

The initial expectation of Pennsylvania policymakers was that federal funds from the $29.3 billion allocation by the U.S. Congress for homeland security in the 2002 budget would be available to implement state, regional, and county projects. The 2003 budget request for homeland security was increased to $37.7 billion. State plans proceeded on this basis, and but were essentially put on hold, waiting for federal funds.[5] As months went by with little distribution of federal funds to support the recommended state actions, the homeland security agenda for the state began to falter for several reasons.

First, the slow economy resulted in a major shortfall of tax revenues for the Commonwealth of Pennsylvania. The state faced a significant budget shortfall in Fiscal Year 2002, and struggled to meet its basic commitments, excluding additional costs for homeland security measures. The state had pledged $200 million in expenditures for homeland security, but little more than $25 million has actually been spent. Security for the Capitol Complex in Harrisburg was upgraded at a cost of $18 million, but other recommendations for upgrades in equipment and training for emergency personnel have been deferred.

In June 2003, nearly twenty months after 9-11, more than $14 million of the expected federal funding arrived in the state.[6] During the waiting period, federally announced emergency alerts required the deployment of emergency response personnel to protect critical facilities such as nuclear plants. These requirements placed heavy burdens on county and municipal jurisdictions that were already coping with major budget deficits. As budget deficits mounted for county and municipal jurisdictions, regional policies were put on hold.

D. Search for Workable Strategies Within Constraints

Workable strategies that increase security at less cost is a continuing issue for metro regions. In many agencies, the process of reviewing existing policies and practices has resulted in more thoughtful allocation of time and resources, which has enhanced monitoring procedures and analysis of data for security purposes. While this effort is beneficial, it has been carried out on a voluntary basis and has not had the systematic effect of a rigorous, statewide program. State funds have now been released to the regional working groups, counties, and municipalities, but the amount does not meet the actual need.[7]

E. Continuing Debate Over Priorities for Action

The scarcity of funding available for domestic security initiatives from federal and state sources has fostered a continuing debate over priorities for action. Governor Schweiker assigned first priority to upgrading training and equipment for emergency response personnel,[8] but the financial costs for this strategy are high. In contrast, a small but significant group of agency personnel, university researchers, and executives from private organizations have recommended making investments in information technology, where small amounts of resources would achieve significant gains in desired security functions. The argument is that well-placed improvements in information technology would lessen the risk of having to use more expensive equipment and training. This approach would rely on information technology as its primary vehicle for organizational learning, and would use this technology to increase speed, reliability, and access to information for organizations that are responsible for monitoring threats to the community.

IV. OBSTACLES, DILEMMAS, AND OPPORTUNITIES FOR ENHANCING SECURITY

The policies and practice for increasing domestic security in Pennsylvania are still evolving. Yet, the experience of state practice to date suggests that a number of obstacles, dilemmas, and opportunities will characterize this process. How these conditions are defined and what actions are taken to meet them will shape the future of homeland security in the metropolitan regions of the state, and will likely affect the alternatives for neighboring states as well. These conditions are interdependent, and actions taken in reference to overcome an obstacle may well exacerbate a dilemma or thwart an opportunity.

A. Obstacles

Three major obstacles are likely to hinder the development of a coherent policy of homeland security in metropolitan regions:

- The lack of funding to support the initiatives in developing the infrastructure and training needed for a comprehensive, integrated, multiorganizational approach to conducting the detailed vulnerability assessments at organizational and jurisdictional levels.
- Even with sufficient funding, developing a common regional approach will require major shift in agency perspectives and problem-solving strategies.
- The lack of a well-developed information infrastructure, particularly at county and municipal jurisdictions, inhibits the learning process that is essential to mobilizing regional education and training programs for homeland security. Until this investment is made, it will be difficult to achieve the horizontal as well as vertical integration of information that is essential for a multiorganizational response to security threats.

B. Dilemmas

Three dilemmas are critical to the emergence of a clear, coherent policy for security and the capacity of the state to manage its own risk. The first dilemma is the tension between the emergency management community and the small but significant group that represents the intelligence and analysis approach. Exacerbated by budget shortfalls and late distribution of federal funds, the clash in priorities and practice will be critical to developing an integrated approach to security measures.

The second dilemma is that granting a higher priority to either approach over the other will not only set back the development of the alternative, but also hinder the advancement of the approach given priority. Performance in both emergency management and intelligence gathering and analysis would suffer, if one is developed separately or in a more advanced form than the other.

The third dilemma is determining where the locus of authority should lie among the jurisdictions. The emergency management community asserts that the locus of authority should lie at the municipal level, a bottom-up approach. The intelligence community, however, seeks to develop a comprehensive view of threat across the Commonwealth. While not exactly "top down," this view represents a macro perspective that acknowledges communities exposed to greater risk require greater investment, while others exposed to lesser risk might achieve an acceptable level of security with less investment of resources.

C. Opportunities

The interaction among the participating groups has generated new opportunities as well. These opportunities need to be recognized, understood, and accepted before they can actually be realized in action. If grasped, they represent a means of overcoming the obstacles and resolving the dilemmas. If missed, they set the process of developing a coherent strategy for homeland security back another step, sending the process off on a different trajectory.

The most critical opportunity is to use well-designed information technology to bridge the emergency management and intelligence communities. Defining homeland security as a regional problem requires both a well-developed capacity for first response and an advanced capability to detect, identify, and communicate risk for multiorganizational response. The problem of security can only be solved by informed coordination among public, private, and nonprofit organizations.

The second opportunity is to use information technology as a vehicle to support the detailed tasks of risk assessment, inventory of existing equipment and databases, classification of existing emergency plans, jurisdictional policies, organizational practices, and performance criteria. Managing risk via multiorganizational response both reduces cost and shifts responsibility to a wider community in sharing the burden as well as mobilizing action.

Third, knowledge acquired through the assessment of hazards and vulnerabilities for the region represents an opportunity to develop models of potential demand and compare it against models of known capacity, drawing upon the inventory of equipment, personnel, training, and criteria for performance for the region. It would mean accepting shared responsibility for performance among the participating organizations and commitment to a common goal.

The interdependence of the obstacles, dilemmas, and opportunities that characterize the still evolving practice of homeland security requires an adaptive approach to this complex set of interacting organizations and conditions. Traditional hierarchical approaches to managing risk in this dynamic environment are almost certain to fail. Developing sociotechnical networks that support interaction among organizations at different levels of responsibility and authority would provide a framework for monitoring, action, feedback, and adjustment in practice needed to adapt to changes in the degree of exposure to risk.

V. AN EMERGING STRATEGY FOR HOMELAND SECURITY

In the 20 months since the traumatic events of September 11, 2001, a strategy is emerging that appears promising for metro regions in Pennsylvania and other states. The details of this strategy are still being defined, but the outline appears strong. Four main elements appear to characterize this emerging strategy:

1. Regional task forces that group counties and cities into geospatial units for preparedness

activities such as risk assessment, training, and exercises;

2. priority given to improving the response capacity of emergency personnel;

3. recognition that information technology offers a means of improving performance of emergency personnel, along with training and equipment; and

4. acknowledgment that a learning strategy constitutes a fundamental approach to managing risk in uncertain environments.

Threats to the security of the population and infrastructure of metropolitan regions will continue, if not from acts of deliberate disaster, then from natural and technological hazards. Developing strategies of monitoring and managing such risks, as well as the technical and organizational infrastructure to support rapid, effective action when they occur, is a fundamental responsibility of governance. To date, tasks of intelligence gathering, analysis, and sharing are least developed at the regional level, but are the most critical for rapid advance in preparedness for emergency personnel and the public at large.

Managing shared risk is an ongoing process, and one that must be monitored by an informed and concerned citizenry. To the extent that metro regions can develop a common framework for addressing hazards–deliberate, natural, and technological–it will achieve greater efficiency and effectiveness. This strategy implies a flexible, adaptive approach to managing risk in a complex, interdependent environment that includes public, private, and nonprofit organizations.

ENDNOTES

1. United States Congress. Public Law 104–201. *Defense Against Weapons of Mass Destruction Act of 1966 and National Defense Authorization Act for Fiscal Year 1997*, September 23, 1996. Volume 110, Statutes at Large, p. 2422.

2. White House. 1998. Presidential Decision Directive-62, "Protection Against Unconventional Threats to the Homeland and Americans Overseas." May 22.

3. Conrad, Eric R. 2002. "Developing Digital Neural Networks for Worldwide Disease Tracking and Prevention." Harrisburg, PA: Department of Environmental Protection.

4. The final report of the governor's Task Force on Security is available through the PA PowerPort at www.state.pa.us. Using key word: "Homeland Security."

5. *The New York Times*, New York, NY. Feb. 13, 2003, p. A1.

6. Pennsylvania Emergency Management Agency. 2003. "PEMA Director Announces Federal Grant Awards to Nine Counter Terrorism Task Forces." Available at www.state.pa.us. Using key word: "Homeland Security." Accessed on August 12, 2003.

7. Lav, Iris J. 2002. "State Fiscal Conditions Continue to Deteriorate: Federal Assistance Badly Needed." Center on Budget and Policy Priorities. http://www.cbpp.org/9/20/02sfp.htm

8. Pennsylvania Office of Homeland Security. 2002. Creating a Secure Homeland: A Report on Pennsylvania's Progress. November 22. www.homelandsecurity.state.pa.us/homelandsecurity/cwp/view.asp

DISCUSSION QUESTIONS

1. Describe the challenge to domestic security in terms of current threats to regional, national, and global security.

2. What was the state of domestic preparedness in Pennsylvania against threats of deliberate actions to harm its citizens and infrastructure before September 11, 2001?

3. What were the major actions taken in Pennsylvania to define a policy for homeland security after September 11, 2001? What was its state of implementation as of the writing of this chapter?

4. Perform research to determine your state's approach to homeland security on a regional

basis. Compare it to that of Pennsylvania as described in this chapter.

5. Identify the major obstacles, dilemmas, and vulnerabilities that confront policymakers as they seek to balance actions to counter security threats against protection for civil liberties.

6. Assess the emerging strategy for homeland security in metropolitan regions. What barriers exist to creating regional approaches to homeland security challenges?

7. What do you see as the best way for metro regions to achieve greater efficiency and effectiveness in homeland security measures?

8. How can metro regions develop an intergovernmental learning strategy and a common framework for addressing hazards–deliberate, natural, and technological? What steps do you suggest to facilitate such an approach?

The US Army Corps of Engineers (USACE) assist in the logistics of generator, ice, water distribution throughout Virginia. FEMA Photo by Melissa Ann Janssen.

Section III

PARTNERING FOR HOMELAND SECURITY

Chapter 7

NEW PARTNERSHIPS FOR HOMELAND SECURITY POLICY DEVELOPMENT AND APPLICATION: GOVERNMENT, PRIVATE SECTOR, AND HIGHER EDUCATION

MONICA TEETS FARRIS

The tragic events of September 11, 2001, emphasized to all Americans the necessity of protecting our homeland against potential terrorist acts. To meet this challenge, various entities are partnering with the goals of improving coordination and most effectively managing resources throughout the United States. The Homeland Security Act of 2002, signed on November 25, 2002, tasks the Department of Homeland Security (DHS) with the following mission: Protect the United States from further terrorist attacks, reduce our vulnerability to terrorism, and minimize the damage from possible terrorist attacks and natural disasters (Haddow & Bullock, 2003, p. 213). This mission requires cooperation among many federal agencies that previously worked independently. Agencies such as the Federal Emergency Management Agency (FEMA), the U.S. Customs Service, Immigration and Naturalization, and the National Domestic Preparedness Office, just to name a few, are now positioned to collaborate under the umbrella of DHS (for more information see the U.S. Department of Homeland Security Strategic Plan found at www.dhs.gov).

In addition to the newly formed federal partnerships resulting from the Homeland Security Act, hazard researchers argue that for our society to be strong and resilient, partnerships must also be forged with entities such as universities, private businesses, and community-based organizations (28th Annual Hazards Research and Applications Workshop, 2003). One such collaborative endeavor is the subject of this chapter. Specifically, it is a partnership comprised of a local government, a university, and a private business. Arguably partnerships such as this are the result of many changes that have recently taken place including various shifts evident in disaster management strategies and technological advances that provide a connection between these entities (Disaster Preparedness Resources Centre, 1998; Miletti, 1999; Pine, 2004).

I. SHIFTS IN DISASTER MANAGEMENT STRATEGIES

Per Salter (cited in Disaster Preparedness Resources Centre, 1998, p. 179), many shifts in disaster management strategies have taken place, including a shift from government being reactive to proactive, from a single agency approach to partnerships, from a single science-driven to

---

Note: Preparation of the manuscript was supported through an EDI/Special Project Grant: B-01-SP-LA-029 from the U.S. Department of Housing and Urban Development (HUD) and the Center for Hazards Assessment, Response, and Technology (CHART), University of New Orleans. The author would also like to acknowledge Dr. Shirley Laska for her invaluable comments relating to this work.

a multidisciplinary approach, from planning and communicating *to* communities to planning and communicating *with* communities.

The shift from a reactive approach to a proactive one allows the aspects of planning and mitigation to become the focus of disaster policy. Historically, the focus has been on response and recovery. We are now seeing government and private industry promoting the benefits of mitigation policies and community planning (Pearce, 2003; Schapley & Schwartz, 2001).

A shift from a single science-driven approach to a multidisciplinary one emphasizes the need for various perspectives to be represented in disaster management policies. In fact, researchers have illustrated the importance of considering various dimensions of hazards including economics, social sciences, public administration, and various technical and professional fields such as engineering and law when developing hazard-related policies. For instance, researchers have found that factors such as social influences, relationships, and social networks have a significant influence on certain aspects of emergency management including decisions to evacuate and the processing of threat warnings (Riad, Waugh, & Norris, 2001; Perry, Lindell, & Greene, 1981; Drabek, 1997). It has also been demonstrated that socioeconomics influence how certain communities are impacted by disasters (Pinkowski, 2001; Bullard, 1994; Phillips, 1990). Effective land use and planning lessen the likelihood of certain areas becoming hazardous sites and the impact of potential events (Pinkowski, 2001). As multiple societal aspects influence disaster management policies, partnerships of experts with varying perspectives would arguably be most valuable in developing policies.

Another change found in disaster planning focuses on including the public in the planning and response process contrary to the traditional view of the public as a problem to be managed. Over the years, disaster researchers have emphasized the need for public involvement (28th Annual Hazards Research and Applications Workshop, 2003; Pearce, 2003). Specifically, it is increasingly recommended that government officials should include communities in planning efforts and maintain constant communication lines with communities at all stages of disaster management (Pearce, 2003; Miletti, 1999; Newport & Jawahar, 2003). Miletti argues that it is important for "local

resilience and responsibility" to be stressed and that community planning and public participation must be considered to accomplish this (1999, p. 2). Since the events of 9-11, the concept of involving the public in disaster management has received renewed attention in policy development.

Pearce (2003) argues that involving communities during the planning stages increases the likelihood of emergency management officials actually finding solutions that are reasonable and will be supported by the citizenry. Emergency management that emphasizes community involvement is exemplified in the emergency management plans developed for individual neighborhood clusters with input of citizens in Washington, D.C. (See http://dcema.dc.gov for individual plan details).

To increase the level of security, government policies have actually encouraged the involvement of citizens. An example of government policy supporting community involvement is the establishment of Citizen Corps. Citizen Corps, a major component of the USA Freedom Corps initiated by President George W. Bush in 2002 in response to 9-11, was developed to assist in the coordination of community volunteer programs and to provide opportunities for citizens to volunteer in various programs to make their communities safer (for more information on this program see www.citizencorps.gov).

Project Impact (U.S. Fire Administration, 2004)[1] also exemplified government policy that encouraged private and public partnerships at the local level with an emphasis on community involvement. The Project Impact initiative provided funding to 250 communities designated by FEMA with the goal of creating "disaster-resistant communities." The funds granted by this project allowed for the establishment of various community-based mitigation projects including hazard identification, risk assessments, structural mitigation, and activities that support public/private partnerships and/or public education. This project not only emphasized the importance of collaborations among the public and private sectors but also among federal agencies as demonstrated by the technical assistance provided to Project Impact by the National Oceanic and Atmospheric Association (NOAA) and the U.S. Geologic Survey (USGS). Furthermore, Project Impact also relied heavily on a private company for Geographical Information Systems (GIS) support (see CFDA 83.551 for details on Project Impact).

II. CHANGES IN TECHNOLOGY

With the merging of computing and telecommunication technologies, "intelligent cities" are being created across the United States. Within these cities, technologies like geographic information systems and wireless networks allow departments, like emergency management and planning and fire and police that traditionally acted alone, to collaborate with other departments. Departments such as these are now becoming dependent on each other for information vital to their planning and operation efforts. Additionally, for these intelligent cities to be successful, research recommends that government officials must not only focus on coordinating individual agencies and departments but must also foster relationships with nongovernmental entities such as the community and the private sector (Stanley & Waugh, 2001).

Overall, advances in technology have also led to a "greater interconnectedness" of government, private business, and not-for-profit agencies (Pine, 2004, p. 1). Pine (2004) argues that this "interconnectedness" will eventually lead to changes in the traditional boundaries of these once distinct groups. As the connectivity becomes easier, these groups will examine the potential advantages of partnering with another. Of course, one of the greatest benefits of establishing new partnerships is the potential for maximizing available resources.

III. PARTNERSHIPS WITH UNIVERSITIES

Considering the shifts in disaster management, technological advances, and the strengths of universities, increasing numbers of partnerships between universities and government agencies are to be expected. Research facilities including those found at the University of California, University of Colorado at Boulder, the University of Delaware, Florida International University, the University of Illinois, and Texas A & M University have developed vast expertise in natural and technological hazards. Researchers at such universities argue that terrorism should be managed as another hazard to be added to the list of hazards already being examined by these research facilities as part of an all-hazard approach. Hence, methods used to manage threats from natural and technological hazards may be applied to the threats posed by terrorism (Waugh, 2001). In fact, a multihazard approach is recommended over a single hazard approach. Recommendations made over a decade ago suggested that emergency managers take advantage of the commonalities found among emergency functions related to various hazards to meet their objectives (McLoughlin, 1985). The value of the all-hazards approach is now being echoed with a renewed strength (Workshop on Emergency Management in the Homeland Security Environment, 2003).

Universities have also had the distinct ability to serve their communities while at the same time serving their states and the federal government. Academic institutions accomplish this in various ways including acting as repositories for numerous funds related to federal economic and social investment. As a result of the billions of dollars in funding that universities receive from various federal agencies, their research has contributed a significant amount to American progress evident in many areas including hazard research (Comerio, 2000). For instance, in 2002, the Louisiana Veterinary Medical Diagnostic Laboratory (LVMDL) at Louisiana State University School of Veterinary Medicine was one of 14 state diagnostic labs funded by the U.S. Department of Agriculture (USDA) to create an animal health network to enhance homeland security efforts in the animal industry in hopes of protecting economic impact of this industry (www.lsu.edu). This particular grant exemplifies the notion that ongoing federal support creates facilities that are ready to respond to specific societal needs including increased security.

Collaborations between universities and the government help to connect research findings to the actual practice of emergency management. Thus, best practices and theories developed may be applied to disaster management in terms of policy development, operations, and administration. The participation of a university facilitates a more systematic approach to disaster management and allows research to support the operations of emergency management (Britton, 1999). Additionally, the practice of linking academic research to the practice of emergency management has led emergency management to be considered a subject of college-level classes, degree programs, and professional certificates (Britton, 1999). Arguably, this fact has contributed to the professionalization of emergency management.

In fact, the importance of the academic community to homeland security efforts has been supported by government policy as exemplified by the DHS initiative of establishing university-based Homeland Security Centers of Excellence. The department's plan is to create a university-based system comprised of the nation's best scholars in various homeland security-related disciplines to aid in their efforts of protecting the nation in its fight against terrorism. The first of these centers is being established at the University of Southern California (U.S. Department of Homeland Security, 2003).

Moreover, DHS-FEMA has also established the Disaster Resistant University program (DRU). The goal of this program is to assist universities in developing a hazard mitigation program in hopes of reducing risk to students, faculty, staff, and physical assets. The requirements of this program actually encourage partnerships among university and community stakeholders (e.g., local, state, and federal government agencies, nonprofit agencies and the private sector) (see "Building a Disaster-Resistant University," August 2003, FEMA).

Universities play a significant role in their respective communities and have a responsibility to educate their communities. Universities bring this mission and the experience of providing information and training to any collaboration. In fact, the Office of Domestic Preparedness (ODP) relies on the National Domestic Preparedness Consortium (NDPC) to identify, develop, test, and provide training to state and local emergency responders. The NDPC includes three university-based facilities housed at Louisiana State University, New Mexico Tech, and Texas A&M University in addition to two federal facilities, ODP's Center for Domestic Preparedness in Anniston, Alabama, and the Department of Energy's Nevada Test Site (see http://www.ojp.usdoj.gov/odp/training.htm for more details).

IV. PARTNERING WITH PRIVATE INDUSTRY

The strength of partnerships has been clearly recognized by researchers since the government at the federal and state level began partnering with universities. These partnerships are now expanding to include local governments and other stakeholders including the private sector. As an integral part of any community, it is suggested that private businesses must be included in partnerships formed with the goal of increasing the strength and resilience of society (28th Annual Hazards Research and Applications Workshop, 2003).

Indeed, many researchers have argued the importance of collaborating with the private sector. For instance, researchers examining the use of geographic information systems (GIS) have argued that by developing partnerships among government, academic, and business sectors, the visibility of GIS and its advantages will likely increase. Additionally, cross-sector mentoring relationships can also be developed with the goal of each sector becoming more proficient in the use of GIS (Wilhelmi & Brunskill, 2003). The importance of GIS to disaster research is exemplified in its capacity to allow users to combine geographic, spatial, and locational data with other data including population characteristics, environmental conditions, evacuation routes, land use, hazardous materials information, and resource data, just to name a few (Tierney, Lindell & Perry, 2001; Gunes & Kovel, 2000; Waugh, 1995).

Although the private sector is often at a disadvantage, relative to the public sector, in regards to resources available for extensive research projects, it can still play an integral role in a partnership with the public sector. For instance, government and universities have the resources necessary to conduct research in various fields. However, results of this research are not always utilized by the public. By forming partnerships among these groups, information and other assets (e.g., knowledge of the marketplace and effective marketing strategies) can be easily shared among the groups enabling new technologies to emerge for use by the public (Lyons-Johnson, 1998). By utilizing the more abstract results of university research, private companies often have the opportunity to finish a product or develop a more usable form of a technology more suitable for general use.

Opportunities for collaborative efforts involving universities and the private sector have been made possible by government policies such as those that provide federal and state funding to develop research and technology parks such as the one found at the University of New Orleans. Parks such as these provide opportunities for collaborations among university research centers, government facilities, and the private sector.[2] Again, much like

university research centers, many of these research and technology parks were created before 9-11 but are now poised to respond to pressing issues such as homeland security.

Due to the various strengths of government, universities, and the private sector, partnerships involving the three entities can contribute greatly to the field of disaster management (considered to include homeland security) (White House 2003(2)).[3] These strengths include government's resources and its political will and power to implement policies; university resources such as research experience, funding, knowledge of hazards research, education, and training experience; and the private sector's knowledge of the marketplace and its experience in developing products for use by the public. Combining these strengths can aid in developing a rather comprehensive emergency management process.

V. CASE STUDY

The following discusses a specific partnership that evolved from a forward-thinking Louisiana city wanting to prepare for potential threats following 9-11. This partnership includes the city of Kenner, Louisiana, a university, and a private company. Based on the aforementioned changes in disaster management, technological advances and the advantages of partnering with universities and private industry, a partnership such as this one is arguably a strategic as well as a natural one.

Considering the fact that emergencies are local and must be handled first by the local government, the city of Kenner teamed with the Center for Hazards Assessment, Response, and Technology (CHART) of the University of New Orleans (UNO) to assist them in improving their ability to respond quickly to emergency events. The city of Kenner, with a population of 70,517 (U.S. Census Bureau, 2000) and home to a major airport, was somewhat ahead of its time in its approach to emergency management. In addition to the Louis Armstrong International Airport, Kenner is home to other potential risks including Interstate 10 and the Mississippi River, both of which are major corridors for the transportation of hazardous materials

and as well as being located adjacent to densely populated neighborhoods.

Although Kenner is included within a larger parish (county), local officials felt that they must do everything possible to prepare its emergency responders and citizens for a potential local emergency event. The city of Kenner was also motivated by its own disaster experience–the 1982 crash of Pan American Flight 759 that killed 145 people on board the flight and 8 people on the ground. With these thoughts in mind, Kenner officials were convinced that they needed to act proactively to the new threats contrary to many cities that have a reactive philosophy. Fortunately, Kenner was not only forward thinking but also fortunate enough to have the tax base funding to request that a university assist in their preparedness efforts.

The project with Kenner included three major components. These included identifying the vulnerable facilities and infrastructure within the city, facilitating a process by which an emergency response plan was created, and implementing emergency exercises to improve the preparedness and response capabilities of Kenner's emergency response agencies.

The evolving appreciation of and commitment to technology in the field of emergency management led to the inclusion of a private Information Technology services and consulting company in the partnership. This IT company assisted CHART in developing a geographical information system (GIS) known as E3R (Emergency Response and Risk Reduction) for use by Kenner administrators and emergency responders. E3R is an easy-to-use application that allows its users to view an interactive and rather comprehensive map of Kenner comprised of multiple data layers relevant to risk assessment and emergency response, as the title implies. E3R organizes related groups of Kenner facilities into GIS layers. These include businesses, schools, government buildings, utilities, transportation assets, places where large crowds may gather, medical and health facilities, and evacuation routes. In addition to the location of these facilities, E3R also contains contact information including names and phone numbers to be used in the event of an emergency and indicates whether or not a facility has hazardous materials on site. These layers of data were carefully selected with the assistance of applicable Kenner department heads to ensure that data only relevant to risk assessment and emergency response were included to avoid notions of data overload.

Vulnerability assessments of major facilities were conducted by identifying potential hazards found within a 1-mile radius of each critical facility. Potential hazards included facilities that may be targets of terrorism and/or potential sites of hazardous chemical accidents such as buildings that contained hazardous materials, major transportation routes by which hazardous materials are transported (e.g., the Mississippi River, Interstate 10, and the railroads), the sewage treatment plant, underground pipelines, and government facilities. Furthermore, critical data contained in the application known as CAMEO (Computer-Aided Management of Emergency Operations) is also integrated into E3R. This allows responders to easily obtain hazardous chemical-related information in the event of an accidental or purposeful release. ALOHA [Areal Locations of Hazardous Atmospheres], another component of the CAMEO suite, is also accessible through E3R. ALOHA allows users to plot possible chemical air plumes resulting from a release.[4]

Overall, E3R is intended to assist Kenner officials in effectively and efficiently identifying and responding to a variety of hazards including technological hazards, acts of terrorism, hurricanes, and other extreme weather events. E3R should also allow responders to better coordinate their actions considering the fact that relevant information is available to all responders in the same format as well as city administrators. This eases communication and coordination efforts of responders. Additionally, by having information pertinent to potential emergency events easily accessible to emergency responders, their response time will also likely be decreased. The information contained in E3R is securely housed on the city's network and is accessible only through the use of passwords.

CHART is also working with Kenner to create an Emergency Operations Plan. Prior to now, the city had operated under the parish (county) plan during emergency events. Because of the goal of increasing community capacity to respond rapidly, city administrators wanted their own plan. The plan follows the strongly recommended multihazard approach (28th Annual Hazards Research and Applications Workshop, 2003; Workshop on Emergency Management in the Homeland Security Environment, 2003; Waugh, 2001) by including preparedness and response methods that are applicable to natural, technological, and manmade disasters. It also integrates the responsibilities of all potential emergency responders including the following agencies: police, fire, public works, inspection and code enforcement, planning, and information systems management. In addition to responsibilities, the plan also contains resource information that will be updated regularly for use in the event of an emergency. The plan was also created with state of Louisiana and Jefferson parish Emergency Plans as guidelines. Hence, Kenner's plan will assist the city in coordinating its efforts with both the state and the parish. Kenner employees may access the plan in hard-copy form or through electronic means. An electronic version was developed for ease of modification of the plan's contents and for ease of access by all city agencies.

CHART is now working with the city to coordinate emergency exercises and drills that will include all Kenner first responders as well as others including Jefferson parish, the airport, emergency medical services, representatives of local utilities, private companies, and citizens.

Finally, the project facilitated by this partnership of government, the university, and private industry also included the citizens of Kenner. The citizens were initially included in this project through a Community Continuity Conference sponsored by the city of Kenner and CHART. Continuity conferences such as these often focus on businesses; however, as a result of this partnership, the concept of continuity was made more inclusive. Participants of the conference included churches, schools, local businesses, and citizens who were provided information on the general status of homeland security, business resilience, legal aspects of business continuity,

and emergency preparedness tips for the protection of information technology. A meeting is also planned with the citizens of Kenner to allow them to provide comments on the Emergency Response Plan.

With the assistance of CHART, citizens were also included in the planning process through the use of citizen focus groups. Separate focus groups were held comprised of residents recognized as citizen leaders representing the four major geographic areas of the city. Participants were asked to identify problems other than crime that they recognized as potential threats to their communities. The results of these groups were submitted to local officials and were considered throughout the planning efforts. Meetings to review the Emergency Plan will also be held with key facilities and schools throughout Kenner.

VI. CONCLUSION

Overall, the advantages of this partnership of government, a university, and a private company to the emergency preparedness efforts of the city of Kenner are quite evident. First, CHART is a research center whose staff has experience in social science research of natural and technological hazards with a focus on individuals, communities, and related political, social, and economic processes.[5] Arguably, sociological concepts "bridge the gap" between emergency management operations and administration (Carroll, 2001). In other words, social concepts such as political relationships and communications between actors influence disaster policy in terms of type and manner in which services are provided by emergency responders (i.e., operations) and how these services are supported (i.e., administration).

Also, by involving these three entities, a more systematic approach was taken in the emergency management effort. Research and best practices developed collaboratively by government, academia, and the private sector helped guide and strengthen the overall process. Another result of this collaboration is the recognition of the importance of the planning process versus the end product–the plan itself (Dynes, 1982). In fact, Wolensky and Wolensky (1990) found that one of the most

consistent problems in the planning stage is "inadequate conceptualization of the planning process." The efforts of the collaboration helped to overcome this challenge and enforced the notion that the Emergency Plan process is an ongoing one that will include continuous updating and training. The creation of the Emergency Plan document is merely shorthand for a process of evolving the community's emergency response capacity. Additionally, the principle of emphasizing the process over the product was exemplified throughout the development of E3R. The process of gathering information, the inclusion of key agency participants, and the coordination of people and agencies were continuously emphasized as integral to emergency management efforts.

In fact, E3R actually facilitated the emergency management process in various ways. For instance, by including key agencies in the process from its inception, these agencies realized that it was in their best interest (i.e., in terms of political power and future planning efforts) to approve requests for data from their domains to be included in E3R (Harris & Weiner, 1998). Considering these process outcomes, E3R is referred to as an emergency response and risk reduction program rather than a new technology or product. Furthermore, relationships between the city and other entities such as the airport were also strengthened as a result of the planning process because the process brought key stakeholders to the table in the important and shared interests of homeland security.

Also, the university and its affiliates provided a multidisciplinary team to this partnership. Specifically, academics in the following disciplines aided in the Kenner project: sociology, political science, urban planning, geography, and law. The inclusion of a private IT company contributed to the technological aspects of the project including the development of E3R in a usable format for emergency responders. As a result, various perspectives were represented and the strengths of the three entities guided the process.

Considering the current powerful status of homeland security policies and the related funding opportunities, there may be many more prospects for collaboration among government, universities, and the private sector. Arguably, supporting partnerships such as these will broaden the approach taken to develop disaster-related policies and to confront disaster management issues (Pine, 2004). Hence, such collaborations should only enhance the field of disaster management generally, as well as benefitting the involved entities.

REFERENCES

Britton, Neil R. (1999). "Whither the Emergency Manager?" *International Journal of Mass Emergencies and Disasters*, 17:223–235.

Bullard, R.D. (1994). *Dumping in Dixie: Race, Class, and Environmental Quality*. Boulder, CO: Westview Press.

Carroll, John. (2001). "Emergency Management on a Grand Scale" In Ali Farazmand (Ed.), *Handbook of Crisis and Emergency Management*, New York: Marcel Dekker, Inc.

Comerio, Mary C. (April 1, 2000). "The Economic Benefits of a Disaster Resistant University: Earthquake Loss Estimation for UC Berkeley." *Institute of Urban and Regional Development. IURD Working Paper Series*. Paper WP-2000-02.

Disaster Preparedness Resources Centre. (January 1998). The Mitigation Symposium: Towards a Canadian Mitigation Strategy, Comprehensive Symposium Proceeding, University of British Columbia, Vancouver, BC.

Dynes, Russell R. (1982). "Problems in Emergency Planning." *Energy*, 8:653–660.

FEMA Mitigaton Diversion (August 2003). "Building a Disaster Resistant University." Available online at http://www.fema.gov/ fima/dru.shtm

Federal Emergency Management Agency, Mitigation Division. (January 2004). "Disaster Resistant Universities." Available online at http://www.fema.gov/ fima/dru.shtm

Gunes, A. Ertug & Kovel, Jacob P. (2000). "Using GIS in Emergency Management Operations," *Journal of Urban Planning and Development*, 126: 136–149.

Haddow, George D. & Bullock, Jane A. (2003). *Introduction to Emergency Management*. New York: Butterworth-Heinemann.

Harris T. & Weiner, D. (1998). "Empowerment, marginalization, and community-integrated GIS." *Cartography and Geographic Information Systems*, 25(2), pp. 217–234.

Lyons-Johnson, Dawn. (1998). "Public-Private Partnership Boosts Public Benefits." *Agricultural Research*, 46: 4–7.

McLoughlin, D. (1985). "A framework for integrated emergency management." *Public Administration Review*, 45:165–172.

Miletti, Dennis. (1999). *Disasters by Design: A Reassessment of Natural Hazards in the United States*. Washington, D.C.: Joseph Henry Press.

Newport, Jeyanth K. & Jawahar, G.P. (2003). "Community participation and public awareness in disaster mitigation." *Disaster Prevention and Management*, 12:33–36.

Pearce, Laurie. (2003). "Disaster Management and Community Planning, and Public Participation: How to Achieve Sustainable Hazard Mitigation." *Natural Hazards* 28:211–228.

Perry, R. W., Lindell, M.K. & Greene, M.R. (1981). *Evacuation Planning in Emergency Management*. Lexington, MA: D.C. Health.

Phillips, Brenda. (1990). "Gender as a Variable in Emergency Response." In R. Bolin (Ed.), *The Loma Prieta Earthquake: Studies of Short-Term Impacts*, pp. 84–90. Boulder: Institute of Behavioral Science, University of Colorado.

Pine, John C. (2004). "Research Needs to Support the Emergency Manager of the Future." *Journal of Homeland Security*. 1(1), p. 1.

Pinkowski, Jack. (2001). "Planning for prevention: Emergency preparedness and planning to lessen the potential for crisis" in Ali Farazmand (Ed.), *Handbook of Crisis and Emergency Management*, New York: Marcel Dekker, Inc.

Riad, Jasmin K., Waugh, Jr., William Lee & Norris, Fran H. (2001). "The psychology of evacuation in the design of policy" in Ali Farazmand (Ed.), *Handbook of Crisis and Emergency Management*, New York: Marcel Dekker, Inc.

Schapley, Patricia M. & Schwartz, Lorena. (2001). "Coastal hazard mitigation in Florida." In Ali Farazmand (Ed.), *Handbook of Crisis and Emergency Management*, New York: Marcel Dekker, Inc.

Stanley, Ellis M. Sr. & Waugh, Jr., William Lee (2001). "Emergency managers for the new millennium." In Ali Farazmand (Ed.), *Handbook of Crisis and Emergency Management*, New York: Marcel Dekker, Inc.

Tierney, Kathleen J., Lindell, Michael K. & Perry, Ronald W. (2001). *Facing the unexpected: Disaster pre- pareness and response in the United States.* Washington, D.C.: Joseph Henry Press.

28th Annual Hazards Research and Applications Workshop, (July 13–16, 2003). Held in Boulder, Colorado.

U.S. Census Bureau (2000). Available online at www.factfinder.census.gov

U.S. Department of Homeland Security. (January 2004.) "U.S. Department of Homeland Security Strategic Plan." Available online at http://www.dhs.gov

U.S. Department of Homeland Security. (November 25, 2003.) "University of Southern California Chosen as First Homeland Security Center for Excellence." Available online at http://www.dhs.gov/dhspublic/display?theme=43&content=3018&print=true

U.S. Fire Administration. (March 2004.) "83.551 Project Impact: Building disaster resistant communities." Department of Homeland Security. Available online at http://usfa.fema.gov/fire-service/grants/federal/fedguide/cfda/cfda83551.html

Waugh, William L. Jr. (1995). "Geographic Information Systems: The case of disaster management." *Social Science Computer Review*, 13: 422–431.

Waugh, William L., Jr. (2001). "Managing terrorism as an environmental hazard." In Ali Farazmand (Ed.), *Handbook of Crisis and Emergency Management*, New York: Marcel Dekker, Inc.

The White House. "Homeland Security Presidential Directive/HSPD 5." (February 28, 2003). Available online at http://whitehouse.gov/news/releases/2003/02/20030228-9.html

The White House. "Homeland Security Presidential Directive/HSPD 8." (December 17, 2003). Available online at http://www.whitehouse.gov/news/releases/2003/12/20031217-6.html

Wilhelmi, Olga V. & Brunskill, Jeffrey C. (2003). "Geographic Information Systems in weather climate and impacts." *Bulletin of the American Meteorological Society*, 84:1409–1414.

Wolensky, Robert P. & Wolensky, Kenneth C. (1990). "Local government's problem with disaster manage- ment: A literature review and structural analysis," *Policy Studies Review*, 9(4), pp. 703–725.

Workshop on Emergency Management in the Homeland Security Environment. (November 19–20, 2003). Held by the George Washington University/ICDRM, in Washington, D.C.

ENDNOTES

1. Although the federal government no longer funds Project Impact, the initial funding provided the nec- essary funds to several communities to establish dis- aster mitigation programs that still exist today but are supported by other funding sources. Additionally, FEMA is now providing funding to selected universities nationwide as part of the Disaster Resistant University program (for details on this program see http://www.fema.gov/fima/dru.shtm).

2. See http://www.latechnologyguide.com for infor- mation on the UNO R & T Park.

3. See Homeland Security Presidential Directive/HSPD 5 found at http://whitehouse.gov/news/releases/2003/02/20030228-9.html and Homeland Security Presidential Directive/HSPD 8 found at http://www.whitehouse.gov/news/releases/2003/12/20031217-6.html

4. CAMEO was created by EPA's Chemical Emergency Preparedness and Prevention Office (CEPPO) and the National Oceanic and Atmospheric Administration Office of Response and Restoration (NOAA).

5. http://www.uno.edu/~chart/

DISCUSSION QUESTIONS

1. Why are new partnerships for homeland security being created?
2. On what levels are such partnerships being created? Who are the members of these new partnerships?
3. What are the advantages and disadvantages in creating new partnerships among institutions of higher learning, units of government, and the private sector?
4. How have disaster management strategies shifted over the years?
5. Describe how citizen involvement in preparedness has changed over time.
6. How have technological developments changed preparedness?
7. Describe the roles of universities and the private sector in preparedness. How are these roles developing?
8. What did you find to be most surprising about the case study described in this chapter?
9. What factors facilitated the partnership in the case study?
10. Discuss how your institution of higher learning, local government, and private sector entities might collaborate in a manner similar to the Kenner, LA, case study. What are the hazards in your area that such an alliance might address? How could such a partnership leverage the resources available to the stakeholders? What barriers do you see to such a common approach in your own area?

Chapter 8

PARTNERING WITH THE DEPARTMENT OF DEFENSE FOR IMPROVED HOMELAND SECURITY

GREGORY M. HUCKABEE

ARTICLE IV, Section 4. The United States shall guarantee to every State in this Union a republican Form of Government, and shall protect each of them against Invasion; and on application of the Legislature, or of the Executive (when the Legislature cannot be convened) against domestic Violence.[1]

Our world is changing in ways our forebearers never could imagine. Although there are magnificent achievements connected with increasing globalization and the contagious spread of freedom, there are risks as well. The shadow of September 11, 2001, looms large over the moment as well as the 1995 bombing of the Alfred P. Murrah Federal Building in Oklahoma City. Such lawless incidents may visit our nation once more if we cease to be vigilant. After all, as an earlier eighteenth-century patriot observed, "Eternal vigilance is the price of freedom."[2]

Preparation for the unknown is admittedly a daunting task, but a republic's first duty is security for its citizens. To that end, the Department of Defense (DoD) has that mission, and many more for some time. Between 1998 and 2000 alone, DoD provided support for an average of 73 events per year for civil authorities facing natural and manmade disasters.[3] When dealing with an unknown threat, versatility and flexibility are characteristics vital to an effective and timely response. With an almost $400 billion annual budget, the nation has every right to expect much from these national resources. With over 1.1 million servicemen and women on active duty, supported by another almost 1 million National Guard and reservists, DoD capabilities run from water purification to electrical generation, to engineering, to the full complement of medical services. This is what the DoD can and does bring to the civil support table. But how does an organization constantly preparing to fight and win the nation's wars approach domestic civil support operations? These are very distinct missions requiring different training, organizational, and operational approaches.

The purpose of this chapter is to examine four questions. First, what role does DoD play in the current Federal Response Plan (FRP) and the new National Response Plan (NRP)?[4] Second, when is the DoD authorized to respond to emergency and ongoing manmade disasters? Third, how does DoD carry out its mission to support state and local government during all phases of emergency management (mitigation, preparedness, response, and recovery)? And fourth, are there any restrictions that Congress and the Chief Executive have placed on the use of the armed forces in civil support operations?

Note: The author is indebted to the assistance of Mr. George Gillette, Office of General Counsel, Defense Threat Reduction Agency, and Mr. Bradford Barz, Graduate Assistant, University of South Dakota, without whose tremendous assistance this chapter would not be possible.

I. THE PECKING ORDER

For the armed forces, the leadership question of who is in charge is an important one, especially when it comes to a civil support operation. While soldiers, sailors, airmen, and marines are trained to kill people and break things, that skill set may not be entirely appropriate to a domestic operation. As mentioned in the introduction, versatility and flexibility are indispensable characteristics of an effective national defense. But how do state and local authorities access those skills in a time of state or local emergency?

Let us start at the top of legal authority and work our way down. The U.S. Constitution empowers Congress "to make Rules for the Government and Regulation of the land and naval forces."[5] The very next clause provides that Congress can call "forth the Militia to execute the Laws of the Union, suppress Insurrections, and repel Invasions." As the Supreme Court of the United States has noted:

> The Constitution gives to Congress the power, among others, to declare war and suppress insurrection, and the latter power is not limited to victories in the field and the dispersion of insurgent forces: it carries with it inherently rightful authority to guard against an immediate renewal of conflict, and to remedy the evils growing out of its rise and progress.[6]

Faced with al Quaida, Taliban, and other would-be insurgents, constitutional authority makes it clear the Congress may use the armed forces at home to defend the country and protect Americans. A terrorist attack can, however, blur the lines between an act of war and a simple crime, albeit one with terrible consequences. While Congress has the authority to respond to an attack with military forces, is not a state primarily responsible for law enforcement activities during an emergency or disaster? Is not an Oklahoma City bombing or World Trade Center crash fundamentally a violation of state criminal law authorizing a state law enforcement response, at least initially?

During the preliminary phases of a domestic weapons of mass destruction (WMD) event, the response may be initiated both at the local level and the federal level. Degrees of federal involvement in the initial response phase through the recovery phase will vary depending on the type of crisis and the ability of the local and state authorities to manage it. Generally, first responders at the state and local level manage the initial consequences of such an event, with the support of the state's emergency management agency. Regarding the law enforcement response, the Tenth Amendment to the Constitution makes clear that in most all cases, the states are primarily responsible for police enforcement activities during an emergency or disaster.[7] Although there is an exception involving a federal primary responsibility, distance and time routinely make the state and local law enforcement authorities the first responders. The norm is that these authorities will shoulder initial responsibility for dealing with the law enforcement challenge. As noted in the following discussion, however, the Federal Bureau of Investigation (FBI) often will take over the law enforcement lead in responding to manmade disasters that are the result of terrorism and/or criminal activities in violation of federal law.

Where law and order is continuing to be threatened and additional support is required, the governor would likely activate state National Guard forces, acting under state authority, as occurred in New York during the aftermath of September 11, 2001. If state and local resources are inadequate to manage the law enforcement aspects of a disaster or emergency, to include protecting lives and property, the state governor has the option under the Justice Assistance Act of requesting emergency assistance from the United States attorney general. Federal law enforcement assistance that may be provided includes equipment, intelligence, personnel, and training.[8] All well and good, but how exactly does the state obtain the assistance of the armed forces? Are there special considerations that apply to requests for DoD support for law enforcement matters?

The Stafford Act is Congress's basic authority for U.S. agencies, to include the Department of Defense, to provide timely and effective federal support in response to local and state needs.[9] Under the Stafford Act, federal assistance may be provided when the state governor requests support because state personnel and resources are inadequate to mount an effective response. The Stafford Act provides for assistance by the federal government to the states in the event of natural or other disasters. It defines major disasters and emergencies; and addresses disaster relief programs, disaster preparedness assistance, hazard mitigation, and federal assistance for losses sustained in disasters.

When the president declares a major disaster or emergency, this activates a coordinated federal response under the draft National Federal Response Plan (as noted, the NRP replaces the Federal Response Plan).[10] The DoD worships plans, and the Federal Response Plan (FRP) as well as the NRP defines who gets to come to the disaster from the federal government, and what their specific role is in the coordinated federal response. The FRP and the NRP translate legal requirements into operational principles and procedures. Both set out incident management primary and support roles and responsibilities among federal agencies, to include the DoD, by assigning emergency support functions. Those emergency support functions are: transportation, communication, public works and engineering, firefighting, information and planning, mass care, resource support, health and medical services, urban search and rescue, hazardous materials, food, and energy. The FRP was reissued in January 2003 to reflect passage of the Homeland Security Act of 2002 and the creation of the Department of Homeland Security. The NRP was finalized in late 2004 as covered in more detail in chapter 4.

To make it crystal clear as to who is responsible for emergency support functions within his bureaucratic empire of seemingly endless agencies and departments, the president issued Executive Order 12656. This order establishes primary and support functions to be performed during any national security emergency of the United States, develops plans for performing these functions, and develops the capability to execute those plans.[11] DoD is assigned primary responsibility for military response; national mobilization; damage assessment; military support to civil and private sector, (including authorized police-type law enforcement activities) within authority; response to all hazards related to nuclear weapons, materials, and devices; through the Secretary of the Army, managing and allocating all usable waters within U.S. jurisdiction; and stockpile of storage and critical materials.[12]

A second but independent legal source authorizing use of military forces in support of law enforcement is provided by The Defense Against Weapons of Mass Destruction Act.[13] Section 2313 of the act directs the Secretary of Defense to designate an official within the Defense Department as the DoD executive agent to coordinate the DoD assistance to federal, state, and local entities in responding to a WMD event. The Secretary of Defense has designated the Assistant Secretary of Defense for Homeland Defense (ASD/HD) as this executive agent.[14] The DoD executive agent is responsible for coordinating DoD assistance with federal, state, and local officials in responding to threats involving nuclear, chemical, and biological weapons.

With both these statutory authorities in place, it is essential to understand the chain of command. Who directs what may be provided under these authorities is of interest to state and local authorities. The Homeland Security Act of 2002 designates the Department of Homeland Security (DHS) as the lead federal agency for coordinating disaster and emergency response and recovery assistance with state and local authorities.[15] Under this congressional delegation of authority, DHS is the Primary Agency/Lead Federal Agency, and the DoD plays a supporting role only.[16] The DoD is a supporting agency, and with one exception,[17] is never a Primary Agency (PA) or Lead Federal Agency (LFA), while the DHS is the supported federal agency.

Under both the NRP and its predecessor, the FRP, within the DHS, the Federal Emergency Management Agency (FEMA) is responsible for coordinating the support activities and response assistance provided by all other federal agencies. When the federal government is responding to a terrorist or criminal act, however, the FBI serves as the primary or lead federal agency.

Homeland Security Presidential Directive 5 (HSPD 5) details the United States' policy in combating terrorism and reaffirmed the lead agencies for the management of various aspects of the counterterrorism effort. The document recognizes that states have primary responsibility in responding to terrorist incidents, including WMD events, and the federal government provides assistance as required. The Presidential Directive does away with the artificial distinction between crisis management and consequence management. The NRP[18] and its operational portion, the National Incident Management System (NIMS),[19] establish a national approach to handling emergencies and disasters.

NIMS utilizes the Incident Command System (ICS) in the field. Under ICS, a chain of command ensures an orderly line of authority. It also emphasizes unity of command, which ensures that each person has a designated supervisor. This approach clarifies reporting relationships. In events involving multiple jurisdictions and agencies, unified command lets agencies work together effectively, while keeping intact individual agency authority, responsibility, and accountability.

Under the NRP, the Secretary of Defense authorizes Defense Support of Civil Authorities (DSCA) for domestic incidents as directed by the President or when consistent with military readiness operations and appropriate under the circumstances and law. The Secretary of Defense retains command of military forces under DSCA, as with all other situations and operations.[20] For military forces, command runs from the President to the Secretary of Defense to the Commander of the combatant command to the commander of the forces. The "Unified Command" concept utilized by civil authorities is distinct from the military chain of command.[21] The Secretary of Defense maintains command of military forces used in the support role.

The NRP creates the Interagency Incident Management Group (IIMG) as a Federal headquarters-level multiagency coordinating group to facilitate strategic Federal domestic incident management for Incidents of National Significance. DoD is a member of the core group staffing for the IIMG.

The Homeland Security Operations Center (HSOC) is the primary national focal point for domestic incident management operational coordination and situational awareness. DoD provides a representative to HSOC.

The FBI's Strategic Information and Operations Center (SIOC) is the control center for all Federal intelligence, law enforcement, and investigative law enforcement activities related to domestic terrorist incidents or credible threats. It connects directly with the HSOC and IIMG. The SIOC houses the National Joint Terrorism Task Force (NJTTF).

Federal assistance is provided by means of Emergency Support Functions (ESFs). The ESF organization provides a modular structure to deploy the precise components that can best address the incident's requirements. ESFs may be activated for Stafford Act and non-Stafford Act implementation of the NRP. DoD is not the Primary Response Agency for any of the ESFs. Rather, it is a Support Agency for all ESFs. This makes sense, given DoD's significant manpower and material resources.

In the field, the Joint Field Office (JFO) is a multiagency coordination center that is established locally. The JFO is commanded by a Principal Federal Official (PFO) who works closely with a Federal Coordinating Officer (FCO), a State Coordinating Office (SCO) and Senior Federal Officials. The FCO manages federal assets on an ongoing basis. The structure of the JFO will vary, depending on the type of event involved.[22]

The PFO represents the Secretary of DHS. The FCO manages and coordinates Federal resource support activities related to Stafford Act disasters and emergencies. As such, it makes sense that the FCO should be a FEMA employee, but this is not set in stone. The FCO identifies federal sources of needed assistance and authorizes reimbursement for this support on request. The FCO generally does so in support of the state emergency management agency (EMA).

If appointed by DoD, the Defense Coordinating Officer (DCO) serves as DoD's single point of contact at the JFO. Generally, requests for Defense Support of Civil Authorities originating at the JFO go through the DCO. The DCO may have a Defense Coordinating Element (DCE), which consists of a staff as well as military liaison officers to facilitate coordination and support to activated ESFs. Particular responsibilities of the DCO normally include processing requirements for military support, forwarding mission assignments to the proper military organizations through DoD-designated channels, and assigning military liaisons, as appropriate, to activated ESFs.

As noted, the role that DoD plays in providing assistance to state and local authorities in WMD and terrorism incidents is most always that of a supporting agency. Scenes from the movie *Under Siege*, whereby U.S. armed forces seize New York City and impose martial law exercising command and control over everyone and everything from the FBI to law enforcement, is pure Hollywood– unlawful, unconstitutional, and improbable. The prior review reveals a sophisticated federal legal and operational tiered system of response authority that carefully places DoD and the armed forces in a supporting role to civil authority. This is how the federal pecking order of authority works.

The prior review reveals a sophisticated federal legal and operational tiered system of response authority that carefully places DoD and the armed forces in a supporting role to civil authority. This is how the federal pecking order of authority works. But does it really? The Missourian reader asks, "show me."

After the 1995 Oklahoma City bombing, the FBI assumed command and control as the LFA over the incident site based on primary federal interest–federal U.S. courthouse property. In this role, the FBI requested DoD support. The U.S. military deployed about 800 active and reserve personnel, while the Oklahoma National Guard provided 465. The military support included medical and rescue teams, structural experts, and air and ground transportation.[23]

After the September 11, 2001, attacks, DoD provided FEMA 657 active duty personnel to support response operations at the Pentagon and the World Trade Center. Most of the active duty support at the World Trade Center came from the 387 personnel manning the hospital ship *Comfort*, but it also included a Defense Coordinating Element (DCE, which will be discussed in detail later), a medical mobilization center, logistics support (airlift), and subject matter experts on demolitions and remote sensing operations.[24]

A congressional Advisory Panel to Assess Domestic Response Capabilities for Terrorism Involving WMD reports that with its size, nation-wide disposition, and inherent capabilities, the army, including the Army National Guard, can be expected to provide most of the military support in the event of future attacks with chemical, biological, radiological, or nuclear (CBRN) weapons.[25] The RAND Corporation (a private company that performs outside studies for Congress, DoD, and other agencies), estimates that an army response could range from approximately 4,000 soldiers for a small biological or radiological attack, to more than 20,000 in response to a large-scale anthrax attack in which more than 15,000 people have been exposed.[26] As this example demonstrates, the legal and tiered authority response system operates as designed with effective civilian control over military resources.

II. WHEN DOES THE FLAG GO UP?

A. Immediate Response

Understanding where DoD fits in as a supporting federal agency and resource provider begins with the legal and operational structure of the NRP/FRP. State and local authorities should be curious to learn when this vaunted cavalry might be expected to arrive to snatch victory from the jaws of a WMD or terrorist disaster. When one stands at Ground Zero viewing the rubble of two gigantic skyscrapers filled with the business of life, the carnage of such a disaster overwhelms the human senses. Any survivor of a WMD incident will testify–it is impossible to get there too quickly to assist in consequence management operations. When can DoD assist state and local authorities?

Remember how much the military adores planning? There are military plans and implementing directives for just about every conceivable WMD or terrorist scenario. Let us be more specific and divide the discussion into two situations. The first situation addresses immediate response authority, and the second discusses a state request for federal assistance.

Consider a military unit at Fort Totten or any installation within the vicinity of New York City on September 11, 2001. Having lost numerous city firemen in battling the collapse of two skyscrapers, the city fire chief calls all military installations asking for military assistance. Based on our previous review, is the appropriate and legal response from the military "I regret to inform you, but under the Stafford Act you must first make your request to the New York state governor, who in turn must make a request to the president to declare this terrorist incident a national disaster. Once the president makes that declaration, then he can send in the FBI or, if the FBI transitions the situation to a CM, they can transfer LFA authority to FEMA, who will appoint a Federal Coordinating Officer (FCO). This FCO will then contact the state emergency management agency to receive support requests. FEMA will then assign those support requests according to previously designated emergency support functions in the FRP. If FEMA needs medical supplies and fire equipment support from DoD, they will contact their Defense Coordinating Officer (DCO), normally a colonel. He will then task appropriate DoD agencies, one of which may or may not be this installation or unit. Until then, we wait. Does that answer your question?" Is this how the system really works?

While the playwrights Gilbert and Sullivan would have a field day with such an inflexible response, there is a way around the bureaucratic paradigm previously mentioned. As in the fire support request illustration, when there is an immediate need for DoD assistance, it may be provided. Based on authority in Art. IV, section 4 of the U.S. Constitution stated at the beginning of this chapter, the Federal Civil Defense Act of 1950,[27] and the National Emergencies Act,[28] military leaders have immediate response authority, independent from the Stafford Act.

As implemented by a Department of Defense Directive, DoD can contribute substantial resources to disaster and emergency recovery and response, provided other resources are unavailable.[29] Contribution by DoD must not interfere with DoD's ability to perform its primary mission or adversely affect military preparedness. Imminently serious conditions resulting from any civil emergency or attack may require immediate attention by military commanders, or by responsible officials of other DoD agencies to (1) save lives; (2) prevent human suffering; or (3) mitigate great property damage.[30]

When such conditions exist and time does not permit prior approval from higher headquarters, local commanders and responsible officials of other DoD components are authorized to take necessary action to respond to requests of civil authorities.[31] Thus, when assistance to state or local authorities is needed most, when it positively, absolutely is needed to ameliorate imminent serious conditions, the cavalry can charge without delay.[32] The Missourian is back. "Show me," he says. "What can your vaunted DoD cavalry really provide with respect to mitigation, preparedness, response, and recovery?" Under applicable DoD directives, the Defense Department support can include:

(1) Rescue, evacuation, and emergency medical treatment of casualties, maintenance or restoration of emergency medical capabilities, and safeguarding of public health;

(2) Emergency restoration of public services (including firefighting, water, transportation, communications, power, and fuel);

(3) Emergency clearance of debris, rubble, and ordinance from public facilities and other areas to permit rescue or movement of people and restoration of essential services;

(4) Recovery, identification, registration, and disposal of the dead;

(5) Monitoring and decontaminating of radiological, chemical, and biological effects; controlling contaminated areas; and reporting through national warning and hazardous control systems;

(6) Roadway movement control and planning;

(7) Safeguarding, collecting, and distributing food, essential supplies, and material on the basis of critical priorities;

(8) Facilitating the reestablishment of civil government functions.[33]

Still unconvinced, the heavyweight question is posed, "So who is going to pay for all this before we go spreading all this goodwill around?" While military assistance should be provided to civil agencies on a cost-reimbursable basis if possible, it should not be delayed or denied because of the inability or unwillingness of the requester to make a commitment to reimburse the DoD.[34] Unfortunately, Congress does not make appropriations to DoD for possible military support to civil authorities in WMD disasters. However, FEMA routinely reimburses DoD pursuant to the Stafford Act for DoD support funds expended, especially when lives were at stake.

B. Declaration of a National Disaster when Requested by a State

For a variety or reasons, immediate response may not always be available. The state may be able to bring resources to bear in the short term to save lives and protect property. In a disaster of any magnitude, however, it may become clear that the state's resources are insufficient to deal with the longer-term needs of those affected by a disaster. A less expedient but more comprehensive federal response involves a formal state request for a presidential disaster declaration and federal assistance under the Stafford Act. Generally, Stafford Act assistance is rendered upon request from the state governor provided certain conditions are met. The governor must certify that the state lacks the resources and capabilities to manage the consequences of the event without federal assistance. Once an emergency or major disaster is declared under the provisions of the Stafford Act, the president may authorize any of the resources specified in the act. In addition, the act provides that the president may authorize DoD resources before the president has declared a national emergency or disaster, as long as he has received a request from a governor as being necessary to save lives and property.[35] In a WMD event, this will not be difficult.

C. Unilateral Presidential Action

Without any state request, the National Emergencies Act empowers the chief executive to declare a national emergency of his own in order to exercise any emergency power. The proclamation of national emergency, or an executive order, must state the statutory authorities or powers he proposes to use. During the national emergency any power or authority the president exercises under it terminates on the date specified in the proclamation or by joint congressional resolution terminating it, whichever occurs earlier.[36] Emergency power authority also terminates automatically one year after the president declares it, or if he fails to provide timely notification to Congress that it is to remain in effect. President Bush exercised this authority on September 14, 2001, when he issued Proclamation 7463, declaring a

national emergency due to the terrorist attacks of September 11. Among the emergency powers he gained were authority to reapportion funds; suspend officer personnel laws (thus retaining in military service those due to be separated or retired); waive military strength limitations (thus calling to active duty and paying more military forces than authorized by Congress); to order the Ready Reserve to active duty; and order Coast Guard officers on the retired list to active duty.[37] Normally such actions would require congressional approval.

D. Emergencies Involving Federal Primary Responsibility

While our federal system leaves police power functions to the states, if the emergency involves a matter for which the federal government has exclusive or primary responsibility and authority, the president may use DoD resources as he deems appropriate. The 1995 Oklahoma City federal building bombing and subsequent DoD CM support is an example of such authority's exercise.[38] Other post-September 11 examples include deployment of military personnel for border security operations. These involved federalizing 1,600 National Guardsmen to augment the U.S. Border Patrol, the Immigration and Naturalization Service, and the U.S. Customs Service in missions that lasted six months.[39] Until such time as these agencies could recruit and train additional personnel, DoD forces assisted these agencies in the performance of their duties.

III. HOW DOES DOD PLAY FRIENDLY?

When your primary mission is to fight and win the nation's wars, domestic civil support operations are not part of basic training, or even advanced training for that matter. In fact, it requires on-the-job-training. As noted next, DoD has had a lot of training in responding to disasters in the United States. Given the ability to respond, how does DoD process specific requests and execute a mission for civil support from the FBI, FEMA, or White House? We are back to planning. There is always a military process for every military

adventure. Knowing how that process works enables the states and local authorities to anticipate what DoD can and cannot do to aid them. Unclassified information in the public domain provides operational opportunities to obtain DoD support services in the most expeditious manner.

A. The Organization: Why Me?

Military support to civil authority is not a new mission for DoD. When natural disaster strikes such as hurricanes, wildfires, floods, or earth-quakes, the states routinely call on the federal government for assistance, and FEMA calls on DoD to provide a plethora of medical, engineering, transportation, and logistic services. Whether it is Hurricanes Andrew in 1992, Marilyn in 1995, Mitch in 1998; the National Democratic or Republican Conventions of 2000; the Summer Olympics of 1996 or Winter Olympics of 2002, the Presidential Inauguration of 2001; or the National Scout Jamboree of 2001, all required tremendous support to state and local authorities by DoD.[40] Whereas some DoD civil support operations are planned in advance, and others provided by Mother Nature are not, the type of support remains the same. Locations, conditions, and numbers served may vary, but the basic functions are the same–life support missions. WMD and terrorist events are just another disaster in many respects. The prospect of chemical, biological, radiological, nuclear radiation, and high explosives (CBRNE) add new challenges to the basic civil support mission.

B. Command Structure: Who is on First?

As has been explained, there is one person charged with coordinating the federal response (to include any military assistance) to a domestic WMD event or other national disaster–the Federal Coordinating Officer (FCO).[41] The FCO is FEMA's local command and control on-the-scene director. All federal agency representatives report to work for him. When a request for assistance comes in, the FCO coordinates with the other federal agencies that can provide assistance. After determining which agency is best able to provide needed support, the FCO issues mission assignments, called Requests for Assistance (RFA). Perhaps most importantly, the FCO also makes a commitment to reimburse the selected federal agency when he gives these RFAs to the appropriate agency representatives. For the FBI, the on-scene representative is the Special Agent in Charge. This is the nonmilitary side of the federal coin.

How does the Defense Department response structure look? In the event of a major manmade (e.g., terrorist) or natural disaster that is of sufficient magnitude that state and local authorities are insufficient to adequately cope and military assistance is needed, the military response would, in most cases, resemble the following.

First, a disaster response-trained Defense Coordinating Officer, or DCO, would be designated, usually based on his proximity to the site of the disaster. Usually an army colonel, DCOs regularly participate in disaster exercises with their federal and state emergency response counterparts. In a real national disaster situation, the DCO and his support team, called the Defense Coordination Element (DCE), would deploy and co-locate with the FCO and the other representatives from the responding federal agencies.

The DCO's role is to be the single voice of the Defense Department in responding to requests for military support that have been given by state, local, or other federal officials to the FCO. DCE members supporting the DCO are tasked with keeping up on the availability of DoD resources in their area of responsibility (e.g., the number of army water trucks at a nearby army installation, or the readiness and equipment of an engineering battalion at a marine corps base in the next state). The DCO will rely on his DCE and other support elements as they are provided (discussed next), to help him properly advise the FCO as to whether the military can provide requested equipment/support on a timely basis. The DCO, will however, also evaluate requests for military resources to help ensure that no state or local or other federal resources are being overlooked. A governor may prefer to use a U.S. Army helicopter to fly over a disaster, rather then expend state funds for an Air Guard aircraft, but simply saving the state money is not a proper basis for the military to provide that support.

Depending on the location of the incident and the severity of the disaster, other military units may deploy to an area close enough to the site to allow them to best support the response; but they routinely locate far enough away to avoid adding an additional burden on the local infrastructure. As with the DCO and his DCE support team, these units ultimately are under the command and control of Northern Military Command (NORTHCOM) because it has been given responsibility for managing most military disaster response operations in the United States.

Currently, there are primarily three units that plan, train, and exercise for this support function: Joint Task Force–Civil Support (JTF-CS), which is directly under NORTHCOM, JTF-CS-EAST, and JTF-CS-WEST. JTF-CS is usually held in reserve, and the others, as their names imply, deploy based on whether the incident site is east or west of the Mississippi River.

These JTF units bring additional information about the availability of military resources and assets to aid in the response effort, as well as logistics and communications support to ensure the smooth flow of military support to the affected area. They also offer subject matter experts who can assist with a variety of matters such as medical issues relating to, for example, a Chem-Bio or nuclear incident, the possible spread of a chemical or a radioactive plume, and expedient ways to decontaminate people or structures. While they mostly are comprised of army soldiers, the other armed services contribute personnel as well. State and local officials will generally have little or no contact with these JTF-CS units, and only limited contacts with the DCOs because, as noted, the official liaison between the federal government and the state and local authorities is the FCO. On the other hand, informal communication between DCE members and various state and local officials can be useful so that they can anticipate areas of particular need and begin examining if it makes sense to request DoD assistance.

There is an additional aspect of this process that must be understood. As has been noted, responding to a domestic disaster is simply not the main mission of the military, and it can be expected that the global war on terrorism and other military operations will continue to be a drain on military resources. Accordingly, there needs to be a central clearinghouse where requests for disaster response military support from state, local, and other federal entities can be considered in the context of overall military operations. Currently, the Joint Director of Military Support Missions (JDOMS) is tasked with this role, with input from the Assistant Secretary of Defense for Homeland Defense.[42]

Moreover, in a variety of situations, approval of the Secretary of Defense may be required before JDOMS can authorize the use of military resources for domestic support. Thus, there may be a valid need and an approved RFA with a reimbursement commitment from FEMA, but because the military resources are needed elsewhere, JDOMS or the Secretary of Defense may not authorize the military support.

C. Train to Fight: DoD Loves the Primary Agency/Lead Federal Agency (LFA)

Basic training for civil support is the DoD Emergency Preparedness Course (DODEPC) conducted several times a year around the country. A week long in nature, its curriculum features everything from classification of domestic emergencies to types of emergency response; local, state, and federal response sequencing; civil disturbance response; WMD response; *posse comitatus*, to FEMA operations. Both enlisted and officer personnel who will participate as members of DCEs and headquarters' task forces controlling DoD responses in the field, are required to attend and obtain DODEPC certification. In addition, all DCEs are required to conduct at least two exercises annually.

First, U.S. Army has 11 DCEs geographically dispersed within its 27-state area, so no DCE is far from a potential civil support location. It is important to note that DCEs are augmented with at least one judge advocate (uniform lawyer) who is also DODEPC trained.[43] Why a lawyer? As we will see later, there are some functions DoD has been prohibited by Congress from performing. It is the responsibility of the judge advocate to advise the commander/DCO of all laws and regulations affecting performance of the DoD mission.[44] The judge advocate is but one safeguard to ensure DoD gets it legally correct from the start. Other personnel are augmented depending on the nature of the mission they are providing for civil support. Each DCE is able to deploy to a disaster site within 12 hours of notification. A lead element deploys within 3 hours of alert to prepare for arrival of the main body.

D. The Battle: Bring on the Impossible

The phone rings on the watch officer's desk at NORTHCOM's Operations Center. It is the Joint

Chiefs of Staff Operations Center in the Pentagon calling to execute a civil support mission in Jackson, Tennessee. Terrorists set off a nuclear blast on the Madrid Seismic Quake fault line creating a chain reaction earthquake along the Mississippi River. The resulting earthquake is endangering large population centers, such as Memphis, along both sides of the tributary. The Tennessee governor requested a declaration of national disaster, which the president is making as we speak. Execute, execute. The watch officer calls Forces Command in Atlanta requesting deployment of a DCO with his DCE immediately from both First and Fifth Armies to provide civil support to FEMA on both sides of the Mississippi River. The Forces Command Operations Center contacts both First and Fifth Army operations centers requesting deployment of DCEs. DCOs are alerted to deploy with their 15-soldier DODEPC certified DCEs. Eight hours later, the teams arrive in their respective areas of operation. FEMA appoints an FCO for the Jackson, Tennessee, area. Upon arrival, he meets with the Tennessee Director of the Emergency Management Agency (TEMA). The TEMA director requests assistance in a number of areas, the most pressing being the nuclear blast area, which local responders are not able to handle.

The FCO calls an immediate meeting of all federal agency representatives. With the DCO from First Army in attendance, he begins discussing requests for state assistance (RFAs) from FEMA. FEMA will issue written mission RFAs to respective federal agencies immediately by fax. These are the official FEMA taskings that include a Mission Control Number that is required when seeking reimbursement from FEMA. No control number means no authorization from FEMA to undertake the mission. This in turn means no FEMA reimbursement. If the requested support activities are undertaken without FEMA reimbursement, the result could be an Anti-Deficiency Act violation, that is, spending appropriated funds for an unauthorized purpose.

The FCO asks the DCO what DoD has that can help state and local authorities remediate the blast area. The military is called on most often to perform these missions because it moves and organizes large numbers of trained personnel to provide a coordinated response to incidents such as this. The military has also developed specialized capabilities (particularly medical, engineering, and chemical, biological, radiological, nuclear, and high-yield explosive [CBRNE] weapon response capabilities). These capabilities either do not exist at the state level or do not exist in sufficient quantities.[45] In responding to the question about available DoD assets, the DCO informs the FCO that the marines have a CBRNE unit that can assess, mitigate, and remediate to a limited degree, in the most serious areas. They can be on-site in 8 hours. The FCO responds by requesting that they be alerted and notes that the mission RFA will be on the wire momentarily.

On his way back to his DCE headquarters, the lieutenant governor stops the DCO and asks if he can provide several helicopters to fly a number of his city and village mayors to assess damage to their communities. Can the state or local civil authorities directly task DoD?

With the single "immediate response" necessity exception previously discussed, no state or local authority can circumvent FEMA or the Primary Agency (PA) or Lead Federal Agency (LFA). All taskings must come through the LFA to supporting federal agencies. If a request comes directly from a state official, the appropriate response for the DCO is to connect the state official with the FEMA FCO. In WMD and disaster incidents, emotions can run high because no amount of federal support can arrive quick enough. The president's personal representative and coordinator for all federal agency effort is the PA/LFA FCO. There is no authority to circumvent his role. He alone coordinates and commands the WMD and disaster scene for all federal agencies, and DoD is just one.

This tiered system works effectively if allowed to function as designed with trained personnel. Without trained DoD personnel, the interface is sometimes strained, because it is not the normal military methodology of operations. However, the armed forces specialize in doing the difficult immediately, the seemingly impossible the next day. They know how to provide disaster civil support to state and local authorities in a timely, compassionate, and effective manner.

IV. DOD LAW ENFORCEMENT ACTIONS: WHEN A SHERIFF IS NEEDED

As one Secretary of State observed in a crisis, "If we cannot use the American military, what good are they?" When the going gets tough, there is always an emotional impulse to throw the problem at the armed forces and let them fix it. While seductive in nature, there are historical, operational, and legal policies that show why this is an inappropriate course of action. The appropriate response is to follow the NRP/FRP. It is foreseeable there may be circumstances when the armed forces are needed to provide law enforcement support, such as the 1992 Los Angeles riots or the Hurricane Andrew looter breakout in Florida.[46]

While weapons, force, and violence are not unknown concepts to the armed forces, unleashing the power of the U.S. military on a foreign battlefield such as Afghanistan or Iraq is one thing, but exercise of such force within the domestic homeland is quite another. Despite an early nineteenth-century tradition of using the American military as a constabulary and frontier police force, post-Civil War military occupation experience led to a movement to restrict use of the armed forces for law enforcement activities. Subsequent enactment of the *Posse Comitatus* Act of 1878 is viewed by many as a means to prevent the military from interfering with civil law, and an attempt to end the use of federal troops to police state elections in ex-confederate states.[47] Another view holds the *Posse Comitatus* Act (PCA) was enacted to protect the military from having to assist law enforcement when requested to aid in the enforcement of civil law.[48] Despite its historical origins, the act remains to this day a restriction on the use of the armed forces in law enforcement activities:

> Whoever, except in cases and under circumstances expressly authorized by the Constitution or of Congress, willfully uses any part of the Army or Air Force as a posse comitatus or otherwise to execute the laws shall be fined under this title or imprisoned not more than two years, or both.[49]

Posse comitatus simply means the power of the county.[50] At first read, it would appear that under this statute, the armed forces are out of the law enforcement business. However, the part of the statute "except in cases and under circumstances expressly authorized by the Constitution or of Congress" has provided opportunities for Congress to create numerous exceptions that have become the norm, rather than true exceptions to the general prohibition policy. Would you believe Congress has created twelve exceptions to date? What exceptions has Congress created that state and local authorities in need of law enforcement support should know?

A. The Insurrection Act: When the Party Gets Out of Hand

Back to Tennessee and the Madrid Seismic Quake WMD explosion. Communications are disrupted and due to the tremendous loss of life and casualties, state and local law enforcement cannot begin to cope with the looting, violence, and rioting that has broken out and is growing in the Memphis area. State authorities are unable to provide coordinated relief assistance until security and order are restored. The Tennessee National Guard is already committed to Mississippi levy reconstruction to prevent wholesale flooding. The governor calls the White House for federal troops. One presidential advisor cautions the president that "the *Posse Comitatus* Act prohibits the use of the military in exactly this type of law and disorder situation. Tennessee is on its own. The southern states asked for this prohibition; now they can live with it." Another more scholarly advisor points out, "Mr. President, Congress did authorize an exception to the PCA by subsequent passage of the Insurrection Act. This Act provides that when a state legislature or governor asks the president for assistance in suppressing an insurrection, the president may call upon the military to suppress the insurrection.[51] This sounds like an insurrection to me, and I believe Tennessee's governor agrees that is what he has on his hands."

But let us assume a slightly different set of facts to illustrate a different military response authority. Assume the Tennessee governor and legislature are casualties of this WMD event and unable to make such a law enforcement request to the president. Another provision of the Insurrection Act authorizes the president to call upon the military without first receiving a request from any state official if it becomes impracticable to enforce the laws of the United States.[52] Examples of how this occurs would be lawlessness that affects opening, access to, and operation of the federal courts in Tennessee. How about operation of the U.S. post offices?

Yet a third source of military response authority is provided in the Insurrection Act. The president may call upon the military whenever the insurrection deprives any part or class of people a constitutional right, privilege, immunity, or protection.[53] Can commerce be affected in Tennessee without lawless interference? How about access to Social Security, welfare, and food stamp offices? During the civil rights era, this authority was used to employ federal troops to enforce admission of minorities to southern state universities.

In all three Insurrection Act exceptions to the *Posse Comitatus* Act, prior to using the military, the president is required to "immediately order the insurgents disperse and retire peaceably" within a limited time.[54] This is where the phrase "being read the riot act" originated.

B. Chemical-Biological WMD: When Gas and Bugs Get Loose

During an emergency involving a biological or chemical WMD weapon, if military assistance is necessary for the immediate protection of human life, and civilian law enforcement officers are not capable of taking action, the military may assist in arrests, searches and seizures, and any direct participation in the collection of intelligence for law enforcement purposes.[55] Again, no request is needed from the state; the president may take action on his own. However, there must first be a request from the attorney general to the Secretary of Defense for law enforcement assistance before this exception to the PCA will apply to military personnel.

C. Transactions Involving Nuclear Materials: When Dr. Strangelove Visits

The attorney general may request DoD to provide assistance during an emergency situation involving

radiological materials that pose a serious threat to the interests of the United States. Two conditions must be met before military forces may be used: (1) enforcement of the law would be seriously impaired if the assistance was not provided; and (2) civilian law enforcement personnel are not capable of enforcing the law.[56] Assistance authorized under this section includes arrests, searches and seizures, and such other activity as is incidental to enforcement of this section, or protection of persons or property from conduct that violates this section.[57] This authority has been used to guard nuclear facilities.

D. Execution of Quarantine and Health Laws: The Unthinkable

Movies educate us on the possible, not always the probable. Dustin Hoffman's movie '*Outbreak*' portrays what an infectious Ebola virus might do to a community. This is a subject that terrifies public health officials, resulting in little public information about the legalities of state or federal quarantines. There is a 1915 law, however, authorizing military forces to faithfully aid in the execution of quarantines and other restraints established by the health laws of any state respecting any vessels arriving in, or bound to, any port or district.[58]

While quarantines traditionally are a state public health matter, in order to contain infectious diseases, the federal government has enacted regulations regarding quarantine procedures. The federal government may restrict the movement of persons suspected of carrying specified communicable diseases in order to prevent interstate spread of disease.[59] The diseases for which quarantine is authorized are listed in presidential Executive Order 13295, issued April 4, 2003. While the military is not mentioned in any of these regulations, using the Federal Primary Responsibility authority, the president could use the armed forces to assist in enforcing quarantine restrictions at airports, seaports, and state borders.

E. Emergency Authority: When All Else Fails

Under Article IV of the Constitution, this authority is reserved for extremely extraordinary circumstances and used in strict accordance under a DoD Directive. This authority is reserved for civil disturbances. Military forces may only be used: (1) when necessary to prevent loss of life or wanton destruction of property, or to restore governmental functioning and public order. This emergency authority only applies when there is a sudden and unexpected civil disturbance, such as earthquake, fire, flood, or other such calamity endangering life, and duly constituted local authorities are unable to control the situation and circumstances preclude obtaining prior authorization by the president;[60] or (2) when duly constituted state or local authorities are unable or decline to provide adequate protection for federal property or federal governmental functions.[61] Military forces are authorized in support of this civil disturbance situation as necessary to protect federal property or functions. As previously noted in section II.A., Immediate Response Authority may also allow for military assistance as a last resort, but likewise, only under very narrow circumstances (e.g., when required to prevent the imminent loss of life).[62]

F. Military Purpose Doctrine: Duty, Duty, Always Duty

Actions taken to further a primary military purpose, regardless of incidental benefits to civilian authorities, are not violations of the *Posse Comitatus* Act. Examples include investigations and actions related to a commander's inherent authority to maintain law and order on a military installation or facility, actions related to enforcement of the Uniform Code of Military Justice or administrative proceedings, protection of classified military information and equipment, protection of DoD personnel, DoD equipment, official guests of DoD, and any other actions that are primarily for a military or foreign affair's purpose.[63] A good example of the military purpose exception to the PCA that easily could occur in a disaster scenario would be using military police to direct traffic for a military convoy. A military convoy carrying relief supplies to hurricane victims could safely travel through an urban area where traffic lights were blown down. No PCA violation would occur (provided the military relief was properly being supplied pursuant to a valid RFA from the PA/LFA).

While there are six additional exceptions to the *Posse Comitatus* Act, none on them are germane to state and local civil support activities. Nevertheless, there are other clarifications to the act that are not considered exceptions, but constitute indirect law enforcement support that should be of interest to state and local authorities.

G. Indirect DoD Law Enforcement Support: Back-up

Congress enacted authority for DoD assistance to law enforcement officials providing the level of DoD participation does not rise to the level of "searches, seizures, arrest and similar activities, unless authorized by law."[64] The armed forces may provide federal, state, and local civilian law enforcement officials any information collected during the normal course of military training or operations that may be relevant to a violation of any federal, or state law.[65] Military aviation photographs of training activities, facilities, or exercises that reveal illegal activity, or radio or intelligence data obtained in the normal course of operations, do not constitute illegal direct assistance and may be provided.

Equipment, base facilities, or research facilities may be provided to any federal, state, or local civilian law enforcement official for law enforcement purposes. This includes training facilities, sensors, protective clothing, and antidotes in preparing for or responding to an emergency involving chemical or biological agents.[66] Examples range from access to military firing ranges, chemical decontamination chambers, armor vests, and helmets. The FBI borrowed everything from tanks, armored personnel carriers, and armored vests and helmets for its assault on the Branch Davidians in Waco, Texas.

The armed forces can provide training to federal, state, and local law enforcement in the operation and maintenance of any equipment.[67] In addition, military personnel are authorized to maintain and operate equipment for federal, state, and local law enforcement officials relieving them of the logistics burden so they can focus on operational activity.[68]

There are two conditions for providing any of this indirect support by DoD. The first condition requires that such support must not adversely affect the military preparedness of the United States.[69] The armed forces are in the business of national defense and indirect support can only be provided if it does not affect operational readiness. The second condition involves the Economy Act.

This federal statute requires that any civilian law enforcement for which support is provided must reimburse DoD for that support.[70] There are no free lunches when it comes to DoD support as required by the Economy Act.

V. CONCLUSION

In business, knowing your client has much to do with making a sale. When state and local officials seek DoD assistance in emergency management phases of mitigation, preparedness, response, and recovery, understanding how DoD operates is key to a smooth partnership. Knowing how DoD functions within a much larger Homeland Defense framework, the civil support functions it can provide, and the methods by which those services are obtained, can pay countless dividends.

Time is always of the essence in emergency response operations. It is true that knowledge is

power. Understanding the importance of the Federal Response Plan and where DoD fits in its operation provides context for knowing what can be expected from DoD resources. Knowing how DoD is organized to provide WMD and terrorist incident civil support increases the state and local civil support knowledge base of what and who DoD brings to the fight. DoD possesses enormous resources, but like any organization, especially during a WMD event, understanding the delivery system for those resources and interfacing with that system has everything to do with timely arrival of critical services.

VI. SUMMARY

1. What role does DoD play in the NRP/FRP?
   - It is a force provider, virtually never the primary or lead federal agency.
2. When is DoD authorized to respond to a WMD or terrorist event?
   - Where there is insufficient time for higher authority approval, local military commanders may always provide an immediate response for civil support to state and local authorities.
   - Where time allows, and the state governor makes a request to the president for support, under the PA/LFA of DHS/FEMA or the FBI, DoD will respond to any tasking.
   - The president may declare a national emergency on his own and direct DoD to respond to it.
   - The president, with respect to an emergency involving a federal primary responsibility, may direct use of DoD's armed forces.
3. How does DoD perform its civil support mission? By following the NRP/FRP and supporting the PA/LFA in completing all assigned and properly approved taskings in the most expeditious manner possible.

4. How do state and local civil support authorities partner with DoD to obtain DoD assistance, and then work with DoD forces providing support?
   - By making specific requests through its State Emergency Management Agency to the PA/LFA, and by establishing local liaison officers to team with DoD DCE officials once they have been tasked with the civil support mission.
5. What restrictions has Congress placed on DoD?
   - Armed forces may not be used to conduct law enforcement activities under the *Posse Comitatus* Act.
   - Exceptions are:
     (1) If an insurrection occurs and assistance is requested by the state;
     (2) If an insurrection interferes with the exercise of a federal function;
     (3) If an insurrection interferes with the exercise of a federal right;
     (4) If an emergency involving a biological or chemical WMD weapon endangers human life and local civilian law enforcement authorities are not capable of taking action;

(5) If an emergency involving radiological materials impairs enforcement of the law, and civilian law enforcement officers are incapable of enforcing the law;

(6) If an emergency requires a federal quarantine action;

(7) If a civil disturbance endangers life or property or a government function, and

state authority is unable to protect federal property or functions;

(8) Actions taken to further a primary military purpose;

(9) Indirect logistic support, equipment, or training, can be provided on a cost reimbursement basis.

ENDNOTES

1. U.S. CONST.
2. John Philpott Curran, Speech Upon Right of Election (July 10, 1790).
3. IV. Implementing the National Strategy, the Fourth Annual Report to the President and the Congress of the Advisory Panel to Assess Domestic Response Capabilities for Terrorism Involving Weapons of Mass Destruction, Dec. 15, 2002. (Hereafter National Strategy.)
4. The NRP is drafted in accordance with HSPD-5, which provides for the establishment of a single "all-discipline, all hazards" National Response Plan to consolidate the various U.S. government prevention, preparedness, response, and recovery plans. The NRP will specifically replace the current Federal Response Plan. Homeland Security Presidential Directive 5, "Management of Domestic Incidents," February 28, 2003.
5. U.S. Const. IV, §8, cl.14.
6. Raymond v. Thomas, 91 U.S. 712 (1875).
7. "The powers not delegated to the United States by the Constitution, nor prohibited by it to the states, are reserved to the states respectively, or to the people." Tenth Amendment to the Constitution of the United States of America.
8. Justice Assistance Act of 1984, 42 U.S.C. §10501, *et seq.* (2002). The Act is implemented by 28 CFR §65.
9. The Robert T. Disaster Relief and Emergency Assistance Act as amended. 42 U.S.C. §5192a.
10. The implementing regulations of the Stafford Act may be found at 44 CFR Part 206 (2002).
11. E.O. 12656 (Nov. 18, 1988).
12. *Id.*
13. 50 U.S.C. §2301 *et seq.* (2002).
14. Pub. L. 107-314, Bob Stump National Authorization Act of Fiscal Year 2002 (NDAA 2003), Dec. 2, 2002.
15. Pub. L. 107-296 (Nov. 25, 2002).
16. The FRP uses the term "Lead Federal Agency," while the NRP uses "Primary Agency."
17. There is one exception where the Defense Department is the Primary or Lead Federal Agency–an accident involving a nuclear weapon while that weapon is in the control of the Department of Defense. The Federal Radiological Emergency Response Plan (May 1, 1996) at II-1.
18. National Response Plan, found on line at: http://www.dhs.gov/interweb/assetlibrary/NRP_FullText.pdf.
19. The implementation document, the "National Incident Management System" 139 pp., was issued on March 1, 2004, by DHS.
20. NRP at 10.
21. *Id.*
22. NRP at 28–33.
23. After Action Report for Oklahoma City Bombing Incident of April 19, 1995, Headquarters, Fifth U.S. Army, Fort Sam Houston (Aug. 17, 1995).
24. Department of the Army, Office of the Director of Military Support, Information Paper, "DoD Support to the Events of and Subsequent to Sept. 11th, 2001" (undated).
25. *Supra* note 3, National Strategy, at 90.
26. Richard Brennan, "U.S. Army Finds Its Role at Home Up for Grabs," *Rand Review*, Vol. 26, No. 2, (Summer 2002) at 47; and Eric V. Larson and John E. Peters, "Preparing the U.S. Army for Homeland Security: Concepts, Issues, and Options (Santa Monica RAND, 2001), at 167.
27. 50 U.S.C. §2251, *et seq.* (1950).
28. 50 U.S.C §1601, *et seq.* (2002).
29. Dept. of Defense Directive (DoDD) 3025.1, Military Support to Civil Authorities, January 15, 1993.
30. *Id.* at 4.5.1.
31. *Id.*
32. As discussed in Section E.5 of this chapter, under other, very narrow circumstances involving the potential loss of life.
33. *Supra* note 29 at 4.5.4.
34. *Id.* at 4.52.
35. 42 U.S.C. §5121, *et seq.*, §5170(c).
36. 50 U.S.C. §1601, *et.seq.* (2002).
37. Proclamation 7363 of September 14, 2001.

38. The Robert T. Stafford Disaster Relief and Emergency Assistance Act, as amended, 42 U.S.C. §5121, *et seq.*, (2002), §5191.
39. *Supra* note 3, National Strategy, at 100. *See also* George Cahlink, "Identity Crisis: The National Guard is Torn Between Two Missions," *Government Executive*, September 2002, available at http: 207.27.3.29/features/0902/0902.2s5.htm.
40. *Id.* at 88.
41. U.S. Army Forces Command, *Command Readiness Program Handbook*, Sep. 1998, at 23.
42. Deputy Secretary of Defense Memorandum (March 25, 2003), Implementation Guidance Regarding the Office of the Assistant Secretary of Defense for Homeland Defense.
43. Joint Task Force Consequence Management Standing Operating Procedures, Dec. 2002, at K-2 (2002).
44. Joint Task Force and Response Task Force-East Standard Operating Procedures, Aug. 2001, at H-1, 2.
45. *Supra* note 3, National Strategy, at 87.
46. *Id.* at 88.
47. United States v. Allred, 867 F.2d 856 (1989).
48. United States v. Harley, 796 F.2d 112 (1986).
49. 18 U.S.C. §1385 (2002).
50. *Webster's Third International Dictionary*, Unabridged, Merriam-Webster, Inc., 1993.
51. 10 U.S.C. §331.
52. *Id.* at §332.
53. *Id.* at §333.
54. *Id.* at §334.
55. 10 U.S.C. §382; 18 U.S.C. §175a; 18 U.S.C. §2332e.
56. 18 U.S.C. §831 (e).
57. *Id.* at 831(e) (3).
58. 42 U.S.C. §97; 42 CFR Part 70 (2002); 42 CFR Part 71 (2002).
59. 42 U.S.C. §264.
60. DoD Directive 3025.12, Military Assistance for Civil Disturbances (MACDIS), Feb. 4, 1994, at 4.2.2.1.
61. *Id.* at 4.2.2.2.
62. *Supra* note 29.
63. DoD Directive, DoD Cooperation with Civilian Law Enforcement Officials, Jan. 15, 1986, at E.41.2.1.1. to 1.6.
64. 10 U.S.C. §375.
65. 10 U.S.C. §371.
66. 10 U.S.C. §372.
67. 10 U.S.C. §373.
68. 10 U.S.C. §374.
69. 10 U.S.C. §376.
70. 31 U.S.C. §1535.

DISCUSSION QUESTIONS

Rapid City, South Dakota, is selected to be the host city for the upcoming Prairie Olympic Winter Games to be conducted at nearby Terry and Deer Peaks. While there are only 2,500 athletes, there are over 1,000,000 spectators who have come to watch the games. Approximately 10,000 local, state, and some federal security personnel are responsible for maintaining law and order at the sites. During the Games, a mysterious influenza breaks out and thousands of visitors overwhelm local medical facilities. Rumors spread that a lethal agent has been released by unknown terrorists that starts a mass exodus away from the Rapid City area. Highly contagious but undiagnosed to date by local medical authorities, county public health officials request assistance. You are a WMD consultant under contract to the Rapid City Olympic Committee and confronted with the following requests for information:

1. Who has initial legal response authority, and why? What immediate assistance can DoD provide, if called upon?
2. Who has authority to declare and enforce quarantine?
3. If local law enforcement authority is overwhelmed, what law enforcement support may DoD provide?
4. If state authorities are unable, for whatever reason, to make a decision and implement a plan imposing quarantine around Rapid City, can any other agency take necessary and appropriate action?
5. If local law enforcement authority desires to maintain control of quarantine operations, but need aviation, armored personnel carriers, communications, intelligence, roadblocks, and related logistic support, how do they obtain it?
6. What hazards do you see in your local area that might require DoD resources during an emergency response?
7. What potential problems do you see in use of DoD resources in the aftermath of an event that creates severe civil unrest?
8. What steps can local government take in advance of a crisis to help ensure smooth integration of DoD resources?

An anti-war protestor's sign rests below a makeshift memorial outside of the Camp Pendleton, CA. main gate Sept. 27, 2003. Members of the North County Coalition for Peace and Justice protested against Operation Iraqi Freedom, but said they supported the troops. USMC Photo by Sgt. L.A. Salinas.

Section IV

CIVIL RIGHTS ISSUES

Chapter 9

INSATIABLE APPETITE: THE GOVERNMENT'S DEMAND FOR NEW AND UNNECESSARY POWERS AFTER SEPTEMBER 11

AMERICAN CIVIL LIBERTIES UNION REPORT

Public Law 107-56 bears an extravagant title: The Uniting and Strengthening America by Providing Appropriate Tools Required to Intercept and Obstruct Terrorism Act. Its acronym–the USA PATRIOT Act–seems calculated to intimidate. Indeed, the legislative process preceding the law's enactment featured both rhetoric and procedures designed to stifle voices of opposition. Soon after the tragic September 11 terrorist attacks, Attorney General John Ashcroft transmitted to Congress a proposal containing the Justice Department's wish list of new police powers, including dramatic new authority to obtain sensitive private information about individuals, eavesdrop on conversations, monitor computer use, and detain suspects without probable cause, all with diminished judicial oversight. Ashcroft demanded that his proposal be enacted within three days, and, when that deadline was not met, he suggested publicly that members of Congress would be responsible for any terrorist attack that occurred during the bill's pendency. Congress passed the far-reaching law after abbreviated debate, handing Ashcroft virtually all the investigative tools he sought and several he had not even asked for. Yet the government's hunger for new powers was not satisfied. Soon after passage of the USA PATRIOT Act, Justice Department spokeswoman Mindy Tucker declared: "This is just the first step. There will be additional items to come."[1]

Additional items have come, some in the form of peremptory executive actions. Officials have detained hundreds of Middle Eastern and South Asian men and engaged in dragnet questioning of thousands of others without individualized suspicion. The Bush administration has asserted unilateral authority to establish secret military tribunals and breach attorney–client communications without a court order. It has even locked up American citizens in military brigs without charging them with a crime and has argued they should have no access to the courts. When challenged, government officials insist their actions represent a natural reordering of the balance between liberty and security. While the loss of liberty is apparent, there is surprisingly little evidence that the new powers will actually enhance security. The loss of liberty associated with these new measures takes various forms, but can be distilled into three basic overarching themes:

- An unprecedented and alarming new penchant for government secrecy and abandonment of the core American principle that a government for the people and by the people must be transparent to the people.
- A disdain for the checks and balances that have been a cornerstone of American democracy for more than 225 years. Specifically, the administration has frequently bypassed Congress, while both the executive and legislative branches have weakened the judiciary's authority to check government excesses.

Note: Found online at: http://www.aclu.org/SafeandFree/SafeandFree.cfm?ID=10623&c=207

- A disrespect for the American value of equality under the law. Government enforcement strategies that target suspects based on their country of origin, race, religion, or ethnicity pose a serious threat to the civil liberties of citizens and noncitizens alike.

A year after the attacks, the administration continues to augment its bulging statutory arsenal and members of Congress seem all too anxious to accommodate these unceasing demands. Attorney General John Ashcroft authorized the Federal Bureau of Investigation (FBI) to spy on First Amendment activities of religious and political organizations in the United States even when they are suspected of doing nothing wrong. The Customs Service secured legal authority to engage in routine searches of packages sent overseas in the U.S. mail. A pending Homeland Security bill already approved by the House would allow state and local police to obtain sensitive intelligence information developed by federal agents, even as legal protections against the dissemination of such information are weakened. The Justice Department is implementing an electronic tracking system for noncitizens and it has asked Congress for an additional expansion of its intelligence surveillance powers. The American Civil Liberties Union (ACLU) has sought to counter these dangerous developments through legislative advocacy, public education, and litigation. From the moment the administration put forth its proposals, the ACLU's Washington National Office worked intensively to moderate the excesses of the USA PATRIOT Act. The output of legislative analyses, background briefing documents, and letters to law and policymakers increased dramatically. The legislative communications unit fielded upwards of 8,000 individual press calls in a three-month period, making it one of the busiest nongovernmental media relations operations in the country. The Washington field staff mobilized ACLU members in opposition to the new measures, generating hundreds of thousands of letters to the Capitol and the administration. Meanwhile, ACLU Executive Director Anthony Romero, ACLU President Nadine Strossen, and other officials brought the struggle to protect civil liberties to the nation's airwaves and testified on numerous occasions before House and Senate committees urging that Congress reclaim its constitutional mandate to reign in overbroad executive branch policies adopted in the wake of September 11.

Working with other organizations, the ACLU has also brought its arguments to the courts, filing lawsuits to uncover information about hundreds of detainees, challenge a new law prohibiting noncitizens from working as airport screeners, and obtain public access to immigration hearings. The ACLU continues to insist that the dichotomy between security and liberty is false: We believe that we can be both safe *and* free, and that government policies should not be based on the myth that liberties must be curtailed to protect the public. One of the most important missions of the ACLU and other civil and human rights groups in this time of crisis is public education: calling attention to the alarming antiliberty trend in a range of government actions since September 11. In furtherance of that goal, this report catalogues some of the new and unnecessary powers the government has granted itself over the last twelve months, and describes other new powers the administration still seeks or that Congress is contemplating. It then highlights ways in which these new laws and regulations threaten the bedrock values of liberty, equality, and government accountability on which the nation was founded.

I. THE EVER-EXPANDING ARSENAL

When commercial airplanes struck the twin towers of the World Trade Center on September 11, 2001, Americans literally did not know what had hit them. In quick succession a third plane hit the Pentagon and a fourth crashed in Pennsylvania. Over the course of the morning there were rumors of numerous other plane crashes, car bombs, and explosions near government buildings. The White House reported that Air Force One was itself a target. In those confusing hours, no one could be sure of the magnitude of the threat confronting the United States or what drastic means might be needed to repel it. No one could assert confidently that new government powers were unnecessary to prevent the next brutal hijacking or the next skyscraper from crumbling. But within days, the contours of the challenge became clearer. Congress promptly responded to the attacks with two measures that built upon current legal authorities. First, it appropriated substantial new funds for existing security agencies to carry out their ongoing duties. Second, it enacted a "Use of Force" resolution authorizing the president to deploy the nation's standing armed forces against the terrorists overseas who had launched the attacks. President Bush made aggressive use of the civilian and military personnel already at his disposal. American military forces launched a campaign against the instigators of the attack in their home base of Afghanistan, destroyed the terrorists' infrastructure and toppled the repressive regime that had harbored them. At the same time, domestic law enforcement agencies mobilized to guard against additional attacks at home. Accomplishments in the war on terrorism have been achieved using statutory tools and other assets available to the government prior to September 11. Our technological superiority on the battlefield, the hard work of domestic public safety officers, and the vigilance of ordinary citizens have all contributed. These advantages were available instantly in a moment of crisis. A 342-page bill was not needed to mobilize the nation's abundant resources. Yet the campaign to enlarge federal police powers has taken on a life of its own. There is no evidence that statutory gaps facilitated the September 11 attacks, but that has not stopped the administration and Congress from amassing an overabundance of new laws, executive orders, and regulations to inflate the government's previously ample authority to defend the country. Anxious to be seen as responsive to public fears, politicians are passing laws for the sake of passing laws rather than to meet any genuine security concerns. The battle in Afghanistan is largely won, but there is no end in sight to the battle over the Constitution. Even during times of crisis, requests for new government powers should bear some relation to the nature of the threat they are designed to counter. Before obtaining new powers, government officials should be required to demonstrate that (1) the new power is necessary to thwart

future attacks; and (2) the benefit of the new power outweighs its adverse effect on liberty.

To be sure, there have been other scares since September 11, and there may well be future terror attacks as the administration has warned. But the basic formula governing consideration of proposals to award the president new antiterror powers should remain the same: Will the proposed new power really enhance security? If so, does the anticipated gain outweigh any loss of liberty that will result? Weighing the civil liberties' implications of new government powers makes it more likely that we will emerge from this period in our nation's history both safe *and* free.

A. The USA PATRIOT Act

A mere two days after the attack, influential members of the Senate Judiciary Committee led by Ranking Member Orrin Hatch (R-UT) proposed a floor amendment to a routine spending bill that would have expanded the government's authority to intercept oral and electronic communications. Although no hearings had been held on the proposal, Hatch explained that he wanted to arm the government with "the right tools to hunt down and find the cowardly terrorists who wreaked such havoc two days ago."[2] Judiciary Committee Chairman Pat Leahy (D-VT) urged a more deliberative process, but Senator Jon Kyl (R-AZ) voiced impatience: "Our constituents are calling this a war on terrorism. In wars, you don't fight by a Marquis of Queensberry rules."[3] The amendment passed quickly and the stampede was on. One week after the attack, Attorney General John Ashcroft transmitted to the Congress an omnibus antiterrorism proposal. In addition to expanded wiretap authority, the Justice Department sought new authority to detain suspicious immigrants indefinitely and without charge, new powers for government agents to obtain financial and other records without probable cause, expanded powers to forfeit assets of suspects, and lower barriers to the involvement of intelligence agencies in domestic law enforcement. Ashcroft declared that his massive proposal should be enacted within three days. The congressional debate that followed was not as abbreviated as the administration requested, although it might as well have been because the attorney general eventually secured nearly all of the powers he requested. The judiciary committees in the House and Senate convened a hearing on the proposal, but Ashcroft made himself available to the panels for only about an hour. In the Senate, the bill moved directly to the floor without a committee vote. Majority Leader Tom Daschle (D-SD) sought unanimous consent to pass the bill without amendment, but Senator Russell Feingold (D-WI) insisted on offering amendments, each of which was promptly tabled with only a few votes of support. In the House, the Republican-led Judiciary Committee debated the proposal and amended it to incorporate additional civil liberties' protections. Acting with rare unanimity, the deeply partisan committee adopted that version of the bill, but the administration persuaded the House leadership to rewrite the bill in the middle of the night before the floor debate to conform the text more closely to Ashcroft's specifications. There was no official conference committee meeting of senators and representatives to reconcile differences between the two bills: instead, a small group of members and administration officials met behind closed doors to negotiate the package. Final passage of the 342-page legislation occurred just as the anthrax scare paralyzed Congress. Most members of Congress had no access to their offices and no opportunity to read the bill. Critiques of the bill's civil liberties implications provided by the ACLU and other like-minded groups and citizens were virtually ignored in the frantic environment. The USA PATRIOT Act showers abundant new law enforcement powers on federal agents. Most of its provisions are not limited to terrorism offenses, but instead apply to all federal investigations; in fact, the Justice Department had unsuccessfully sought many of the proposals well before September 11 to bolster routine drug cases and other nonterrorism investigations. Some skeptical members of Congress argued for a sunset provision under which the law would expire in several years, forcing congressional reconsideration under less frenzied conditions. In the end, a four-year sunset applies to only a handful of the eavesdropping sections in one part of the ten-part bill. Among the most far-reaching provisions in the law are the following:

- It permits the attorney general to incarcerate or detain noncitizens based on mere suspicion,

and to deny readmission to the United States of noncitizens (including legal, long-term permanent residents) for engaging in speech protected by the First Amendment.
- It minimizes the power of the courts to prevent law enforcement authorities from illegally abusing telephone and Internet surveillance in both antiterrorism investigations and ordinary criminal investigations of American citizens.
- It expands the authority of the government in both terrorism and nonterror investigations to conduct so-called "sneak and peek" or "black bag" secret searches, which do not require notification of the subject of the search.
- It grants the FBI–and, under new information-sharing provisions, many other law enforcement and intelligence agencies–broad access to highly personal medical, financial, mental health, and student records with only the most minimal judicial oversight.
- It permits law enforcement agents to investigate American citizens for criminal matters without establishing probable cause based on an assertion that the investigation is for "intelligence purposes."
- It puts the CIA firmly back in the historically abusive business of spying on Americans by giving the director of Central Intelligence broad authority to target intelligence surveillance in the United States.[4]
- It contains an overbroad definition of domestic terrorism. The new definition is so vague that the government could designate lawful advocacy groups–such as Operation Rescue or Greenpeace–as terrorists and subject them to invasive surveillance, wiretapping, and harassment and then criminally penalize them for what had been constitutionally protected political advocacy.

The immigration provisions of the bill are also expansive. They empower the attorney general to detain a noncitizen if he believes there are "reasonable grounds to believe" the individual may be a threat to national security. The suspect may be detained for seven days before criminal or deportation charges are brought, but thereafter may be detained indefinitely in six-month increments without meaningful judicial review. (As -

narrow as these protections are, the administration has essentially ignored them in its subsequent actions.)

President Bush signed the USA PATRIOT Act into law on October 26. Yet even while negotiating with members of Congress about the scope of new authorities in the bill, the administration was pushing the limits of its existing powers by practicing widespread preventive detention of Arab and South Asian men and planning a series of nonstatutory initiatives to expand executive supremacy.

B. Spying on Americans

On May 30, 2002, Attorney General Ashcroft announced that he had rewritten the guidelines that govern FBI domestic surveillance. The Ashcroft guidelines sever the tie between the start of investigative activities and evidence of crime. Ashcroft's guidelines give the FBI a green light to send undercover agents or informants to spy on worship services, political demonstrations, and other public gatherings and in Internet chat rooms without even the slightest evidence that wrongdoing is underfoot. The surveillance guidelines that Ashcroft rewrote were adopted in the 1970s after disclosures that the FBI and CIA had operated widespread domestic surveillance programs—known as COINTELPRO, COMINFIL, and Operation CHAOS—to monitor activists such as Dr. Martin Luther King, Jr.[5] In response to reports that Ashcroft intended to rewrite the guidelines, the ACLU Washington National Office distributed a report on the FBI's excesses in its scheme to discredit Dr. King that led, in part, to adoption of the original guidelines.[6] The new guidelines call for utilizing twenty-first-century methods—such as data mining to pull together intimate details of a person's life activities—to carry out 1960s-era spying on domestic groups. The Ashcroft guidelines also diminish FBI headquarters' oversight of its field offices. In so doing, they invite abuses that result from rogue investigations.

C. Detention of Noncitizens

Immediately following September 11, some 75 men, largely of Arab and South Asian origin, were rounded up and held in secretive federal custody. Lacking evidence to prove that these detainees were involved in the plot to destroy the World Trade Center, the government relied on minor immigration violations to justify their continued incarceration. The number of detainees grew steadily through September and October, and by early November, 1,147 people were being held in connection with the investigation, according to the Justice Department. At that point the department declared it would no longer release a tally of detainees. To this date, despite repeated requests from members of Congress and the media, the administration has failed to present a full public accounting of the prisoners.

The American Civil Liberties Union and other organizations have filed suit under the Freedom of Information Act seeking a meaningful report on the detainees. Papers filed by the government in response to the suit reveal that a number of the detainees were held without any civil or criminal charges being filed against them for weeks or even as long as two months.[7] On August 2, a federal court ordered the government to release the names of the nearly 1,200 people detained since September 2001. In her order, U.S. District Judge Gladys Kessler wrote, "Unquestionably, the public's interest in learning the identity of those arrested and detained is essential to verifying whether the government is operating within the bounds of law."[8]

The ACLU filed another lawsuit in New Jersey state court seeking access under New Jersey law to information about the state's Immigration and Naturalization Service detainees (INS). The lower court ordered disclosure of information about the detainees and criticized the government's reticence to disclose basic information about the detainees, saying in its ruling that secret arrests are "odious to democracy." The Department of Justice then successfully undercut the court's ruling by adopting a new regulation barring INS detention contractors from complying with state freedom of information laws requiring disclosure of information about immigration detainees.[9]

In late November 2001, shortly before Assistant Attorney General Michael Chertoff testified before a Senate committee, the Justice Department grudgingly released minimal information about the detainees, such as a list of their countries of origin. But the disclosure omitted the names of detainees, the location of their detention, the charges against them, and whether they were represented by counsel. Some of the detainees held without bond had overstayed their visas or committed other technical violations of the immigration laws that would rarely result in incarceration prior to September 11. Others were held without bond as "material witnesses," but witnesses are very rarely incarcerated in ordinary criminal cases; it has become clear that these individuals are not, in fact, witnesses, but rather suspects against whom no formal charges could be lodged for lack of evidence. For example, a Catholic citizen of the Ivory Coast named Tony Oulai was detained in various federal facilities for months following his September 14 arrest without charges, without evidence of his affiliation with terrorist organizations, and largely without access to an attorney.[10]

Most of the detainees were of Arab or South Asian descent and almost all were Muslims. In effect, the government had executed a dragnet, rounding up men who bore superficial similarities to those who had carried out the September 11 attacks. By mid-December authorities conceded that only a handful of the hundreds of detainees were still suspected of terrorism, and only one–Zacarias Moussaoui–has actually been charged with conduct relating to September 11.[11] By early March some of the detainees had been released or deported,[12] but a full year later, it appears that scores of these young men remain in custody.

Those detainees charged with crimes or held as material witnesses are entitled to court-appointed lawyers and to have their circumstances reviewed by an independent federal judge. Those held on violations of visa status and other civil immigration offenses do not obtain appointed counsel and their cases are heard by administrative law judges within the Justice Department. A rule change permits the government to hold a noncitizen without charge for an undefined "reasonable" period, and another rule change–implemented without public comment–gives the government authority to maintain custody of noncitizens even if an immigration judge has ordered them freed.[13]

Ironically, the United States is a signatory to the International Covenant on Civil and Political Rights, which limits the period of custody allowed before a detainee must be brought in front of a judge to only a "few days."[14] The arbitrary and indefinite detention of noncitizens plainly violates this international accord. Already, the government detained one person in solitary confinement for more than eight months without bringing him before a magistrate or letting him see a lawyer.[15]

In another judicial repudiation of the Department of Justice's overzealous detention activities, a federal judge recently ruled against the use of the "material witness" statute to justify the detention of persons innocent of wrongdoing. The court ordered the release of a Jordanian student being held as a material witness, saying that the government cannot use the statute to coerce testimony. The government has appealed that ruling, and convinced one other federal court that its position is correct.[16] And the dragnet continues to widen. In an internal memo made public earlier this year, the Department of Justice explicitly adopted a policy of selective immigration enforcement. Certain immigrants who have overstayed their visas are now targeted for speedy deportation based on their of national origin.[17] While the attorney general has defended the large-scale roundup of young Arab and South Asian men on national security grounds, even former FBI officials have questioned the effectiveness of a strategy so dependent on national origin profiling.[18]

A year after the campaign of preventive detention began, its sponsors have failed to demonstrate that the vast majority of those ensnared in the net were criminals, much less terrorists.

D. Detention of Citizens

The administration's detention-without-trial campaign has even ensnared U.S. citizens. Upon discovering that Yaser Esam Hamdi, one of the men captured in Afghanistan and detained at Guantanamo Bay, Cuba, was born in the United States, the government transferred him to a military brig, denied him access to counsel, failed to charge him with a crime, and asserted that no court could review its actions. Then, on June 20, in a dramatic live speech from Moscow, the attorney general announced that another American had been labeled an "enemy combatant" by the president, removed from the criminal justice system, and placed in a military brig for an indefinite period. On television, Ashcroft accused Abdullah al-Muhajir (who is also known as Jose Padilla) of scouting targets in the United States for a dirty bomb attack. In court, al-Muhajir was accused of nothing. He was removed to military detention only days before the expiration of the 30-day period the court had given the government to charge or release him. As if to underline the apparent lack of evidence to charge al-Muhajir with a crime, White House officials reportedly surprised by Ashcroft's announcement issued an alternate, less alarming statement about the arrest.[19]

This assault on the rights of American citizens to be free from detention without charge or trial flies in the face of constitutional guarantees and a specific statute prohibiting the same.[20] And there is no limiting principle to suggest that Hamdi and al-Muhajir are not the first of many citizens to be subjected to such summary treatment.

E. Dragnet Questioning and Fingerprinting of Immigrants

While one group of Middle Eastern and South Asian immigrants was detained, a much larger group of them was singled out for questioning. On November 9, 2001, Attorney General Ashcroft unveiled a plan to interview some 5,000 young men who had entered the United States within the past two years from specified countries. As those interviews were winding down in mid-March, the attorney general extended the program to 3,000 more Middle Eastern and South Asian immigrants who had more recently entered the United States. Ashcroft conceded that the list was compiled without particularized suspicion of any of these men. It was apparent they were targeted for law enforcement attention because of their country of origin.

In many parts of the country, local police carried out the questioning despite the fact that few such officers are trained to conduct terrorist investigations. The Department of Justice provided a list of questions to guide the interviews, covering such matters as the subject's employment and sources of income, foreign travel, reaction to terrorism, and sympathy for terrorists. Some local police departments balked at the request to

conduct the interviews because the scheme violated state laws or local policies against profiling based on race or national origin.[21]

Attorney General Ashcroft also announced a massive new program to fingerprint over 100,000 Arab and Muslim immigrants suspected of no wrongdoing.[22] Earlier in the year both President Bush and Attorney General Ashcroft had vowed to end racial profiling, but neither proffered a persuasive argument as to why the mass questioning and fingerprinting of these immigrants did not constitute blatant reliance on this discredited practice. These programs engender mistrust and resentment in Arab-American communities and among immigrants generally. In addition, the attorney general has not to date provided any evidence either program has been effective in identifying new suspects in the September 11 attacks or preventing other acts of terror.

F. Military Tribunals

On November 13, 2001, the president issued an order in his capacity as commander in chief investing himself with unprecedented authority to try individuals suspected of terror-related activity in a military tribunal rather than a civilian court.[23]

In this order the president asserted the authority to try by military commission any noncitizen suspected of being a terrorist, aiding a terrorist, or harboring a terrorist. The option could be exercised against legal immigrants in the United States, even those arrested by domestic law enforcement agencies. The president reserved for himself the exclusive discretion to invoke the tribunal option against any particular suspect. In effect, the president decides who will be entitled to constitutional rights and who will not.

The president's order provoked immediate controversy on procedural grounds. First, it came on the heels of a legislative process, however abbreviated, in which the question of how long immigrant suspects could be held without access to the courts was the subject of careful compromise. That compromise was embodied in section 412 of the USA PATRIOT Act, but the tribunal order essentially negated the new law's meager protections. Second, President Bush acted unilaterally, without congressional authorization or even consultation.

Supporters of the concept cited the precedent of President Roosevelt's order to try Nazi saboteurs by military tribunal, but Roosevelt had acted pursuant to a declaration of war and with statutory authority, since repealed, that authorized the procedure.

Some of the rules of the tribunal are spelled out in the president's order and others were put in place in a March 21, 2002, order issued by Secretary of Defense Donald Rumsfeld. The orders were criticized for disregard for procedures needed for reliable fact-finding. The orders make it clear that military officers handpicked by the president, Rumsfeld, or their designees would serve as judges and jurors. Only a two-thirds vote would be needed for conviction in all but capital cases, where unanimity would be required. The trials may be held in secret.

Evidence may be withheld from the defendant and the defendant's civilian lawyer, regardless of whether disclosure would reveal classified information. Under the orders, no court–federal, state, or international–is allowed to review the military commission's proceedings. While limited habeas corpus review may be available should the proceedings be conducted in the United States, the Defense Department apparently intends to conduct the proceedings abroad, and the government recently convinced a federal judge that no U.S. court has jurisdiction to hear a challenge to detentions at a U.S. military base in Guantanamo Bay, Cuba.[24] The administration has even indicated that it may hold the Guantanamo detainees indefinitely without even a trial before a military tribunal, and reserves the right to continue to detain persons indefinitely even if a military tribunal finds them not guilty of all charges.

The breadth of the order's scope is extraordinary. International law contemplates reliance on military justice in the zone of combat. But the order is not limited to, for example, al Quaida fighters captured in the caves of Tora Bora and transported to Guantanamo Bay. Instead it applies to all individuals the president has reason to believe may have "aided or abetted" or "conspired to commit" terrorism "or acts in preparation therefore." It applies to someone the president has a reason to believe has "knowingly harbored" or aided a terrorist. It does not apply to American citizens but potentially applies to any of the 18 million foreign-born legal residents of the United States.[25]

G. Attorney–Client Privilege

On October 31, 2001, the Justice Department published in the *Federal Register* a new regulation authorizing prison officials to monitor communications between detainees and their lawyers without obtaining a court order.[26] Here, as with the military tribunal regulations, the administration bypassed Congress altogether. By pursuing this authority unilaterally instead of including it among the surveillance authorities it sought from Congress in the USA PATRIOT Act, which had been signed into law only days before, the new regulation was promulgated. The administration's antiterror campaign eroded constitutional checks and balances. Under prior law, monitoring of attorney–client communications could occur if the government obtained a court order based on probable cause to believe that communication with an attorney was being used to facilitate a new crime or for foreign intelligence purposes. However, in the October 31 regulation, the attorney general bestowed on himself discretion to monitor communications without a court order. The regulation became effective immediately, with public comment to follow implementation. The new authority is an unjustified exception to the well-recognized confidentiality of attorney–client communications. That privilege is intended to encourage candor in such communications to ensure effective representation by defense counsel. To date, it appears that this new power has been exercised only once in which a court order had already authorized a wiretap, suggesting that the regulation was never needed to fill a real gap in current law. But of course the mere threat of government intrusions in the attorney–client relationship, even if never carried out, undermines the trust between lawyers and clients and chills their communications.

H. New Secrecy Measures

Attorney General Ashcroft has earned ridicule by spending $8,000 in public funds to cover a revealing Art Deco statue in the Great Hall of the Justice Department. Less well known are the attorney general's persistent efforts to shield the administration's controversial policies from public view.

As described earlier, the administration's failure to respond to reasonable requests under the Freedom of Information Act led to a lawsuit by the ACLU and others seeking basic information about September 11 detainees. More generally, since September 11 the attorney general has reversed prior Justice Department guidance and counseled executive branch agencies to resist FOIA requests; instead of requiring that information be released except when its disclosure would result in some harm, Attorney General Ashcroft has directed that information be withheld whenever possible under the statute, regardless of whether disclosure would be harmful.[27] Within the Department of Justice, the attorney general has instituted new secret procedures for cases before immigration judges. In a memo to his fellow judges dated September 21, 2001, Chief Immigration Judge Michael J. Creppy declared that certain hearings would be closed to the public and that information about such cases could not be disclosed to anyone outside the immigration court.

On January 2, 2002, House Judiciary Committee ranking member John Conyers (D-MI) was turned away when he sought to attend a court hearing involving one of his constituents, Rabih Haddad. Soon after, Conyers, the ACLU, and a number of news outlets filed a lawsuit challenging this unconstitutional practice in the Haddad case. A federal district court judge rejected in no uncertain terms the government's argument that all such hearings should be closed on a blanket basis for reasons of national security. And a federal appeals court, declaring, "Democracies die behind closed doors," issued a resounding affirmation on August 26. The ACLU filed another lawsuit challenging the closure of immigration hearings more broadly, and that case is pending. Ashcroft has also created an interagency task force, the first in two decades, to review administrative and criminal sanctions for the leak of classified information. Media organizations and watchdog groups have argued that such actions discourage whistleblowers and undermine legitimate efforts to hold government agencies accountable, but the attorney general is undeterred.[28] The FBI even went so far as to ask members of Congress–who were themselves investigating the FBI's performance prior to September 11–to submit to lie detector tests in connection with the FBI's investigation of one alleged leak. Many members declined out of fear of inaccurate results. Experts expressed doubt about Congress's ability to investigate the FBI's performance leading up to the September 11 attacks while the FBI was investigating the members of Congress conducting the investigation.[29]

Finally, the administration has asked Congress to broadly shield from public disclosure information businesses voluntarily submit to the government that they mark secret. Congress seems poised to reject this overly broad proposal to protect "critical infrastructure" information in favor of a more limited compromise, because the original proposal would have shielded corporate inaction or wrongdoing from public disclosure.

Frustrated with the administration's regime of secrecy, the ACLU on August 21, 2002, filed a new FOIA request seeking information on 14 different categories of Justice Department records. The ACLU FOIA request mirrors questions posed by House Judiciary Committee Chairman James Sensenbrenner (R-WI) and Ranking Minority Member John Conyers (D-MI). Sensenbrenner, in fact, has expressed such great frustration with Attorney General Ashcroft that he has threatened to subpoena the Justice Department to turn over information about how it is utilizing the powers granted it by the USA PATRIOT Act. In an interview with National Public Radio, Sensenbrenner said that the Ashcroft Justice Department has been the least cooperative of any in his 24-year tenure on the Judiciary Committee.[30]

Chairman Sensenbrenner is not alone in questioning this Justice Department. In a remarkable decision made public in August 2002, the secret Foreign Intelligence Surveillance Court explicitly rejected Ashcroft's efforts to eliminate federal "bright line" protections against having prosecutors direct intelligence investigations to use them for criminal prosecutions. Although the decision says the Justice Department expended "considerable effort justifying deletion of that bright line," it emphatically added, "the Court is not persuaded." The decision decisively demonstrates that Congress should reject two proposals pending in the Senate Intelligence Committee to reduce the level of proof the government must provide to the surveillance court to obtain an intelligence warrant. As the ACLU stated, "the intelligence court's opinion shows that the Department of Justice has abused the intelligence powers it already has and should not be showered with more until it addresses the problems the court identified."

The administration's preference for secrecy extends beyond the war on terrorism. Even before September 11, Vice President Dick Cheney had rebuffed lawful requests by the General Accounting Office for documents relating to his energy policy task force. And in November, President Bush issued an executive order limiting the release of presidential documents from past administrations, notwithstanding a statute that appears to mandate public availability. Finally the administration has restricted the amount of information available to the public on agency Websites, even though, according to the Federation of American Scientists, much of the information removed "appears to have little bearing on the terrorist threat."[31] An apt summary of the administration's hostility to open government comes from Representative Dan Burton, Republican Chair of the House Government Reform Committee, who has criticized the Bush administration's invocation of executive privilege in refusing to turn over documents subpoenaed by Congress. Burton observed that "[a]n iron veil is descending over the executive branch."[32]

II. ADDITIONAL MEASURES ON THE HORIZON

The mammoth USA PATRIOT Act expanded government powers in ways that will diminish liberty for years to come, and the subsequent executive branch actions pose additional challenges. But even the policies now on the books may be dwarfed in significance by the far-reaching activities that the federal government is contemplating but has not yet undertaken. Even now, some six months after the attack, the pressure to add new ammunition to the federal law enforcement arsenal has not abated.

A. Surveillance

Many of the proposed new government powers under consideration in Congress and elsewhere involve increased surveillance authority. Only weeks after passage of the USA PATRIOT Act and before that law's provisions were fully implemented, the Justice Department asked Congress for an additional major expansion of electronic surveillance powers.[33]

The USA PATRIOT Act granted the FBI broad access to records about individuals maintained by third parties, such as businesses and libraries.[34] According to a study by the University of Illinois, such powers have been used by law enforcement officials to seek information from 85 libraries about their patrons.[35] The attorney general declared that the frequency of his use of this power is classified, and refused to disclose this information to key members of Congress.[36]

New technology tends to magnify the intrusive nature of government surveillance, and a number of new surveillance proposals partake of technological developments. For example, President Bush has proposed a high-tech tracking system for noncitizens involving biometric equipment of unproven efficacy.[37] And a leading Democratic congressman has suggested that the postal service should reduce the anonymity of mail service, perhaps issuing encoded stamps that could be traced back to the purchaser.[38]

Not content with the new broad surveillance powers he granted FBI agents himself, Attorney General Ashcroft announced a new program to recruit millions of Americans to spy for the government. "Operation TIPS" would train truckers, utility workers, postal workers, and local cable, gas, and electric technicians to report activities they deem suspicious to a special Department of Justice hotline. Once revealed as an effort to evade warrant procedures by having workers with access to private homes snoop for the government, the program was roundly condemned. Some critics dubbed it a government-sanctioned peeping Tom program while others equated it with George Orwell's *1984* and with the former East German Stasi, a secret police service that recruited thousands to spy on dissidents and compile dossiers about them.[39]

Members of Congress moved quickly to head off the program. House Majority Leader Dick Armey (R-TX) is attempting to outlaw the program by means of an amendment to the Homeland Security Act.[40] The administration, however, is intent on going forward with what it has called a scaled-back version of the program. In addition, the long-standing campaign to establish a system of national identification cards has gained new momentum in the wake of September 11. Current proposals typically incorporate new technology into the card in what its proponents call efforts to guard against forgery, but doubts about the concept's effectiveness and fears of the abuses it may breed remain.[41]

Some in Congress have proposed measures to standardize driver's licenses nationwide, proposals that have provoked an unusual alliance among such ideologically divergent groups as the ACLU and the Eagle Forum to decry the proposals as de facto national IDs. A House bill, introduced by Reps. Jim Moran (D-VI) and Tom Davis (R-VI), and a Senate counterpart, soon to be introduced by Sen. Dick Durbin (D-IL), would implement such a system.[42] Remarkably, even the apolitical National Research Council has expressly identified the driver's license standardization scheme as a "nationwide identity system" and raised questions about its effectiveness.[43]

B. State and Local Insatiable Appetites

The federal government is not alone in seeking to augment its powers in the aftermath of September 11. According to *Time* magazine, 46 state legislatures planned to debate antiterrorism bills in 2002, many expanding local law enforcement powers.[44] Among the ways in which federal antiterror policies have begun to influence state laws is in challenges to principles of open government. A number of state legislatures have limited public access to government documents in the name of public safety.[45] California and other states are exploring new wiretap laws that mirror federal statutes.[46] Meanwhile a number of local jurisdictions, including the District of Columbia, are expanding their network of surveillance cameras. According to D.C. officials, the city's grid links hundreds of government video cameras that routinely monitor streets, metro stations, schools, and other government facilities.[47] Other cities are aggressively experimenting with facial recognition technology. In Congress, the pending Homeland Security bill would relax privacy safeguards by enabling state and local police to obtain virtually all of the sensitive intelligence information developed by federal agents. Vast law enforcement databases containing detailed information about suspects and law-abiding citizens alike would be shared seamlessly among all enforcement agencies. The widespread dissemination of personal information about private citizens, even among law enforcement agencies, is inevitably prone to abuse. These concerns are especially relevant given the additional powers granted to the CIA in the USA PATRIOT Act, which essentially put the agency back in the business of spying on Americans. Basic civil liberties are imperiled if state and local law enforcement agencies are able to acquire information gathered by the CIA without normal constitutional restrictions.

III. CHALLENGES TO AMERICAN VALUES

Some of the new statutes, rules, and executive orders adopted in the last year may be benign while others are obviously troublesome. In any event, there has been little showing that the post 9-11 avalanche of laws, in the aggregate, make America safer. And, while the benefit of these measures is hard to discern, there is no question that they exact a profound cost to civil liberties and core constitutional values. Would efforts to prevent terrorism be any less successful if in the weeks after the attacks Congress had merely appropriated funds for existing agencies, authorized the deployment of troops to Afghanistan, and the executive branch had simply exercised its extant pre-September 11 powers?

A. The Threat to Patriotic Dissent

Looming over other threats is the threat that those who voice opposition to government policies will be branded unpatriotic. The most basic of all American values, one that buttresses all others, is the First Amendment right to express dissenting views about government actions. Attorney General Ashcroft has a different view. Testifying before the Senate Judiciary Committee on December 6, 2001, the attorney general stated, in his prepared remarks, "To those who scare peace-loving people with phantoms of lost liberty, my message is this: Your tactics only aid terrorists, for they erode our national unity and diminish our resolve. They give ammunition to America's enemies and pause to America's friends." This threat, although chilling, was hollow. If the attorney general hoped to silence critics of the administration's antiterror tactics he has plainly failed because public concern about those tactics is growing, not waning. Yet it appears that the attorney general's sentiment has been translated into action. Reports have emerged recently of federal agents investigating an art museum that exhibited materials on American covert operations and government secrets, a student who displayed a poster critical of President Bush's position on the death penalty, and a San Francisco weightlifter who publicly criticized the administration, among others.[48]

B. The Threat to Liberty

Individual liberty is the central precept of our system of government, but new government powers challenge that value in both extreme and subtle ways. One of the most significant attacks on individual liberty in the name of antiterrorism is the government's lengthy detention of individuals whose conduct has not warranted such a deprivation. At one time more than a thousand individuals were jailed in reaction to September 11. Today that number is smaller, but the Justice Department still refuses to provide a precise accounting. Some may deserve to be detained for criminal conduct, but many do not. Conservative columnist Stuart Taylor, who has defended a number of the new antiterror measures, observes:

> Not since the World War II internment of Japanese-Americans have we locked up so many people for so long with so little explanation. The same logic that made it prudent to err on the side of

overinclusiveness in rounding up suspects after the crimes of September 11 makes it imperative to ensure that these people are treated with consideration and respect, that they have every opportunity to establish their innocence and win release, and that they do not disappear for weeks or months into our vast prison-jail complex without explanation.[49]

A more long-term infringement of liberty is posed by the loss of privacy that will result from many of the provisions in the USA PATRIOT Act and related measures. The new authorities interfere with the right to privacy by making it easier for the government to conduct surveillance, listen in on conversations, obtain sensitive financial, student, and medical records, and otherwise track the daily activities of individuals. Subjecting individuals to intrusive police questioning without particularized suspicion is an additional deprivation of liberty that has flourished in recent months. The potential for such deprivation increased with the decision to allow the CIA to, once again, compile dossiers on ordinary Americans and then–through new information-sharing provisions–distribute that information throughout the law enforcement and intelligence communities.

Defenders of liberty do not take issue with the minor inconveniences that accompany many current security measures. Few Americans quarrel, for example, with reasonable screening procedures in airports such as luggage matching and strict control of secure areas to prevent weapons from being carried onto airplanes. Rather, the debate is about measures, like the USA PATRIOT Act, that represent genuine encroachments on privacy. Opinion polls suggest that a growing number of Americans are unwilling to sacrifice core values in the fight against terrorism, especially without proof that any particular measure is likely to be effective. Before it may scrutinize such personally sensitive materials as medical records, school records, banking records or an individual's Internet use, the government should be required to demonstrate in a particularized fashion that such scrutiny is necessary to achieve safety. That balance, of course, is embodied in the Fourth Amendment, which prohibits "unreasonable" searches and seizures and authorizes the government to intrude on privacy only on a finding of probable cause by a neutral judge.

The new enforcement powers conferred by Congress and assumed by the Justice Department reflect impatience with the Fourth Amendment, and its embodiment of the fundamental American conviction that individual liberty is accorded the benefit of the doubt when enforcing criminal law. The surveillance authorities in the USA PATRIOT Act undermine the role of the courts as the protectors of the individual against unfair and unwarranted government scrutiny or harassment. And the new Ashcroft surveillance guidelines reflect the view that dissent is to be feared and monitored, not protected under the First Amendment.

C. The Threat to Equality

The Constitution guarantees equal protection of the laws. It prohibits the government from establishing different sets of rules for similarly situated groups without a compelling reason. Citizenship is a characteristic on which some distinctions may be made, but not others. For example, noncitizens may not vote in federal elections but they are entitled to equal treatment, due process, and other constitutional protections by virtue of their presence in the country.

It is striking how many of the new restrictions and investigative tactics distinguish between citizens and noncitizens. Many of the government's actions, such as the military tribunal framework, the dragnet interviews, and of course the immigration-related detentions, all apply to noncitizens but not citizens. Also, new rules prohibit noncitizens from serving as airline screeners and limit the jobs noncitizens may perform at certain federal facilities. The broad premise of this distinction is that noncitizens pose a threat to Americans that citizens do not. That the 19 men who hijacked planes last September were noncitizens makes this premise superficially appealing, but in fact citizenship is a highly unreliable proxy for evidence of dangerousness.

First, at least one of the al Quaida members convicted in the trial arising from the terror attack on U.S. embassies in Africa was an American citizen (Wadih el-Hage), and at least two American citizens have been apprehended as suspected Taliban soldiers (John Walker Lindh and Yaser Esam Hamdi). Second, the president has made clear that the war on terrorism is not limited to al Quaida and the Taliban but encompasses all who utilize violence to intimidate civilian populations. By that measure, there have been numerous U.S. citizen-terrorists, including Timothy McVeigh whose bombing of the federal building in Oklahoma City was the bloodiest act of terrorism on U.S. soil prior to September 11.

Although some citizens are terrorists, a more important fact is that the overwhelming majority of noncitizens are not terrorists. Of the millions of noncitizens residing in the United States legally or illegally, only an infinitesimally small number of them have been tied to September 11 or other terror plots. As a statistical matter, citizenship status reveals essentially nothing about likely involvement in terrorism. Factoring in age and gender by focusing on young, male noncitizens does not meaningfully narrow the targeted class.

The pattern of detentions, the efforts to selectively deport out-of-status noncitizens and the dragnet effort to question 8,000 young Arab and South Asian men and fingerprint 100,000 more constitute profiling on the basis of national origin. Profiling is a flawed law enforcement tactic and a flawed tactic in the war on terrorism. It is inefficient and ineffective because it squanders limited law enforcement resources based on a factor that bears no statistically significant relationship to wrongdoing. Also, unwarranted focus on noncitizens as a class engenders hostility and resentment in immigrant communities. Yet it is precisely those communities in which law enforcement agencies are now seeking to recruit agents, hire translators, and search for suspicious behavior. An undue investigative focus on noncitizens threatens to spill over into governmental or nongovernmental harassment of citizens who happen to look foreign or who have foreign-sounding names. Already the federal government's reliance on a national origin dragnet has spawned similar tactics: Detectives in New York City's warrant squad have prioritized their activities by culling through computers for petty crime suspects with Middle Eastern-sounding names.[50] And on more than 200 college campuses investigators have contacted administrators to collect information about students from Middle Eastern countries and have approached foreign students without notice to conduct "voluntary" interviews.[51] Reliance on mere noncitizenship as a distinguishing characteristic is not just ineffective law enforcement; it is also anathema to American values. Vice President Cheney has said that those who kill innocent Americans would get "the kind of treatment we believe they deserve" because such people do not deserve "the same guarantees and safeguards that would be used for an American citizen going through the normal judicial process."[52] The vice president's dichotomy between "an American citizen" and "those who kill innocent Americans" is dangerously misleading. Citizenship is simply not a trait that distinguishes those who kill innocent Americans from those who do not.

D. The Threat to Constitutional Checks and Balances

The administration's actions since enactment of the USA PATRIOT Act betray a serious disrespect for the role of Congress. That law emerged from a flawed legislative process, and a number of the subsequently announced initiatives were never even discussed with Congress. For example, painstaking negotiations with Congress over the circumstances under which noncitizens could be detained in the name of national security led to enactment of section 412 of the act, which limits detentions to seven days before the individual must be brought before a judge to face immigration or criminal charges. However, just after enactment, the administration unveiled its military tribunal proposal, permitting indefinite detention of noncitizens without any review by an independent judicial officer.

Now the designation of certain individuals as enemy combatants renders even the meager protections of the military tribunal regulations inoperative. Moreover, both the USA PATRIOT Act and the subsequent executive actions undermine the role of the judiciary in overseeing the exercise of executive authority. The act essentially codifies a series of shortcuts for government agents. Under many of its provisions, a judge exercises no review function whatsoever; the court must issue an order granting access to sensitive information on mere certification by a government official. The act reflects a distrust of the judiciary as an independent safeguard against abuse of executive authority.

This trend is particularly apparent in the electronic surveillance provisions of the act. For example, the USA PATRIOT Act subjects surveillance of Internet communications to a minimal standard of review. This surveillance would reveal the persons with whom one corresponded by e-mail and the Websites one visited. Law enforcement agents may access this information by merely certifying that the information is relevant to an ongoing investigation. The court must accept the law enforcement certification; the judge must issue the order even if he or she finds the certification factually unpersuasive. The subsequent executive actions are even more flawed in this regard. The regulation allowing for monitoring of attorney–client communications was promulgated to bypass the courts, since prior to its promulgation government agents could only engage in such monitoring if they obtained a court-issued warrant and now they may act on their own suspicions without judicial review. And the military tribunal order and military detention of American citizens constitute pure court-stripping by removing federal judges from the process altogether.

These initiatives misunderstand the role of the judiciary in our constitutional system. They treat the courts as an inconvenient obstacle to executive action rather than an essential instrument of accountability. The framers of the Constitution understood that legislative and judicial checks on executive authority are important bulwarks against abusive government. It is true that the president plays a heightened role as commander in chief in defending the nation against foreign threats, but current circumstances do not render ordinary constitutional constraints on his role inoperative or unnecessary.

E. The Threat to Open Government

In our democracy, executive and legislative actions derive legitimacy from the fact that they emerge from a process that is deliberative and largely open to the public, at least through the media, but many of the new antiterrorism measures fail this fundamental test. As described earlier, much of the USA PATRIOT Act was negotiated out of public view. Key stages of the legislative process—committee vote, floor debate, and conference—were either short-circuited or skipped altogether. Similarly, the executive order concerning attorney–client communications and the presidential order authorizing military tribunals were developed in secret with no opportunity for public debate about their efficacy or wisdom before their promulgation.

At the same time, secrecy permeates the process by which hundreds of young Arab and South Asian men have been detained by the government. One reason the justice system must be open to the public is to ensure that the government affords individuals due process consistent with the Constitution and applicable statutes. One detainee was held for eight months without being brought before a judge. Georgetown Law Professor David Cole has observed: "In open proceedings the government would never get away with holding a person for three weeks without bringing charges. The only reason they have gotten away with it is these proceedings have been conducted under a veil of secrecy."[53]

The administration's FOIA policies threaten to usher in a new era of government secrecy. While the attorney general invoked the threat to terrorism in his directive limiting FOIA compliance, the order covers all government information, much of which has no national security or law enforcement connection whatsoever. As a result, all executive branch activities will be less open and less accountable under this new regime.

To be sure, there is a need for some secrecy in times of crisis. No one advocates the disclosure of documents that might endanger troops on the battlefield. However, secrecy appears to be a hallmark of the Bush administration's every move, even in the development of policies that should emerge from the crucible of public scrutiny and in the adjudication of charges against individuals.

F. The Threat to the Rule of Law

It is often said that ours is a government of laws, not those who inhabit high office at any given moment. Americans may trust or admire such individuals, but their enduring faith is reserved for certain fundamental legal principles and traditions that emanate from our Constitution: that the federal government is one of limited, enumerated powers; that the Congress makes the law, the president executes the law, and the judiciary interprets the law; that criminal suspects are innocent until proven guilty and entitled to various procedural protections during the process of adjudicating guilt.

Many of the new powers assumed by the president and his officers since September 11 run counter to these principles. For example, the detention of Americans in military brigs, and the contemplated procedures for noncitizens facing military tribunals skirt the rule of law. Department of Defense guidelines governing the tribunals shows marked and alarming deviation from traditional courts-martial. First, while the Pentagon has codified tribunal procedures in a less offensive fashion than opponents originally feared, the tribunals still—unacceptably—lack a clear appeals process. The guidelines essentially give the final word on the accused's fate to the president or the Secretary of Defense. Also, the guidelines confer complete discretion on the president or the Secretary of Defense to hold the tribunals in secrecy. Finally, in a surreal twist, it appears that the government will still be able to detain suspects acquitted by the tribunals indefinitely. In the final analysis, the main difference between the tribunals and courts-martial is that nothing is binding with the tribunals. The administration has given itself unlimited discretion to compose the rules for the tribunals as they go—an affront to the American tradition of impartial procedures to protect individual rights from the caprice of persons in authority.

American citizens are treated no better. According to the Bush administration, the president need only sign an order labeling an American citizen an enemy combatant to begin a process in which the citizen can be held indefinitely—without charge and without a right to see a lawyer—until the war on terrorism has ended. And the administration argues that no court can review the president's designation of an enemy combatant. Other facets of the war on terrorism also undermine the rule of law. Secret detentions, the unreviewable assertion of executive authority, the deployment of law enforcement agents against groups of people without particularized suspicion, recruiting ordinary Americans to spy on their neighbors–these are the hallmarks of undemo-cratic, strong-arm governments, not the two-century-old American democracy. Resorting to such tactics, even temporarily or in limited contexts, is cause for serious concern.

One reason for concern is that the new powers, especially many of the investigative tools in the USA PATRIOT Act, are not limited to the pursuit of terrorists. Even those that are reserved for ter-rorism investigations may be used in contexts that the drafters of the act never contemplated. The label terrorism is notoriously elastic; it has recently come to light that the Department of Justice cate-gorizes as terrorism such garden-variety crimes as erratic behavior by people with mental illness,

passengers getting drunk on airplanes, and con-victs rioting to get better prison food.[54]

In recent decades the United States has styled itself a champion of international human rights, and has encouraged the development of civilian legal institutions and the rule of law in countries throughout the world. For example, the State Department has pressured Egypt to abandon mili-tary tribunals in that country's war on terrorism, and has also criticized the secret trials that fre-quently characterize the justice systems in South America and China. What force will those criti-cisms have if the United States avails itself of these shortcuts even though its civilian courts are fully functional and open for business?

IV. CONCLUSION

America, more so than at any time in the past three decades, stands at a crossroads. The adminis-tration has invoked historical precedents to justify its wartime tactics, and in doing so has brought key segments of American society and politics to the brink of repeating much in our history that we have come to regret. It is true that throughout American history–from the eighteenth-century Alien and Sedition Acts to the suspension of habeas corpus during the Civil War to the Palmer Raids and the internment of Japanese-Americans during World War II–constitutional protections have taken a back seat to national security. With the benefit of hindsight, Americans have regretted such asser-tions of new government powers in times of crisis.

It is especially true that immigrants and others, citizens and noncitizens alike, have been mis-treated in wartime. The disgraceful internment of Japanese-Americans remains a stain on our national honor. That is surely not a precedent on which the administration would want to rely. Concepts of due process, military justice, and inter-national human rights have advanced substantially since World War II. Departure from these princi-ples has detrimental consequences for the war on terrorism. European allies, already wary of extra-diting suspects to the United States because of opposition to the death penalty, have now expressed misgivings about the possibility of mili-tary tribunals and other measures.[55]

Some national leaders downplay these con-cerns, saying that wartime limitations on civil liberties are temporary and normal conditions will return once hostilities end. However, the war on terrorism, unlike conventional wars, is not likely to come to a public and decisive end. Both Home-land Security Director Tom Ridge and the newly appointed drug czar John Walters recently equated the war on terrorism with the nation's continuing wars on drugs and crime, so restrictions on civil liberties may be with us for a very long time. So long, in fact, that they may change the character of our democratic system in ways that very few Americans desire.

In the absence of a broader sunset provision in the USA PATRIOT Act, and since the subsequent orders and regulations are of indefinite duration, Congress must be vigilant in monitoring imple-mentation of these new authorities. These powers have been structured in a manner that limits the role judges would ordinarily play in ensuring that enforcement agencies abide by constitutional and statutory rules. Without judicial oversight, there is a real danger that the war on terrorism will have domestic consequences that are inconsistent with American values and ideals. It is as *New York Times* columnist Bob Herbert has written:

We have a choice. We can fight and win a just war against terrorism, and emerge with the greatness of the United States intact. Or, we can win while running roughshod over the principles of fairness and due process that we claim to cherish, thus shaming ourselves in the eyes of the world—eventually, when the smoke of fear and anger finally clears—in our own eyes as well.[56]

ENDNOTES

1. Dreyfuss, "John Ashcroft's Midnight Raid," *Rolling Stone*, November 22, 2001.
2. 148 Cong. Rec. S9372 (daily ed. September 13, 2001).
3. Id. at S9374.
4. Dreyfuss, "Spying on Ourselves," *Rolling Stone*, March 28, 2002.
5. Johnston & Van Natta, "Ashcroft Seeking to Free F.B.I. to Spy on Groups," *New York Times*, December 1, 2001.
6. Johnson, "The Dangers of Domestic Spying by Federal Law Enforcement," ACLU Washington National Office, 2002. The report is available online at http://www.aclu.org/news/2002/ n011702d.html
7. Eggen, "Delays Cited in Charging Detainees," *Washington Post*, January 15, 2002 at A1.
8. *CNSS v. U.S. Dept. of Justice*, (D.D.C. Aug. 02, 2002) available at http://news.findlaw.com/cnn/docs/terrorism/cnssvdoj080202ord.pdf
9. Fainaru, "N.J. Appeals Court Upholds Secret Detentions," *Washington Post*, June 13, 2002, at A18.
10. Goldstein, "I Want to Go Home," *Washington Post*, January 26, 2002 at A1. Oulai has since been ordered deported and was convicted of making false statements to immigration agents.
11. "Officials Winnow Suspect List," *Washington Post*, December 14, 2001.
12. Fainaru and Goldstein, "U.S. is Quickly Repatriating Pakistanis Held After Sept. 11," *Washington Post*, March 8, 2002.
13. Lewis, "It Can Happen Here," *New York Times*, December 1, 2001.
14. Purohit, "Testimony Before the U.S. Civil Rights Commission on the Civil Rights Impact of the Implementation of the USA PATRIOT Act of 2001," Lawyers Committee for Human Rights, April 24, 2002.
15. Fainaru, "Suspect Held 8 Months Without Seeing Judge," *Washington Post*, June 12, 2002 at A1.
16. On July 11, a federal judge in Manhattan permitted the government to detain an unidentified person as a material witness who had important information and who might flee if released. Swanson, "Indefinite detentions OK, judge rules," *Chicago Tribune*, July 12, 2002, at page 8.
17. Eggen, "Deportee Sweep Will Start with Mideast Focus," *Washington Post*, February 8, 2002.
18. McGee, "Ex-FBI Officials Criticize Tactics on Terrorism," *Washington Post*, November 28, 2001. In the same article, prominent former law enforcement officials question the effectiveness of the dragnet questioning of 5,000 young men from Arab countries, discussed later in this report.
19. Johnson & Locy, "Threat of 'Dirty Bomb' Softened: Ashcroft's Remarks Annoy White House," *USA Today*, June 12, 2002, at A1.
20. 18 U.S.C. §4001.
21. Butterfield, "Police are Split on Questioning of Mideast Men," *New York Times*, November 22, 2001.
22. Schmitt, "Ashcroft Proposes Rules for Foreign Visitors," *New York Times*, June 5, 2002.
23. 66 Fed. Reg. 57831 (2001).
24. Tucker, "Judge Denies Detainees in Cuba Access to U.S. Courts," *Washington Post*, August 1, 2002, at A10.
25. Section 2(a)(1) of Military Order appearing at 66 Fed. Reg. 57831 (2001).
26. 66 Fed. Reg. 55062 (October 31, 2001).
27. Associated Press, "Ashcroft Urges Caution With FOIA Requests," *Washington Post*, October 17, 2001.
28. "Ashcroft Creates Interagency Force on Security Leaks," *Washington Times*, December 6, 2001. The panel was established pursuant to the Intelligence Authorization Act (Pub. L. 107-108).
29. Newton, "Lawmakers Balk at Polygraph Request," *AP Online*, August 2, 2002.
30. NPR: Morning Edition, "Analysis: House Judiciary Committee threatening to subpoena John Ashcroft for the Justice Department's failure to detail its use of the USA PATRIOT Act." September 9, 2002.
31. The Federation of American Scientists position can be found at http://www.fas.org/terrorism/is/index.html, and on April 11, 2002, Rep. Burton and 22 other members introduced legislation (H.R. 4187) that would override President Bush's order restricting release of old presidential documents.
32. Abrams, "Burton Asks Investigation into Justice Figures on Terrorist Convictions," *Associated Press*, December 19, 2001.

33. McGee, "Bush Team Seeks Broader Surveillance Powers," *Washington Post*, December 2, 2001. Some of these new provisions were included in last year's Intelligence Authorization bill (Pub. L. 107-108), but others remain pending.

34. Pub. L. 107-56, Section 215.

35. Kennedy, "Reading? Somebody May Be Watching," *Los Angeles Times*, July 29, 2002, at E3.

36. Letter from Attorney General Ashcroft to Rep. James Sensenbrenner and Rep. John Conyers, Jr., July 26, 2002, p. 4.

37. Allen and Miller, "Bush Proposes Tracking System for Non-Citizens," *Washington Post*, January 26, 2002.

38. Interview with Rep. Henry Waxman (D-CA) on *All Things Considered* (National Public Radio), December 11, 2001.

39. Sorokin, "Planned Volunteer-Informant Corps Elicits '1984' Fears," *Washington Times*, July 16, 2002.

40. H.R. 5005, "Homeland Security Act of 2002," Section 771.

41. O'Harrow and Krim, "National ID Card Gaining Support," *Washington Post*, December 17, 2001.

42. Testimony of ACLU Legislative Counsel Katie Corrigan Before the House Transportation Subcommittee on Highways and Transit on Driver's License Security Issues, available at http://www.aclu.org/congress/l090502a.html

43. "IDs–Not That Easy: Questions about Nationwide Identity Systems," National Research Council,

44. "46 States Debate Anti-Terror Legislation," *Time*, January 21, 2002.

45. Cha, "Risks Prompt U.S. to Limit Access to Data," *Washington Post*, February 24, 2002.

46. Bustillo and Vogel, "Legal Advice Sinks Davis' Wiretap Bill," *Los Angeles Times*, January 16, 2002.

47. Hsu, "D.C. Forms Network of Surveillance," *Washington Post*, February 17, 2002.

48. Axtman, "Political Dissent Can Bring Federal Agents to Door," *Christian Science Monitor*, January 8, 2002.

49. Taylor, *Legal Times*, November 19, 2001.

50. Purdy, "Bush's New Rules to Fight Terror Transform the Legal Landscape," *New York Times*, November 25, 2001.

51. Id.

52. Waldmeir, "Attack on Afghanistan Investigation," *Financial Times*, November 15, 2001.

53. Eggen, "Delays Cited in Charging Detainees," *Washington Post*, January 15, 2002, at A1.

54. Fazlollah and Nicholas, "U.S. Overstates Arrests in Terrorism," *Philadelphia Inquirer*, December 16, 2001.

55. Reid, "Europeans Reluctant to Send Terror Suspects to U.S.," *Washington Post*, November 29, 2001.

56. Herbert, "The Witch Hunt," *New York Times*, December 3, 2001.

Computer Science and Telecommunications Board, 2002.

DISCUSSION QUESTIONS

1. What do you see as the most important parts of the USA PATRIOT Act as described in this chapter? Why are they so critical?

2. How have the tensions between civil liberties and civil order changed in the aftermath of the USA PATRIOT Act?

3. What is your position on the USA PATRIOT Act? Defend your perspective.

4. How does the USA PATRIOT Act alter the role of the courts in the prevention of terrorism? What do you think the courts' role should be? Explain your answer.

5. Read and analyze the *Hamdi, Padilla*, and *Rasul* cases in Appendices F, G, and H. What issues in this chapter do they resolve? What matters do the cases not address?

6. What kind of issues, if any, do you see as not appropriate for judicial oversight? Why might the courts not be the appropriate forums to address such issues?

7. The chapter quotes Attorney General John Ashcroft as saying, "To those who scare peace-loving people with phantoms of lost liberty, my message is this: Your tactics only aid terrorists, for they erode our national unity and diminish our resolve. They give ammunition to America's enemies and pause to America's friends." How do you evaluate Mr. Ashcroft's words? Do you feel that you have lost liberty in the wake of 9-11? Describe how you personally have been affected, if at all, by the USA PATRIOT Act.

8. In the aftermath of the beginning of every war, civil liberties always seem to diminish in the interest of increased national security. Why does this occur? Explain why you think the chapter is overreacting to the situation or not.

Chapter 10

ANTITERRORISM INVESTIGATIONS AND THE FOURTH AMENDMENT AFTER SEPTEMBER 11, 2001

TESTIMONY OF PAUL ROSENZWEIG

Hearing Before the Subcommittee on the Constitution of the Committee on the Judiciary, House of Representatives, 180th Congress First Session, May 20, 2003

My perspective on this matter, then, is that of a lawyer and a prosecutor with a law enforcement background, not that of technologist or an intelligence officer/analyst. I should hasten to add that much of my testimony today is based upon a series of papers I have written on various aspects of this topic and testimony I have given before other bodies in Congress, all of which are available at The Heritage Foundation Website (www.heritage.org). For any who might have read this earlier work, I apologize for the familiarity that will attend this testimony. Repeating myself does have the virtue of maintaining consistency–I can only hope that any familiarity with my earlier work on the subject does not breed contempt.

It is commonplace for those called to testify before Congress to commend the representatives or senators before whom they appear for their wisdom in recognizing the importance of whatever topic is to be discussed–so much so that the platitude is often disregarded as mere puffery. Today, however, when I commend this Subcommittee for its attention to the topic at hand–the difficulty of both protecting individual liberty and enabling our intelligence and law enforcement organizations to combat terror–it is no puffery, but rather a heartfelt view. I have said often since September 11 that the civil liberty/national security question is the single most significant domestic legal issue facing America today, bar none. And, as is reflected in my testimony today, in my judgment one of the most important components of a responsible governmental policy addressing this difficult question will be the sustained, thoughtful, nonpartisan attention of America's elected leaders in Congress. Nothing is more likely, in my judgment, to allow America to find the appropriate balance than your engagement in this issue.

What I would like to do today is assist your consideration of this question by sharing with you some general legal analysis on the scope of the Fourth Amendment as it might apply in this context. I then offer some theoretical principles that you might consider in structuring your thinking. Finally, in an effort to avoid being too theoretical, I'd like to apply those principles to the concrete issues of data mining in the Total Information Awareness (TIA) program and the revised FBI investigative guidelines.

Let me first give you a short, pithy answer to the question posed by the title of today's hearing: Where and when can the government go to prevent terrorist attacks? The short answer is: As a matter of constitutional law, virtually anywhere

---

Note: Paul Rosenzweig is a Senior Legal Research Fellow in the Center for Legal and Judicial Studies at The Heritage Foundation and Adjunct Professor of Law at George Mason University. He graduated from the University of Chicago Law School and was the former law clerk to Judge Anderson of the U.S. Court of Appeals for the Eleventh Circuit. Rosenzweig also served as a prosecutor in the Department of Justice and elsewhere, prosecuting white-collar offenses.

that any other member of the public can go. The more difficult and interesting question is how best should those efforts be regulated as a matter of public policy so as to increase our ability to combat terror while minimizing any infringement on American liberty interests.

I. FOURTH AMENDMENT PRINCIPLES

Under settled modern Fourth Amendment jurisprudence, law enforcement may secure without a warrant (through a subpoena) an individual's bank records, telephone toll records, and credit card records, to name just three of many sources of data. Other information in government databases (e.g., arrest records, entries to and exits from the country, and driver's licenses) may be accessed directly without even the need for a subpoena.

In 1967, the Supreme Court said that the Fourth Amendment protects only those things in which someone has a "reasonable expectation of privacy" and, concurrently, that anything one exposes to the public (i.e., places in public view or gives to others outside of his own personal domain) is not something in which he has a reasonable expectation of privacy—that is, a legally enforceable right to prohibit others from accessing or using what one has exposed. So, for example, federal agents need no warrant, no subpoena, and no court authorization to:

- have a cooperating witness tape a conversation with a third party (because the third party has exposed his words to the public);
- attach a beeper to someone's car to track it (because the car's movements are exposed to the public);
- fly a helicopter over a house to see what can be seen; or
- search someone's garbage.

Thus, an individual's banking activity, credit card purchases, flight itineraries, and charitable donations are information that the government may access because the individual has voluntarily provided it to a third party. According to the Supreme Court, no one has any constitutionally based enforceable expectation of privacy in them. The individual who is the original source of this information cannot complain when another entity gives it to the government. Some thoughtful scholars have criticized this line of cases, but it has been fairly well settled for decades.

Congress, of course, may augment the protections that the Constitution provides and it has with respect to certain information. There are privacy laws restricting the dissemination of data held by banks, credit companies, and the like. But in almost all of these laws (the census being a notable exception), privacy protections are good only as against other private parties; they yield to criminal, national security, and foreign intelligence investigations. Thus, the extent of privacy protection is mostly a creature of legislation, not constitutional provisions.

One important caveat or note should be made here—in the foregoing discussion I have spoken principally of the restrictions that apply to domestic law enforcement officials. Important additional restrictions continue to exist on the authority of foreign intelligence agencies to conduct surveillance or examine the conduct of American citizens. Conversely, however, the courts have recognized that in the national security context the requirements of the Fourth Amendment apply somewhat differently than they do in the context of domestic law enforcement. Since the issues before the Subcommittee today are, as I understand it, principally focused on domestic law enforcement activity—potential domestic uses of TIA and the FBI's investigative guidelines—I will simply note the distinction here and then, for purposes of discussion, allude to it no further.

II. OVERARCHING PRINCIPLES

Since I conclude that, for the most part, limitations on law enforcement are likely to be the product of policy rather than constitutional law, let me next share with you some general thoughts about how cautious yet effective governmental action can, in my view, be implemented. Fundamental legal principles and conceptions of American government should guide the configuration of our intelligence and law enforcement efforts rather than the reverse. The precise contours of any rules relating to the use of any new technology or new program will depend, ultimately, on exactly what the new program is capable of or intended to accomplish–the more powerful the system or program, the greater the safeguards necessary. As a consequence, the concerns of civil libertarian critics should be fully voiced and considered while any research program is underway.

In general, unlike civil libertarian skeptics, I believe that new intelligence and law enforcement information gathering and information analytical systems can (and should) be constructed in a manner that fosters both civil liberty and public safety. We should not say that the risks of such systems are so great that any effort to construct them should be dispensed with. Rather, in my view, the proper course is to ensure that certain overarching principles animate and control the architecture of any new program and provide guidelines that will govern implementation of the program in the domestic environment.

THE COMMON DEFENSE. Let me make one important preliminary point: Most of the debate over new intelligence systems focuses on perceived intrusions on civil liberties, but Americans should keep in mind that the Constitution weighs heavily on both sides of the debate over national security and civil liberties. The president and congressional policymakers must respect and defend the individual civil liberties guaranteed in the Constitution when they act, but there is also no doubt that they cannot fail to act when we face a serious threat from a foreign enemy.

The Preamble to the Constitution acknowledges that the United States government was established in part to provide for the common defense. The war powers were granted to Congress and the president with the solemn expectation that they would be used. Congress was also granted the power to "punish . . . Offenses against the Law of Nations," which include the international law of war, or terrorism. In addition, serving as chief executive and commander in chief, the president also has the duty to "take Care that the Laws be faithfully executed," including vigorously enforcing the national security and immigration laws. Thus, as we assess questions of civil liberty I think it important that we not lose sight of the underlying end of government–personal and national security. I do not think that the balance is a zero-sum game, by any means. However, it is vital that we not disregard the significant factors weighing on both sides of the scales.

CIVIL LIBERTY. Of course, just because the Congress and the president have a constitutional obligation to act forcefully to safeguard Americans against attacks by foreign powers does not mean that every means by which they might attempt to act is necessarily prudent or within their power. Core American principles require that any new counterterrorism technology deployed domestically should be developed only within the following bounds:

- No fundamental liberty guaranteed by the Constitution can be breached or infringed upon.
- Any increased intrusion on American privacy interests must be justified through an understanding of the particular nature, significance, and severity of the threat being addressed by the program. The less significant the threat, the less justified the intrusion.
- Any new intrusion must be justified by a demonstration of its effectiveness in diminishing the threat. If the new system works poorly by, for example, creating a large number of false positives, it is suspect. Conversely, if there is a close fit between the technology and the threat (that is, for example, if it is accurate and useful in predicting or thwarting terror), the technology should be more willingly embraced.
- The full extent and nature of the intrusion worked by the system must be understood and appropriately limited. Not all intrusions are justified simply because they are effective. Strip searches at airports would prevent people from boarding planes with weapons, but at too high a cost.
- Whatever the justification for the intrusion, if there are less intrusive means of achieving the same end at a reasonably comparable cost, the less intrusive means ought to be preferred. There is no reason to erode Americans' privacy

when equivalent results can be achieved without doing so.

- Any new system developed and implemented must be designed to be tolerable in the long term. The war against terror, uniquely, is one with no immediately foreseeable end. Thus, excessive intrusions may not be justified as emergency measures that will lapse upon the termination of hostilities. Policymakers must be restrained in their actions; Americans might have to live with their consequences for a long time.

From these general principles can be derived certain other more concrete conclusions regarding the development and construction of any new technology:

- No new system should alter or contravene existing legal restrictions on the government's ability to access data about private individuals. Any new system should mirror and implement existing legal limitations on domestic or foreign activity, depending on its sphere of operation.
- Similarly, no new system should alter or contravene existing operational system limitations. Development of new technology is not a basis for authorizing new government powers or new government capabilities. Any such expansion should be independently justified.
- No new system that materially affects citizens' privacy should be developed without specific authorization by the American people's representatives in Congress and without provisions for their oversight of the operation of the system.
- Any new system should be, to the maximum extent practical, tamperproof. To the extent the prevention of abuse is impossible, any new system should have built-in safeguards to ensure that abuse is both evident and traceable.
- Similarly, any new system should, to the maximum extent practical, be developed in a manner that incorporates technological improvements in the protection of American civil liberties.
- Finally, no new system should be implemented without the full panoply of protections against its abuse. As James Madison told the Virginia ratifying convention, "There are more instances of the abridgment of the freedom of the people by gradual and silent encroachments of those in power than by violent and sudden usurpations."

III. "DATA MINING"–TOTAL INFORMATION AWARENESS TODAY

To that end, let me first discuss the concept of data mining and more particularly the Total Information Awareness program (TIA)–a program that has been widely misunderstood. (For more detail on the program I refer you to a paper I coauthored with my Heritage colleague, Michael Scardaville, "The Need to Protect Civil Liberties While Combating Terrorism: Legal Principles and the Total Information Awareness Program," The Heritage Foundation, Legal Memorandum No. 6 [February 2003].)

A. Data Analysis

First, and foremost, I think that much of the public criticism has obscured the fact that TIA is really not a single program. Virtually all of the attention has focused on the data mining aspects of the research program, but far more of the research effort is being devoted to providing tools for enhanced data analysis. In other words, TIA is not, as I understand it, about bypassing existing legal restrictions and providing governmental agencies with access to new and different domestic information sources. Rather, it is about providing better tools to enable intelligence analysts to more effectively and efficiently analyze the vast pool of data already at their disposal–in other words to make our analysts better analysts. These tools include, for example, a virtual private network linking existing counterterrorism intelligence agencies. It would also include, for example, research into a machine translation capability to automatically render Arabic into English. While these developments certainly pose some threat to civil liberty because any enhancement of governmental capability is inherently such a threat, they are categorically different than the data-mining techniques that most concern civil libertarians. The threat to civil liberty is significantly less and the potential gain from their development is substantial.

Thus, my first concrete recommendation to you is to not paint with too broad a brush–the distinction between collection and analysis is a real and important one that, thus far, Congress has failed to adequately recognize. Earlier this year, Congress passed an amendment, the so-called Wyden Amendment, which substantially restricts TIA development and deployment. That restriction applies broadly to all programs under development by The Defense Advanced Research Projects Agency (DARPA). That's a mistake. The right answer is not for Congress to adopt a blanket prohibition. Rather, Congress should commit to doing the hard work of digging into the details of TIA and examining its operation against the background of existing laws and the existing terrorist threats at home and abroad.

We have already seen some of the unintended but pernicious effects of painting with such a broad brush. Recently at a forum conducted by the Center for Strategic Policy, DARPA officials discussed how the Wyden Amendment had short-circuited plans to sign a Memorandum of Understanding (MOU) with the FBI. The FBI, as this Subcommittee knows, is substantially behind the technological curve and is busily engaged in updating its information technology capabilities. The MOU under consideration would have enabled the FBI to join in the counterterrorism Virtual Private Network (VPN) being created by the TIA program. Again, the VPN is not a new data collection technology–it is a technology to enhance data analysis by allowing information sharing. Other counterterrorism agencies with exclusively foreign focus are already part of the VPN–the Central Intelligence Agency (CIA) and Denver International Airport (DIA), for example. Although the Department of Defense (DoD) has not reached a final interpretation of the Wyden Amendment, the lawyers at DoD were sufficiently concerned with its possible scope that they directed DARPA to not sign the MOU with the FBI. As a consequence one of our principal domestic counterterrorism agencies is being excluded from a potentially valuable network of information sharing. Extrapolating from this unfortunate precedent, it is

likely that the Wyden Amendment will have the effect of further balkanizing our already unwieldy domestic counterintelligence apparatus. The same law will probably be interpreted to prohibit the Department of Homeland Security from joining the network, as well as the counterterrorism agencies of the various states. In short, as Senator Richard C. Shelby (R. AL) has written of TIA:

> The TIA approach thus has much to recommend it as a potential solution to the imperative of deep data access and analyst empowerment within a 21st-century Intelligence Community. If pursued with care and determination, it has the potential to break down the parochial agency information "stovepipes" and permit nearly pure *all* source analysis for the first time—yet without unmanageable security difficulties. If done right, moreover, TIA would be infinitely scalable: expandable to as many databases as our lawyers and policymakers deem to be appropriate.

> TIA promises to be an enormously useful tool that can be applied to whatever data we feel comfortable permitting it to access. How broadly it will ultimately be used is a matter for policymakers to decide if and when the program bears fruit. It is worth emphasizing, however, that TIA would provide unprecedented value even if applied exclusively within the current intelligence community—as a means of finally providing analysts deep but controlled and accountable access to the databases of collection and analytical agencies alike. It would also be useful if applied to broader U.S. government information holdings, subject to laws restricting the use of tax return information, census data, and other information. Ultimately, we might choose to permit TIA to work against some of the civilian "transactional space" in commercially available databases that are already publicly and legally available today to marketers, credit card companies, criminals, and terrorists alike. The point for civil libertarians to remember is that policymakers can choose to restrict TIA's application however they see fit: It will be applied only against the data streams that our policymakers and our laws permit.

Put more prosaically, it remains for this Congress to decide how widely the analytical tools to be provided by TIA are used; but it is imperative that Congress understand that the tools themselves are distinct from the databases to which they might have access.

B. Data Collection: Structural Limitations

As for concerns that the use of new data collection technologies will intrude on civil liberties by affording the government access to new databases, I certainly share those concerns. The question then is how best to ensure that any domestic use of TIA (or, frankly, any other intelligence gathering program) does not unreasonably intrude on American domestic civil liberties. There are several operational principles that will effectively allow the use of TIA while not substantially diminishing American freedom. Among these are the following requirements:

REQUIRE CONGRESSIONAL AUTHORIZATION. In light of the underlying concerns over the extent of government power, it is of paramount importance that there be formal congressional consideration and authorization of the TIA program, following a full public debate, before the system is deployed. Some of the proposed data-querying methods (for example, the possibility for access to nongovernment, private databases, which is discussed in the next section) would require congressional authorization in any event. But, more fundamentally, before any program like TIA—with both great potential utility and significant potential for abuse— is implemented, it ought to be affirmatively approved by the American people's representatives. Only through the legislative process can many of the restrictions and limitations suggested later in this testimony be implemented in an effective manner. The questions are of such significance that they should not be left to executive branch discretion alone.

MAINTAIN STRINGENT CONGRESSIONAL OVERSIGHT. In connection with the congressional authorization of TIA, Congress should also commit at the outset to a strict regime of oversight of the TIA program. This would include periodic reports on TIA's use once developed and implemented, frequent examination by the U.S. General Accounting Office, and, as necessary, public hearings on the use of TIA. Congressional oversight is precisely the sort of check on executive power that is necessary to ensure that TIA-based programs are implemented in a manner consistent with the appropriate limitations and restrictions. Without effective oversight, these restrictions are mere parchment barriers. While potentially problematic, one can be hopeful that congressional oversight in this key area of national concern will be bipartisan, constructive, and thoughtful. Congress has an interest in preventing any dangerous encroachment on civil liberties by an executive who might misuse TIA.

My colleagues at The Heritage Foundation have written extensively on the need for reorganization of the congressional committee structure to meet the altered circumstances posed by the war on terrorism and the formation of the Department of Homeland Security. Oversight of any program developed by TIA would most appropriately be given either to the committee that, after reorganization, had principal responsibility for oversight of that department or, if TIA is limited to foreign intelligence applications, to the two existing intelligence committees.

CONSTRUCT TIA TO PERMIT REVIEW OF ITS ACTIVITIES. To foster the requisite oversight and provide the American public with assurances that TIA is not being used for inappropriate purposes, the TIA program must incorporate as part of its basic structure an audit trail system that keeps a complete and accurate record of activities conducted using the technology. To the maximum extent practical, the audit system should be tamperproof. To the extent it cannot be made tamperproof, it should be structured in a way that makes it evident whenever anyone has tampered with the audit system. Only by providing users, overseers, and critics with a concrete record of its activity can TIA-developed technology reassure all concerned that it is not being misused.

LIMIT THE SCOPE OF ACTIVITIES FOR WHICH QUERIES OF DOMESTIC NONGOVERNMENT DATABASES MAY BE USED. TIA is a technological response to the new, significant threat of terrorism at home and abroad. After September 11, no one can doubt that domestic law enforcement and foreign intelligence agencies face a new challenge that poses a qualitatively greater threat to the American public than any other criminal activity.

U.S. foreign counterintelligence efforts are responding to a new and different form of terrorism and espionage. It is appropriate, therefore, that the use of TIA to query nongovernment databases be limited to the exigent circumstances that caused it to be necessary. Technology being developed for TIA to build models, query and correlate data, and uncover potential terrorist activity should be used (whether for law enforcement or intelligence purposes) only to investigate terrorist, foreign intelligence, or national security activities, and the TIA technology should never be used for other criminal activity that does not rise to this level.

It is important to be especially wary of "mission creep," lest this new technology become a routine tool in domestic law enforcement. It should not be used to fight the improperly named war on drugs, combat violent crime, or address other sundry problems. Although certainly issues of significant concern, none of these are so grave or important as the war on terrorism. Given the bona fide fears of increased government power, any systems that might be derived from TIA should be used only for investigations where there is substantial reason to believe that terrorist-related activity is being perpetrated by organizations whose core purpose is domestic terrorism.

The legislation authorizing TIA should enact this limitation. Congress should, therefore, specify that use of the TIA system is limited to nongovernment data inquiries that are certified at a sufficiently high and responsible level of government to be necessary to accomplish the antiterrorism objectives of the United States. Only if, for example, a Senate-confirmed officer of the Department of Justice, Homeland Security, FBI, or CIA (such as an assistant attorney general or the FBI director) certifies the objectives of the query based on a showing of need should one be made.

LIMIT ACCESS TO THE RESULTS OF THE SEARCH. A corollary to the need to limit authority to initiate an analysis using TIA is an equivalent necessity to limit access to the findings of any resulting analysis. It would be unacceptable, for example, for the data and analysis derived from a TIA query (or, for that matter, a CAPPS II query), and linked to an individual identity, to be available to every Transportation Security Administration screener at every airport. Assuredly, after high-level analysis substantiated the utility of the information, it could be used to create watch lists and other information that can be shared appropriately within the responsible agencies. Until that time, however, access to the results of a TIA search should be limited by the authorizing legislation to a narrow group of analysts and high-level officials in those intelligence, counterintelligence, and law enforcement agencies.

DISTINGUISH BETWEEN USE OF TIA IN EXAMINING DOMESTIC AND FOREIGN ACTIVITIES. In practice, it will be possible to use whatever technology the TIA program develops to unearth terrorist activity or conduct counterintelligence activity both abroad and domestically. Existing law places significant restrictions on intelligence and law enforcement activity that addresses the conduct of American citizens or occurs on American soil. Conversely, fewer restrictions exist for the examination of the conduct of non-Americans abroad.

The development of TIA is not a basis for disturbing this balance and changing existing law. Thus, even if Congress ultimately chooses to prohibit the implementation of TIA for any domestic law enforcement purpose whatsoever (a decision that would be unwise), it would be a substantial expansion of existing restrictions on the collection of foreign intelligence data were it to extend that prohibition to use of the technology with respect to overseas databases containing information on noncitizens. At a minimum, in considering TIA, Congress should ensure that, consistent with existing law, any program developed under TIA will be used in an appropriate manner for foreign intelligence and counterintelligence purposes.

IMPOSE CIVIL AND CRIMINAL PENALTIES FOR ABUSE. Most important, all of these various prohibitions must be enforceable. Violations of whatever prohibitions Congress enacts should be punishable by the executive branch through its administrative authority. Knowing and willful violations should be punishable as crimes. These forms of strong punishment are a necessary corollary of any TIA authorization.

In addition, Congress should enlist the third branch of government–the courts–to serve as a further check on potential abuse of TIA. As is detailed next, the courts will be involved in challenges to TIA information requests. To ensure effective oversight of the use of TIA by the courts, Congress should also authorize a private right of civil action for injunctive relief, attorneys' fees, and (perhaps) monetary damages by individuals aggrieved by a violation of the restrictions Congress imposes.

SUNSET THE AUTHORIZATION. Any new law enforcement or intelligence system must withstand the test of time; it must be something that the American public can live with since the end of the war on terrorism is not immediately in sight. Congress should be cautious, therefore, in implementing a new system of unlimited duration. It is far better for the initial authorization of TIA to expire after a fixed period of time so that Congress may evaluate the results of the research program, its costs (both public and private), and its long-term suitability for use in America. A sunset provision of five years would be ample time for Congress to gather concrete information on the program. With such information, Congress will be in a position to continue, modify, or terminate the program, as it deems appropriate.

C. Data Collection: Legal Limitations

As I noted earlier, the existing legal structure and the overarching principles that I see in American law lead to a singular legal recommendation for the structure and operation of TIA:

TIA should be implemented only in a manner that mirrors existing legal restrictions on the government's ability to access data about private individuals—nothing more and nothing less.

This recommendation may be particularized in the following ways:

TIA SHOULD NOT HAVE ACCESS TO PROTECTED GOVERNMENTAL DATABASES. Most government databases (e.g., arrest records and driver's licenses) contain information about an individual that is accessible to the government and in which the individual has no reasonable expectation of privacy. Linking such information through TIA technology should not be subject to any greater restriction than that applied to its initial inclusion in the local, state, or federal government database from which the information is retrieved. By contrast, some existing governmental databases (like

the census database) cannot be used for purposes other than those for which they were created. Others (like the IRS database on taxpayer returns) can be accessed only with a special court order.

In authorizing the development of TIA technology, Congress should make it clear that information from existing government databases may be queried using TIA structured query programs only to the extent that the government already lawfully has access to the data. The creation of TIA-based networks should not be viewed as an excuse or opportunity to remove existing restrictions on the use of particularly sensitive individual data.

INFORMATION FROM PRIVATE DOMESTIC DATA-BASES SHOULD BE ACCESSED ONLY AFTER NOTICE TO THE DATA HOLDER. A similar limitation should also apply to queries made of private, nongovernment databases from which the government seeks information. Where predication for an investigation (whether criminal or foreign intelligence) exists, law enforcement or intelligence authorities should have the ability to secure data about an individual or pattern of conduct from private databases just as they do under current law.

Thus, with appropriate predication and/or court authorization (if the law requires), the government should be able to secure data from banks, credit card companies, and telephone companies about the conduct of specified individuals or about specified classes of transactions, but existing warrant and subpoena requirements should not be changed. Such data gathering should be done only at the retail level when a particularized basis for investigation exists.

More important, in each instance where data is sought from a private database, the holder of the data should be notified prior to securing the data and (as in the context of a subpoena today) have the capacity to interpose an objection to the data query to the same extent the law currently permits. The law today does not provide a mechanism by which such information requests may be made other than by subpoena. Thus, in authorizing a TIA-based investigative system, Congress should require that any aspects of TIA seeking data from private databases should operate in a manner similar to that in contemporary subpoena practice.

As this analysis makes evident, one should strongly oppose any effort to incorporate in TIA the ability to gather private database information at the wholesale level (e.g., all bank transactions processed by Citibank). One should also strongly oppose any TIA-based system that allows access to privately held data without notice to (and the opportunity to object by) the data holder. In short, the development of TIA technology and the war on terrorism is not a justification for the routine incorporation of all private data and information in a single government database.

TIA IS NOT A JUSTIFICATION FOR CREATING NEW GOVERNMENT DATABASES. Given the clear distinction that the law enacts between access to government and access to private, nongovernment databases, a further cautionary note is in order. In order to evade the legal strictures limiting access to information in private databases, the government might be tempted, in effect, to institutionalize the information it deems relevant by enacting new data-reporting requirements to capture in government databases information that now exists only in private databases to which access is less ready. The first such proposal may already have been made: that Americans flying abroad be required to provide their travel itineraries to the Transportation Security Administration upon their departure from America.

The expansion of existing government databases should be resisted except on a showing of extraordinary need. The government already collects too much information about Americans on a day-to-day basis. While many government programs require the collection of such data to permit them to operate, one should not create databases where no program requiring their creation exists—otherwise, there is the risk of wholesale evasion of existing legal restrictions on the use of information in private databases. Initiatives such as the new itinerary-collection program should be evaluated independently to determine their necessity and utility.

THERE MUST BE ABSOLUTE PROTECTION FOR FUNDAMENTAL CONSTITUTIONALLY PROTECTED ACTIVITY. The gravest fear that most Americans have about TIA is that it might be used to transmit queries about and assemble dossiers of information on political opponents. One should not discount these fears as they rest on all-too-recent abuses of governmental power. If a system developed based

on TIA technology is used to enable an effort to harass antiwar demonstrators or gather information on those who are politically opposed to the government's policies (as the FBI used its investigative powers to do in the 1960s and 1970s), such abuse should be terminated immediately.

This prospect is not, however, sufficient to warrant a categorical rejection of all of the benefits to the war on terrorism that TIA technology might provide. TIA can be developed without these abuses, and aspects of the technology under investigation in fact hold the promise of enhancing civil liberties. Still, it is imperative that any implementing legislation has concrete, verifiable safeguards against the misuses of TIA. These should include, for example, an absolute prohibition on accessing databases relating to support of political organizations that propagate ideas—even ones favorable to terrorist regimes—absent compelling evidence that the organizations also aid terrorist conspirators with monetary, organizational, and other support not protected by the First Amendment. There must be an absolute prohibition on accessing databases relating solely to political activity or protest.

TIA SHOULD BUILD PRIVACY PROTECTIONS INTO ITS ARCHITECTURE. Finally, it should be recognized that access to data is not necessarily equated with a loss of privacy. To be sure, it may in many instances amount to the same thing, but it need not. There is, for example, a sense in which the automated screening of personal data by computer enhances privacy: It reduces the arbitrariness or bias of human screening and ensures that an individual's privacy will be disrupted by human intervention only in suspicious cases.

In addition, those developing TIA can be required to construct a system that initially disaggregates individual identifiers from pattern-based information. Only after the pattern is independently deemed to warrant further investigation should the individual identity be disclosed. So, for example, only after a query on the bulk purchase of the precursors of Ricin poison turned up a qualifying series of purchases linked to a single individual would the individual's name be disclosed to terrorism analysts.

Thus, everyone on both sides of the discussion should welcome one aspect of TIA, the Genisys Privacy Protection program. The Genisys program is developing filters and other protections to keep a person's identity separate from the data being evaluated for potential terrorist threats. In authorizing TIA, Congress should mandate that a trusted third party rather than an organization's database administrator control these protections.

IV. FBI INVESTIGATIVE GUIDELINES

Let me turn now briefly to the new FBI investigative guidelines. Many of the principles I have applied to TIA are equally relevant to any consideration of the recent changes in the FBI's investigative guidelines. I will not burden the record by repeating my analysis in its entirety here.

There are, however, aspects of the FBI's guidelines that suggest the need for heightened sensitivity to the potential for an infringement on protected constitutional liberties. As you will recognize from my testimony I have generally been supportive of the potential inherent in the development of the TIA system. In part, that reflects my belief in the benefits of technology. It also reflects my conviction that existing Supreme Court precedent, dating back to the 1960s, accurately captures the scope of the constitutional privacy protection embodied in the Fourth Amendment: The Constitution affords no additional protection to information that an individual has made available to other individuals or institutions. Privacy concerns relating to the further distribution of such information are matters of policy and legislative concern, not constitutional law. Similarly, the FBI guidelines raise no Fourth Amendment concerns, insofar as they authorize the FBI to collect publicly available information from public databases and/or public meetings.

PROTECTING CONSTITUTIONAL LIBERTIES. Nonetheless, the FBI guidelines do implicate potential threats to atleast two fundamental liberty interests guaranteed by the Constitution. Most obviously, the Supreme Court has long recognized a freedom of political association and the threat to that freedom posed by requiring organizations to identify their members. Second, many of the indicators that might be used to identify potential subjects of a terrorist investigation are also indicators that, in other circumstances, are potentially the products of protected First Amendment activity–in other words, although FBI investigative techniques are not intended to impinge on free political speech or association, they may have the collateral effect of doing so.

Thus, there is a significant risk that a maladministered system will impinge upon fundamental constitutional liberties. I am not, however, one to say that the risk of such impingement means abandonment of the program–especially not in light of the potentially disastrous consequences of another terrorist attack in the United States. I do, however, believe that some fairly stringent steps are necessary to provide the requisite safeguards for minimizing inadvertent or abusive infringements of civil liberty in the first instance and correcting them as expeditiously as possible. Those steps would include some or all of the following (many of which mirror recommendations I have already made with respect to TIA):

• The FBI's use of these new investigative guidelines should be subject to extensive, continuous congressional oversight. By this I do not mean the mere reporting of raw data and numbers–I mean that, at least as a spot check, Congress should examine individual, closed cases (if necessary using confidential procedures to maintain classified status) to assure itself that the investigative guidelines are not being misused. In other words, the database contemplated by the FBI guidelines should, under limited circumstances, be subject to congressional scrutiny;

• Authorization for criminal intelligence investigations under the FBI's guidelines should, in all circumstances, be in writing such that the FBI's internal system creates an audit trail for the authorization of investigations with potential First Amendment implications. Only through detailed recordkeeping can the use and/or abuse of investigative authority be reviewed;

- The FBI's new guidelines generally authorize the use of all lawful investigative techniques for both general crimes investigations and criminal intelligence investigations. There should be an especial hesitancy, however, in using the undisclosed participation of an undercover agent or cooperating private individual to examine the conduct of organizations that are exercising core First Amendment rights. When an organization is avowedly political in nature (giving that phrase the broadest definition reasonable) and has as its sole mission the advocacy of a viewpoint or belief, we should be especially leery of ascribing to that organization criminal intent, absent compelling evidence to that effect.

- There should, as well, be a hesitancy in visiting public places and events that are clearly intended to involve the exercise of core First Amendment rights, as the presence of official observers may chill expression. This is not to say that no such activity should ever be permitted—it is, however, to suggest the need for supervisory authorization and careful review before and after the steps are taken. Conversely, existing court consent decrees that expressly prohibit all such activity (as is currently the case in New York City) should be revisited.

- No American should be the subject of a criminal investigation solely on the basis of his exercise of a constitutionally protected right to dissent. An indication of threat sufficient to warrant investigation should always be based on significant intelligence suggesting actual criminal or terrorist behavior.

Privacy

Although the FBI's guidelines authorize preliminary inquiries through the use of public information resources, many Americans fear that these inquiries will result in the creation of personalized dossiers on dissenters. As it appears now, there are no explicit provisions in the guidelines for the destruction of records from preliminary inquiries that produce no evidence sufficient to warrant a full-scale investigation. One possible amendment to the guidelines that would ameliorate many privacy concerns would be an explicit provision providing for such destruction or archiving with limited retrieval authority.

One other brief point should be made about privacy—in many ways the implementation of the FBI guidelines is not an unalloyed diminution of privacy. Rather it is the substitution of one privacy intrusion (into certain public spheres) for other privacy intrusions (into more private spheres, perhaps through other investigative means). It may also substitute for increased random investigations or the invidious use of racial, national origin, or religious classifications. Here one cannot make broad value judgments—each person weighs the utility of his or her own privacy by a different metric. However, I do venture to say that for many Americans the price of a little less public privacy might not be too great if it resulted in a little more personal privacy.

DISCUSSION QUESTIONS

1. The author states that "the civil liberty/national security question is the single most significant domestic legal issue facing America today, bar none." Do you agree? Why is the matter of such central concern?

2. Contrast the views in this chapter with those in the previous chapter from the ACLU. Which positions most closely resemble your own? Explain why you endorse one perspective over the other.

3. The author states that "the extent of privacy protection is mostly a creature of legislation, not constitutional provisions." Do you agree? What are the implications for privacy if this statement is true?

4. What privacy protections do you see as important enough that they must be protected, whether by legislation or constitutional provision? Why are these protections of such import?

5. The author states that "new intelligence and law enforcement information gathering and information analytical systems can (and should) be constructed in a manner that fosters both civil liberty and public safety." Do you agree? What are the challenges in pursuing this goal?

6. What is your opinion of the Total Information Awareness program (TIA)? Examine the safeguards the author proposes for the program. Do you believe them to be sufficient? Why or why not?

7. How can a government determined to use the results of a program such as TIA to control its political opponents be prevented from doing so? What additional safeguards might you suggest?

Chapter 11

THE USA PATRIOT ACT, MONEY LAUNDERING, AND SUSPICIOUS ACTIVITY REPORTS FROM FINANCIAL INSTITUTIONS

KRISTEN S. NOLAN

The Uniting and Strengthening America by Providing Appropriate Tools Required to Intercept and Obstruct Terrorism Act of 2001, better known as the USA PATRIOT Act (the "Patriot Act"), was enacted on October 26, 2001. It was swiftly drafted and passed a mere six weeks after the terrorist acts on the World Trade Center on September 11, 2001. The USA PATRIOT Act was designed to "deter and punish terrorist acts in the United States and around the world, to enhance law enforcement investigatory tools, and for other purposes."[1] The USA PATRIOT Act has ten titles that affect various laws.[2] Title III is the International Money Laundering Abatement and Antiterrorist Financing Act of 2001 ("Title III").

One of Title III's stated purposes is "to increase the strength of United States measures to prevent, detect, and prosecute international money laundering and the financing of terrorism."[3] Terrorism and money laundering are problems that bank compliance officers think about every day. Every incoming check or wire, every outflow of cash or securities, every new account that is opened, must be reviewed to ensure that it is not related to one of these crimes. There are various laws that govern financial institutions[4] and impose a requirement to report the foregoing transactions to law enforcement when they raise suspicions of a violation of the law. This chapter will briefly discuss the definition of money laundering and terrorism and the relationship between the two crimes. It will also discuss the regulatory framework that applies and just one of the many issues the USA PATRIOT Act raises; one's right to privacy with respect to their financial records.

I. WHAT IS MONEY LAUNDERING?

Money laundering is the way criminals take proceeds from illegal activities and get it back into circulation so that it no longer appears to be from illegal activities. It is "a process in which assets obtained or generated by criminal activity are moved or concealed to obscure the link between the crime and the assets."[5] Not only are the activities that generate funds that need to be laundered illegal, but money laundering is itself a violation of the law:[6] "Money laundering is one of the most critical problems facing law enforcement today."[7]

It is estimated that money laundering is a "$1 trillion per year problem."[8]

Money laundering does more than just facilitate and support organized crime. It can lead to "unpredictable changes in money demand, prudential risks to the soundness of financial institutions and financial systems, contamination effects on legal financial transactions and increased volatility of international capital flows and exchange rates due to unanticipated cross-border transfers."[9] Money laundering can also lead to the

---

Note: Kristen Nolan is a fourth-year evening division student at the Widener University School of Law.

notion that those sectors affected are "under the control and influence of organized crime."[10]

Money laundering is not a simple concept. There are three basic phases of money laundering; placement, layering, and integration.[11] Placement is the structuring of cash into various financial institutions in such a way as to avoid detection.[12] Placement may include actions such as deposits, wire transfers, purchasing money orders and travelers' checks, and any other transaction that those laundering feel would evade detection.[13] Layering is the process by which layers of transactions are placed into the financial system, often through international banks, to pass funds through multiple hands to create distance between the source of the funds and the ultimate destination.[14] Integration is the process by which what is now clean money is reentered into the economy.[15]

II. WHAT IS TERRORISM?

Terrorism is difficult to define.[16] There are various federal statutes that define terrorism. Yet Chapter 12 of the United States Code (the "Code"), does not contain a definition of terrorism. The sections of the USA PATRIOT Act that amend Chapter 12 of the Code do not provide a definition of the term. Thus, financial institutions must turn to other laws or regulations for guidance in determining whether an activity is related to terrorism.

The USA PATRIOT Act addressed the definition of terrorism in another context: "Section 802 of [the Patriot Act] added a new definition of 'domestic terrorism' under 18 U.S.C. §2331. Section 411 amended 8 U.S.C. §1182(a)(3) of the Immigration and Nationality Act to include other definitions relating to terrorism, including a definition of 'engage in terrorist activity' and 'terrorist organization.'"[17] Title 18 of the Code already defined the term international terrorism as any act that is a criminal violation and is designed to influence the government, intimidate the citizens of the United States, or affect the working of the government through assassination or kidnapping.[18] The USA PATRIOT Act merely amended the definition to state that terrorism can be affected through actions designed to "affect the conduct of a government by mass destruction, assassination, or kidnapping"[19] and added a definition of domestic terrorism to be activities that:

> involve acts dangerous to human life that are a violation of the criminal laws . . . intended—(i) to intimidate or coerce a civilian population; (ii) to influence the policy of a government by intimidation or

coercion; or (iii) to affect the conduct of a government by mass destruction. . . ."[20]

The definitions of international and domestic terrorism provide a broad base by which to judge whether an act is terrorism or not.

Yet other sections of the Code define terrorism in a slightly different manner. Elsewhere, "the term 'terrorism' means premeditated, politically motivated violence perpetrated against noncombatant targets by subnational [*sic*] groups or clandestine agents."[21] Another definition can be found when reviewing the Federal Bureau of Investigation's definition: "[t]errorism includes the unlawful use of force and violence against persons or property to intimidate or coerce a government, the civilian population, or any segment thereof, in furtherance of political or social objectives."[22] Yet another definition can be in the Code as an act that attempts to "influence or affect the conduct of government by intimidation or coercion, or to retaliate against government conduct" and also violates any number of sections of the Code, including sections dealing with the safety of aircraft, hostages, or homicides.[23]

The Financial Action Task Force (FATF) defines a terrorist act to be one "which constitutes an offence within the scope of, and as defined in one of the following treaties: Convention for the Suppression of Unlawful Seizure of Aircraft (1970), . . . and the International Convention for the Suppression of Terrorist Bombings (1997); and (ii) any other act intended to cause death or serious bodily injury to a civilian, or to any other person not taking an active part in the hostilities . . . or to compel a Government or an international organization to do or to abstain from doing any act."[24]

One theme is constant throughout these definitions. The theme is best illustrated by reviewing some nonlegal definitions. One professional group defines terrorism as having "[t]he primary objective . . . 'to intimidate a population, or to compel a Government of an international organisation [*sic*] to do or abstain from doing any act.' "[25] The Merriam-Webster dictionary defines terrorism as "the systematic use of terror especially as a means of coercion."[26] No matter which definition is correct, terrorism is an act that instills fear through violence and it affects lots of people throughout the world.

III. HOW ARE MONEY LAUNDERING AND TERRORISM RELATED?

Terrorism and money laundering are linked.[27] Like money laundering, terrorism is a global problem.[28] Terrorists need money to fund their operations. They cannot merely open a business to generate revenue: "Terrorists, as well as drug traffickers and other criminal organizations, need to launder money. It takes money to purchase weapons and explosives or take lessons at flight school. It takes money to get terrorists to their targets, and then into hiding."[29] Since 1995, the Office of Foreign Asset Control by the Department of Treasury has blocked over $3.8 billion in assets from investors around the world.[30] Because financing flight school or other terrorist necessities is not cheap,[31] terrorists often use illegitimate means to get funding: "From a technical perspective, the methods used by terrorists and their associates to generate funds from illegal sources differ little from those used by traditional criminal organizations [*sic*]."[32]

Terrorism is linked to money laundering through the other characteristics that are necessary for one to be successful at either crime: "[C]riminal acts of violence, such as the horrific terrorist attacks of September 11 need more than just cunning leadership and dedicated followers to be successful."[33] Leadership and having dedicated followers are cornerstones of organized crime, a group proficient at money laundering. The connection is recognized by many. Former Secretary of the Treasury Jimmy Gurulé stated that:

> [terrorist] undertakings also require extensive financial funding. . . . Although the complexities of money laundering have long been associated with concealing the true nature of proceeds generated from the drug cartels, the tragedies of September 11 also underscore the need for aggressive and vigilant anti-money laundering efforts which target . . . funds earmarked for terror.[34]

Further, "[t]he 'life blood' of any profit-generating criminal activity, the laundering process allows narcotics traffickers, terrorists, perpetrators of financial fraud, and every other criminal enterprise to perpetuate, and to live lavishly from, their illegal activity."[35] Even the agency charged with preventing money laundering implicitly recognized some connection, for "[a]fter September 11, 2001, the FATF expanded its mission beyond money laundering and agreed to focus its expertise on the worldwide effort to combat terrorist financing."[36]

Terrorist money, like that which needs to be laundered, often starts out legitimate.[37] "Although it would seem logical that funding from legitimate sources would not need to be laundered, there is nevertheless often a need for the terrorist group to obscure or disguise links between it and its legitimate funding sources. It follows then that terrorist groups must similarly find ways to launder these funds in order to be able to use them without drawing the attention of authorities. In examining terrorist-related financial activity, FATF experts have concluded that terrorists and their support organizations generally use the same methods as criminal groups to launder funds."[38] Moreover, "[i]nternational terrorist groups need money to attract, support, and retain adherents throughout the world as well as to secure the loyalty of other groups that share the same goals. Thus, they need to devise schemes to raise, collect, and distribute money to operatives preparing for attacks."[39]

Like money laundering, terrorist funds may be detected through careful monitoring of financial institutions and financial transactions: "[Terrorist] fundraising schemes and the movement of money internationally makes the terrorist funds vulnerable to detection if we have the safeguards in place."[40] "The FBI has aggressively pursued groups, individuals, and networks that provide financing for terrorism worldwide."[41]

Terrorists generally get their funding from two primary sources.[42] Funds will generally come from states or large organizations that can afford to support terrorists.[43] Terrorists will also generate income through crimes, directly raising the need for money laundering:[44] "Terrorist activities are sometimes funded from the proceeds of illegal activities, and perpetrators must find ways to launder the funds in order to use them without drawing the attention of authorities."[45] "[M]oney laundering, and the defects in financial transparency on which money launderers rely, are critical to the financing of global terrorism and the provision of funds for terrorist attacks[.]"[46] Notwithstanding all the attempts to catch terrorist activities, the "FATF indicates that identifying terrorist financing activity is unlikely, absent dealings with known terrorists or terrorist organizations. As a result, financial institutions should focus on ascertaining whether transactions are unusual, suspicious, or otherwise indicative of criminal or terrorist activity."[47]

IV. REGULATORY FRAMEWORK

In the United States, there are various regulatory agencies that govern the operations of financial institutions. These agencies promulgated regulations related to money laundering.[48] The Office of the Comptroller of the Currency (the OCC) regulates national banks. The Office of Thrift Supervision (the OTS) regulates federal savings associations.[49] The Financial Crimes Enforcement Network (FINCen) is a bureau of the Treasury.[50] FinCEN "plays a key role in the . . . effort to stop financial crimes and the flow of money to terrorist organizations. FinCEN works with the financial community[51] to support local, state, and federal law enforcement and intelligence agencies to help prevent the abuse of our financial system by criminals and terrorists."[52] However, it is the FATF that has the "primary responsibility for developing a worldwide anti-money laundering framework, in close cooperation with relevant international organizations."[53]

There are numerous laws that govern financial institutions. First, the Bank Secrecy Act was passed in 1970.[54] Then, "[i]n 1992, Congress passed the Annunzio-Wylie Money Laundering Act, giving the Secretary of the Treasury the power to require banks and other financial institutions to report suspicious transactions to the appropriate authorities."[55] The latest law in the fight against money laundering is also a law designed to thwart terrorism; the USA PATRIOT Act.[56]

The USA PATRIOT Act has already impacted money laundering and terrorism: "The [Patriot Act] gave us the tools we needed to integrate our law enforcement and intelligence capabilities to win the war on terror. It allowed the Department of Justice to use the same tools from the criminal process on terrorists that we use to combat mobsters or drug dealers."[57] The success of the financial portions of the act has led to the freezing of over $125 million and 600 accounts around the world.[58]

V. HOW DOES PREVENTING MONEY LAUNDERING PREVENT TERRORISM?

There are two potential ways that the anti-money laundering procedures of financial institutions could catch terrorist activity. First, terrorist funds might be invested by someone on the OFAC list[59] and through the know-your-customer rules,[60] terrorist money would be identified. Then, the assets may be flagged, frozen, and/or ultimately seized.[61]

Second, the methods by which terrorist organizations that generate income through criminal activities would need to be cleaned to avoid detection. Reporting of activities that may be money laundering could start an investigation by legal authorities. Hopefully, assets will be seized and criminal activity prevented. If terrorists' assets are seized and they have no money, it will be hard for them to fund acts of destruction.

Reporting Requirements, SARs

Financial institutions, which include national banks, savings associations, and other banking entities, are required to report any activity believed to be a possible violation of the law.[62] The violations are not limited to money laundering or other financial-related crime. Any activity that may be suspicious to the financial institution and could lead to any crime is subject to the reporting requirements. Thus, terrorist activities are included in those that are reported if detected or suspected.

VI. PREVENTING BOTH TERRORISM AND VIOLATIONS OF THE RIGHT TO PRIVACY: SUSPICIOUS ACTIVITY REPORTS

The primary reporting tool for activity believed to be terrorist in nature of money laundering is the Suspicious Activity Report (SAR).[63] The Annunzio-Wylie Anti-Money Laundering Act gave the Secretary of the Treasury the authority to require reports of suspicious activities.[64] A SAR is required whenever a bank suspects a possible criminal violation involving the transactions at the bank and when a dollar threshold is met or a bank insider is involved in the transaction.[65] The requirement for a SAR is not limited to activities such as money laundering.

Statutes provide that SARs are required when "they have a high degree of usefulness in criminal, tax, or regulatory investigations or proceedings, or in the conduct of intelligence or counterintelligence activities, including analysis, to protect against international terrorism."[66] Financial institutions must file the SAR within a certain time of the discovery of the suspicious activity.[67] Moreover, the USA PATRIOT Act's

> sections of the final version . . . which expand the definition of Specified Unlawful Activities for Money Laundering are a crucial component of the [Patriot Act]. We all know that in order to crush terrorism in all its forms, it will be necessary for us to put an end to the money laundering which is essential to the financing of terrorists' networks. In order for our legislation to be effective, our laws against money laundering must have the widest possible scope.[68]

SARs are confidential.[69] Even criminal defendants who would normally be entitled to see all the evidence that is used to convict them are not entitled to see copies of SARs that have been filed, reporting activities that the financial institutions believed suspicious:[70] "Congress and the regulatory agencies made SARs privileged, and courts have refused to order an exception to that privilege, even if necessary to raise an affirmative defense."[71] The financial institution that reports a suspicious activity in a SAR is prohibited from disclosing that the SAR was filed, or the information in the SAR.[72]

The information in the SAR is sensitive.[73] SARs must contain private information about banks' customers. SARs must include the name and address of the institution making the report.[74] It must also contain the name, address, social security number, date of birth, occupation, and identification form and number[75] of the suspect. It must include all information that the institution has available about the transaction causing the report.[76]

Law enforcement activities require SARs to be confidential.[77] The detection of illegal activities is a delicate process. Disclosure of a SAR could "compromise an ongoing law enforcement investigation, tip off a criminal wishing to evade detection, or reveal the methods by which banks are able to detect suspicious activity."[78] For SARs to be an effective tool, banks must be free to file them, without fear of retribution by the individual(s) named in the SAR.

Retribution by the individual(s) would make banks hesitate when deciding whether to file a SAR. Thus, "banks may be reluctant to prepare an SAR if it believes that its cooperation may cause its customers to retaliate. Moreover, the disclosure of an SAR may harm the privacy interests of innocent people whose names may be contained therein."[79] The protection from liability for banks that disclose information predates the USA PATRIOT Act.[80] Moreover, the courts have noted that they do not have the power to order disclosure of the SAR, in fact "courts have an obligation to prevent disclosures of privileged information."[81]

Implicit in the contract between the bank and its customer is the notion that no information may be disclosed by the bank concerning the customer's account. The same contract would provide that "unless authorized by law or by the customer or depositor, the bank must be held liable for breach of the implied contract."[82] But SARs, the USA PATRIOT Act, money laundering, and terrorism give rise to many debates over personal rights and the need to prevent crimes. The right to privacy is squarely within the realm of those debates.

The debate over where one's right to privacy comes from is not the subject of this chapter. The Constitution does not specifically enumerate a right to privacy. The right to privacy is raised by plaintiffs and defendants when discussing many rights.[83] Although many argue that the right to be let alone is fundamental,[84] it is not an absolute right.

Various arguments have been used to justify the lack of a right to privacy concerning their financial records. First, some argue that anyone who voluntarily discloses information to a third party surrenders the right to keep such information private.[85] Papers such as those turned over or maintained by a bank are not private or within the protected zone of privacy.[86] Second, any imposition on one's right to privacy is justified in certain circumstances, such as preventing acts of terrorism.[87] Third, the statutes that impose the liability shield for the banks and prohibit disclosure of the SAR

also clearly require the filing of SARs.[88] Thus, if a bank believes that someone is involved in terrorism, reports the information in a SAR, and an investigation ensues that reveals no basis or grounds for arrest or prosecution, any customer feeling adverse effects of the investigation has no recourse.[89]

To provide protection for individuals, the Right to Financial Privacy Act (RFPA) was passed:[90] "The centerpiece of federal statutory efforts to protect individual privacy is the federal Right to Financial Privacy Act of 1978."[91] RFPA defines financial institution as "any office of a bank, savings bank, card issuer . . . industrial loan company, trust company, savings association, building and loan, or homestead association (including cooperative banks), credit union, or consumer finance institution, located in any State or territory of the United States. . . ."[92] RFPA prohibits banks from disclosing "the information contained in the financial records of any customer"[93] unless an exception is found.

The disclosure in a SAR is one such exception.[94] One of the purposes of Title III is "to clarify the terms of the safe harbor from civil liability for filing suspicious activity reports."[95] Subtitle B of Title III amends the Bank Secrecy Act, which was the primary law governing money laundering and suspicious activities for banks.[96] Section 352(a) adds to 31 USC 5318(g)(3) a liability shield for financial institutions who disclose information in connection with possible violations of the law, from privacy actions by those whose information is disclosed. Infringing on the right to privacy even more, the disclosure itself is confidential.

The confidentiality of disclosure has been upheld.[97] In *United States v. Holihan*, a criminal defendant charged with embezzlement sought disclosure via subpoena of any SAR that might have been filed. The subpoena also sought the supporting information contained in various employees' personnel files. The court reviewed the relevant statutes, prohibiting the disclosure and found no ambiguity in the requirement to uphold the SAR statute. The court noted that the Annunzio-Wylie Act prohibits disclosure of SARs. Moreover, since SARs are confidential, one "need not disclose any information establishing the existence or contents of any SAR files as to any such employee."[98] Further, the court noted that not only was the SAR privileged, but the court lacked the authority to order disclosure.[99]

The latest case to discuss the confidentiality of the SAR, *Whitney National Bank v. Karam*, also upheld the confidentiality of the SAR. The bank was protected against discovery "into any SARs filing and into communications and information exchanged between the Whitney Bank Parties and law enforcement or governmental officials or agencies pertaining to suspected illegal activities relating to or arising out of defendants' activities and transactions. . . ."[100]

Currency transaction report (CTR) jurisprudence is the basis for upholding SAR reporting as constitutional. Previously, the Supreme Court held that the failure to notify a suspect "that a CTR was filed did not violate the fourth Amendment."[101] Reasoning that the defendant and the bank were both parties to the transaction reported, the defendant "had no legitimate 'expectation of privacy' concerning information contained in Bank record, and no Fourth Amendment protected interest in the Bank records."[102] The Fourth Amendment does not protect one from banks disclosing information under the Bank Secrecy Act.[103]

Not all courts agree that there is no right to keep financial records private.[104] Some states have rejected this notion "relying upon their own state constitutions to hold that bank customers have a legitimate expectation of privacy in their bank records."[105] Conversely, many states have passed laws designed to protect that right, recognizing that the right is not inherent in the federal or their state constitutions.[106] The law provides:

> Nothing in this chapter shall preclude any financial institution . . . from notifying a Government authority that such institution . . . has information which may be relevant to a possible violation of any statute or regulation. Such information may include only the name or other identifying information concerning any individual, corporation, or account involved in and the nature of any suspected illegal activity. Such information may be disclosed notwithstanding

any constitution, law, or regulation of any State or political subdivision thereof to the contrary.[107]

The act of reporting information by financial institutions to the government has been challenged since the inception of the requirement. In *Stark v. Connally*, the court held that the reporting of foreign transactions were not constitutional violations.[108] However, due to the nature of the information required in the reports of domestic transactions, the information is not limited to information about the banks' own records; there is a "degree of privacy in [bank] matters and that such an expectation is one that society has been prepared to recognize as 'reasonable.'"[109] However, the government's need for the information persisted. In 1974, *Stark* was overturned.

The *Shultz* court reversed *Stark*, finding the filing of a currency transaction report constitutional.[110] The plaintiff in *Shultz* argued that the reporting requirements under the Bank Secrecy Act violated the fourth Amendment as an unreasonable search and seizure.[111] However, rationalizing that the bank is a party to the transactions, the bank's reporting of the information is not an unreasonable search.[112] Thus, the reporting requirements were upheld.[113]

The passage of the USA PATRIOT Act merely brings an old issue to the surface again. The tension between an individual's right to privacy and the government's need for certain information has been discussed since the passage of the Bank Secrecy Act, which was passed in 1970.[114] The Bank Secrecy Act, as amended,[115] required financial institutions to monitor for and report various activities, especially anti-money laundering, even before the USA PATRIOT Act was dreamed of. However, even before the Bank Secrecy Act, financial institutions reported information pertaining to various transactions; so long as the financial institution thought that the transaction was the basis for concern for the institution.[116] Yet the reporting,[117] and the confidentiality of the reporting,[118] has been repeatedly upheld. Unlike the Annunzio Wylie Anti-Money Laundering Act, the USA PATRIOT Act requires the disclosure of information to authorities in "situations where notification has been made to the Secretary of the Treasury and where terrorism or money laundering is suspected."[119]

VII. CONCLUSION

The USA PATRIOT Act did not really break new ground by including Title III. It merely enhanced the provisions already applicable to banks. Through SARs and compliance programs to detect and report money laundering and other suspicious activity, terrorism will face obstacles in managing and cleaning United States currency in domestic institutions. Blocking terrorist assets will make it difficult for terrorists to carry out their plans.

While the SAR might seem to violate one's right to privacy, it is a necessary and effective tool for law enforcement to detect and prosecute terrorism. The debate over whether the SAR is a violation of one's fourth Amendment rights will likely continue. However, the jurisprudence seems fairly settled; there is a reasonable need for the SAR and there are many arguments as to why they are permissible. Hopefully, the ability of financial institutions to report suspicious activities in SARs will continue to outweigh any possible infringement of one's right to privacy.

ENDNOTES

1. USA PATRIOT Act, Pub. L. No. 107-56, 115 Stat. 272 (2001).

2. The act amends various laws, including the Bank Secrecy Act, the Antiterrorism and Effective Death Penalty Act of 1996, the Foreign Intelligence Surveillance Act of 1978, the Illegal Immigration Reform and Immigrant Responsibility Act of 1996, the Federal Rules of Criminal Procedure, and the Wiretapping Act. Moreover, it linked terrorism to organized crime in an unusual way by "amend[ing] RICO to include terrorism-related offenses as predicate acts" (*The European Community v. RJR Nabisco Inc.*, 355 F.3d. 123, 127 (2nd Cir. 2004).

3. USA PATRIOT Act, Pub. L. No. 107-56, 115 Stat. 279 (2001).

4. For purposes of this chapter, the term financial institution includes national banks, savings associations, state chartered trust companies, credit unions, and other banklike entities.

5. *The IMF and the Fight Against Money Laundering and the Financing of Terrorism: A Fact Sheet* (April 2003), http://www.imf.org

6. 18 U.S.C. §1965 (2004).

7. Robert S. Pasley, *Privacy Rights v. Anti-Money Laundering Enforcement*, 6 N.C. Banking Inst. 147, 148 (April 2002).

8. International Federation of Accountants, *Anti-Money Laundering, 2nd Edition*, (March 2004), *at* http://www.ifac.org

9. *The IMF and the Fight Against Money Laundering and the Financing of Terrorism: A Fact Sheet* (April 2003), http://www.imf.org

10. *Id.*

11. *Id.*

12. *Id.*

13. *Id.*

14. *Id.*

15. *Id.*

16. "There is no single, universally accepted definition of terrorism. There are many reasons for this (not the least of which is the cliche 'one man's terrorist is another's freedom fighter'). Even different agencies of the U.S. government have different working definitions. Most definitions usually have common elements, though, oriented around terrorism as the systematic use of physical violence—actual or threatened—against noncombatants but with an audience broader than the immediate victims in mind, to create a general climate of fear in a target population, in order to effect [sic] some kind of political and/or social change. Terrorism by nature is difficult to define. Acts of terrorism conjure emotional responses in the victims (those hurt by the violence and those affected by the fear) as well as in the practitioners. Even the U.S. government cannot agree on one single definition. The old adage, "One man's terrorist is another man's freedom fighter" is still alive and well. Listed below are several definitions of terrorism. For the purposes of the Terrorism Research Center, we have adopted the definition used by the Federal Bureau of Investigation." Terrorism Research Center, at http://www.terrorism.com/modules.php?op=modload&name=FAQ&file=index&myfaq=yes&id_cat=1&categories=General+Questions&parent_id=0#1

17. *United States v. Graham*, 275 F.3d 490, 542 (6th Cir. 2001).

18. Section 802(a)(1) of the USA PATRIOT Act.

19. 18 U.S.C. §2331(1)(b)(iii) (2004).

20. 50 U.S.C. §1701(1) (2004).

21. *Graham*, 275 F. 3d at 542 (citing 22 U.S.C. §2656f).

22. *Id.* (citing (28 C.F.R. 0.85(*l*)).

23. 18 U.S.C. 2332b(g)(5) (2004).

24. Financial Action Task Force on Money Laundering, The Forty Recommendations (2003). Available online at http://www1.oecd.org/fatf/40Recs_en.htm

25. AL-2002-4, Financial Action Task Force for Financial Institutions in Detecting Terrorist Financing (Office of the Comptroller of the Currency, May 16, 2002) (citing Article 2. International Convention for the Suppression of the Financing of Terrorism. 9 December, 1999).

26. Available at http://www.webster.com/cgi-bin/dictionary?book=Dictionary&va=terrorism. Last visited April 12, 2004. (The dictionary's definition of terror is simple; it discusses fear and violence. *Id.*)

27. International Federation of Accountants, *Anti-Money Laundering, 2nd Edition*, (March 2004), at http://www.ifac.org. "Governments and [intergovernmental organizations] now believe that there may be links between the proceeds of foreign official corruption and terrorist financing and the crime of money laundering." *Id.*

28. Approximately 3,066 died in the attacks on September 11, 2001 (http:www/nightlightfund.org/people.html).

29. Robert S. Pasley, *Privacy Rights v. Anti-Money Laundering Enforcement*, 6 N.C. Banking Inst. 147, 149 (April, 2002).

30. Terrorism Asset Report, Annual Report to the Congress on Assets in the United States of Terrorist Countries and International Terrorism Program designees (2002), p. 1.

31. As of April 12, 2004, a professional pilot course is $25,995 at Airman Flight School in Norman, Oklahoma, (http://www.airmanflightschool.com) and the Harrisburg Jet Center states that "[t]he cost of a private pilot certificate varies by section of the country and from school to school, but prices range from $5,500 to $6,500 or more." See http://www.harrisburgjetcenter.com/hjc/flight_school/faq/flight school_faq.htm#cost

32. AL 2002-4, Financial Action Task Force Guidance for Financial Institutions in Detecting Terrorist Financing (Office of the Comptroller of the Currency, May 16, 2002).

33. Robert S. Pasley, *Privacy Rights v. Anti-Money Laundering Enforcement*, 6 N.C. Banking Inst. 147, 154 (April 2002) (quoting Secretary of the Treasury Gurule).

34. *Id.*

35. F.D.I.C. FIL-70-96 (Financial Crimes Enforcement Network, 1996).

36. *The IMF and the Fight Against Money Laundering and the Financing of Terrorism: A Fact Sheet* (April 2003), http://www.imf.org. "The [FATF] is an intergovernmental body whose purpose is the development and promotion of policies to combat money laundering. The FATF currently consists of 29 countries and two international organizations." *Id.*

37. "In addition, the events of September 11, 2001, and the many subsequent acts of terrorism around the world have prompted a whole new emphasis and 'war' on terrorist financing, frequently referred to as 'money laundering in reverse'–i.e., money that starts out legitimate and grows 'dirty' in its ultimate purpose." International Federation of Accountants, *Anti-Money Laundering, 2nd Edition*, (March 2004), at http://www.ifac.org

38. AL 2002-4, Financial Action Task Force Guidance for Financial Institutions in Detecting Terrorist Financing (Office of the Comptroller of the Currency, May 16, 2002).

39. Dept. Treas. News Release, Keynote Address of Deputy Assistant Secretary Juan C. Zarate Before the Investment Company Institute, "Securing the Financial System Against Rogue Capital" (November 10, 2003).

40. *Id.*

41. Executive Summary: Attacking Terrorist Networks at Home and Abroad found at http://www.whitehouse.gov/homeland/progress/full.html. "The FBI uncovered facts showing that the Benevolence International Foundation (BIF) and Global Relief Foundation (GRF), Islamic charities holding themselves out to be conduits for directing aid to the poor and needy of the Islamic world, were actually conduits for funding Islamic fighters engaged in battle throughout the world, including Chechnya. BIF and GRF have been designated as global terrorist entities, and their international organizations have been successfully disrupted and dismantled." *Id.*

42. AL 2002-4, Financial Action Task Force Guidance for Financial Institutions in Detecting Terrorist Financing, (Office of the Comptroller of the Currency, May 16, 2002).

43. *Id.* The OCC notes that sources such as the personal fortunes of terrorists themselves, such as Osama bin Laden who is believed to have funded al Quaida, are included in this type of fundraising. *Id.*

44. *Id.* The OCC suggests that kidnapping, extortion, robbery, and narcotics trafficking are attractive crimes for terrorist groups. *Id.*

45. *The IMF and the Fight Against Money Laundering and the Financing of Terrorism: A Fact Sheet* (April 2003), http://www.imf.org

46. USA PATRIOT Act, Pub. L. No. 107-56, 115 Stat. 272 (2001), codified as 31 U.S.C. §5311.

47. AL 2002-4, Financial Action Task Force Guidance for Financial Institutions in Detecting Terrorist Financing, (Office of the Comptroller of the Currency, May 16, 2002).

48. Pursuant to the Bank Secrecy Act, the Department of the Treasury is authorized to promulgate record-keeping and reporting regulations that govern the activities of financial institutions. *California Bankers Association v. Shultz,* 416 U.S. 21, 25–26 (1974).

49. 12 U.S.C. §1462a establishes the OTS.

50. 31 U.S.C. §310 established FinCEN in 1990 and authorizes FinCEN to investigate and identify financial criminal activities.

51. One additional agency, not discussed is the Office of Foreign Asset Control (OFAC). OFAC is "the lead agency for the blocking of assets of terrorism-supporting countries and international terrorist organizations." Terrorism Asset Report, Annual Report to the Congress on Assets in the United States of Terrorist Countries and International Terrorism Program designees (2002), p. 1.

52. Dept. Treas. News Release, "Bush Administration Announces Budget Increase to Help Fight Terrorist Financing and Financial Crime," January 16, 2004.

53. *The IMF and the Fight Against Money Laundering and the Financing of Terrorism: A Fact Sheet* (April, 2003), http://www.imf.org. The article goes on to explain that the International Money Fund has "long been involved in international efforts to combat money laundering, and over the last year and a half it has intensified its activities significantly and extended them to combating the financing of terrorism." *Id.*

54. "While reports [disclosing certain information about transactions] had been required by previous regulations issued by the Treasury Department, it was felt that more precise and detailed reporting requirements were needed." *State v. Schultz,* 850 P.2d 818, 827 (Kan. 1993). Moreover, one of the first types of reporting required was the currency transaction report (CTR), still used today for reporting transactions that exceed $10,000 by various institutions.

55. *Cotton v. Privatebank and Trust Company,* 235 F. Supp. 2d 809, 812 (N.D. Ill. 2002) (citing *Nevin v. Citibank,* 107 F. Supp. 2d 333, 340 (S.D.N.Y. 2000). The case also notes that "[t]he Act was passed as Pub.L. No. 102-550, 106 Stat. 4044, and is codified as amended in scattered sections of the United States Code." *Id.*

56. The USA PATRIOT Act, passed soon after September 11, is seen by the banking industry as "the latest anti-money laundering statute" designed to "attempt to improve the security of our country against international terrorism." Robert S. Pasley, *Privacy Rights v. Anti-Money Laundering Enforcement,* 6 N.C. Banking Inst. 147 (April, 2002).

57. Attorney General John Ashcroft, Testimony before the United States House of Representatives Committee on the Judiciary (June 5, 2003). Available online at http://www.usdoj.gov/ag/testimony/2003/0605003ag/houseremarks.htm

58. This was as of June 2003. *Id.*

59. The USA PATRIOT Act also discusses the requirement of a list. However, the regulatory agencies did not have additional details to provide to registrants about how the lists would work.

60. See e.g., 31 C.F.R. 103. Financial institutions are required to gather information such as name, date of birth, and physical address for those opening accounts.

61. 31 U.S.C. §5332(c) (2004).

62. 31 U.S.C. §5318(g)(1) authorizes the promulgation of implementing regulations. See e.g., 12 C.F.R. §563.180 (2004), the OTS regulation. While this paper discusses the requirements specific to banking entities, money services businesses, currency dealers, casinos and card clubs, securities and futures broker-dealers are currently required to file SARs, and there is discussion that insurance companies and mutual fund operators should file them. PowerPoint presentation from FinCEN. P. 5

63. The Currency Transaction Report (CTR) is still required when transactions of $10,000 or more are processed. 31 C.F.R. §103.22 (2004). The contents of a CTR are often similar to the SAR, and vice versa. However, each is required under different circumstances and an activity that implicates one will not necessarily implicate the other.

64. *Cotton,* 235 F. Supp. 2d at 812.

65. 12 C.F.R. §21.22(c) (2004).

66. 31 U.S.C. §5311 (2004).

67. A SAR must be filed no later than 30 calendar days after the detection if the suspect is identified and no later than 60 calendar days after the detection if no suspect was identified. 30 C.F.R. 103.18 (2004).

68. *The European Community v. Japan Tobacco, Inc.,* 186 F. Supp. 2d 231, 239 (E.D.N.Y. 2002).

69. See e.g., 12 C.F.R. 21.11 (k) (2004). This regulation states that "SARs are confidential. Any national bank or person subpoenaed or otherwise requested to disclose a SAR or the information contained in a SAR shall decline to produce the SAR or to provide

any information that would disclose that a SAR has been prepared of files. . . ." *Id.* There are similar code sections that apply to each type of financial institution.

70. *Whitney National Bank v. Karam*, No. CIV.A. H-02-2250, 2004 WL 414969, at *3 (S.D. Tex., 2004).

71. *Cotton*, 235 F. Supp. 2d at 814. (Citing *Gregory v. Bank One, Indiana, N.A.*, 200 F. Supp. 2d 1000, 1003 (S.D. Ind. 2002) holding that the confidentiality could not be waived by the reporting institution).

72. 31 U.S.C. §5318(g)(2) (2004).

73. See Exhibit A for a copy of TD F 90-22.47, the SAR form used by the Department of the Treasury and all banking institutions.

74. See, *infra*, n. 73.

75. For example, the financial institution must state whether a driver's license or passport was used to identify the suspect, and list the number and issuing authority for the identifier. See, *infra* n. 73.

76. See, *infra*, n. 73.

77. *Cotton*, 235 F. Supp. 2d at 815.

78. *Id.*

79. *Id.*

80. 31 U.S.C. §5318(g)(1) was not amended by the USA PATRIOT Act.

81. *Gregory v. Bank One, Indiana, N.A.*, 200 F. Supp. 2d 1000, 1003 (S.D. Ill. 2002).

82. Robert S. Pasley, *Privacy Rights v. Anti-Money Laundering Enforcement*, 6 N.C. Banking Inst. 147, 176–177 (April, 2002).

83. *Lawerence v. Texas* 539 U.S. 558 (2003) (sexual preference); *Vernonia School District*, 515 U.S. 646 (1995) (drug testing in schools); *Whisenhunt v. Spradlin* 464 U.S. 965 (1983) (dating a fellow employee); *H.L. v. Matheson* 450 U.S. 398 (1981) (abortion); *United States v. Miller*, 425 U.S. 435 (1976) (bank records).

84. Privacy is often seen as the "right to be let alone–the most comprehensive of rights and the right most valued by civilized men." *Olmstead v. U.S.*, 277 U.S. 438, 478 (1928) (Brandeis's dissent).

85. "The Court noted it consistently has held that an individual 'has no legitimate expectation of privacy in information he voluntarily turns over to third parties.'" *Schultz*, 850 P.2d at 824 (citations omitted). This case dealt with telephone records. The court also noted here that the right to privacy could be read into the state constitution, but the court declined to do so.

86. *Miller*, 425 U.S. 435.

87. "In summary, the Patriot Act provides helpful additions and amendments to the [Bank Secrecy Act], especially those provisions that support enhanced due diligence with regard to high-risk accounts, that restrict obviously high-risk transactions, and that allow for increased sharing between banks in order to better protect the industry to eliminate fraud. As set forth above, these provisions do not appear to unduly affect any privacy rights and are particularly important as demonstrated by the horrible terrorist attacks of September 11, 2001." Robert S. Pasley, *Privacy Rights v. Anti-Money Laundering Enforcement*, 6 N.C. Banking Inst. 147, 211 (April, 2002).

88. 31 U.S.C. 5318(a)(1) (2004).

89. Whitney was a defamation case where the court said that the bank is immune from any civil liability resulting from the filing of the SAR. *Whitney*, 2004 WL 414969 at *3.

90. Another federal statute providing some privacy rights to customers of financial institutions is the Gramm-Leach Bliley Act, passed in November 1999. However, the intent of Title V of this act was to prohibit financial institutions from sharing "non-public personal information" to third parties, unless it is shared with the customer's consent or under certain narrow exceptions. The impact of this title may be best known because of the privacy notices that consumers now receive at the establishment of a relationship with a financial institution and then annually, typically in one of the periodic statements received from the institutions.

91. Robert S. Pasley, *Privacy Rights v. Anti-Money Laundering Enforcement*, 6 N.C. Banking Inst. 147, 217 (April 2002) (quoting L. Richard Fischer, The Law of Financial Privacy 4-2-4-4 (A.S. Pratt & Sons) (2001)).

92. 12 U.S.C. §3401(1) (2004).

93. 12 U.S.C. §3402 (2004).

94. 12 U.S.C. §3403(c) (2004).

95. USA PATRIOT Act, Pub. L. No. 107-56, 115 Stat. 298 (2001).

96. USA PATRIOT Act, Pub. L. No. 107-56, 115 Stat. 320 (2001).

97. *Whitney National Bank*, 2004 WL 414969.

98. *United States v. Holihan*, 248 F. Supp. 2d 179, 187 (W.D.N.Y., 2003).

99. *Holihan*, 248 F. Supp. 2d. at 187.

100. *Whitney National Bank*, 2004 WL 414969 at *1.

101. *United States v. Kaatz*, 705 F.2d 1237, 1242 (10th Cir. 1983).

102. *Kaatz*, 705 F.2d at 1242 (citations omitted).

103. *Miller*, 425 U.S. 435.

104. *People v. Jackson*, 116 Ill. App. 3d (Ill. App. 1983); *Burrows v. Superior Court*, 529 P.2d 590 (Cal. 1975); *Charnes v. DiGiacomo*, 612 P.2d 1117 (Colo. 1980).

105. 850 P.2d at 828. (citing *Burrows v. Superior Court*, 13 Cal.3d 238, 118 Cal. Rptr. 166, 529 P.2d 590;

Charnes v. DiGiacomo, 200 Colo. 94, 612 P.2d 1117 (1980) (en banc); *Winfield v. Div. of Pari-Mutuel Wagering,* 477 So.2d 544 (Fla.1985); *People v. Jackson,* 116 Ill.App.3d 430, 72 Ill. Dec. 153, 452 N.E.2d 85 (1983); *Com. v. DeJohn,* 486 Pa. 32, 403 A.2d 1283 (1979), *cert. denied* 444 U.S. 1032, 100 S.Ct. 704, 62 L.Ed.2d 668 (1980); *State v. Thompson,* 810 P.2d 415 (Utah 1991)). However, the court here also noted that approximately one-third of the states at that time had already passed an equivalent to the RFPA. *Id.* at 832.
106. *Schultz,* 850 P. 2d. at 831. "About one third of the fifty states have enacted a state equivalent of the Right to Financial Privacy Act." *Id.*
107. 12 U.S.C. §3403(c).
108. *Stark v. Connally,* 347 F. Supp. 1242, 1246 (N.D. Ca. 1972).
109. *Stark,* 347 F. Supp. at 1249.
110. *Shultz,* 416 U.S. 21 (overruling *Stark v. Connally*).
111. *Id.* at 42.
112. *Id.* at 66–70.
113. The plaintiff raised other constitutional claims; all were dismissed, and are not relevant to the topic of this chapter.
114. Robert S. Pasley, *Privacy Rights v. Anti-Money Laundering Enforcement,* 6 N.C. Banking Inst. 147, 192 (April, 2002).
115. Numerous laws have amended the Bank Secrecy Act including "the Comprehensive Crime Control Act of 1984; the Money Laundering Control Act of 1986; the Anti-Drug Abuse Act of 1988; the Depository Institution Money Laundering Amendment Act of 1990; the Annunzio-Wylie Anti-Money Laundering Act of 1992; the Money Laundering Suppression Act of 1994;" and the USA PATRIOT Act have all amended the Bank Secrecy Act. Robert S. Pasley, *Privacy Rights v. Anti-Money Laundering Enforcement,* 6 N.C. Banking Inst. 147, 198–199 (April, 2002) (footnotes omitted).
116. Robert S. Pasley, *Privacy Rights v. Anti-Money Laundering Enforcement,* 6 N.C. Banking Inst. 147, 193 (April, 2002).
117. *United States v. Katz,* 705 F.2d 1237 (10th Cir. 1983).
118. *Whitney National Bank,* 2004 WL 414969.
119. Robert S. Pasley, *Privacy Rights v. Anti-Money Laundering Enforcement,* 6 N.C. Banking Inst. 147, 207 (April, 2002).

DISCUSSION QUESTIONS

1. What is money laundering?
2. How private should one's financial records be?
3. Should there be any difference in the privacy given to individual financial records and corporate financial records? Explain your answer.
4. What differences does the article identify between treatment of funds that may be associated with terrorist organizations and those that may be associated with other types of criminal enterprise? Should there be any differences in accounting for such funds?
5. Describe the link between money laundering and terrorism.
6. Explain your understanding of the connection between drug traffickers and terrorists. To what extent do you believe the actions college students should be affected, if at all, by this relationship? Explain your answer.
7. What is your opinion of the confidentiality requirements for SARs?
8. What potential problems, if any, could an innocent individual face due to the confidentiality requirements for SARs?

Airport security in Denver, August 7, 2004. WC Nicholson photo.

Section V

CHALLENGES FOR TRANSPORTATION

Chapter 12

MASS TRANSIT AND HOMELAND SECURITY: POLICY ISSUES

EVA LERNER-LAM

I. WHY IS PUBLIC TRANSIT SECURITY A CHALLENGE?

A. The Open Nature of Public Transit Makes It an Attractive Target

Transit's purpose is to provide a means of transportation for the general public.[1] Bus, minibus, commuter rail, heavy rail, light rail, ferry, and other public transportation systems seek to optimize operations by providing a network of multimodal systems. Transfer locations are designed to provide rapid access between high-capacity systems, resulting in high volumes of riders in concentrated spaces. Ironically, the same concentrations and flows of riders that enable a public transit network to operate efficiently make it difficult to establish hard perimeters and screening points, and thus create crucial vulnerabilities for security threats and attacks. Passengers do not need to present identification or itineraries, and even the most basic baggage screening would quickly impede passenger flow. As observed by the Federal Transit Administration:[2]

Transit is designed and operated as an open environment—it is by its very nature a high-risk, high-consequence target for terrorists. More than 9.5 billion passengers a year ride our transit systems. Some of the largest transit systems report that more than 1,000 people a minute enter their largest intermodal facilities during rush hour. Transit subways travel under key government buildings, business centers, and harbors. Worldwide, transit has been a frequent terrorist target, including bombings in the London and Paris subways, the Sarin gas attack in Tokyo, and bus bombings in Israel."

— *FTA Briefing: Update on the Status of FTA Security Initiatives, January 3, 2003*

B. Multijurisdictional Environments Require Aggressive Coordination, Cooperation, and Funding

Most transit systems typically serve many cities, counties, and even states, and transit lines often cross multiple jurisdictional boundaries. Each municipality maintains its own first responders—police force, fire, and emergency medical crews—and every time

Note: Eva Lerner-Lam has 27 years of experience in transportation planning, operations, research and policy making. Founder and president of the Palisades Consulting Group, Inc. (www.palisadesgroup.com), she leads many national technical committees focused on transportation security. She has served in several key public sector positions, including director of planning and operations for the San Diego Metropolitan Transit Development Board and member of the New Jersey Transit Corporation Board of Directors, and has received numerous professional awards and honors. She is a graduate and past trustee of Princeton University, and earned a master's degree in Civil Engineering/Transportation Systems Division from the Massachusetts Institute of Technology. This chapter was reviewed by Charles Barker, Ron Heil, George Kovatch Ron Libengood, and Ellen Thompson. Many of their suggestions were incorporated into the text. Although the author of this chapter is grateful for their careful review and well-considered comments and suggestions, she assumes full responsibility for any errors or omissions.

a transit vehicle crosses a jurisdictional boundary, a new set of first responders–each with their own set of operating procedures and communications equipment–comes into play. In addition, public transit requires infrastructure, including motor fuel, electricity, and computer systems, each of which is operated by separate and distinct regional providers. Multijurisdictional coordination is critical at all stages of assessment, preparation, planning, drills, live response, and recovery, and it must occur at all levels of command. In rural areas, with their broad geographic coverage and scarce resources, such coordination may be extremely challenging and difficult to achieve if cooperation is not aggressively encouraged and funded. Without an effective response program, risk and consequences will be greater.

C. Multimodal Interactions Can Increase Vulnerability and Consequences

Public transit works best when different modes link with one another to provide broad geographic coverage, although frequently each separate mode operates under its own set of rules and regulations, and answers to different authorities. This increases the vulnerability of transit agencies by making the sharing of intelligence difficult and providing many more opportunities for security threats to infiltrate screened facilities and vehicles. For example, an urban bus terminal may have many bus companies, public and private, accessing its loading and unloading bays. With the nation on heightened alert, each bus company is expected to provide a measure of security (pre-trip inspection of vehicles for left packages, suspicious devices detected inside or under the vehicles, passengers behaving in a suspicious manner, etc.). Unfortunately, the overall security of the facility is only as good as the weakest link in the system; that is, the security of the whole is only as good as the security provided by the bus company with the least effective security procedures. The attacks on September 11, 2001, provide a good example–terrorists used airports that were perceived to have less effective security than others from which to launch their attacks.

Furthermore, local disruptions in service provided by one modal agency can have cascading effects on other service to which it connects. The Port Authority Trans-Hudson (PATH) service that carried passengers between Hoboken, NJ, and the World Trade Center in Manhattan was severely damaged on September 11, 2003, and attack-related evacuation and access between New Jersey and lower Manhattan for hundreds of thousands of commuters was shifted during response and recovery phases to other crossing providers, creating substantial changes in commuter travel patterns and difficult operating challenges for transit service providers.[3] In addition, as systems begin recovery operations, the timing of the resumption of normal service on one system may impact the recovery of the others, and the corresponding transitions in security measures may open up vulnerabilities in overall system security.

II. TYPES OF PUBLIC TRANSIT SECURITY THREATS

There are many types of security threats against which public transit agencies must prepare: armed assault, hostage taking, chemical release onboard, explosive on-board, chemical outside, and explosive/sabotage outside. In addition, transit systems are becoming more dependent on automated communications and technology systems, and there is growing potential for cyber security intrusion using cell phones, laptops, or wireless technologies to disrupt operations in critical systems such as transit vehicle command and control, vehicle interlock systems, and personnel identification.

Each of these scenarios requires a different set of vulnerability assessments, preparation, planning, drills, live response, and recovery procedures.[4] Furthermore, for each of these, as in the September 11, 2001, attacks in New York City and Washington, DC, and the ongoing attacks in commercial and entertainment establishments in England, Israel, Malaysia, and other terrorist targets around the world, it is important to consider the willingness of the attacker to commit suicide as an element of the attack. This changes the nature of all aspects of vulnerability assessment, preparation, planning, drills, live response, and recovery efforts prior to the suicide missions in the United States on September 11, 2001. In addition to precluding the possibility of an escape route that could be used by victims of the attack, the lack of a live perpetrator completely eliminates the option of negotiation with the attacker to spare the lives of victims.

III. PUBLIC TRANSIT SECURITY POLICY

Since September 11, 2001, there has been a tremendous effort by the public transit community to prepare, prevent, respond, and recover from future security threats and attacks.

A. A Systems Approach

Federal agencies and regional, state, and local providers of public transit services have approached post-September 11, 2001, strategically, with a series of policy initiatives guided by an overall systems approach. Organizationally, this was emphasized at the federal level by the formation of the Transportation Security Administration (TSA), an attempt to unify security policy, procedures, and communications of all transportation modes.

The systems approach emphasizes the integration of security into every aspect of transit programs, operations, and infrastructure. Specifically, it requires "coherent security systems that are well integrated with transportation operations and are deliberately designed to deter terrorists even as they selectively guard against and prepare for terrorist attacks."[5] In addition, the concept of layered security systems is an important one, characterized by "an interleaved and concentric set of security features . . . that cannot be breached by the defeat of a single security feature–such as a gate or guard–as each layer provides backup for the others, so that impermeability of individual layers is not required."[6]

B. Safety and Security First

Today's emphasis on security is similar to the emphasis on safety that began about two decades ago in transit. Now, "safety first" is a common theme that exists in all aspects of a transit agency's operations, and in the future security must be first as well. The System Security and Emergency Preparedness Plans that the Federal Transit Administration is encouraging transit agencies to adopt are intended to provide a framework for creating a new emphasis on security.[7]

C. Collaboration and Coordination

Close collaboration and coordination with other public agencies is critical to effective public transit security policy. Agency personnel must develop strong working relationships with personnel from other agencies before an attack, not during one. Integrated planning of facilities and operations help to prevent or mitigate threats and attacks, and tabletop exercises and drills can be used to bring related agency personnel together to work out threat and attack scenarios and alternative response strategies. Ideally, once those strategies are identified and tested, all personnel should "practice, practice, practice" to ensure a high level of response and recovery capability.

D. Role of Technology

Technology can enhance an agency's ability to detect reconnaissance prior to an attack and the attack itself as well as improve communications for evacuation coordination and recovery. However, technologies such as chemical detection devices, employee smart card identification systems, vehicle location systems, radio and other wireless communications systems all require substantial amounts of interjurisdictional planning, integration, maintenance, and training. Technologies can enhance existing collaborative and cooperative relationships within and among transit agencies and related government and private partners; however, procuring technology for technology's sake without a strong set of working relationships can lead to misspending of funds. For example, there are several Web-based software systems available for first responders and government agencies to supervise and monitor emergency response to incidents. However, each system requires data to be entered in different, proprietary formats. Therefore, if several jurisdictions within a response zone have different Web-based software systems for emergency response supervision and monitoring, it will be necessary to somehow integrate the data so that all systems can receive and interpret the same information. Oftentimes, that integration is simply too difficult or expensive to accomplish, and the systems remain "stovepiped" and unable to interact with neighboring jurisdictions and agencies.

To the extent that technology in the form of intelligent systems can be leveraged to assist in the efforts of transit agencies to conduct "smart" reconnaissance, detection, emergency communications and response, evacuation, and recovery, the existence of the National ITS Architecture and its supporting standards and protocols provides a strong framework within which vendors and purchasers of technology systems can work toward interoperability.[8] However, no amount of technology or even planning for implementation of the technology, can replace the fundamental need for human collaboration and cooperation at the operating level within and among different responding organizations.

E. Transit as a First Responder

In acknowledgment of the first responder role in evacuation of people that transit plays in a security emergency, the transit community determined that, at least for the transit community, the Department of Homeland Security's color-coded warning advisory system should include two additional colors besides the five colors otherwise in force: black for "under attack" and purple for "recovery." The two additional colors and their respective actions are:[9]

- Black: Indicates that an attack is underway against a specific transit agency or within the agency's immediate geographic area. The Black state is entered only when an attack has occurred. Black includes the immediate postattack time period when the transit agency may be responding to casualties, assisting in evacuations, inspecting and securing transit facilities, or helping with other tasks directed by the local emergency management authority.
- Purple: Indicates the recovery of transit service after an attack has occurred. Purple includes restoration of levels of service, routes, and schedules; repairing or reopening facilities; adjustment of staff work schedules and duty assignments; responding to customer inquiries about services; and other activities necessary to restore transit service. The Purple state follows the Black state and may also exist for short time periods when the agency is transitioning from a higher threat condition to a lower threat condition (e.g., from Red to Orange). The Purple state will coexist with the prevailing threat condition. In other words, business recovery (Purple) will be accomplished while maintaining the prevailing readiness status (e.g., Orange protective measures).

— *Federal Transit Administration, Policy Statement 2003*

IV. KEY STRATEGIES

There are four key strategies for addressing security threats and attacks against transit facilities, employees, and customers: prepare, prevent, respond, and recover.

A. Prepare

Transit agencies prepare for security threats and attacks by having security plans in place and by training their employees and educating their customers about observing and reporting suspicious activities. In addition, certain procedures are instituted based on the national threat level, as expressed by the Homeland Security Warning System color codes.

System Security and Emergency Preparedness Plans (SSEPPs) are basic tools used to develop effective security and emergency management programs. The plans are intended to be integrated into each agency's emergency policies, as well as their respective acquisition and procurement processes. They are also intended to promote coordination with local public safety personnel and emergency responders, emphasizing drills and exercises.[10]

The National Transit Institute and the Transportation Safety Institute offer courses for transit personnel to become trained in dealing with various aspects of transit security. The courses are subsidized by the U.S. Department of Transportation.[11] Emergency planning drills and exercises involving related agencies are also strongly encouraged by the federal government:[12]

> Tabletop and functional drills are conducted at least once every six months and full-scale exercises, coordinated with regional emergency response providers, are performed at least annually.
> —Federal Transit Administration, Top 20 Security Program Action Items, 2003

B. Prevent

Prevention involves many elements, including upgraded detection and deterrence capabilities, (such as employee credentialing systems and updated locking systems), visible and undercover security patrols and aggressive reconnaissance and monitoring of suspicious behavior. Incorporation of Crime Prevention Through Environmental Design (CPTED) concepts into transit terminal facility design can be an effective tool in preventing security risks and vulnerability.[13]

In addition, transit employees and customers are being asked to be vigilant and provide a layer of prevention themselves. Transit Watch is a new nationwide safety and security awareness program designed to encourage the active participation of transit passengers and employees in maintaining a safe transit environment.[14] Modeled after the highly successful Neighborhood Watch campaign, the Transit Watch campaign was developed in collaboration with industry partners, including the American Public Transportation Association (APTA), the Community Transportation Association of America (CTAA), the Amalgamated Transit Union (ATU), and the Transportation Security Administration (TSA).

C. Respond

Transit response to security threats and attacks requires close coordination with many peer organizations; local, state, federal, and regional jurisdictions; emergency management teams; emergency hospitals; utility services; and other infield support teams in the affected area. Peer organizations (including over-the-road commercial bus, paratransit, bus, commuter rail, light rail, ferries, and subways), local law enforcement, fire and emergency medical crews, and specially tasked regional emergency teams all need to share updated contact information (name, title, position, responsibility, phone, cell phone, e-mail address, etc.) and drill and practice together in tabletop and field exercises regularly in order to remain ready to respond. There are many training programs, handbooks, and manuals provided by U.S. DOT and other sources.

It is important to note that when an area is under attack, transit is expected to play a crucial role in evacuation, and is therefore considered an integral member of the overall emergency response team, alongside police, fire, and emergency medical crews.

D. Recover

Transit plays a critical role in supporting local economies and has a direct impact on safety and quality of life. A rapid restoration of service is important. Depending on the size and nature of the attack, recovery may take weeks, months, and sometimes years. Transit's role in recovery efforts consists of restoring service and accommodating changes in customer travel patterns resulting from the attack.

V. TRANSIT INITIATIVES

Due to the nature of transit's vulnerability to all types of security threats and attacks, transit operators have always had security procedures in place.

With the September 11, 2001, suicide attacks on the homeland, however, the Federal Transit Administration took swift steps to enhance already existing procedures and established five key transit initiatives, including the development of a 20-point security program to assess, prepare, drill, respond, and recover;[15] threat and vulnerability assessments of 37 of the largest and highest risk transit agencies;[16] deployment of technical teams to assist agencies in implementing major components of a systematic security program;[17] tabletop and full-scale drills with regional emergency responders to test and improve security and emergency response plans;[18] accelerated deployment of technology;[19] and training and outreach to transit employees and management.[20]

Prior to these initiatives, however, it was necessary to set the tone and framework for collaboration and coordination among fire, police, and medical emergency responders and transit. To this end, the Federal Transit Administration held a very successful series of workshops around the nation in 2002–2003 entitled Connecting Communities. In all, 17 regional forums were held and nearly 1,300 individuals, including representatives of 125 transit agencies and their community partners, participated in the forums. The forums provided a framework and foundation for future forums that can be hosted at the local, state, and regional levels.

On the research side, the Transit Cooperative Research Program of the National Academy of Sciences Transportation Research Board took quick action and sponsored a series of research projects that provided a core set of transit security reference materials for transit operators.[21]

In addition, an Information Sharing and Analysis Center (ISAC) for transit, where transit agencies can share security information about evolving terrorist threats or ongoing information system attacks, was established at the American Public Transportation Association.[22]

Mass Transit has also been included in the Department of Homeland Security's Transportation Security Administration (TSA), although TSA has yet to assume full responsibility for the security of any transportation mode other than aviation. TSA and FTA are currently developing a memorandum of understanding that will define each agency's roles and responsibilities for transit security.[23]

VI. CHALLENGES AND FUTURE POLICY DIRECTIONS

A. Federal

According to the Government Accounting Office, insufficient funding is the most significant challenge in making transit systems as safe and secure as possible.[24] Funding security improvements is challenging due to tight budget environments, competing budget priorities, and the prohibition on transit agencies that serve areas with populations of 200,000 or more from using federal urbanized area formula funds for operating expenses.

In considering the federal government's role in funding transit safety and security initiatives, the Government Accounting Office identified several issues that need to be addressed, including (1) developing federal funding criteria, (2) determining the roles of stakeholders in funding transit security, and (3) selecting the appropriate federal policy instruments to deliver assistance that may be deemed necessary by policymakers (e.g., grants, tax incentives, etc.).[25]

B. Regional and State

By far the most challenging issue at the regional and state levels is the need to ensure collaboration and cooperation between and among the many different agencies and jurisdictions that make up a regional area. Lack of funding, differing technologies and operating procedures, inefficient means of updating key personnel contact information all contribute to the formidable obstacles to regional readiness to prepare for, prevent, respond to, and recover from major security threats and attacks. Progress has been made to varying degrees, but it is difficult to see how sustained efforts can be maintained without substantial funding support for regular tabletop and field exercises, practice drills, and training sessions.

C. Local

By the beginning of 2004, with some modest funding assistance from the Federal Transit

Administration, most transit agencies have prepared or are in the process of preparing System Security and Emergency Preparedness Plans to guide them in their planning and implementation of security systems and procedures. The challenge at the local level will be for them to maintain a high level of diligence in maintaining and upgrading those plans over time. In a difficult economy and more frequent color-code alerts, finding the funding to support the desired level of diligence will become increasingly problematic.

D. Technology Interoperability Challenges

At all governmental levels and across many professional disciplines and public service sectors, there exist significant challenges in achieving technological interoperability, that is, the ability to communicate information between and among the many proprietary technology devices that are used to collect, compile, and synthesize data and information for each respective entity. The lack of interoperability standards in radio communications at the World Trade Center site on September 11, 2001, between fire, police, and emergency crews has been the subject of close scrutiny, but it is symptomatic of most technology applications in public transit: Basic information architectures and their supporting standards and protocols are only beginning to be established for many technologies critical to successful planning, prevention, response, and recovery efforts. The National Intelligent Transportation Systems (ITS) Architecture and its supporting standards and protocols are a big step in the right direction[26] and transit has played a key role in the development and implementation of that architecture and its standards and protocols. However, there is much more work that must be done to achieve true interoperability in the field.

VII. CONCLUSION

By its open and accessible nature, and with its high concentrations of people transferring between vehicles and facilities operated by different modes throughout large geographic areas, transit is particularly vulnerable to security threats and attacks. Different threats present different challenges in terms of preparation, prevention, response, and recovery, and each threat requires thorough assessment, training, drills, and exercises. Collaboration and coordination are critical elements in the development of an integrated response to increased magnitude and number of security threats, especially in light of ever-tightening budgets, the need for interoperability of technologies intended to enhance security, and the ripple effect of threats and attacks in our interconnected society.

Although much progress has been made since the attacks on our homeland on September 11, 2001, there is still much more to do. Transit's strategic response to the tragedy has been to deal with the challenges with a systems approach, reaching out to related agencies and working hard within the transit sector to develop strong communications and collaborative relationships in order to leverage scarce resources and maximize effectiveness against security threats and attacks. With its key initiatives focused on planning, coordination, training, education, drills and exercises, and deployment of technology, transit has taken important first steps toward protecting its employees, customers, and physical assets.

ENDNOTES

1. In this chapter, public transit refers to modes commonly known as urban passenger transportation, including urban and over-the-road bus, minibus, commuter rail, heavy rail, light rail, and ferry services. It does not include airlines, airports, cruise lines, or seaports, which are governed by very different characteristics and operating principles.

2. See FTA Safety and Security Website at http://transit-safety.volpe.dot.gov/Security/Default.asp

3. Vulnerabilities in the days, weeks, and months following a major attack are particularly of concern, because all systems are typically operating in recovery mode. Therefore, close attention should be paid to the systemwide integrity of security measures in force by the network of public transit providers operating in recovery mode after an attack.

4. For example, see *Chemical Plant Bomb Threat Planning Handbook*, by Critical Intervention Services, Inc., March 2002, which describes bomb threat management protocols for buildings and *Standard Protocols for Managing Security Incidents Involving Surface Transit Vehicles*, March 2003, which describes threat management protocols for transit vehicles.

5. See page 1, Executive Summary, Special Report 270 of the Transportation Research Board, *Deterrence, Protection and Preparation: The New Transportation Security Imperative*.

6. Ibid.

7. "Public Transportation System Security and Emergency Preparedness Planning Guide," Federal Transit Administration, January 2003 (http://transit-safety.volpe.dot.gov/Security/SecurityInitiatives/Top20/1%20-%20Management%20and%20Accountability/1%20-%20Written%20Security%20and%20Emergency%20Plans/default.asp)

8. For more information on the National ITS Architecture, see http://itsarch.iteris.com/itsarch/

9. See FTA Transit Threat Level Response Recommendation Policy Statement at http://transit-safety.volpe.dot.gov/Security/SecurityInitiatives/ThreatLevel/default.asp

10. See *Public Transportation System Security and Emergency Preparedness Planning Guide*, 2003. http://transit-safety.volpe.dot.gov/Publications/default.asp#Security

11. See National Transit Institute: http://www.ntionline.com and Transportation Safety Institute: http://www.tsi.dot.gov/

12. See http://transit-safety.volpe.dot.gov/Security/SecurityInitiatives/Top20/5%20-%20Audits%20and%20Drills/16%20-%20On-going%20Drills%20and%20Exercises/default.asp

13. See Crime Prevention Through Environmental Design: http://www.cpted.net/default.html

14. See Transit Watch: http://transit-safety.volpe.dot.gov/Security/SecurityInitiatives/Items/transit-watch.asp

15. See FTA Top 20 Security Program Action Items for Transit Agencies: Self-Assessment Checklist (http://transit-safety.volpe.dot.gov/Security/SecurityInitiatives/Top20/checklist.asp)

16. Listed at: Transit Security Briefing: Update on the Status of FTA Security Initiatives, January 3, 2003 http://transit-safety.volpe.dot.gov/Security/Default.asp. Multidisciplinary teams including experts in antiterrorism, security, and transit operations assessed the readiness of the largest and highest risk transit agencies. Based on these assessments, FTA provided specific feedback to individual agencies on how to improve their security systems and reduce vulnerabilities, as well as information on best practices to all transit agencies.

17. Ibid. Emergency response planning and technical assistance teams were deployed to the top 50–60 transit agencies to help them to implement the major components of a systematic security program.

18. Ibid. Grants of up to $50,000 were awarded to 83 transit agencies to conduct tabletop and full-scale drills with regional emergency responders to test and improve their security and emergency response plans.

19. Ibid. FTA accelerated the deployment and testing of the PROTECT system for chemical detection in subway systems. In addition, research funds were refocused to conduct 11 short-term, quick payoff research projects identified by the transit industry.

20. Ibid and U. S. Department of Transportation, Federal Transit Administration, Issue No. 34, Office of Safety and Security, *Transit Security Newsletter*, January 2003 http://transit-safety.volpe.dot.gov/security/newsletters/html/vol34/page7.asp. A new 2-hour security awareness course for frontline employees and supervisors is being delivered nationwide.

21. See TCRP Security Project J-10: http://www4.trb.org/trb/crp.nsf/All+Projects/TCRP+J-10.

22. See press releases from the American Public Transportation Association and the Federal Transit Administration: http://www.apta.com/media/releases/isac_2003.cfm and http://transit-safety.volpe.dot.gov/Security/SecurityInitiatives/Items/isac.asp

23. See page 3, United States General Accounting Office, Testimony Before the Subcommittee on Housing and Transportation, Committee on Banking, Housing, and Urban Affairs, U.S. Senate September 18, 2002, Mass Transit Challenges in Securing Transit Systems, Statement of Peter Guerrero, Director, Physical Infrastructure Issues: http://www.gao.gov/new.items/d021075t.pdf

24. Ibid., p. 3.

25. Ibid., p. 3.

26. See National ITS Architecture, http://itsarch.iteris.com/itsarch/

DISCUSSION QUESTIONS

You are a resident of a medium-sized suburb in a large metropolitan area with a population of several million people. You have been active in community affairs, and have coached several youth athletic teams to regional and state championships.

Recently, your mayor appointed you to be a citizen member of a regional task force on public transportation security. The task force consists of the chief of police from the metropolitan transit agency, several police chiefs from neighboring towns (not yours), several emergency medical team professionals (one from your town), and a deputy chief of the state highway patrol. The task force is set to meet next week for the first time, and will meet once every three months until further notice. Your term of service is two years.

1. What authority should the task force possess? How should it view transit security in the context of overall security concerns? What should its perspective be on technological approaches to security concerns?
2. What do you hope to accomplish on the task force during your tenure?
3. The task force chair has asked each of the members to consider nominating two additional task force members. Whom will you nominate? (Hint: what groups are missing from the current task force roster?)
4. What will you do between now and the first meeting to prepare yourself to represent your fellow citizens?
5. What do you think will be the hardest part of your volunteer service on the task force?
6. What do you see as the most vulnerable parts of the mass transit system? What solutions can you propose to address the issues?

Chapter 13

POST-9-11 CHALLENGES FOR AVIATION SECURITY

FRANK J. COSTELLO

Aviation is the frontline of homeland security. Aviation is both vulnerable and vital. Whatever else is said about the September 11 tragedies, they were not the products of technologically complex strategies. At their roots, they were well thought-out, violent acts of thuggery. September 11 also emphasized that aircraft are potential weapons with the ability to create tremendous secondary damage. A fully fueled, large transport category aircraft is a threat to anything and anyone on the ground, even the largest man-made structures. At the same time, the aviation industry is a crucial part of the U.S. economy. The total economic impact of U.S. civil aviation is estimated to exceed $900 billion annually, or roughly 9 percent of our gross national product, and to account for over 11 million jobs.[1] When the events of September 11 shut down the industry, the entire U.S. economy was put at risk.

For these reasons, aviation has been, and probably always will be, a primary target of terrorists. This is the terrible truth that underscores aviation security and that has compelled so many actions that, prior to September 11, would have been unthinkable. If aviation cannot be made secure, homeland security itself will fail.

This chapter briefly reviews the history of U.S. aviation security, then examines the general legal framework both for existing measures and for measures likely to be taken in the future. It is not intended to be either a primer on or critical analysis of existing security measures.

I. A BRIEF HISTORY OF U.S. AVIATION SECURITY

You do not have to be much over the age of 40 to remember when an airport was an open, friendly venue where passengers could be met on the ramp and the only access restrictions were those related to safety. This changed with the Cuban revolution and the introduction of aircraft hijacking to our lexicon.

On May 1, 1961, a National Airlines flight was hijacked to Cuba. Congress responded to this and other incidents later that year with enactment of the Air Piracy Act.[2] When the incidence of hijackings increased in the early 1970s,[3] the Federal Aviation Administration (FAA) responded by creating the Sky Marshal program (formally

Note: Frank Costello is a managing partner of Zuckert, Scoutt & Rasenberger, L.L.P., a Washington, D.C., law firm with 40 years of experience in handling regulatory, international, legislative, and litigation matters, primarily in transportation industries. The firm's aviation practice encompasses virtually every aspect of that industry. Mr. Costello currently serves as chairman of the Aviation Committee of the American Bar Association's Section of Public Utility, Communications and Transportation Law. Mr. Costello is admitted to practice in the District of Columbia. He is a graduate of Dartmouth College (1965) and the Georgetown University Law Center (1970). Shannon Moyer, an associate in the firm, assisted in the preparation of this chapter.

reconstituted in 1985 as the Federal Air Marshal program).

Ironically, it was a notorious nonpolitical aircraft hijacking that finally prompted greater airport security. On November 24, 1971, a passenger named D. B. Cooper parachuted from a Northwest Airlines flight after demanding and receiving a large cash ransom. He never was found. This prompted the FAA to require universal screening of passengers and their carry-on baggage, effective January 5, 1973. The decision was made to (i) rely on magnetometer screening for weapons and (ii) place the responsibility for the screening functions with the airlines who, in turn, largely relied on private contractors. In 1974, Congress directed the FAA to require X-ray screening of all carry-on baggage.[4] With various modifications and additions, this was the system in place on September 11, 2001.

While security remained constant, the world became a much more dangerous place. Aircraft and airports became targets of terrorists rather than simply means of transportation or instruments of barter for political extremists. On December 21, 1988, Pan Am Flight 103, a Boeing 747 departing from London, exploded over Lockerbie, Scotland. The explosion killed all 259 passengers and crew and 11 people on the ground. One response to this tragedy was the creation of the President's Commission on Aviation Security and Terrorism (the Lockerbie Commission). The report of the Lockerbie Commission severely faulted the existing security system[5] and made a number of recommendations, including the rapid deployment of explosive detection systems. Many of these recommendations were included in the Aviation Security Improvement Act of 1990.[6] FAA implementation of the Lockerbie Commission's recommendations proceeded at a measured pace, hampered by slower than expected research and lower than expected funding. By the mid-1990s, the FAA had certified the basic CAT scan based explosive detection system now familiar to airline passengers, but it lacked the funds to deploy those devices in large numbers.

In December 1994, a bomb exploded on a Philippine Airlines flight, killing one passenger. The subsequent investigation revealed a plot to place explosive devices on as many as one dozen U.S. airline aircraft operating in the Pacific. On July 17, 1996, TWA Flight 800, a Boeing 747 destined for Paris, exploded over Long Island Sound shortly after departure from JFK International Airport. A bomb was suspected as the cause, although the explosion eventually was attributed to a mechanical problem.[7] Five weeks later, the president established the White House Commission on Aviation Safety and Security (the Gore Commission).

The Gore Commission's Final Report, issued more than four and one-half years before the September 11 tragedies, contained this prescient language:

> The Federal Bureau of Investigation, the Central Intelligence Agency, and other intelligence sources have been warning that the threat of terrorism is changing in two important ways. First, it is no longer just an overseas threat from foreign terrorists. People and places in the United States have joined the list of targets, and Americans have joined the ranks of terrorists. The bombings of the World Trade Center in New York and the Federal Building in Oklahoma City are clear examples of the shift, as is the conviction of Ramzi Yousef for attempting to bomb twelve American airliners out of the sky over the Pacific Ocean. The second change is that in addition to well-known, established terrorist groups, it is becoming more common to find terrorists working alone or in ad-hoc groups, some of whom are not afraid to die in carrying out their designs.

> When terrorists attack an American airliner, they are attacking the United States. They have so little respect for our values—so little regard for human life or the principles of justice that are the foundation of American society—that they would destroy innocent children and devoted mothers and fathers completely at random.

> Today's aviation security is based in part on the defenses erected in the 1970s against hijackers and on recommendations made by the Commission on Aviation Security and Terrorism. . . . Improvements in aviation security have been complicated because government and industry often found themselves at odds, unable to resolve disputes over financing, effectiveness, technology, and potential impacts on operations and passengers.[8]

The Gore Commission recommended increased federal funding for security-related capital improvements and increased FAA supervision of security.[9] That this largely did not occur is a result of several miscalculations. All parties, both governmental and private, tended to underestimate the general intelligence reflected here and overestimate the effectiveness of existing security in addressing the threat, which was perceived as a hijacking or a bombing.[10] When balancing the enormous direct and indirect costs of increased security against that perceived threat, security lost. All parties also tended to overestimate the ability of the intelligence community to identify specific threats. In that sense, the thwarted Pacific Rim bombing campaign of Ramzi Yousef was, to some extent, a negative incentive to increased security.[11]

The security paradigm was shattered on September 11, 2001. A system designed to prevent armed hijacking and bombing was unable to prevent suicidal mob action. None of the names of the September 11 terrorists were on a watch list. That is not surprising since "the number of individuals subject to such special security instructions issued by the FAA was less than 20 compared to the tens of thousands of names identified in the State Department's TIPOFF watch list [today]." Nine of the nineteen September 11 terrorists were selected by CAPPS for additional screening, but the additional screening was limited to searching their checked baggage for explosives. Formal and informal screening guidelines in place at that time allowed a passenger to carry onto the aircraft a pocket utility knife with a less than 4-inch blade.[12] As summarized bluntly by the 9-11 Commission, the September 11 terrorists "did not count on a sloppy screener. All 19 hijackers were able to pass successfully through checkpoint screening to board their flights. They were 19 for 19. They counted on beating a weak system."[13]

The congressional response was immediate. The Aviation and Transportation Security Act, Pub. L. No. 107-71 (the Security Act) was enacted on November 19, 2001. The heart of the Security Act was the creation of the largest federal law enforcement agency in history, the Transportation Security Administration (TSA), originally part of the Department of Transportation and now a part of the Department of Homeland Security (DHS).[14]

Although the TSA has responsibility for securing all modes of transportation, most of its initial efforts have been directed to aviation. Congress directed the TSA to federalize security at the 429 airports in the United States certificated by the FAA to receive schedule airline service.[15] The TSA opened its doors on December 28, 2001, and today has approximately 60,000 employees, including nearly 56,000 airport screeners who are better paid and better trained than their privately employed predecessors.

The passenger screening process is now directed at any object or device that potentially could be used by a terrorist. Passenger watch lists have been expanded exponentially. Explosive detection systems have been deployed at most certificated airports, and all checked baggage passes through those systems or is subject to trace detection, explosive-sniffing dogs and/or hand inspection. Airport perimeters and other sensitive areas have been better secured, and persons with unescorted access to such areas have undergone background checks. Cockpit doors have been hardened, and Federal Air Marshals, who used to number under one hundred, now number in the thousands and ride both domestic and international flights. Intelligence has been coordinated and numerous other nonpublic measures have been implemented.

Although issues remain with respect to specific areas such as cargo security and general aviation, there is no doubt that aviation today is substantially more secure than it was even one year ago. The downside has been the cost. The direct cost of aviation-related security measures runs, by most estimates, in excess of five billion dollars per year paid from the general treasury, taxes imposed on passengers at the rate of $2.50 per segment (up to $5 per one-way flight), and taxes imposed on airlines generally at the level of their security costs in 2000. The indirect cost in terms of inconvenience to passengers and loss of business to the airlines is very difficult to measure, but no one doubts, particularly if you are a frequent flyer, that the cost is high. There also is little doubt that the security measures in place today, driven in substantial part by technology and political perceptions, will change over time. Aviation security will remain a work in progress.

II. THE LEGAL FRAMEWORK

Congress legislates, the FAA, the TSA, and other agencies regulate, and the airlines implement, security measures with little thought to the legal bases for their actions. This is not to suggest that any existing measures are unlawful, but questioning the legal authority for any action is a productive exercise. This chapter looks at five general legal areas relating to aviation security: the authority of the federal government to regulate; issues arising from the federalized screening process; the security responsibilities of private parties; international legal obligations; and the sensitive issue of privacy, an issue whose resolution may well shape the future not only of aviation security but of all homeland security.

A. The Authority of the Federal Government to Regulate Aviation Security

The near plenary power of the Congress to regulate interstate and foreign commerce, consistent with the broad constitutional purpose of ensuring "domestic tranquility," provides the underpinning for all federal legislative and regulatory actions with respect to aviation security.[16] However, there is more at work, a principle that will not be found in the Constitution but which applies in any judicial review of such actions–the maxim "better safe than sorry."[17]

Courts rarely express it this way, but it is a fact that any court is loath to overturn a legislative or regulatory action that addresses aviation safety, of which security is a particularly sensitive subset. A good example is the FAA requirement that U.S. commercial pilots retire at age 60. This rule does not apply to private pilots or pilots of smaller commercial aircraft, and many foreign airlines permit their pilots to fly into their 60s. There is scant empirical or even anecdotal evidence to support the rule and much evidence to the contrary. Yet the rule has withstood repeated judicial challenges because of the "better safe than sorry" maxim. In a 1997 D.C. Circuit decision rejecting such a challenge, Judge Wald, in a dissenting/concurring opinion, stated it bluntly: Deference accorded an agency "is most

acute in regard to safety determinations, given the potential catastrophic effects of inadequate safety regulations, and it is difficult to imagine an agency decision which judges would be more disposed to accept than one that implicates aviation safety."[18]

The restrictions placed on aviation in the Washington, D.C., metropolitan area after September 11 provide a case study. At 9:30 a.m. on September 11, 2001, the FAA closed all U.S. airspace. That airspace was reopened at 11:00 a.m. on September 14, with several exceptions. The most notable exception was the Washington, D.C., airspace, effectively closing Ronald Reagan Washington National Airport and three small general aviation airports in the Maryland suburbs.[19] Reagan Washington National was partially reopened to scheduled airline service on October 4 (and fully opened to pre-September 11 airline service levels seven months later), but all general aviation operations were banned (and remained so at the time this chapter was written). Prior to September 11, general aviation averaged 60,000 operations per year at Reagan Washington National. The three general aviation airports were reopened on February 13, 2002, but with restrictions that substantially limited their operations. From a legal standpoint, the most interesting thing about these restrictions is not why they were imposed but how.[20]

"A citizen of the United States has a public right of transit through the navigable airspace."[21] While the FAA can create special zones with security-based restrictions, it must do so in a way that "encourages and allows maximum use of navigable airspace."[22] The FAA also is bound by the due process requirements of the Administrative Procedure Act, including the ability of all interested persons to comment on proposed regulatory actions before those actions are implemented; the duty of the FAA to explain fully both its proposed and final actions and to conduct the requisite economic analyses; and the duty of the FAA to avoid arbitrary and capricious actions.[23] Finally, if there is a substantial, direct, and continued interference with the continued use and enjoyment of a right, just compensation might be due under the Fifth Amendment.

The restrictions imposed on the Washington area airports met almost none of these requirements, yet, with the exception of an unsuccessful due process "takings" claim,[24] they never were challenged in court. With one minor exception,[25] the restrictions were imposed through the issuance of Notices to Airmen, a unilateral procedure otherwise reserved for short-term emergency measures or technical matters. But while recourse to the courts may not have been viewed as practical relief, the affected parties took the merits of their cases to Congress. Vision 100 contained two provisions directed at providing relief. Section 817 authorized the Department of Transportation (DOT) to make up to $100 million in grants to general aviation entities (including the three general aviation airports, business aircraft operators, and service companies) for security costs incurred and revenues foregone as a result of the post-September 11 restrictions. Section 823 directed the DHS to develop and implement a plan for reopening Reagan Washington National to general aviation. An argument could be made that the legislative result is not too different from the best result that could have been expected in court, with the caveat that the $100 million in compensation, although authorized, has not yet been appropriated.

While judicial challenges to federal security-based actions may be unlikely, it is possible that there may be challenges on federal preemption grounds to similar actions by state and local authorities. Several states have expressed an interest in imposing special security requirements on pilots, and some local airport authorities have imposed security restrictions on aircraft operators, for example, wheel locks. While none of these have risen to the level of litigation to date, the unanswered question is the extent to which the federal government has completely occupied the field of aviation security, thus precluding nonfederal regulation.[26]

B. The Federalized Screening Process

The Fourth Amendment right to be secure in person and property against unreasonable searches and seizures largely is lost once a passenger enters the TSA screening line at an airport. Routine border searches, with the border including international airport terminals, long have been presumptively reasonable under the Fourth Amendment.[27] As one court recently noted, "The events of

September 11, 2001, only emphasize the heightened need to conduct searches at this nation's international airports."[28]

A security-specific search at a domestic or international airport is considered reasonable under the Fourth Amendment if, in good faith, "it is no more extensive or intensive than necessary, in light of current technology, to detect weapons or explosives," and the passenger may avoid the search by electing not to fly.[29] While other justifications for this position can be advanced, for example, there is no reasonable expectation of privacy when preparing to board an aircraft,[30] it rests for the most part on the theory that once a passenger enters the security line and places his or her baggage on the X-ray conveyor belt or checks a bag, there is implied consent to a search.[31] Implied consent, which exists at common law, also has been codified.[32]

Fourth Amendment issues aside, passengers do have the right to be treated fairly and without discrimination. In August 2002, TSA agents on a flight from Atlanta to Philadelphia subdued an unruly passenger and directed all other passengers not to move until the aircraft had landed and the unruly passenger had been removed. When the TSA agents reboarded the aircraft after removing the unruly passenger, they seized one of the seated passengers, handcuffed him, and took him to a police station where he was booked and placed in a cell. He was not allowed to leave for four hours, with the only explanation that "we didn't like the way you look." That passenger, a physician and lieutenant colonel in the U.S. Army Reserve, brought suit against the TSA. The case was settled in June 2003 with the TSA agreeing to (i) submit a report to the court "setting forth all of the changes in their policies and training procedures regarding the allegations in the complaint," (ii) provide a written apology from the TSA Administrator, and (iii) pay $50,000 to plaintiff.[33]

C. The Security Responsibilities of Private Parties

Although airport screening has been federalized, airlines and other private parties still have substantial responsibilities with respect to security. The TSA has followed the regulatory scheme it inherited from the FAA, modified to reflect the requirements of the Security Act and subsequent legislation. That scheme consists of regulations laying down the general requirements for each segment of aviation–airports, U.S. airlines, non-U.S. airlines, general aviation and indirect air carriers (freight forwarders)–with the details for airports and airlines left to classified security programs that are filed with and approved by the TSA.[34] In addition, for U.S. airports and U.S. airlines, fingerprint-based criminal history record checks (CHRCs) are required for flight crews and all employees with unescorted access to secure areas, basically anyone with a badge at an airport.[35] As of mid-2003, a clearinghouse administered by the American Association of Airport Executives had processed one million CHRCs for airline and airport employees.[36]

These requirements aside, the foundation for all aviation safety is the principle that "the pilot-in-command of an aircraft is directly responsible for, and is the final authority as to, the operation of that aircraft."[37] Derived from admiralty law, this principle makes certain that final decisions with respect to safety are taken by the captain, not by a committee. Additionally, the pilot-in-command is the Inflight Security Coordinator with responsibility for supervising the airline's security program while the aircraft is under his or her command.[38] Superimposed over these requirements are two statutory directions:(i) an airline may not carry a passenger or his or her baggage if that passenger has refused to be screened; and (ii) an airline may refuse to carry a passenger or his or her baggage if it decides that such carriage "is, or might be, inimical to safety."[39]

These responsibilities are driven by the need and desire to assure security to the maximum extent possible. But the exercise of these responsibilities can carry serious legal consequences. For one thing, they create public expectations that can translate into legal liability. The post-September 11 litigation is an example of such expectations at work.

The Air Transportation Safety and System Stabilization Act of 2001, enacted within weeks of the September 11 tragedies,[40] created two separate tracks for the processing of claims by the victims and their representatives "for damages arising out of the hijacking and subsequent crashes." One track is administrative, with claims processed by a Special Master and paid by the United States.[41]

The other track is litigation, with all claims to be brought in the Southern District of New York. Lawsuits were filed by some of the victims and their representatives against American, United, and Boeing (the Aviation Defendants) and the owners and managers of the World Trade Center. The Aviation Defendants moved to dismiss with respect to the victims on the ground, arguing that the injuries they suffered were beyond the scope of any reasonable duty that may have been owed. The district court denied the motions:

> Ours is a complicated and specialized society. We depend on others charged with special duties to protect the quality of the water we drink and the air we breathe, to bring power to our neighborhoods, and to enable us to travel with a sense of security over bridges, through tunnels and via subways. We live in the vicinity of busy airports, and we work in tall office towers, depending on others to protect us from the willful desire of terrorists to do us harm. Some of those on whom we depend for protection are the police, fire and intelligence departments of local, state and national governments. Others are private companies, like the Aviation Defendants. They perform their screening duties, not only for those boarding airplanes, but also for society generally. It is both their expectation, and ours, that the duty of screening was performed for the benefit of passengers and those on the ground, including those present in the Twin Towers on the morning of September 11, 2001."[42]

A similar issue can arise when a discretionary action taken in the name of security provokes claims of discrimination by a passenger. This is one of those difficult areas where it is the perception of the facts, and not the facts themselves, which drive the positions of both parties. There have been numerous instances in which an airline has denied boarding to a passenger or removed a passenger on the basis of security concerns. Those concerns may have been no more than suspicions based on reports from other passengers or airline or airport staff.[43] The issue almost always comes down to whether the passenger was profiled because of his or her apparent ethnicity, religion, or nationality.

The section 44902(b) authority of an airline to refuse to transport a passenger it decides "is or might be inimical to safety" creates a qualified immunity for the airline for such action. "Such a refusal cannot give rise to a claim for damages under either federal or [state] law unless the carrier's decision was arbitrary and capricious."[44] In general,

> The test of whether or not the airline properly exercised its power under [§44902] to refuse passage to an applicant or ticket-holder rests upon the facts and circumstances of the case as known to the airline at the time it formed its opinion and made its decision and whether or not the opinion and decision were rational and reasonable and not capricious or arbitrary in the light of those facts and circumstances.[45]

When the person making the decision acts on the basis of a representation made by a third party, neither the decision maker nor the court need look beyond that representation.[46] Finally, the objective assessment to be made by the court should take "into account all the circumstances surrounding the decision, including the (perhaps limited) facts known at the time; the time constraints under which the decision is made; and, not least, the general security climate in which the events unfold."[47]

In all of these cases, the court essentially is applying a "what if" test—what would I have done had I been in the position of the captain or other decision maker? This is the product of both the practical reality and the section 44902(b) qualified immunity of the airline. The DOT, on the other hand, has urged a "but for" test:

> Use the "but/for" test to help determine the justification for your actions. Ask yourself, *But for this person's perceived race, ethnic heritage, or religious orientation, would I have subjected this individual to additional safety or security scrutiny?* If the answer is "no," then the action may violate civil rights laws.[48]

This is a classic civil rights formulation, but these are not classic civil rights cases. For example, in April 2003, the DOT's enforcement staff filed an administrative complaint against American Airlines alleging that in nine instances immediately following September 11, 2001, and in one instance the follow-

ing year, American denied boarding to passengers because they were or were perceived to be "of Arab, Middle Eastern or South Asian descent, and/or Muslim."[49] The complaint alleged that these instances violated the prohibition against status-based discrimination in air transportation[50] and sought civil penalties and a cease and desist order.

The American case was settled in a nonpublished order, but an undocketed matter against United involving similar allegations was settled with a published consent decree on nearly identical terms.[51] The consent decree contained the following language:

> The Enforcement Office recognizes that the September 11 terrorist attacks were unprecedented and clearly created a difficult situation for the airline industry, acting pursuant to FAA-approved security programs, in trying to protect passengers and crew from further attacks. . . . Even though the Enforcement Office does not dispute that the [airline's] employees involved believed they were acting to ensure the safety and security of passengers and crew, the Enforcement Office believes some passengers were denied boarding or removed from flights in a manner inconsistent with the carrier's nondiscrimination obligations under Federal law.

No civil penalties were imposed and no finding of illegality was made in either case.

D. International Legal Obligations

Although U.S. citizens and property were the primary victims of the September 11 attacks, no one doubts that terrorism is a problem for all nations. Nonetheless, the United States sometimes legislates and regulates as if it were the only concerned nation. Controversies over placing armed law enforcement officers on certain flights of non-U.S. airlines, the timing of cockpit door strengthening, the mandatory provision of passenger name records by non-U.S. airlines, and the biometric identification requirements of the US-VISIT program and the Border Security Act are just some of the U.S. actions that have created controversy abroad.

There is a legal framework for addressing air transportation security at the international level, albeit a somewhat sketchy one. The Chicago

Convention,[52] to which the United States and 187 other nations are signatories, speaks only indirectly to security. Pursuant to Article 9, a nation can restrict access to the aircraft of other nations for military or other exceptional purposes, provided that it does so without regard to the nationality of the aircraft. However, the Chicago Convention also created the International Civil Aviation Organization (ICAO), an arm of the United Nations, and authorized ICAO to promulgate general standards and recommendations for the conduct of international air transportation. ICAO's Annex 17 to the Chicago Convention provides that each contracting state "shall cooperate with other States in order to adopt their respective national civil aviation security programmes, as necessary,"[53] and sets forth minimal security procedures for screening and related security measures, for example, standards for biometrically encoded passports. This is, at most, a rough blueprint for security and a vehicle for international cooperation.

Some of the bilateral air transport agreements that the United States has with individual nations are more explicit. The "Open Skies" agreements, most of which have been executed in the last 10 years, typically contain an aviation security clause. Apart from promoting cooperation and communication, the clause contains the following language:

> Each Party agrees to observe the security provisions required by the other Party for entry into, for departure from, and while within the territory of that other Party and to take adequate measures to protect aircraft and to inspect passengers, crew, and their baggage and carry-on items, as well as cargo and aircraft stores, prior to and during boarding or loading. Each Party shall also give positive consideration to any request from the other Party for special security measures to meet a particular threat.[54]

The clause allows a Party to take interim action to withhold, limit, or condition the operating authority of another states' airlines pending consultations. Again, this does not impose much in the way of obligations over those already existing under the Chicago Convention or as a matter of practice.

The U.S. controls the world's largest air transportation market and that gives it both a leadership role and the leverage to support that role. If the United States is viewed as overstepping in some areas, the best, and often only, solution for other nations is to take it to the diplomatic level.[55] With the shared goal of improving security, most issues can be worked out.

E. Privacy

Although privacy is the flashpoint for many security issues, a legal analysis begins with the fact that there is no unfettered constitutional right to anonymity. At most, there is a qualified right to anonymity in certain First Amendment contexts that implicate the freedoms of speech and association.[56] Justice Douglas's often quoted dictum that "the right to be let alone is indeed the beginning of all freedom" ignores both the highly unusual nature of that case (it involved the authority of a public service commission to allow a transit company to have live radio broadcasts on its vehicles) and the rest of that dictum: "One who enters any public place sacrifices some of his privacy. My protest is against the invasion of his privacy over and beyond the risks of travel."[57] At the present time, the risks of travel are great and the sacrifice of some privacy would appear to be reasonable.

The Supreme Court further weakened any claimed right to anonymity in *Hiibel v. Nevada*, 124 S.Ct. 2451. 72 U.S.L.W. 4509 (June 21, 2004). Although this case had nothing directly to do with security, if you believe, as many do, that positive identification is essential to infrastructure security,[58] *Hiibel* is a linchpin case. The court was presented with a challenge to a state law that criminalized the failure to provide identification during a Terry stop, that is, a police stop based on a reasonable suspicion but on less than probable cause. Petitioner raised both a Fourth Amendment search and seizure issue and a Fifth Amendment self-incrimination issue. Amici joined in, focusing on the Fifth Amendment issue and a claimed constitutional right to anonymity. The five-justice majority had little problem disposing with the Fourth Amendment issue, but it did take its time with respect to self-incrimination. It declined to hold that a person's name is nontestimonial in all circumstances and, therefore, never can invoke the Fifth Amendment privilege. At the same time, it made clear that such a unique situation would rarely, if ever, occur:

> One's identity is, by definition, unique; yet it is, in another sense, a universal characteristic. Answering a request to disclose a name is likely to be so insignificant in the scheme of things as to be incriminating only in unusual circumstances. . . . Even witnesses who plan to invoke the Fifth Amendment privilege answer when their names are called to take the stand.

This would appear to dispose of the argument that there is an unbounded right to anonymity, and would appear to allow mandatory positive identification in most security contexts. Only Justice Stevens, dissenting, would have held that providing identification is a testimonial act in all circumstances. The other dissenters would have held that asking for identification exceeded the Fourth Amendment boundaries of a Terry stop.[59]

Positive identification is any system that provides a sure way to know that the person standing at the entrance is who he or she claims to be and what such identification means. The technology exists to biometrically encode an ID to positively match it with the bearer and to search data banks to determine that person's relevant history.[60] But once you have truly positive means of identification, what do you do with it? Three proposed uses are, or were, the TWIC, trusted passenger, program and much maligned CAPPS II programs.

The DOT is leading the effort to establish a standardized Transportation Worker Identification Credential (TWIC). The TWIC would be an "electronic personal card or similar device that will positively identify transportation workers (including government workers, contractor, and private sector employees) who require unescorted physical and logical access to secure areas and functions of the transportation system . . . supported by a single integrated and secure network of databases."[61] If implemented, TWIC would provide positive identification for several million transportation workers. Perhaps because it is tied to a job function rather than travel, TWIC has not raised privacy concerns.

The trusted passenger program has been more controversial. Section 109(a)(3) of the Security Act directed the TSA to "establish requirements to implement trusted passenger programs and use available technologies to expedite the security screening of passengers who participate in such programs, thereby allowing security screening personnel to focus on those passengers who should be subject to more extensive screening." The essence of such a program is that a "trusted" passenger should receive a lesser degree of scrutiny than a person not in the program. There are a number of similar programs in existence today at selected U.S. locations and for specific purposes.[62]

Trusted passenger programs have been criticized on policy and efficacy grounds. Those issues will continue to be debated in public forums, but there would appear to be nothing per se unconstitutional with such programs. If a highly intrusive search of a passenger and his or her baggage does not violate the Fourth Amendment in part because the passenger can avoid the search by not taking the flight, then a voluntary program that simply requires a lesser level of screening for passengers who volunteer to provide certain information plainly is constitutional. In the summer of 2004, trusted passenger evolved into the Registered Traveler program. At the time this chapter was written, the program was being beta-tested utilizing airline frequent flyer program members at five domestic airports.

The most controversial of all security screening programs has been CAPPS II. As originally implemented in 1997, and still applied today, computer-assisted passenger prescreening (CAPPS) uses travel-related characteristics, for example, a one-way ticket or a cash purchase, to identify passengers for additional screening. In January 2003, following a congressional directive,[63] the TSA proposed to revise the program to include more detailed and personal information about each passenger.[64] That effort, known as CAPPS II, became the center of a national debate on privacy and security.

On August 1, 2003, the TSA issued an interim final notice under the Privacy Act, detailing how CAPPS II would work and reflecting substantial changes to the original proposal:[65] Once you make a reservation or purchase a ticket, the passenger name record created by the airline or booking agency would be electronically transmitted to the TSA.

This generally consists of your name, home address, telephone number, and itinerary. The TSA would transmit selected parts of this data to a commercial data provider who, in turn, would give the TSA a numeric score for each passenger.[66] The commercial data providers would not use credit or health information (which leaves the question of what they would use). Once the TSA gets the scores, it would run the passenger name records through national security, law enforcement, and immigration files. The final product would be placing the passenger in one of three categories: low risk for normal screening; unknown risk for heightened screening; and high risk for a "passenger with identifiable links to terrorism" and notification to "law enforcement or other appropriate authorities." The purpose of CAPPS II was commendable—to improve security while reducing the security screening hassle for many passengers.[67] Nonetheless, concerns raised on privacy, discrimination, and due process grounds made it a political liability. Vision 100 put CAPPS II on hold. Sections 607 and 608 prohibited DHS from implementing CAPPS II on anything other than a test basis until it could certify to Congress that a number of specific privacy and due process concerns had been addressed. DHS was directed to report to Congress on these issues, and GAO had to submit its own report and recommendations. The GAO Report was issued on February 12, 2004 (GAO-04-385, *Aviation Security: Computer-Assisted Passenger Prescreening System Faces Significant Implementation Challenges* [2004] or the (GAO Report). GAO found that "TSA currently is behind schedule in testing and developing initial increments of CAPPS II, due in large part to delays in obtaining passenger data needed for testing from air carriers because of privacy concerns," and "its new completion date is unknown."[68]

In September 2004, DHS and TSA abandoned CAPPS II and introduced the Secured Flight Program in its place. The program contemplates using airline-generated passenger name records (PNRs) to support computerized searching of federal watch lists. As a first step, TSA ordered all U.S. airlines to produce all PNRs generated for flights in June 2004. This data will be used to test the automated watch list screening, but TSA will also

"test the use of commercial data to identify instances in which passengers' identifying passenger information is inaccurate or incorrect." Basically, this is similar to CAPPS II but without reliance on commercial data-mining by third-party contractors, the most controversial feature of the earlier program. Think of it as CAPPS 1.5.

Ironically, as CAPPS II was being abandoned, the litigation surrounding earlier efforts to test portions of the program largely was dismissed. The first such cases to reach a disposition involved Northwest. In December 2001, Northwest was requested by NASA's Ames Laboratory to provide a 3-month sample of its PNRs. NASA told Northwest that it would examine the PNRs to explore whether such data could be used to develop better passenger screening and threat assessment tools. At that time, Northwest's Website made a number of privacy representations concerning passenger information, including: Northwest would not sell individual customer names or other private information to third parties; Northwest would comply with law enforcement requests or requirements; and when a reservation was made, "Northwest would provide only the relevant information required by the car rental agency, hotel, or other involved third party to ensure the successful fulfillment of your travel arrangements." Northwest provided the requested PNRs to NASA.

Northwest faced two legal challenges when the release of the PNRs was disclosed. First, a number of class actions were brought on various grounds. Second, the Electronic Privacy Information Center (EPIC) filed an unfair or deceptive practice complaint with the DOT. The class actions were the first to be dismissed. The court handling the class actions brought in Minnesota and Tennessee found that: (i) no claims were viable under the Electronic Communications Privacy Act or the Fair Credit Reporting Act; (ii) state law claims under Minnesota's Deceptive Trade Practices Act and for negligent misrepresentation were preempted by the Airline Deregulation Act; (iii) trespass-related claims were baseless; and (iv) contract-related claims failed because Northwest's purported privacy policy vested discretion in Northwest and, in any event, there were no provable damages (*In re Northwest Airlines Privacy Litigation*, 2004 U.S. Dist.

LEXIS 10580 [D. Minn. June 6, 2004]).[69] The DOT was next to act, dismissing the EPIC complaint on the grounds that

> Northwest's privacy policy did not unambiguously preclude it from sharing data with the federal government; that, even if it did, such a promise would be unenforceable as against public policy, as Northwest is required by law to make such records available to the Department and to other federal agencies "upon demand"; and that, in this case, the record contains no evidence of actual or likely harm to those passengers who provided Northwest with the data that it shared.

Third-Party Enforcement Complaint of The Electronic Privacy Information Center Against

Northwest Airlines, Inc., DOT Order 2004-9-13 (September 10, 2004).

In a related matter, in December 2003, the European Union reached agreement with the United States over the sharing of passenger name records required by U.S. law. The United States originally wanted non-U.S. airlines to submit in advance the complete passenger name records (the basic information recorded at the time a reservation is made and/or the ticket is sold) for all passengers on flights to or from the United States. The EU resisted on privacy grounds. The agreement limited the amount of information to be collected, limited the storage of such data to 42 months (the United States initially wanted the data saved for 7 years) and provided that this information could not be used in CAPPS II unless agreed upon at a later date.[70]

III. CONCLUSION

The aviation security system is being constructed on legal grounds that are solid, or at least solid enough, to withstand most challenges. That should lend encouragement both to providers and beneficiaries of aviation security. However, that should not be the end of the inquiry. The system also lends itself to the possibility of abuse in the form of discrimination, denials of due process, and unreasonable invasions of privacy. That is not a criticism. It is a fact. Effective security is an intrusion into what most of us view as our

personal prerogatives, whether we define those as constitutional rights, as privacy, or simply as convenience.

The challenge is to devise security systems that are effective but, at the same time, minimally intrude and do not compromise access to our national air transportation system. Common sense is a valuable tool, but so is the rule of law. Lawyers within and without the government must do their best to assure that the perceived interests of security do not supercede the rule of law.

ENDNOTES

1. Vision 100–Century of Aviation Reauthorization Act, Pub. L. No. 108-176, §4(3) (2003) ("Vision 100").
2. The Air Piracy Act makes it a federal crime, with punishment ranging from 20 years to death, to seize or exercise control of an aircraft if it is done by "force, violence, threat of force or violence, or any form of intimidation, and with wrongful intent." The jurisdictional bases for the law are so broad as to include almost any hijacking incident involving a U.S.-registered aircraft, within U.S. airspace, with a U.S. national onboard or with the hijacker otherwise in U.S. custody. 49 U.S.C. §§46501 and 46502. The Air Piracy Act also included the provision

   authorizing an airline to refuse to carry a passenger who it believes is "inimical to safety." 49 U.S.C. §44902(b).
3. In 1970, 1971, and 1972, there were, respectively, 25, 25, and 26 hijackings of U.S. airlines. Subsequent to 1972, there were only three years in which this number was in the double digits (1979, 1980, and 1983) and there were no such hijackings from 1992 through September 10, 2001. FAA, Office of Civil Aviation Security, *Criminal Acts Against Civil Aircraft* (1996 and 2000).
4. Antihijacking and Air Transportation Security Acts, Pub. L. No. 93-366 (1974).

5. Ironically, the ability of the victims' representatives to avoid the compensatory damages limitations of the Warsaw Convention was predicated on their showing that Pan Am had *not* followed the FAA requirements, i.e., that it had X-rayed the unaccompanied baggage when a physical inspection had been required. *In re Air Disaster at Lockerbie, Scotland*, 37 F.3d 804 (2d Cir. 1994). The court's opinion, however, gives a good sense of how confused those regulations, and the FAA's instructions to carriers, were at that time.

6. Pub. L. No. 101-604 (1990). The act included an 18-month deadline for developing and testing an explosive detection system for baggage.

7. The National Transportation Safety Board (NTSB) determined that the probable cause was an explosion of the center wing fuel tank caused by ignition within the tank. The ignition most likely was caused by a short circuit. Accident Report NTSB/AAR-00/03 (August 23, 2000).

8. *Final Report of the White House Commission on Aviation Safety and Security* (February 12, 1997).

9. Some additional security measures were implemented, e.g., Computer-Assisted Passenger Prescreening System (CAPPS), a program begun in 1997 to identify passengers and their baggage through travel-related characteristics for a higher level of screening. The FAA also instituted, but never completed, a rulemaking to require certification of private screening companies.

10. "Despite the documented shortcomings of the screening system, the fact that neither a hijacking nor a bombing had occurred domestically in over a decade was perceived by many within the system as a confirmation that it was working." National Commission on Terrorist Attacks on the United States, Staff Statement No. 3, at 7 (January 27, 2004) ("9-11 Commission Staff Statement No. 3").

11. "Historically, explosives on aircraft had taken a heavy death toll, hijackings had not. So, despite continued foreign hijackings leading up to 9-11, the U.S. aviation security system worried most about explosives." 9-11 Commission Staff Statement No. 3, at 5.

12. *Id.*, at 6–9.

13. *Id.*, at 9.

14. Homeland Security Act of 2002, Pub. L. No. 107-296 (2002). A little noticed provision of the Homeland Security Act, section 424, allows the DHS to "sunset" the TSA after November 24, 2004.

15. The Security Act had two small concessions to those favoring privatization: a 3-year pilot program for not more than five airports; and an opt-out to begin in November 2004. Under either program, the screeners have to be hired, trained, tested, and, most importantly, paid to TSA standards, which makes it largely a zero-sum game for the airports. Additionally, the TSA to date has been unwilling to accept any liability. There are five airports in the pilot program, but it is not expected that many other airports will seek to opt-out and use private screeners.

16. *See, e.g.*, 49 U.S.C. §44903(b) (the FAA and TSA are authorized to "prescribe regulations to protect passengers and property on an aircraft").

17. This is not undercut by the right to travel, the doctrine that "the nature of our Federal Union and our constitutional concepts of personal liberty unite to require that all citizens be free to travel throughout the length and breadth of our land uninhibited by statutes, rules or regulations which unreasonably burden or restrict this movement." *Saenz v. Roe*, 526 U.S. 489, 499 (1999), *quoting, Shapiro v. Thompson*, 394 U.S. 618, 629 (1969). The "unreasonableness" requirement creates a necessary, and broad, exception to this right. Moreover, some courts have held that a restriction on a single mode of travel cannot invoke this principle even if it is unreasonable. *See, e.g., Miller v. Reed*, 176 F.3d 1202, 1205 (9th Cir. 1999) and cases cited therein.

18. *Professional Pilots Federation v. Federal Aviation Administration*, 118 F.3d 758, 776 (D.C. Cir. 1997).

19. These included College Park Airport. Opened in 1909 to accommodate Wilbur Wright's Type A military trainer, it was the home of the first Army Aviation School (1911) and the first U.S. airmail operation (1918). Until the morning of September 11, it was the world's oldest continuously operated airport.

20. It generally is acknowledged that in imposing the restrictions on Washington area airspace, the FAA was acting as the proxy for the U.S. Secret Service.

21. 49 U.S.C. §40103(a)(2).

22. 49 U.S.C. §40103(b)(3).

23. 5 U.S.C. §§553 and 706(2).

24. In *Air Pegasus of D.C. v. United States*, 60 Fed. Cl. 448 (2004), the operator of a heliport near Capitol Hill that was closed for a year after September 11 by FAA operating restrictions brought a "takings" claim. The Court of Federal Claims granted the government's motion for summary judgment, ruling that "any business associated with the airline business is under sovereign control by the United States government and activities within the Washington, D.C., geographic area are subject to pervasive regulation. No property right exists to

25. The FAA did conduct a brief rulemaking proceeding regarding the restricted reopening of the three general aviation airports. *See*, 67 *Fed. Reg.* 7538 (2002).

26. For example, in *Rubin v. United Air Lines, Inc.*, 96 Cal. App. 4th 364 (Cal. Ct. App. 2002) the court held that a state law tort claim brought by a passenger removed from an aircraft because of unruly behavior was preempted not by the "rates, routes and service" preemption of the Airline Deregulation Act, 49 U.S.C. §41713(b)(1), but by the authority given an airline to refuse to transport a passenger on the grounds that such carriage might be "inimical to safety." 49 U.S.C. §44902(b).

27. "[W]here the risk to public safety is substantial and real, blanket suspicionless searches calibrated to the risk may rank as 'reasonable'—for example, searches now routine at airports and at entrances to courts and other official buildings." *Chandler v. Miller*, 520 U.S. 305, 323 (1997). *See also, City of Indianapolis v. Edmond*, 531 U.S. 32, 47–48 (2000); *United States v. Montoya de Hernandez*, 473 U.S. 531, 537 (1985); *United States v. Ramsey*, 431 U.S. 606, 616 (1977); *United States v. Yang*, 286 F.3d 940, 944 (7th Cir. 2003).

28. *Yang*, 286 F.3d.at 944, n.1.

29. *Torbet v. United Air Lines, Inc.*, 298 F.3d 1087, 1089 (9th Cir. 2002).

30. A "reasonable expectation of privacy" is a prerequisite to application of the Fourth Amendment. *Katz v. United States*, 389 U.S. 347, 351 (1967).

31. *See, e.g., United States v. Henry*, 615 F.2d 1223, 1228 (9th Cir. 1980); *United States v. Freeland*, 562 F.2d 383, 385 (6th Cir. 1977). Most of the case law on airport screening was developed before passage of the Security Act, which now requires that all passengers and all baggage (carry-on and checked) be screened by federal employees for both weapons and explosives. 49 U.S.C. §§44901(a) and 44901(c)–(e). The standard for passenger compliance approaches strict liability. *Zoltanski v. Federal Aviation Administration*, 372 F.3d 1195 (10th Cir. 2004) (There is no scienter requirement in the passenger screening regulations.)

32. 49 U.S. §44902(c).

33. *Rajcoomar v. United States*, E.D. Pa., Case No. 2:03-cv-02294-JF (electronic docket, Complaint and Settlement Order).

34. 49 C.F.R. §§542 (airports), 1544 (U.S. airlines), 1546 (non-U.S. airlines), 1548 (indirect air carriers) and 1550 (general aviation).

35. 49 C.F.R. §§1542.209 and 1544.229 and 1544.230. Other provisions reflect congressional fine tuning of the security process, *e.g.*, the Arming Pilots Against Terrorism Act which was part of the Homeland Security Act and is codified at 49 U.S.C. §44921. Under this provision, the TSA has established a program to deputize, train, and arm volunteer U.S. airline pilots.

36. Press Release, American Association of Airport Executives, *AAAE's Transportation Security Clearinghouse Hits One Million Mark* (July 16, 2003). The AAAE's clearinghouse is the largest program for processing CHRCs.

37. 14 C.F.R. §91.3. The pilot-in-command also has complete control over and responsibility for all passengers and crew "without limitation." 14 C.F.R. §121.537(d)).

38. 49 C.F.R. §1544.215(c).

39. 49 U.S.C. §§44902(a) and (b).

40. Pub. L. No. 107-42 (2001).

41. The cut-off date for filing administrative claims was December 22, 2003. The Special Master reported that timely claims had been filed on behalf of approximately 95% of the total eligible victims. *See* http://www.usdoj.gov/victimcompensation/comp_deceased.html

42. *In Re September 11 Litigation*, 280 F.Supp.2d 279, 292–3 (S.D. N.Y. 2003). The court emphasized that "[t]his is a very early point in the litigation. There has been no discovery, and defendant's motions to dismiss accept, as they must, all allegations of the complaints." *Id.*, at 301.

43. The Security Act encourages reporting by providing immunity from civil liability to any person reporting a "suspicious transaction" to law enforcement personnel or airport or airline security personnel. 49 U.S.C. §44941(a).

44. *Schaeffer v. Cavallero*, 54 F.Supp.2d 350, 351 (S.D.N.Y. 1999). *See also, Williams v. Trans World Airlines*, 509 F.2d 942, 948 (2d Cir. 1975).

45. *Id.*

46. *Christel v. AMR Corp.*, 222 F.Supp.2d 335, 340 (E.D.N.Y. 2002) (The captain is "entitled without further inquiry to rely upon a flight attendant's representations that a conflict with a passenger might distract the flight attendant from performing his or her safety-related duties.") *See also, Al-Qudhai'een v. America West Airlines, Inc.*, 267 F.Supp.2d 841 (S.D. Ohio 2003); *Rubin v. United Air Lines, Inc.*, 96 Cal App. 4th 364, 376–83 (Cal. Ct. App. 2002).

47. *Dasrath v. Continental Airlines, Inc.*, 228 F.Supp.2d 531, 539 (D.N.J. 2002). Although the court denied the defendant's motion to dismiss, it noted that

public navigable airspace. Therefore, no property right over the navigable airspace above the leased area at the South Capitol Street Heliport can attach to the lessee, Air Pegasus." *Id.* at 459.

"Plaintiff's burden will be a heavy one considering the heightened actual dangers arising from the increased risk of terrorist acts, the catastrophic consequences in the case of air travel of the failure to detect such acts in advance, and the necessity that pilots make safety decisions on short notice without the opportunity to make extensive investigations." *Id.*, at 540.

48. DOT Industry Letter, *Nondiscrimination in Inspection and Security Duties* (October 12, 2001) (emphasis in original).

49. DOT Docket OST-2003-15046.

50. 49 U.S.C. §40127. The complaint also alleged that these instances constituted unreasonable discrimination in foreign air transportation, a failure to provide safe and adequate transportation and an unfair or deceptive trade practice. 49 U.S.C. §§41310, 41702 and 41712.

51. DOT Order 2003-11-13 (2003).

52. Convention on International Civil Aviation, *opened for signature*, December 7, 1944, 61 Stat. 1180, 15 U.N.T.S. 295 (ratified August 9, 1946).

53. *Id.*, Art. 3.2.1.

54. *See, e.g.*, Protocol between the Government of the United States of America and the Government of the Republic of Italy to Amend the Air Transport Agreement of June 22, 1970, Art.4.4 (December 6, 1999). The United States currently has "Open Skies" air transport agreements with 59 nations.

55. Retaliatory action is difficult except in unusual circumstances, *e.g.*, Rio de Janeiro, where the local judiciary required arriving U.S. citizens to be photographed and fingerprinted in retaliation for similar requirements imposed on Brazilians visiting the United States.

56. *See, e.g., NAACP v. Alabama*, 357 U.S. 449 (1958). Even in that context, the court recognizes that there may be compelling state interests compelling disclosure. *Id.*, at 463–6.

57. *Public Utilities Commission v. Pollak*, 343 U.S. 451, 468 (1952).

58. The believers include the National Commission on Terrorist Attacks Upon the United States, which strongly endorsed the use of biometric identifiers at all borders and infrastructure gateways. *The 9-11 Commission Report*, Executive Summary, at 19.

59. *Also see, Gilmore v. Ashcroft*, 2004 U.S. Dist. LEXIS 4869 (N.D. Cal. March 19, 2004), dismissing an action brought by a passenger who refused to provide identification at the gate.

60. The General Accounting Office has identified four technologies—fingerprint recognition, iris recognition, hand geometry, and facial recognition—each of which has been deployed, at least on a small scale, at airports throughout the world. General Accounting Office, *Aviation Security: Registered Traveler Program Policy and Implementation Issues* GAO-03-253, Appendix III (November 2002) (GAO Report).

61. See, Department of Transportation, Research & Special Projects Administration Contract Announcement, available at http://www.rspa.dot.gov/baa02baa0005.html

62. Within the U.S., the SENTRI/PORTPASS, INSPASS, and NEXUS programs at selected U.S. border points and airports use biometrics to positively identify and expedite passengers entering the U.S. *GAO Report*, Appendix IV. The most ambitious program–US-VISIT (United States Visitor and Immigrant Status Indicator Technology)–went into effect in January 2004 at the 115 U.S. international airports and 14 major seaports and is scheduled to be operational at all ports of entry by December 31, 2005. Under this statutorily mandated program, every person entering the United States who is not a U.S. citizen or an authorized resident of the United States is fingerprinted and photographed digitally on both entry and exit. Apart from checking this information against a database of known and suspected terrorists, this information becomes part of the visitor's travel records. Press Release, Department of Homeland Security, *US-VISIT Fact Sheet* (December 5, 2003). It is expected that over 70% of the persons subjected to this program will be airline passengers. Finally, the Border Security Act required that citizens of the nations in the visa waiver program must have biometrically encoded passports by October 26, 2004. Pub. L. No. 107-173, §303(c)(1) (2001). In May 2003, ICAO promulgated standards for encoding passports with facial recognition technology. Few, if any, of those nations, who account for nearly 70% of all U.S. visitors, will be able to meet the October 26 deadline, and the deadline has since been extended.

63. Security Act, §136, codified at 49 U.S.C. §44903(I)(2).

64. 68 *Fed. Reg.* 2101 (2003).

65. 68 *Fed. Reg.* 45265, 45266 (2003).

66. Maintenance of confidentiality by third-party commercial data providers is an issue. In September 2003, it was disclosed that some passenger information voluntarily provided by Jet Blue to the Defense Department to test the data mining capabilities of one such company had been publicly disclosed. Although it was not directly related to CAPPS II, it undermined confidence in the program. In early

2004, Northwest faced similar criticism for sharing some older passenger data with NASA in a data-mining test.

67. The GAO Report, footnote 65, *infra.*, notes TSA's estimate that 15% of passengers currently require additional screening under CAPPS, "compared to an expected 1 to 3 percent under CAPPS II." *Id.*, at 9.

68. *Id.*, at 4.

69. The remaining class action against Northwest in North Dakota subsequently was dismissed. *Dyer v. Northwest Airlines Corporation*, District of North Dakota Case No. A1-04-033, Memorandum Order dated September 8, 2004.

70. Press Release, Department of Homeland Security, *Fact Sheet: Homeland Security and European Commission Reach PNR Accord* (December 16, 2003).

DISCUSSION QUESTIONS

1. Why is aviation security such a central element of our homeland security efforts?

2. Describe the evolution of aviation security until 9-11. What factors have driven its development?

3. What steps have been taken since 9-11 to improve aviation security? Have we done enough? What steps remain to be taken? How do you prioritize future steps to improve aviation security?

4. How well does federalized airport screening work? What is your opinion of the Transportation Security Administration? What is your opinion of re-privatizing airport security?

5. What are the legal responsibilities of the airlines and airports for aviation security?

6. Do you view international legal controls promoting aviation security as adequate? Why or why not? What additional steps would you suggest to improve international legal controls?

7. What is your opinion of the Computer-Assisted Passenger Prescreening System (CAPPS) and CAPPS II? Do you believe that such programs provide the added security that is their goal? How might they be improved?

8. What is the proper balance between the privacy of air travelers and security concerns? What suggestions do you have to help ensure that the balance between these factors is properly maintained?

9. Compare the security concerns discussed in this chapter with the similar discussions in the civil liberties portion of this book. How can all of the concerns expressed in these chapters be reconciled with one another?

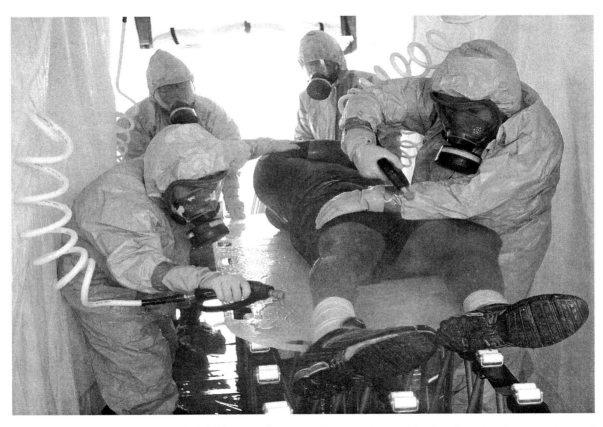

Naval Hospital, Guam (Jun. 26, 2003)–Hospital Corpsman decontaminate a simulated victim during a chemical biological and radiological (CBR) drill. US Navy photo by Hospital Corpsman 3rd Class Raolito M. Pambid. (RELEASED)

Section VI

WEAPONS OF MASS DESTRUCTION

Chapter 14

NATURAL DISASTERS AND WEAPONS OF MASS DESTRUCTION: POLICY ISSUES AND IMPLICATIONS

ANNE STRACK ANGELHEART

As the last decade of the twentieth century drew to a close, Americans enjoyed the greatest ever array of federal, private, and charitable resources used in support of disaster relief. This did not prevent devastating disasters from occurring (such as Hurricane Andrew, the Northridge earthquake, or the Mississippi River floods), but it did provide a variety of methods for the victims to use in restoring the fabric of their communities. Soon after the turn of the twenty-first century, however, a new type of disaster–a catastrophic terrorist attack–demanded a reevaluation of federal disaster policy in order to reduce the potential for harm from this threat.

This chapter summarizes the changes in federal disaster policy and the concomitant changes in disaster outcomes over the last century. It also discusses the changes in disaster prevention and mitigation efforts with respect to extreme terrorist attacks. There are two major sections: The Changing Dynamics of Disaster Response and When Terrorism Creates a Disaster.

I. THE CHANGING DYNAMICS OF DISASTER RESPONSE

Disasters, by definition, are distinguished by their impact on human society (Smith, 1996; Tobin & Montz, 1997). Disasters follow a discernable cycle. The seven elements of this cycle often overlap (rather than occurring as separate and distinct phases). These elements are detection, protection, prevention, preparation, mitigation, response, and recovery. Most disaster management activities focus on the last four elements of a disaster. For instance, the Federal Emergency Management Agency (FEMA) has been promoting a strategy of comprehensive emergency management that involves preparedness, mitigation, response, and recovery.

Generally speaking, the greater the degree of disruption to society the more severe the disaster. The distinction between a disaster and a nondisaster is often made along one of three lines:

- Human suffering
- Structural damage
- Political declaration

The first two refer to the impact of the event itself. Human impacts are not just death or injury, but also disrupted social networks or substantially altered day-to-day routines. These effects are more severe if major infrastructure elements

Note: Anne Strack Angelheart is a graduate of the University of Florida, where she earned her B.A., M.A. and Ph.D. in Geography with specializations in Economic Geography and Natural Hazards. She has taught at the University of North Carolina at Charlotte and the University of Florida. Her publications include "Business Response to Natural Disaster: A Case Study of the Response by Firms in Greenville, North Carolina, to Hurricane Floyd."

are out of service (e.g., electricity, phones, roads). Disaster impacts on the social and structural environments can interact, escalating the cumulative effect of the disastrous event. On the other hand, an event that has been politically defined as a disaster may or may not, in fact, have resulted in significant disruption of a community's normal activities. A political declaration does provide a community with access to a greater volume of disaster recovery resources.

II. CHANGE IN DISASTER IMPACTS

Like the event itself, the root causes of a disaster are complex and ever-changing. A disaster results from interactions between the natural environment (air, land, sea), the built environment (e.g., roads, bridges, buildings), and the socioeconomic environment (a human population and its traits, such as age, income, education, and attitudes about risk).

Until recent decades, the death toll and casualty counts were prominent in describing a disaster's impact. Although this is still true in descriptions of disastrous events in lesser developed countries, these numbers are not as frequently referred to when reporting a disaster's severity in the developed world. Here, the figures most prominently used refer to the financial cost of a disaster; this, in turn, is largely a reflection of the structural damage inflicted by the event, and the resulting economic disruptions as well.

Although the death toll and casualty counts from disastrous events among more developed nations have been substantially reduced in recent decades, this is due to physical changes to the natural landscape, as well as improved forecast and warning technologies. These technological or structural improvements are costly to produce and implement. Then again, the reduction in human suffering is remarkable. Yet, the detection, mitigation, and preparation advancements that reduced the human toll are not without inherent disadvantages. Such advancements may create:

- A false sense of security among residents living in a hazard-prone area,
- A perceived amenity that attracts even more people to the vulnerable area,
- A greater risk of disaster to a nearby community, and
- A more extreme catastrophe if the structural improvements or warning/forecasting system fails.

Take a dam, for example. A well-designed and well-built dam can reduce the risk of flooding of those communities below the dam. No longer believing flooding to be a significant danger, new people may move to the area to take advantage of boating, fishing, or other amenities created by the dam. By storing large volumes of water in the dam's reservoir, the flow rate and erosion patterns of the river (both up and downstream of the dam) are altered. In severe or prolonged heavy rain events the dam operators may not have enough time to gradually release the reservoir's stored water in order to prevent the rainfall from overtopping the dam. In such a case, the communities upstream from the dam may flood as the water backs up the river. The communities downstream may have flash floods if the dam operators open the flood gates to release a large volume of the reservoir's water in order to prevent the excess water damaging the dam. Or the dam may rupture or collapse entirely, sending a tidal wave downstream—inundating those communities with more water than if the dam had never been built at all.

Achieving the right balance between the natural, built, and social environments has been the clarion call of disaster professionals for years (Anderson & Woodrow, 1989; Haas, Kates, & Bowden, 1977; Mileti, 2000; Tobin & Montz, 1997). But there are influential factors that are difficult to change.

A. Politics and Media in American Disaster Recovery

At the outset of the twentieth century, the federal government seldom involved itself in disaster recovery activities. Establishing the Disaster Loan Corporation in 1939 was Congress's initial attempt to provide disaster relief. Congress was responding to public outcry in the wake of the Great

Depression, as well as the suffering endured in the wake of multiple floods in the 1920s and 1930s, and the 1933 Long Beach earthquake. Throughout the first half of the twentieth century, however, the federal government's limited disaster relief procedures ensured that private charities (including the Red Cross) performed most of the relief activities themselves. The government intervened "only when the scale of the disaster was beyond the capacity of the Red Cross" (Comerio, 1998, 199; Platt, 1999).

In 1950, Congress passed two acts that would alter federal disaster relief: The Federal Disaster Act of 1950 and the Civil Defense Act of 1950. The Federal Disaster Act established the basis for federal and state governments to share the costs of disaster assistance. The Civil Defense Act stipulates that states and localities assume responsibility for disaster preparedness. These two acts establish the framework for government disaster assistance, particularly with respect to repairing or replacing damaged or destroyed infrastructure (Comerio, 1998; Mileti, 2000; Platt, 1999). Since 1950, the federal government has expanded its policies.

In authorizing federal disaster relief, the government created a federal disaster aid program with the intent of supplementing state and local recovery efforts by aiding local governments. Currently, the federal government extends disaster support (via disaster relief loans) to private businesses and individuals. This is accomplished by the Small Business Administration (SBA), which was created in 1953. The initial intent of federal support was to supplement insurance, in addition to charities', states', and local governments' relief efforts. Uncle Sam's helping hand would create a safety net that would prevent communities from being destroyed altogether.

As the decades following WWII passed, Congress increased the range of disaster assistance available. Today, federal intervention in disaster recovery provides a community with access to an array of federal assistance programs, which are coordinated by FEMA.[1] These include SBA Disaster Loans, U.S. Department of Agriculture (USDA) Disaster Programs, and Department of Housing and Urban Development (HUD) Community Development Block Grants (CDBGs). These programs not only facilitate reconstruction, mitigation, and economic (re)development

activities, but they can also provide additional disaster response resources (e.g., temporary shelters, medical support, and emergency communications systems).

Federal assistance was further expanded by the 1988 Stafford Disaster Relief and Emergency Assistance Act. The Stafford Act allows the president to authorize assistance for disaster preparedness efforts as well as for mitigation, response, and recovery from a disaster. With respect to preparedness, funding can be authorized without a disaster having occurred. Indeed, the 2000 Disaster Mitigation Act created a National Predisaster Mitigation Fund through which local governments can obtain financial and technical assistance in implementing strategies to reduce losses from future disasters.[2] Funding for the other three phases of a disaster is provided as part of the federal (presidential) disaster declaration. Since the 1988 Stafford Act increased the political leverage to be gained by offering federal disaster assistance, there has been a dramatic rise in the number of presidentially declared disaster areas in the United States (Comerio, 1998; Mileti, 2000; Platt, 1999).

Usually, a state requests that the president declare the impacted area a disaster area. After reviewing the impact information provided, the president may decide the situation does not justify a disaster declaration. Prior to 1988, the average number of presidentially declared disasters in any given year was about two-thirds of those requested for such a declaration. Between 1988 and 1998 the number of declarations has steadily risen. In fact, in the election years of 1992 and 1996, the president declared disasters in more than four-fifths of the events requested (Platt, 1999).

The increasing number of politically defined disaster has occurred in tandem with the expansion of press coverage of disasters. Media reports on disasters tend to vary based on the media organization's primary audience. Local media typically provide detailed information for victims and residents (e.g., shelter locations). National and international media tend to report on the event's most dramatic aspects. The visual images from national or international news sources will particularly emphasize the devastation of the disaster (Fischer, 1998; Tobin & Montz, 1997). These images evoke a powerful altruistic response among the media's audience. The stage is thus set for a politician to don a hero's mantle and step into this scene declaring his determination to make as many resources available as possible to assist the victims.[3] The media receives a good public response, the politician receives good coverage, and the affected area receives additional disaster relief. The biggest drawback to increased media coverage and disaster assistance is the changing expectations of disaster victims. Decades ago, victims had little expectation of outside help for a variety of reasons. These included poor communication methods (that limited the outside world's awareness of the event) and limited resources at state and federal levels. Frequently today more and more victims expect that Uncle Sam will help restore the victim to his predisaster sense of well-being. This is not true, but the expectation still grows.

B. The American Military and Domestic Disaster Recovery

The provision of disaster recovery support has evolved from a heavy reliance on charitable organizations to substantial reliance on insurance, along with state and federal government assistance (Mileti, 2000; NRC, 1999; Platt, 1999). Yet there was one resource whose scope of disaster assistance activities Uncle Sam limited: the active duty military service. While National Guard and reserve units are called up in times of emergency, such as in the wake of a disaster, most of these personnel are not serving on active duty status in the military. Additionally, the United States Army Corps of Engineers (USACE) provides significant support in developing and implementing new techniques for use in limiting flood and earthquake damages. But USACE represents only a tiny fraction of the number of active duty service members in the army.

Despite military reluctance to adopt a "first responder to disaster" focus as part of its overall national mission (Anderson, 1970; Lay, 1993), the military's successful intervention during the aftermath of Hurricane Andrew encouraged many to suggest military interventions in all large-scale domestic disasters (U.S. Senate, 1993). Hurricane Andrew's impact on South Florida and Louisiana in 1992 exceeded local, state, and FEMA capabilities. It was an especially difficult period for FEMA, as Hurricane Iniki ravaged Hawaii only days after Andrew ripped through the Florida peninsula and then plowed inland from Louisiana. The military were called in to establish emergency shelters, food kitchens, provide sentries, and other support for local recovery efforts. The military's response was not without flaws (Yelvington, 1997). Nonetheless, their response was noteworthy for its speed and its resources (e.g., food, water, tents, cots, and bedding).

Reluctance on the part of the military to assume first-responder responsibilities in the wake of a disaster is primarily due to concerns that resources used (human and materiel) in disaster response cannot be withdrawn from disaster duties and redeployed to support other military duties elsewhere (Anderson, 1970; Lay, 1993). If a significant volume of the military's resources were in use at a disaster zone, it could leave the country (or its overseas outposts) vulnerable to attack (Lay, 1993; Schrader, 1993). Other difficulties in using military resources include limited number of appropriately trained service members and legal issues regarding jurisdiction and authority (Schrader, 1993). This does not mean that the military opposes providing disaster relief—merely that it is conservative in its enthusiasm for such additional duties.

C. Who Pays?

As disaster costs mount and victims' expectations rise, sooner or later the question must be asked: Who's paying for recovery and reconstruction? Much of the financial estimates of a disaster's cost are based on a combination of insurance estimates (e.g., cars, homes, building contents) and repair or replacement estimates of public structures (e.g., government buildings, roads, bridges). The rest is modeled on the financial costs of economic disruption. This includes job losses and business closures (either temporary or permanent closures) (Comerio, 2000; NRC, 1999).

Some efforts have been made to reduce the federal cost of disaster assistance. For instance, there are national insurance programs, such as the National Flood Insurance Program (NFIP). In addition, a community affected by disaster is required to undertake measures to lessen or mitigate the potential losses from a future disaster in order to receive federal assistance. Such measures include more stringent building code enforcement and land use planning. However, a community's attempts to reduce its hazards is quite often in conflict with the community's own development goals. As a result, the effectiveness of government disaster mitigation programs is strongly debated (Dyer, 1999; Dyer & McGoodwin, 1999; Mileti, 2000; Platt, 1999).

In addition, because of how the media reports on federal assistance programs, there are several misconceptions among the public regarding the federal government's role in disaster recovery. Of the two most common, the first is that FEMA is the primary provider of aid. Federal aid is offered by up to 26 different federal agencies, depending on the type of assistance needed. FEMA coordinates the interaction between local and state governments and these agencies. FEMA also coordinates the application process between federal agencies and affected local businesses, disaster victims, and impacted governments. For example, a victim that has lost his home may receive financial assistance from the SBA rather than FEMA–even though the victim was not a business owner. The second common misconception is that FEMA (or the federal government) will provide enough assistance for the victims to return to their predisaster level of well-being (Tobin & Montz, 1997). The expectation of assistance contributes to the backlash against the government that typically occurs a few weeks after the disaster event itself (Oliver-Smith, 1999; Platt, 1999; Tobin & Montz, 1997).

At the household level, there are strong socio-economic factors that indicate which disaster victims will be able to finance their own recovery efforts, and which will not. The better educated and/or more wealthy tend to have access to enough financial support (such as insurance, savings, investments, new bank loans) to cover the costs of any necessary repairs or reconstruction. Victims at the opposite end of the economic spectrum have fewer initial resources, little or no collateral, and little or no experience with the process of obtaining a loan. These victims make up the bulk of aid recipients (Comerio, 1998; Tobin & Montz, 1997). In an effort to reduce the federal government's financial disaster recovery costs, the government is reducing assistance to those victims who have received disaster aid in the past and then repositioned themselves back in harm's way, only to become a repeat disaster victim. (The almost back-to-back floodings of the Mississippi River in the 1990s dramatically demonstrated this, as some flood victims used their assistance money to rebuild their homes or businesses in flood-prone locations, only to be flooded out again.) Furthermore, with the new millenium, there has been a decided shift away from recovery and toward prevention or protection in anticipation of terrorist-induced disaster.

III. WHEN TERRORISM CREATES A DISASTER

The magnitude of some terrorist attacks is so great that they are, in themselves, disasters. The collapse of the World Trade Center towers on September 11, 2001, is the prime example. Terrorism creates a difficult wrinkle in the web of disaster planning, preparation, recovery, and mitigation. With many natural disasters (hurricanes and volcanic eruptions are just two), one can develop models to help in predicting vulnerable areas and the severity of impact based on a variety of different scenarios. So, too, for manmade (technological) hazards, such as chemical spills, oil spills, and radiation leaks. Terrorism, on the other hand, operates along a different set of principles. Natural or technological hazards usually have a spatial aspect that can be easily determined—where are people most vulnerable? From there it can be determined:

- who the vulnerable people are,
- why they are in such a vulnerable area,
- how vulnerable they are, and
- how their vulnerability can be lessened.

In contrast, terrorists depend heavily on publicity of their acts. There are a number of reasons for this, including:

- To increase support for the terrorist group by demonstrating a 'successful' attack,
- To serve as a recruitment tool,

- To inspire allegiance or to improve morale of the group's members,
- To fan the flames of an egocentric leader, and
- To frighten the targeted group into yielding to the group's demands.

To accomplish this, terrorists typically attack targets with either a symbolic value, or in a manner guaranteed to garner media coverage. Thus, they are more likely to attack in urban locations rather than rural ones. They may attack politicians, judges, journalists, or others who publicly oppose the group's objectives. They may also attack innocent civilians in ordinary settings (such as a marketplace, a nightclub, or a bus) in order to frighten the public as a whole (Combs, 2003; Hudson, 1999).

A. Fear and Communication

Some of the ways in which an event can increase the public's fear is illustrated in Table 14.1. For example, earthquakes occur with little or no warning; severe earthquakes can be terrifying due to their unexpected and destructive nature. On the other hand, advance warning of tropical storms and hurricanes allows the public to assess their risk and respond accordingly. This warning system allows the potential victim a degree of control over their circumstances, which, in turn, reduces their fear.

In contrast, a terrorist group that deploys a Weapon of Mass Destruction (WMD) in a surprise attack maximizes the public's fear. It is unexpected. The public (and perhaps the emergency response personnel) has little or no experience with the substance released (or its effects). The public does not know how to behave to minimize

their own exposure. In some communities, law enforcement and other emergency personnel may not be able to effectively quarantine victims or communicate with the public to limit exposure to, or the spread of, the contaminating agent (Fitzgerald, Sztajnkrycer, & Crocco, 2003). Therefore, there is a sense of no control over the situation, and the outcome can be calamitous. (The terrorist attack on the Tokyo subway, in which Sarin gas–a nerve agent–was released in an attempt to murder thousands, is such an example.) Add to this that such an attack is also a crime scene, with its need to restrict media and public access to the details of the event, and the potential for instilling terror in the public is enormous.

An important technique in reducing public fear and restoring normalcy after any disastrous event is effective risk communication. The media and other information sources must be utilized to convey to the public the nature of the risk to them, the methods for reducing their exposure to the risk, and the potential outcome if they do not attempt to protect themselves from the risk. This is most effectively conveyed if the spokesperson is someone whom the audience feels it can trust. In some circumstances, a government representative may not be deemed a credible source of information. One reason for this is that the government may be perceived as withholding information from the public. Restricting access to information about a terrorist attack may prevent the terrorists from refining the method of attack. It may also prevent copycat crimes from occurring. However, withholding information may aggravate the public perception of vulnerability, which helps the terrorists achieve one of their objectives. It is an unfortunate conundrum that the government must grapple with.

Table 14.1
DISASTER TRAITS THAT INFLUENCE PUBLIC FEAR

Less Fear	More Fear
Not a Catastrophic Outcome	Potentially Catastrophic Outcome
Forewarned about Event	Unexpected Event
Familiar with Event	Unfamiliar with Event
Educated about Risk	Uneducated about Risk
Sense of Control over Outcome	No Sense of Control over Outcome

Source: Ropeik & Gray, 2002.

B. Preventing Terrorism and Protecting the Public

The difficulty in assessing the risk of terrorist attack lies, in part, in determining who or what the target is. A frequent form of terrorism is a perpetual series of unexpected small attacks that keep the public in fear. Each of these attacks is not individually disruptive enough to warrant a disaster declaration, but there are three possible scenarios in which a terrorist event (or series of closely occurring events) could be disastrous:

- If there are a huge number of casualties,
- If there is a shortage of resources, destruction of infrastructure, or significant disruption of normalcy, or
- If it relies on a method that maximizes public panic by using substances with which the public is unfamiliar and which the emergency responders are not prepared to remedy.

The 2001 attack on the World Trade Center towers fulfilled the first two criteria. The third criteria may be met by an attack that uses chemical, biological, or nuclear substances, such as accomplished with WMDs in order to inflict high casualties with minimal risk to the attacker (Champion & Mattis, 2003; Noji, 2000).

Terrorism creates many new wrinkles in federal disaster policy. Unlike natural or other human-caused events (e.g., an oil spill), terrorism relies on premeditated malice cloaked in secrecy. The human agent's involvement makes it difficult to predict or prevent an event. Finding predictive variables for more traditional disasters (such as hurricanes, volcanic eruptions, dam breaks) has been the realm of scientists. With terrorism, the search to predict and prevent attacks is more often

the duty of law enforcement and medical personnel. Likewise, there is a substantial shift in emphasis in terms of addressing this potential disaster. Previous federal disaster policy typically concentrated on preparing for, or mitigation, response, and recovery from natural and technological disasters. With terrorism, the policy goals are to predict and/or prevent attacks. (Strategies to minimize or alleviate the impact are still being developed, but this is a less desirable outcome than preventing the attack altogether.)

These changes in disaster objectives have resulted in significant changes in federal policy (although it is still too early into the war on terror to know if the changes are harbingers of more to come, or if they are merely temporary). Government policy with respect to natural or technological (nonterrorist) disasters frequently focused on regulating or modifying land or buildings to lessen the risk and/or the impact of a disaster. Since the collapse of the World Trade Center towers, the government's efforts to reduce the risk of terrorism within the United States has resulted in new regulations regarding human behavior and law enforcement techniques (e.g., the USA PATRIOT Act). Additionally, all federal agencies with law enforcement activities, as well as those with disaster response functions have been restructured under a new federal department: the Department of Homeland Security (DHS).

Some of the regulatory changes that have occurred since the war on terror began are in the process of legal challenges. As with challenges to policies regarding natural or technological disasters, these legal rulings will help delineate the boundary between individual, community, and government duties and obligations. Clearly, though, federal involvement in disaster response will continue to increase in light of this new form of disaster.

IV. CONCLUSION

Federal efforts to reduce human suffering from natural and technological disasters have been successful and expensive. It has also created an unrealistic expectation among victims: the belief that the government will restore their lives back to their predisaster level of well-being. The risk of

a terrorist-caused disaster creates many new difficulties for the federal government. Detection involves scrutinizing the behavior of individuals and groups rather than the behavior and interactions of environmental features. Detection also requires regulating the behavior of individuals and groups rather than the standards of land use or construction in order to limit the potential losses from a disaster. The unique attributes of a potentially catastrophic terrorist attack are requiring

governments, aid groups, and individuals to reevaluate their risk, their strategies for avoiding harm, and their methods for coping with the aftermath.

REFERENCES

Anderson, Mary B. & Woodrow, Peter J. (1989). *Rising from the Ashes: Development Strategies in Times of Disaster*. Boulder: Westview Press.

Anderson, William A. (1970). "Military Organizations in Natural Disaster: Established and Emergent Norms." *American Behavioral Scientist*, 13: 415–422.

Averch, Harvey, & Dluhy, Milan J. (1997). "Crisis Decision Making and Management." Peacock, Morrow, & Gladwin, (Eds.). *Hurricane Andrew: Ethnicity, Gender and the Sociology of Disasters*, pp. 75–91. New York: Routledge.

Champion, David R. & Mattis, Ronald E. (2003). "Terrorism, Weapons of Mass Destruction and Deterrence." *Criminal Justice Studies*, 16:1, 29–37.

Combs, Cindy C. (2003). *Terrorism in the Twenty-First Century, 3rd ed.*, Upper Saddle River, NJ: Prentice Hall.

Comerio, Mary C. (Spring, 2000). "Paying for the Next Big One." *Issues in Science and Technology*, 65–72.

Comerio, Mary C. (1998). *Disaster Hits Home: New Policy for Urban Housing Recovery*. Berkeley: University of California Press.

Dyer, Christopher L. (1999). "The Phoenix Effect in Post-Disaster Recovery: An Analysis of the Economic Development Administration's Culture of Response to Hurricane Andrew." In Oliver-Smith & Hoffman, (Eds.). *The Angry Earth, Disaster in Anthropological Perspective*, pp. 278–300. New York: Routledge.

Dyer, Christopher L., & McGoodwin, James R. (1999). "'Tell Them We're Hurting': Hurricane Andrew, the Culture of Response, and the Fishing Peoples of South Florida and Louisiana." In Oliver-Smith & Hoffman, (Eds.). *The Angry Earth, Disaster in Anthropological Perspective*, pp. 213–232. New York: Routledge.

Fischer, Henry W. III. (1998). *Response to Disaster: Fact versus Fiction and Its Perpetuation (The Sociology of Disasters), 2nd ed.*, Lanham, MD: University Press of America.

Fitzgerald, Denis J., Sztajnkrycer, Matthew D. & Crocco, Todd J. (2003). "Chemical Weapon Functional Exercise–Cincinnati: Observations and Lessons Learned from a "Typical Medium-Sized" City's Response to Simulated Terrorism Utilizing Weapons

of Mass Destruction." *Public Health Reports*, 118: 205–214.

Haas, J. Eugene, Kates, Robert W. & Bowden, Martyn J. (Eds.). (1977). *Reconstruction Following Disaster*. Cambridge, MA: The MIT Press.

Hudson, Rex A. (1999). *The Sociology and Psychology of Terrorism: Who Becomes a Terrorist and Why?* Washington, DC: Library of Congress Report. http://www.loc.gov/rr/frd/terrorism.html

Lay, Col. Robert Jr. (April 13–16, 1993). *Role of the Military*, Proceedings of the 15th Annual National Hurricane Conference, Orlando, FL.

Mileti, Dennis S. (2000). *Disaster by Design: A Reassessment of Natural Hazards in the United States*. Washington, DC: National Academy Press.

National Research Council (NRC). (1999). *The Impacts of Natural Disasters: A Framework for Loss Estimation*. Washington, DC: National Academy Press.

Noji, Eric K. (2000). "Biological Agents as Natural Hazards and Bioterrorism as a "New" Natural Disaster Threat." *Natural Hazards Observer* (25, 2): 1–3.

Oliver-Smith, Anthony. (1999). "The Brotherhood of Pain: Theoretical and Applied Perspectives on Post-Disaster Solidarity." In Oliver-Smith & Hoffman, (Eds.). *The Angry Earth, Disaster in Anthropological Perspective*, pp. 156–172. New York: Routledge.

Platt, Rutherford H. (Ed.). (1999). *Disasters and Democracy: The Politics of Extreme Natural Events*. Washington, DC: Island Press.

Ropeik, D. & Gray, G. (2002). *Risk: A Practical Guide for Deciding What's Really Safe and What's Really Dangerous in the World Around You*. Boston: Houghton Mifflin.

Schrader, John Y. (1993). *The Army's Role in Domestic Disaster Support: An Assessment of Choices*. RAND Report: US Army.

Smith, Keith. (1996). *Environmental Hazards, Assessing Risk and Reducing Disaster 2nd ed.*, New York: Routledge.

Tobin, Graham A. & Burrell E. Montz. (1997). *Natural Hazards, Explanation and Integration*. New York: The Guilford Press.

United States Senate. (1993). *Federal disaster policy and future of Federal Emergency Management Agency, Special Hearing 103-207, Subcommittee of the Committee on Appropriations, U.S. Senate, 103rd Congress, 1st session,*

January 27, 1993. Washington, DC: U.S. Government Printing Office.

Yelvington, Kevin A. (1997). "Coping in a Temporary Way: The Tent Cities." Peacock, Morrow, & Gladwin, (Eds.). *Hurricane Andrew: Ethnicity, Gender and the Sociology of Disasters*, pp. 92–115. New York: Routledge.

ENDNOTES

1. In 1979, Congress established the Federal Emergency Management Agency (FEMA). FEMA's goal was to help streamline and coordinate disaster programs, but three large programs are still independent of FEMA:
   - SBA disaster loan program
   - Farmer's Home Administration (FHA) recovery loan program
   - US Army Corps of Engineers (USACE) flood control program

   (Comerio, 1998, Platt, 1999).

2. The 2000 Disaster Mitigation Act also restricts federal assistance if an otherwise eligible public or private facility had been repaired following more than one disaster in the preceding 10 years, and if the repairs failed to mitigate future disaster losses.

3. For a noteworthy description of how this interplay of events can backfire, see Averch and Dluhy's (1997) description of the initial interaction among various government and media organizations during the immediate aftermath of Hurricane Andrew in South Florida.

DISCUSSION QUESTIONS

1. What are the elements of a disaster?
2. Which impacts are more likely to predominate in a natural disaster, and which in a WMD event?
3. Describe the effects of technological improvements on the physical structures that we build. List ways that technology has improved preparedness steps. What are the challenges posed by these improvements?
4. What effect has the media had on disaster preparedness, response, and recovery?
5. Who pays for recovery and reconstruction? Discuss the economic effects of choices regarding who bears these costs.
6. How do terrorist attacks differ from other types of hazards? What implications do these differences have for preparedness steps? What tensions underlie decisions regarding preparedness for WMD terrorism events and natural disasters?
7. How much preparedness is enough? How can we measure the proper amounts to apply to preparedness for different types of hazard?
8. What types of hazard might affect your community? Prioritize among these risks. Explain where you would direct limited resources, and on what basis you would make the decisions.

Chapter 15

BIOTERRORISM DEFENSE: CURRENT COMPONENTS AND CONTINUING CHALLENGES

LESLIE GIELOW JACOBS

Although biological warfare has existed since antiquity,[1] bioterrorism has only recently become a real and recognized national and homeland security threat. United States policymakers are now scrambling to put into place the components of a comprehensive and effective bioterrorism defense. Protecting the homeland against dangerous weapons threats is not a new challenge. Established policy models exist to protect against the threat posed both by conventional weapons and Weapons of Mass Destruction (WMD). Additionally, policy measures implemented in the recent surge to combat terrorism generally expand the focus of these objectives beyond nations to non-nation groups and individuals, and outside the battlefield to civilian targets, both abroad and domestic.

Many of the generic defense policy measures serve bioterrorism defense goals as well, but they are incomplete. Crucial differences between biological weapons and other weapons threats means that, although it can follow the same general template, bioterrorism defense policy must be different both in emphasis and in its specifics from all other aspects of homeland defense. Both terrorists and the biological agents that they may use move stealthily in camouflage, reproduce rapidly, and are constantly adapting and mutating to overcome countermeasures employed against them. Bioterrorism defense policymakers must address these continuing challenges.

This chapter will first place the bioterrorism threat in historical context. Next, it will briefly describe the components of current bioterrorism defense. This chapter will then discuss some of the crucial differences between biological and other weapons and the continuing challenges that these differences pose for policymakers crafting bioterrorism defense.

I. THE CONTEXT

Hostile use of biological agents and toxins has a long history. Animal carcasses in wells, pus-lined peepholes, and smallpox-laden clothing[2] were some of the early biological weapons. Nations have sporadically used biological weapons during war.[3] The United States actively researched and developed offensive biological weapons from World War II through the late 1960s, but claims never to have used them.[4] In 1969, the United States renounced biological weapons,[5] and then joined the Biological Weapons Convention of 1972 (BWC).[6]

Although the BWC forbids development, use, or stockpiling of biological weapons, signatory nations have widely violated its provisions. In 1992, President Boris Yeltsin confirmed the existence of a massive biological weapons development program

Note: Professor of Law, University of Pacific, McGeorge School of Law. Thanks to Kim Clarke and Scott Sommerdorf for their excellent research assistance.

in the former Soviet Union and the accidental release of anthrax from one of the plants that had occurred in 1979.[7] In 1995, Iraqi authorities acknowledged that they had an ongoing biological weapons program at the beginning of the first Gulf War.[8] A 1993 Office of Technology Assessment report lists 15 countries as suspected of manufacturing biological weapons: Iran, Iraq, Libya, Syria, North Korea, Taiwan, Israel, Egypt, Vietnam, Laos, Cuba, Bulgaria, India, China, and Russia.[9]

In addition to use by nations, the threat of biological weapons in the hands of non-nation terrorists has become increasingly clear. In 1984, members of the Rajneeshee cult in Oregon laced salad bars with salmonella to affect a local election. The attack was undetected through disease tracing, but was revealed a year later by several cult members who informed the government.[10] During the 1990s, the Aum Shinrikyo cult made numerous attempts at biological and chemical weapon attacks, including the successful release of sarin gas in the Toyko subway.[11] In 1995, Larry Wayne Harris, a white supremacist lab technician, used forged letterhead to order and receive plague culture from a Maryland biomedical supply firm.[12] Apparently, these biological materials were widely available upon request. Several years earlier, a United States biomedical supply firm had sent pathogen samples to Saddam Hussein's Iraq as well.[13] According to United States officials, its invasion of Afghanistan disrupted the early conceptual stage of an al Quaida program to develop chemical and biological weapons.[14] Domestic attacks occurred in October 2001 when someone sent letters containing anthrax to news organizations and government offices in New York and Washington, DC. A total of 22 cases resulted, primarily among postal workers who handled the infected letters. Five victims died.[15] Although the anthrax is suspected to have

originated in one of several United States laboratories,[16] the crime remains unsolved.

Recent events also demonstrate the security threat infectious diseases pose, whether intentionally introduced or naturally occurring. The AIDS epidemic rages unchecked in sub-Saharan Africa and other parts of the developing world. In 2000, President Clinton declared AIDS a national security threat.[17] A 2003 RAND Corporation report argues that naturally occurring infectious diseases present national and human security threats around the world.[18] And, in spring 2003, China's efforts to conceal a novel respiratory disease outbreak in one of its provinces unraveled as plane travelers spread it throughout the world. Strong intervention by the World Health Organization and other governments, along with China's belated cooperation, brought the epidemic under control. The severe acute respiratory syndrome (SARS) outbreak, however, provides a window on how events would unfold in the event of a bioterrorism attack, specifically the impact of global travel and trade on the spread of infectious diseases, and the panic, chaos, and social and economic disruption that disease can cause. The widespread and publicly visible use of personal control mechanisms to limit the spread of SARS also brought civil liberties issues, which had been largely forgotten during the last century, to the fore.

Despite this chain of events, the risk of a devastating bioterrorism attack is difficult to estimate. Considerations on both sides affect terrorist motivations to choose biological weapons.[19] Moreover, a range of factors will affect the impact of any particular attack.[20] Still, terrorist interest in using biological weapons against the United States is certain.[21] This recognition has spurred United States policymakers to begin the work of creating and implementing the components of an effective and comprehensive bioterrorism defense.

II. THE COMPONENTS

The components of current bioterrorism defense are designed to implement a number of broad policy goals. These are deterring and punishing creation, acquisition, or use of biological weapons; limiting proliferation of weapons

and the materials and information that may be used to create them; protecting bioterrorism targets; and preparing to respond to an attack. These measures are both international and domestic in scope.

Internationally, the Biological Weapons Convention of 1972 (BWC) outlaws development, acquisition, or stockpiling of biological weapons, but unlike the International Atomic Energy Agency with respect to nuclear weapons,[22] no agency has the authority to inspect to verify compliance with the BWC prohibitions. The United Nations has played a role in enforcing and verifying compliance with unconventional weapons prohibitions, most recently in Iraq after the 1992 Gulf War. In spring 2003, however, the United States rejected these efforts. Citing intelligence demonstrating an ongoing WMD, including biological weapons, program, and links between Iraq and terrorists, the United States established preemptive war as a bioterrorism defense policy tool.[23] With respect to other nations, most recently Libya after the Iraq war, diplomacy without use of force has achieved the bioterrorism defense disarmament objective.[24] Export restrictions limit access of nations and non-nation actors outside the United States to materials and information that may be used to produce biological weapons.[25] In the nations of the former Soviet Union, a federal government program works to dispose of the materials and relocate the experts engaged in WMD production so that the tools to create such weapons are not available to terrorists.[26]

Domestically, a broad range of policy measures address bioterrorism defense. The Biological Weapons Anti-Terrorism Act of 1989 implements the BWC, and makes it a crime to knowingly create, keep, or transfer any biological agent, toxin, vector, or delivery system "for use as a weapon" or to knowingly assist a foreign state or any organization to do so.[27] Other statutes more generally criminalize international and domestic terrorism.[28]

Several pieces of legislation and their implementing regulations track and limit access to "select agents" that could be used in a bioterrorism attack.[29] New visa programs track and limit access by aliens to select agents and research activities that might pose a bioterrorism threat.[30] Although no federal law criminalizes dissemination of privately generated biological research information, as the Atomic Energy Act does with respect to nuclear research,[31] a number of actual and proposed policy measures may restrict dissemination of research results in other ways.[32]

Federal legislation also provides funding and orders various agencies to coordinate with state and local governments and private entities both to protect likely targets, which include transportation systems, water systems, and the food supply, and to prepare to respond to a bioterrorism attack.[33] The latter efforts include training first responders, improving bioterrorism surveillance and information exchange, stockpiling vaccines and antidotes, and implementing a smallpox preparedness program.[34] Additionally, the Centers for Disease Control and Prevention commissioned creation of a Model State Emergency Health Powers Act, which provides a template for states to update their statutory authorities to respond to a bioterrorism attack.[35]

Legislative and executive efforts to add new components to the bioterrorism defense arsenal continue.[36] Efforts by federal agencies and state and local governments to implement the bioterrorism defense mandates of statutes and presidential directives is ongoing. In all of these efforts, policymakers must identify and address the differences between biological and other weapons that pose continuing challenges to bioterrorism defense.

III. THE CONTINUING CHALLENGES

Biological weapons are different in a number of ways from both conventional weapons and other WMD, especially nuclear weapons, around which existing weapons defense polices have been designed.[37] These differences shape the current components of bioterrorism defense and pose continuing challenges to it.

A. Detecting and Deterring Biological Weapons Development and Use

A primary objective of weapons defense is to deter violations by maintaining a credible and ongoing ability to detect and punish weapons development or acquisition. Several aspects of biological weapons materials pose a continuing challenge to achieving this objective.

A primary aspect that confounds bioterrorism defense is the dual use dilemma, which means that the substances, equipment, and knowledge necessary to make biological weapons are the same as those used in legitimate, highly beneficial research and development in university and commercial laboratories across the United States and throughout the world.[38] In fact, the same experiments that could lead to the creation of a deadly biological disease weapon may be necessary to discover the cure. For example, enhancing the virulence of a pathogen can both lead to a more potent weapon and test a cure.[39] Advances in aerosolization techniques can perfect the delivery of a bioweapon as well as beneficial inhalation vaccines.[40]

Compounding the dual use dilemma is the fact that the materials and equipment necessary to make a biological weapon are small and often easily obtainable, even directly in nature.[41] The materials can be easily transported either by legitimate commercial transportation or by smuggling.[42] Production does not require a large infrastructure. The equipment can be obtained piece by piece and assembled in a small area,[43] and the activities do not otherwise emit telltale signs that can be detected by surveillance.

Recent events in the international arena illustrate the difficulties that both the dual use dilemma and the easily concealable nature of biological weapons pose to detecting and punishing weapons violations. The United States rejected a proposed verification and compliance protocol that would have added teeth to the BWC on the grounds that widespread legitimate uses of agents and equipment that could create biological weapons renders inspections, especially by an international agency, ineffective.[44] Intelligence, the United States asserted, is a more accurate means to detect violations.[45] The United States again rejected international agency inspections and relied on intelligence to justify its war to disarm Iraq.[46] However, despite extensive searching, WMD have not been found, and the United States chief weapons inspector testified before a Senate committee that, in his opinion, they would not be.[47] Because of their small size, biological weapons are at the center of

administration officials' claims that, although searches have not yet been successful, prohibited WMD may still be found.[48]

The BWC stalemate and the legitimacy crisis occasioned by the failure to find the expected biological and other weapons in Iraq have broader implications for bioterrorism defense. Effective national and homeland defense requires notice of bioterrorism threats before an attack. The continuing challenge is to identify an accurate and credible means of detecting biological weapons activities.

Inspectors can be part of a detection arsenal. As they apparently did in Iraq, inspections, if authorized, could play a role in containing weapons activities by nations. However, they do not reach individuals and non-nation groups that pose the primary bioterrorism threat. Moreover, even in the case of nuclear weapons activities, which are subject to international inspections, nations such as South Africa, Iran, North Korea, and Libya have successfully hidden their activities from the world.[49]

Accurate intelligence must supplement inspections as a means of early biological weapons activities detection. Since September 11, 2001, and after the Iraq war, it has become clear that intelligence gathering needs to reach wider and deeper to infiltrate and understand the objectives, motivations, and communications of foreign persons and entities that threaten national security.[50] Recruiting agents of other nationalities, with foreign language abilities and understanding of other cultures, addresses the terrorism threat generally.[51] With respect to the more specific bioterrorism threat, improved intelligence means wider and deeper access to and understanding of the objectives, motivations, and communications of scientists and other specialists who possess the expertise and materials to create biological weapons. Biological scientists and the government are currently interacting to find ways to improve United States intelligence about activities that could assist terrorists to develop or acquire biological weapons.[52] It is this type of enhanced command over information in the fast-paced and complex field of microbiology and its applications that may enhance the government's ability to detect bioterrorism threats before they materialize.

Another objective of weapons defense is to deter their use by credibly demonstrating that if used, the perpetrator will be identified and punished. A crucial difference between biological and other weapons–the delay between an attack and its manifestation as disease–complicates this objective. Specifically, the delay between an attack and its manifestation means that identifying when a bioterrorism attack has occurred is itself a defense challenge.[53] Obviously, the best time to detect an attack is before it hits the population. Germs, however, are transparent. Even special sensors can only detect certain pathogens and cannot be placed everywhere.[54] The delay is thus an inevitable challenge. Once an attack hits the population, a problem with detection is that bioterrorism agents can be expected to produce symptoms that mimic those of existing, naturally occurring diseases.[55] Information combined from a number of sources is necessary to identify a pattern that indicates an unusual agent or outbreak. Combining this information to detect an attack takes time. So, too, does tracing an outbreak back to its source once an attack is identified. These multiple delays present a further defense challenge, as they increase the likelihood that a perpetrator will escape undetected.

The policy challenge is to make a bioterrorism attack traceable. Select agent controls help serve this objective by identifying potential sources of dangerous biological agents and so making current supplies traceable to their source. DNA records refine the tracing,[56] but to be complete, these controls must be implemented internationally as well.[57] Even tracking systems may not be enough to locate a perpetrator. The anthrax used in the October 2001 attacks has been traced to several United States laboratories, but no arrests have been made.[58] Experts have also called for measures that would cut the time between an attack and the source diagnosis.[59] DNA fingerprints provide the information, but existing laboratories may be overwhelmed in an attack. New laboratories with the ability to do high-speed analyses of samples from around the world would add credibility to a claim that pathogens used in a bioterrorism attack could be traced quickly.[60] This credibility is an important aspect of deterrence, which is a crucial aspect of bioterrorism defense.

B. Achieving Nonproliferation

The dual use dilemma profoundly complicates the biological weapons nonproliferation objective. While a national policy goal is to forbid biological weapons development and acquisition, another objective is simultaneously to encourage scientific advances and the exchange of scientific knowledge that may help humanity in myriad ways, including countering the bioterrorism threat itself. That the same activities may lead to humane or horrible ends means that the government must walk a tightrope between encouraging openness and imposing controls.

The goals of nonproliferation and encouraging scientific advances are in inevitable tension. So that intelligence agencies can assess the security danger, nonproliferation requires disclosure, at least to the government, of potentially dangerous scientific activities and exchanges before they happen, and then, to control the danger, secrecy, and exchange limits after a development has occurred. Promoting scientific advances requires precisely the opposite sequence. Secrecy comes first, before and during scientific activities, to protect professional or commercial incentives. Openness follows as the development is advertised to the world for critical evaluation or profit. Achieving one objective necessarily threatens the other. Specifically with respect to advertising scientific achievements, homeland security demands limits; good science depends upon proliferation.

The secrecy/openness debate affects all aspects of nonproliferation policy. Scientists and universities have been heavily involved in commenting on proposed select agent and access controls.[61] The rules currently in effect reflect their input. Still, the new restrictions take time and money away from beneficial scientific research and thus hamper it.[62]

Enforcing the new controls has provoked controversy as well. As one example, the United States recently prosecuted Dr. Thomas Butler, a microbiologist at Texas Tech University for violating these provisions. According to Butler, he discovered 30 vials of plague missing, and reported that to the government, as is currently required by law.[63] The government's response was an exhaustive search by the Federal Bureau of Investigation, arrest of Butler, indictment of him on 69 counts, most of which did not relate to the plague incident, and a trial in which Butler was convicted of numerous counts,[64] none of which related to the bioterrorism defense provisions or the loss of the plague cultures. Numerous prominent scientists, along with the Human Rights Committee of the National Academy of Sciences, protested that Butler's treatment was excessive and unfair.[65] The government defended its activities as appropriately scaled to counter the bioterrorism threat.[66]

Implementation of systems to control access of foreigners to United States laboratories has led to laments by research universities and institutions that the cumbersome process and its delay is causing them to lose access to important and talented foreign scientists.[67] United States research institutes rely on foreign students to provide a significant part of the workforce that has established the United States as the world leader in scientific research and technology development.[68] New programs that dramatically increase the time and paperwork required to bring foreign students to the United States threaten to compromise this status as talented scientists choose to go elsewhere.[69]

The prospect of information controls has stirred scientists deeply. Scientists themselves are divided about whether information controls, either by the government or voluntarily imposed by scientific journals or organizations,[70] are appropriate. On the one hand, some scientists criticized the decision of the top scientific journals to censor dangerous information, even if the power were to be rarely used.[71] On the other hand, scientists criticized the decision of their colleagues to conduct and publish research that could be used to enhance smallpox as a biological weapon.[72] The result of the research, argued those who did it, would be to enhance bioterrorism defenses.[73]

Scientists and others even differ over whether publishing information that may assist production of biological weapons is, in fact, more dangerous than suppressing it.[74] Only one federal court has enjoined publication of scientific information because of the national security threat posed by it.[75] Although the court relied on the danger inherent in releasing "The H-Bomb Secret: How We Got It, Why We're Telling It," the writer sought to publish it to expose national security vulnerabilities and

encourage nonproliferation.[76] The question of whether information controls are appropriate as a policy matter, even if they survive constitutional hurdles, remains a continuing challenge.

C. Preparing to Respond to a Bioterrorism Attack

The delay between a bioterrorism attack and its manifestation as a disease complicates response. One consequence of the delay is the potentially expanded impact of a bioterrorism attack. Dispersal techniques are difficult to perfect, and may limit the initial impact of a bioterrorism attack.[77] Nevertheless, that the medium is disease provides a unique advantage to the terrorist–during the delay between attack and manifestation, victims may become vectors or carriers of the disease, so that the impact continues and grows beyond the initial impact. The world's experiences with AIDS, and more recently, with SARS, illustrate how the victim-as-vector phenomenon combined with global mobility exponentially increase the devastation that the appearance of a single novel and dangerous pathogen may wreak.

Additionally, the delay between attack and manifestation, and the victim-as-vector phenomenon, mean that response to a bioterrorism attack will likely require intrusions on the personal liberties of civilians not required with the use of other types of weapons. Government use of these mechanisms, such as testing, contact tracing, vaccination, and isolation or quarantine, will create tension between it and both the victim and nonvictim population, and so further complicate bioterrorism defense.

The federal government's response to these policy challenges has been to prepare to respond to the aftermath of a bioterrorism attack. The government has held a number of exercises in various cities to reveal strengths and weaknesses in response capacities.[78] In addition to preparing to respond to its physical impact, the government is preparing to respond to the psychological effects of a bioterrorism attack as well. Accurate communication during an event, along with pre-event communication to prepare the public for the possibility and results of bioterrorism, aim to reduce the panic and terror that will follow an attack.[79] The continuing challenge for the government is to walk the tightrope between adequately preparing the public for an attack, and inducing the panic and terror that perpetrators aim for through heightened or hyped preparation.

D. Risk Assessment and Resource Allocation

The perplexing question with respect to bioterrorism response is how deep and how wide to go. At both of these levels, the fundamental issue is resource allocation. The response required to a bioterrorism attack is to contain and cure disease. The question is what resources should be allocated to counter a possible bioterrorism attack when naturally occurring diseases and other public health threats wreak havoc daily in the United States and elsewhere.[80] Although there is some overlap between bioterrorism preparation activities and those that promote public health generally, it is far from complete.[81] Because the federal government provides so much of state and local public health funding, its decision to reallocate priorities toward bioterrorism response drains funds available to address other diseases and public health threats, with respect to prevention, treatment, and scientific research.[82]

The continuing challenge is to balance the risk and potential devastation of a bioterrorism attack against the toll taken by other public health threats that could be addressed. Scientists are working on ways to alleviate this tension. One of these is to develop countermeasures that are not disease-specific. Instead, they bolster immunity generally to respond to an attack, and so address a wider range of disease problems.[83]

Further complicating the issue is that because detecting the identity and source of the disease is an important element of response, policymakers cannot draw a bright line between intentionally inflicted and naturally occurring infectious diseases. At the onset, where a particular outbreak falls may not be immediately apparent.[84] Moreover, even a naturally occurring disease outbreak, such as SARS, which threatened to gain a United States foothold, can cause panic, result in chaos, and undermine the many structures of society, thereby creating the conditions that threaten homeland security in the same way as an intentional act. So, even from a security viewpoint, expenditures must reach beyond preparing for bioterrorism to, at least in some respects, address the threat posed by infectious disease.

The truism that germs don't respect borders expands the potential scale of response even further. Some argue that devastating diseases in other nations threaten United States national security even if transmission to this country is not a credible threat.[85] The Clinton administration declared AIDS in Africa a national security threat for this reason.[86] Even absent this argument, the fact is that a bioterrorism attack or infectious disease outbreak in another nation could threaten to spread to the United States.[87] In such a situation, protecting homeland security could mean assisting a disease response abroad. This prospect dramatically augments the potential scale of response. Under this view, the United States must be prepared to provide vaccines, antibiotics, and other assistance elsewhere, while maintaining stocks sufficient to protect the nation.

There are no easy answers to the resource allocation dilemma. While public health workers, scientists, and others lament an overwhelming focus on bioterrorism defense at the expense of routine killers,[88] the danger on the other side is that policymakers and the public will become complacent about a threat that does not immediately materialize and so create the conditions for a bioterrorism disaster.[89] A continuing policy challenge is to strike this balance.

IV. CONCLUSION

A bioterrorism defense infrastructure is now in place. The need to address bioterrorism as a homeland security threat arises from a historical context in which both terrorists and biological agents are more prevalent, more dangerous, and more difficult to identify and understand. The components of bioterrorism defense address the special aspects of biological agents used as weapons. Still, efforts to adapt and adjust these components to respond to the rapidly developing and changing activities of terrorists and the scientists who may work wittingly or unwittingly to terrorists' advantage is ongoing. Policymakers face continuing challenges as they strive to create a complete and effective system of bioterrorism defense.

ENDNOTES

1. COMMITTEE ON RESEARCH STANDARDS AND PRACTICES TO PREVENT THE DESTRUCTIVE APPLICATION OF BIOTECHNOLOGY, NATIONAL RESEARCH COUNCIL OF THE NATIONAL ACADEMIES, BIOTECHNOLOGY RESEARCH IN AN AGE OF TERRORISM 33 (2004) [hereinafter COMMITTEE ON RESEARCH STANDARDS].

2. Skyler Cranmer, *Assessing Biological Weapons: Threat, Proliferation, and Countermeasures*, 5 INT'L REL. J. 247 (2003); Thomas C. Shevory, *Disease, Criminality and State Power: Evolving Legal Rhetorics and Cultural Constructions*, Prepared for Presentation at the Foundations Workshop on Political Myths, Rhetoric, and Symbolism, Aug. 30–Sept. 3, 2000, *at* http://wearcam.org/envirotech/disease criminality and state powerDRAFTA.htm (last visited Feb. 22, 2004).

3. Prior to and during World War II, Japan conducted experiments with anthrax, meningitis, cholera, and plague on prisoners of war in a compound called United 731. Japan also used biological weapons in attacks against Chinese cities. Thomas V. Inglesby, *The Germs of War; How Biological Weapons Could Threaten Civilian Population*, WASHINGTON POST, Dec. 9, 1999, at H1. Germany has been accused of infecting livestock with anthrax and glanders, both highly infectious diseases, during World War I. COMMITTEE ON RESEARCH STANDARDS, *supra*, note 1, at 20.

4. This work began within the Chemical Warfare Service at Camp Detrick in Frederick, Maryland, and subsequently expanded to three other locations. The program employed thousands of personnel, who worked with a variety of human, animal, and plant pathogens to develop offensive weapon capabilities. COMMITTEE ON RESEARCH STANDARDS, *supra*, note 1, at 20–21 *citing* U.S. DEPARTMENT OF THE ARMY, 1 U.S. ARMY ACTIVITY IN THE U.S. BIOLOGICAL WARFARE PROGRAMS 1-3 (1977).

5. President Richard Nixon, Remarks Announcing Decisions on Chemical and Biological Defense Policies and Programs (Nov. 25, 1969), *at* http://www.nixonfoundation.org/Research Center/1969_pdf_files/1969_0462.pdf ("[I]n the field of chemical warfare, I hereby reaffirm that the United States will never be the first country to use chemical weapons to kill. And I have also extended this renunciation to chemical weapons that incapacitate.").

6. The Convention on the Prohibition of the Development, Production and Stockpiling of Bacteriological (Biological) and Toxin Weapons and on their Destruction, Apr. 10, 1972, 26 U.S.T. 583.

7. *The September 11th Sourcebooks: Volume V: Anthrax at Sverdloysk, 1979*. The National Security Archive, National Security Archive Electronic Briefing Book No. 61 (Robert A. Wampler and Thomas S. Blanton, eds., Nov. 15, 2001), *at* http://www.gwu.edu/~nsarchiv/NSAEBB/NSAEBB61/index2.html (last visited Feb. 22, 2004); "Plague War; The 1979 Anthrax Leak in Sverdlovsk," *Frontline*, *at* http://www.pbs.org/wgbh/pages/frontline/shows/plague/sverdlovsk/ (last visited Feb. 22, 2004).

8. Kenneth Katzman, *Iraq: Compliance, Sanctions, and U.S. Policy*, Congressional Research Service Issue Brief for Congress (February 27, 2002) at CRS-4, http://fpc.state.gov/documents/organization/9041.pdf (last visited Feb. 22, 2004).

9. OFFICE OF TECHNOLOGY ASSESSMENT, PRO-LIFERATION OF WEAPONS OF MASS DESTRUCTION: ASSESSING THE RISKS 82 (1993), http://www.wws.princeton.edu/cgibin/byteserv.prl/~ota/disk 1/1993/9341.PDF (last visited Feb. 22, 2004).

10. Ian Katz, "The Mystic and the Mayhem; When the Bhagwan's followers took on the people of Antelope there could only be one Winner," *THE GUARDIAN* (LONDON), Aug. 1, 1994, at T2 ("Public health experts tested the salad bars but found different strains of bacteria, making it difficult to establish whether the food had been laced with germs. It was only later, when the sect began to disintegrate, that several Rajneeshis told police that they had sprayed the salad bars with salmonella.").

11. In April 1990, the Aum Shinrikyo failed in their attempt to spray botulinum germs in Central Tokyo, two American Navy bases, and the Narita airport. Their attempt to use the same toxin in the Tokyo subways in 1995 also failed. The cult sprayed

anthrax in a residential neighborhood in Tokyo on two occasions, without anyone becoming ill. It successfully employed sarin gas on two occasions: the first being in the city of Matsumoto in 1994, and the second being in the Tokyo subway system in 1995. William J. Broad, "Sowing Death; How Japan Germ Terror Alerted World," *New York Times*, May 26, 1998, at A2.

12. "Plague Charge is Denied," *New York Times*, June 1, 1995, at B10 ("Mr. Harris, who has said he belongs to white separatist groups, said he had been developing antidotes for the plague because of the potential invasion of germ-carrying rats from Iraq.").

13. Philip Shenon, "Threats and Responses: The Bioterror Threat; Iraq Links Germs for Weapons to U.S. and France," *New York Times*, Mar. 16, 2003, at A18.

14. "Malaysia Orders Terror Suspect Held, says he had more to tell about al-Quaida," *USA Today*, Jan. 28, 2004, *at* http://www.usatoday.com/news/world/2004-01-28-mal-terror_x.htm (last visited Feb. 22, 2004).

15. Daniel B. Jernigan et al., "Investigation of Bioterrorism Related Anthrax, United State 2001: Epidemiologic Findings," 8 *Emerging Infectious Diseases* 1 (October 2002), http://www.cdc.gov/ncidod/EID/vol18no10/pdf/02-0353.pdf (last visited Feb. 22, 2004).

16. William J. Broad and David Johnston, "A Nation Challenged: The Anthrax Trail; U.S. Inquiry Tried, but Failed, to Link Iraq to Anthrax Attack," *New York Times*, Dec. 22, 2001, at A1.

17. President William J. Clinton, Proclamation 7382–World AIDS Day, 2000, *Weekly Comp. Pres. Doc.* 2949 (Nov. 30, 2000) ("Because the spread of HIV has reached catastrophic proportions in many areas of our global community, AIDS has become a national and international security threat.").

18. See Jennifer Brower and Peter Chalk, *The Global Threat of New and Reemerging Infectious Diseases: Reconciling U.S. National Security and Public Health Policy* (2003).

19. See Audrey Kurth Cronin, *Terrorist Motivations for Chemical and Biological Weapons Use: Placing the Threat in Context*, Congressional Research Service Report for Congress (March 28, 2003), http://www.fas.org/irp/crs/RL31831.pdf (last visited Feb. 22, 2004).

20. *Id.*

21. *Id.*; see also Mike Allen, "Chemical, Nuclear Arms Still 'Major Threat,' Cheney Says," *Washington Post*, Dec. 17, 2003, at A15 (remarks by Vice President Cheney, warning that "the major threat"

facing the nation is the possibility that terrorists could detonate a biological or nuclear weapon in a U.S. city).

22. The International Atomic Energy Association (IAEA) is the verification authority for the Treaty for the Nonproliferation of Nuclear Weapons. Pursuant to safeguard agreements entered into with more than 140 countries, the IAEA is authorized to inspect the nuclear facilities in these countries. See generally IAEA, The International Atomic Energy Association main page, at http://www.iaea.org (last visited Feb. 22, 2004).

23. President George W. Bush, State of the Union Address (Jan 28, 2003), at http://www.whitehouse.gov/news/releases/2003/01/20030128-19.html (last visited Feb. 22, 2004) ("Let there be no misunderstanding: If Saddam Hussein does not fully disarm, for the safety of our people and for the peace of the world, we will lead a coalition to disarm him.").

24. President George W. Bush, Remarks on Libya Pledges to Dismantle WMD Programs (Dec. 19, 2003), *at* http://www.whitehouse.gov/news/releases/2003/12/20031219-9.html (last visited Feb. 22, 2004) ("Our understanding with Libya came about through quiet diplomacy.").

25. 22 U.S.C. §§2798, 5603, 5605(a) (2000). The export of dual-use items, those that have both a civilian and military application, are regulated by the International Economic Emergency Powers Act, 50 App. U.S.C. §2410c (2000).

26. The United States provides this assistance through the Nunn-Lugar Cooperative Threat Reduction Program, authorized by 22 U.S.C. §5951 (2000).

27. 18 U.S.C. §175(a) (2000).

28. 18 U.S.C. §2331 et seq. (2000).

29. Pub. L. No. 104-132 §511(d) & (e), 110 Stat. 1214, 1284–85 (1996); 42 C.F.R. pt. 72 (2002); 18 U.S.C. §175b(a) (Supp I 2001); 42 U.S.C.A. §262a (West 2003); 7 U.S.C.A. §8401 (West Supp. 2003); 67 Fed. Reg. 76908 (2002).

30. The Visas Condor program checks the applicant's name against a number of government databases and denies visas to applicants suspected of having terrorist connections. Richard Boucher, Daily Press Briefing of State Department (September 24, 2002) (transcript available at http://www.state.gov/r/pa/prs/dpb/2002/13645.htm) (last visited Feb. 22, 2004). The State Department has created a Technology Alert List that identifies specialized research activities designated on a visa application that will result in a further intelligence review. U.S. State Department, *Technology Alert List*, at

http://foia.state.gov/masterdocs/09fam/0940031X1. pdf (last visited Feb. 22, 2004). In May 2002, the White House proposed the creation of an Interagency Panel for Advanced Science and Security that would screen foreign graduate students, postdoctoral fellows and scientists who apply for visas to study in sensitive topics on U.S. campuses.

31. 42 U.S.C. §2271 et seq. (2000).

32. When entering into a contract with a university or research institution, government agencies can designate the project as classified and impose conditions on the release of the information generated. Recently, agencies have extended the scope of secrecy to prepublication review requirements on contract research. Anne Marie Borrego, "Colleges See More Federal Limits on Research," *The Chronicle of Higher Education*, Nov. 1, 2002 at 24; Dana A. Shea, *Report for Congress: Balancing Scientific Publication and National Security Concerns: Issues for Congress*, at http://www.fas.org/irp/crs/RL31695. pdf (January 10, 2004) (last visited Feb. 22, 2004). In response to concerns expressed by the research institutes, the Bush administration has reaffirmed that research information that is not classified will be publicly available. *See* Spencer Abraham, Secretary of Energy, *Memorandum for Heads of all Departmental Elements on National Security Decision Directive-189* (May 12, 2003), at http://www. fas.org/sgp/othergov/doe/sec051203.pdf (last visited Mar. 1, 2004).

33. 42 U.S.C.A. §§247d-6, 247d-7b, 300hh-11(b), 300hh-11-12 (West 2003); 21 U.S.C.A. §356-1 (West Supp. 2003).

34. 21 U.S.C.A. §356-1 (West Supp. 2003).

35. The Center for Law and the Public's Health at Georgetown and Johns Hopkins Universities, *The Model State Emergency Health Powers Act*, 2001, at http://www.publichealthlaw.net/MSEHPA/MSEHPA2.pdf (last visited Feb. 22, 2004).

36. For example, the president proposed Project BioShield in early 2003. President George W. Bush, "President Details Project BioShield" (Feb. 3, 2003), at http://www.whitehouse.gov/news/releases/2003/02/print/20030203.html (last visited Feb. 22, 2004) (describing the features of Project BioShield, which include developing and making available modern, effective drugs and vaccines to protect against attack by biological and chemical weapons or other dangerous pathogens). Both the Senate and the House of Representatives introduced legislation to authorize the Project in that session of Congress. In August, 2003, the House of Representatives passed its version of the bill. Brian Vastag, "Project Bioshield Moves Ahead," 290 *The Journal of the American Medical Association (JAMA)* 590 (Aug. 6, 2003), http://jama.amaassn.org/cgi/content/full/290/14/1844 (last visited Mar. 1, 2004).

37. Christopher F. Chyba, "*Towards Biological Security,*" *FOREIGN AFFAIRS*, May–June 2002, at 122.

38. COMMITTEE ON RESEARCH STANDARDS, *supra* note 1, at 18.

39. "Mousepox Virus or Bioweapon?," *BBC WORLD SERVICE*, Jan. 17, 2004, at http://www.bbc.co.uk/worldservice/sci_tech/highlights/010117_mousepox.shtml (last visited Feb. 22, 2004).

40. Gigi Kwik et al., "Biosecurity: Responsible Stewardship of Bioscience in an Age of Catastrophic Terrorism," 1 *BIOSECURITY AND BIOTERRORISM: BIODEFENSE STRATEGY, PRACTICE AND SCIENCE* 27, 29 (2003).

41. For example, the toxin ricin can, with some expertise, be extracted from castor beans, a readily accessible plant. Donald G. McNeil, Jr., "Ricin on Capital Hill: The Poison; Ricin, Made from Castor Beans, Can be Lethal but has Drawbacks as a Weapon," *NEW YORK TIMES*, Feb. 4, 2004, at A18; "The Recipe for Ricin: Examining the legend," *National Security Notes*, Feb. 20, 2004, George Smith, Ed., at http://www.global security.org/org/nsn/index.html (last visited Feb. 24, 2004). Scientists also fear that common illnesses, such as the flu, could be mutated to become a biological weapon. Delthia Ricks, "The Flu Factor in Bioterrorism," *NEWSDAY*, Sept. 23, 2003, at A35. Terrorist groups may also try to obtain samples of deadly viruses during an outbreak, such as the Aum Shinrikyo cult, which tried to obtain the Ebola virus during an outbreak in Zaire. Andrew C. Revkin, "Arrests Reveal Threat of Biological Weapons," *NEW YORK TIMES*, Feb. 21, 1998, at A7.

42. Ceci Connolly, "Science Groups Protest Researcher's Treatment; Scientist Couldn't Account for all Plague Specimens," *WASHINGTON POST*, Aug. 28, 2003, at A2; *see also 60 Minutes: The Case Against Dr. Butler* (CBS Television Broadcast, Oct. 19, 2003) [hereinafter *60 Minutes*].

43. Judith Miller et al., "U.S. Germ Warfare Research Pushes Treaty Limits," *NEW YORK TIMES*, Sept. 4, 2001, at A1 ("Pentagon experts assembled a germ factory in the Nevada desert from commercially available materials. Pentagon officials said the project demonstrated the ease with which a terrorist or rogue nation could build a plant that could produce pounds of the deadly germs.").

44. *Biological Weapons Convention Protocols: Status and Implications: Hearing Before the Subcommittee on National Security, Veterans Affairs, and International Relations of the House Comm. On Gov't Reform*, 107th Cong. (2001) (testimony of Edward Lacey, Principal Deputy Assistant Secretary, Verification and Compliance, Department of State).

45. *Id.*

46. President George W. Bush, *supra* note 23.

47. "Former Chief Inspector Testifies on Iraq WMD," *FOX NEWS*, Jan 28, 2004, *available at* http://www.foxnews.com/printer_friendly_story/0,3566,109701,00.html (last visited Feb. 22, 2004).

48. Peter Slevin, "Powell Voices Doubts About Iraqi Weapons," *WASHINGTON POST*, Jan. 25, 2004, at A14; David E. Sanger, "Administration's Message on War in Iraq Now Strikes Discordant Note," *NEW YORK TIMES*, Feb. 7, 2004, at A8; Douglas Jehl and Eric Schmitt, "Rumsfeld and Tenet Defending Assessment of Iraqi Weapons," *NEW YORK TIMES*, Feb. 5, 2004, at A1.

49. Thom Shanker and David E. Sanger, "North Korea Hides New Nuclear Site, Evidence Suggest," *NEW YORK TIMES*, July 20, 2003, at A1; Mark Landler, "U.N. Atom Agency Gives Iran Both a Slap and a Pass," *NEW YORK TIMES*, Nov. 27, 2003, at A22; David E. Sanger and Neil MacFarquhar, "Bush to Portray Libya as Example," *NEW YORK TIMES*, Jan. 20, 2004, at A1; Michael R. Gordon, "Giving up Those Weapons: After Libya, Who is Next?," *NEW YORK TIMES*, Jan. 1, 2004, at A10.

50. James Risen, "Report Faults C.I.A.'s Recruitment Rules," *NEW YORK TIMES*, July 18, 2002, at A14; Bruce Berkowitz, "The Nation: Terrorists Talk; Why All that Chatter Doesn't Tell Us Much," *NEW YORK TIMES*, Feb. 16, 2003, at A5; Douglas Jehl, "Tenet Concedes Gaps in C.I.A. Data on Iraqi Weapons," *NEW YORK TIMES*, Feb. 6, 2004, at A1.

51. Douglas Jehl, "The Struggle for Iraq: Intelligence; C.I.A. Needs to Learn Arabic, House Committee Leader Says," *NEW YORK TIMES*, Nov. 5, 2003, at A14.

52. Directorate of Intelligence, Central Intelligence Agency, *The Darker Bioweapons Future*, Nov. 3, 2003, at http://www.fas.org/irp/cia/product/bw1103.pdf (last visited Mar. 1, 2004).

53. "SARS Could be Biological Weapon: Experts," *ABC ONLINE*, April 11, 2003, at http://www.abc.net.au/news/newsitems/s830628.htm (last visited Feb. 22, 2004) [hereinafter *ABC ONLINE*]; Delthia Ricks, *supra* note 41; Eric Sabo, "Mad Cow as Bioterrorism?," *THE SCIENTIST*, Jan. 15, 2004, at

http://www.biomedcentral.com/news/20040115/04 (last visited Feb. 22, 2004).

54. JASON, The MITRE Corp., *Biodetection Architectures*, at http://www.fas.org/irp/agency/dod/jason/biodet.pdf (last visited Feb. 22, 2004).

55. Ceci Connolly, "Flu, Anthrax Similarities Stir Concern," *WASHINGTON POST*, Oct. 26, 2001, at A17; Tracy Wheeler, "SARS, flu tough to tell apart," *THE NATIONAL FLU SURVEILLANCE NETWORK*, at http://www.fluwatch.com/output news_1.cfm?pageid = 65&ID=188 (last visited Feb. 22, 2004).

56. Marilyn W. Thompson, "DNA Analysis of Ricin Could Track Source," *WASHINGTON POST*, Feb. 8, 2004, at All.

57. Alex Kirby, "Better Bio-Weapons Controls Urged," *BBC NEWS*, Jan. 19, 2004, *at* http://news.bbc.co.uk/2/hi/science/nature/3403957.stm (last visited Feb. 22, 2004).

58. Broad and Johnston, *supra* note 16.

59. See Scott P. Layne, "Virtually Assured Detection and Response: Utilizing Science, Technology, and Policy against Bioterrorism," *in BIOLOGICAL THREATS AND TERRORISM: Assessing the Science and Response Capabilities* 211 (S.L. Knobler et al., eds., 2002).

60. *Id.* at 212–14.

61. Carly Geehr, "Profs Criticize U.S. Patriot Act," *Stan. Daily*, Nov. 8, 2002, *at* http://daily.stanford.edu/tempo?page=content&id=9438&repository=0001 article (last visited Feb. 22, 2004); Albert H. Teich, "Will Science Become Another Victim of 9-11?," *at* http://www.aaas.org/news/releases/2003/0408teich2.shtml (last visited Feb. 22, 2004); Peg Brickley, "Sweeping Controls on Select Agents," *THE SCIENTIST*, Dec. 12, 2002, *at* http://www.biomedcentral.com/ news/20021212/06/ (last visited Feb. 22, 2004).

62. Judith Miller, "New Biolabs Stir Debate Over Secrecy and Safety," *NEW YORK TIMES*, Feb. 10, 2004, at F1.

63. *60 Minutes, supra* note 42.

64. Lee Hockstader, "Texas Plague Expert Convicted of Fraud," *WASHINGTON POST*, Dec. 2, 2003, at A2.

65. Connolly, *supra* note 42; *60 Minutes, supra* note 42; John Dudley Miller, "More Support for Butler: New York Academy of Sciences Criticizes Government Treatment of Plague Researcher," *THE SCIENTIST*, Sept. 22, 2003, at http://www.biomedcentral.com/news/20030922/07 (last visited Feb. 22, 2004).

66. Kenneth Chang, "Scientists' Panel Defends Researcher in Bacteria Smuggling Case," *NEW YORK TIMES*, Aug. 30, 2003, at A16.

67. Michael Stroh, "Tougher Visa Rules to Stop Terrorism Hamper Research; Many Foreign

Scientists Delayed or Prevented from Coming to the U.S.," *Baltimore Sun*, July 13, 2003, at 1A.

68. International students comprised 36 percent of all graduate enrollments in United States science and engineering fields in 2000, according to data from the Commission on Professionals in Science and Technology (CPST). Ginger Pinholster, American Association for the Advancement of Science, "Fear of 'Foreigners' May Slow Scientific Progress," June 6, 2003, at http://www.aaas.org/news/releases/2003/0606xeno.shtml (last visited Feb. 22, 2004).

69. David Malakoff, "Security Rules Leave Labs Wanting More Guidance," 299 *Science* 1175 (Feb. 21, 2003).

70. In 2002, the American Society for Microbiology was one of the first associations to issue policy guidelines for publishing material of a sensitive nature in their journals. American Society for Microbiology, *Policy Guidelines of the Publications Board of the ASM in the Handling of Manuscripts Dealing with Microbiological Sensitive Issues* (August 2002), at http://journals.asm.org/misc/Pathogens and Toxins.shtml (last visited Feb. 22, 2004). In early 2003, editors and authors of the leading science journals released a statement setting out tenets governing the publication of potentially dangerous articles. Journal Editors and Authors Group, "Uncensored Exchange of Scientific Results," 100 *Proceedings of the National Academy of Sciences* 1464 (Feb. 18, 2003), http:// www.pnas.org/cgi/content/full/100/4/1464 (last visited Feb. 22, 2004).

71. Tina Hesman, "Critics Question Journals' Bow to Security," *St. Louis Dispatch*, Feb. 23, 2003, at B5.

72. Rick Weiss, "Engineered Virus Related to Smallpox Evades Vaccine," *Washington Post*, Nov. 1, 2003, at A1 ("The lead researcher, virologist Mark Buller of Saint Louis University, said he has already heard from many people distressed about his work, details of which he presented at a scientific meeting in Geneva recently. 'I've received all this hate mail,' he said.").

73. *Id.*

74. William J. Broad, "A Nation Challenged: Domestic Security; U.S. is Tightening Rules on Keeping Scientific Secrets," *New York Times*, Feb. 17, 2002, at A1; Diana Jean Schemo, "Sept. 11 Strikes at Labs' Doors," *New York Times*, Aug. 13, 2002, at F1; Willie Schatz, "*Science Publishing Versus Security: Meeting Explores Balance Between Openness and Defense of Sensitive Data,*" *The Scientist*, Jan. 13, 2003, at http://www.biomedcentral.com/news/20030113/07/(last visited Feb. 22, 2004).

75. *United States v. Progressive,* 467 F. Supp. 990, 996 (W.D. Wis. 1979), *appeal dismissed* 610 F. 2d 819 (7th Cir. 1979).

76. *Id.* at 994.

77. Ceci Connolly, "Smallpox Vaccine Comes Full Circle," *Washington Post,* March 16, 2003, at A28.

78. The government held Top Official (TOPOFF) Exercises, including a simulated plague outbreak, in May 2000, and an exercise simulating the release of smallpox entitled *Dark Winter* in 2001. Scott R. Lillibridge, Special Assistant to the Secretary for National Security and Emergency Management, Dept. of Health and Human Services, *HHS Bioterrorism Preparedness*, Statement of Testimony before the House Subcommittee on Oversight and Investigations, Committee on Energy and Commerce (Oct. 10, 2001), at http://www.hhs.gov/asl/testify/t011010a.html (last visited Feb. 22, 2004). The government held further exercises (TOPOFF 2) in Seattle and Chicago in spring 2003. Frank James and Gary Washburn, "Simulated attacks called valuable; Terror exercises exposed flaws in communications," *Chicago Tribune*, Dec. 20, 2003, at C16.

79. Thomas A. Glass and Monica Schoch-Spana, "Bioterrorism and the People: How to Vaccinate a City against Panic," 34 *Clinical Infectious Diseases* 217 (2002).

80. When the 2004 influenza strain proved to be unexpectedly virulent, shortages of the vaccination caused many people to go into "semi-panic mode." Avi Salzman, "The Flu Steps in and the Wary Wait," *New York Times*, Dec. 14, 2003, at N3. In the early 1990s, federal health officials warned that tuberculosis, a disease they hoped to have eradicated by 2010, was on the increase rather than decrease. The experts say they began losing the war with the disease when financial support for the disease was cut in the mid-1980s. Lawrence K. Altman, "Americans Aren't Being Protected Against Tuberculosis Panel Says," *New York Times*, Dec. 7, 1991, at sec. 1, p. 17.

81. One example of an activity that does not confer collateral benefits on other public health efforts is stockpiling vaccines and antidotes to prepare for a bioterrorism attack. While stockpiling is necessary to prevent lack of supply and the panic it would engender in the event of an attack, it drains funds from a limited pool. The 2004 flu vaccine shortage demonstrates the dilemma. Companies overprepared vaccine for 2003, and so prepared less for the 2004 season. Lawrence K. Altman, "U.S. Considers Importing Influenza Vaccine," *New York Times*, Dec. 10, 2003, at A27. When a more virulent strain struck widely, the public rushed to be

vaccinated and drained supplies, which could not be replenished.

82. Ceci Connolly, "Smallpox Campaign Taxing Health Resources; Program Siphons Funds, Staffing from Other Projects, State and Local Officials Say," WASHINGTON POST, March 10, 2003, at A4; Lawrence K. Altman, "Smallpox Effort Putting Drain on Care, Local Agencies Warn," CHICAGO TRIBUNE, Jan. 5, 2003, at C13.

83. Directorate of Intelligence, *supra* note 52.

84. *ABC ONLINE, supra* note 53.

85. Cronin, *supra* note 19 at ii. ("Although it can have a powerful psychological impact, past [chemical and biological weapons] use by terrorists has been rare and has not caused a large number of casualties,

especially compared to other weapons. Terrorist attacks are deliberately designed to surprise, so no trend analysis will ever perfectly predict them, especially in the contemporary international climate.").

86. BROWER AND CHALK, *supra* note 18.

87. Chyba, *supra* note 37.

88. Connolly, *supra* note 82; Stephen Smith, "Anthrax vs. the Flu as State Governments Slash their Public Health Budgets, Federal Money is Pouring in for Bioterror Preparedness," BOSTON GLOBE, July 29, 2003, at C1.

89. Marilynn Marchione, "Nation steps up its bioterrorism preparations; Year after anthrax attacks, health agencies have more tests, vaccines," MILWAUKEE J. SENTINEL, Sept. 15, 2002, at 1A.

DISCUSSION QUESTIONS

1. Weapons of Mass Destruction include nuclear, chemical, and biological weapons. Identify how different characteristics of these types of weapons require different measures to prevent and respond to an attack.

2. What do you see as the biggest challenges posed by the threat of bioterrorism? How would you deal with the threat if you were in charge?

3. Consider the complications that the dual use dilemma presents. Are there some types of scientific information that should not be published? Are there certain types of scientific experiments that should not be done? How should these things be defined and who should define them?

4. What international measures are necessary to supplement United States bioterrorism defense? How should they be implemented?

5. In the event of a bioterrorism attack, would mass quarantine such as portrayed in the movie *Outbreak* be appropriate? Would it be feasible? What civil liberties issues would arise?

6. How should the government prepare in advance to respond to an infectious disease epidemic, either naturally occurring or intentionally inflicted?

7. How should limited resources be allocated among bioterrorism and other public health threats?

8. In what ways do bioterrorism defense measures also address other disease threats?

9. In what ways does bioterrorism defense spending detract from other public health goals?

Chapter 16

UNDERSTANDING THE "DIRTY BOMB" AND ITS POLICY IMPLICATIONS

MICHAEL P. DONOHUE

The use of traditional nuclear weapons has been part of the American psyche for well over 50 years.[1] For many of the most recent years the concern revolved around unsubstantiated rumors that the Soviet Union had manufactured and subsequently lost a number of small suitcase sized nuclear bombs.[2] Public concern regarding nuclear weapons and terrorist activity in the United States was primarily focused on the assumed existence of these small conventional-type nuclear weapons.[3] However, on May 8, 2002, that public focus shifted with the revelation that terrorist organizations, including al Quaida, had been attempting and may have even built a type of nuclear weapon called a "dirty bomb."[4] On that date it was revealed that a former youth gang member and Muslim convert named Jose Padilla had been arrested in Chicago by the U.S. Department of Justice on suspicion of attempted domestic terrorism.[5] Specifically, U.S. officials had developed intelligence that linked Padilla to the al Quaida terrorist group and their plan to build and detonate a radioactive "dirty bomb" in the United States.[6] Although the potential manufacture, acquisition, or eventual use of a traditional thermonuclear device as a *Weapon of Mass Destruction* (WMD) has been seen as a remote possibility, most current speculation today surrounds the more probable use of radioactive materials in a "dirty bomb" as a *Weapon of Mass Contamination.*[7] This chapter will attempt to explore some of the details of what a "dirty bomb" is, how a terrorist might access the necessary nuclear materials to build such a bomb, what organizations and countries have already attempted to build or detonate a dirty bomb, what the federal and state response to this type of nuclear disaster might encompass, cleanup issues after a detonation, medical treatments following exposure to the radioactive debris, and finally, some thoughts on what improvements might be made to help prevent a dirty bomb from being built or detonated in the United States in the first place.

I. THE DIRTY BOMB

A. Nature of the Dirty Bomb

A "dirty bomb" is essentially a device that combines a conventional explosive, like dynamite, with radioactive materials to form a type of hybrid nuclear weapon.[8] These weapons are technically known as a Radiological Dispersion Devices (RDD).[9] These devices use mechanical and/or explosive means to spread highly radioactive materials over an area in an effort to contaminate that area for years, possibly centuries.[10] Because these weapons damage by dispersing radioactivity,

---

Note: Michael P. Donohue is a fourth-year evening division student at the Windener University School of Law.

the radioactive material used in a dirty bomb necessarily takes the physical form of powder or pellets so that the nuclear material can be spread over an area by the detonation of the conventional explosive.[11]

This so-called dirty bomb is a different kind of device than that which usually comes to mind when the words nuclear weapon are mentioned. Traditional nuclear weapons essentially involve a detonation that causes the uncontrolled fission or splitting of atoms. For example, the nuclear weapons detonated over the Japanese cities of Hiroshima and Nagasaki during World War II[12] and the California/Nevada deserts during the 1950s[13] were conventional nuclear weapons using nuclear fission as the destructive force. Conventional nuclear weapons do their damage primarily through mass destruction of large areas resulting from a fission-induced blast, and only damage secondarily through nuclear fallout and contamination.[14] RDDs or dirty bombs on the other hand do their damage primarily by spreading and contaminating smaller areas with radioactive material and only secondarily damage through the blast of their traditional explosives.[15] Essentially, the primary use of a dirty bomb is to terrify by inducing fear and panic by dispersing through the air nuclear material to contaminate people and property.[16] Thus, while a dirty bomb will not have the capacity to destroy everything in its immediate vicinity, it will have the capacity to deliver "significant negative social, financial, and emergency management impacts" on local communities, states, and the nation.[17]

B. Makings of a Dirty Bomb

A dirty bomb is the type of nuclear-based weapon you build if you do not have the ability or resources to construct a conventional-type nuclear device.[18] Essentially, you wrap radioactive material with the most powerful explosive you can find.[19] The process is fairly straightforward provided a terrorist or some other person has access to a supply of traditional explosives and radioactive material.[20] The question then becomes what kind of radioactive material is potentially usable in a dirty bomb and where are the most likely places a terrorist might obtain this material. The answers are somewhat surprising.

Over the course of the last decade, there have been nearly 200 cases of terrorist and criminal incidents involving the smuggling or attempted procurement of radioactive materials.[21] However, not all radioactive materials are suitable for use in dirty bombs. Only those materials that can be reduced to powder or pellet form can be effectively dispersed through the air by way of an explosion.[22] Dr. Charles Ferguson, a scientist in residence at the Center for Nonproliferation Studies in Washington DC, reports that there are at least seven radioactive isotopes that pose inherent radiological security risks in the context of dirty bombs.[23] These isotopes are americium-241, californium-252, cesium-137, cobalt-60, iridium-192, plutonium-238, and strontium-90.[24] Each of these isotopes is artificially produced in a nuclear reactor.[25] Three of these isotopes, americium-241, cobalt-60 and cesium-137, are particularly well suited to use in a dirty bomb because of their potential for conversion into a dispersible form, the ease of availability, and the somewhat lengthy amount of time it takes for the radioactivity to subside.[26] These various radioactive isotopes have been widely used throughout the world for decades in hospitals, factories, and laboratories for the treatment of cancer, food sanitation, safety devices, and coastal navigation.[27] Thus, there are potentially millions of sources worldwide and controls to prevent them from being lost or stolen are poor in over 100 countries.[28]

For example, in September of 1987, a scrap yard worker in Goiania, Brazil, brought home and opened a lead canister scavenged from a medical device abandoned at a former cancer treatment center.[29] Inside the can was sparkling blue radioactive cesium.[30] The material was passed around from home to home for about a week, exposing over 112,000 people to the radioactivity.[31]

The situation in the former Soviet Union is even more serious. The General Accounting Office reported in June of 2003 that thousands of containers of radioactive materials that could be used to build dirty bombs are missing throughout the region. For example, in December of 2001, three woodcutters in Lja, Georgia, found heat emanating from two lead containers they found in the woods.[32] The woodcutters took the containers back to their camp to use as a heat source and within hours had become ill with radiation sickness.[33] What they had found were the remains of two abandoned Soviet-era radiothermal generators, each holding a flashlight size core of strontium-90, enough strontium to equal the amount of radiation released at Chernobyl during that nuclear accident.[34]

In August of 2003, a 44-year-old elementary school teacher from Bangkok was arrested for attempting to sell .035 ounces of cesium-137, which had been kept at the home of a Thai air force officer prior to his death, for $240,000.[35] The cesium's lead container was marked with Soviet-era designations and was thought to have been in Thailand for at least seven years.[36]

More recently, during the Iraq War, seven of Iraq's main nuclear facilities were extensively looted.[37] In particular, the Tuwaitha Nuclear Storage Facility near Baghdad was looted of a minimum of 22 pounds of uranium.[38] Other sites in Iraq were looted of cesium, strontium, and cobalt.[39] No one is sure where these materials are currently stored or whether they are still even in Iraq.[40]

In the United States, radioactive materials are in use in over 100 nuclear power plants and are contained in several million medical and industrial devices.[41] For instance, cobalt-60 is used by hospitals in radiation therapy and in the food-processing industry; cesium-137 is used in medical gauges and radio therapy machines, and americium is used in smoke detectors.[42] While the Nuclear Regulatory Commission (NRC) is responsible for the licensing and regulation of these devices, there is no national database for tracking the included radioactive materials.[43] According to the International Atomic Energy Agency (IAEA), U.S. companies since 1996 have lost approximately 1,500 radiation sources, 750 of which have never been recovered.[44] The NRC estimates that approximately one licensed source of radioactive material is lost or orphaned each day.[45] For example, in March of 1998, 19 tubes of cesium were discovered missing from a hospital in North Carolina.[46] Despite an extensive search by local, state, and federal officials using sophisticated detection equipment, the cesium was never recovered.[47]

There is even the strong and very potential possibility of purchasing dirty bomb usable material from legal suppliers in the open market.[48] Radioactive materials can and are purchased fairly easily in the overseas markets from legitimate suppliers who are under no absolute requirement to verify the license of the U.S. end user.[49] In fact, the United Nations International Atomic Energy Agency (IAEA) reported that "more than 100 countries 'may have no minimum infrastructure in place to properly control radiation sources.'"[50] Furthermore, there are apparently few real stumbling blocks for getting the material into the country[51] although that state of affairs appears to be changing.[52]

Other possibilities for gaining access to nuclear materials in the United States focus less on actual possession of radioactive material and more on acquiring access to targets of existing material for dispersal. For example, the federal government has for some years been planning to move the nation's radioactive waste to a central geologic site in the Yucca Mountains of the Southern Nevada desert.[53] Currently, there is approximately 70,000 metric tons of radioactive material to be placed at the site.[54] The material must be transported by rail and truck from sites scattered across the nation both commercial and military.[55] The Department of Energy's own environmental impact statement suggests that the process will take years to complete at three to six shipments per day, 365 days per year, over 25 or more years.[56] This radioactive material is so hazardous that it must be shielded from the environment for 10,000 years.[57] These shipments represent a substantial source of radioactive material for dispersal even though the federal government has downplayed its danger.[58] The issue of "terrorist vulnerable" transportation of nuclear materials has in the past evoked strong feelings between the states and the federal government over the likelihood of danger from terrorist attack on transported radioactive material.[59] That controversy is likely to continue.

Thus, there are a multitude of potential sources for radioactive material available for use in a dirty bomb domestically, through overseas smuggling, and legal purchase. The vast numbers of lost domestic sources coupled with the almost overwhelming overseas problems, particularly in Russia, are extremely troubling. The potential for a terrorist disaster is seemingly enormous and the likelihood of an attempt should never be discounted given the hard lessons learned of terrorist ingenuity after the Oklahoma City and World Trade Center disasters.

II. POTENTIAL EFFECTS OF A DIRTY BOMB DETONATION

Currently, the most available estimates suggest that only one country has ever successfully built and detonated a dirty bomb.[60] In 1987, Iraq successfully detonated a test device but abandoned the program because the radioactive fallout was apparently not sufficient to be an effective military weapon.[61] Other groups have come close to detonation of a dirty bomb. In December of 1995, Chechen separatists placed a shielded cancer treatment device containing cesium-137 surrounded by dynamite in a Moscow park.[62] The separatists alerted the Russian authorities as to the bomb's location but the bomb itself was never detonated.[63]

In the late 1990s, Osama bin Laden's al Quaida organization failed in its attempt to produce and detonate a dirty bomb while training in the Sudan. However, information recently found in the caves of Afghanistan and corroborated by al Quaida prisoners strongly suggests the organization may have another dirty bomb with which to threaten the world.[64] With so much current interest in radiological dispersal devices by terrorist organizations, the question becomes what would be the potential effect on people and property from a successful detonation of a dirty bomb here in the United States.

It is generally conceded that a dispersal-type radiological attack like a dirty bomb would in fact result in a number of deaths.[65] However, the detonation of this type of device in an urban area would not result in the hundreds of thousands of fatalities that could be caused by even a crude fission-based nuclear weapon.[66] Rather, the physical effects of a dirty bomb are centered on long-term contamination of people and property.[67]

Contamination of property with fallout from a dirty bomb would result in significant economic losses. A report from the Center for Technology

and National Security Policy at the National Defense University estimated that the economic impact of a dirty bomb could easily surpass the impact made by the terrorist attacks in New York on September 11, 2001.[68] The report notes that while a majority of the cleanup expense for the September 11 tragedy was paid through insurance, no such coverage exists for the cleanup of radiological debris.[69] As an example, 50 grams of cesium-137 detonated with as little as 10 pounds of dynamite could potentially contaminate an area of 40 city blocks.[70] A dirty bomb manufactured out of a single one-inch by one-foot rod of cobalt-60, commonly found all over the United States in food irradiation plants, could potentially contaminate approximately three hundred city blocks.[71] In each case, if decontamination were not possible, the area would have to be abandoned for decades resulting in tremendous property and economic losses.[72]

Potential health injuries to persons exposed to radiological contamination resulting from a dirty bomb would also be significant. Health injuries from radiological contamination generally take two forms; deterministic injuries and stochastic injuries.[73] Deterministic injuries are injuries characterized by outward signs of exposure to radioactive contaminates like radiation sickness and burns.[74] Stochastic injuries are latent unidentifiable injuries in which it is not possible to accurately determine whether a person exposed to radiological contamination will develop an associated disease or illness like cancer.[75] Thus, the health effects of a dirty bomb detonation are both immediate and delayed with the increased potential for health issues well past the period after the release of the radiological contaminate.

III. RESPONSE TO A DIRTY BOMB

A. Governmental

Virtually all governmental units have some type of plan in place to address a radiological disaster.[76] Attempting to discuss, even in a general way, the

myriad variations of local and state radiological response plans is well outside the scope of this chapter. However, all local and state governmental units look to the federal government and the Federal Radiological Emergency Response Plan

(FRERP) for assistance when the effects of a radiological disaster overwhelm their abilities and resources to deal with the emergency. Thus, I will limit the scope of this section to a very brief discussion of the federal response under the FRERP.

The Federal Radiological Emergency Response Plan is the operational plan that assists federal agencies in the discharge of their statutorily mandated responsibility of rendering assistance during a peacetime radiological emergency.[77] This plan was originally developed by the Federal Emergency Management Agency (FEMA) with the assistance of 17 other federal agencies.[78] The FRERP was made effective on May 8, 1996.[79] FEMA and the FRERP were transferred to the Department of Homeland Security on November 27, 2002, under the Homeland Security Act as an attempt to unify all federal agency actions related to disasters, accidents, and terrorism, including nuclear contamination disasters like a dirty bomb detonation.[80]

The FRERP plan itself is incorporated as part of the National Response Plan which establishes the overall process and procedures "for the systematic, coordinated and effective delivery of federal assistance" to address the consequences of federally declared disasters and emergencies.[81] Under the National Response Plan (FRP), FEMA is tasked as the lead agency to implement and manage the Federal Radiological Emergency Response Plan's *nonradiological* support efforts during a radiological disaster.[82] Concurrent *radiological* support efforts are generally tasked to the Environmental Protection Agency under the FRP as the lead agency to implement and manage the federal response when the radiological contamination is from unknown sources like a dirty bomb.[83] Each of these lead agencies has the ability to utilize any number of other federal agencies to carry out the needs of the lead agency's response.[84] Generally speaking, each subordinate federal agency that is providing support for either radiological or nonradiological issues will remain active in that role until the "conditions of the emergency have stabilized and immediate actions to protect public health and safety and property have been accomplished."[85]

Thus, based on the very limited discussion above, the federal response to a dirty bomb disaster will generally hinge on whether the local or state response to the radiological contamination becomes overwhelmed to the point of outstripping the local and state resources. Once the local and state resources are deemed inadequate, a federal disaster can be declared and the FRERP can be activated. Lead agencies are then informed, and actions to protect people, health, and property are taken by the federal agencies to assist the local and state governments.

B. Cleanup

Effective cleanup procedures for dealing with the aftermath of a dirty bomb are problematic.[86] Currently, there is no way to neutralize radioactive materials that have been dispersed by a dirty bomb.[87] Furthermore, there are no proven methods to effectively and completely decontaminate existing buildings or areas of land by isolation and/or removal of contaminated material.[88] The problem is complicated because several of the radiological materials that could be used in a dirty bomb like cesium and cobalt can chemically bind to concrete, asphalt, and soil.[89] Other materials would simply lodge in the crevices of buildings and sidewalks becoming almost impossible to remove given the overwhelming number of potential places for contaminate settlement.[90] Decontamination options include aggressive removal of radiological contaminates by abrasive, chemical, or hydro blasting.[91] However, even assuming these techniques would effectively remove the radiological contamination, each process presents its own inherent problems.[92] Water washes would create massive amounts of radioactive and thus toxic runoff that could potentially spread contamination well beyond the immediate effected area.[93] Abrasive blasting and chemical washes have similar disposal and containment issues.[94]

Some experts believe that the most viable method of cleanup is to tear down contaminated buildings and remove the soil from affected areas,[95] but this method of decontamination is not without problems. The Gonada accident is potentially the best example of the problems inherent in this method of cleanup.[96] Decontamination was possible only with destruction and removal of buildings and soil but equipment, training, and disposal issues, including accidents involving the trucks transporting the contaminated material, became major challenges.[97] Even today, after extensive cleanup and re-cleanup procedures were completed, some areas still remain contaminated and the general thought is that there is probably no way to absolutely and completely clean the area of radioactive material.[98]

C. Medical Treatment

In general, there are three elementary principles of protection for all radiological disasters.[99] Minimization of the time you spend in a contaminated area, maximization of the distance between yourself and the contamination, and maximization of shielding between yourself and the contamination.[100] When this tripartite of safety is not possible or effective, medical treatment is absolutely necessary.[101]

Most medical treatment for exposure to radiological fallout from a dirty bomb focuses initially on decontamination of the outer body and treatment of external and internal deterministic injuries received through direct exposure to contaminate material that has been ingested, inhaled, or absorbed through the skin.[102] Treatment for internal contamination is focused on attempts to reduce the radiation exposure received by the internal organs and associated structures.[103] Thus, treatments focus on decontamination by flushing out as many of the internal organs as possible.

For a number of years, the internal use of potassium iodide (KI) was one of the more publicly touted measures for protection against radiological exposure.[104] The problem with this blanket use of potassium iodide as a treatment is that it is only effective if the isotope involved is radioactive iodine and the potassium iodide was taken prior to exposure.[105] As discussed earlier, radioactive iodine has not been identified as an isotope that would lend itself to dirty bomb use either because of availability problems or dispersal problems. Thus, the general use of potassium iodide as a preventative or posttreatment for all radiological

exposures would be ineffective for most if not all dirty bomb detonations.[106] Fortunately, there have been some medical advancements in the field of internal treatment for radiological contamination.

In 2003, the FDA approved the use of two chemical compounds for the treatment of internal radiological contamination of the body. In early 2003, the FDA announced that ferric hexacyanoferrate or Prussian Blue, could be an effective treatment for cesium-137 and thallium exposure.[107] Prussian Blue is a color pigment first synthesized in 1704. The pigment has been medically investigated for treatment of radiological contamination since the 1960s because of its discovered ability to trap thallium or cesium contamination in the intestine, interrupt its absorption into the body, facilitating removal by excretion and thus reducing internal levels of radioactivity.[108] In September of 2003, the FDA announced their conclusions that another family of compounds, pentetate calcium trisodium and pentetate zinc trisodium, were effective in isolating, binding through chelation, and facilitating removal through the urinary tract plutonium, americium, and curium from the body.[109] However, while these treatments are available and claimed effective, many experts do not regard them as a panacea and recommend a healthy skepticism regarding the medical effectiveness of either compound until there has been adequate testing.[110] There are other more involved treatment options available but decontamination of both the external and internal structures of the body are the first-line defenses.[111]

Treatment is just the tip of the medical iceberg. Other incidental issues lie just under the surface including cross-contamination of other patients, doctors, and health care workers; disposal of the eliminated waste material; and contamination of the treatment equipment.[112] One thing should be clear: radiological decontamination and postexposure treatment are not well defined, highly effective, or well practiced and those facts add to the unknown and thus the terror of the threat.

IV. CONCLUSION

It is apparent that there are definite weaknesses in the current system that makes the use of a dirty bomb in this country both appealing and possible

to a terrorist. There are probably no perfect solutions to this ongoing issue but there are actions to take in which we can improve our chances in the area of detection and prevention. The following nonexclusive suggestions may be ways in which we can make our country less attractive to a would-be dirty bomber.

First, it is absolutely imperative that we severely limit access to radiological materials. Cradle-to-grave oversight by one central agency with plenary authority over all domestic production, foreign importation, and domestic use and disposal of radioactive materials should be adopted. This agency must have a full array of enforcement actions available to meet its mandate of public protection including both civil and criminal penalties. Strict adherence to agency authority should be the legal duty of care for anyone who is working with radiological materials.

Second, we should substantially increase funding to provide the strictest port and border security in the world. Every mode of transportation and cargo that enters into the country should be subjected to a screening by radiation detection and X-ray equipment. In terms of port activity, funding for these programs should necessarily come at the expense of those who wish to avail themselves of our domestic market. Just the consistent and frequent use of these tests should go a long way in discouraging some would-be terrorists bent on importing their materials of terror into the United States.

Third, we should make it a point to increase funding to organizations that are the front-line educators of those who would be expected to respond to a radiological disaster. It is unethical and immoral to ask those tasked with the job of responding to this kind of a disaster to do so without a good faith effort to properly train and equip them.

Finally, we should ensure an adequate supply of whatever medications are currently thought to be helpful in the treatment and prevention of sickness and disease resulting from exposure to a dirty bomb.

In conclusion, there is much work to be done if we wish to be truly proactive in our quest to deter, prevent, or respond to the dirty bomb threat. The issue of radiological exposure is both real and possible, which makes it all the more frightening. Constant and continual diligence and an ever improving system of detection and prevention may be the best approach to the dirty bomb scenario.

ENDNOTES

1. See Kia Bird & Martin Sherwin, "The First Line Against Terorism," *Washington Post*, Dec. 12, 2001, at A35.
2. Tony Karon, "The 'Dirty Bomb' Scenario," *Time Magazine*, June 10, 2002.
3. See *Id*.
4. *Id*.
5. See, *Padilla v. Bush*, 233 F. Supp. 2d 564 (S.D.N.Y. 2002).
6. Charles Lane, "Court Accepts Case of 'Dirty Bomb' Suspect," *Washington Post*, February 21, 2004 at A4.
7. James J. Ballard & Kristine Mullendore, (February 2003). "Weapons of Mass Victimization, Radioactive Waste Shipments, and Environmental Laws; Policy Making and First Responders," *American Behavioral Scientist*, 46(6), p. 770.
8. *Fact Sheet: Dirty Bombs*, United States Nuclear Regulatory Commission, available at www.nrc.gov/reading-rm/doc-collections/fact-sheets/dirty-bombs.html, last visited on February 25, 2004.
9. *Id*.
10. James J. Ballard & Kristine Mullendore, (February 2003). "Weapons of Mass Victimization, Radioactive Waste Shipments, and Environmental Laws; Policy Making and First Responders," *American Behavioral Scientist*, 46(6), p. 766, 770.
11. See, *Fact Sheet: Dirty Bombs*, Center for Disease Control and Prevention, available at www.cdc.gov/radiation, last visited on February 25, 2004.
12. *Id*.
13. See Peter Jennings & Todd Brewster, *The Century*, pp. 280–281 (Doubleday Books, 1998). In 1951, the government began a series of atomic tests in the California/Nevada deserts. Mushroom clouds became a regular part of the Las Vegas skyline. Nearly 50 years later, the federal government admitted that the fallout from those tests may have caused up to 75,000 cases of thyroid cancer.
14. See supra note 11.
15. See *Id*.

16. Peter D. Zimmerman & Cheryl Loeb, (January 2004). "Dirty Bombs: The Threat Revisited," *Defense Horizons* 38, p. 2.

17. James J. Ballard & Kristine Mullendore, (February 2003). "Weapons of Mass Victimization, Radioactive Waste Shipments, and Environmental Laws; Policy Making and First Responders," *American Behavioral Scientist*, 46(6), pp. 766, 770.

18. Dr. David Whitehouse, *Analysis: Making a "dirty bomb*," BBC News World Americas, available at http://newsvote.bbc.co.uk/1/hi/world/americas, last visited on February 25, 2004.

19. *Facts about "dirty bombs" for Industrial Hygienists*, The American Industrial Hygiene Association, available at http://www.aiha.org/GovernmentAffairs-PR/html/pr-dirtybomb.htm, last visited on February 25, 2004.

20. Dr. David Whitehouse, *Analysis: Making a "dirty bomb*," BBC News World Americas, available at http://newsvote.bbc.co.uk/1/hi/world/americas, last visited on February 25, 2004.

21. *Id.*

22. See *Fact Sheet: Dirty Bombs*, Center for Disease Control and Prevention, available at www.cdc.gov/radiation, last visited on February 25, 2004.

23. Charles Ferguson, Tahseen Kazi & Judith Perera, *Commercial Radioactive Sources: Surveying the Security Risks*, Occasional Paper No. 11, Center for Nonproliferation Studies, available at www.cns.miis.edu/pubs/opapers/op11/index.htm, last visited on February 14, 2004.

24. *Id.*

25. *Id.*

26. Federation of American Scientist, available at www.fas.org/nuke, last visited on February 30, 2004. For example, cesium's radioactivity has a half life of 30 years, which simply means that after 30 years, fully half of the original radioactivity of cesium remains as undecayed and thus dangerous. After 30 more years, one quarter of the original radiation remains. This 30-year pattern continues until all of the radiation has decayed.

27. Peter D. Zimmerman & Cheryl Loeb, "Dirty Bombs: The Threat Revisited," *Defense Horizons* 38, January 2004 at 2.

28. Rob Edwards, "Millions of Dirty Bomb Sources," NewScentist.com news service, June 25, 2002, available at www.newscientist.com/news/print.jsp?id=ns99992455 last visited on February 25, 2004.

29. Lexi Krock & Rebecca, "NOVA: Dirty Bombs, Chronology of Events," available at www.pbs.org/wgbh/nova/dirtybomb/chrono.html, last visited on February 25, 2004.

30. *Id.*

31. *Id.*

32. *Id.*

33. Lexi Krock & Rebecca, "NOVA: Dirty Bombs, Chronology of Events," available at www.pbs.org/wgbh/nova/dirtybomb/chrono.html, last visited on February 25, 2004.

34. *Id.*

35. James Hookway, "Unusual Suspect: Thai Principle had Cesium for Sale," *Wall Street Journal* (*Eastern Edition*), August 1, 2003 at A1.

36. Id.

37. Brett Wagner, "What Happened to Looted Iraqi Nuclear Material," *USA Today*, October 6, 2003, p. 23.

38. Andy Oppenheimer, "Dirty Bombs for the Taking," *World News Today*, July 2003, at p. 10.

39. Brett Wagner, "What Happened to Looted Iraqi Nuclear Material," *USA Today*, October 6, 2003, p. 23.

40. *Id.*

41. See *The Regulation and Use of Radioisotopes in Today's World*, U.S. Nuclear Regulatory Commission, available at http://www.nrc.gov/reading-rm/doc-collections/nuregs/brouchures/br0217/r1/br0217r1.pdf, last visited on April 15, 2004.

42. Henry Kelly, Michael Levi, Robert Nelson & Jaime Yassif, "Dirty Bombs: Response to a Threat," FAS Public Interest Report, 55 *Journal of the Federation of American Scientists* 6, March/April 2002.

43. Peter D. Zimmerman & Cheryl Loeb, "Dirty Bombs: The Threat Revisited," *Defense Horizons* 38, January 2004, p. 2.

44. International Atomic Agency (IAEA) at www.iaea.org/worldatom

45. Peter D. Zimmerman & Cheryl Loeb, "Dirty Bombs: The Threat Revisited," *Defense Horizons* 38, January 2004, p. 2.

46. Lexi Krock & Rebecca, "NOVA: Dirty Bombs, Chronology of Events," available at www.pbs.org/wgbh/nova/dirtybomb/chrono.html, last visited on February 25, 2004.

47. *Id.*

48. Supra note 45 at 3.

49. Peter D. Zimmerman & Cheryl Loeb, "Dirty Bombs: The Threat Revisited," *Defense Horizons* 38, January 2004, p. 3.

50. *Facts about "dirty bombs" for Industrial Hygienists*, The American Industrial Hygiene Association, available at http://www.aiha.org/GovernmentAffairs-PR/html/pr-dirtybomb.htm, last visited on February 25, 2004.

51. Supra note 49.

52. *See* 69 *Federal Register* 3698. On January 26, 2004, the NRC issued 69 FR 3698 which amended its regulations on packaging and transporting radioactive material to be compatible with the more comprehensive and traceable standards used by the International Atomic Energy Agency.

53. James J. Ballard & Kristine Mullendore, (February 2003). "Weapons of Mass Victimization, Radioactive Waste Shipments, and Environmental Laws; Policy Making and First Responders," *American Behavioral Scientist*, 46(6), pp. 766, 771.

54. *Id.*

55. *Id.* at 772.

56. James J. Ballard & Kristine Mullendore, (February 2003). "Weapons of Mass Victimization, Radioactive Waste Shipments, and Environmental Laws; Policy Making and First Responders," *American Behavioral Scientist*, 46(6), pp. 766, 772. (citing Department of Energy (1999), *Final Environmental Impact Statement for a Geological Repository for the Disposal of Spent Nuclear Fuel and High-level Radioactive Waste at Yucca Mountain, Nye County, Nevada* (DOE/EIS-0250D), Washington DC: U.S. Department of Energy, Office of Civilian Radioactive Waste Management).

57. *Id.*

58. *Id,* at 775–777.

59. *See United States Department of Energy v. Hodges*, 255 F. Supp. 2d 539 (D.S.C 2002). South Carolina Governor Jim Hodges attempted to block shipments of radioactive weapons grade plutonium to sites located within his state by declaring a state of emergency. He cited his concerns regarding the potential use of the shipments as a source of radioactive "dirty bomb" material and the recent "detention of a person suspected of 'planning to build and explode a radioactive dirty bomb'" as his reasons for interfering with the shipments. His attempt to block those shipments ultimately failed.

60. James Hookway, "Unusual Suspect: Principle Had Cesium For Sale," *Wall Street Journal (Eastern Edition)*, August 1, 2003, A1.

61. *Id.*

62. Andy Oppenheimer, "A Sickening Episode: Nuclear Looting in Iraq and the Global Threat From Radiological Weapons," 73 *Disarmament Diplomacy*, October–November 2003 available at http://www.acronym.org.uk/dd/dd73/73op03.htm, last visited on March 21, 2004.

63. See *Id.*

64. "Nuclear Material Found in al-Quaida Caves, Officials Say," *Knight-Ridder Newspapers* (Dec. 21, 2001) available at http://www.nci.org/01/12/22-04.htm, last visited on March 20, 2004.

65. Henry Kelly, Michael Levi, Robert Nelson & Jaime Yassif, "Dirty Bombs: Response to a Threat," FAS Public Interest Report, 55 *Journal of the Federation of American Scientists* 6, March/April 2002.

66. *Id.*

67. See *Id.*

68. "NDU Study Examines Impact of Dirty Bombs," DFI International, Homeland Security: Update, January 22, 2004, p. 2. Available at http://updates.dfi-intl.com, last visited on March 18, 2004.

69. *Id.*

70. Supra note 65 at 7.

71. *Id.* In this example, a cesium-based dirty bomb was theoretically detonated near the Capitol in Washington DC requiring the abandonment of the National Gallery of Art, the Capitol, Supreme Court, and the Library of Congress.

72. *Id.* This particular fact pattern was modeled on a detonation of a cobalt-based dirty bomb in downtown Manhattan. The economic result of having to abandon the area was estimated in the trillions of dollars.

73. Peter D. Zimmerman & Cheryl Loeb, "Dirty Bombs: The Threat Revisited," *Defense Horizons* 38, January 2004, p. 2.

74. *Id.*

75. *Id.*

76. See Mason Booth, "Mock Dirty Bomb "Detonated" as Homeland Security Drill Begins," *Red Cross In the News*, available at http://www.redcross.org/news/ds/terirism.html, last visited on February 25, 2004. On May 13, 2003, in Seattle, Washington, emergency managers and first responders held an extensive 2-day dirty bomb drill that focused on state and local responses to a radiological disaster.

77. *Federal Register, FEMA: Federal Radiological Emergency Response Plan*, available at http://www.nrt.org/production/nrt/home.nsf, last visited on March 17, 2004.

78. *Id.* at I(B)(1)-(17). These other federal agencies include the Departments of Agriculture, Commerce, Defense, Energy, Health and Human Services, Housing and Urban Development, Interior, Justice, State, Transportation, and Veterans Affairs, as well as the Environmental Protection Agency, Federal Emergency Management Agency, General Services Administration, National Aeronautics and Space Administration, National Communications System and the Nuclear Regulatory Commission. Each of

the agencies has responsibilities and capabilities that specifically pertain to radiological emergencies and can be utilized by state and local governments under FRERP to deal with a radiological disaster that outstrips the local and state ability to effectively respond.

79. *Id.*

80. William C. Nicholson, *Emergency Response and Emergency Management Law*, 255 n.18. (Charles Thomas Publisher, 2003).

81. *Id.* at 238.

82. *Federal Register, FEMA: Federal Radiological Emergency Response Plan*, available at http://www.nrt.org/ production/nrt/home.nsf, last visited on March 17, 2004. Nonradiological support is support that is not directly related to radiological monitoring and assessment.

83. *Id.* at II(D)(3)(b).

84. *Id.* at II(E)(1)(a).

85. *Id.* at II(E)(5)(a).

86. Peter D. Zimmerman & Cheryl Loeb, "Dirty Bombs: The Threat Revisited," *Defense Horizons* 38, January 2004, p. 9.

87. *NOVA: Dirty Bomb, Ask The Expert* (March 5, 2003), available at http://www.pbs.org/wgbh/nova/dirty-bomb/ferg-030305.html, last visited on February 25, 2004.

88. Peter D. Zimmerman & Cheryl Loeb, "Dirty Bombs: The Threat Revisited," *Defense Horizons* 38, January 2004, p. 9; *NOVA: Dirty Bomb, Ask The Expert* (March 5, 2003), available at http:// www.pbs.org/wgbh/nova/dirtybomb/ferg-030305. html, last visited on February 25, 2004.

89. Henry Kelly, Michael Levi, Robert Nelson & Jaime Yassif, *Dirty Bombs: Response to a Threat*, FAS Public Interest Report, 55 *Journal of the Federation of American Scientists*, 7, March/April 2002.

90. *Id.*

91. See generally, Jamie Yasif, "U.S. Unprepared for "Dirty Bomb" Aftermath," *Defense News*, April 28, 2003 available at http://www.fas.org/ssp/docs/ 030428-defnews.htm, last visited on February 25, 2004.

92. *Id.*

93. See *Id.*

94. See *Id.*

95. Peter D. Zimmerman & Cheryl Loeb, "Dirty Bombs: The Threat Revisited," *Defense Horizons* 38, January 2004, p. 9.

96. *Case Study: Accidental Leakage of Cesium-137 in Goiania, Brazil, in 1987*, Available at www.nbc-med.org/sitecontent/medref/onlineref/ casestudies/csgoiania.html, last visited on April 15, 2004.

97. *Id.* These problems ensued in part because the National Commission on Nuclear Energy badly underestimated the severity of the cleanup issues before them.

98. Marco Antonio Sperb Leite & L. David Roper, *The Goiannia Radiation Incident: A Failure of Science and Society*, 1988, available at www. ants.bev.net/roper-david/gri.htm, last visited on April 12, 2004.

99. *NOVA: Dirty Bomb, Ask The Expert* (March 5, 2003), available at http://www.pbs.org/wgbh/nova/dirty-bomb/ferg-030305.html, last visited on February 25, 2004.

100. *Id.*

101. See generally, *Department of Homeland Security Working Group on Radiological Dispersal Device (RDD) Preparedness, Medical Preparedness and Response Sub-Group*, May 1, 2003 version.

102. *Id.* at 3–4.

103. *Id* at 19.

104. *Id.* at 61–63.

105. *Department of Homeland Security Working Group on Radiological Dispersal Device (RDD) Preparedness, Medical Preparedness and Response Sub-Group*, May 1, 2003 version, at 61–63.

106. *Id.*

107. *Guidance for Industry on Prussian Blue for Treatment of Internal Contamination with Thallium or Radioactive Cesium*, 68 *Federal Register* 5645 (February 4, 2003). The FDA used as guidance for their conclusions regarding Prussian Blue's effectiveness as a treatment for radiological exposure the published reports of the 1987 Goinia, Brazil, incident in which 46 patients with heavy internal contamination with cesium-137 saw reductions in the effective half life of the radiation levels of between 43 and 63 percent. The pigment is currently marketed commercially by a German company as Radiogardase®.

108. *Id.*

109. *Guidance for Industry on Pentetate Calcium Trisodium and Pentetate Zinc Trisodium for Treatment of Internal Contamination with Plutonium, Americum and Curium*, 68 *Federal Register* 53984 (September 15, 2003).

110. *NOVA: Dirty Bomb, Ask The Expert* (March 5, 2003), available at http://www.pbs.org/wgbh/nova/dirty-bomb/ferg-030305.html, last visited on February 25, 2004.

111. See generally, *Department of Homeland Security Working Group on Radiological Dispersal Device (RDD) Preparedness, Medical Preparedness and Response Sub-Group*, May 1, 2003 version, for a more thorough look at some available treatments for radiation contamination.

112. *Id.*

DISCUSSION QUESTIONS

1. What challenges do a dirty bomb pose to our security systems that other types of WMD do not?

2. What advantages might a terrorist see in using a dirty bomb?

3. What approaches do you suggest to improve our ability to prevent use of a dirty bomb? Explain your answer, discussing both internal and international approaches.

4. Evaluate current governmental preparedness plans for a dirty bomb as described in the chapter. How might they be improved?

5. Describe the steps that you believe a city should take upon receiving a threat to use a dirty bomb.

6. What would your own reaction be to a dirty bomb threat? Explain why you would act in this manner.

7. How might your local unit of government act in advance of a dirty bomb to improve the chances of its citizenry to survive?

8. After people have been exposed to the aftermath of the dirty bomb, what can be done to assist them in the short and long term?

Iraqi and coalition troops patrol together. July 16, 2004. DoD photo by Tech. Sgt. Scott Reed, U.S. Air Force.

Section VII

FOREIGN POLICY ASPECTS
OF HOMELAND SECURITY

Chapter 17

TWO YEARS LATER: WORLD OPINION; FOREIGN VIEWS OF U.S. DARKEN SINCE SEPT. 11

By RICHARD BERNSTEIN; Contributing to this report were JAMES BROOKE, FRANK BRUNI, ALAN COWELL, IAN FISHER, JOSEPH KAHN, CLIFFORD KRAUSS, MARC LACEY, JANE PERLEZ, CRAIG S. SMITH, and MICHAEL WINES.

September 11, 2003, Thursday, Late Edition–Final Section A; Page 1; Column 1; Foreign Desk
BERLIN, September 10

In the two years since September 11, 2001, the view of the United States as a victim of terrorism that deserved the world's sympathy and support has given way to a widespread vision of America as an imperial power that has defied world opinion through unjustified and unilateral use of military force.

"A lot of people had sympathy for Americans around the time of 9-11, but that's changed," said Cathy Hearn, 31, a flight attendant from South Africa, expressing a view commonly heard in many countries. "They act like the big guy riding roughshod over everyone else."

In interviews by *Times* correspondents from Africa to Europe to Southeast Asia, one point emerged clearly: The war in Iraq has had a major impact on public opinion, which has moved generally from post-9-11 sympathy to post-Iraq antipathy, or at least to disappointment over what is seen as the sole superpower's inclination to act preemptively, without either persuasive reasons or United Nations approval.

To some degree, the resentment is centered on the person of President Bush, who is seen by many of those interviewed, at best, as an ineffective spokesman for American interests and, at worst, as a gunslinging cowboy knocking over international treaties and bent on controlling the world's oil, if not the entire world.

Foreign policy experts point to slowly developing fissures, born at the end of the Cold War, that exploded into view in the debate leading up to the Iraq war. "I think the turnaround was last summer, when American policy moved ever more decisively toward war against Iraq," said Josef Joffe, co-editor of the German weekly *Die Zeit*. "That's what triggered the counteralliance of France and Germany and the enormous wave of hatred against the United States."

The subject of America in the world is of course complicated, and the nation's battered international image could improve quickly in response to events. The Bush administration's recent turn to the United Nations for help in postwar Iraq may represent such an event.

Even at this low point, millions of people still see the United States as a beacon and support its policies, including the war in Iraq, and would, given the chance, be happy to become Americans themselves.

Some regions, especially Europe, are split in their view of America's role: The governments and, to a lesser extent, the public in former Soviet-bloc countries are much more favorably disposed to American power than the governments and the public in Western Europe, notably France and Germany.

Note: Copyright 2003 The New York Times Company, *The New York Times*, Reprinted by permission.

In Japan, a strong American ally that feels insecure in the face of a hostile, nuclear-armed North Korea, there may be doubts about the wisdom of the American war on Iraq. But there seem to be far fewer doubts about the importance of American power generally to global stability.

In China, while many ordinary people express doubts about the war in Iraq, anti-American feeling has diminished since September 11, 2001, and there seems to be greater understanding and less instinctive criticism of the United States by government officials and intellectuals. The Chinese leadership has largely embraced America's "war on terror."

Still, a widespread and fashionable view is that the United States is a classically imperialist power bent on controlling global oil supplies and on military domination.

That mood has been expressed in different ways by different people, from the hockey fans in Montreal who boo the American national anthem to the high school students in Switzerland who do not want to go to the United States as exchange students because America is not "in." Even among young people, it is not difficult to hear strong denunciations of American policy and sharp questioning of American motives.

"America has taken power over the world," said Dmitri Ostalsky, 25, a literary critic and writer in Moscow. "It's a wonderful country, but it seized power. It's ruling the world. America's attempts to rebuild all the world in the image of liberalism and capitalism are fraught with the same dangers as the Nazis taking over the world."

Frenchman Jean-Charles Pogram, 45, a computer technician, said, "Everyone agrees on the principles of democracy and freedom, but the problem is that we don't agree with the means to achieve those ends. The United States can't see beyond the axiom that force can solve everything, but Europe, because of two world wars, knows the price of blood."

Lydia Adhiamba, a 20-year-old student at the Institute of Advanced Technology in Nairobi, Kenya, said the United States "wants to rule the whole world, and that's why there's so much animosity to the U.S."

The major English language daily newspaper in Indonesia, *The Jakarta Post*, recently ran a prominent article titled, "Why Moderate Muslims are Annoyed with America," by Sayidiman Suryohadiprojo, a prominent figure during the Suharto years.

"If America wants to become a hegemonic power, it is rather difficult for other nations to prevent that," he wrote. "However, if America wants to be a hegemonic power that has the respect and trust of other nations, it must be a benign one, and not one that causes a reaction of hate or fear among other nations."

BUSH AS SALESMAN

Crucial to global opinion has been the failure of the Bush administration to persuade large segments of the public of its justification for going to war in Iraq.

In striking contrast to opinion in the United States, where polls show a majority believe there was a connection between Saddam Hussein and al Quaida terrorists, the rest of the world remains skeptical.

That explains the enormous difference in international opinion toward American military action in Afghanistan in the months after September 11, which seemed to have tacit approval as legitimate self-defense, and toward American military action in Iraq, which is seen as the arbitrary act of an overbearing power.

Perhaps the strongest effect on public opinion has been in Arab and Muslim countries. Even in relatively moderate Muslim countries like Indonesia and Turkey, or countries with large Muslim populations, like Nigeria, both polls and interviews show sharp drops in approval of the United States.

In unabashedly pro-American countries like Poland, perhaps the staunchest American ally on Iraq after Britain, polls show 60 percent of the people oppose the government's decision to send 2,500 troops to Iraq.

For many people, the issue is not so much the United States as it is the Bush administration, and what is seen as its arrogance. In this view, a different set of policies and a different set of public statements from Washington could have resulted in a different set of attitudes.

"The point I would make is that with the best will in the world, President Bush is a very poor salesman for the United States, and I say that as someone who has no animus against him or the United States," said Philip Gawaith, a financial communications consultant in London. "Whether it's al Quaida or Afghanistan, people have just felt that he's a silly man, and therefore they are not obliged to think any harder about his position."

TRYING TO DEFINE "THREAT"

But while the public statements of the Bush administration have not played well in much of the world, many analysts see deeper causes for the rift that has opened. In their view, the Iraq war has not so much caused a new divergence as it has highlighted and widened one that existed since the end of the Cold War. Put bluntly, Europe needs America less now that it feels less threatened.

Indeed, while the United States probably feels more threatened now than in 1989, when the Cold War ended, Europe is broadly unconvinced of any imminent threat.

"There were deep structural forces before 9-11 that were pushing us apart," said John J. Mearsheimer, professor of political science at the University of Chicago and the author of *The Tragedy of Great Power Politics.* "In the absence of the Soviet threat or of an equivalent threat, there was no way that ties between us and Europe wouldn't be loosened.

"So, when the Bush administration came to power, the question was whether it would make things better or worse, and I'd argue that it made them worse."

"In the Cold War you could argue that American unilateralism had no cost," Professor Mearsheimer continued. "But as we're finding out with regard to Iraq, Iran, and North Korea, we need the Europeans and we need institutions like the U.N. The fact is that the United States can't run the world by itself, and the problem is, we've done a lot of damage in our relations with allies, and people are not terribly enthusiastic about helping us now."

Recent findings of international surveys illustrate those divergences. A poll of 8,000 people in Europe and the United States conducted by the German Marshall Fund of the United States and Compagnia di Sao Paolo of Italy found Americans and Europeans agreeing on the nature of global threats but disagreeing sharply on how they should be dealt with.

Most striking was a difference over the use of military force, with 84 percent of Americans but only 48 percent of Europeans supporting force as a means of imposing international justice.

In Europe overall, the proportion of people who want the United States to maintain a strong global presence fell 19 points since a similar poll last year, from 64 percent to 45 percent, while 50 percent of respondents in Germany, France, and Italy express opposition to American leadership.

Many of the difficulties predated September 11, of course. Eberhard Sandschneider, director of the German Council on Foreign Relations, listed some in a recent paper: "Economic disputes relating to steel and farm subsidies; limits on legal cooperation because of the death penalty in the United States; repeated charges of U.S. 'unilateralism' over actions in Afghanistan; and the U.S. decisions on the ABM Treaty, the Kyoto Protocol, the International Criminal Court, and the Biological Weapons Protocol."

"One could conclude that there is today a serious question as to whether Europe and the United States are parting ways," Mr. Sandschneider writes.

From this point of view, as he and others have said, the divergence will not be a temporary phenomenon but permanent.

A recent survey by the Pew Global Attitudes Project showed a growth of anti-American sentiment in many non-European parts of the world. It found, for example, that only 15 percent of Indonesians have a favorable impression of the United States, down from 61 percent a year ago.

Indonesia may be especially troubling to American policymakers, who have hoped that, as a country with an easygoing attitude toward religion, it would emerge as a kind of pro-American Islamic model.

But since September 11, a virulent group of extremists known as Jemaah Islamiyah has gained strength, attacking in Bali and Jakarta and making the country so insecure that President Bush may skip it during an Asian trip planned for next month.

One well-known mainstream Indonesian Muslim leader, Din Syamsuddin, an American-educated vice president of a Islamic organization that claims 30 million members, calls the United States the "king of the terrorists" and refers to President Bush as a "drunken horse."

This turn for the worse has occurred despite a $10 million program by the State Department in which speakers and short films showing Muslim life in the United States were sent last fall to Muslim countries, including Indonesia.

A RESIDUE OF GOOD WILL

Still, broad sympathy for the United States exists in many areas. Students from around the world clamor to be educated in America. The United States as a land of opportunity remains magnetic.

Some analysts point out that the German Marshall Fund study actually showed a great deal of common ground across the Atlantic.

"Americans and Europeans still basically like each other, although such warmth has slipped in the wake of the Iraq war," Ronald Asmus, Philip P. Everts and Pierangelo Isernia, analysts from the United States, the Netherlands, and Italy, respectively, wrote in an article explaining the findings. "Americans and Europeans do not live on different planets when it comes to viewing the threats around them."

But there is little doubt that the planets have moved apart. Gone are the days, two years ago, when 200,000 Germans marched in Berlin to show solidarity with their American allies, or when *Le Monde*, the most prestigious French newspaper, could publish a large headline, "We Are All Americans." More recently, Jean Daniel, the editor of the weekly *Nouvel Observateur*, published an editorial entitled, "We Are Not All Americans."

For governments in Eastern Europe, September 11 has forced a kind of test of loyalties. Romania, Hungary, Bulgaria, the Czech Republic, and Poland have felt themselves caught between the United States and the European Union, which they will soon be joining.

Here, too, the war in Iraq seems to have been the defining event, the division of Europe into "new" and "old" halves, defined by their willingness to support the American-led war.

Most Eastern European countries side with the European Union majority on such questions as the International Criminal Court, which is opposed by the Bush administration, while helping in various ways with the Iraq war. Poland and Romania have sent troops and Hungary has permitted training of Iraqis at a military base there.

But even if the overall mood in the former Soviet Bloc remains largely pro-American, recent polls have shown some slippage in feelings of admiration.

"We would love to see America as a self-limiting superpower," said Janusz Onyszkiewicz, a former Polish defense minister.

Perhaps the administration's decision to turn to the United Nations to seek a mandate for an international force in Iraq reflects a new readiness to exercise such restraint. The administration appears to have learned that using its power in isolation can get very expensive very quickly.

But the road to recovering global support is likely to be a long one for a country whose very power—political, economic, cultural, military—makes it a natural target of criticism and envy.

Even in Japan, where support for America remains strong, the view of the United States as a bully has entered the popular culture. A recent cartoon showed a character looking like President Bush in a stars and stripes vest pushing Japanese fishermen away from a favorite spot, saying, "I can fish better."

DISCUSSION QUESTIONS

1. Do you agree with the article's view that relations have deteriorated with long-time allies in the aftermath of the September 11, 2001, attacks?
2. In your opinion, where does the responsibility lie for this situation?
3. The article mentions that the United States probably feels more threatened now than in 1989, when the Cold War ended, but that Europe is broadly unconvinced of any imminent threat. Why do these attitudes exist?
4. Describe steps that you think would improve the United States' relations with other nations. What are the positive and negative aspects to the approaches you advocate?
5. What do you believe the limits are, if any, on the United States' control of its international actions?
6. If you believe limits are appropriate, who should set them? Who should enforce them?
7. Do you believe that the United States should be subject to the same standards as other nations? Defend your answer.

Chapter 18

GOP CONGRESSMAN: WAR WAS A MISTAKE

August 19, 2004

REPRESENTATIVE DOUG BEREUTER (R.-NEVADA)

It is a painful and disturbing process, but America and everyone involved in the decision-making and oversight process (the Executive Branch and Congress) must learn from the errors and failures related to waging a war against Saddam Hussein's Iraq and the aftermath of that war. The toll in American military casualties and those of civilians, physical damages caused,

financial resources spent, and the damage to the support and image of America abroad, all demand such an assessment and accounting. Certainly, all the facts and impacts are not yet apparent, and the violence and financial and diplomatic costs of the Iraqi aftermath continue to accumulate. However, I must give this account before I leave Congress on August 31, 2004.

I. APPARENT INTELLIGENCE FAILURES

The first, and most basic, conclusion is that it appears there was a massive failure or misinterpretation of intelligence concerning the Weapons of Mass Destruction (WMD) programs and supply stocks of Saddam, both by the American agencies and leading decision makers, but also on the part of allies and other leading countries. The fact that Saddam had used chemical weapons against Iran and Iraqi Kurds, that chemical weapons and biological and nuclear development programs were discovered after the first Gulf War, and that Saddam so strenuously resisted unfettered international inspection efforts in recent years all contributed to the general conclusion that he had reconstructed his chemical weapons stock and was weaponizing biological agents. There was also the suspicion that his efforts to surreptitiously import certain dual-use technology were part of an effort to reconstitute his nuclear development program.

The conclusion generally reached was that he had at least some of these types of WMD and that he would use them again against countries of the neighborhood. Even more directly troubling to America was the concern that he would share them with terrorist groups. It was a combination of these conclusions and fears that were the primary justification for the preemptive military action against Iraq. Most importantly, however, it was the fear that his WMD would be shared with terrorists when it served his purposes. These concerns caused this member of Congress to vote to authorize the use of military force by the president, even preemptive military force, if the conditions specified in House Joint Resolution 114 of October 2002 were judged by the president to have been met. That resolution that authorized the use of military force was passed by large majorities in both houses of Congress, and I believe that for most members

Note: This letter to Congressman Bereuter's constituents may be found on the Web at: http://www.antiwar.com/orig/bereuter.php?articleid=3385

the element of a WMD-terrorist link was a key factor.

Evidence that substantial Iraqi chemical and biological WMD stocks existed at the time the war began or that they covertly had been destroyed just before the conflict began still may be discovered. Certainly, there were such chaotic conditions after the "military war" ended, with huge weapons dumps and laboratories left unguarded or undiscovered for months, that evidence and supplies could have been hidden or destroyed. However, revelations in the unredacted portions of reports recently released by the Senate Select Committee on Intelligence point to a massive intelligence failure by the American and foreign intelligence agencies, and even more disturbingly, leave unresolved whether inadequate or questionable elements of intelligence and sources of intelligence were used to justify military action.

(Many members of the House Permanent Select Committee on Intelligence, on which I serve, have also reached some of the same conclusions as the Senate Committee–and that includes me.)

Knowing now what I know about the reliance on the tenuous or insufficiently corroborated intelligence used to conclude that Saddam maintained a substantial WMD arsenal, *I believe that launching the preemptive military action was not justified.* However, the inability of the administration to clearly establish a link between al Quaida and Saddam, despite the intimations of various administration leaders like Vice President Dick Cheney, is no surprise to me. In my floor statement of October 8, 2002, during the debate on the "military use of force" resolution, I said, "The administration cannot yet present incontrovertible evidence of a link between al Quaida and Saddam."

II. SKEWING OF INTELLIGENCE TO JUSTIFY THE WAR?

Of course, one of the major controversies yet remaining is whether key individuals in the administration skewed the intelligence made available to them to justify military action against Saddam's Iraq or, whether coerced, intimidated, or sympathetic American intelligence analysts and managers gave them the findings they seemed to want in order to justify military action. The Senate Select Intelligence Committee reports finding no evidence of such pressure and I do not believe that individual members of the House Committee have such evidence. Left unresolved for now is whether intelligence was intentionally misconstrued to justify military action. That would be difficult to determine definitively without a smoking gun.

III. PREPARATIONS FOR WAR AND THE AFTERMATH

Here, I first refer you to an excerpt from my floor statement during the October 8, 2002, debate on House Joint Resolution 114. You will note that I raised four questions of the administration illustrative of additional questions that could be asked, in an attempt to determine whether "the Executive Branch had given adequate consideration and provided contingency planning and resources" for a military action against Iraq and its aftermath, and if not, to stimulate such consideration before any military action was taken against Iraq. I can only conclude now that it failed on questions #1, #3, and #4.

I was very interested to read Paul Krugman's column in *The New York Times* of April 23,

2004, because his words, which follow, succinctly mirrored my own thoughts:

> Just as experts on peacekeeping predicted before the war, the invading force was grossly inadequate to maintain postwar security. And this problem was compounded by a chain of blunders: doing nothing to stop the postwar looting, disbanding the Iraqi Army, canceling local elections, appointing an interim council dominated by exiles with no political base and excluding important domestic groups. The lessons of the last few weeks are that the occupation has never recovered from those early errors. The insurgency, which began during those early months of chaos, has spread.

Of course, the insurgency has grown dramatically since Krugman wrote those words in April. While the American military deaths have declined from the highest levels of April and May during the U.S. offensive against the terrorists, there is still an average of 50 tragic U.S. military deaths per month at the time this is being written.

It should be noted, too, that the administration received many warnings not to make those very errors. Perhaps the warning most frequently given by reputable sources was to avoid disbanding the Iraqi army, but to instead immediately reconstitute it. Many of those Iraqi army personnel became insurgents or, at best, disenchanted. Now that army and police forces are being trained and deployed, they are targets for the organized and increasingly motivated insurgency. The same is the case for the Iraqis who have assumed leadership roles at the national or local level; that violence has intensified since the handover in late June.

In my view, another fundamental and predictable failure was placing the responsibility for reconstruction and interim governance in the hands of the Department of Defense. The State Department, and particularly its Agency for International Development, would no doubt have handled these responsibilities more expeditiously and economically, and with less questionable procurement and contractual practices. These are responsibilities normally assigned to State, and it has a better experience base for such programs.

Finally, I would reiterate the frequent criticism that the American and coalition forces were inadequate in number to take effective control of Iraq when the initial military action was completed. This was a misjudgment from the top levels of the Defense Department and contrary to the estimates

of the former U.S. Army chief of staff who was sharply criticized by the DoD civilian leadership. Of course, that inadequacy was accentuated by both the unexpected rejection by Turkey for the movement of one U.S. Army division across that country to enter northern Iraq and by the unwillingness of a number of European countries to supply troops for the coalition because of their opposition to the war.

The Middle East neighborhood and the rest of the world are no doubt safer from attack and subversion now that Saddam has been removed from power. The oppressed Kurdish and Shiite Iraqis no longer have to fear for their lives from his government, and the same is true of other Iraqis whom he punished as enemies of the state.

Was the preemptive military strike to remove Saddam in America's best interest? That is a question that receives a sharply divided response in our country with the trend being against the preemptive military action we launched. I've reached the conclusion, retrospectively, now that the inadequate intelligence and faulty conclusions are being revealed, *that all things being considered, it was a mistake to launch that military action*, especially without a broad and engaged international coalition. The cost in casualties is already large and growing, and the immediate and long-term financial costs are incredible. Our country's reputation around the world has never been lower and our alliances are weakened. From the beginning of the conflict it was doubtful that we for long would be seen as liberators, but instead increasingly as an occupying force. Now we are immersed in a dangerous, costly mess and there is no easy and quick way to end our responsibilities in Iraq without creating bigger future problems in the region and, in general, in the Muslim world.

DISCUSSION QUESTIONS

1. Former Congressman Bereuter refers to multiple "errors and failures related to waging a war against Saddam Hussein's Iraq and the aftermath of that war." Do you agree with his overall theme? Why or why not?

2. He refers to a "massive intelligence failure" regarding Iraq's possession of Weapons of Mass Destruction, and identifies that failure as being

common to all our allies. What should be done in the aftermath of such a failure to prevent its reoccurrence?

3. He states: "Knowing now what I know about the reliance on the tenuous or insufficiently corroborated intelligence used to conclude that Saddam maintained a substantial WMD arsenal, *I believe that launching the preemptive*

military action was not justified." To what extent is such a statement helpful to our leaders as they evaluate future steps in Iraq? What effect do you anticipate such language having on our troops who are in harm's way in Iraq?

4. The author refers to "the inability of the administration to clearly establish a link between al Quaida and Saddam." Do you agree with this evaluation? Should it have an effect on our Iraq policy? Why or why not? What should future steps be regarding Iraq and al Quaida if such a link cannot be established?

5. Congressman Bereuter is of the opinion that "left unresolved for now is whether intelligence was intentionally misconstrued to justify military action." What effect, if any, should a resolution of this question have on future policy toward Iraq?

6. The author criticizes the disbanding of the Iraqi army. Describe the possible benefits and costs of leaving the Iraqi army intact.

7. Another concern is the lack of preparedness for the aftermath of the war and leaving rebuilding to the Department of Defense rather than the State Department. What are the arguments on both sides of such a decision?

8. Other commentators as well as Congressman Bereuter have criticized the number of troops deployed in Iraq as too small to keep order during reconstruction. Why do you believe that we went in with the numbers we did? What other options might the Bush administration have utilized to either increase the number of troops or made a large number of troops less important?

9. Overall, knowing what was generally available at the time of the Iraqi incursion, was it the right thing to do? Why or why not?

10. How has your opinion changed, if it has, regarding whether our Iraq adventure is a good idea?

11. What should our next steps be in Iraq? What should our long-term goals be for that country?

12. What should be our next steps in the war on terror overall?

13. Is it possible to win a war on terror? Explain how this can be accomplished.

Chapter 19

PRESIDENT BUSH DISCUSSES IRAQ

Another lesson of September 11, I said if we see a threat, we must deal with it before it fully materializes. We saw a threat in Iraq. And let me tell you why; not only the intelligence say there was a threat there, but we remembered the history of the man [Saddam Hussein]. He was a sworn enemy of America. Terrorists were able to–and terrorist networks were able to–operate in and out of his country. Remember Abu Nidal? He was the guy that killed the man, an American citizen, because he was Jewish. His network was there inside of Iraq. Zarqawi, who's still running around in Iraq, his network was in Iraq. He is a–Saddam was a fellow who paid the families of suicide bombers. That's one of the–suiciding to kill innocent people as an act of terror. He paid the families as an incentive to do so. He had used Weapons of Mass Destruction. Remember that? He had used them on his own people. He had used them against countries in his neighborhood. He was a source of instability. He was a threat, and we saw him as a threat.

Now, the United States Congress looked at the same intelligence I looked at, the exact same intelligence, and came to the same conclusion. Members of both political parties looked at the intelligence. My opponent [John Kerry] looked at the very same intelligence and came to the same conclusion. (Applause.) The United Nations–remember I went to the U.N., and said, you have forever condemned him. You've told him to get rid of his weapons, yet nothing has happened, so let's try her one more time. And the United Nations looked at the intelligence, saw a threat, and passed a resolution, 15 to nothing. That was what the Security Council said. They said, disclose, disarm, or face serious consequences.

And so, the world spoke, and again, he defied us. And not only did he defy us, he systematically deceived the inspectors. You remember the period of time, we said, well, let's give the inspectors the chance to work. We agreed, until we found out he was deceiving them. What he was trying to do was buy time. Why? Because he wanted to reconstitute a weapons program. He wanted to make sure he had the capacity to make weapons. And if he had any, like we thought he did, he didn't want anybody to find them. That's why. I had a choice to make then. Forget the lessons of September 11, trust a madman, or take action to defend our country. Every time, I will defend America. (Applause.)

We are safer–we are safer and the world is better off because Saddam is sitting in a prison cell. I want to share something with you. Committing troops into harm's way is the most difficult decision a president can make. That decision must always be last resort. That decision must be done when our vital interests are at stake, but after we've tried everything else. There must be a compelling national need to put our troops into harm's way. I felt that. I felt we had a compelling national need. I know we had tried diplomacy. I knew that diplomacy at this point couldn't possibly work because he had no intention of listening to demands of the free world. And when you put your troops in harm's way, you better have the best–the best equipment, the best support, and the best possible pay. (Applause.)

Note: Excerpt from August 5, 2004, speech. (Found online at: http://www.whitehouse.gov/news/releases/2004/08/20040805-12.html)

That's why I went to the Congress and said—last September—said, we need more money for our troops, $87 billion more money. Some of it was for reconstruction, most of it was for the troops, over $60 billion for the troops—Humvees, spare parts, body armor, the things necessary that you would want. If you are a mom or dad—we probably got a mom or dad here whose child is in Iraq—you want your son or daughter to have the best. Thank you, appreciate you.

There were two senators—there were 12 senators who voted against more funding for the troops, two of whom are my opponent and his running mate. (Applause.)

I don't know if you heard the explanation. He said, "I actually did vote for the $87 billion before I voted against it." (Laughter.) That's not the way most folks speak in Ohio. (Applause.) As the Commander-in-Chief, I'll see to it our troops have the best—the best possible pay, the best possible training, the best possible equipment to defend the United States of America. (Applause.) Thank you all. By the way, I know we've got some veterans here. Thanks for setting such a good example for those who wear our uniform today. (Applause.) I appreciate your service.

The world is changing. This is an historic time. Freedom equals peace. Listen, we've done the hard work, and there's more hard work to do. But I want you to know that we're headed for a peaceful world. That's my hope. My hope is that young children can grow up in a peaceful world. My hope is that we never have to live another day like we did on September 11. (Applause.)

And you achieve peace by spreading freedom. That's what America believes. (Applause.) And that's hard work. Free nations are peaceful nations. Free nations, nations that listen to the aspirations of their people, are nations in which it's hard to recruit people willing to kill themselves for a radical philosophy. That's what Americans believe. We believe that freedom is the Almighty God's gift to every man and woman in this world. (Applause.)

And therefore, our strategy for peace is to do everything we can to protect the homeland, by being on the offense against an enemy, but it's also to spread liberty. These are historic times. That's why it's vital we stand with those who love freedom in Afghanistan and Iraq. Now, it's not easy to be a free society in a place like Iraq—it's just not. You can understand why: these people were brutalized. There were mass graves of thousands of—of a thousand citizens.

I'll tell you an interesting story, and it's one that touched my heart. Seven people came to the Oval Office, seven Iraqi men. Walking in that Oval Office, by the way, is a pretty interesting experience—the kind of place people say outside and say, when I get in I'm going to tell him what-for. And they walk in, they get overwhelmed by the Oval Office, say, many, you're looking good, Mr. President. (Laughter.)

These people came in and they said, liberator. I said, you don't need to thank me, you need to thank the American people. You need to thank the mothers and fathers of those, and the husbands and wives of those who served to free you. (Applause.) They had something in common besides being Iraqi men—all of them had their right hands cut off by Saddam Hussein. That's the society that we've liberated. You know why? Because his currency had devalued and he needed a scapegoat. So he found seven small businessmen. For example, one of them was a jeweler and he told me, he said, I sold dinars to buy—I think he said euros—to buy gold so I could make a watch. And so what they were looking for, the authority, Saddam and his thugs were looking for people who sold dinars that caused the currency to be devalued at that particular moment. They put them in prison, and he cut off their right hands and burned an X in their forehead. So in come seven guys who have got an X in their forehead. The good news is that they had been discovered by an American named Marvin Zindler, from Houston, and he had a foundation to help people from around the world. They flew them into Houston. These seven guys had new hands, new prosthesis. (Applause.)

A guy took my Sharpee, wrapped his new fingers and wrote, "God bless America," in Arabic. (Applause.) What a contrast, what a contrast in societies—on the one hand, a society that was so brutalized by a dictator that he could just say, I'm going to cut off their hands; to a society which says, we want to heal you, no matter who you are, no matter your religion, no matter where you're from. We believe in human dignity and human rights in the United States of America. (Applause.)

There's good people now running those countries: Karzai and Allawi. Allawi, I'm told, woke up one night in London to a axe-wielding group of men that had been sent by Saddam Hussein to kill him with an axe. He got away from the axe-wielding thugs severely wounded. In other words, this guy has seen the worst of tyranny, and now he's leading the country. He believes in a free Iraq. He believes in a self-governing Iraq. He believes in listening to the aspirations of the people. And he's plenty tough to do the job.

And so we've got to stand with these people, see, because, you know what, a free world—a free Iraq in a part of the world that's desperate for freedom is an historic opportunity. Maybe I can put it to you best this way: You know, my dad, I'm sure some of your dads, fought in World War II against Japan. And right after World War II there was a movement to rebuild Japan, so it would be a self-governing nation. Some doubted whether that was possible. Some people in our country, they said, why are you wasting your time; why worry about a self-governing Japan? Fortunately, there were some optimists, some people who believed in the power of liberty to change

societies and lives who stood the line, and finally succeeded. We succeeded in helping Japan self-govern.

So I'm having Kobe beef one night with Prime Minister Koizumi. He's the Prime Minister of Japan and a good friend of mine. We're talking about how to keep the peace. We're talking about how to deal with Mr. Kim Jong-il of North Korea—people are starving, by the way, and who want to try to blackmail the free world with a nuclear weapon. And here we are talking about peace. That's what we're talking about. See, free societies are peaceful societies. Someday, an American president will be talking to a duly-elected leader of Iraq, talking about the peace, and America will be better for it. (Applause.)

And the people of Iraq are watching carefully right now. Are we going to be a country of our word? When we say we believe people should be free, are we willing to stand by our word? Or are we going to go timid and weary and afraid of the barbaric behavior of a few? I want to be your president for four more years because I believe that freedom can change the world and the world will be more peaceful.

DISCUSSION QUESTIONS

1. President Bush states "We are safer—we are safer and the world is better off because Saddam is sitting in a prison cell." Do you agree or disagree? Explain your answer.
2. President Bush states that there was a "compelling national need to put our troops into harm's way" in Iraq. Explain why you think he is right or wrong.
3. At the beginning of the Iraq War, President Bush says "I had a choice to make then. Forget the lessons of September 11, trust a madman, or take action to defend our country." Do you agree with his description of the choice at that time? What other choices might have been

available to him at that time. Explain the advantages and disadvantages of the options available.
4. President Bush states, "a free Iraq in a part of the world that's desperate for freedom is an historic opportunity." Do you agree that the Middle East is desperate for freedom? Why or why not?
5. What do you think the eventual outcome of the Iraq War will be, and why?
6. Compare President Bush's explanation of why we are in Iraq with Representative Bereuter's evaluation of the war. Which do you find more compelling, and why?

The future will require sacrifice on the part of civilians and members of the armed services alike. Lance Cpl. Darryl J. Toquinto holds the Purple Heart medal he was awarded Sept. 17 during a ceremony aboard Camp Lejeune, N.C. Toquinto received the award for a gunshot wound he received fighting Taliban insurgents in Afghanistan while deployed there with the 22nd Marine Expeditionary Unit (Special Operations Capable). Photo by: Gunnery Sgt. Keith A. Milks.

Section VIII

FUTURE CHALLENGES FOR HOMELAND SECURITY

Chapter 20

RESTRUCTURING MANAGEMENT OF NATIONAL SECURITY INTELLIGENCE

Part 1

HOW TO DO IT? A DIFFERENT WAY OF ORGANIZING THE GOVERNMENT

As presently configured, the national security institutions of the U.S. government are still the institutions constructed to win the Cold War. The United States confronts a very different world today. Instead of facing a few very dangerous adversaries, the United States confronts a number of less visible challenges that surpass the boundaries of traditional nation–states and calls for quick, imaginative, and agile responses.

The men and women of the World War II generation rose to the challenges of the 1940s and 1950s. They restructured the government so that it could protect the country. That is now the job of the generation that experienced 9-11. Those attacks showed, emphatically, that ways of doing business rooted in a different era are just not good enough. Americans should not settle for incremental, ad-hoc adjustments to a system designed generations ago for a world that no longer exists.

We recommend significant changes in the organization of the government. We know that the quality of the people is more important than the quality of the wiring diagrams. Some of the saddest aspects of the 9-11 story are the outstanding efforts of so many individual officials straining, often without success, against the boundaries of the possible. Good people can overcome bad structures. They should not have to.

The United States has the resources and the people. The government should combine them more effectively, achieving unity of effort. We offer five major recommendations to do that:

- unifying strategic intelligence and operational planning against Islamist terrorists across the foreign-domestic divide with a National Counterterrorism Center;
- unifying the intelligence community with a new National Intelligence Director;
- unifying the many participants in the counterterrorism effort and their knowledge in a network-based information-sharing system that transcends traditional governmental boundaries;
- unifying and strengthening congressional oversight to improve quality and accountability; and
- strengthening the FBI and homeland defenders.

Source: **The 9-11 Commission Report: Final Report of the National Commission on Terrorist Attacks Upon the United States**, Chapter 13 (Found on the Web at http://a257.g.akamaitech.net/7/257/2422/22jul20041130/www.gpoaccess. gov/911/pdf/sec 13.pdf)

I. UNITY OF EFFORT ACROSS THE FOREIGN-DOMESTIC DIVIDE

A. Joint Action

Much of the public commentary about the 9-11 attacks has dealt with "lost opportunities," some of which we reviewed in Chapter 11. These are often characterized as problems of "watchlisting," of "information sharing," or of "connecting the dots." In Chapter 11 we explained that these labels are too narrow. They describe the symptoms, not the disease.

In each of our examples, no one was firmly in charge of managing the case and able to draw relevant intelligence from anywhere in the government, assign responsibilities across the agencies (foreign or domestic), track progress, and quickly bring obstacles up to the level where they could be resolved. Responsibility and accountability were diffuse.

The agencies cooperated, some of the time. But even such cooperation as there was is not the same thing as joint action. When agencies cooperate, one defines the problem and seeks help with it. When they act jointly, the problem and options for action are defined differently from the start. Individuals from different backgrounds come together in analyzing a case and planning how to manage it.

In our hearings we regularly asked witnesses: Who is the quarterback? The other players are in their positions, doing their jobs. But who is calling the play that assigns roles to help them execute as a team?

Since 9-11, those issues have not been resolved. In some ways joint work has gotten better, and in some ways worse. The effort of fighting terrorism has flooded over many of the usual agency boundaries because of its sheer quantity and energy. Attitudes have changed. Officials are keenly conscious of trying to avoid the mistakes of 9-11. They try to share information. They circulate—even to the president—practically every reported threat, however dubious.

Partly because of all this effort, the challenge of coordinating it has multiplied. Before 9-11, the CIA was plainly the lead agency confronting al Quaida. The FBI played a very secondary role.

The engagement of the Departments of Defense and State was more episodic.

- Today the CIA is still central. But the FBI is much more active, along with other parts of the Justice Department.
- The Defense Department effort is now enormous. Three of its unified commands, each headed by a four-star general, have counterterrorism as a primary mission: Special Operations Command, Central Command (both headquartered in Florida), and Northern Command (headquartered in Colorado).
- A new Department of Homeland Security combines formidable resources in border and transportation security, along with analysis of domestic vulnerability and other tasks.
- The State Department has the lead on many of the foreign policy tasks we described in Chapter 12.
- At the White House, the National Security Council (NSC) now is joined by a parallel presidential advisory structure, the Homeland Security Council.

So far we have mentioned two reasons for joint action—the virtue of joint planning and the advantage of having someone in charge to ensure a unified effort. There is a third: the simple shortage of experts with sufficient skills. The limited pool of critical experts—for example, skilled counterterrorism analysts and linguists—is being depleted. Expanding these capabilities will require not just money, but time.

Primary responsibility for terrorism analysis has been assigned to the Terrorist Threat Integration Center (TTIC), created in 2003, based at the CIA headquarters but staffed with representatives of many agencies, reporting directly to the director of central intelligence. Yet the CIA houses another intelligence "fusion" center: the Counterterrorist Center that played such a key role before 9-11. A third major analytic unit is at Defense, in the Defense Intelligence Agency. A fourth, concentrating more on homeland vulnerabilities, is at the Department of Homeland Security. The FBI is in the process of building the analytic capability it has long lacked, and it also has the Terrorist Screening Center.[1]

The U.S. government cannot afford so much duplication of effort. There are not enough experienced experts to go around. The duplication also places extra demands on already hard-pressed single-source national technical intelligence collectors like the National Security Agency.

B. Combining Joint Intelligence and Joint Action

A "smart" government would integrate all sources of information to see the enemy as a whole. Integrated all-source analysis should also inform and shape strategies to collect more intelligence. Yet the Terrorist Threat Integration Center, although it has primary responsibility for terrorism analysis, is formally proscribed from having any oversight or operational authority and is not part of any operational entity, other than reporting to the director of central intelligence.[2]

The government now tries to handle the problem of joint management, informed by analysis of intelligence from all sources, in two ways.

- First, agencies with lead responsibility for certain problems have constructed their own interagency entities and task forces in order to get cooperation. The Counterterrorist Center at CIA, for example, recruits liaison officers from throughout the intelligence community. The military's Central Command has its own interagency center, recruiting liaison officers from all the agencies from which it might need help. The FBI has Joint Terrorism Task Forces in 84 locations to coordinate the activities of other agencies when action may be required.
- Second, the problem of joint operational planning is often passed to the White House, where the NSC staff tries to play this role. The national security staff at the White House (both NSC and new Homeland Security Council staff) has already become 50 percent larger since 9-11. But our impression, after talking to serving officials, is that even this enlarged staff is consumed by meetings on day-to-day issues,

sifting each day's threat information and trying to coordinate everyday operations.

Even as it crowds into every square inch of available office space, the NSC staff is still not sized or funded to be an executive agency. In Chapter 3 we described some of the problems that arose in the 1980s when a White House staff, constitutionally insulated from the usual mechanisms of oversight, became involved in direct operations. During the 1990s Richard Clarke occasionally tried to exercise such authority, sometimes successfully, but often causing friction.

Yet a subtler and more serious danger is that as the NSC staff is consumed by these day-to-day tasks, it has less capacity to find the time and detachment needed to advise a president on larger policy issues. That means less time to work on major new initiatives, help with legislative management to steer needed bills through Congress, and track the design and implementation of the strategic plans for regions, countries, and issues that we discuss in Chapter 12.

Much of the job of operational coordination remains with the agencies, especially the CIA. There Director of Central Intelligence (DCI) Tenet and his chief aides ran interagency meetings nearly every day to coordinate much of the government's day-to-day work. The DCI insisted he did not make policy and only oversaw its implementation. In the struggle against terrorism these distinctions seem increasingly artificial. Also, as the DCI becomes a lead coordinator of the government's operations, it becomes harder to play all the position's other roles, including that of analyst-in-chief.

The problem is nearly intractable because of the way the government is currently structured. Lines of operational authority run to the expanding executive departments, and they are guarded for understandable reasons: the DCI commands the CIA's personnel overseas; the Secretary of Defense will not yield to others in conveying commands to military forces; the Justice Department will not give up the responsibility of deciding whether to seek arrest warrants. But the result is that each agency or department needs its own intelligence apparatus to support the performance of its duties. It is hard to "break down stovepipes" when there are so many stoves that are legally and politically entitled to have cast-iron pipes of their own.

Recalling the Goldwater–Nichols legislation of 1986, Secretary Rumsfeld reminded us that to achieve better joint capability, each of the armed services had to "give up some of their turf and authorities and prerogatives." Today, he said, the executive branch is "stovepiped much like the four services were nearly 20 years ago." He wondered if it might be appropriate to ask agencies to "give up some of their existing turf and authority in exchange for a stronger, faster, more efficient government-wide joint effort."[3] Privately, other key officials have made the same point to us.

We therefore propose a new institution: a civilian-led unified joint command for counterterrorism. It should combine strategic intelligence and joint operational planning.

In the Pentagon's Joint Staff, which serves the chairman of the Joint Chiefs of Staff, intelligence is handled by the J-2 directorate, operational planning by J-3, and overall policy by J-5. Our concept combines the J-2 and J-3 functions (intelligence and operational planning) in one agency, keeping overall policy coordination where it belongs, in the National Security Council.

Recommendation: We recommend the establishment of a National Counterterrorism Center (NCTC), built on the foundation of the existing Terrorist Threat Integration Center (TTIC). Breaking the older mold of national government organization, this NCTC should be a center for joint operational planning and joint intelligence, staffed by personnel from the various agencies. The head of the NCTC should have authority to evaluate the performance of the people assigned to the Center.

Such a joint center should be developed in the same spirit that guided the military's creation of unified joint commands, or the shaping of earlier national agencies like the National Reconnaissance Office, which was formed to organize the work of the CIA and several defense agencies in space.

NCTC–Intelligence. The NCTC should lead strategic analysis, pooling all-source intelligence, foreign and domestic, about transnational terrorist organizations with global reach. It should develop net assessments (comparing enemy capabilities and intentions against U.S. defenses and countermeasures). It should also provide warning. It should do this work by drawing on the efforts of the CIA, FBI, Homeland Security, and other departments and agencies. It should task collection requirements both inside and outside the United States.

The intelligence function (J-2) should build on the existing TTIC structure and remain distinct, as a national intelligence center, within the NCTC. As the government's principal knowledge bank on Islamist terrorism, with the main responsibility for strategic analysis and net assessment, it should absorb a significant portion of the analytical talent now residing in the CIA's Counterterrorist Center and the DIA's Joint Intelligence Task Force-Combatting Terrorism (JITF-CT).

NCTC–Operations. The NCTC should perform joint planning. The plans would assign operational responsibilities to lead agencies, such as State, the CIA, the FBI, Defense and its combatant commands, Homeland Security, and other agencies. The NCTC should not direct the actual execution of these operations, leaving that job to the agencies. The NCTC would then track implementation; it would look across the foreign-domestic divide and across agency boundaries, updating plans to follow through on cases.[4]

The joint operational planning function (J-3) will be new to the TTIC structure. The NCTC can draw on analogous work now being done in the CIA and every other involved department of the government, as well as reaching out to knowledgeable officials in state and local agencies throughout the United States.

The NCTC should not be a policymaking body. Its operations and planning should follow the policy direction of the president and the National Security Council.

Consider this hypothetical case. The NSA discovers that a suspected terrorist is traveling to Bangkok and Kuala Lumpur. The NCTC should draw on joint intelligence resources, including its own NSA counterterrorism experts, to analyze the identities and possible destinations of these individuals. Informed by this analysis, the NCTC would then organize and plan the management of the case, drawing on the talents and differing kinds of experience among the several agency representatives assigned to it—assigning tasks to the CIA overseas, to Homeland Security watching entry points into the United States, and to the FBI. If military assistance might be needed, the Special Operations Command could be asked to develop an appropriate concept for such an operation. The NCTC would be accountable for tracking the progress of the case, ensuring that the plan evolved with it, and integrating the information into a warning. The NCTC would be responsible for being sure that intelligence gathered from the activities in the field became part of the government's institutional memory about Islamist terrorist personalities, organizations, and possible means of attack.

In each case the involved agency would make its own senior managers aware of what it was being asked to do. If those agency heads objected, and the issue could not easily be resolved, then the disagreement about roles and missions could be brought before the National Security Council and the president.

NCTC–Authorities. The head of the NCTC should be appointed by the president, and should be equivalent in rank to a deputy head of a cabinet department. The head of the NCTC would report to the national intelligence director, an office whose creation we recommend below, placed in the executive office of the president. The head of the NCTC would thus also report indirectly to the president. This official's nomination should be confirmed by the Senate and he or she should testify to the Congress, as is the case now with other statutory presidential offices, like the U.S. trade representative.

To avoid the fate of other entities with great nominal authority and little real power, the head of the NCTC must have the right to concur in the choices of personnel to lead the operating entities of the departments and agencies focused on counterterrorism, specifically including the head of the Counterterrorist Center, the head of the FBI's Counterterrorism Division, the commanders of the Defense Department's Special Operations Command and Northern Command, and the State Department's coordinator for counterterrorism.[5] The head of the NCTC should also work with the director of the Office of Management and Budget in developing the president's counterterrorism budget.

There are precedents for surrendering authority for joint planning while preserving an agency's operational control. In the international context, NATO commanders may get line authority over forces assigned by other nations. In U.S. unified commands, commanders plan operations that may involve units belonging to one of the services. In each case, procedures are worked out, formal and informal, to define the limits of the joint commander's authority.

The most serious disadvantage of the NCTC is the reverse of its greatest virtue. The struggle against Islamist terrorism is so important that any clear-cut centralization of authority to manage and be accountable for it may concentrate too much power in one place. The proposed NCTC would be given the authority of planning the activities of other agencies. Law or executive order must define the scope of such line authority.

The NCTC would not eliminate interagency policy disputes. These would still go to the National Security Council. To improve coordination at the White House, we believe the existing Homeland Security Council should soon be merged into a single National Security Council. The creation of the NCTC should help the NSC staff concentrate on its core duties of assisting the president and supporting interdepartmental policymaking.

We recognize that this is a new and difficult idea precisely because the authorities we recommend for the NCTC really would, as Secretary Rumsfeld foresaw, ask strong agencies to "give up some of their turf and authority in exchange for a stronger, faster, more efficient government-wide joint effort." Countering transnational Islamist terrorism will test whether the U.S. government can fashion more flexible models of management needed to deal with the twenty-first-century world.

An argument against change is that the nation is at war, and cannot afford to reorganize in midstream. But some of the main innovations of the 1940s and 1950s, including the creation of the Joint Chiefs of Staff and even the construction of the Pentagon itself, were undertaken in the midst of war. Surely the country cannot wait until the struggle against Islamist terrorism is over.

"Surprise, when it happens to a government, is likely to be a complicated, diffuse, bureaucratic thing. It includes neglect of responsibility, but also responsibility so poorly defined or so ambiguously delegated that action gets lost."[6] That comment was made more than 40 years ago, about Pearl Harbor. We hope another commission, writing in the future about another attack, does not again find this quotation to be so apt.

II. UNITY OF EFFORT IN THE INTELLIGENCE COMMUNITY

In our first section, we concentrated on counterterrorism, discussing how to combine the analysis of information from all sources of intelligence with the joint planning of operations that draw on that analysis. In this section, we step back from looking just at the counterterrorism problem. We reflect on whether the government is organized adequately to direct resources and build the intelligence capabilities it will need not just for countering terrorism, but for the broader range of national security challenges in the decades ahead.

A. The Need for a Change

During the Cold War, intelligence agencies did not depend on seamless integration to track and count the thousands of military targets–such as tanks and missiles–fielded by the Soviet Union and other adversary states. Each agency concentrated on its specialized mission, acquiring its own information and then sharing it via formal, finished reports. The Department of Defense had given birth to and dominated the main agencies for technical collection of intelligence. Resources were shifted at an incremental pace, coping with challenges that arose over years, even decades.

We summarized the resulting organization of the intelligence community in Chapter 3. It is outlined below.

1. Members of the U.S. Intelligence Community

Office of the Director of Central Intelligence, which includes the Office of the Deputy Director of Central Intelligence for Community Management, the Community Management Staff, the Terrorism Threat Integration Center, the National Intelligence Council, and other community offices

The Central Intelligence Agency (CIA), which performs human source collection, all-source analysis, and advanced science and technology

National intelligence agencies:

- National Security Agency (NSA), which performs signals collection and analysis
- National Geospatial-Intelligence Agency (NGA), which performs imagery collection and analysis
- National Reconnaissance Office (NRO), which develops, acquires, and launches space systems for intelligence collection
- Other national reconnaissance programs

2. Departmental Intelligence Agencies

- Defense Intelligence Agency (DIA) of the Department of Defense
- Intelligence entities of the Army, Navy, Air Force, and Marines
- Bureau of Intelligence and Research (INR) of the Department of State
- Office of Terrorism and Finance Intelligence of the Department of Treasury
- Office of Intelligence and the Counterterrorism and Counterintelligence Divisions of the Federal Bureau of Investigation of the Department of Justice
- Office of Intelligence of the Department of Energy
- Directorate of Information Analysis and Infrastructure Protection (IAIP) and Directorate of Coast Guard Intelligence of the Department of Homeland Security

The need to restructure the intelligence community grows out of six problems that have become apparent before and after 9-11:

1. **Structural barriers** to performing joint intelligence work. National intelligence is still organized around the collection disciplines of the home agencies, not the joint mission. The importance of integrated, all-source analysis cannot be overstated. Without it, it is not possible to "connect the

dots." No one component holds all the relevant information.

By contrast, in organizing national defense, the Goldwater–Nichols legislation of 1986 created joint commands for operations in the field, the Unified Command Plan. The services–the Army, Navy, Air Force, and Marine Corps–organize, train, and equip their people and units to perform their missions. Then they assign personnel and units to the joint combatant commander, like the commanding general of the Central Command (CENTCOM). The Goldwater–Nichols Act required officers to serve tours outside their service in order to win promotion. The culture of the Defense Department was transformed, its collective mind-set moved from service-specific to "joint," and its operations became more integrated.[7]

2. **Lack of common standards and practices across the foreign-domestic divide**. The leadership of the intelligence community should be able to pool information gathered overseas with information gathered in the United States, holding the work–wherever it is done–to a common standard of quality in how it is collected, processed (e.g., translated), reported, shared, and analyzed. A common set of personnel standards for intelligence can create a group of professionals better able to operate in joint activities, transcending their own service-specific mind-sets.

3. **Divided management of national intelligence capabilities**. While the CIA was once central to our national intelligence capabilities, following the end of the Cold War it has been less able to influence the use of the nation's imagery and signals intelligence capabilities in three national agencies housed within the Department of Defense: the National Security Agency, the National Geospatial-Intelligence Agency, and the National Reconnaissance Office. One of the lessons learned from the 1991 Gulf War was the value of national intelligence systems (satellites in particular) in precision warfare. Since that war, the department has appropriately drawn these agencies into its transformation of the military. Helping to orchestrate this transformation is the undersecretary of defense for intelligence, a position established by Congress after 9-11. An unintended consequence of these developments has been the far greater demand made by Defense on technical systems, leaving the DCI less able to influence how these technical resources are allocated and used.

4. **Weak capacity to set priorities and move resources**. The agencies are mainly organized around what they collect or the way they collect it, but the priorities for collection are national. As the DCI makes hard choices about moving resources, he or she must have the power to reach across agencies and reallocate effort.

5. **Too many jobs**. The DCI now has at least three jobs. He is expected to run a particular agency, the CIA. He is expected to manage the loose confederation of agencies that is the intelligence community. He is expected to be the analyst-in-chief for the government, sifting evidence and directly briefing the president as his principal intelligence adviser. No recent DCI has been able to do all three effectively. Usually what loses out is management of the intelligence community, a difficult task even in the best case because the DCI's current authorities are weak. With so much to do, the DCI often has not used even the authority he has.

6. **Too complex and secret**. Over the decades, the agencies and the rules surrounding the intelligence community have accumulated to a depth that practically defies public comprehension. There are now 15 agencies or parts of agencies in the intelligence community. The community and the DCI's authorities have become arcane matters, understood only by initiates after long study. Even the most basic information about how much money is actually allocated to or within the intelligence community and most of its key components are shrouded from public view.

The current DCI is responsible for community performance but lacks the three authorities critical for any agency head or chief executive officer: (1) control over purse strings, (2) the ability to hire or fire senior managers, and (3) the ability to set standards for the information infrastructure and personnel.[8]

The only budget power of the DCI over agencies other than the CIA lies in coordinating the budget requests of the various intelligence agencies into a single program for submission to Congress. The overall funding request of the 15 intelligence entities in this program is then presented to the president and Congress in 15 separate volumes.

When Congress passes an appropriations bill to allocate money to intelligence agencies, most of their funding is hidden in the Defense Department in order to keep intelligence spending secret. Therefore, although the House and Senate Intelligence committees are the authorizing committees for funding of the intelligence community, the final budget review is handled in the Defense Subcommittee of the Appropriations committees. Those committees have no subcommittees just for intelligence, and only a few members and staff review the requests.

The appropriations for the CIA and the national intelligence agencies–NSA, NGA, and NRO–are then given to the Secretary of Defense. The Secretary transfers the CIA's money to the DCI but disburses the national agencies' money directly. Money for the FBI's national security components falls within the appropriations for Commerce, Justice, and State and goes to the attorney general.[9]

In addition, the DCI lacks hire-and-fire authority over most of the intelligence community's senior managers. For the national intelligence agencies housed in the Defense Department, the Secretary of Defense must seek the DCI's concurrence regarding the nomination of these directors, who are presidentially appointed. But the Secretary may submit recommendations to the president without receiving this concurrence. The DCI cannot fire these officials. The DCI has even less influence over the head of the FBI's national security component, who is appointed by the attorney general in consultation with the DCI.[10]

B. Combining Joint Work with Stronger Management

We have received recommendations on the topic of intelligence reform from many sources. Other commissions have been over this same ground. Thoughtful bills have been introduced, most recently a bill by the Chairman of the House Intelligence Committee Porter Goss (R-Fla.), and another by the ranking minority member, Jane Harman (D-Calif.). In the Senate, Senators Bob Graham (D-Fla.) and Dianne Feinstein (D-Calif.) have introduced reform proposals as well. Past efforts have foundered, because the president did not support them; because the DCI, the Secretary of Defense, or both opposed them; and because some proposals lacked merit. We have tried to take stock of these experiences, and borrow from strong elements in many of the ideas that have already been developed by others.

Recommendation: The current position of Director of Central Intelligence should be replaced by a National Intelligence Director with two main areas of responsibility: (1) to oversee national intelligence centers on specific subjects of interest across the U.S. government and (2) to manage the national intelligence program and oversee the agencies that contribute to it.

First, the National Intelligence Director should oversee national intelligence centers to provide all-source analysis and plan intelligence operations for the whole government on major problems.

One such problem is counterterrorism. In this case, we believe that the Center should be the intelligence entity (formerly TTIC) inside the National Counterterrorism Center we have proposed. It would sit there alongside the operations management unit we described earlier, with both making up the NCTC, in the executive office of the president. Other national intelligence centers–for instance, on counterproliferation, crime and narcotics, and China–would be housed in whatever department or agency is best suited for them.

The National Intelligence Director would retain the present DCI's role as the principal intelligence adviser to the president. We hope the president will come to look directly to the directors of the national intelligence centers to provide all-source analysis in their areas of responsibility, balancing the advice of these intelligence chiefs against the contrasting viewpoints that may be offered by department heads at State, Defense, Homeland Security, Justice, and other agencies. Second, the National Intelligence Director should manage the national intelligence program and oversee the component agencies of the intelligence community. (Figure 20.1)[11]

The National Intelligence Director would submit a unified budget for national intelligence that reflects priorities chosen by the National Security Council, an appropriate balance among the varieties of technical and human intelligence collection

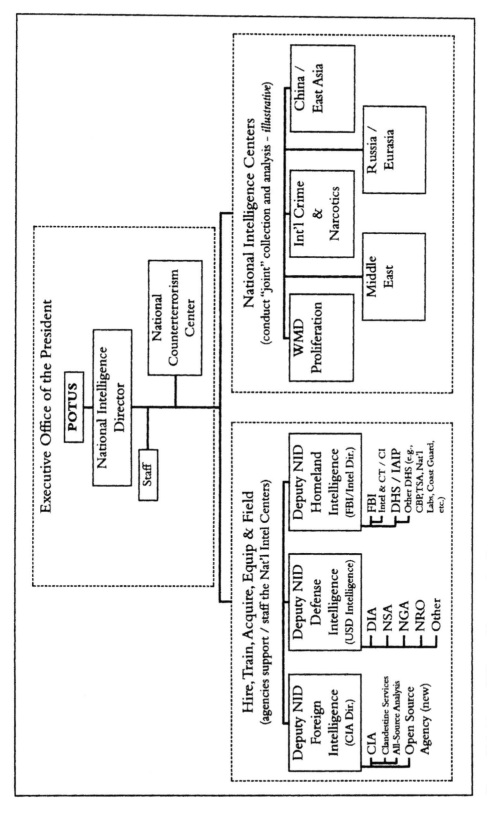

Figure 20.1. Unity of Effort in Managing Intelligence

and analysis. He or she would receive an appropriation for national intelligence and apportion the funds to the appropriate agencies, in line with that budget, and with authority to reprogram funds among the national intelligence agencies to meet any new priority (as counterterrorism was in the 1990s). The National Intelligence Director should approve and submit nominations to the president of the individuals who would lead the CIA, DIA, FBI Intelligence Office, NSA, NGA, NRO, Information Analysis and Infrastructure Protection Directorate of the Department of Homeland Security, and other national intelligence capabilities.[12]

The National Intelligence Director would manage this national effort with the help of three deputies, each of whom would also hold a key position in one of the component agencies.[13]

- foreign intelligence (the head of the CIA)
- defense intelligence (the undersecretary of defense for intelligence)[14]
- homeland intelligence (the FBI's executive assistant director for intelligence or the undersecretary of homeland security for information analysis and infrastructure protection).

Other agencies in the intelligence community would coordinate their work within each of these three areas, largely staying housed in the same departments or agencies that support them now.

Returning to the analogy of the Defense Department's organization, these three deputies–like the leaders of the Army, Navy, Air Force, or Marines–would have the job of acquiring the systems, training the people, and executing the operations planned by the national intelligence centers.

And, just as the combatant commanders also report to the Secretary of Defense, the directors of the national intelligence centers–for example, for counterproliferation, crime and narcotics, and the rest–also would report to the National Intelligence Director.

The Defense Department's military intelligence programs–the joint military intelligence program (JMIP) and the tactical intelligence and related activities program (TIARA)–would remain part of that department's responsibility.

C. Unity of Effort in Managing Intelligence

The National Intelligence Director would set personnel policies to establish standards for education and training and facilitate assignments at the national intelligence centers and across agency lines. The National Intelligence Director also would set information-sharing and information technology policies to maximize data sharing, as well as policies to protect the security of information.

Too many agencies now have an opportunity to say no to change. The National Intelligence Director should participate in an NSC executive committee that can resolve differences in priorities among the agencies and bring the major disputes to the president for decision.

The National Intelligence Director should be located in the executive office of the president. This official, who would be confirmed by the Senate and would testify before Congress, would have a relatively small staff of several hundred people, taking the place of the existing community management offices housed at the CIA.

In managing the whole community, the National Intelligence Director is still providing a service function. With the partial exception of his or her responsibilities for overseeing the NCTC, the National Intelligence Director should support the consumers of national intelligence–the president and policymaking advisers such as the Secretaries of State, Defense, and Homeland Security and the attorney general.

We are wary of too easily equating government management problems with those of the private sector. But we have noticed that some very large private firms rely on a powerful CEO who has significant control over how money is spent and can hire or fire leaders of the major divisions, assisted by a relatively modest staff, while leaving responsibility for execution in the operating divisions.

There are disadvantages to separating the position of National Intelligence Director from the job of heading the CIA. For example, the National Intelligence Director will not head a major agency of his or her own and may have a weaker base of support. But we believe that these disadvantages are outweighed by several other considerations:

- The National Intelligence Director must be able to directly oversee intelligence collection inside the United States. Yet law and custom has counseled against giving such a plain domestic role to the head of the CIA.
- The CIA will be one among several claimants for funds in setting national priorities. The National Intelligence Director should not be both one of the advocates and the judge of them all.
- Covert operations tend to be highly tactical, requiring close attention. The National Intelligence Director should rely on the relevant joint mission center to oversee these details, helping to coordinate closely with the White House. The CIA will be able to concentrate on building the capabilities to carry out such operations and on providing the personnel who will be directing and executing such operations in the field.
- Rebuilding the analytic and human intelligence collection capabilities of the CIA should be a full-time effort, and the director of the CIA should focus on extending its comparative advantages.

Recommendation: The CIA Director should emphasize (a) rebuilding the CIA's analytic capabilities; (b) transforming the clandestine service by building its human intelligence capabilities; (c) developing a stronger language program, with high standards and sufficient financial incentives; (d) renewing emphasis on recruiting diversity among operations officers so they can blend more easily in foreign cities; (e) ensuring a seamless relationship between human source collection and signals collection at the operational level; and (f) stressing a better balance between unilateral and liaison operations.

The CIA should retain responsibility for the direction and execution of clandestine and covert operations, as assigned by the relevant national intelligence center and authorized by the National Intelligence Director and the president. This would include propaganda, renditions, and nonmilitary

disruption. We believe, however, that one important area of responsibility should change.

Recommendation: Lead responsibility for directing and executing paramilitary operations, whether clandestine or covert, should shift to the Defense Department. There it should be consolidated with the capabilities for training, direction, and execution of such operations already being developed in the Special Operations Command.

Before 9-11, the CIA did not invest in developing a robust capability to conduct paramilitary operations with U.S. personnel. It relied on proxies instead, organized by CIA operatives without the requisite military training. The results were unsatisfactory.

Whether the price is measured in either money or people, the United States cannot afford to build two separate capabilities for carrying out secret military operations, secretly operating standoff missiles, and secretly training foreign military or paramilitary forces. The United States should concentrate responsibility and necessary legal authorities in one entity.

The post-9-11 Afghanistan precedent of using joint CIA-military teams for covert and clandestine operations was a good one. We believe this proposal to be consistent with it. Each agency would concentrate on its comparative advantages in building capabilities for joint missions. The operation itself would be planned in common.

The CIA has a reputation for agility in operations. The military has a reputation for being methodical and cumbersome. We do not know if these stereotypes match current reality; they may also be one more symptom of the civil-military misunderstandings we described in Chapter 4. It is a problem to be resolved in policy guidance and agency management, not in the creation of redundant, overlapping capabilities and authorities in such sensitive work. The CIA's experts should be integrated into the military's training, exercises, and planning. To quote a CIA official now serving in the field: "One fight, one team."

Recommendation: Finally, to combat the secrecy and complexity we have described, the overall amounts of money being appropriated for national intelligence and to its

component agencies should no longer be kept secret. Congress should pass a separate appropriations act for intelligence, defending the broad allocation of how these tens of billions of dollars have been assigned among the varieties of intelligence work.

The specifics of the intelligence appropriation would remain classified, as they are today. Opponents of declassification argue that America's enemies could learn about intelligence capabilities by tracking the top-line appropriations figure. Yet the top-line figure by itself provides little insight into U.S. intelligence sources and methods. The U.S. government readily provides copious information about spending on its military forces, including military intelligence. The intelligence community should not be subject to that much disclosure. But when even aggregate categorical numbers remain hidden, it is hard to judge priorities and foster accountability.

III. UNITY OF EFFORT IN SHARING INFORMATION

Information Sharing

We have already stressed the importance of intelligence analysis that can draw on all relevant sources of information. The biggest impediment to all-source analysis–to a greater likelihood of connecting the dots–is the human or systemic resistance to sharing information.

The U.S. government has access to a vast amount of information. When databases not usually thought of as intelligence, such as customs or immigration information, are included, the storehouse is immense. However, the U.S. government has a weak system for processing and using what it has. In interviews around the government, official after official urged us to call attention to frustrations with the unglamorous back office side of government operations.

In the 9-11 story, for example, we sometimes see examples of information that could be accessed–like the undistributed NSA information that would have helped identify Nawaf al Hazmi in January 2000, but someone had to ask for it. In that case, no one did. Or, as in the episodes we describe in Chapter 8, the information is distributed, but in a compartmented channel. Or the information is available, and someone does ask, but it cannot be shared.

What all these stories have in common is a system that requires a demonstrated need to know before sharing. This approach assumes it is possible to know, in advance, who will need to use the information. Such a system implicitly assumes that the risk of inadvertent disclosure outweighs the benefits of wider sharing. Those Cold War assumptions are no longer appropriate. The culture of agencies feeling they own the information they gathered at taxpayer expense must be replaced by a culture in which the agencies instead feel they have a duty to the information–to repay the taxpayers' investment by making that information available.

Each intelligence agency has its own security practices, outgrowths of the Cold War. We certainly understand the reason for these practices. Counterintelligence concerns are still real, even if the old Soviet enemy has been replaced by other spies. However, the security concerns need to be weighed against the costs. Current security requirements nurture overclassification and excessive compartmentation of information among agencies. Each agency's incentive structure opposes sharing, with risks (criminal, civil, and internal administrative sanctions) but few rewards for sharing information. No one has to pay the long-term costs of overclassifying information, although these costs–even in literal financial terms–are substantial. There are no punishments for not sharing information. Agencies uphold a "need-to-know" culture of information protection rather than promoting a "need-to-share" culture of integration.[15]

Recommendation: Information procedures should provide incentives for sharing to restore a better balance between security and shared knowledge.

Intelligence gathered about transnational terrorism should be processed, turned into reports, and distributed according to the same quality standards, whether it is collected in Pakistan or in Texas.

The logical objection is that sources and methods may vary greatly in different locations. We therefore propose that when a report is first created, its data be separated from the sources and methods by which they are obtained. The report should begin with the information in its most shareable but still meaningful form. Therefore the maximum number of recipients can access some form of that information. If knowledge of further details becomes important, any user can query further, with access granted or denied according to the rules set for the network—and with queries leaving an audit trail in order to determine who accessed the information. But the questions may not come at all unless experts at the "edge" of the network can readily discover the clues that prompt to them.[16]

We propose that information be shared horizontally, across new networks that transcend individual agencies.

- The current system is structured on an old mainframe, or hub-and-spoke, concept. In this older approach, each agency has its own database. Agency users send information to the database and then can retrieve it from the database.
- A decentralized network model, the concept behind much of the information revolution, shares data horizontally too. Agencies would still have their own databases, but those databases would be searchable across agency lines. In this system, secrets are protected through the design of the network and an information rights management approach that controls access to the data, not access to the whole network. An outstanding conceptual framework for this kind of "trusted information network" has been developed by a task force of leading professionals in national security, information technology, and law assembled by the Markle Foundation. Its report has been widely discussed throughout the U.S. government, but has not yet been converted into action.[17]

Recommendation: The president should lead the government-wide effort to bring the major national security institutions into the information revolution. He should coordinate the resolution of the legal, policy, and technical issues across agencies to create a "trusted information network."

No one agency can do it alone. Well-meaning agency officials are under tremendous pressure to update their systems. Alone, they may only be able to modernize the stovepipes, not replace them.

Only presidential leadership can develop government-wide concepts and standards. Currently, no one is doing this job. Backed by the Office of Management and Budget, a new National Intelligence Director empowered to set common standards for information use throughout the community, and a Secretary of Homeland Security who helps extend the system to public agencies and relevant private-sector databases, a government-wide initiative can succeed.

White House leadership is also needed because the policy and legal issues are harder than the technical ones. The necessary technology already exists. What does not are the rules for acquiring, accessing, sharing, and using the vast stores of public and private data that may be available. When information sharing works, it is a powerful tool. Therefore the sharing and uses of information must be guided by a set of practical policy guidelines that simultaneously empower and constrain officials, telling them clearly what is and is not permitted.

"This is government acting in new ways, to face new threats," the most recent Markle report explains. "And while such change is necessary, it must be accomplished while engendering the people's trust that privacy and other civil liberties are being protected, that businesses are not being unduly burdened with requests for extraneous or useless information, that taxpayer money is being well spent, and that, ultimately, the network will be effective in protecting our security." The authors add: "Leadership is emerging from all levels of government and from many places in the private sector. What is needed now is a plan to accelerate these efforts, and public debate and consensus on the goals."[18]

IV. UNITY OF EFFORT IN THE CONGRESS

A. Strengthen Congressional Oversight of Intelligence and Homeland Security

Of all our recommendations, strengthening congressional oversight may be among the most difficult and important. So long as oversight is governed by current congressional rules and resolutions, we believe the American people will not get the security they want and need. The United States needs a strong, stable, and capable congressional committee structure to give America's national intelligence agencies oversight, support, and leadership.

Few things are more difficult to change in Washington than congressional committee jurisdiction and prerogatives. To a member, these assignments are almost as important as the map of his or her congressional district. The American people may have to insist that these changes occur, or they may well not happen. Having interviewed numerous members of Congress from both parties, as well as congressional staff members, we found that dissatisfaction with congressional oversight remains widespread.

The future challenges of America's intelligence agencies are daunting. They include the need to develop leading-edge technologies that give our policymakers and warfighters a decisive edge in any conflict where the interests of the United States are vital. Not only does good intelligence win wars, but the best intelligence enables us to prevent them from happening altogether.

Under the terms of existing rules and resolutions the House and Senate intelligence committees lack the power, influence, and sustained capability to meet this challenge. While few members of Congress have the broad knowledge of intelligence activities or the know-how about the technologies employed, all members need to feel assured that good oversight is happening. When their unfamiliarity with the subject is combined with the need to preserve security, a mandate emerges for substantial change.

Tinkering with the existing structure is not sufficient. Either Congress should create a joint committee for intelligence, using the Joint Atomic Energy Committee as its model, or it should create

House and Senate committees with combined authorizing and appropriations powers.

Whichever of these two forms are chosen, the goal should be a structure–codified by resolution with powers expressly granted and carefully limited–allowing a relatively small group of members of Congress, given time and reason to master the subject and the agencies, to conduct oversight of the intelligence establishment and be clearly accountable for their work. The staff of this committee should be nonpartisan and work for the entire committee and not for individual members.

The other reforms we have suggested–for a National Counterterrorism Center and a National Intelligence Director–will not work if congressional oversight does not change too. Unity of effort in executive management can be lost if it is fractured by divided congressional oversight.

Recommendation: Congressional oversight for intelligence–and counterterrorism–is now dysfunctional. Congress should address this problem. We have considered various alternatives: A joint committee on the old model of the Joint Committee on Atomic Energy is one. A single committee in each house of Congress, combining authorizing and appropriating authorities, is another.

The new committee or committees should conduct continuing studies of the activities of the intelligence agencies and report problems relating to the development and use of intelligence to all members of the House and Senate.

We have already recommended that the total level of funding for intelligence be made public, and that the national intelligence program be appropriated to the National Intelligence Director, not to the Secretary of Defense.[19]

We also recommend that the intelligence committee should have a subcommittee specifically dedicated to oversight, freed from the consuming responsibility of working on the budget.

The resolution creating the new intelligence committee structure should grant subpoena authority to the committee or committees. The majority party's representation on this committee should never exceed the minority's representation by more than one.

Four of the members appointed to this committee or committees should be a member who also serves on each of the following additional committees: Armed Services, Judiciary, Foreign Affairs, and the Defense Appropriations subcommittee. In this way the other major congressional interests can be brought together in the new committee's work.

Members should serve indefinitely on the intelligence committees, without set terms, thereby letting them accumulate expertise.

The committees should be smaller—perhaps seven or nine members in each house—so that each member feels a greater sense of responsibility, and accountability, for the quality of the committee's work.

The leaders of the Department of Homeland Security now appear before 88 committees and subcommittees of Congress. One expert witness (not a member of the administration) told us that this is perhaps the single largest obstacle impeding the department's successful development. The one attempt to consolidate such committee authority, the House Select Committee on Homeland Security, may be eliminated. The Senate does not have even this.

Congress needs to establish for the Department of Homeland Security the kind of clear authority and responsibility that exist to enable the Justice Department to deal with crime and the Defense Department to deal with threats to national security. Through not more than one authorizing committee and one appropriating subcommittee in each house, Congress should be able to ask the Secretary of Homeland Security whether he or she has the resources to provide reasonable security against major terrorist acts within the United States and to hold the Secretary accountable for the department's performance.

Recommendation: Congress should create a single, principal point of oversight and review for homeland security. Congressional leaders are best able to judge what committee should have jurisdiction over this department and its duties. But we believe that Congress does have the obligation to choose one in the House and one in the Senate, and that this committee should be a permanent standing committee with a nonpartisan staff.

B. Improve the Transitions Between Administrations

In Chapter 6, we described the transition of 2000–2001. Beyond the policy issues we described, the new administration did not have its deputy cabinet officers in place until the spring of 2001, and the critical subcabinet officials were not confirmed until the summer—if then. In other words, the new administration—like others before it—did not have its team on the job until at least six months after it took office.

Recommendation: Since a catastrophic attack could occur with little or no notice, we should minimize as much as possible the disruption of national security policymaking during the change of administrations by accelerating the process for national security appointments. We think the process could be improved significantly so transitions can work more effectively and allow new officials to assume their new responsibilities as quickly as possible.

Before the election, candidates should submit the names of selected members of their prospective transition teams to the FBI so that, if necessary, those team members can obtain security clearances immediately after the election is over.

A president-elect should submit lists of possible candidates for national security positions to begin obtaining security clearances immediately after the election, so that their background investigations can be complete before January 20.

A single federal agency should be responsible for providing and maintaining security clearances, ensuring uniform standards, including uniform security questionnaires and financial report requirements, and maintaining a single database. This agency can also be responsible for administering polygraph tests on behalf of organizations that require them.

A president-elect should submit the nominations of the entire new national security team, through the level of undersecretary of cabinet departments, not later than January 20. The Senate, in return, should adopt special rules requiring hearings and votes to confirm or reject national security nominees within 30 days of their submission. The Senate should not require confirmation of such executive appointees below Executive Level 3.

The outgoing administration should provide the president-elect, as soon as possible after election day, with a classified, compartmented list that catalogues specific, operational threats to national security; major military or covert operations; and pending decisions on the possible use of force. Such a document could provide both notice and a checklist, inviting a president-elect to inquire and learn more.

V. ORGANIZING AMERICA'S DEFENSES IN THE UNITED STATES

A. The Future Role of the FBI

We have considered proposals for a new agency dedicated to intelligence collection in the United States. Some call this a proposal for an "American MI-5," although the analogy is weak–the actual British Security Service is a relatively small worldwide agency that combines duties assigned in the U.S. government to the Terrorist Threat Integration Center, the CIA, the FBI, and the Department of Homeland Security.

The concern about the FBI is that it has long favored its criminal justice mission over its national security mission. Part of the reason for this is the demand around the country for FBI help on criminal matters. The FBI was criticized, rightly, for the overzealous domestic intelligence investigations disclosed during the 1970s. The pendulum swung away from those types of investigations during the 1980s and 1990s, although the FBI maintained an active counterintelligence function and was the lead agency for the investigation of foreign terrorist groups operating inside the United States.

We do not recommend the creation of a new domestic intelligence agency. It is not needed if our other recommendations are adopted–to establish a strong national intelligence center, part of the NCTC, that will oversee counterterrorism intelligence work, foreign and domestic, and to create a National Intelligence Director who can set and enforce standards for the collection, processing, and reporting of information.

Under the structures we recommend, the FBI's role is focused, but still vital. The FBI does need to be able to direct its thousands of agents and other employees to collect intelligence in America's cities and towns–interviewing informants, conducting surveillance and searches, tracking individuals, working collaboratively with local authorities, and doing so with meticulous attention to detail and compliance with the law. The FBI's job in the streets of the United States would thus be a domestic equivalent, operating under the U.S. Constitution and quite different laws and rules, to the job of the CIA's operations officers abroad.

B. Creating a New Domestic Intelligence Agency Has Other Drawbacks

The FBI is accustomed to carrying out sensitive intelligence collection operations in compliance with the law. If a new domestic intelligence agency were outside of the Department of Justice, the process of legal oversight–never easy–could become even more difficult. Abuses of civil liberties could create a backlash that would impair the collection of needed intelligence.

Creating a new domestic intelligence agency would divert attention of the officials most responsible for current counterterrorism efforts while the threat remains high. Putting a new player into the mix of federal agencies with counterterrorism responsibilities would exacerbate existing information-sharing problems.

A new domestic intelligence agency would need to acquire assets and personnel. The FBI already has 28,000 employees; 56 field offices, 400 satellite offices, and 47 legal attaché offices; a laboratory, operations center, and training facility; an existing network of informants, cooperating defendants, and other sources; and relationships with state and local law enforcement, the CIA, and foreign intelligence and law enforcement agencies.

Counterterrorism investigations in the United States very quickly become matters that involve violations of criminal law and possible law enforcement action. Because the FBI can have agents working criminal matters and agents working intelligence investigations concerning the same international terrorism target, the full range of investigative tools against a suspected terrorist can be considered within one agency. The removal of the wall that existed before 9-11 between intelligence and law enforcement has opened up new opportunities for cooperative action within the FBI.

Counterterrorism investigations often overlap or are cued by other criminal investigations, such as money laundering or the smuggling of contraband. In the field, the close connection to criminal work has many benefits.

Our recommendation to leave counterterrorism intelligence collection in the United States with the FBI still depends on an assessment that the FBI–if it makes an all-out effort to institutionalize change–can do the job. As we mentioned in Chapter 3, we have been impressed by the determination that agents display in tracking down details, patiently going the extra mile and working the extra month, to put facts in the place of speculation. In our report we have shown how agents in Phoenix, Minneapolis, and New York displayed initiative in pressing their investigations.

FBI agents and analysts in the field need to have sustained support and dedicated resources to become stronger intelligence officers. They need to be rewarded for acquiring informants and for gathering and disseminating information differently and more broadly than usual in a traditional criminal investigation. FBI employees need to report and analyze what they have learned in ways the Bureau has never done before.

Under Director Robert Mueller, the Bureau has made significant progress in improving its intelligence capabilities. It now has an Office of Intelligence, overseen by the top tier of FBI management. Field intelligence groups have been created in all field offices to put FBI priorities and the emphasis on intelligence into practice. Advances have been made in improving the Bureau's information technology systems and in increasing connectivity and information sharing with intelligence community agencies.

Director Mueller has also recognized that the FBI's reforms are far from complete. He has outlined a number of areas where added measures may be necessary. Specifically, he has recognized that the FBI needs to recruit from a broader pool of candidates, that agents and analysts working on national security matters require specialized training, and that agents should specialize within programs after obtaining a generalist foundation. The FBI is developing career tracks for agents to specialize in counterterrorism/counterintelligence, cyber crimes, criminal investigations, or intelligence. It is establishing a program for certifying agents as intelligence officers, a certification that will be a prerequisite for promotion to the senior ranks of the Bureau. New training programs have been instituted for intelligence-related subjects.

The Director of the FBI has proposed creating an Intelligence Directorate as a further refinement of the FBI intelligence program. This directorate would include units for intelligence planning and policy and for the direction of analysts and linguists.

We want to ensure that the Bureau's shift to a preventive counterterrorism posture is more fully institutionalized so that it survives beyond Director Mueller's tenure. We have found that in the past the Bureau has announced its willingness to reform and restructure itself to address transnational security threats, but has fallen short–failing to effect the necessary institutional and cultural changes organization-wide. We want to ensure that this does not happen again. Despite having found acceptance of the director's clear message that counterterrorism is now the FBI's top priority, two years after 9-11 we also found gaps between some of the announced reforms and the reality in the field. We are concerned that management in the field offices still can allocate people and resources to local concerns that diverge from the national security mission. This system could revert to a focus on lower-priority criminal justice cases over national security requirements.

Recommendation: A specialized and integrated national security workforce should be established at the FBI consisting of agents, analysts, linguists, and surveillance specialists who are recruited, trained, rewarded, and retained to ensure the development of an institutional culture imbued with a deep expertise in intelligence and national security.

The president, by executive order or directive, should direct the FBI to develop this intelligence cadre.

Recognizing that cross-fertilization between the criminal justice and national security disciplines is vital to the success of both missions, all new agents should receive basic training in both areas. Furthermore, new agents should begin their careers with meaningful assignments in both areas.

Agents and analysts should then specialize in one of these disciplines and have the option to work such matters for their entire career with the Bureau. Certain advanced training courses and assignments to other intelligence agencies should be required to advance within the national security discipline.

In the interest of cross-fertilization, all senior FBI managers, including those working on law enforcement matters, should be certified intelligence officers.

The FBI should fully implement a recruiting, hiring, and selection process for agents and analysts that enhances its ability to target and attract individuals with educational and professional backgrounds in intelligence, international relations, language, technology, and other relevant skills.

The FBI should institute the integration of analysts, agents, linguists, and surveillance personnel in the field so that a dedicated team approach is brought to bear on national security intelligence operations.

Each field office should have an official at the field office's deputy level for national security matters. This individual would have management oversight and ensure that the national priorities are carried out in the field.

The FBI should align its budget structure according to its four main programs—intelligence, counterterrorism and counterintelligence, criminal, and criminal justice services—to ensure better transparency on program costs, management of resources, and protection of the intelligence program.[20]

The FBI should report regularly to Congress in its semiannual program reviews designed to identify whether each field office is appropriately addressing FBI and national program priorities.

The FBI should report regularly to Congress in detail on the qualifications, status, and roles of analysts in the field and at headquarters. Congress should ensure that analysts are afforded training and career opportunities on a par with those offered analysts in other intelligence community agencies.

The Congress should make sure funding is available to accelerate the expansion of secure facilities in FBI field offices so as to increase their ability to use secure e-mail systems and classified intelligence product exchanges. The Congress should monitor whether the FBI's information-sharing principles are implemented in practice.

The FBI is just a small fraction of the national law enforcement community in the United States, a community comprised mainly of state and local agencies. The network designed for sharing information, and the work of the FBI through local Joint Terrorism Task Forces, should build a reciprocal relationship, in which state and local agents understand what information they are looking for and, in return, receive some of the information being developed about what is happening, or may happen, in their communities. In this relationship, the Department of Homeland Security also will play an important part.

The Homeland Security Act of 2002 gave the undersecretary for information analysis and infrastructure protection broad responsibilities. In practice, this directorate has the job to map "terrorist threats to the homeland against our assessed vulnerabilities in order to drive our efforts to protect against terrorist threats."[21] These capabilities are still embryonic. The directorate has not yet developed the capacity to perform one of its assigned jobs, which is to assimilate and analyze information from Homeland Security's own component agencies, such as the Coast Guard, Secret Service, Transportation Security Administration, Immigration and Customs Enforcement, and Customs and Border Protection. The Secretary of Homeland Security must ensure that these components work with the Information Analysis and Infrastructure Protection Directorate so that this office can perform its mission.[22]

C. Homeland Defense

At several points in our inquiry, we asked, "Who is responsible for defending us at home?" Our national defense at home is the responsibility, first, of the Department of Defense and, second, of the

Department of Homeland Security. They must have clear delineations of responsibility and authority.

We found that North American Aerospace Defense Command (NORAD), which had been given the responsibility for defending U.S. airspace, had construed that mission to focus on threats coming from outside America's borders. It did not adjust its focus even though the intelligence community had gathered intelligence on the possibility that terrorists might turn to hijacking and even use of planes as missiles. We have been assured that NORAD has now embraced the full mission. Northern Military Command has been established to assume responsibility for the defense of the domestic United States.

Recommendation: The Department of Defense and its oversight committees should regularly assess the adequacy of Northern Command's strategies and planning to defend the United States against military threats to the homeland.

The Department of Homeland Security was established to consolidate all of the domestic agencies responsible for securing America's borders and national infrastructure, most of which is in private hands. It should identify those elements of our transportation, energy, communications, financial, and other institutions that need to be protected, develop plans to protect that infrastructure, and exercise the mechanisms to enhance preparedness. This means going well beyond the pre-existing jobs of the agencies that have been brought together inside the department.

Recommendation: The Department of Homeland Security and its oversight committees should regularly assess the types of threats the country faces to determine (a) the adequacy of the government's plans—and the progress against those plans—to protect America's critical infrastructure and (b) the readiness of the government to respond to the threats that the United States might face.

We look forward to a national debate on the merits of what we have recommended, and we will participate vigorously in that debate.

Part 2

EXECUTIVE ORDERS ISSUED IN RESPONSE TO THE 9-11 COMMISSION REPORT

EXECUTIVE ORDER 13354 OF AUGUST 27, 2004

National Counterterrorism Center

By the authority vested in me as president by the Constitution and laws of the United States of America, including section 103(c)(8) of the National Security Act of 1947, as amended (Act), and to protect the security of the United States through strengthened intelligence analysis and strategic planning and intelligence support to operations to counter transnational terrorist threats against the territory, people, and interests of the United States of America, it is hereby ordered as follows:

Section 1. Policy. (a) To the maximum extent consistent with applicable law, agencies shall give the highest priority to (i) the detection, prevention, disruption, preemption, and mitigation of the effects of transnational terrorist activities against the territory, people, and interests of the United States of America, (ii) the interchange of terrorism information among agencies, (iii) the interchange of terrorism information between agencies and appropriate authorities of states and local governments, and (iv) the protection of the ability of agencies to acquire additional such information.

(b) Agencies shall protect the freedom, information privacy, and other legal rights of Americans in the conduct of activities implementing section 1(a) of this order.

Sec. 2. Establishment of National Counterterrorism Center. (a) There is hereby established a National Counterterrorism Center (Center).

(b) A director of the Center shall supervise the Center.

(c) The director of the Center shall be appointed by the director of Central Intelligence with the approval of the president.

(d) The director of Central Intelligence shall have authority, direction, and control over the Center and the director of the Center.

Sec. 3. Functions of the Center. The Center shall have the following functions:

(a) serve as the primary organization in the United States Government for analyzing and integrating all intelligence possessed or acquired by the United States Government pertaining to terrorism and counterterrorism, excepting purely domestic counterterrorism information. The Center may, consistent with applicable law, receive, retain, and disseminate information from any federal, state, or local government, or other source necessary to fulfill its responsibilities concerning the policy set forth in Section 1 of this order; and agencies authorized to conduct counterterrorism activities may query Center data for any information to assist in their respective responsibilities;

(b) conduct strategic operational planning for counterterrorism activities, integrating all instruments of national power, including diplomatic, financial, military, intelligence, homeland security, and law enforcement activities within and among agencies;

(c) assign operational responsibilities to lead agencies for counterterrorism activities that are consistent with applicable law and that support strategic plans to counter terrorism. The Center shall ensure that agencies have access to and receive intelligence needed to accomplish their assigned activities. The Center shall not direct the execution of operations. Agencies shall inform the National Security Council and the Homeland Security Council of any objections to designations and assignments made by the Center in the planning and coordination of counterterrorism activities;

(d) serve as the central and shared knowledge bank on known and suspected terrorists and international terror groups, as well as their goals, strategies, capabilities, and networks of contacts and support; and

(e) ensure that agencies, as appropriate, have access to and receive all-source intelligence support needed to execute their counterterrorism plans or perform independent, alternative analysis.

Sec. 4. Duties of the director of Central Intelligence. The director of Central Intelligence shall:

(a) exercise the authority available by law to the director of Central Intelligence to implement this order, including, as appropriate, the authority set forth in section 102(e)(2)(H) of the Act;

(b) report to the president on the implementation of this order, within 120 days after the date of this order and thereafter not less often than annually, including an assessment by the director of Central Intelligence of:

(1) the effectiveness of the United States in implementing the policy set forth in Section 1 of this order, to the extent execution of that policy is within the responsibilities of the director of Central Intelligence;

(2) the effectiveness of the Center in the implementation of the policy set forth in Section 1 of this order, to the extent execution of that policy is within the responsibilities of the director of Central Intelligence; and

(3) the cooperation of the heads of agencies in the implementation of this order; and

(c) ensure the performance of all-source intelligence analysis that, among other qualities, routinely considers and presents alternative analytical views to the president, the vice president in the performance of executive functions, and other officials of the executive branch as appropriate.

Sec. 5. Duties of the director of the Center. In implementing the policy set forth in Section 1 of this order and ensuring that the Center effectively performs the functions set forth in Section 3 of this order, the director of the Center shall:

(a) access, as deemed necessary by the director of the Center for the performance of the Center's functions, information to which the director of the Center is granted access by section 6 of this order;

(b) correlate, analyze, evaluate, integrate, and produce reports on terrorism information;

(c) disseminate transnational terrorism information, including current terrorism threat analysis, to the president, the vice president in the performance of executive functions, the Secretaries of State, Defense, and Homeland Security, the attorney general, the director of Central Intelligence, and other officials of the executive branch as appropriate;

(d) support the Department of Homeland Security, and the Department of Justice, and other appropriate agencies, in fulfillment of their responsibility to disseminate terrorism information, consistent with applicable law, executive orders and other presidential guidance, to state and local government officials, and other entities, and coordinate dissemination of terrorism information to foreign governments when approved by the director of Central Intelligence;

(e) establish both within the Center, and between the Center and agencies, information systems and architectures for the effective access to and integration, dissemination, and use of terrorism information from whatever sources derived;

(f) undertake, as soon as the director of Central Intelligence determines it to be practicable, all functions assigned to the Terrorist Threat Integration Center;

(g) consistent with priorities approved by the president, assist the director of Central Intelligence in establishing requirements for the intelligence community for the collection of terrorism information, to include ensuring military force protection requirements are met;

(h) under the direction of the director of Central Intelligence, and in consultation with heads of agencies with organizations in the intelligence community, identify, coordinate, and prioritize counterterrorism intelligence requirements for the intelligence community; and

(i) identify, together with relevant agencies, specific counterterrorism planning efforts to be initiated or accelerated to protect the national security.

Sec. 6. Duties of the Heads of Agencies. (a) To implement the policy set forth in Section 1 of this order:

(i) the head of each agency that possesses or acquires terrorism information:

(A) shall promptly give access to such information to the director of the Center, unless prohibited by law (such as section 103(c)(7) of the Act or Executive Order 12958, as amended) or otherwise directed by the president;

(B) shall cooperate in and facilitate the production of reports based on terrorism information with contents and formats that permit dissemination that maximizes the utility of the information in protecting the territory, people, and interests of the United States; and

(C) shall cooperate with the director of Central Intelligence in the preparation of the report to the president required by Section 4 of this order; and (ii) the head of each agency that conducts diplomatic, financial, military, homeland security, intelligence, or law enforcement activities relating to counterterrorism shall keep the director of the Center fully and currently informed of such activities, unless prohibited by law (such as section 103(c)(7) of the Act or Executive Order 12958, as amended) or otherwise directed by the president.

(b) The head of each agency shall, consistent with applicable law, make available to the director of the Center such personnel, funding, and other resources as the director of Central Intelligence, after consultation with the head of the

agency and with the approval of the director of the Office of Management and Budget, may request. In order to ensure maximum information sharing consistent with applicable law, each agency representative to the Center, unless otherwise specified by the director of Central Intelligence, shall operate under the authorities of the representative's agency.

Sec. 7. Definitions. As used in this order:

(a) the term "agency" has the meaning set forth for the term "executive agency" in Section 105 of Title 5, United States Code, together with the Department of Homeland Security, but includes the Postal Rate Commission and the United States Postal Service and excludes the Government Accountability Office;

(b) the term "intelligence community" has the meaning set forth for that term in Section 3.4(f) of Executive Order 12333 of December 4, 1981, as amended;

(c) the terms "local government", "state", and, when used in a geographical sense, "United States" have the meanings set forth for those terms in Section 2 of the Homeland Security Act of 2002 (6 U.S.C. 101); and

(d) the term "terrorism information" means all information, whether collected, produced, or distributed by intelligence, law enforcement, military, homeland security, or other United States Government activities, relating to (i) the existence, organization, capabilities, plans, intentions, vulnerabilities, means of finance or material support, or activities of foreign or international terrorist groups or individuals, or of domestic groups or individuals involved in transnational terrorism; (ii) threats posed by such groups or individuals to the United States, United States persons, or United States interests, or to those of other nations; (iii) communications of or by such groups or individuals; or (iv) information relating to groups or individuals reasonably believed to be assisting or associated with such groups or individuals.

[General Provisions Omitted]

GEORGE W. BUSH
THE WHITE HOUSE
August 27, 2004

EXECUTIVE ORDER 13355 OF AUGUST 27, 2004

Strengthened Management of the Intelligence Community

By the authority vested in me as president by the Constitution and laws of the United States of America, including Section 103(c)(8) of the National Security Act of 1947, as amended (Act), and in order to further strengthen the effective conduct of United States intelligence activities and protect the territory, people, and interests of the United States of America, including against terrorist attacks, it is hereby ordered as follows:

Section 1. Strengthening the Authority of the director of Central Intelligence. The director of Central Intelligence (director) shall perform the functions set forth in this order to ensure an enhanced joint, unified national intelligence effort to protect the national security of the United States. Such functions shall be in addition to those assigned to the director by law, executive order, or presidential directive.

Sec. 2. Strengthened Role in National Intelligence. Executive Order 12333 of December 4, 1981, as amended, is further amended as follows:

(a) Subsection 1.5(a) is amended to read:

"(a)(1) Act as the principal adviser to the president for intelligence matters related to the national security;

"(2) Act as the principal adviser to the National Security Council and Homeland Security Council for intelligence matters related to the national security; and

(b) Subsection 1.5(b) is amended to read:

"(b)(1) Develop such objectives and guidance for the intelligence community necessary, in the director's judgment, to ensure timely and effective collection, processing, analysis, and dissemination of intelligence, of whatever nature and from whatever source derived, concerning current and potential threats to the security of the United States and its interests, and to ensure that the National Foreign Intelligence Program (NFIP) is structured adequately to achieve these requirements; and

"(2) Working with the intelligence community, ensure that United States intelligence collection activities are integrated in:

(i) collecting against enduring and emerging national security intelligence issues;

(ii) maximizing the value to the national security; and

(iii) ensuring that all collected data is available to the maximum extent practicable for integration, analysis, and dissemination to those who can act on, add value to, or otherwise apply it to mission needs."

(c) Subsection 1.5(g) is amended to read:

"(g)(1) Establish common security and access standards for managing and handling intelligence systems, information, and products, with special emphasis on facilitating:

"(A) the fullest and most prompt sharing of information practicable, assigning the highest priority to detecting, preventing, preempting, and disrupting terrorist threats against our homeland, our people, our allies, and our interests; and

"(B) the establishment of interface standards for an interoperable information-sharing enterprise that facilitates the automated sharing of intelligence information among agencies within the intelligence community.

"(2) (A) Establish, operate, and direct national centers with respect to matters determined by the president for purposes of this subparagraph to be of the highest national security priority, with the functions of analysis and planning (including planning for diplomatic, financial, military, intelligence, homeland security, and law enforcement activities, and integration of such activities among departments and agencies) relating to such matters.

"(B) The countering of terrorism within the United States, or against citizens of the United States, our allies, and our interests abroad, is hereby determined to be a matter of the highest national security priority for purposes of subparagraph (2)(A) of this subsection."

"(3) Ensure that appropriate agencies and departments have access to and receive all-source intelligence support needed to perform independent, alternative analysis."

(d) Subsection 1.5(m) is amended to read:

"(m)(1) Establish policies, procedures, and mechanisms that translate intelligence objectives and priorities approved by the president into specific guidance for the intelligence community.

"(2) In accordance with objectives and priorities approved by the president, establish collection requirements for the intelligence community, determine collection priorities, manage collection tasking, and resolve conflicts in the tasking of national collection assets (except when otherwise directed by the president or when the Secretary of Defense exercises collection tasking authority under plans and arrangements approved by the Secretary of Defense and the director) of the intelligence community."

"(3) Provide advisory tasking concerning collection of intelligence information to elements of the United States government that have information collection capabilities and are not organizations within the intelligence community.

"(4) The responsibilities in subsections 1.5(m)(2) and

(3) apply, to the maximum extent consistent with applicable law, whether information is to be collected inside or outside the United States."

(e) Subsection 1.6(a) is amended to read:

"(a) The heads of all departments and agencies shall:

"(1) Unless the director provides otherwise, give the director access to all foreign intelligence, counterintelligence, and national intelligence, as defined in the Act, that is relevant to transnational terrorist threats and Weapons of Mass Destruction proliferation threats, including such relevant intelligence derived from activities of the FBI, DHS, and any other department or agency, and all other information that is related to the national security or that otherwise is required for the performance of the director's duties, except such information that is prohibited by law, by the president, or by the attorney general acting under this order at the

direction of the president from being provided to the director. The attorney general shall agree to procedures with the director pursuant to Section 3(5)(B) of the Act no later than 90 days after the issuance of this order that ensure the director receives all such information;

"(2) support the director in developing the NFIP;

"(3) ensure that any intelligence and operational systems and architectures of their departments and agencies are consistent with national intelligence requirements set by the director and all applicable information sharing and security guidelines, and information privacy requirements; and

"(4) provide, to the extent permitted by law, subject to the availability of appropriations, and not inconsistent with the mission of the department or agency, such further support to the director as the director may request, after consultation with the head of the department or agency, for the performance of the director's functions."

Sec. 3. Strengthened Control of Intelligence Funding. Executive Order 12333 is further amended as follows:

(a) Subsections 1.5(n), (o), and (p) are amended to read as follows:

"(n)(1) Develop, determine, and present with the advice of the heads of departments or agencies that have an organization within the intelligence community, the annual consolidated NFIP budget. The director shall be responsible for developing an integrated and balanced national intelligence program that is directly responsive to the national security threats facing the United States. The director shall submit such budget (accompanied by dissenting views, if any, of the head of a department or agency that has an organization within the intelligence community) to the president for approval; and

"(2) Participate in the development by the Secretary of Defense of the annual budgets for the Joint Military Intelligence Program (JMIP) and the Tactical Intelligence and Related Activities (TIARA) Program.

"(o)(1) Transfer, consistent with applicable law and with the approval of the director of the Office of

Management and Budget, funds from an appropriation for the NFIP to another appropriation for the NFIP or to another NFIP component;

"(2) Review, and approve or disapprove, consistent with applicable law, any proposal to: (i) reprogram funds within an appropriation for the NFIP; (ii) transfer funds from an appropriation for the NFIP to an appropriation that is not for the NFIP within the intelligence community; or (iii) transfer funds from an appropriation that is not for the NFIP within the intelligence community to an appropriation for the NFIP; and

"(3) Monitor and consult with the Secretary of Defense on reprogrammings or transfers of funds within, into, or out of, appropriations for the JMIP and the TIARA Program.

"(p)(1) Monitor implementation and execution of the NFIP budget by the heads of departments or agencies that have an organization within the intelligence community, including, as necessary, by conducting program and performance audits and evaluations;

"(2) Monitor implementation of the JMIP and the TIARA Program and advise the Secretary of Defense thereon; and

"(3) After consultation with the heads of relevant departments, report periodically, and not less often than semiannually, to the president on the effectiveness of implementation of the NFIP Program by organizations within the intelligence community, for which purpose the heads of departments and agencies shall ensure that the director has access to programmatic, execution, and other appropriate information."

Sec. 4. Strengthened Role in Selecting Heads of Intelligence Organizations. With respect to a position that heads an organization within the intelligence community:

(a) if the appointment to that position is made by the head of the department or agency or a subordinate thereof, no individual shall be appointed to such position without the concurrence of the director;

(b) if the appointment to that position is made by the president alone, any recommendation to the

president to appoint an individual to that position shall be accompanied by the recommendation of the director with respect to the proposed appointment; and

(c) if the appointment to that position is made by the president, by and with the advice and consent of the Senate, any recommendation to the president for nomination of an individual for that position shall be accompanied by the recommendation of the director with respect to the proposed nomination.

Sec. 5. Strengthened Control of Standards and Qualifications. The director shall issue, after coordination with the heads of departments and agencies with an organization in the intelligence community, and not later than 120 days after the date of this order, and thereafter as appropriate, standards and qualifications for persons engaged in the performance of United States intelligence activities, including but not limited to:

(a) standards for training, education, and career development of personnel within organizations in the intelligence community, and for ensuring compatible personnel policies and an integrated professional development and education system across the intelligence community, including standards that encourage and facilitate service in multiple organizations within the intelligence community and make such rotated service a factor to be considered for promotion to senior positions;

(b) standards for attracting and retaining personnel who meet the requirements for effective conduct of intelligence activities;

(c) standards for common personnel security policies among organizations within the intelligence community; and

(d) qualifications for assignment of personnel to centers established under Section 1.5(g)(2) of Executive Order 12333, as amended by Section 2 of this order . . .

[Technical corrections omitted.]

GEORGE W. BUSH
THE WHITE HOUSE
August 27, 2004

EXECUTIVE ORDER 13356 OF AUGUST 27, 2004

Strengthening the Sharing of Terrorism Information to Protect Americans

By the authority vested in me as president by the Constitution and laws of the United States of America, and in order to further strengthen the effective conduct of United States intelligence activities and protect the territory, people, and interests of the United States of America, including against terrorist attacks, it is hereby ordered as follows:

Section 1. Policy. To the maximum extent consistent with applicable law, agencies shall, in the design and use of information systems and in the dissemination of information among agencies:

(a) give the highest priority to (i) the detection, prevention, disruption, preemption, and mitigation of the effects of terrorist activities against the territory, people, and interests of the United States of America, (ii) the interchange of terrorism information among agencies, (iii) the interchange of terrorism information between agencies and appropriate authorities of states and local governments, and (iv) the protection of the ability of agencies to acquire additional such information; and

(b) protect the freedom, information privacy, and other legal rights of Americans in the conduct of activities implementing subsection (a).

Sec. 2. Duty of Heads of Agencies Possessing or Acquiring Terrorism Information. To implement the policy set forth in Section 1 of this order, the head of each agency that possesses or acquires terrorism information:

(a) shall promptly give access to the terrorism information to the head of each other agency that has counterterrorism functions, and provide the terrorism information to each such agency in accordance with the standards and information sharing guidance issued pursuant to this order, unless otherwise directed by the president, and consistent with (i) the statutory responsibilities of the agencies providing and receiving the information, (ii) any guidance issued by the attorney general to fulfill the policy set forth in subsection 1(b) of this order, and (iii) other applicable law, including Section 103(c)(7)

of the National Security Act of 1947, Section 892 of the Homeland Security Act of 2002, Executive Order 12958 of April 17, 1995, as amended, and Executive Order 13311 of July 29, 2003;

(b) shall cooperate in and facilitate production of reports based on terrorism information with contents and formats that permit dissemination that maximizes the utility of the information in protecting the territory, people, and interests of the United States; and

(c) shall facilitate implementation of the plan developed by the Information Systems Council established by Section 5 of this order.

Sec. 3. Preparing Terrorism Information for Maximum Distribution within Intelligence Community. To assist in expeditious and effective implementation by agencies within the intelligence community of the policy set forth in Section 1 of this order, the director of Central Intelligence shall, in consultation with the attorney general and the other heads of agencies within the intelligence community, set forth not later than 90 days after the date of this order, and thereafter as appropriate, common standards for the sharing of terrorism information by agencies within the intelligence community with (i) other agencies within the intelligence community, (ii) other agencies having counterterrorism functions, and (iii) through or in coordination with the Department of Homeland Security, appropriate authorities of state and local governments. These common standards shall improve information sharing by such methods as:

(a) requiring, at the outset of the intelligence collection and analysis process, the creation of records and reporting, for both raw and processed information including, for example, metadata and content, in such a manner that sources and methods are protected so that the information can be distributed at lower classification levels, and by creating unclassified versions for distribution whenever possible;

(b) requiring records and reports related to terrorism information to be produced with multiple versions at an unclassified level and at varying levels of classification, for example on an electronic tearline basis, allowing varying degrees of access by other agencies and personnel commensurate with their particular security clearance levels and special access approvals;

(c) requiring terrorism information to be shared free of originator controls, including, for example, controls requiring the consent of the originating agency prior to the dissemination of the information outside any other agency to which it has been made available, to the maximum extent permitted by applicable law, executive orders, or presidential guidance;

(d) minimizing the applicability of information compartmentalization systems to terrorism information, to the maximum extent permitted by applicable law, executive orders, and presidential guidance; and

(e) ensuring the establishment of appropriate arrangements providing incentives for, and holding personnel accountable for, increased sharing of terrorism information, consistent with requirements of the nation's security and with applicable law, executive orders, and presidential guidance.

Sec. 4. Requirements for Collection of Terrorism Information Inside the United States. (a) The attorney general, the Secretary of Homeland Security, and the director of Central Intelligence shall, not later than 90 days after the date of this order, jointly submit to the president, through the assistants to the president for National Security Affairs and Homeland Security, their recommendation on the establishment of executive branch-wide collection and sharing requirements, procedures, and guidelines for terrorism information to be collected within the United States, including, but not limited to, from publicly available sources, including nongovernmental databases.

(b) The recommendation submitted under subsection (a) of this section shall also:

(i) address requirements and guidelines for the collection and sharing of other information necessary to protect the territory, people, and interests of the United States; and

(ii) propose arrangements for ensuring that officers of the United States with responsibilities for protecting the territory, people, and interests of the United States are provided with clear, understandable, consistent, effective, and lawful procedures and guidelines for the collection, handling, distribution, and retention of information.

Sec. 5. Establishment of Information Systems Council. (a) There is established an Information Systems Council (Council), chaired by a designee of the director of the Office of Management and Budget, and composed exclusively of designees of: the Secretaries of State, the Treasury, Defense, Commerce, Energy, and Homeland Security; the attorney general; the director of Central Intelligence; the director of the Federal Bureau of Investigation; the director of the National Counterterrorism Center, once that position is created and filled (and until that time the director of the Terrorism Threat Integration Center); and such other heads of departments or agencies as the director of the Office of Management and Budget may designate.

(b) The mission of the Council is to plan for and oversee the establishment of an interoperable terrorism information sharing environment to facilitate automated sharing of terrorism information among appropriate agencies to implement the policy set forth in Section 1 of this order.

(c) Not later than 120 days after the date of this order, the Council shall report to the president through the assistants to the president for National Security Affairs and Homeland Security, on a plan, with proposed milestones, timetables for achieving those milestones, and identification of resources, for the establishment of the proposed interoperable terrorism information sharing environment. The plan shall, at a minimum:

(i) describe and define the parameters of the proposed interoperable terrorism information sharing environment, including functions, capabilities, and resources;

(ii) identify and, as appropriate, recommend the consolidation and elimination of current programs, systems, and processes used by agencies to share terrorism information, and recommend as appropriate the redirection of existing resources to support the interoperable terrorism information sharing environment;

(iii) identify gaps, if any, between existing technologies, programs, and systems used by agencies to share terrorism information and the parameters of the proposed interoperable terrorism information sharing environment;

(iv) recommend near-term solutions to address any such gaps until the interoperable terrorism information sharing environment can be established;

(v) recommend a plan for implementation of the interoperable terrorism information sharing environment, including roles and responsibilities, measures of success, and deadlines for the development and implementation of functions and capabilities from the initial stage to full operational capability;

(vi) recommend how the proposed interoperable terrorism information sharing environment can be extended to allow interchange of terrorism information between agencies and appropriate authorities of states and local governments; and

(vii) recommend whether and how the interoperable terrorism information sharing environment should be expanded, or designed so as to allow future expansion, for purposes of encompassing other categories of intelligence and information.

Sec. 6. Definitions. As used in this order:

(a) the term "agency" has the meaning set forth for the term "executive agency" in Section 105 of title 5, United States Code, together with the Department of Homeland Security, but includes the Postal Rate Commission and the United States Postal Service and excludes the Government Accountability Office;

(b) the terms "intelligence community" and "agency within the intelligence community" have the meanings set forth for those terms in Section 3.4(f) of Executive Order 12333 of December 4, 1981, as amended;

(c) the terms "local government," "state," and, when used in a geographical sense, "United States," have the meanings set forth for those terms in Section 2 of the Homeland Security Act of 2002 (6 U.S.C. 101); and

(d) the term "terrorism information" means all information, whether collected, produced, or distributed by intelligence, law enforcement, military, homeland security, or other United States government activities, relating to (i) the existence, organization, capabilities, plans, intentions, vulnerabilities, means of finance or material support, or activities of foreign or international terrorist groups or individuals, or of domestic groups or individuals involved in transnational terrorism; (ii) threats posed by such groups or individuals to the United States, United States persons, or United States interests, or to those of other nations; (iii) communications of or by such groups or individuals; or (iv) information relating to groups or individuals reasonably believed to be assisting or associated with such groups or individuals.

[General Provisions Omitted]

GEORGE W. BUSH
THE WHITE HOUSE
August 27, 2004

Part 3

9-11 COMMISSION REPORT
IMPLEMENTATION LEGISLATION

In the wake of the 9-11 Commission's Report, a number of bills have been introduced to make its recommendations a reality. One of these was put forth on September 7, 2004, when a bipartisan group of senators introduced *S.2274: A bill to implement the recommendations of the National Commission on Terrorist Attacks Upon the United States, and for other purposes.* The bill's goals include creating a strong national intelligence director with budgetary and personnel authority over 15 intelligence agencies. Sponsoring senators expect the *9-11 Commission Report Implementation Act* to be enacted before the November elections. Senate sponsors include Senators Evan Bayh, D-Ind.; Joe Lieberman, D-Conn.; John McCain, R-Ariz.; and Arlen Specter, R-Pa. In the House, Representatives Carolyn Maloney, D-N.Y. and Christopher Shays, R-Conn. introduced similar legislation.

The Commission's proposals are all incorporated in the 280-page bill. The legislation proposes only relatively minor changes. The 9-11 Commission's final report and recommendations state that the U.S. intelligence community was too disjointed and did not have a person in command of directing resources, centralizing intelligence, and make certain of information sharing.

Senator Bayh said, "It remains to be seen whether we can rise above bureaucratic inertia, turf jealousies, and divisions within Congress and the executive branch" to pass the law. "This proposal emphasizes accountability and that is something that is long overdue," he continued. "As far as I know, following the tragedies that led to 9-11 and following the mistakes that were made on Weapons of Mass Destruction in Iraq, no one has been fired, no one has been admonished, no one has been demoted."

The legislation introduced to implement the 9-11 Commission's recommendations includes:

H.R.5024: To implement the recommendations of the National Commission on Terrorist Attacks on the United States by establishing the position of National Intelligence Director, by establishing a National Counterterrorism Center, by making other improvements to enhance the national security of the United States, and for other purposes.
Sponsor: Rep. Pelosi, Nancy [CA-8] (introduced 9/8/2004)
H.R.5040: To implement the recommendations of the National Commission on Terrorist Attacks Upon the United States, and for other purposes.
Sponsor: Rep. Shays, Christopher [CT-4] (introduced 9/9/2004)
S.2774: A bill to implement the recommendations of the National Commission on Terrorist Attacks Upon the United States, and for other purposes.
Sponsor: Sen. McCain, John [AZ] (introduced 9/7/2004)
S.AMDT.3631 to **H.R.4567** To require the Secretary of Homeland Security to allocate formula-based grants to state and local governments based on an assessment of threats and vulnerabilities and other factors that the Secretary considers appropriate, in accordance with the recommendation of the 9-11 Commission.
Sponsor: Sen. Clinton, Hillary Rodham [NY] (introduced 9/14/2004)

ENDNOTES

1. The Bush administration clarified the respective missions of the different intelligence analysis centers in a letter sent by Secretary Ridge, DCI Tenet, FBI Director Mueller, and TTIC Director Brennan to Senators Susan Collins and Carl Levin on April 13, 2004. The letter did not mention any element of the Department of Defense. It stated that the DCI would define what analytical resources he would transfer from the CTC to TTIC no later than June 1, 2004. DCI Tenet subsequently told us that he decided that TTIC would have primary responsibility for terrorism analysis but that the CIA and the Defense Intelligence Agency would grow their own analysts. TTIC will have tasking authority over terrorism analysts in other intelligence agencies, although there will need to be a board to supervise deconfliction. George Tenet interview (July 2, 2004). We have not received any details regarding this plan.

2. "TTIC has no operational authority. However, TTIC has the authority to task collection and analysis from intelligence community agencies, the FBI, and DHS through tasking mechanisms we will create. The analytic work conducted at TTIC creates products that inform each of TTIC's partner elements, as well as other federal departments and agencies as appropriate." Letter from Ridge and others to Collins and Levin, April 13, 2004.

3. Donald Rumsfeld prepared statement, March 23, 2004, p. 20.

4. In this conception, the NCTC should plan actions, assigning responsibilities for operational direction and execution to other agencies. It would be built on TTIC and would be supported by the intelligence community as TTIC is now. Whichever route is chosen, the scarce analytical resources now dispersed among TTIC, the Defense Intelligence Agency's Joint Interagency Task Force–Combatting Terrorism (JITF-CT), and the DCI's Counterterrorist Center (CTC) should be concentrated more effectively than they are now.

   - The DCI's Countertertorist Center would become a CIA unit, to handle the direction and execution of tasks assigned to the CIA. It could have detailees from other agencies, as it does now, to perform this operational mission. It would yield much of the broader, strategic analytic duties and personnel to the NCTC. The CTC would rely on the restructured CIA (discussed in Section 13.2) to organize, train, and equip its personnel.

   - Similarly, the FBI's Counterterrorism Division would remain, as now, the operational arm of the Bureau to combat terrorism. As it does now, it would work with other agencies in carrying out these missions, retaining the JTTF structure now in place. The Counterterrorism Division would rely on the FBI's Office of Intelligence to train and equip its personnel, helping to process and report the information gathered in the field.

   - The Defense Department's unified commands–SOCOM, NORTHCOM, and CENTCOM–would be the joint operational centers taking on DOD tasks. Much of the excellent analytical talent that has been assembled in the Defense Intelligence Agency's JITF-CT should merge into the planned NCTC.

   - The Department of Homeland Security's Directorate for Information Analysis and Infrastructure Protection should retain its core duties, but the NCTC should have the ultimate responsibility for producing *net* assessments that utilize Homeland Security's analysis of domestic vulnerabilities and integrate all-source analysis of foreign intelligence about the terrorist enemy.

   - The State Department's counterterrorism office would be a critical participant in the NCTC's work, taking the lead in directing the execution of the counterterrorism foreign policy mission.

The proposed National Counterterrorism Center should offer one-stop shopping to agencies with counterterrorism and homeland security responsibilities. That is, it should be an authoritative reference base on the transnational terrorist organizations: their people, goals, strategies, capabilities, networks of contacts and support, the context in which they operate, and their characteristic habits across the life cycle of operations–recruitment, reconnaissance, target selection, logistics, and travel. For example, this Center would offer an integrated depiction of groups like al Quaida or Hezbollah worldwide, overseas, and in the United States.

The NCTC will not eliminate the need for the executive departments to have their own analytic units. But it would enable agency-based analytic units to become smaller and more efficient. In particular, it would make it possible for these agency-based analytic units to concentrate on analysis that is tailored to their agency's specific responsibilities.

A useful analogy is in military intelligence. There, the Defense Intelligence Agency and the service production agencies (like the Army's National Ground Intelligence Center) are the institutional memory and reference source for enemy order of battle, enemy organization, and enemy equipment. Yet the Joint Staff and all the theater commands still have their own J-2s. They draw on the information they need, tailoring and applying it to their operational needs. As they learn more from their tactical operations, they pass intelligence of enduring value back up to the Defense Intelligence Agency and the services so it can be evaluated, form part of the institutional memory, and help guide future collection.

In our proposal, that reservoir of institutional memory about terrorist organizations would function for the government as a whole, and would be in the NCTC.

5. The head of the NCTC would thus help coordinate the operational side of these agencies, like the FBI's Counterterrorism Division. The intelligence side of these agencies, such as the FBI's Office of Intelligence, would be overseen by the National Intelligence Director we recommend later in this chapter.

6. The quotation goes on: "It includes gaps in intelligence, but also intelligence that, like a string of pearls too precious to wear, is too sensitive to give to those who need it. It includes the alarm that fails to work, but also the alarm that has gone off so often it has been disconnected. It includes the unalert watchman, but also the one who knows he'll be chewed out by his superior if he gets higher authority out of bed. It includes the contingencies that occur to no one, but also those that everyone assumes somebody else is taking care of. It includes straightforward procrastination, but also decisions protracted by internal disagreement. It includes, in addition, the inability of individual human beings to rise to the occasion until they are sure it is the occasion—which is usually too late. . . . Finally, as at Pearl Harbor, surprise may include some measure of genuine novelty introduced by the enemy, and some sheer bad luck." Thomas Schelling, foreword to Roberta Wohlstetter, *Pearl Harbor: Warning and Decision* (Stanford University Press, 1962), p. viii.

7. For the Goldwater-Nichols Act, see Pub. L. No. 99-433, 100 Stat. 992 (1986). For a general discussion of the act, see Gordon Lederman, *Reorganizing the Joint Chiefs of Staff: The Goldwater-Nichols Act of 1986* (Greenwood, 1999); James Locher, *Victory on the Potomac: The Goldwater-Nichols Act Unifies the Pentagon* (Texas A&M University Press, 2003).

8. For a history of the DCI's authority over the intelligence community, see CIA report, Michael Warner ed., *Central Intelligence; Origin and Evolution* (CIA Center for the Study of Intelligence, 2001). For the director's view of his community authorities, see DCI directive, "Director of Central Intelligence Directive 1/1: The Authorities and Responsibilities of the Director of Central Intelligence as Head of the U.S. Intelligence Community," November 19, 1998.

9. As Norman Augustine, former chairman of Lockheed Martin Corporation, writes regarding power in the government," As in business, cash is king. If you are not in charge of your budget, you are not king." Norman Augustine, *Managing to Survive in Washington: A Beginner's Guide to High-Level Management in Government* (Center for Strategic and International Studies, 2000), p. 20.

10. For the DCI and the Secretary of Defense, see 50 U.S.C. § 403-6(a). If the director does not concur with the Secretary's choice, then the Secretary is required to notify the president of the director's nonconcurrence. Ibid. For the DCI and the attorney general, see 50 U.S.C. § 403-6(b)(3).

11. The new program would replace the existing National Foreign Intelligence Program.

12. Some smaller parts of the current intelligence community, such as the State Department's intelligence bureau and the Energy Department's intelligence entity, should not be funded out of the national intelligence program and should be the responsibility of their home departments.

13. The head of the NCTC should have the rank of a deputy national intelligence director, e.g., Executive Level II, but would have a different title.

14. If the organization of defense intelligence remains as it is now, the appropriate official would be the undersecretary of defense for intelligence. If defense intelligence is reorganized to elevate the responsibilities of the director of the DIA, then that person might be the appropriate official.

15. For the information technology architecture, see Ruth David interview (June 10, 2003). For the necessity of moving from need-to-know to need-to-share, see James Steinberg testimony, October 14, 2003. The director still has no strategy for removing information-sharing barriers and—more than two years since 9-11—has only appointed a working group on the subject. George Tenet prepared statement, March 24, 2004, p. 37.

16. The intelligence community currently makes information shareable by creating "tearline" reports, with the nonshareable information at the top and

then, below the "tearline," the portion that recipients are told they can share. This proposal reverses that concept. All reports are created as tearline data, with the shareable information at the top and with added details accessible on a system that requires permissions or authentication.

17. See Markle Foundation Task Force report, *Creating a Trusted Information Network for Homeland Security* (Markle Foundation, 2003); Markle Foundation Task Force report, *Protecting America's Freedom in the Information Age* (Markle Foundation, 2002) (both online at www.markle.org).

18. Markle Foundation Task Force report, *Creating a Trusted Information Network* p. 12. The pressing need for such guidelines was also spotlighted by the Technology and Privacy Advisory Committee appointed by Secretary Rumsfeld to advise the Department of Defense on the privacy implications of its Terrorism Information Awareness Program. Technology and Privacy Advisory Committee report, *Safeguarding Privacy in the Fight Against Terrorism* (2004) (online at www.sainc.com/ tapac/TAPAC_Report_Final_5-10-04.pdf). We take

no position on the particular recommendations offered in that report, but it raises issues that pertain to the government as a whole– not just to the Department of Defense.

19. This change should eliminate the need in the Senate for the current procedure of sequential referral of the annual authorization bill for the national foreign intelligence program. In that process, the Senate Armed Services Committee reviews the bill passed by the Senate Select Committee on Intelligence before the bill is brought before the full Senate for consideration.

20. This recommendation, and measures to assist the Bureau in developing its intelligence cadre, are included in the report accompanying the Commerce, Justice and State Appropriations Act for Fiscal Year 2005, passed by the House of Representatives on July 7, 2004. H.R. Rep. No. 108–576, 108th Cong., 2d sess. (2004), p. 22.

21. Letter from Ridge and others to Collins and Levin, April 13, 2004.

22. For the directorate's current capability, see Patrick Hughes interview (April 2, 2004).

DISCUSSION QUESTIONS

1. Pick one of the 9-11 Commission's recommendations described in the text with which you agree, and one with which you disagree. Why do you hold the positions that you do? What improvements would you suggest for the recommendation with which you agree? How would the recommendation with which you disagree need to be changed for it to be acceptable to you?

2. What are the barriers to coordinating antiterrorism information between domestic and foreign intelligence agencies? Include in your answer both our agencies (FBI, DHS, CIA, NSA, etc.) and agencies of foreign governments (such as Mossad, MI-6, and Russian intelligence).

3. What are the barriers to establishment of a National Counterterrorism Center (NCTC) as the Commission recommends? Discuss how Executive Order 13355 responds to the Commission's recommendations. Where do they differ? Why do they differ? Which approach do you think better, and why?

4. Is the government organized adequately to direct resources and build the intelligence capabilities it will need not just for countering terrorism, but for the broader range of national security challenges in the decades ahead? What improvements would you suggest?

5. The report states that "Of all our recommendations, strengthening congressional oversight may be among the most difficult and important." Do you agree or disagree, and why?

6. What should the future role for the FBI be regarding terrorism?

7. What arguments are there for and against creating a new agency to provide for antiterrorism at home?

8. Examine Executive Order 23356 reorganizing the oversight of the intelligence community. Discuss how it responds to the Commission's recommendations. Where do they differ? Why do they differ? Which approach do you think better, and why?

9. Perform research to find out the current state of intelligence supervision in the federal

government. Compare it to the Commission's recommendations and the Executive Order of August 27, 2004, in Part 2 of this chapter.

10. Describe the barriers to information sharing mentioned by the 9-11 Commission. Do you agree that sharing intelligence information is a good idea? What do you see as the biggest challenges to information sharing? What do you see as the best ways to share information?

11. Examine Executive Order 13357 strengthening terrorism information sharing. Discuss how it responds to the Commission's recommendations. Where do they differ? Why do they differ? Which approach do you think better, and why?

12. Perform research to find out the current state of intelligence supervision and information sharing in the federal government. Compare it to the Commission's recommendations and the Executive Order of August 27, 2004.

13. Pick one of the bills submitted in response to the report. Read the bill, and describe the bill's goals. Discuss how well it responds to the report. Perform research to find out the current status of the bill you chose. Be prepared to discuss the implications of that bill for how our government prepares for and responds to terrorism.

14. What barriers do you see to prompt implementation of the Commission's recommendations?

15. Create your own additional recommendation for improving the way our government protects us from terrorism. Explain why you believe that your idea should be adopted. What possible challenges might your idea face in becoming a national standard?

Chapter 21

THE FUTURE OF HOMELAND SECURITY

WILLIAM C. NICHOLSON

The future of homeland security will be informed by its past. Although the history of homeland security is a relatively short one, it is very rich in documentary material, in large part because the topic is so all encompassing. The mission statement for the federal Department of Homeland Security sets general parameters for the subject. For better or worse, it focuses on terrorism and leaves the other missions of constituent agencies to mere "also ran" status. The consequences of this concentration are seen on a daily basis in our nation.

The most direct predecessor agency to the Department of Homeland Security (DHS) is the Federal Emergency Management Agency (FEMA). The lessons of FEMA's history could benefit DHS if the latter agency were willing to learn from its predecessor's experience. DHS has been willing to learn in some areas, although in others DHS personnel apparently believe that their mission and responsibilities are without precedent.

In enacting the National Response Plan (NRP) and National Incident Management System (NIMS), DHS failed at first to adequately consider the need to achieve consensus with the groups the documents were to regulate. Internally, DHS has seen an ongoing debate regarding the nature of its mission. A law enforcement-dominated focus on terrorism as the agency's main mission appears to have triumphed over those who wish to see FEMA's previous all-hazards approach continued.

Funding decisions appear to support this conclusion. While antiterrorism monies continue to grow, the Bush administration has proposed cuts to the Emergency Management Preparedness Grants and FIRE Grants. These programs support general preparedness, rather than antiterrorism alone. The budget for the FEMA Higher Education Project has been slashed by 75%. The Higher Ed Project is perhaps the most highly leveraged expenditure of federal training dollars, supporting as it does college- and university-level education for emergency management. Thanks to the Project's efforts, during the ten years of its existence, the number of programs nationally has grown from fewer than a handful to over 113, with an additional 100 considering joining their ranks. The Higher Education Project uses an all-hazards approach, however, which may be an important reason for its deemphasis. Meanwhile, billions are spent on unproven antiterrorism training initiatives.

The law enforcement focus under DHS significantly impacts local emergency management agencies. Law enforcement dominates in many communities and states, moving in lock step with those at DHS who view terrorism as the overriding priority. Local emergency management has seen its voice shrink even as funds have been diverted from multiple use areas such as hazardous materials teams to law enforcement-specific projects that have very little application outside a policing function. Many propets to late to terrorism alone.

DHS needs to do a better job of improving preparedness. Emergency responder funds are bogged down in the distribution chain. Many eligible organizations have yet to see all their funding from as much as two years ago. As noted earlier, the Department of Homeland Security is afflicted with internal strife. As time passes, however, priorities should become clearer and the agency will hopefully better define its mission.

Should the emphasis on terrorism at the expense of all other hazards continue, significant negative effects may be anticipated. Decreased mitigation funding means lowered readiness for natural hazards. All jurisdictions may be affected by terrorism, but all jurisdictions will be affected by natural disasters.

Beginning in Federal Fiscal Year 2005, Homeland Security Presidential Directive (HSPD) 5 requires adoption of NIMS, to the extent permitted by law, for providing federal preparedness assistance through grants, contracts, or other activities. Through the NIMS Integration Center, the DHS Secretary will develop standards and guidelines for determining whether a state or local entity has adopted NIMS. Adoption of nationwide certification standards for responders should proceed in a cooperative manner if the desires of the responsible folks at DHS prevail. Emergency managers and hospital emergency room personnel are now regarded as first responders, and regulation of their activities is to be expected. Adoption of NFPA 1600 (2004 Edition) may eventually be anticipated to occur nationwide, with resulting standardization of emergency response and emergency management standards. NFPA 1600 applies to the private sector as well. Concern regarding potential liabilities will encourage the private sector, in which the vast majority of our national critical infrastructure resides, to become compliant with the NFPA 1600 benchmark.

One positive effect of the NRP and NIMS is their promotion of mutual aid and regional approaches to preparedness and response. These efforts pre-date the current emphasis on terrorism by a number of years. The National Emergency Management Association (NEMA) had been promoting the Emergency Management Assistance Compact (EMAC) since well before Congress enacted it in 1996. Clearly, the trend toward more cooperation and mutual aid will continue.

Programs like FEMA's Project Impact, which encouraged the public and private sectors to work together to make their communities more disaster resistant, fostered other types of partnering. Again, DHS has built on these proven concepts. The Department of Defense (DoD) has long been one of the most important federal sources of assistance in the aftermath of disasters. DHS has worked with the DoD to refocus its efforts on terrorism preparedness and response activities.

The military's munitions are ever more sophisticated. They are far more accurate and more lethal, meaning that the military can now do more with far fewer members than in the past. While this development is good news for the primary mission of protecting the United States from foreign adversaries, the secondary mission of support for the civilian sector in the aftermath of disasters may suffer. The reason for this is that the type of post disaster support needed is manpower and heavy equipment oriented, rather than being focused on lethality. Trucks, earthmovers, and bodies to fill sandbags are typical needs.

Civil liberties in the aftermath of 9-11 have been a source of continuing concern from a wide variety of Americans. The USA PATRIOT Act granted significant powers to the executive branch, which has pushed the envelope as far as possible in seeking to find, apprehend, and imprison potential terrorists. Many worry, however, that the net is cast too widely and that its mesh is too small, with the result that people are snared who should not be, and, once caught, are incapable of demonstrating that they should be released. The USA PATRIOT Act contains numerous limitations on civil rights that address the daily lives of all Americans and allow ever-increasing intrusion by the federal government into matters that have historically been confidential. Perhaps most troubling is the act's lessening of judicial oversight of intelligence-gathering activities, even as those actions have increased markedly. The implied belief that judicial oversight somehow results in lower security indicates a mistrust of our judicial branch of government. These conflicts will doubtless continue.

The antimoney laundering portions of the USA PATRIOT Act plug loopholes that previously allowed terrorists, drug dealers, and other criminals to move funds in a relatively unfettered manner. This part of the act will doubtless continue to exist, even if some of the other parts of the law are changed or repealed.

The events of 9-11 directly impacted our transportation infrastructure. Prevention of future terrorist acts is a high priority for providers of transportation services as well as for the federal government. Mass transit, with its requirement for moving large volumes of people efficiently and promptly, faces significant and costly needs for improving policing of suspicious persons and physical safety of patrons and equipment. The challenges of providing security and rapidly moving people appear to be in direct conflict. Identity checks and other steps take time and slow the flow of passengers significantly. The attacks on morning commuters in Madrid, Spain, in spring 2004 illustrate the potential vulnerability of mass transit passengers.

9-11 immediately affected the commercial aviation population, as it involved using airliners as flying bombs to destroy buildings and kill thousands of innocent people. The industry took immediate, severe hits on income at the same time that it faced tough new requirements to improve security. The challenges for transportation providers will continue to evolve, even as existing problems are addressed. The major reason for this is that terrorists clearly view transportation, with its concentration of target populations, as a prime target for attacks.

The use of Weapons of Mass Destruction (WMD) is perhaps the most worrisome of potential terrorist activities. Again, this concern pre-dates creation of DHS. FEMA and the Office of Justice Programs provided WMD preparedness training during the 1990s. While terrorism attacks differ in significant ways from natural disasters, they possess significant similarities as well. One potential source of trauma is the fact that terrorists wish to terrorize; therefore, maximum infliction of casualties is high on their list of goals. This contrasts with natural disasters, where mitigation and preparedness efforts have, by and large, succeeded in reducing deaths. Many have predicted that terrorists will succeed in a WMD attack on the United States.

Bioterrorism defense is a huge challenge. Creating a comprehensive and effective national defense requires a massive effort. Both terrorists and biological agents move in secrecy, seek to duplicate themselves quickly, and are continually altering themselves to counter defenses. The precursor equipment requirements to create bioweapons may look innocent and be fairly easy to obtain. Some varieties of the weapons themselves may be easily concealed and transported.

Therefore, truly countering bioterrorism will require efforts that cross international borders. Some lessening of national concepts of sovereignty may be required for efficient controls. Such an approach would be resisted in many quarters, but it may hold the best hope for the future.

A less sophisticated, but no less real, threat is the so-called dirty bomb. The materials needed to construct such a weapon are readily available. While a radiation-enhanced explosive apparatus would not come near to equaling the destructive effects of a thermonuclear device, it could cause significant and very persistent economic and health damage. The vast number of untracked radiation sources worldwide makes rather likely the use of a dirty bomb. DHS is currently working with the private sector to improve detection capabilities to prevent use of such weapons. Expenditures for this and other expensive technological responses to terrorism threats will doubtless be ongoing into the future.

Successfully dealing with terrorism within our borders requires winning the struggle against global terrorism. To do so, we must have allies. We have worked to isolate al Quaida by attacking and removing their Taliban sponsors from power in Afghanistan. Allegedly, by removing Saddam Hussein in Iraq, we deprived al Quaida of a strong supporter. Yet we cannot do these things alone. We have a coalition in Afghanistan and a smaller group of supporters in Iraq. To succeed, we must understand that mutual aid is needed on the international stage no less than between local units of government. We also need to appreciate that, in diplomacy as in emergency management, the best money spent goes for mitigation rather than response.

One key reality that influences all future planning for homeland security is the fact that we are at war with terrorism. All indications are that the United States will continue to be at risk from Islamic fundamentalist terrorists. Although it is better to fight them overseas than here, we must realize that they are not a monolithic block of universally anti-American terrorists. We must strive to better understand their motivations and consider what steps we might take to provide young Islamists with alternatives to terrorism. That basically signifies that we must work to develop opportunities for peaceful progress and hope for their future.

The 9-11 Commission's recommendations include significant changes in the federal government's structure aimed at improving our national preparedness for terrorism. Many entrenched special interests and powers in Washington, DC, face lessened power under the Commission's proposals. Some responses to the Commission's work were watered-down versions of its recommendations. These could have actually resulted in a nation less well-prepared for terrorism than we would be if things had been left as they were before the Commission's report. The Intelligence Reform and Terrorism Prevention Act of 2001 addresses many of the Commission's concerns, but does not Streamline Congressional oversight.

It is essential to anticipate threats and act before they can become imminent. To do so, however, our nation must have good intelligence. To date, our intelligence system has been severely challenged and found wanting. Human intelligence must be improved. Ongoing efforts to accomplish that goal are underway, but success will take time.

President Bush decided to declare war on terrorism in general rather than on al Quaida in particular. Eliminating al Quaida as an example to other terrorist groups would have given us a winnable mission rather than an open-ended commitment. In the future, the United States may consider declaring war on specific groups as credible evidence of their threat becomes known. Declaring war on terrorism may only serve to unite enemies who might otherwise have stayed divided and focused on their existing local adversaries.

Iraq is arguably separate from the war on terrorism. The United States entered that war for reasons and under timing that now seem less clear than when they were first presented to the American people. No matter how incorrect the decision to invade might have been, we are committed. The Vietnam experience illustrates the pitfalls of not persevering until we have created a stable situation. Although clearly not a progressive leader by any stretch of the imagination, Saddam Hussein kept order in Iraq through fear, and forced ethnic factions to tow the line. As a secular regime, he also provided a balance to the religious states in the region. One undesirable possible outcome would be

for the United States to tire of the Iraqi adventure and leave precipitously, leaving a void in power to be filled by religious zealots. Clearly in some form or another, the United States will continue to be involved in Iraq, either as an ally to a regime evolving toward democracy, or as an opponent to a new religious state, possibly in league with Iran.

Unfortunately, the decision to enter Iraq before finishing the job in Afghanistan shows a questionable understanding of international politics. Spreading our forces too thin in Iraq and Afghanistan demonstrates the limits that constrain even the sole superpower on the planet. The result of showing any weakness on our part is encouragement of those who do not have our best interests at heart.

Perhaps the most important legacy of the struggle for homeland security may be economic. Billions of dollars have been appropriated, and this spending, combined with large tax cuts to the most wealthy people and corporations, has resulted in the economy moving from a healthy surplus to the greatest deficits in the history of our nation. Furthermore, the choices on how these funds are to be spent affects the quality of life for all Americans. In the emergency management context, preparedness for the natural disasters that have grown ever more frequent has suffered. Viewed from the broader perspective of national opportunity, spending our treasure for homeland security means that those funds are not available to address national challenges like deteriorating cities and schools that are stripping out important classes like art, music, and physical education, even as they produce mediocre graduates.

The biggest trial for homeland security may be maintaining the effort on an ongoing basis. Our actions may have exacerbated the challenges we face, but those dangers are real. The longer we go without a terrorist attack, however, the more likely the American people are to believe that the risk has become lower. This is similar to the situation faced by emergency management, where a disaster-free period nearly always results in lower funding and decreased prominence of the mission. Unfortunately, it is almost a certainty that terrorists will continue to do their best to destroy our way of life. Preventing them from succeeding while at the same time addressing our nation's many other needs will be the greatest challenge for the future.

DISCUSSION QUESTIONS

1. Of all the homeland security policy issues discussed in this book, which do you believe to be the most important? Explain your answer.
2. How should we balance our priorities as we plan for the variety of hazards that face our nation?
3. What area of preparedness do you believe needs the greatest additional effort?
4. Prioritizing in one area of preparedness means that funds spent there are not available for other important uses. Which emergency preparedness and emergency response activities should get first crack at available funds?
5. Which parts of our total federal budget should be the source of funds for homeland security?
6. How will your personal behavior change as a result of what you have learned in this class?
7. During the next decade, how do see homeland security issues evolving? Will new threats arise?
8. What do you anticipate causing the greatest demand on our emergency response capabilities in the next decade, natural or manmade disasters? Explain your answer.
9. In the aftermath of 9-11, our nation embarked on new foreign commitments, putting troops in Afghanistan and Iraq to replace their governments. What do you believe that these actions foretell about future homeland security efforts beyond our borders?
10. What is the most valuable thing you have learned from this book?
11. How has your understanding of the policy issues in homeland security changed as a result of reading this book?

APPENDICES

Appendix A

HOMELAND SECURITY-ORIENTED WEBSITES

American College of Emergency Physicians
www.acep.org
The American College of Emergency Physicians (ACEP) exists to support quality emergency medical care, and to promote the interests of emergency physicians.

American Police Beat
http://www.apbweb.com/index.html
The online voice on the Nation,s police community.

British Intelligence
www.mi5.gov.uk/
The official Website of the Security Service (MI5).

Center for Defense Information
http://www.cdi.org/
The Center for Defense Information is a non-partisan, nonprofit organization committed to independent research on the social, economic, environmental, political, and military components of global security.

Centers for Disease Control and Prevention
http://www.cdc.gov/
CDC Website informs about bioterrorism issues, including anthrax.

Chemical and Biological Information Analysis Center
http://www.cbiac.apgea.army.mil/
Established in 1986, the CBIAC serves as the Department of Defense focal point for information related to Chemical and Biological Defense (CBD) technology.

Chemical Emergency Preparedness and Prevention Office
http://www.epa.gov/swercepp/
EPA's CEPPO provides leadership, advocacy, and assistance to: 1) Prevent and prepare for chemical emergencies; 2) Respond to environmental crises; and 3) Inform the public about chemical hazards in their community. Includes chemical hazard terrorism information.

CNN News
http://www.cnn.com/WORLD/
Provides up-to-date, breaking news stories.

Cops on Line
http://www.copsonline.com/index_2.htm
A real cop site by real cops.

Counterterrorism Office: U.S. Department of State
http://www.state.gov/s/ct/
Works to support U.S. counterterrorism policy.

Counterterrorism/Weapons of Mass Destruction Training Links
http://www.fbi.gov/hq/td/academy/ctwork12.htm
FBI terrorism training links.

Customs Cyber Security Center
http://www.customs.gov/enforcem/cyber.htm
The U.S. Customs Service, Office of Investigations, has established the Cyber Smuggling Center.

Department of Homeland Security
http://www.dhs.gov/dhspublic/
Official site featuring homeland security news, research and technology, threats and protection, links to subagencies, and more.

Federal Bureau of Investigation
http://www.fbi.gov/homepage.htm
FBI site offers many resources.

Federal Emergency Management Agency
http://www.fema.gov/
The FEMA Website is loaded with information on preparedness for all hazards.

Federation of American Scientists
	http://www.fas.org/
The Federation of American Scientists conducts analysis and advocacy on science, technology, and public policy.

Homeland Security Newsletter
	http://www.homelandsecurity.org/bulletin/current_bulletin.htm
Provides timely information on homeland security issues.

Indiana State Emergency Management Agency
	http://www.in.gov/sema/
Contains a variety of information on state-level emergency and terrorism preparedness.

Institute for Advanced Study of Information Warfare
	http//:www.infowar.com
Cyberterrorism information site.

Institute for Homeland Security
	http://www.homelandsecurity.org/
Provides executive education and public awareness of the challenges to homeland security in the 21st century.

International Association of Emergency Managers
	http://www.iaem.com/index.html
Professional emergency managers from around the world.

International Conference of Building Officials (ICBO)
	http://www.icbo.org/
ICBO has developed building and construction codes for more than 75 years.

International Policy Center for Counterterrorism
	http://www.ict.org.il/
ICT is a research institute and thinktank dedicated to developing innovative public policy solutions to international terrorism.

Medical, Emergency, Rescue and Global Information Rescue Network
	http://www.merginet.com/
The longest-running emergency provider Website (since 1996), Merginet concentrates on EMS issues.

Moxie Safety Resources
	http://www.moxietraining.com/oshalinks/bioterrorism_state.htm
Website connecting to multiple other sites.

National Association of Amusement Ride Safety Officials (NAARSO)
	http://naarso.com/
The National Association of Amusement Ride Safety Officials is composed of Amusement Ride Inspectors representing jurisdictional agencies, insurance companies, private consultants, safety professionals, and federal government agencies.

National Association of EMS Physicians
	http://www.naemsp.org/
The National Association of EMS Physicians is an organization of physicians and other professionals who provide leadership and foster excellence in out-of-hospital emergency medical services.

National Association of State EMS Directors
	http://www.nasemsd.org/
The National Association of State EMS Directors is the lead national organization for EMS.

National Association of State Fire Marshals (NASFM)
	http://www.firemarshals.org/
NASFM is a very small organization–51 members.

National Conference of State Legislatures
	(http://www.ncsl.org/programs/press/2001/freedom/stateaction.htm)
A resource for state legislators and others interested in developments on the state side. Contains model legislation.

National Emergency Management Association (NEMA)
	http://www.nemaweb.org/index.cfm
NEMA is the professional association of state, pacific and caribbean insular state emergency management directors.

National Institute for Occupational Safety and Health (NIOSH)
	http://www.cdc.gov/niosh/homepage.html
The National Institute for Occupational Safety and Health (NIOSH) is the federal agency

responsible for conducting research and making recommendations for the prevention of work-related disease and injury. The Institute is part of the Centers for Disease Control and Prevention (CDC).

NIOSH conducts the Firefighter Fatality Investigation and Prevention Program. The reports are an invaluable safety and liability prevention source.

> http://www.cdc.gov/niosh/firehome.html

National Fire Protection Association (NFPA)

> http://www.nfpa.org/Home/index.asp
> The mission of the international nonprofit NFPA is to reduce the worldwide burden of fire and other hazards on the quality of life by providing and advocating scientifically based consensus codes and standards, research, training, and education.

National Highway Traffic Safety Administration–EMS Division (NHTSA)

> http://www.nhtsa.dot.gov/people/injury/ems/
> The goal of NHTSA's EMS Division is to develop/enhance comprehensive emergency medical service systems to care for the injured patients involved in motor vehicle crashes.

National Interagency Civil-Military Institute (NICI)

> http://www.nici.org/
> NICI is a field operating activity of The National Guard Bureau. NICI provides free training, information, and research services for professionals, civic leaders, and public servants on domestic military support capabilities in public safety/disaster preparedness.

National Response Center (NRC)

> http://www.nrc.uscg.mil/index.htm
> The NRC is the sole federal point of contact for reporting oil and chemical spills.

National Safety Council

> http//:www.nsc.org
> The National Safety Council is the nation's leading advocate for safety and health.

National Weather Service

> http//:www.iwin.nws.noaa.gov
> A user-friendly interface to the weather.

Office for Domestic Preparedness

> http://www.ojp.usdoj.gov/odp
> USDOJ Website contains useful terrorism preparedness information.

Office of Homeland Security

> http://www.whitehouse.gov/homeland
> A link through the White House to the Office of Homeland Security.

Oklahoma City National Memorial Institute for the Prevention of Terrorism

> http://www.mipt.org/index.html
> The Oklahoma City National Memorial Institute for the Prevention of Terrorism is dedicated to preventing and reducing terrorism and mitigating its effects.

Page, Wolfberg & Wirth

> www.pwwemslaw.com
> Page, Wolfberg & Wirth is a national EMS, ambulance, and medical transportation industry law firm.

Terrorism Questions and Answers

> http://www.terrorismanswers.com/home/
> Information from the Council on Foreign Relations.

Transportation Security Administration

> http://www.tsa.dot.gov/
> The Transportation Security Administration protects the nation's transportation systems to ensure freedom of movement for people and commerce.

UCS United We Stand

> (http://www.courts.state.ny.us/september11.htm)
> New York Unified Court System Website contains important and helpful information on planning for courthouse safety.

U.S. Army Soldier and Biological Chemical Command (SBCCOM)

> http://www.sbccom.army.mil/
> The mission of the U.S. Army Soldier and Biological Chemical Command's (SBCCOM's) Homeland Defense Business Unit is to enhance the response capabilities of military, federal, state, and local emergency responders to terrorist

incidents involving Weapons of Mass Destruction (WMD).

U.S. Fire Administration (USFA)
http://www.usfa.fema.gov/
As an entity of the Federal Emergency Management Agency, the mission of the USFA is to reduce life and economic losses due to fire and related emergencies, through leadership, advocacy, coordination, and support.

U.S. Army Corps of Engineers
http://www.usace.army.mil/
The mission of the U.S. Army Corps of Engineers is to provide quality, responsive engineering services to the nation.

U.S. Department of Energy
http://www.energy.gov/
The Department of Energy's overarching mission is enhancing national security.

U.S. Geological Survey
http://www.usgs.gov/
USGS provides accurate scientific information to help prevent and recover from natural disasters.

U.S. Nuclear Regulatory Commission (NRC)
http://www.nrc.gov/
The NRC regulates U.S. commercial nuclear power plans and regulates civilian use of nuclear materials.

Trial Lawyers Care: Free Legal Help for 9-11 Victims
http://www.911lawhelp.org
Website details assistance for 9-11 victims provided pro bono by trial lawyers of the New York Bar. Interesting information for other postdisaster legal assistance.

Emergency Plans

Note: Due to security concerns, some federal plans are no longer found on the Web.
Biological and Chemical Terrorism: Strategic Plan for Preparedness and Response
http://www.cdc.gov/mmwr/preview/mmwrhtml/rr4904a1.htm

CDC, National Center for Infectious Diseases: Strategic Plan
http://www.cdc.gov/ncidod/emergplan/1toc.htm

Department of Health and Human Services, Health and Medical Services Support Plan for the Federal Response to Acts of Chemical/Biological (C/B) Terrorism
http://ndms.dhhs.gov/CT_Program/Response_Planning/C-BHMPlan.pdf

Federal Response Plan
http://www.fema.gov/ rrr/frp/

Indiana Emergency Response Commission Online Policy Manual
http://www.state.in.us/ierc/manual/index.htm

Indiana State Comprehensive Emergency Management Plan
http://www.in.gov/sema/ema/ cemp.html

National Oil and Hazardous Substances Pollution Contingency Plan (commonly referred to as the National Contingency Plan or NCP)
http://tis.eh.doe.gov/oepa/guidance/cwa/ncp_rev.pdf for overview, see: http://www.epa.gov/oilspill/ncpover.htm

Other Resources

Current FEMA Instructions and Manuals: Alphabetical Index
http://www.fema.gov/library/ alphaman.shtm

Federal Insurance and Mitigation Administration (FIMA), manages the National Flood Insurance Program and oversees FEMA's mitigation programs
http://www.fema.gov/fima/

Society for College and University Planning
http://www.scup.org/

State and Local Guide (SLG) 101: Guide for All-Hazard Emergency Operations Planning
http:// www.fema.gov/rrr/gaheop.shtm

Understanding Your Risks: Identifying Hazards and Estimating Losses (FEMA 386-2)
http:// www.fema.gov/fima/planning_toc3.shtm

Appendix B

LIST OF ACRONYMS

APHIS Animal and Plant Health Inspection Service
CBO Community-Based Organization
CDRG Catastrophic Disaster Response Group
CERCLA Comprehensive Environmental Response, Compensation, and Liability Act
CERT Community Emergency Response Team
CFO Chief Financial Officer
CI/KR Critical Infrastructure/Key Resources
CMC Crisis Management Coordinator
CNMI Commonwealth of the Northern Mariana Islands
CONPLAN U.S. Government Interagency Domestic Terrorism Concept of Operations Plan
CSG Counterterrorism Security Group
DCE Defense Coordinating Element
DCO Defense Coordinating Officer
DEST Domestic Emergency Support Team
DFO Disaster Field Office
DHS Department of Homeland Security
DMAT Disaster Medical Assistance Team
DMORT Disaster Mortuary Operational Response Team
DOC Department of Commerce
DOD Department of Defense
DOE Department of Energy
DOI Department of the Interior
DOJ Department of Justice
DOL Department of Labor
DOS Department of State
DOT Department of Transportation
DPA Defense Production Act
DRC Disaster Recovery Center
DRM Disaster Recovery Manager
DSCA Defense Support to Civil Authorities
DTRIM Domestic Threat Reduction and Incident Management

EAS Emergency Assistance Personnel or Emergency Alert System
EOC Emergency Operations Center
EPA Environmental Protection Agency
EPCRA Emergency Planning and Community Right-to-Know Act
EPLO Emergency Preparedness Liaison Officer
EPR Emergency Preparedness and Response
ERL Environmental Research Laboratories
ERT Environmental Response Team (EPA)
ERT-A Emergency Response Team–Advance Element
ERT-N National Emergency Response Team
ESF Emergency Support Function
ESFLG Emergency Support Function Leaders Group
EST Emergency Support Team
FAS Freely Associated States
FBI Federal Bureau of Investigation
FCO Federal Coordinating Officer
FEMA Federal Emergency Management Agency
FIRST Fedeal Incident Response Support Team
FMC Federal Mobilization Center
FNS Food and Nutrition Service
FOC FEMA Operations Center
FOG Field Operations Guide
FRC Federal Resource Coordinator
FRERP Federal Radiological Emergency Response Plan
FRP Federal Response Plan
GAR Governor's Authorized Representative
GIS Geographical Information System
GSA General Services Administration
HHS Department of Health and Human Services
HQ Headquarters
HSAS Homeland Security Advisory System
HSC Homeland Security Council

HSOC Homeland Security Operations Center
HSPD Homeland Security Presidential Directive
IAIP Information Analysis and Infrastructure Protection
IC Incident Command
ICP Incident Command Post
ICS Incident Command System
IIMG Interagency Incident Management Group
IMT Incident Management Team
INRP Initial National Response Plan
IOF Interim Operating Facility
ISAO Information-Sharing and Analysis Organization
JFO Joint Field Office
JIC Joint Information Center
JIS Joint Information System
JOC Joint Operations Center
JTF Joint Task Force
JTTF Joint Terrorism Task Force
MAC Entity Multiagency Coordinating Entity
MACC Multiagency Command Center
MERS Mobile Emergency Response Support
MOA Memorandum of Agreement
MOU Memorandum of Understanding
NAHERC National Animal Health Emergency Response Corps
NASA National Aeronautics and Space Administration
NAWAS National Warning System
NCP National Oil and Hazardous Substances Pollution Contingency Plan
NCR National Capital Region
NCS National Communications System
NCTC National Counterterrorism Center
NDMS National Disaster Medical System
NEP National Exercise Program
NGO Nongovernmental Organization
NICC National Infrastructure Coordinating Center
NICC National Interagency Coordinating Center
NIMS National Incident Management System
NIPP National Infrastructure Protection Plan
NIRT Nuclear Incident Response Team
NJTTF National Joint Terrorism Task Force
NMRT National Medical Response Team
NOAA National Oceanic and Atmospheric Administration
NRC Nuclear Regulatory Commission

NRCC National Response Coordination Center
NRCS Natural Resources Conservation Service
NRP National Response Plan
NRT National Response Team
NSC National Security Council
NSP National Search and Rescue Plan
NSSE National Special Security Event
NVOAD National Voluntary Organizations Active in Disaster
NWCG National Wildland Coordinating Group
OIA Office of the Assistant Secretary for Information Analysis
OSC On-Scene Coordinator
OSHA Occupational Safety and Health Administration
OSLGCP Office of State and Local Government Coordination and Preparedness
PCC Policy Coordinating Committee
PDA Preliminary Damage Assessment
PDD Presidential Decision Directive
PFO Principal Federal Official
POC Point of Contact
RA Reimbursable Agreement
RAMP Remedial Action Management Program
RCP Regional Contingency Plan
RCRA Resource Conservation and Recovery Act
REPLO Regional Emergency Preparedness Liaison Officer
RFI Request for Information
RISC Regional Interagency Steering Committee
RRCC Regional Resource Coordination Center
RRT Regional Response Team
ROC Regional Operations Center
SAC Special Agent-in-Charge
SAR Search and Rescue
SCC Secretary's Command Center (HHS)
SCO State Coordinating Officer
SFLEO Senior Federal Law Enforcement Official
SFO Senior Federal Official
SIOC Strategic Information and Operations Center
SOG Standard Operating Guideline
SOP Standard Operating Procedure
START Scientific and Technical Advisory and Response Team
TSA Transportation Security Administration

TSC Terrorist Screening Center
TTIC Terrorism Threat Integration Center
US&R Urban Search and Rescue
USACE U.S. Army Corps of Engineers
USCG U.S. Coast Guard
USDA U.S. Department of Agriculture

USSS U.S. Secret Service
VMAT Veterinarian Medical Assistance Team
WAWAS Washington Area Warning System
WMD Weapons of Mass Destruction
(National Response Plan November 16, 2004–APPENDIX 2)

Appendix C

LEGAL AUTHORITIES AND REFERENCES FOR THE NATIONAL RESPONSE PLAN (NRP)

The principal authorities that guide the structure, development, and implementation of the NRP are statutes, Executive orders, and Presidential directives. Congress has provided the broad statutory authority necessary for the NRP, and the President has issued Executive orders and Presidential directives to supply authority and policy direction to departments and agencies of the Executive Branch. Among the major statutes, orders, and directives relevant to the NRP are those summarized below.

A. Statutes and Regulations

1. **The Homeland Security Act of 2002**, Pub. Law 107-296, 116 Stat. 2135 (2002) (codified predominantly at 6 U.S.C. §§101-557 and in other scattered sections of the U.S.C.) established the Department of Homeland Security with the mandate and legal authority to protect the American people from the continuing threat of terrorism. In the act, Congress assigned DHS the primary missions to:
   - Prevent terrorist attacks within the United States;
   - Reduce the vulnerability of the United States to terrorism at home;
   - Minimize the damage and assist in the recovery from any attacks that may occur, and
   - Act as the focal point regarding natural and manmade crises and emergency planning.

   The Homeland Security Act gives the Secretary of Homeland Security full authority and control over the Department and the duties and activities performed by its personnel, and it vests the Secretary with the broad authority necessary to fulfill the Department's statutory mission to protect the American homeland. This statutory authority, combined with the President's direction in HSPD-5, supports the NRP's unified, effective approach to domestic prevention, preparedness, response, and recovery activities.

   Responsibilities in the Homeland Security Act of particular relevance to the development and execution of the NRP include the following:
   a. Preparedness of the United States for acts of terrorism. Executed through the DHS OSLGCP, this responsibility includes coordinating preparedness efforts at the Federal level, and working with State, local, tribal, parish, and private-sector emergency response providers on matters pertaining to combating terrorism.
   b. Response to terrorist attacks, major disasters, and other emergencies. Executed through the Directorate of Emergency Preparedness and Response, this responsibility includes:
      - Consolidating existing Federal emergency response plans into a single, coordinated national response plan;
      - Building a comprehensive national incident management system to respond to such attacks and disasters;
      - Ensuring the effectiveness of emergency response providers to terrorist attacks, major disasters, and other emergencies;
      - Providing the Federal Government's response to terrorist attacks, major disasters, and emergencies, including managing such response; and

- Coordinating Federal response resources in the event of a terrorist attack, major disaster, or emergency.

c. Coordination of homeland security programs with State and local government personnel, agencies, and authorities and with the private sector. Executed through the DHS OSLGCP and the Private Sector Office, this responsibility includes:

- Coordinating to ensure adequate planning, training, and exercise activities;
- Coordinating and consolidating appropriate Federal Government communications and systems of communications; and
- Distributing or coordinating the distribution of warnings and information.

d. Risk analysis and risk management. The DHS/IAIP has primary authority for threat and event risk analysis and risk management within DHS, although other DHS organizations—such as the U.S. Secret Service, the OSLGCP, and the Border and Transportation Security Directorate—also engage in risk management. DHS/IAIP responsibilities include:

- Analyzing and integrating information from all available sources to identify, assess, detect, and understand terrorist threats against the United States;
- Carrying out comprehensive assessments of the vulnerabilities of the key resources and critical infrastructure, including risk assessments to determine the risks posed by particular types of terrorist attacks within the United States;
- Identifying priorities for and recommending protective and support measures for such infrastructure by all concerned;
- Developing a comprehensive national plan (the National Infrastructure Protection Plan (NIPP)) for securing critical infrastructure and key resources, such as power and telecommunications; and
- Conducting risk assessments and vulnerability assessments after other agencies have conducted those studies and ranked top items based on those studies.

e. Preventing the entry of terrorists and the instruments of terrorism into the United States. Executed through the Border and Transportation Security Directorate, this responsibility includes:

- Securing the borders, territorial waters, ports, terminals, waterways, and air, land, and sea transportation systems of the United States; and
- Carrying out immigration enforcement functions.

2. **The Robert T. Stafford Disaster Relief and Emergency Assistance Act**, 93 Pub. L. No. 288, 88 Stat. 143 (1974) (codified as amended at 42 U.S.C. §§5121-5206, and scattered sections of 12 U.S.C., 16 U.S.C., 20 U.S.C., 26 U.S.C., 38 U.S.C. (2002)) establishes the programs and processes for the Federal Government to provide disaster and emergency assistance to States, local governments, tribal nations, individuals, and qualified private nonprofit organizations. The provisions of the Stafford Act cover all hazards including natural disasters and terrorist events. Relevant provisions of the Stafford Act include a process for Governors to request Federal disaster and emergency assistance from the President. The President may declare a major disaster or emergency:

- If an event is beyond the combined response capabilities of the State and affected local governments; and
- If, based on the findings of a joint Federal-State-local PDA, the damages are of sufficient severity and magnitude to warrant assistance under the act. (Note: In a particularly fast-moving or clearly devastating disaster, DHS/EPR/FEMA may defer the PDA process until after the declaration.)

a. If an emergency involves a subject area for which the Federal Government exercises exclusive or preeminent responsibility and authority, the President may unilaterally direct the provision of emergency assistance under the Stafford Act. The Governor of the affected State will be consulted if practicable.

b. DHS/EPR/FEMA can pre-deploy personnel and equipment in advance of an imminent Stafford Act declaration to reduce immediate threats to life, property, and public health and safety, and to improve the timeliness of disaster response.

c. During the immediate aftermath of an incident which may ultimately qualify for assistance under the Stafford Act, the Governor of the State in which such incident occurred may request the President to direct the Secretary of Defense to utilize the resources of the DOD for the purpose of performing on public and private lands any emergency work that is made necessary by such incident and that is essential for the preservation of life and property. If the President determines that such work is essential for the preservation of life and property, the President shall grant such request to the extent the President determines practical. Such emergency work may only be carried out for a period not to exceed 10 days.

d. The Stafford Act directs appointment of an FCO by the President. The FCO is designated by the DHS Under Secretary for Emergency Preparedness and Response to coordinate the delivery of Federal assistance to the affected State, local, tribal governments and disaster victims.

e. Federal agencies must avoid duplicating resources and benefits for disaster victims. Disaster victims are responsible for repayment of Federal assistance duplicated by private insurance, or other Federal programs, or when they have been otherwise compensated for their disaster-related losses.

f. All authorities under the Stafford Act granted to the Secretary of Homeland Security in the Homeland Security Act have been redelegated to the Under Secretary of EPR through Delegation No. 9001.

3. **The Public Health Security and Bioterrorism Preparedness and Response Act of 2002**, Pub. L. No. 107-188, 116 Stat. 294 (2002) (codified in scattered sections of 7 U.S.C., 18 U.S.C., 21 U.S.C., 29 U.S.C., 38 U.S.C., 42 U.S.C., and 47 U.S.C. (2002)), is designed to improve the ability of the United States to prevent, prepare for, and respond to bioterrorism and other public health emergencies. Key provisions of the act, 42 U.S.C. §247d and §300hh among others, address the development of a national preparedness plan by HHS designed to provide effective assistance to State and local governments in the event of bioterrorism or other public health emergencies; operation of the National Disaster Medical System to mobilize and address public health emergencies; grant programs for the education and training of public health professionals and improving State, local, and hospital preparedness for and response to bioter-rorism and other public health emergencies; streamlining and clarifying communicable disease quarantine provisions; enhancing controls on dangerous biological agents and toxins; and protecting the safety and security of food and drug supplies.

4. **The Defense Production Act of 1950**, 64 Stat. 798 (1950) (codified as amended by the **Defense Production Act Reauthorization of 2003**, Pub. L. 108-195, 117 Stat. 2892 (2003) at 50 U.S.C. app. §§2061-2170 (2002)) are the primary authorities to ensure the timely availability of resources for national defense and civil emergency preparedness and response. Among other things, the DPA authorizes the President to demand that companies accept and give priority to government contracts that the President "deems necessary or appropriate to promote the national defense." The DPA defines "national defense" to include critical infrastructure protection and restoration, as well as activities authorized by the emergency preparedness sections of the Stafford Act. Consequently, DPA authorities are available for activities and measures undertaken in preparation for, during, or following a natural disaster or accidental or man-caused event. The Dpartment of Commerce has redelegated DPA authority under Executive Order 12919, National Defense Industrial Resource Preparedness, June 7, 1994, as amended, to the Secretary of Homeland Security to place, and upon application, to authorize State and local governments to place, priority-rated contracts in support of Federal, State, and local emergency preparedness activities.

5. **The Economy Act**, 31 U.S.C. §§1535-1536 (2002), authorizes Federal agencies to provide goods or services on a reimbursable basis to other Federal agencies when more specific statutory authority to do so does not exist.

6. **The Posse Comitatus Act**, 18 U.S.C. §1385 (2002), prohibits the use of the Army or the Air Force for law enforcement purposes, except as otherwise authorized by the Constitution or statute. This prohibition applies to Navy and Marine Corps personnel as a matter of DOD policy. The primary prohibition of the Posse Comitatus Act is against direct involvement by active duty military personnel (to include Reservists on active duty and National Guard personnel in Federal service) in traditional law enforcement activities (to include interdiction of vehicle, vessel, aircraft, or other similar activity; directing traffic; search or seizure; an arrest, apprehension, stop and frisk, or similar activity). (**Note exception under the Insurrection Statutes.**) Exceptions to the Posse Comitatus Act are found in 10 U.S.C. §§331-335 (2002) and other statutes.

7. **The National Emergencies Act**, 50 U.S.C. §§1601-1651 (2003), establishes procedures for Presidential declaration and termination of national emergencies. The act requires the President to identify the specific provision of law under which he or she will act in dealing with a declared national emergency and contains a sunset provision requiring the President to renew a declaration of national emergency to prevent its automatic expiration. The Presidential declaration of a national emergency under the act is a prerequisite to exercising any special or extraordinary powers authorized by statute for use in the event of national emergency.

8. **The Comprehensive Environmental Response, Compensation, and Liability Act**, 42 U.S.C. §§9601-9675 (2002), and the Federal Water Pollution Control Act (Clean Water Act), 33 U.S.C. §§1251-1387 (2002), established broad Federal authority to respond to releases or threats of releases of hazardous substances and pollutants or contaminants that may present an imminent and substantial danger to public health or welfare and to discharges of oil. The National Oil and Hazardous Substances Pollution Contingency Plan, 40 CFR Part 300 (2003), was developed to ensure coordinated and integrated response by departments and agencies of the Federal Government to prevent, minimize, or mitigate a threat to public health or welfare posed by discharges of oil and releases of hazardous substances, pollutants, and contaminants.

9. **The Cooperative Forestry Assistance Act of 1978**, 16 U.S.C. §§2101-2114 (2002) authorizes the Secretary of Agriculture to assist in the prevention and control of rural fires, and to provide prompt assistance whenever a rural fire emergency overwhelms, or threatens to overwhelm, the firefighting capabilities of the affected State or rural area.

10. **The Communications Act of 1934**, 47 U.S.C. §§151-615b (2002), provides the authority to grant special temporary authority on an expedited basis to operate radio frequency devices. It would serve as the basis for obtaining a temporary permit to establish a radio station to be run by a Federal agency and broadcast public service announcements during the immediate aftermath of an emergency or major disaster. 47 U.S.C. §606 (2002) provides the authority for the NCS to engage in emergency response, restoration, and recovery of the telecommunications infrastructure.

11. **The Insurrection Act**, 10 U.S.C. §§331-335 (2002). Recognizing that the primary responsibility for protecting life and property and maintaining law and order in the civilian community is vested in State and local governments, the Insurrection Statutes authorize the President to direct the armed forces to enforce the law to suppress insurrections and domestic violence. Military forces may be used to restore order, prevent looting, and engage in other law enforcement activities.

12. **The Defense Against Weapons of Mass Destruction Act**, 50 U.S.C. §§2301-2368 (2003), is intended to enhance the capability of the Federal Government to prevent and respond to terrorist incidents involving WMD. Congress has directed that DOD provide certain expert advice to Federal, State, and local agencies with regard to WMD, to include domestic terrorism rapid response teams, training in emergency response to the use or threat of use of WMD, and a program of testing and improving the response of

civil agencies to biological and chemical emergencies.

13. **Emergencies Involving Chemical or Biological Weapons.** Pursuant to 10 U.S.C. §382 (2002), in response to an emergency involving biological or chemical WMD that is beyond the capabilities of civilian authorities to handle, the Attorney General may request DOD assistance directly. Assistance that may be provided includes identifying, monitoring, containing, disabling, and disposing of the weapon. Direct law enforcement assistance– such as conducting an arrest, searching or seizing evidence of criminal violations, or direct participation in the collection of intelligence for law enforcement purposes–is not authorized unless such assistance is necessary for the immediate protection of human life and civilian law enforcement officials are not capable of taking the action, and the action is otherwise authorized.

14. **Emergencies Involving Nuclear Materials.** In emergencies involving nuclear materials, 18 U.S.C. §831(e)(2002) authorizes the Attorney General to request DOD law enforcement assistance–including the authority to arrest and conduct searches, without violating the Posse Comitatus Act–when both the Attorney General and Secretary of Defense agree that an "emergency situation" exists and the Secretary of Defense determines that the requested assistance will not impede military readiness. An emergency situation is defined as a circumstance that poses a serious threat to the United States in which (1) enforcement of the law would be seriously impaired if the assistance were not provided, and (2) civilian law enforcement personnel are not capable of enforcing the law. In addition, the statute authorizes DOD personnel to engage in "such other activity as is incident to the enforcement of this section, or to the protection of persons or property from conduct that violates this section."

15. **Volunteer Services.** There are statutory exceptions to the general statutory prohibition against accepting voluntary services under 31 U.S.C. §1342 (2002) that can be used to accept the assistance of volunteer workers. Such services may be accepted in "emergencies involving the safety of human life or the protection of property." Additionally, provisions of the Stafford Act, 42 U.S.C. §§5152(a), 5170a(2) (2002), authorize the President to, with their consent, use the personnel of private disaster relief organizations and to coordinate their activities.

Under the Congressional Charter of 1905, 36 U.S.C. §§300101-300111 (2002), the American Red Cross and its chapters are a single national corporation. The Charter mandates that the American Red Cross maintain a system of domestic and international disaster relief. The American Red Cross also qualifies as a nonprofit organization under section 501(c)(3) of the Internal Revenue code.

16. **The Public Health Service Act**, 42 U.S.C. §§201 et seq. Among other things, this act provides that the Secretary of HHS may declare a public health emergency under certain circumstances (see 42 U.S.C. §247d), and that the Secretary is authorized to develop and take such action as may be necessary to implement a plan under which the personnel, equipment medical supplies, and other resources of the Department may be effectively used to control epidemics of any disease or condition and to meet other health emergencies and problems. (See 42 U.S.C. §243.) The Public Health Service Act authorizes the Secretary to declare a public health emergency (42 U.S.C. 247d) and to prepare for and respond to public health emergecies (42 U.S.C. 300hh). The Secretary is further empowered to extend temporary assistance to States or localities to meet health emergencies. During an emergency proclaimed by the President, the President has broad authority to direct the services of the Public Health Service (42 U.S.C. §217). Under that section, the President is authorized to "utilize the [Public Health] Service to such extent and in such manner as shall in his judgment promote the public interest." Additionally, under 42 U.S.C. §264, the Secretary is authorized to make and enforce quarantine regulations "necessary to prevent the introduction, transmission, or

spread of communicable diseases" from foreign countries into the States or possessions, or from one State or possession to another. The diseases for which a person may be subject to quarantine must be specified by the President through an Executive Order.

17. **The Veterans Affairs Emergency Preparedness Act of 2002**, Pub. L. No. 107-287, 116 Stat. 2024 (2002) (amending and codifying various sections of 38 U.S.C.). 38 U.S.C. §1785(2003), if funded, directs the VA and DOD to develop training programs for current health-care personnel and those emergency/medical personnel in training in the containment of nuclear, biological, and chemical attacks and treatment of casualties. It authorizes the Secretary of Veterans Affairs to furnish hospital care and medical services to individuals responding to, involved in, or otherwise affected by a disaster or emergency during and immediately following a disaster or emergency declared by the President under the Robert T. Stafford Disaster Relief and Emergency Assistance Act, or a disaster or emergency in which the NDMS is activated.

18. **The Atomic Energy Act of 1954**, 42 U.S.C. §§2011-2297 (2003), and the Energy Reorganization Act of 1974, 5 U.S.C. §§5313-5316, 42 U.S.C. §§5801-5891 (2002) provide the statutory authority for both the DOE and the NRC, and the foundation for NRC regulation of the Nation's civilian use of byproduct, source, and special nuclear materials to ensure adequate protection of public health and safety, to promote the common defense and security, and to protect the environment.

19. **The Price-Anderson Amendments Act of 1988**, Pub. L. No. 100-408, 102 Stat. 1066 (1988) (amending the Atomic Energy Act of 1954 and codified at 42 U.S.C. §§2014, 2210, 2273, 2282a (2003)), provides for indemnification of governments and individuals affected by nuclear incidents.

20. **Furnishing of Health-Care Services to Members of the Armed Forces during a War or National Emergency**, 38 U.S.C. §8111A (2002). During and immediately following a period of war, or a period of national emergency declared by the President or the Congress that involves the use of the Armed Forces in armed conflict, the Secretary of Veterans Affairs may furnish hospital care, nursing home care, and medical services to members of the Armed Forces on active duty. The Secretary may give a higher priority to the furnishing of care and services to active duty Armed Forces than others in medical facilities of the Department with the exception of veterans with service-connected disabilities.

21. **The Resource Conservation and Recovery Act of 1976**, 42 U.S.C. §§6901-6986 (2002), which was passed as an amendment of the Solid Waste Disposal Act of 1965, Pub. L. 89-272, 79 Stat. 997 (1965), gave the EPA the authority to control hazardous waste from "cradle to grave." This includes the generation, transportation, treatment, storage, and disposal of hazardous waste. RCRA also set forth a framework for the management of nonhazardous wastes.

22. **The Occupational Safety and Health Act**, 29 U.S.C. §§651-678 (2002), among other things, assures safe and healthful working conditions for working men and women by authorizing enforcement of the standards developed under the act; by assisting and encouraging the States in their efforts to assure safe and healthful working conditions; by providing for research, information, education, and training in the field of occupational safety and health.

23. **The Maritime Transportation Security Act**, Pub. L. No. 107-295, 116 Stat. 2064 (2002) (codified at 46 U.S.C. §§70102-70117 and scattered sections of the U.S.C.), requires sectors of the maritime industry to implement measures designed to protect America's ports and waterways from a terrorist attack.

24. **Flood Control and Coastal Emergencies**, 33 U.S.C. §701n (2002) (commonly referred to as Public Law 84-99), authorizes the USACE an emergency fund for preparation for emergency response to natural disasters, flood fighting and rescue operations, rehabilitation of flood control and hurricane protection structures, temporary restoration of essential

public facilities and services, advance protective measures, and provision of emergency supplies of water. The USACE receives funding for such activities under this authority from the Energy and Water Development Appropriation.

25. **The Oil Pollution Act of 1990**, Pub. L. No. 101-380, 104 Stat. 484 (1990) (codified as amended at 33 U.S.C. §§1203, 1223, 1321, 2701-2761 and various other sections of the U.S.C. (2002)), improved the Nation's ability to prevent and response to oil spills by establishing provisions that expand the Federal Government's ability, and provides the money and personnel necessary to respond to oil spills. The act also created the national Oil Spill Liability Trust Fund.

26. **The Clean Air Act**, 42 U.S.C. §§7401-7671q (2002) and 40 CFR §80.73 (2003). The EPA may temporarily permit a refiner, importer, or blender to distribute nonconforming gasoline in appropriate extreme or unusual circumstances (e.g., an Act of God) that could not have been avoided. EPA may seek DOE's advice on fuel supply situations when deciding whether to grant a request to distribute nonconforming gasoline.

27. **The Public Utilities Regulatory Policies Act of 1978**, Pub. L. No. 95-617, 92 Stat. 3117, (1978) (codified at scattered sections of 15 U.S.C., 16 U.S.C., 30 U.S.C., 42 U.S.C., 43 U.S.C.(2002)) and the Powerplant and Industrial Fuel Use Act of 1978, Pub. L. No. 95-620, 92 Stat. 3289 (1978) (codified as amended at 42 U.S.C. §§8301-8484 (2002)). The President has authority to prohibit any powerplant or major fuel-burning installation from using natural gas or petroleum as a primary fuel during an emergency.

28. **The Federal Power Act**, 16 U.S.C. §§791a-828c, 824a(c) (2002), 10 C.F.R. §205.370 (2003). The Secretary of Energy has authority in an emergency to order temporary interconnections of facilities and/or the generation and delivery of electric power.

29. **The Department of Energy Organization Act**, Pub. L. No. 95-91, 91 Stat. 567 (1977) (codified predominately at 42 U.S.C. §§7101-7385o (2002)), and the Federal Power Act, 16 U.S.C. §§791a-828c (2002), 10 CFR §§205.350, 205.353 (2003). DOE has authority to obtain current information regarding emergency situations on the electric supply systems in the United States.

30. **The Department of Energy Organization Act**, Pub. L. No. 95-91, 91 Stat. 567 (1977) (codified predominately at 42 U.S.C. §§7101-7385o (2002)), 10 CFR §§205.350, 205.353 (2003), and the **Federal Energy Administration Act of 1974**, 15 U.S.C. §§761-790h (2002). DOE and the National Association of State Energy Officials (NASEO) have agreed that DOE will develop, maintain, and distribute a contact list of State and Federal individuals responsible for energy market assessment and energy emergency responses, and that the States will participate in the effort by providing timely assessments of energy markets to DOE and other States in the event of an energy supply disruption.

31. **The Energy Policy and Conservation Act**, 42 U.S.C. §§6201-6422 (2002), as amended by the Energy Policy Act of 1992, Pub. L. No. 102-486, 106 Stat. 2776 (1992) (as amended and codified in scattered sections of the U.S.C.). The President may, in an emergency, order Federal buildings to close and/or conserve energy.

32. **Transportation of Hazardous Material**, 49 U.S.C. §§5101-5127 (2002). Improves the regulatory and enforcement authority of the Secretary of Transportation to provide adequate protection against the risks to life and property inherent in the transportation of hazardous material in commerce.

33. **The Ports and Waterways Safety Act of 1978**, Pub. L. No. 95-474, 92 Stat. 1471 (1978) (amending Pub. L. No. 92-340 and codified at 33 U.S.C. §§1222-1232 and 46 U.S.C. §§214, 391a (2002)). The Secretary of Transportation has authority to establish vessel traffic systems for ports, harbors, and other navigable waterways, and to control vessel traffic in areas determined to be hazardous (e.g., due to vessel congestion). In such emergency situations, DOE may be asked to advise the U.S. Coast Guard on "priority" vessel movements to expedite delivery of needed energy supplies.

34. **The Energy Policy and Conservation Act**, 42 U.S.C. §§6231-6247 (2002). DOE is authorized to create and maintain a Strategic Petroleum Reserve (SPR) and the President is authorized to order a drawdown of the Reserve in emergency circumstances defined in the act.

35. **The Energy Policy and Conservation Act**, 42 U.S.C. §§6250c (2002). DOE is authorized to create and maintain a Northeast Home Heating Oil Reserve and the President is authorized to order a drawdown of the reserve in emergency circumstances defined in the act.

36. **The Natural Gas Policy Act of 1978**, 15 U.S.C. §§3301-3432 (2002). DOE can order any interstate pipeline or local distribution company served by an interstate pipeline to allocate natural gas in order to assist in meeting the needs of high-priority consumers during a natural gas emergency.

37. **The Powerplant and Industrial Fuel Use Act of 1978**, 42 U.S.C. §§8301-8484 (2002). The President has authority to allocate coal (and require the transportation of coal) for the use of any powerplant or major fuel-burning installation during an energy emergency.

38. **The Low Income Home Energy Assistance Act of 1981**, 42 U.S.C. §§8621-8629 (2002). HHS has discretionary funds available for distribution under the Low Income Home Energy Assistance Program (LIHEAP), according to the criteria that relate to the type of emergency that precipitates their need. DOE may advise HHS on the fuel supply situation for such emergency funding.

39. **The Small Business Act**, 15 U.S.C. §§631-651e (2002). The mission of the Small Business Administration is to maintain and strengthen the Nation's economy by aiding, counseling, assisting, and protecting the interests of small businesses and by helping families and businesses recover from incidents such as major disasters, emergencies, and catastrophes.

40. **The Immigration Emergency Fund (IEF)** was created by section 404(b)(1) of the Immigration and Nationality Act. The IEF can be drawn upon to increase INS's enforcement activities, and to reimburse States and localities in providing assistance as requested by the Secretary of the DHS in meeting an immigration emergency declared by the President.

41. **The Animal Health Protection Act of 2002**, 7 U.S.C. 8310, consolidates all of the animal quarantine and related laws and replaces them with one flexible statutory framework. This act allows APHIS Veterinary Services to act swiftly and decisively to protect U.S. animal health from a foreign pest or disease.

42. **28 CFR §0.85** designates the FBI as the agency with primary responsibility for investigating all crimes for which it has primary or concurrent jurisdiction and which involve terrorist activities or acts in preparation of terrorist activities within the statutory jurisdiction of the United States. This would include the collection, coordination, analysis, management and dissemination of intelligence and criminal information as appropriate.

B. Executive Orders

1. **Executive Order 12148**, 44 Fed. Reg. 43239 (1979), as amended by Exec. Order 13286, 68 Fed. Reg. 10619 (2003), designates DHS as the primary agency for coordination of Federal disaster relief, emergency assistance, and emergency preparedness. The order also delegates the President's relief and assistance functions under the Stafford Act to the Secretary of Homeland Security, with the exception of the declaration of a major disaster or emergency.

2. **Executive Order 12656**, 53 Fed. Reg. 47491 (1988), Assignment of Emergency Preparedness Responsibilities, as amended by Exec. Order 13286, 68 Fed. Reg. 10619 (2003), assigns lead and support responsibilities to each of the Federal agencies for national security emergency preparedness. The amendment designates DHS as the principal agency for coordinating programs and plans among all Federal departments and agencies.

3. **Executive Order 13354**, 69 Fed. Reg. 53589 (2004), National Counterterrorism Center, establishes policy to enhance the interchange of terrorism information among agencies and creates the National Counterterrorism Center to

serve as the primary Federal organization in the U.S. Government for analyzing and integrating all intelligence information posed by the United States pertaining to terrorism and counterterrorism.

4. **Executive Order 13356**, 69 Fed. Reg. 53599 (2004), Strengthening the Sharing of Terrorism Information to Protect Americans, requires the Director of Central Intelligence, in consultation with the Attorney General and the other intelligence agency heads, to develop common standards for the sharing of terrorism information by agencies within the Intelligence Community with 1) other agencies within the Intelligence Community, 2) other agencies having counterterrorism functions, and 3) through or in coordination with the Department of Homeland Security, appropriate authorities of State and local governments.

5. **Executive Order 12580**, 52 Fed. Reg. 2923 (1987), Superfund Implementation, as amended by numerous Executive orders, delegates to a number of Federal departments and agencies the authority and responsibility to implement certain provisions of CERCLA. The policy and procedures for implementing these provisions are spelled out in the NCP and are overseen by the NRT.

6. **Executive Order 12382**, 47 Fed. Reg. 40531 (1982), as amended by numerous Executive orders, President's National Security Telecommunications Advisory Committee (NSTAC). This order provides the President with technical information and advice onnational security telecommunications policy. Up to 30 members from the telecommunications and information technology industries may hold seats on the NSTAC.

7. **Executive Order 12472**, 49 Fed. Reg. 13471 (1984), Assignment of National Security and Emergency Preparedness Telecommunications Functions, as amended by Exec. Order 13286, 68 Fed. Reg. 10619 (2003). This Order consolidated several directives covering NSEP telecommunications into a comprehensive document explaining the assignment of responsibilities to Federal agencies for coordinating the planning and provision of NSEP telecommunications. The fundamental NSEP objective is to ensure that the Federal Government has telecommunications services that will function under all conditions, including emergency situations.

8. **Executive Order 12742**, 56 Fed. Reg. 1079 (1991), National Security Industrial Responsiveness, as amended by Exec. Order 13286, 68 Fed. Reg. 10619 (2003). This order states that the United States must have the capability to rapidly mobilize its resources in the interest of national security. Therefore, to achieve prompt delivery of articles, products, and materials to meet national security requirements, the Government may place orders and require priority performance of these orders.

9. **Executive Order 13284**, 68 Fed. Reg. 4075 (2003), Amendment of Executive Orders, and Other Actions, in Connection With the Establishment of the Department of Homeland Security. This order amended previous Executive orders in order to make provisions for the establishment of DHS.

10. **Executive Order 13286**, 68 Fed. Reg. 10619 (2003), Amendment of Executive Orders, and Other Actions, in Connection With the Transfer of Certain Functions to the Secretary of Homeland Security. This order reflects the transfer of certain functions to, and other responsibilities vested in, the Secretary of Homeland Security, as well as the transfer of certain agencies and agency components to DHS, and the delegation of appropriate responsibilities to the Secretary of Homeland Security.

11. **Executive Order 12333**, 46 Fed. Reg. 59941 (1981), United States Intelligence Activities, designates DOE as part of the Intelligence Community. It further defines counterintelligence as information gathered and activities conducted to protect against espionage, sabotage, or assassinations conducted for or on behalf of foreign powers, organizations or persons, or international terrorist activities. This order specifically excludes personnel, physical, document, or communications security programs from the definition of counterintelligence.

12. **Executive Order 12919**, 59 Fed. Reg. 29625 (1994), National Defense Industrial Resources Preparedness, as amended by Exec. Order 13286, 68 Fed. Reg. 10619 (2003). This order delegates authorities and addresses national defense industrial resource policies and programs under the Defense Production Act of 1950, as amended, except for the amendments to Title III of the act in the Energy Security Act of 1980 and telecommunication authorities under Exec. Order 12472, 49 Fed. Reg. 13471 (1984).

13. **Executive Order 12777**, 56 Fed. Reg. 54757 (1991), Implementation of Section 311 of the Federal Water Pollution Control Act of October 18, 1972, as amended, and the Oil Pollution Act of 1990, as amended by Exec. Order 13286, 68 Fed. Reg. 10619 (2003). Implemented section 311 of the FWPCA as amended by OPA 90.

14. **Executive Order 13295**, 68 Fed. Reg. 17255 (2003), Revised List of Quarantinable Communicable Diseases. Specifies certain communicable diseases for regulations providing for the apprehension, detention, or conditional release of individuals to prevent the introduction, transmission, or spread of suspected communicable diseases.

15. **Executive Order 12196**, 45 Fed. Reg. 12769 (1980), Occupational Safety and Health Programs for Federal Employees. This order sets the OSHA program guidelines for all agencies in the Executive Branch except military personnel and uniquely military equipment, systems, and operations.

C. Presidential Directives

1. **Presidential Decision Directive 39:** U.S. Policy on Counterterrorism, June 21, 1995, establishes policy to reduce the Nation's vulnerability to terrorism, deter and respond to terrorism, and strengthen capabilities to detect, prevent, defeat, and manage the consequences of terrorist use of WMD; and assigns agency responsibilities.

2. **Presidential Decision Directive 62:** Combating Terrorism, May 22, 1998, reinforces the missions of Federal departments and agencies charged with roles in defeating terrorism.

3. **Homeland Security Presidential Directive-1:** Organization and Operation of the Homeland Security Council, Oct. 29, 2001. This directive establishes policies for the creation of the HSC, which shall ensure the coordination of all homeland security-related activities among executive departments and agencies and promote the effective development and implementation of all homeland security policies.

4. **Homeland Security Presidential Directive-2:** Combating Terrorism Through Immigration Policies, Oct. 29, 2001. This directive mandates that, by November 1, 2001, the Attorney General shall create the Foreign Terrorist Tracking Task Force, with assistance from the Secretary of State, the Director of Central Intelligence, and other officers of the Government, as appropriate. The Task Force shall ensure that, to the maximum extent permitted by law, Federal agencies coordinate programs to accomplish the following: 1) deny entry into the United States of aliens associated with, suspected of being engaged in, or supporting terrorist activity; and 2) locate, detain, prosecute, or deport any such aliens already present in the United States.

5. **Homeland Security Presidential Directive-3:** Homeland Security Advisory System, Mar. 11, 2002. This directive established policy for the creation of a Homeland Security Advisory System, which shall provide a comprehensive and effective means to disseminate information regarding the risk of terrorist acts to Federal, State, and local authorities and to the American people. Such a system would provide warnings in the form of a set of graduated "Threat Conditions" that would increase as the risk of the threat increases. At each Threat Condition, Federal departments and agencies would implement a corresponding set of "Protective Measures" to further reduce vulnerability or increase response capability during a period of heightened alert.

6. **Homeland Security Presidential Directive-4:** National Strategy to Combat Weapons of Mass Destruction, Dec. 2002. Sets forth the National Strategy to Combat Weapons of Mass Destruction

based on three principal pillars: (1) Counter-proliferation to Combat WMD Use, (2) Strengthened Nonproliferation to Combat WMD Proliferation, and (3) Consequence Management to Respond to WMD Use. The three pillars of the U.S. national strategy to combat WMD are seamless elements of a comprehensive approach. Serving to integrate the pillars are four cross-cutting enabling functions that need to be pursued on a priority basis: intelligence collection and analysis on WMD, delivery systems, and related technologies; research and development to improve our ability to address evolving threats; bilateral and multilateral cooperation; and targeted strategies against hostile states and terrorists.

7. **Homeland Security Presidential Directive-5:** Management of Domestic Incidents, February 28, 2003, is intended to enhance the ability of the United States to manage domestic incidents by establishing a single, comprehensive national incident management system. In HSPD-5 the President designates the Secretary of Homeland Security as the PFO for domestic incident management and empowers the Secretary to coordinate Federal resources used in response to or recovery from terrorist attacks, major disasters, or other emergencies in specificcases. The directive assigns specific responsibilities to the Attorney General, Secretary of Defense, Secretary of State, and the Assistants to the President for Homeland Security and National Security Affairs, and directs the heads of all Federal departments and agencies to provide their "full and prompt cooperation, resources, and support," as appropriate and consistent with their own responsibilities for protecting national security, to the Secretary of Homeland Security, Attorney General, Secretary of Defense, and Secretary of State in the exercise of leadership responsibilities and missions assigned in HSPD-5. The directive also notes that it does not alter, or impede the ability to carry out, the authorities of Federal departments and agencies to perform their responsibilities under law.

8. **Homeland Security Presidential Directive-6:** Integration and Use of Screening Information, Sept. 16, 2003. In order to protect against terrorism, this directive establishes the national policy to: (1) develop, integrate, and maintain thorough, accurate, and current information about individuals known or appropriately suspected to be or have been engaged in conduct constituting, in preparation for, in aid of, or related to terrorism (Terrorist Information); and (2) use that information as appropriate and to the full extent permitted by law to support (a) Federal, State, local, territorial, tribal, foreign-government, and private-sector screening processes, and (b) diplomatic, military, intelligence, law enforcement, immigration, visa, and protective processes.

9. **Homeland Security Presidential Directive-7:** Critical Infrastructure Identification, Prioritization, and Protection, Dec. 17, 2003. This directive establishes a national policy for Federal departments and agencies to identify and prioritize U.S. critical infrastructure and key resources and to protect them from terrorist attacks.

10. **Homeland Security Presidential Directive-8:** National Preparedness, Dec. 17, 2003. This directive establishes policies to strengthen the preparedness of the United States to prevent and respond to threatened or actual domestic terrorist attacks, major disasters, and other emergencies by requiring a national domestic all-hazards preparedness goal, establishing mechanisms for improved delivery of Federal preparedness assistance to State and local governments, and outlining actions to strengthen preparedness capabilities of Federal, State, and local entities.

11. **Homeland Security Presidential Directive-9:** Defense of United States Agriculture and Food, Jan. 30, 2004. This directive establishes a national policy to defend the agriculture and food system against terrorist attacks, major disasters, and other emergencies.

12. **Homeland Security Presidential Directive-10:** Biodefense for the 21st Century, April 28, 2004. This directive provides a comprehensive framework for the nation's biodefense and, among other things, delineates the roles and responsibilities of Federal agencies and departments in continuing their important work in this area.

13. **National Security Directive 42:** National Policy for the Security of National Security

Telecommunications and Information Systems, July 5, 1990. This directive establishes initial objectives of policies, and an organizational structure to guide the conduct of activities to secure national security systems from exploitation; establishes a mechanism for policy development and dissemination; and assigns responsibilities for implementation.

Appendix D

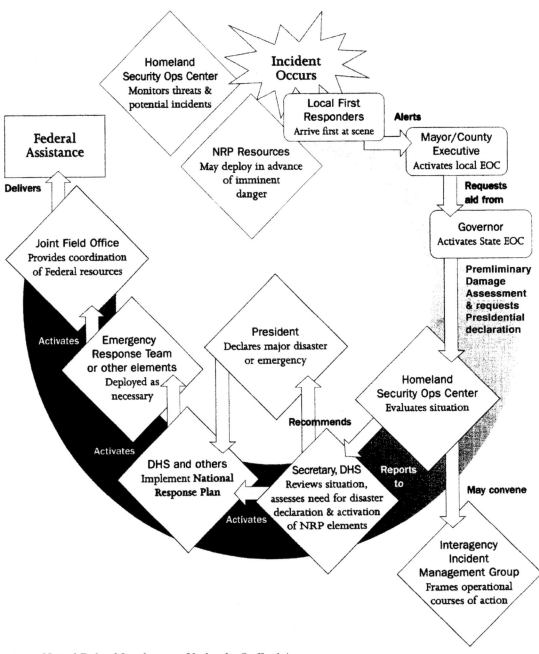

Incident Occurs

Homeland Security Ops Center
Monitors threats & potential incidents

Local First Responders
Arrive first at scene

Alerts

Mayor/County Executive
Activates local EOC

Requests aid from

Governor
Activates State EOC

NRP Resources
May deploy in advance of imminent danger

Federal Assistance

Delivers

Premliminary Damage Assessment & requests Presidential declaration

Joint Field Office
Provides coordination of Federal resources

President
Declares major disaster or emergency

Homeland Security Ops Center
Evaluates situation

Activates

Emergency Response Team or other elements
Deployed as necessary

Recommends

Reports to

May convene

Activates

DHS and others
Implement **National Response Plan**

Secretary, DHS
Reviews situation, assesses need for disaster declaration & activation of NRP elements

Activates

Interagency Incident Management Group
Frames operational courses of action

Overview of Initial Federal Involvement Under the Stafford Act

364

Appendix E

STATE DEFINITIONS OF TERRORISM

1. **Alabama**–Ala. Code 1975 §13A-10-151 (THE ANTITERRORISM ACT OF 2002)
(1) ACT OF (TERRORISM). An act or acts constituting a specified offense as defined in subdivision (4) for which a person may be convicted in the criminal courts of this state, or an act or acts constituting an offense in any other jurisdiction within or outside the territorial boundaries of the United States which contains all of the essential elements of a specified offense, that is intended to do the following: a.) Intimidate or coerce a civilian population. b.) Influence the policy of a unit of government by intimidation or coercion. c.) Affect the conduct of a unit of government by murder, assassination, or kidnapping. (2) MATERIAL SUPPORT OR RESOURCES. Currency or other financial securities, financial services, lodging, training, safehouses, false documentation or identification, communications equipment, facilities, weapons, lethal substances, explosives, personnel, transportation, and other physical assets, except medicine or religious materials. (3) RENDERS CRIMINAL ASSISTANCE. Shall have the same meaning as in Section 13A-10-42. (4) SPECIFIED OFFENSE. A Class A felony, manslaughter, kidnapping in the second degree, assault in the first or second degree, stalking, intimidating a witness, criminal tampering, or any attempt or conspiracy to commit any of these offenses.

2. **Alaska**–2 Alaska Admin. Code 80.110 *citing* 18 U.S.C. sec. 2331
The term "international terrorism" means activities that–(A) involve violent acts or acts dangerous to human life that are a violation of the criminal laws of the United States or of any state, or that would be a criminal violation if committed within the jurisdiction of the United States or of any state; (B) appear to be intended–(i) to intimidate or

coerce a civilian population; (ii) to influence the policy of a government by intimidation or coercion; or (iii) to affect the conduct of a government by mass destruction, assassination, or kidnapping; and (C) occur primarily outside the territorial jurisdiction of the United States, or transcend national boundaries in terms of the means by which they are accomplished, the persons they appear intended to intimidate or coerce, or the locale in which their perpetrators operate or seek asylum.

3. **Arizona**–A.R.S. §13-2301
"Terrorism" means any felony, including any completed or preparatory offense, that involves the use of a deadly weapon or a Weapon of Mass Destruction or the intentional or knowing infliction of serious physical injury with the intent to either: (a) Influence the policy or affect the conduct of this state or any of the political subdivisions, agencies or instrumentalities of this state. (b) Cause substantial damage to or substantial interruption of public communications, communication service providers, public transportation, common carriers, public utilities, public establishments, or other public services.

4. **Arkansas**–A.C.A. §5-54-205
(a) A person commits the offense of terrorism when with the intent to intimidate or coerce a civilian population, influence the policy of a unit of government by using intimidation or coercion, affect the conduct of a unit or level of government by intimidation or coercion, or retaliate against a civilian population or unit of government for a policy or conduct the person: (1) Knowingly commits an act of terrorism within this state; or (2) While outside this state, knowingly commits an act of terrorism that takes effect within this state or produces substantial detrimental effects within this state.(b) Terrorism is a Class Y felony.

5. California–Cal Gov Code §8549.2
"Act of terrorism" means any unlawful harm, attempted harm, or threat to do harm to, any state employee, state property, or the person or property of any person on the premises of any state-occupied building or other property leased or owned by the state.

6. Colorado–28 C.F.R. §0.85
"Terrorism" includes the unlawful use of force and violence against persons or property to intimidate or coerce a government, the civilian population, or any segment thereof, in furtherance of political or social objectives.

7. Connecticut–C.G.S.A. §53a-300
A person is guilty of an act of terrorism when such person, with intent to intimidate or coerce the civilian population or a unit of government, commits a felony involving the unlawful use or threatened use of physical force or violence.

8. Delaware–11 Del. C. §9002 *citing* 18 U.S.C. sec. 2331
"Domestic terrorism" means activities that–(A) involve acts dangerous to human life that are a violation of the criminal laws of the United States or of any state; (B) appear to be intended–(i) to intimidate or coerce a civilian population; (ii) to influence the policy of a government by intimidation or coercion; or (iii) to affect the conduct of a government by mass destruction, assassination, or kidnapping; and (C) occur primarily within the territorial jurisdiction of the United States.

9. District of Columbia–DC ST §22-3152
(1) "Act of Terrorism" means an act or acts that constitute a specified offense as defined in paragraph (8) of this section and that are intended to:

(A) intimidate or coerce a significant portion of the civilian population of
  i. The District of Columbia; or
  ii. The United States; or
(B) Influence the policy or conduct of a unit of government by intimidation or coercion.

(8) "Specified Offense" means:

(A) Murder in the first degree;
(B) Murder in the first degree B placing obstructions upon or displacement of railroads;

(C) Murder of law enforcement officer or public safety employee;
(D) Murder in the second degree;
(E) Manslaughter;
(F) Kidnapping and conspiracy to kidnap;
(G) Assault with intent to kill only;
(H) Mayhem or maliciously disfiguring;
(I) Arson;
(J) Malicious burning, destruction, or injury of another's property, if the property is valued at $500,000 or more; or
(K) An attempt or conspiracy to commit any of the offenses listed in subparagraphs (A) through (J) of this paragraph.

10. Florida–F.S.A. §775-30
As used in the Florida Criminal Code, the term "terrorism" means an activity that: (1)(a) Involves a violent act or an act dangerous to human life which is a violation of the criminal laws of this state or of the United States; or (b) Involves a violation of s. 815.06 ("Offenses against computer users"); and (2) Is intended to: (a) Intimidate, injure, or coerce a civilian population; (b) Influence the policy of a government by intimidation or coercion; or (c) Affect the conduct of government through destruction of property, assassination, murder, kidnapping, or aircraft piracy.

11. Georgia–Ga. Code Ann., §16-4-10
"Domestic terrorism" means any violation of, or attempt to violate, the laws of this state or of the United States which: (1) Is intended or reasonably likely to injure or kill not less than ten individuals as part of a single unlawful act or a series of unlawful acts which are interrelated by distinguishing characteristics; and (2)(A) Is intended to intimidate the civilian population of this state, any of its political subdivisions, or of the United States; (B) Is intended to alter, change, or coerce the policy of the government of this state or any of its political subdivisions by intimidation or coercion; or (C) Is intended to affect the conduct of the government of this state or any of its political subdivisions by use of destructive devices, assassination, or kidnapping.

12. Hawaii–HRS §351-32 *citing* 18 U.S.C. sec. 2331
"Domestic terrorism" means activities that–(A) involve acts dangerous to human life that are a

violation of the criminal laws of the United States or of any state; (B) appear to be intended–(i) to intimidate or coerce a civilian population; (ii) to influence the policy of a government by intimidation or coercion; or (iii) to affect the conduct of a government by mass destruction, assassination, or kidnapping; and (C) occur primarily within the territorial jurisdiction of the United States.

13. **Idaho**–Idaho Code §18-8102
"Terrorism" means activities that: (a) Are a violation of Idaho criminal law; and (b) Involve acts dangerous to human life that are intended to: (i) Intimidate or coerce a civilian population; (ii) Influence the policy of a government by intimidation or coercion; or (iii) Affect the conduct of a government by the use of Weapons of Mass Destruction, as defined in section 18-3322, Idaho Code.

14. **Illinois**–720 ILCS 5/29D-10
"Terrorist act" or "act of terrorism" means: (1) any act that is intended to cause or create a risk and does cause or create a risk of death or great bodily harm to one or more persons; (2) any act that disables or destroys the usefulness or operation of any communications system; (3) any act or any series of two or more acts committed in furtherance of a single intention, scheme, or design that disables or destroys the usefulness or operation of a computer network, computers, computer programs, or data used by any industry, by any class of business, or by five or more businesses or by the federal government, state government, any unit of local government, a public utility, a manufacturer of pharmaceuticals, a national defense contractor, or a manufacturer of chemical or biological products used in or in connection with agricultural production; (4) any act that disables or causes substantial damage to or destruction of any structure or facility used in or used in connection with ground, air, or water transportation; the production or distribution of electricity, gas, oil, or other fuel; the treatment of sewage or the treatment or distribution of water; or controlling the flow of any body of water; (5) any act that causes substantial damage to or destruction of livestock or to crops or a series of two or more acts committed in furtherance of a single intention, scheme, or design which, in the aggregate, causes substantial damage to or destruc-

tion of livestock or crops; (6) any act that causes substantial damage to or destruction of any hospital or any building or facility used by the federal government, state government, any unit of local government or by a national defense contractor or by a public utility, a manufacturer of pharmaceuticals, a manufacturer of chemical or biological products used in or in connection with agricultural production or the storage or processing of agricultural products or the preparation of agricultural products for food or food products intended for resale or for feed for livestock; or (7) any act that causes substantial damage to any building containing five or more businesses of any type or to any building in which ten or more people reside.

15. **Indiana**–IC 35-41-1-26.5
"Terrorism" means the unlawful use of force or violence or the unlawful threat of force or violence to intimidate or coerce a government or all or part of the civilian population.

16. **Iowa**–I.C.A. §708A.1
"Terrorism" means an act intended to intimidate or coerce a civilian population, or to influence the policy of a unit of government by intimidation or coercion, or to affect the conduct of a unit of government, by shooting, throwing, launching, discharging, or otherwise using a dangerous weapon at, into, or in a building, vehicle, airplane, railroad engine, railroad car, or boat, occupied by another person, or within an assembly of people. The terms "intimidate," "coerce," "intimidation," and "coercion," as used in this definition, are not to be construed to prohibit picketing, public demonstrations, and similar forms of expressing ideas or views regarding legitimate matters of public interest protected by the United States and Iowa constitutions.

17. **Kansas**–K.S.A. §74-7301 *citing* 18 U.S.C. sec. 2331
The term "international terrorism" means activities that–(A) involve violent acts or acts dangerous to human life that are a violation of the criminal laws of the United States or of any state, or that would be a criminal violation if committed within the jurisdiction of the United States or of any state; (B) appear to be intended–(i) to intimidate or coerce

a civilian population; (ii) to influence the policy of a government by intimidation or coercion; or (iii) to affect the conduct of a government by mass destruction, assassination, or kidnapping; and (C) occur primarily outside the territorial jurisdiction of the United States, or transcend national boundaries in terms of the means by which they are accomplished, the persons they appear intended to intimidate or coerce, or the locale in which their perpetrators operate or seek asylum.

18. **Kentucky**–KRS §346.020 *citing* 18 U.S.C. sec. 2331

"Domestic terrorism" means activities that–(A) involve acts dangerous to human life that are a violation of the criminal laws of the United States or of any state; (B) appear to be intended–(i) to intimidate or coerce a civilian population; (ii) to influence the policy of a government by intimidation or coercion; or (iii) to affect the conduct of a government by mass destruction, assassination, or kidnapping; and (C) occur primarily within the territorial jurisdiction of the United States.

19. **Louisiana**–LSA-R.S. 14:128.1

Terrorism is the commission of any of the acts enumerated in this subsection, when the offender has the intent to intimidate or coerce the civilian population, influence the policy of a unit of government by intimidation or coercion, or affect the conduct of a unit of government by intimidation or coercion: (1) Intentional killing of a human being. (2) Intentional infliction of serious bodily injury upon a human being. (3) Kidnapping of a human being. (4) Aggravated arson upon any structure, watercraft, or movable. (5) Intentional aggravated criminal damage to property.

20. **Maine**–5 M.R.S. §3360 *citing* 18 U.S.C. sec. 2331

The term "international terrorism" means activities that–(A) involve violent acts or acts dangerous to human life that are a violation of the criminal laws of the United States or of any state, or that would be a criminal violation if committed within the jurisdiction of the United States or of any state; (B) appear to be intended–(i) to intimidate or coerce a civilian population; (ii) to influence the policy of a government by intimidation or coer-

cion; or (iii) to affect the conduct of a government by mass destruction, assassination, or kidnapping; and (C) occur primarily outside the territorial jurisdiction of the United States, or transcend national boundaries in terms of the means by which they are accomplished, the persons they appear intended to intimidate or coerce, or the locale in which their perpetrators operate or seek asylum.

21. **Maryland**–Md. CRIMINAL PROCEDURE Code Ann. §11-801 *citing* 18 U.S.C. sec. 2331

The term "international terrorism" means activities that–(A) involve violent acts or acts dangerous to human life that are a violation of the criminal laws of the United States or of any state, or that would be a criminal violation if committed within the jurisdiction of the United States or of any state; (B) appear to be intended–(i) to intimidate or coerce a civilian population; (ii) to influence the policy of a government by intimidation or coercion; or (iii) to affect the conduct of a government by mass destruction, assassination, or kidnapping; and (C) occur primarily outside the territorial jurisdiction of the United States, or transcend national boundaries in terms of the means by which they are accomplished, the persons they appear intended to intimidate or coerce, or the locale in which their perpetrators operate or seek asylum.

22. **Massachusetts**–ALM GL ch. 258C, §1 *citing* 18 U.S.C. sec. 2331

"Domestic terrorism" means activities that–(A) involve acts dangerous to human life that are a violation of the criminal laws of the United States or of any state; (B) appear to be intended–(i) to intimidate or coerce a civilian population; (ii) to influence the policy of a government by intimidation or coercion; or (iii) to affect the conduct of a government by mass destruction, assassination, or kidnapping; and (C) occur primarily within the territorial jurisdiction of the United States.

23. **Michigan**–M.C.L.A. 750.543b

"Act of terrorism" means a willful and deliberate act that is all of the following: (i) An act that would be a violent felony under the laws of this state, whether or not committed in this state. (ii) An act that the person knows or has reason to know is dangerous to human life. (iii) An act that is intended to intimidate or coerce a civilian population or influence or affect the conduct of government or a unit of government through intimidation or coercion.

24. **Minnesota**–M.S.A. §609.714

A crime is committed to "further terrorism" if the crime is a felony and is a premeditated act involving violence to persons or property that is intended to: (1) terrorize, intimidate, or coerce a considerable number of members of the public in addition to the direct victims of the act; and (2) significantly disrupt or interfere with the lawful exercise, operation, or conduct of government, lawful commerce, or the right of lawful assembly.

25. **Mississippi**–2004 Bill Text MS S.B. 2360, *amending* §33-15-11, Mississippi Code of 1972

The term "terrorism" means activities that involve violent acts or acts dangerous to human life that are intended to and do put another person in fear of serious bodily harm under circumstances manifesting extreme indifference to the value of human life that appear to be intended to intimidate or coerce a civilian population or to affect the conduct of government through the activities.

26. **Missouri**–§595.010 R.S.Mo. *citing* 18 U.S.C. sec. 2331

The term "international terrorism" means activities that–(A) involve violent acts or acts dangerous to human life that are a violation of the criminal laws of the United States or of any state, or that would be a criminal violation if committed within the jurisdiction of the United States or of any state; (B) appear to be intended–(i) to intimidate or coerce a civilian population; (ii) to influence the policy of a government by intimidation or coercion; or (iii) to affect the conduct of a government by mass destruction, assassination, or kidnapping; and (C) occur primarily outside the territorial jurisdiction of the United States, or transcend national boundaries in terms of the means by which they are accomplished, the persons they appear intended to intimidate or coerce, or the locale in which their perpetrators operate or seek asylum.

27. **Montana**–Mont. Code Anno., §53-9-102 *citing* 18 U.S.C. sec. 2331

The term "international terrorism" means activities that–(A) involve violent acts or acts dangerous to human life that are a violation of the criminal laws of the United States or of any state, or that would be a criminal violation if committed within the jurisdiction of the United States or of any state; (B) appear to be intended–(i) to intimidate or coerce a civilian population; (ii) to influence the policy of a government by intimidation or coercion; or (iii) to affect the conduct of a government by mass destruction, assassination, or kidnapping; and (C) occur primarily outside the territorial jurisdiction of the United States, or transcend national boundaries in terms of the means by which they are accomplished, the persons they appear intended to intimidate or coerce, or the locale in which their perpetrators operate or seek asylum.

28. **Nebraska**–R.R.S. Neb. §28-311.01

A person commits terroristic threats if he or she threatens to commit any crime of violence: (a) With the intent to terrorize another; (b) With the intent of causing the evacuation of a building, place of assembly, or facility of public transportation; or (c) In reckless disregard of the risk of causing such terror or evacuation.

29. **Nevada**–NRS §202.4415

"Act of terrorism" means any act that involves the use or attempted use of sabotage, coercion or violence which is intended to: (a) Cause great bodily harm or death to the general population; or (b) Cause substantial destruction, contamination or impairment of: (1) Any building or infrastructure, communications, transportation, utilities or services; or (2) Any natural resource or the environment. 2. As used in this section, "coercion" does not include an act of civil disobedience.

30. **New Hampshire**–2003 Bill Text NH H.B. 212

"Act of terrorism" means (1) an activity that involves a violent act dangerous to human life that is a violation of the criminal laws of the United States or of any state, or that would be a criminal violation if committed within the jurisdiction of the United States or of any state, and appears to be intended to intimidate or coerce a civilian population; (2) to influence the policy of a government by intimidation or coercion; (3) to affect the conduct of a government by assassination or kidnapping.

31. **New Jersey**–N.J.S.A. 2C:38-2
a) A person is guilty of the crime of terrorism if he commits or attempts, conspires or threatens to commit any crime enumerated in subsection c. of this section with the purpose:

(1) to promote an act of terror; or
(2) to terrorize five or more persons; or
(3) to influence the policy or affect the conduct of government by terror; or
(4) to cause by an act of terror the impairment or interruption of public communications, public transportation, public or private buildings, common carriers, public utilities or other public services.

c) The crimes encompassed by this section are: murder pursuant to N.J.S.2C:11-3; aggravated manslaughter or manslaughter pursuant to N.J.S.2C:11-4; vehicular homicide pursuant to N.J.S.2C:11-5; aggravated assault pursuant to subsection b. of N.J.S.2C:12-1; disarming a law enforcement officer pursuant to section 1 of P.L.1996, c. 14 (C.2C:12-11); kidnapping pursuant to N.J.S.2C:13-1; criminal restraint pursuant to N.J.S.2C:13-2; robbery pursuant to N.J.S.2C:15-1; carjacking pursuant to section 1 of P.L.1993, c. 221 (C.2C:15-2); aggravated arson or arson pursuant to N.J.S.2C:17-1; causing or risking widespread injury or damage pursuant to N.J.S.2C:17-2; damage to nuclear plant with the purpose to cause or threat to cause release of radiation pursuant to section 1 of P.L.1983, c. 480 (C.2C:17-7); damage to nuclear plant resulting in death by radiation pursuant to section 2 of P.L.1983, c. 480 (C.2C:17-8); damage to nuclear plant resulting in injury by radiation pursuant to section 3 of P.L.1983, c. 480 (C.2C: 17-9); producing or possessing chemical weapons, biological agents or nuclear or radiological devices pursuant to section 3 of P.L.2002, c. 26 (C.2C: 38-3); burglary pursuant to N.J.S.2C:18-2; possession of prohibited weapons and devices pursuant to N.J.S.2C:39-3; possession of weapons for unlawful purposes pursuant to N.J.S.2C:39-4; unlawful possession of weapons pursuant to N.J.S.2C:39-5; weapons training for illegal activities pursuant to section 1 of P.L.1983, c. 229 (C.2C:39-14); racketeering pursuant to N.J.S.2C:41-1 et seq.; and any

other crime involving a risk of death or serious bodily injury to any person.

32. **New Mexico**–N.M. Stat. Ann. §31-22-3 *citing* 18 U.S.C. sec. 2331
"Domestic terrorism" means activities that– (A) involve acts dangerous to human life that are a violation of the criminal laws of the United States or of any state; (B) appear to be intended–(i) to intimidate or coerce a civilian population; (ii) to influence the policy of a government by intimidation or coercion; or (iii) to affect the conduct of a government by mass destruction, assassination, or kidnapping; and (C) occur primarily within the territorial jurisdiction of the United States.

33. **New York**–NY LEGIS 300 (2001)
"Act of terrorism": (a) for purposes of this article means an act or acts constituting a specified offense as defined in subdivision three of this section for which a person may be convicted in the criminal courts of this state pursuant to article twenty of the criminal procedure law, or an act or acts constituting an offense in any other jurisdiction within or outside the territorial boundaries of the United States which contains all of the essential elements of a specified offense, that is intended to: (i) intimidate or coerce a civilian population; (ii) influence the policy of a unit of government by intimidation or coercion; or (iii) affect the conduct of a unit of government by murder, assassination or kidnapping; or (b) for purposes of subparagraph (xiii) of paragraph (a) of subdivision one of section 125.27 of this chapter means activities that involve a violent act or acts dangerous to human life that are in violation of the criminal laws of this state and are intended to: (i) intimidate or coerce a civilian population; (ii) influence the policy of a unit of government by intimidation or coercion; or (iii) affect the conduct of a unit of government by murder, assassination or kidnapping.

34. **North Carolina**–N.C. Gen. Stat. §15B-2 *citing* 18 U.S.C. sec. 2331
"Domestic terrorism" means activities that– (A) involve acts dangerous to human life that are a violation of the criminal laws of the United States or of any State; (B) appear to be intended– (i) to intimidate or coerce a civilian population; (ii) to influence the policy of a government by

intimidation or coercion; or (iii) to affect the conduct of a government by mass destruction, assassination, or kidnapping; and (C) occur primarily within the territorial jurisdiction of the United States.

35. **North Dakota**–N.D. Cent. Code, §54-23.4-01
citing 18 U.S.C. sec. 2331
"Domestic terrorism" means activities that–(A) involve acts dangerous to human life that are a violation of the criminal laws of the United States or of any State; (B) appear to be intended–(i) to intimidate or coerce a civilian population; (ii) to influence the policy of a government by intimidation or coercion; or (iii) to affect the conduct of a government by mass destruction, assassination, or kidnapping; and (C) occur primarily within the territorial jurisdiction of the United States.

36. **Ohio**–Ohio Code §2909.21
"Act of terrorism" means an act that is committed within or outside the territorial jurisdiction of this state or the United States, that constitutes a specified offense if committed in this state or constitutes an offense in any jurisdiction within or outside the territorial jurisdiction of the United States containing all of the essential elements of a specified offense, and that is intended to do one or more of the following: (1) Intimidate or coerce a civilian population; (2) Influence the policy of any government by intimidation or coercion; (3) Affect the conduct of any government by the act that constitutes the offense.

37. **Oklahoma**–21 Okl.St.Ann. §1268.1
"Terrorism" means an act of violence resulting in damage to property or personal injury perpetrated to coerce a civilian population or government into granting illegal political or economic demands; or conduct intended to incite violence in order to create apprehension of bodily injury or damage to property in order to coerce a civilian population or government into granting illegal political or economic demands. Peaceful picketing or boycotts and other nonviolent action shall not be considered terrorism.

38. **Oregon**–2003 Ore. SB 106
"International terrorism" means activities that: (a) Involve violent acts or acts dangerous to human life that are a violation of the criminal laws of the United States or any state or that would be a criminal violation if committed within the jurisdiction of the United States or of any state; (b) Appear to be intended to: (A) Intimidate or coerce a civilian population; (B) Influence the policy of a government by intimidation or coercion; or (C) Affect the conduct of a government by assassination or kidnapping; and (c) Occur primarily outside the territorial jurisdiction of the United States or transcend national boundaries in terms of the means by which they are accomplished, the persons they appear intended to intimidate or coerce, or the locale in which their perpetrators operate or seek asylum.

39. **Pennsylvania**–35 P.S. §2140.102
"Terrorism" The unlawful use of force or violence committed by a group or individual against persons or property to intimidate or coerce a government, the civilian population, or any segment thereof in furtherance of political or social objectives.

40. **Rhode Island**–R.I. Gen. Laws §12-25-17
citing 18 U.S.C. sec. 2331
"Domestic terrorism" means activities that–(A) involve acts dangerous to human life that are a violation of the criminal laws of the United States or of any State; (B) appear to be intended–(i) to intimidate or coerce a civilian population; (ii) to influence the policy of a government by intimidation or coercion; or (iii) to affect the conduct of a government by mass destruction, assassination, or kidnapping; and (C) occur primarily within the territorial jurisdiction of the United States.

41. **South Carolina**–S.C. Code Ann. §14-7-1630
Terrorism includes activities that: (a) involve acts dangerous to human life that are a violation of the criminal laws of this state; (b) appear to be intended to: (i) intimidate or coerce a civilian population; (ii) influence the policy of a government by intimidation or coercion; or (iii) affect the conduct of a government by mass destruction, assassination, or kidnapping; and (c) occur primarily within the territorial jurisdiction of this State.

42. **South Dakota**–S.D. Codified Laws 22-8-12.
"Act of terrorism" Any person who commits a crime of violence as defined by subdivision 22-1-2 (9) or

an act dangerous to human life including any use of chemical, biological, or radioactive material, or any explosive or destructive device with the intent to do any of the following: (1) Intimidate or coerce a civilian population; (2) Influence the policy or conduct of any government or nation; (3) Affect the conduct of any government or nation by assassination or kidnapping; or (4) Substantially impair or interrupt public communications, public transportation, common carriers, public utilities, or other public services, . . . is guilty of an act of terrorism. A violation of this section is a Class A felony.

43. Tennessee–Tenn. Code Ann. §39-13-803

"Act of terrorism" means an act or acts constituting a violation of this part, any other offense under the laws of Tennessee, or an act or acts constituting an offense in any other jurisdiction within or outside the territorial boundaries of the United States that contains all of the elements constituting a violation of this part or is otherwise an offense under the laws of such jurisdiction, that is intended, directly or indirectly, to: (A) Intimidate or coerce a civilian population; (B) Influence the policy of a unit of government by intimidation or coercion; or (C) Affect the conduct of a unit of government by murder, assassination, torture, kidnapping, or mass destruction.

44. Texas–Tex. Penal Code §22.07

"Terroristic Threat" (a) A person commits an offense if he threatens to commit any offense involving violence to any person or property with intent to: (1) cause a reaction of any type to his threat by an official or volunteer agency organized to deal with emergencies; (2) place any person in fear of imminent serious bodily injury; (3) prevent or interrupt the occupation or use of a building; room; place of assembly; place to which the public has access; place of employment or occupation; aircraft, automobile, or other form of conveyance; or other public place; (4) cause impairment or interruption of public communications, public transportation, public water, gas, or power supply or other public service; (5) place the public or a substantial group of the public in fear of serious bodily injury; or (6) influence the conduct or activities of a branch or agency of the federal government, the state, or a political subdivision of the state.

45. Utah–Utah Code Ann. §63-25a-402 *citing* 18 U.S.C. sec. 2331

"Domestic terrorism" means activities that–(A) involve acts dangerous to human life that are a violation of the criminal laws of the United States or of any state; (B) appear to be intended–(i) to intimidate or coerce a civilian population; (ii) to influence the policy of a government by intimidation or coercion; or (iii) to affect the conduct of a government by mass destruction, assassination, or kidnapping; and (C) occur primarily within the territorial jurisdiction of the United States.

46. Vermont–13 V.S.A. §351 *citing* 18 U.S.C. sec. 2331

"Domestic terrorism" means activities that– (A) involve acts dangerous to human life that are a violation of the criminal laws of the United States or of any state; (B) appear to be intended–(i) to intimidate or coerce a civilian population; (ii) to influence the policy of a government by intimidation or coercion; or (iii) to affect the conduct of a government by mass destruction, assassination, or kidnapping; and (C) occur primarily within the territorial jurisdiction of the United States.

47. Virginia–Va. Code Ann. §18.2–46.4

"Act of terrorism" means an act of violence as defined in clause (i) of subdivision A of 19.2–297.1 (capital murder, murder of the first degree, murder of the second degree, voluntary manslaughter, or involuntary manslaughter) committed with the intent to (i) intimidate the civilian population at large; or (ii) influence the conduct or activities of the government of the United States, a state or locality through intimidation.

48. Washington–2003 Wa. ALS 124

Criminal terrorist acts . . . are acts that significantly disrupt the conduct of government or of the general civilian population of the state or the United States and that manifest an extreme indifference to human life.

49. West Virginia–W. Va. Code §14-2A-3 *citing* 18 U.S.C. sec. 2331

"Domestic terrorism" means activities that– (A) involve acts dangerous to human life that are a violation of the criminal laws of the United States or of any state; (B) appear to be intended–(i) to intimidate or coerce a civilian population; (ii) to influence the policy of a government by intimidation or coercion; or (iii) to affect the conduct of a government by mass destruction, assassination, or kidnapping; and (C) occur primarily within the territorial jurisdiction of the United States.

50. **Wisconsin**–Wis. Stat. §146.50

"Act of terrorism" means a felony under ch. 939 to 951 that is committed with intent to terrorize and is committed under any of the following circumstances: 1. The person committing the felony causes bodily harm, great bodily harm, or death to another. 2. The person committing the felony causes damage to the property of another and the total property damaged is reduced in value by $25,000 or more. For purposes of this subdivision, property is reduced in value by the amount that it would cost either to repair or replace it, whichever is less. 3. The person committing the felony uses force or violence or the threat of force or violence.

51. **Wyoming**–Wyo. Stat. §§1-40-102 *citing* 18 U.S.C. sec. 2331

"Domestic terrorism" means activities that–(A) involve acts dangerous to human life that are a violation of the criminal laws of the United States or of any state; (B) appear to be intended–(i) to intimidate or coerce a civilian population; (ii) to influence the policy of a government by intimidation or coercion; or (iii) to affect the conduct of a government by mass destruction, assassination, or kidnapping; and (C) occur primarily within the territorial jurisdiction of the United States.

Appendix F

AUTHOR'S UPDATE FOR CHAPTER 3

One hazard in writing a book that covers evolving events is that subsequent happenings can alter the situation. Such an event occurred in late February 2005, when US Fire Administrator David R. Paulison addressed a group of fire service leaders on many of the concerns expressed in Chapter 3 of this book regarding funding for the U.S. Fire Administration and the National Emergency Training Center. Due to the information he shared, this Chapter's discussion of funding issues at the USFA and NETC is largely obsolete. People quoted as having concerns regarding the situation have changed their views. The author regrets that this event occurred too late to be incorporated in the body of the text.

Administrator Paulison made several important points, including:

- Funding for the USFA for FY 2006 reflects a $1.3 million increase, and includes funding from the NIMS Integration Center for NIMS/NRP training;
- No students have been turned away from the National Fire Academy, and no courses have been closed. The USFA hopes to increase its capacity for students on the National Emergency Training Center campus by blending distance learning with on-campus learning;
- The NETC will not be closed; and
- Paulison is working to get some of the terrorism training that has moved to the Office for Domestic Preparedness back into the USFA.

Attending fire service leaders adopted the following "Unified Fire Service Findings and Policy Goals:"

- America's fire service must be represented by fire chiefs and other senior fire service officials within the office of the DHS Secretary and throughout the department.
- The USFA must occupy a key position and function in a comprehensive role within DHS proportionate to the responsibilities of the fire service in responding to incidents of terrorism and all-hazards events.
- The Office of Management and Budget and DHS need to recognize and designate the USFA and the NFA as "homeland security-critical" in the federal budgeting process.
- The USFA and the NFA must be fully funded to the authorized levels to support the ongoing mission to reflect contemporary issues and community risks.
- DHS should be required to work more closely with the NFA and state and local fire training academies regarding the use of curriculum and the delivery system for terrorism response training.

For more information, read Pat West, "Financial Check Up," *FIRE CHIEF* (April 1, 2005). Found on line at: http://firechief.com/mag/firefighting_financial_checkup/index.html

Although many fire service concerns have been addressed, the issues cited regarding funding for the FEMA Higher Education Project and the Emergency Management Institute persist.

INDEX

A

Accident 24, 30–33, 36, 40, 42, 46, 73, 124, 132, 154, 263, 277, 279, 354

Afghanistan 169, 181, 184, 189, 263, 278, 290, 291, 299, 315, 340, 341

Al Quaida 160, 186, 191, 263, 275, 278, 290–291, 295, 306, 334, 340–341

Allbaugh, Joe 41–42, 44

Aviation security 234–250

Awareness, public 183

Awareness, terrorism 124, 139, 229

B

Bayh, Evan 333

Bin Laden, Osama 278

Bioterrorism 15, 17, 148, 150, 262–274, 340

Brown, Michael D. 61, 79

Bush, George H.W. 38, 42, 43, 44, 69, 120, 150, 326, 329, 332

Bush, George W. 5, 23, 24, 36, 298–302

Business continuity 74, 81, 155

C

Carter, Jimmy 22–23, 28–33, 35, 39, 42–43, 46

Center for Domestic Preparedness 152

Central Intelligence Agency (CIA) 182, 183, 189, 190, 201, 203, 235, 306–308, 310–312, 314–316, 320

Chemical Stockpile Emergency Preparedness Program (CSEPP) 24, 37–39, 42, 46

Civil Defense 6, 23–28, 36–37, 39, 111, 112, 164, 255

Civil rights 179–208 (See also USAPATRIOT Act)

Clinton, William J. 11, 24, 32, 33–34, 36, 38–39, 41–44, 46, 56, 58, 125, 263, 268

Community Emergency Response Teams (CERT) 117, 120–121, 124

Critical infrastructure 11, 17, 74, 75, 76, 85, 112, 120–122, 129, 131, 187, 323, 339

D

Defense, Department of 28, 35–36, 38, 114, 122, 159–176, 193, 201, 256, 296, 310–312, 322–323, 339 (see also National Response Plan)

Data mining 183, 197, 200–201, 243

"Dirty bomb" (See radiological dispersion device)

Disaster Mitigation Act of 2000 (DMA) 120, 129, 255

Disaster Resistant Universities Program 129, 151–152

E

Emergency Management Assistance Compact (EMAC) 83–84, 339

Emergency Management Higher Education Project 58, 59, 338

Emergency Management Institute 36, 58, 59, 60, 104

Emergency Management Performance Grant (EMPG) 61, 82, 113, 117, 124, 126–128, 130

Emergency Medical Services 12, 17, 73, 113, 114, 117, 155

Evacuation 8, 32, 152, 154, 164, 226–229

Exercising 39, 41, 47, 70, 72, 81, 126, 166, 323

F

Federal Bureau of Investigation (FBI) 6–7, 35, 39–40, 56, 112–113, 115, 117, 119–20, 122, 125, 160–163, 165, 166, 171, 172, 180, 182–184, 187–188, 197–198, 201, 203, 205–207, 210, 212, 235, 266, 305–310, 312, 314, 319–322, 331, 359

Federal Emergency Management Agency (FEMA) 338–340

Department of Homeland Security, role in 123–126

Hazardous materials and 23–55

Local government and 111–136

Nuclear power emergencies and 30–32
Post 9–11 priorities of 56–67
Universities and 149
Federal Radiological Emergency Response Plan
(FRERP) 31, 41–4, 70, 74, 278–279
Federal Response Plan (FRP)32, 38, 40, 43, 48, 56,
71–74, 115, 122, 129, 159, 161, 172
Firefighters 34–36, 44, 58, 59–61, 80, 126
FIRE Grants 45, 61–62, 126, 370
Flood insurance 23, 29, 37, 58, 257
Foreign policy and terrorism 287–302
Funding, local law enforcement role in 126–128

G

Grants 39, 44, 49, 60–62, 79, 84–85, 103–104, 113,
116, 124, 126, 127, 129, 151, 354
Governor's role 26, 29, 73, 81, 84, 93, 103–106, 115,
122, 123, 125, 139, 141, 160–166, 168–169, 172

H

Hazardous materials 23–55, 62, 70, 76–77, 80, 114,
117, 120,121, 124, 127, 132, 152–154, 161, 338,
FEMA role in response to releases of 23–55
Homeland security - see specific topics
Definition 5–22
Future of 338–341
Local government and 111–136
Homeland Security Act of 2002 (HS Act) 5–7, 24,
44, 56, 59, 68, 80, 87, 122–123, 131, 149, 161,
189, 279, 322
Homeland Security, Department of
Border and Transportation Security Directorate
(BTSD) 86
Emergency Preparedness and Response
Directorate 59, 86
Legal basis for 5–9, 69–70, 352–363
Transportation Security Administration (TSA) 59,
70, 79, 87, 119, 121, 203, 205, 227, 229,
230, 236–239, 242–243, 322
Homeland Security Presidential Directives (HSPDs)
HSPD 5 27, 42, 47, 56, 58, 69–70, 72–74, 78–80,
83–85, 103, 123, 129–131, 339, 352
HSPD 7 131
HSPD 8 58, 130–132

I

Immunity 83, 170, 240, 258
Incident command (See National Incident
Management System)
Intelligence 289–302, 305–335

Interagency Incident Management Group 162
International Association of Emergency Managers
(IAEM) 30
Iraq 121, 169, 263–265, 277–278, 340–341
Foreign views of US involvement in 289–293
President Bush discusses 298–302
Representative Bereuter (R-Nevada) views on
294–297

M

Mass transit security 225–233
Meese, Edwin II 31, 39, 42, 43
Metropolitan Medical Strike Teams (MMST)
114–117, 120–121, 123–124, 127, 129, 132–133
Mitigation 17, 27–28, 34, 37, 41, 44, 47, 57–58,
62–63, 71, 72, 73, 76, 78, 82, 111–113, 117,
119–120, 124, 126, 129–130, 131, 133, 150, 152,
159, 161, 164, 172, 253–255, 257, 258, 259,
324, 330, 339, 340
Money Laundering 209–222
Mutual aid 17, 30, 72–73, 79, 83–84, 104, 114, 127,
129, 339, 340

N

National Emergency Management Association
(NEMA) 81, 83, 339
National Emergency Training Center 59–60
National Fire Academy 59, 61
National Fire Protection Association 1600 (NFPA
1600) 80–83, 87, 339
National Oil and Hazardous Substances Pollution
Contingency Plan (National Contingency Plan)
31, 34, 35, 39–41, 70, 72
National Incident Management System (NIMS)
68–108
Compliance standards 103–106
NIMS Integration Center 78–80, 84, 85, 87, 103,
339
Unified Command 162
National Response Plan (NRP) 68–108, 162–169, 279
Defense Coordinating Element 162–163,
166–168, 172, 354
Defense Coordinating Officer 162–169
Federal Coordinating Officer 162–169
Homeland Security Operations Center 72, 162
Joint Field Office 77, 162
Joint Terrorism Task Force 115
Legal basis for 68–70, 352–363
National Joint Terrorism Task Force 162
Principal Federal Official 72, 162, 362
Strategic Information and Operations Center 162

National Security Agency (NSA) 307, 309–312, 314, 316

9–11 Commission 80–81, 105, 236, 324, 333, 341

O

Occupational Safety and Health Administration (OSHA) 130

Office of Domestic Preparedness (ODP) 49, 50, 60–62, 85, 105, 152

P

Pennsylvania Office of Homeland Security 139

Personal Protective Equipment (PPE) 18, 115–116, 126

Planning 17, 18, 24–32, 36–37, 40, 42–44, 46–47, 48, 60, 75–76, 78, 81–83, 104, 113, 116, 118, 120, 124, 126, 129, 131, 132, 137, 150–151, 154, 155–156, 161, 163, 164–165, 183, 226–229, 231, 257, 277, 295, 305–310, 315, 321, 323, 324–327, 340

Posse comitatus 73, 123, 167, 169–172, 355–356

Preparedness 10–12, 14, 17–20, 24, 26, 27–31, 34, 36, 36–37, 39, 40–44, 52, 54, 60–62, 68–75, 78–82, 84–87, 103–105, 111–115, 117, 118, 124–126, 129–133, 138–140, 142–143, 149, 152–156, 159, 161, 164, 167, 172, 227, 228, 231, 253, 255, 264, 323, 338–341

For all hazards 30, 47, 56–62, 69, 70, 73, 78, 86, 87, 111–112, 120, 123–125, 129, 131–133, 151, 161, 338

Presidential Decision Directives
PDD 39 39, 56, 120, 162
PDD 62 39, 120, 131
PDD 63 120

Private sector 28, 58, 68, 72, 74, 75, 67, 80, 120, 131, 139, 150–153, 155–156, 161, 244, 314, 317, 339–340

Project Impact 58, 150, 339

R

Radiological dispersion device ("Dirty bomb") 28, 116, 185, 273–286, 340

Reagan National Airport 237, 238

Reagan, Ronald W. 31–35, 37, 39–40, 43, 46

Recovery 6,8,11, 24, 26–30, 33–34, 40–42, 56, 57, 62, 70–73, 75–76, 78, 81–82, 103, 111–112, 114 124, 132–133, 150, 159–161, 164, 172, 226–229, 231, 253–257, 259

Red Cross 43, 121, 124, 140, 255

Responder Certification 42, 78–81, 83, 84, 167, 321, 339

Response see specific topics

Rulemaking 32, 85–87

S

Stafford Act 32–34, 40–44, 46, 73, 112, 120, 160–161, 163–164, 255, 353–356, 359, 364

State government 5, 8, 72, 106, 130, 255, 257, 278–279, 365–373

Superfund Amendments and Reauthorization Act of 1986 (SARA) 34

Suspicious Activity Reports (SARs) 209–222

T

Total Information Awareness 127, 200–205

U

United States Fire Administration (USFA) 34–36, 59, 79

Uniting and Strengthening America by Providing Appropriate Tools Required to Intercept and Obstruct Terrorism (USA PATRIOT) Act of 2001 7, 16, 17, 128, 179–196, 209–222, 259, 339

Urban Area Security Initiative (UASI) 84, 104, 128–129, 132

Urban Search and Rescue (USAR) Teams 116, 127, 129, 133

V

Volunteers 48, 60, 77, 80, 111, 115, 120, 133, 150, 242, 388

W

Weapons of mass destruction 17–18, 23, 28, 39, 61–62, 68, 79, 113, 114–117, 138, 160–162, 251–286, 294–296, 298, 329, 333, 340

Witt, James Lee 32, 36, 37, 41–43, 56, 58, 61, 62, 125, 129